CRITICAL SURVEY OF
Poetry
Fourth Edition

Topical Essays

CRITICAL SURVEY OF

Poetry

Fourth Edition

Topical Essays

Volume 2
Macedonian Poetry—Structuralist
and Poststructuralist Criticism
Resources
Indexes

Editor, Fourth Edition
Rosemary M. Canfield Reisman
Charleston Southern University

SALEM PRESS
Pasadena, California
Hackensack, New Jersey

Editor in Chief: Dawn P. Dawson

Editorial Director: Christina J. Moose   *Research Supervisor:* Jeffry Jensen
Development Editor: Tracy Irons-Georges   *Research Assistant:* Keli Trousdale
Project Editor: Rowena Wildin   *Production Editor:* Andrea E. Miller
Manuscript Editor: Desiree Dreeuws   *Page Desion:* James Hutson
Acquisitions Editor: Mark Rehn   *Layout:* Mary Overell
Editorial Assistant: Brett S. Weisberg   *Photo Editor:* Cynthia Breslin Beres

Cover photo: Persian poet Firdusi's *Shahnamah* (The Granger Collection, New York)

Some of the essays in this work, which have been updated, originally appeared in the following Salem Press publications, *Critical Survey of Poetry, English Language Series* (1983), *Critical Survey of Poetry: Foreign Language Series* (1984), *Critical Survey of Poetry, Supplement* (1987), *Critical Survey of Poetry, English Language Series, Revised Edition,* (1992; preceding volumes edited by Frank N. Magill), *Critical Survey of Poetry, Second Revised Edition* (2003; edited by Philip K. Jason).

∞ The paper used in these volumes conforms to the American National Standard for Permanence of Paper for Printed Library Materials, X39.48-1992 (R1997).

Library of Congress Cataloging-in-Publication Data

Critical survey of poetry. — 4th ed. / editor, Rosemary M. Canfield Reisman.
    v. cm.
  Includes bibliographical references and index.
  ISBN 978-1-58765-582-1 (set : alk. paper) — ISBN 978-1-58765-763-4 (set : topical essays : alk. paper) — ISBN 978-1-58765-764-1 (v. 1 : topical essays : alk. paper) — ISBN 978-1-58765-765-8 (v. 2 : topical essays : alk. paper)
  1. Poetry—History and criticism—Dictionaries. 2. Poetry—Bio-bibliography. 3. Poets—Biography—Dictionaries. I. Reisman, Rosemary M. Canfield.
  PN1021.C7 2011
  809.1'003--dc22

        2010045095

First Printing

CONTENTS

Complete List of Contents xxi

POETRY AROUND THE WORLD (*cont.*)
Macedonian Poetry 475
Native American Poetry 478
Polish Poetry 489
Postcolonial Poetry 500
Russian Poetry 509
Scandinavian Poetry 526
Serbian Poetry 566
Slovak Poetry 573
Slovenian Poetry 579
Spanish Poetry to 1400 583
Spanish Poetry Since 1400 592
Tibetan Poetry 604

LITERARY MOVEMENTS
Metaphysical Poets 615
Restoration Poetry 620
Romantic Poets 626
Fireside Poets 633
French Symbolists 639
Imagists 644
Modernists 650
Harlem Renaissance 655
Beat Poets 661
Confessional Poets 668
New York School 674
Movement Poets 679

Black Mountain School 684
Green Movement Poets 690

CRITICISM AND THEORY
Criticism from Plato to Eliot 699
Archetypal and Psychological Criticism 719
Cultural Criticism 731
Feminist Criticism 736
Formalistic Criticism 743
Linguistic Criticism 750
Marxist Criticism 760
New Historicism 764
Postcolonial Criticism 769
Queer Theory 774
Structuralist and Poststructuralist Criticism . . . 780

RESOURCES
Explicating Poetry 789
Language and Linguistics 798
Glossary of Poetical Terms 810
Bibliography 823
Guide to Online Resources 851
Time Line 856
Major Awards 865

INDEXES
Geographical Index of Essays 893
Master List of Contents 895
Subject Index 906

COMPLETE LIST OF CONTENTS

VOLUME 1

Publisher's Note v
Contributors ix
Contents xi
Complete List of Contents xiii

POETRY AROUND THE WORLD

African American Poetry 3
African Poetry 15
Asian American Poetry 21
Australian and New Zealand Poetry 30
Canadian Poetry 37
Caribbean Poetry 43
Catalan Poetry 48
Chinese Poetry 54
Croatian Poetry 71
Czech Poetry 78
East German Poetry 87
English and Continental Poetry in the
    Fourteenth Century 98
English Poetry in the Fifteenth Century 120
English Poetry in the Sixteenth Century 130
English Poetry in the Seventeenth Century . . . 144

English Poetry in the Eighteenth Century 160
English and American Poetry in the
    Nineteenth Century 174
English and American Poetry in the
    Twentieth Century 185
European Oral and Epic Traditions 214
French Poetry to 1700 232
French Poetry Since 1700 254
German Poetry to 1800 283
German Poetry: 1800 to Reunification 298
German Poetry Since Reunification 315
Greek Poetry in Antiquity 320
Greek Poetry Since 1820 331
Hungarian Poetry 352
Indian English Poetry 365
Italian Poetry to 1800 377
Italian Poetry Since 1800 393
Japanese Poetry to 1800 412
Japanese Poetry Since 1800 427
Latin American Poetry 435
Latin Poetry 441
Latino Poetry 466

VOLUME 2

Contents xix

POETRY AROUND THE WORLD (*cont.*)

Macedonian Poetry 475
Native American Poetry 478
Polish Poetry 489
Postcolonial Poetry 500
Russian Poetry 509
Scandinavian Poetry 526
Serbian Poetry 566
Slovak Poetry 573
Slovenian Poetry 579
Spanish Poetry to 1400 583

Spanish Poetry Since 1400 592
Tibetan Poetry 604

LITERARY MOVEMENTS

Metaphysical Poets 615
Restoration Poetry 620
Romantic Poets 626
Fireside Poets 633
French Symbolists 639
Imagists 644
Modernists 650
Harlem Renaissance 655
Beat Poets 661

Confessional Poets. 668
New York School 674
Movement Poets 679
Black Mountain School 684
Green Movement Poets 690

CRITICISM AND THEORY
Criticism from Plato to Eliot. 699
Archetypal and Psychological Criticism. 719
Cultural Criticism 731
Feminist Criticism 736
Formalistic Criticism. 743
Linguistic Criticism 750
Marxist Criticism 760
New Historicism 764
Postcolonial Criticism 769

Queer Theory 774
Structuralist and Poststructuralist Criticism . . . 780

RESOURCES
Explicating Poetry 789
Language and Linguistics 798
Glossary of Poetical Terms 810
Bibliography 823
Guide to Online Resources 851
Time Line 856
Major Awards 865

INDEXES
Geographical Index of Essays 893
Master List of Contents 895
Subject Index. 906

CRITICAL SURVEY OF
Poetry

Fourth Edition

Topical Essays

MACEDONIAN POETRY

Like the Slovenes, the Macedonians have had to travel a rocky historical path. After their early state was subjugated in the eleventh century by the Byzantines and, later, by the Turks, they did not enjoy independence until 1945. During those long centuries, however, they were able to maintain their identity, both ethnically and culturally; when conditions became favorable at the end of World War II, they began to produce their own literature.

Despite this long history of oppression, Macedonian culture can trace its heritage back to the earliest Slavic writings, which appeared in the ninth century in the language of the Macedonian Slavs around Salonika. Centering on the lively activity of Macedonian missionaries, led by Klement Ohridski and Naum Ohridski and their disciples, early Macedonian literature was exclusively related to the Church. Indeed, for many centuries, the only Macedonian literature that was not directly connected with the Church was oral folk literature, which was as abundant in Macedonia as in other South Slavic lands. Much of this literature was in poetic form, but because of its oral nature, not much has been preserved. Today, folklorists are making concerted efforts to record and document what remains of this tradition, and at least some of the folk literature that can still be heard has been handed down for generations.

EIGHTEENTH AND NINETEENTH CENTURIES

The first known verses in Macedonian were written by Kiril Pejčinoviḱ-Tetoec (c. 1770-1845). The beginning of known Macedonian poetry coincided with the revival of national awareness and the struggle against the Turks and the Greek clergy, who had tried strenuously to suppress the Macedonian language and the development of Macedonian literature. The next generation of writers included several poets: Jordan Hadži Konstantinov-Džinot (1820-1882), Dimitrije Miladinov (1810-1862), Konstantin Miladinov (1830-1862), Rajko Žinzifov (1839-1877), and Grigor Prličev (1830-1893). The Miladinov brothers were especially active in their efforts to introduce Macedonian in schools and in collecting and publishing folk poetry. For their nationalistic activity, they both died in a prison in Constantinople. Žinzifov, a talented poet and an erudite scholar (he was graduated from Moscow University), was also instrumental in collecting and translating folk poetry, and his own poetry is not without merit. The most talented of these writers was Prličev. As a student of Greek, he wrote in Greek the epic poems *Serdar* (1860; *The Sirdar*, 1973) and *Skender beg* (1861; Skender Bey), which he later translated into Macedonian. He also translated Homer's *Iliad* (c. 750 B.C.E.; English translation, 1611) and *Odyssey* (c. 725 B.C.E.; English translation, 1614) into his native language. The poetry of all of these poets, being so closely connected with the struggle of their people for independence, has more historical than artistic value. By writing in their own language, they helped to preserve it in literature after centuries of suppression. They also drew heavily from folk poetry, bringing that cultural treasure into focus and perhaps saving it from oblivion.

TWENTIETH CENTURY ONWARD

In the creation of Yugoslavia at the end of World War I (the new nation of the Southern Slavs was not known by that name until 1929), the Macedonians were denied their nationality once again. Their writers were again forced to live and write outside their native land, for writing and publishing in Macedonian were not allowed. Among these émigré writers, three stand out: Kosta Racin (1908-1943), Venko Markovski (1915-1988), and Kole Nedelkovski (1912-1943). By far the most important of the three, Racin was the first to publish a collection of poems in Macedonian, *Beli mugri* (1939; white dawns). Here, Racin depicts the plight of his countrymen, who were often forced to go for long periods to other countries, especially the United States, to look for work.

The recognition of Macedonian nationality within Yugoslavia at the end of World War II triggered a burst of cultural and literary activity. A single dialect was chosen to serve as the basis for Macedonia's literary language, and books began to be published in great numbers. More important, several writers and poets of unmistakable talent emerged, laying the foundation of contemporary literature and poetry. Among these, three stand out: Slavko Janevski (1920-2000), Blaźe Koneski (1921-1993), and Aco Šopov (1923-1983).

Janevski's poetry, whether about his war experiences or about his intimate concerns, is characterized by a picturesque quality, originality, boldness, and even a touch of black humor. In form, he is just as bold, imaginative, and innovative. The author of the first Macedonian novel, he is active in other genres, although poetry still seems to be his main interest.

Koneski, an academician who has done pioneering work in the field of the Macedonian language, writes direct, intimate, and meditative poetry. Macedonian motifs—mythical, folkloric, and contemporary—are frequently found in his somewhat traditional and subdued poems. Koneski is a master of controlled pathos and understatement. Šopov published the first Macedonian book of poetry after World War II and thus started, along with Janevski and Koneski, the process of establishing the right of Macedonian poetry to exist.

A subtle lyricist, a sensitive observer, and a poet of intense personal experience, Šopov enriched Macedonian poetry at the very beginning of the new period, thus creating models for the younger poets. He was also one of the first to liberate Macedonian poetry from nonaesthetic criteria in the late 1940's.

After these three poets, the road was open for a large number of remarkably capable poets. Mateja Matevski (born 1929) and Gané Todorovski (born 1929) were the leaders in the second generation of contemporary Macedonian poets. Matevski contributed to the transformation of declarative, descriptive, and confessional Macedonian poetry into a meditative and abstract approach bordering at times on the surreal. Influenced by French poets, he paid great attention to form, attempting to strike a balance between an abundance of impressions and an economy of expression. Todorovski's poetry shows a peculiar sensitivity and strong linguistic ability.

Radovan Pavlovski (born 1936) and Bogomil Gjuzel (born 1939) belong to the third wave of modern Macedonian poets. Pavlovski is a poet of extraordinary im-

agistic invention and an almost animistic approach to the natural world. His images seem to rise out of the unconscious with echoes of folklore and rural life. The sense of nostalgia, of loss, that one experiences in reading his verse recalls the spirit of anonymous folk poetry, yet Pavlovski gives his expression a thoroughly modern and sophisticated tone. Gjuzel is a more contemplative poet, but with equally close ties to his native soil. In his work, one can see the beginnings of a conscious effort to organize the Macedonian experience and sensibility. His poems impress the reader by their formal excellence and the evocative and sensuous quality of his language.

The vitality of the poetic tradition in Macedonia is evident in the fact that every August for almost five decades, the southern Macedonian city of Struga has held an international poetry festival that attracts poets from all over the world, as well as scholars, literary critics, and translators. Struga Poetic Evenings (SPE) was launched in 1962, when several Macedonian poets presented readings in honor of Konstantin and Dimitar Miladinov. By 2009, SPE had become a four-day event, attended by more than eighty poets from fifty countries. The festival always opens with a reading of Konstantin Miladinov's poem "T'ga za jug" ("Longing for the South"). Among the activities that follow are poetry readings and performances, multimedia presentations, symposia, concerts, and the presentation of awards for poetic achievement, among them, the naming of an SPE laureate. The festival is followed by a Caravan of Poetry, a series of poetry readings in other Macedonian cities, which ends in Skopje, where the SPE laureate is made an honorary member of the Macedonian Poetry Association.

BIBLIOGRAPHY

Barac, Antun. *A History of Yugoslav Literature*. Ann Arbor. Mich.: Joint Committee on Eastern Europe Publication Series, 1973. A standard history of all Yugoslav literatures and poetry, including a brief discussion of Macedonian poetry, by a leading literary scholar. Although somewhat outdated, it still provides reliable information, especially of the older periods.

Dimkovska, Lidija. *Do Not Awaken Them with Ham-*

mers. Translated by Ljubica Arsovska and Peggy Reid. Brooklyn, N.Y.: Ugly Duckling Press, 2006. The first of this highly acclaimed writer's four poetry collections to be translated into English. Complicated poems, often humorous, but all infused with the poet's identity as a woman living in Eastern Europe at a time of change.

George, Emery, ed. *Contemporary East European Poetry: An Anthology*. 2d ed. New York: Oxford University Press, 1993. Thirty-two newer poets have been added to this edition of the massive 1983 volume. Macedonian poets are discussed in the introduction to the Yugoslavian section, which includes translated poems by Slavko Janevski, Blaže Koneski, Aco Šopov, Mateja Matevski, and Gané Todorovski.

Janevski, Slavko. *The Bandit Wind: Poems*. Translated by Charles Simic. Takoma Park, Md.: Dryad Press, 1991. A bilingual collection of works by one of Macedonia's most highly regarded poets, noted for his bold experimentation, his vivid characters, and his dreamlike imagery. The translator is a Pulitzer Prize-winning poet.

Kizer, Carolyn. *Carrying Over: Poems from the Chinese, Urdu, Macedonian, Yiddish, and French African*. Translated by Kizer. Port Townsend, Wash.: Copper Canyon Press, 1989. This unusual book consists of entries from the journal of the author, a noted poet, along with her beautifully crafted translations of poems that she found especially appealing. The section on Yugoslavia includes Kizer's prose poem on translation and nine poems translated from Macedonian, six of them by Bogomil Gjuzel and the other three by Radovan Pavlovski, Mateja Matevski, and Anté Popovkski.

Mihailovich, Vasa D. *A Comprehensive Bibliography of Yugoslav Literature in English, 1593-1980*. Columbus, Ohio: Slavica, 1984. Consult also the author's First Supplement, 1981-1985 (1988), the Second Supplement, 1986-1990 (1992), and the Third Supplement, 1991-1998 (1999). All are indispensable research tools.

Osers, Ewald, ed. *Contemporary Macedonian Poetry*. Translated by Eward Osers. London: Kultura/Forest Books, 1991. English translations of works by twenty-five poets, selected from volumes published since the early 1970's.

Padron, Justo Jorge. "Contemporary Poetry in Macedonia." *Equivalences*, no. 17 (1989): 7-21. Interesting views on Macedonian poetry by a Spanish poet and publisher, thus offering an outsider's perspective.

Szporer, Michael. Introduction to *Stremež* 30, nos. 4/5 (1986): 223-239. The editor of an important anthology of Macedonian poetry, Szporer writes down his views and impressions of this poetry, seeing different waves of poetic generations, and including women poets and younger poets hitherto inadequately represented.

Vasa D. Mihailovich
Updated by Rosemary M. Canfield Reisman

NATIVE AMERICAN POETRY

The first humans to inhabit the North American continent are believed to have arrived by crossing the land bridge over the Bering Strait, between ten and perhaps as many as fifty thousand years ago. During the long development of many highly elaborated cultures in the Western Hemisphere, a rich body of literature was produced, the earliest of which manifested itself as spoken, or oral, literature. Of that oral literature, some minute portion has been recorded in written texts and, more recently, in film and audiotape. Within contemporary traditional Indian communities, oral poetry is still being composed and performed.

ORAL TRADITIONS OF THE SOUTH AMERICAN INDIAN

The categories of verbal arts among peoples with oral cultures are not always the same as genres in written literatures. The English category of "verse," for example, has no counterpart in many North American Indian literatures. Speakers of indigenous languages may say, "We have no poetry in our language," meaning that spoken, metered verbal artifacts are not composed; the same languages may, however, have a highly developed song tradition, which will be recognized as comparable to the European concept of lyric. For example, the O'odham (Papago) of southern Arizona maintain that "poetry" as it is defined in English does not exist in their language, but they have many songs. Moreover, songs belong to a special category of verbal production; they are composed in a unique language used only for songs, and special composition processes and performance requirements go along with the production of songs. The following Papago song illustrates some of these characteristics:

> In the great night my heart will go out.
> Towards me the darkness comes rattling,
> In the great night my heart will go out.

The words and music were not consciously composed by the song's "owner" but were received in a dream from a person who had died. "Song dreaming" is a feature of traditional Papago literary composition. The function of the song, as part of a ritual intended to heal the sick and prevent death, is also characteristic of many oral poetic traditions.

LYRIC POETRY

In *Native American Literature* (1985), Andrew Wiget identified two major types of American Indian poetry: lyric poetry and ritual poetry. Lyric poetry, while it may have ritual or religious subject matter, is personal, expressive, and often highly emotional. Although composers and their audiences would be likely to divide songs into very different categories, non-Indian readers of translated lyrics may recognize familiar classifications such as love songs, elegies for grief, or lyrics of exultation and boastfulness. An elegy translated from Tlingit, a language spoken in coastal British Columbia, is by a woman whose brothers were drowned; it alludes to the place and manner of their death as she expresses the grieving emotions of sorrow, denial, and despair: "Your reef has beaten me, Kagwantan's children./ But take pity on me."

Not all lyrics are tied so closely to personal experience or emotion. Like other peoples, Native Americans have a large store of songs identified with various functions of daily living. Some recognizable categories are work songs, such as corn-grinding songs or rowing songs (which accompany the carrying out of repetitious tasks), lullabies, hunting songs, and gambling and game songs, such as the many songs still being composed to accompany the widespread hand game. Numerous traditional corn-grinding songs, some very old, are part of the literatures of the agricultural peoples of the Southwest. This corn-grinding song from the pueblo of Laguna, New Mexico, has characteristic forms and devices:

> I-o-ho, wonder-water,
> I-o-ho, wonder water,
> Life anew to him who drinks!
> Look where southwest clouds are bringing rain;
> Look where southeast clouds are bringing rain!

Like many others, this song contains vocables; these untranslatable syllables or phrases may be remnants of archaic languages, they may be part of the special poetic language reserved for songs, or they may simply be rhythmic units incorporated into the total structure of the song. Rain, water, and clouds appear repeatedly in all the songs and stories from this arid region. Directional signals are important for the continual expression of the people's relationship to the center of their universe; the balancing of southeast and southwest integrates the life of the community with the four cardinal directions.

RITUAL POETRY

Ritual poetry, in relation to lyric poems, is more communal and less personal in expression, composition, and performance. While the actual texts of ritual poems may appear quite short, often elements are intended to be repeated many times. In other cases, individual passages or poems may be part of much larger performance productions, great ceremonies lasting as long as eight or nine days, which could be considered whole poems or dramatic productions in themselves.

Wiget subdivides ritual poetry into integrative, restorative, and transformational modes. Integrative rituals function as rites of passage, assisting the individual to pass safely from one stage of life, or identity, to another. Thus there are ceremonies for birth and naming, for puberty and initiation into adulthood, for death and dying. Among the integrative songs, Wiget also includes healing songs intended to enable the sick or dying individual to make safe passage back to the community.

One of the most widely known healing songs is a lyric that forms part of the Navajo Night Chant. The Night Chant is a major ceremony of healing for the Navajo people; when performed in full it lasts ten days and nights and involves many ceremonial observances such as face and body painting, ingestion of medicines, dry painting of sacred pictures, and feasting and dancing. The poem is sung as part of the ceremonial activities of the third day; the words allude to a particular place, which is said to be the House of Dawn, and also to sacred or holy beings that are part of the spiritual reality of the Navajo people.

The Night Chant ceremony of which the song is a part is performed to cure and reintegrate the individual into a healthy, viable community. The title of N. Scott Momaday's Pulitzer Prize-winning novel, *House Made of Dawn* (1968), comes from this poem; the novel depicts the struggle of an alienated young man to heal himself of deep psychological distress and reintegrate himself into his Pueblo community. In the novel, the poem appears as sung by one of the characters; it becomes part of Abel's healing.

The words of this song, as translated by Washington Matthews, express fundamental Navajo ideas regarding the ideal relationship of the individual to the universe:

> Happily, with abundant dark clouds, may I walk.
> . . . .
> May it be beautiful all around me.
> In beauty it is finished.

The English word "beauty" is used to translate a Navajo term that encompasses concepts of balance, harmony, and movement through time. Balance is expressed in the alternation and repetition of parallel figures and tropes: Dawn and evening light, clouds and showers, and plants and pollen are paired and joined in the poem. The rhetorical pairing and doubling of pairs corresponds to the Navajo conceptualization of the universe: All entities are seen as gendered (hence the poem makes reference to "male rain" and "female rain"), and quaternary patterning in doubled pairs reflects the fundamental cognitive ordering principle. Four directions, four colors, four sacred mountains at the four corners of the world, four sacred plants, and countless other sets of four recur in all forms of Navajo discourse. The magnificent culmination of the poem expresses the sense of motion, centering, and balancing of four in the repositioning of the speaker at the center of a world of beauty: The four significant directions are before, behind, below, and above, and then comes the inclusive "all around."

Restorative poetry is a type Wiget defines as forming part of communal ceremonies devoted to redefining the origins and continuity of the community within the natural world. Such ceremonies characteristically incorporate references to myths of creation and origin; sometimes they are called "world-renewal" ceremonies. Like important rituals in other cultures, ceremonial observances in Native American traditions have some resemblance to dramatic performances. An early attempt to transcribe, describe, and translate such a ceremony of renewal is Alice Fletcher's work in the 1800's with the Hako ceremony of the Pawnee, which honors Mother Corn:

> Loud, loud the young eagles cry, cry, seeing their
> mother come;
> Flies she to them slantwise, flies;
> Then over the nest she hangs, there hovering, stays her
> flight;
> Thanks, thanks as we look we give.
> .   .   .   .
> Then over the nest she drops; there, folding her wings,
> she rests,
> Rests safely within her nest.

The translation reflects both Fletcher's nineteenth century conception of appropriate poetic diction and her attempt to replicate the rhythms she thought she heard in the original Pawnee. The poem displays the acute observation of natural phenomena characteristic of much Native American literature; it vividly renders the sight of the mother eagle approaching the nest, circling and seeming to hover, and finally settling on it. In addition, the poem reflects a particular moment in the ceremony. Fletcher's notes explain to the reader that these texts are part of rites involving feathers, meant to represent nest building and the relationship of parent and child in the founding myth.

Wiget finds transformational ritual and poetry in the Ghost Dance religion and its songs and rites. Such rituals, he maintains, attempt to negotiate passage between the death of some fundamental element in the culture and the origin or birth of a new order. They differ from world-renewal rites, which replicate an original mythic creation of the universe, by introducing the idea of a new reality not referable to the old, original order. Certain syncretic religious forms, such as the Yaqui Easter ceremonies (which incorporate Catholic and traditional motifs) or the North American peyote rite (which combines Mexican, Plains Indian, and Methodist elements) might also be included under this rubric.

Certain features recur characteristically in lyric and ritual poems of Native American cultures. Repetition is obvious and logical as a mnemonic device. The visual and verbal compression of many written translations of lyric texts, mistaken by the early twentieth century Imagist movement as a protomodernist, Native American form of literary Imagism, belies the effect of these texts' performance, for verses are customarily repeated, sometimes as many as thirty-six times. Striking visual imagery based on close observation of the natural world pervades the poems, but translated poems can be difficult to grasp or may mislead the English-speaking reader unfamiliar with their references to occasions of composition or reception or to places with which particular stories are associated. Thus, a song received from an animal or another being in a dream may be spoken in the persona of that creature, as are these lines from a hunting song:

> I ate the thornapple leaves
> And the leaves made me dizzy.
> I drank thornapple flowers
> And the drink made me stagger
> The hunter, Bow-remaining,
> He overtook and killed me,
> Cut and threw my horns away.

Not only are the sung words understood as spoken by the deer, but also the whole song forms part of a ceremony designed to assure a successful hunt by inducing the deer to sacrifice itself to the hunters. Part of the ceremony involves eating a mind-altering drug, *datura*, which the translator here calls "thornapple leaves." This song would be sung by a dancer who assumes the persona of the deer in the ceremony; the language refers simultaneously to the behavior of an actual deer, to the singer's dream, and to the circumstances of the rite.

RECORDING ORAL POETRY

The collection of written texts of Native American oral poetry begins with the preservation of some few of the great codices of the Mayas and the Aztecs of Mexico and Central America; many of these works were transported as curiosities to collections in Europe, and translations into European languages have been attempted from time to time. Serious attempts to transcribe and translate North American oral literatures began in the 1830's, when Henry Rowe Schoolcraft transcribed the legends and myths told to him by his wife and members of her Ojibwa family.

Somewhat later in the century, after the American Civil War, a major movement to record Native American languages and preserve records of native cultures was launched under the sponsorship of major museums, folklore societies, and, especially, the United States government through the Bureau of American Ethnology. The impetus for the project in "salvage ethnography" was a perception that American Indian cultures were inexorably disappearing, and it was important to preserve as much of their remains as possible before the expected end came. The preservationist motive led to collecting of texts primarily for purposes of linguistic study and ethnographic information, rather than as aesthetic objects in their own right. Nevertheless, some of the finest examples of literary translation come from this period; the translations of Matthews from Navajo and the studies of the musician Frances Densmore are particularly noteworthy. Such poems as were translated were published as parts of government reports, bulletins of learned societies, or articles in scholarly journals. From these sources were mined the selections presented in the earliest anthologies of traditional American Indian poetry.

A very early compendium of American Indian literature and song texts is Natalie Curtis's *The Indians' Book* (1907, 1968). Curtis intended her book to permit Indians to speak for themselves as much as possible; she took pains to use graphics by Indian artists, as well as to include musical notation to encourage performance of the songs. Her translation method remains the model for translating such texts today: Her fourfold presentation of each text included a transcription from the original language, a separate transcription with musical notation, an interlinear ("non-grammatical") literal translation, and a more "literary" poem text.

Curtis's collection was followed by *The Path on the Rainbow* (1918), edited by George W. Cronyn and reissued as *American Indian Poetry* (1962). Unlike Curtis, Cronyn did not himself collect the texts he printed from their Indian owners; he reprinted excerpts from the ethnological collections then being published in abundance. He was not particularly knowledgeable about Indian culture or literature, and he sometimes changed

texts he did not understand into something more conformable to his idea of the poetic. He also included non-Indian poems written by contemporaries who had been inspired by the modernist characteristics they perceived in Native American poems. Nevertheless, *The Path on the Rainbow* was the first collection to bring the literary accomplishments of Native American oral poets to the attention of the larger reading public.

Following Curtis and Cronyn, two anthologists working in the 1940's brought out responsibly edited general collections of Native American poetry and prose. Margot Astrov's *The Winged Serpent* (1946), reprinted as *American Indian Prose and Poetry* (1962), included some contextual notes to the texts and fragments she reprinted, as well as a reliable bibliography and helpful introduction. Astrov was the first to reprint the "House Made of Dawn" song from the Night Chant, and it was probably in her collection that Momaday found the poem he placed at the heart of his novel. In 1951, A. Grove Day published *The Sky Clears: Poetry of the American Indians*. Grove Day's book also reprints poems from ethnological and other publications but incorporates them into an extensive discussion of the literary, cultural, and historical backgrounds that form the context for the lyrics; the book is not so much an anthology as it is a scholarly introduction incorporating many texts as examples. This collection has the most comprehensive bibliography of sources for translated poem texts. A later collection of American Indian poetry is John Bierhorst's *The Sacred Path: Spells, Prayers, and Power Songs of the American Indians* (1983).

From the beginnings of such studies, translators, editors, and scholars have been in general agreement that lyric texts from Native American cultures correspond to poetry in English, whereas narrative texts are basically prose productions. In the 1960's, two linguistics specialists challenged this view by offering conceptualizations of Native American narratives as essentially poetic in nature. Dennis Tedlock and Dell Hymes, using different approaches and materials, initiated discussion of an aesthetic and linguistic discourse that they call ethnopoetics.

Tedlock, a field researcher, collected and translated texts from a number of poet-storytellers. The basis for his theory of ethnopoetics, and the illustrative translations, came out of his work with Zuñi storytellers in New Mexico. Tedlock's theory of poetry holds that phonetic components of language, such as pitch, pause, and stress, define the poetic line. He identifies patterning of these elements in Zuñi narratives and asserts that these tales must actually be regarded as narrative poems comparable to ballads or epics in other traditions. The explanation and examples of his theory are worked out in the introduction and texts he compiled in *Finding the Center: Narrative Poetry of the Zuñi Indians* (1972). The texts themselves are printed in Zuñi and English, with typographical cues such as capitals, superscripts, subscripts, and italics to indicate performance elements of pause, pitch, and stress.

Hymes's ethnopoetics theory derives from work with written texts. Hymes worked with texts collected by linguists working with peoples of the Northwest (Oregon, Washington, and British Columbia), notably the collections of Melville Jacobs. The ethnopoetic theory he developed from these works sees poetic patterning in rhetorical configurations of repetition, parallel, and chiasmus at the level of word, phrase, line, and plot element. This analysis led to reconfiguring printed versions of the stories to look less like prose and more like poetry, with parallel elements set off by line divisions and indentation. Many narrative texts that Hymes restructured in this way came to have an apparently dramatic structure, which he sometimes indicates by notations of act and scene divisions. Hymes did not publish an anthology of texts but printed examples of ethnopoetic renderings of stories in his major work *"In Vain I Tried to Tell You": Essays in Native American Ethnopoetics* (1981).

MODERN WRITTEN POETRY

By contrast with the long and rich history of oral poetry, written poetry by Native Americans is of relatively recent date. Two nineteenth century poets are noted by A. LaVonne Brown Ruoff in her introductory book *American Indian Literatures* (1990): John Rollin Ridge and Pauline Johnson. These two poets wrote conventional nineteenth century verse; they were followed in the first half of the twentieth century by writers such as Alexander Posey, who primarily produced fiction, satire, humor, and nonfiction and who wrote lit-

tle if any poetry. After World War II, in the 1950's and 1960's, a Native American Renaissance in literature began to take place; it continued in the 1970's and 1980's with a virtual explosion of poetry by young Native American writers.

NORA MARKS DAUENHAUER

Nora Marks Dauenhauer occupies a unique place among late twentieth century Native American poets. A fluent speaker of Tlingit, Dauenhauer is one of few poets who translate from the classical Native American languages. She undertook a massive project to publish significant works on Tlingit oral literature by the few remaining performers of that literature. She has written and edited many works on Tlingit language and literature, including *Haa Shuká, Our Ancestors: Tlingit Oral Narratives* (1987); *Haa Tuwunáagu Yís, for Healing Our Spirit: Tlingit Oratory* (1990), featuring a dual-language presentation that makes use of a free-verse format to suggest speech performance; and *Haa kusteeyí, Our Culture: Tlingit Life Stories* (1994). Dauenhauer's own poetry reflects an interest in formal experimentation as well as preoccupations of traditional Native American life; "Tlingit Concrete Poem," for example, uses the conventions of concrete poetry as well as mixing Tlingit and English in a visual pun. Her major collections include *The Droning Shaman* (1990) and *Live Woven with Song* (2000).

DUANE NIATUM

Another notable poet from the Pacific Northwest is Duane Niatum, who has published several collections, including *Songs for the Harvester of Dreams* (1981) and *The Crooked Beak of Love* (2000). Niatum also edited the most representative collection of contemporary American Indian poetry, *Harper's Anthology of Twentieth-Century Native American Poetry* (1986), which remained in print through 1999.

N. SCOTT MOMADAY

Although most widely noted as a writer of prose, fiction, and nonfiction, Kiowa writer N. Scott Momaday began his career as a poet. His major collection, *The Gourd Dancer* (1976), shows a variety of influences: the post-Symbolist poetics that intrigued his mentor and friend Yvor Winters; American Romanticism and anti-Romanticism of the nineteenth century, especially in the work of Emily Dickinson, whom

Momaday admires greatly; and oral traditions of both Native American and Euroamerican culture. His poetry finds a place in the meditative-contemplative tradition of Western literature. His complex and highly wrought poem "Before an Old Painting of the Crucifixion" displays characteristics typical of much of Momaday's work: a speaker, positioned before some visible object or vista, who silently contemplates the enigma of phenomena as they appear before him. Momaday's philosophical position in such poems resembles that of Wallace Stevens: Both poets assert the absolute cleavage between knowing mind and intractable external reality, and both affirm the power of the imagination to create coherence and significance beyond the nihilism of the mind-world abyss. Explicitly in interviews, and by implication in his writings, Momaday has expressed admiration for what he sees as the Native American sense of continuity and familiarity with nature; unlike the Romantic Western vision, Momaday says, American Indian philosophy does not see an unbridgeable chasm between mind and matter. His second novel, *The Ancient Child* (1990), an uneven work that contains some of his poetry published elsewhere, explores the possibility of undoing the split and restoring the old continuity with the natural world.

LAGUNA AND ACOMA

The Keresan-speaking pueblos of Laguna and Acoma in New Mexico, and their environs, have been home to four of the most productive younger Native American poets. Leslie Marmon Silko, Simon Ortiz, Paula Gunn Allen, and Carol Lee Sanchez all have family or childhood roots in the area.

LESLIE MARMON SILKO

Leslie Marmon Silko's best-known work, the novel *Ceremony* (1977), appeared a few years after her poetry collection *Laguna Woman* (1974); some of the poems from that volume as well as new works were incorporated into the later mixed-genre book *Storyteller* (1981). Although her theoretical emphasis is on narrative forms and she has spoken extensively on the process of storytelling and its function in maintaining identity and community, Silko's poems often tend to be brief first-person lyrics relying on natural imagery to convey deep personal emotion. An exception is "Story-

telling," which captures in its free-verse rhythms the give-and-take of storytelling in the communal situation as well as the sense of ancient myth that stands behind and lends coherence to chaotic present reality.

SIMON ORTIZ

Simon Ortiz, from the pueblo of Acoma, is unusual in living close to the landscape that inspires him and has informed his sense of generations of continuity with the land. His poetry is often sacramental in its reverence for the mysterious power of the particular place and in its outrage at desecrations perpetrated by materialism and commercialism; yet he reaches out, as in the collection titled *From Sand Creek: Rising in This Heart Which Is Our America* (1981), to embrace a vision of Indian (as distinct from tribal) identity and common purpose. Both this collection and his *After and Before the Lightning* (1994) interweave prose narrative and poetry, the latter to relate his experiences during a winter on the Rosebud Indian Reservation.

PAULA GUNN ALLEN

Paula Gunn Allen, born in New Mexico, maintained her continuity with land and landscape in imagination from the perspective of urban academia. Allen was outspoken in an ongoing project of reclaiming feminist thought from what she saw as middle-class Anglo values; in poems such as "Madonna of the Hills," she sets out to recover and celebrate the strength of women and to subvert facile judgments of victimization and superficial categories of beauty. Allen's major collections of poetry include *Skins and Bones: Poems, 1979-1987* (1988) and *Life Is a Fatal Disease: Collected Poems, 1962-1995* (1997). She also published fiction and criticism.

CAROL LEE SANCHEZ

Carol Lee Sanchez, of Laguna and Lebanese American heritage, is Allen's cousin. The poems of her *Conversations from the Nightmare* (1975), *She) Poems* (1995), and *From Spirit to Matter: New and Selected Poems, 1969-1996* (1997) make highly experimental use of traditional Pueblo and Indian material; "Open Dream Sequence" expresses the nightmare distortions of surrealist art, while "Tribal Chant" explores the question of dual identity in a synthesis of Spanish and English. Like Momaday, Wendy Rose, and Joy Harjo, Sanchez is a visual artist as well as a poet.

OJIBWA AND CHIPPEWA

Louise Erdrich and Gerald R. Vizenor, Ojibwa poets, both have roots in the woodlands area of the Great Lakes, though Erdrich belongs to the displaced Turtle Mountain Chippewa of North Dakota.

LOUISE ERDRICH

Widely recognized for her series of North Dakota novels as well as collaborations with her husband, Michael Dorris, Louise Erdrich published the poetry collections *Jacklight* (1984) and *Baptism of Desire* (1990). Both collections expand her exploration in her fiction of the clashes and dissonances brought about by membership in and loyalty to both Euroamerican and Native American traditions. The two books contain retellings of oral tales featuring the folk hero Potchikoo. The poignant poem series "The Butcher's Wife" in *Jacklight* explores the delicacy of feeling and violent passions of ordinary, unremarkable people. In *Baptism of Desire*, Erdrich celebrates, in a series of poems based on popular hagiographies, the Catholic folk beliefs that provide much of the comedy of her novels; other poems

Louise Erdrich (Michael Dorris)

in this collection express her continuing fascination with various occult symbol systems. Critics note her interest in exploring the tension between Christian and Anishinaabe belief systems, no doubt due to her own experiences as a person of mixed heritage. In 2003, she published *Original Fire: Selected and New Poems*, which contains her earlier poetry collections plus new poems, including a section "Original Fire," in which she focuses on relationships.

GERALD R. VIZENOR

Gerald R. Vizenor is one of the most prolific of American Indian authors, producing journalism, fiction, criticism, screenplays, and autobiography as well as poetry. He has lived in Asia for extended periods, first in Japan with the armed forces and then as a visiting professor in the People's Republic of China, and has incorporated into his work an appreciation for Asian literatures, particularly the very short Japanese form of haiku. *Seventeen Chirps* (1964, 1968) and *Slight Abrasions* (1966) are collections of Vizenor's haiku; appreciation of the imagistic compression of haiku also informs Vizenor's reworking in *Summer in the Spring* (1981) of Densmore's translations of Chippewa lyrics. In 1984, much of Vizenor's poetry was collected in *Matsushima: Pine Islands*.

OTHER NATIVE AMERICAN POETS

Joy Harjo, Carter Revard, and Linda Hogan are joined by a common heritage in Oklahoma, the old Indian Territory.

JOY HARJO

Joy Harjo, a distant relation of Creek writer Alexander Posey, is a musician as well as a painter and poet. Her poetry seeks an organic synthesis of visual and sound effects in what is often a dreamlike sense of metamorphosis and dissolution of cognitive boundaries. "Rainy Dawn," from her major collection *In Mad Love and War* (1990), is one of several prose vignettes in the volume; like many of her poems, it is dedicated to a family member. Later, she wrote two more collections of poetry: *The Woman Who Fell from the Sky* (1994) and *A Map to the Next World* (2000). Harjo, like many other poets, has combined her poetry with performing arts. She performs her work and plays saxophone with her band, Poetic Justice, which was originally envisioned as a musical vehicle to enhance her poetry but has become something more. In one of her later poems, she says, "All acts of kindness are lights in the war for justice." This sums up her theme dealing with politics. Her poetry goes beyond strictly Native American concerns; she explores the common American experience of immigration.

Both Harjo and Hogan, who is from a Chickasaw family, confront difficult social and political questions in their work. Harjo's elegy "For Anna Mae Pictou Aquash . . . ," dedicated to a young Native American woman apparently murdered by the Federal Bureau of Investigation, bears witness to ongoing persecution of those who work on behalf of the dispossessed.

LINDA HOGAN

Linda Hogan's poems frequently take up themes of poverty, deprivation, and injustice. In *Daughters, I Love You* (1981), reprinted in *Eclipse* (1983), she offers a series of meditations on the evil and destruction of the nuclear culture. Her fourth collection of poetry, *Seeing Through the Sun* (1985), is more diverse, as she deals with mixed-blood heritage, human strengths and weaknesses, use of the land, urban life, feminism, and environmentalism. She attempts to synthesize all life in these poems—herself and others, humans and their environment. In 1988, she produced another volume of poems, *Savings*, that deals with the flight of many Native Americans to the cities, where they led frustrated and desperate lives. *The Book of Medicines* (1993) focuses on Hogan's belief that women need to be the primary caretakers of the environment. The poems act as therapeutic prayers to enable humans to clean up and restore their planet. Both Hogan and Harjo offer social criticism through the first-person lyric.

CARTER REVARD

Osage poet Carter Revard, like Momaday, has won academic as well as literary honors. A professor and former Rhodes scholar, he has published fiction, autobiography, and criticism as well as poetry. Also like Momaday a compelling storyteller and enthusiastic raconteur, Revard is often at his best, as in "My Right Hand Don't Leave Me No More," when celebrating memories of his rambunctious, energetic family. Having grown up in the Dust Bowl Oklahoma of the Great Depression, Revard chronicles his experiences from a

childhood of poverty to his status as a respected scholar of medieval literature, using both forms and allusions ranging from Anglo-Saxon alliterative verse to tribal chants in such collections as *An Eagle Nation* (1993) and *Winning the Dust Bowl* (2001).

WENDY ROSE

Wendy Rose and Maurice Kenny express the distinctive sensibility of urban experience. Rose's tribal background is Hopi and Miwok, but her life has been lived in the urban centers of the West Coast. Trained as an anthropologist, she has written from both sides of the studier-and-studied divide of Western scholarship; her poem "Academic Squaw" (from the collection *Academic Squaw: Reports to the World from the Ivory Tower*, 1977) is an acerbic look at the academic world from the point of view of the object of study. One of Rose's most noted collections is *The Halfbreed Chronicles, and Other Poems* (1985); the title section contains a series of poems in which the personas of circus freaks, concentration camp survivors, and other victims offer stinging critiques of Western culture. Rose also produced *Lost Copper* (1986), in which her poems, or songs as some called them, reaffirmed her connection with the earth. In 1993, she issued *Going to War with All My Relations: New and Selected Poems*, and in 1994, *Bone Dance: New and Selected Poems, 1965-1993*, a major collection of selections from her previous collections and new poems. One critic said her poetry is able to "enhance our awareness of the human complexity of our social and moral dilemmas."

MAURICE KENNY

Rose's sometime collaborator Maurice Kenny is Mohawk and an award-winning poet, fiction writer, playwright, editor, and longtime resident of New York City. Kenny has been a publisher, directing the Strawberry Press; his poetry reflects some of the main currents in experimental literature in the mid-twentieth century, especially an affinity with the Beat generation. The opening lines from his "Wild Strawberry" carry resonances of Allen Ginsberg: "And I rode the Greyhound bus down to Brooklyn/ where I sit now eating woody strawberries/ grown on the backs of Mexican farmers." Kenny's work comprises both short and long poems. A book-length poem, *Tekonwatonti, Molly Brant, 1735-1795: Poems of War* (1992), chronicles the experiences of the sister of Mohawk leader Joseph Brant during the French and Indian War; she led her people in cooperation with the British, believing it the best way to preserve their Mohawk land and way of life. Kenny's many collections include *The Mama Poems* (1984) and *Between Two Rivers: Selected Poems, 1956-1984* (1987). Kenny's major poems and prose were collected in 1995 in *On Second Thought*, edited by Joseph Bruchac.

JOSEPH BRUCHAC

Joseph Bruchac, with an Abenaki, Slovak, and English heritage, was raised in the Adirondack foothills in New York. He is not only a well-known editor and chronicler of Native American literature but also a poet, a children's author, and a teller of traditional Native American tales. Like other poets, he has written and performed songs with his own musical group, the Dawn Land Singers. Collections of his poems include *Flow* (1975), *The Good Message of Handsome Lake* (1979), *Near the Mountains* (1987), and *No Borders* (1999). In an attempt to understand poets and their poetry, Bruchac interviewed Native American poets and put the results together in *Survival This Way* (1987). He edited *Returning the Gift* (1994), a book that contains poetry and prose from the first Native American National Writers' Festival, and *Smoke Rising: The Native North American Literary Companion* (1995), an anthology of works by thirty-five Native American writers.

OFELIA ZEPEDA

Ofelia Zepeda, a professor of linguistics, was born and raised near the Tohono O'odham (Papago) and Pima reservations in Arizona. She not only is the foremost authority in Tohono O'odham, having created the first grammar for the language, but also teaches many Native Americans strategies for preserving their vanishing languages. She has published several bilingual collections of her own poetry in English and Tohono O'odham, the most important of which is *Ocean Power* (1995), dealing with the importance of the desert climate to people who live in the arid Southwest. In this collection, she reflects on her life, the natural environment of the Arizona-Mexico border region, the seasons, the meeting of old and new, the past and the present, and the human and natural worlds. The closing poems take as their subject the sea, and the Tohono O'odham's past relationship with the sea. Much of the poetry is in the Tohono O'odham language, with English translations provided. Zepeda has also edited poetry collections, including *When It Rains, Papago and Pima Poetry = Mat hekid o ju: 'O'odham Ha-Ceg̃itodag* (1982), a collection of Papago and Pima poetry.

SHERMAN ALEXIE

Perhaps one of the most visible Native American writers to mainstream audiences is a Spokane/Cœur d'Alene Indian, Sherman Alexie, who grew up on an Indian reservation in Washington State. Soon after he was graduated from college, Alexie published two of his poetry collections: *The Business of Fancydancing: Stories and Poems* (1992) and *I Would Steal Horses* (1992). He shares with other contemporary Native American poets a love of performing his work, so he occasionally does readings and standup performances with musician Jim Boyd, a Colville Indian. Alexie is known for his humor as well as his performance ability. He and Boyd recorded an album, *Reservation Blues*, that contains songs from a novel of the same name that

Sherman Alexie (©Marion Ettlinger)

Alexie published in 1995. In June, 1998, Alexie competed in his first World Heavyweight Poetry Bout, in which he defeated world champion Jimmy Santiago Baca. Because of his poetry, short stories, novels, and screenwriting skills, in 1999, *The New Yorker* recognized Alexie as one of the top writers of the twentieth century. His collection of mixed poetry and prose *One Stick Song* (2000) reveals many of his skills: his ability to handle multiple perspectives and complex psychological subject matter, sense of humor, facility with vivid scene setting, and sweet sarcasm. Alexie gives voice to the feelings of many Native Americans combating society's negative perceptions of them, and the emotions here range from dark humor to anger to grief. His formula "Poetry = Anger × Imagination" is expressed throughout this collection and reflects the experiences and emotions of many Native Americans at the beginning of the twenty-first century.

DEFINING NATIVE AMERICAN

Native Americans or American Indians (the terms themselves are misleading) are no monolithic group: Although contemporary Native American poets are sometimes friends, colleagues, and collaborators, they do not form a distinctive school of poetry. Their formal allegiances are largely to experimental modes, although the first-person free-verse lyric tends to predominate, even in such apparently public modes as satire. Two major motifs can be identified as characteristic: on one hand, an abiding sense of continuity with the land (as distinguished from landscape), and on the other, a pervasive social consciousness stemming from the historical and personal experience of injustice. Ties to land, and meaning derived from survival within a given natural environment, are explicit in the works of poets such as Dauenhauer, Ortiz, and Silko; even urban poets such as Kenny and Rose look to severance from land as the precipitating injustice in their critique of contemporary civilization. Furthermore, in one way or another, each of these poets is engaged with the difficulties and delights of being at once an inheritor of ancient cultural riches and a mediator between worlds of affluence and deprivation. Each is committed to tribal and Indian heritage and sees that heritage as a source of strength for not only Native American people but also the world.

BIBLIOGRAPHY

Erdrich, Heid E., and Laura Tohe, eds. *Sister Nations: Native American Women Writers on Community*. St. Paul: Minnesota Historical Society Press, 2002. Foreword by Winona LaDuke. An anthology of short fiction, poetry, and essays, in which forty-nine women record their experiences as members of Native Americans communities. Includes brief biographies of the contributors and information about their tribes.

Fast, Robin Riley. *The Heart as a Drum: Continuance and Resistance in American Indian Poetry*. Ann Arbor: University of Michigan Press, 1999. The author, who also has written on traditional American poets such as Emily Dickinson, covers the topics of audience, community, "Talking Indian," telling stories, and "Toward a Native Poetics of Contested Spaces."

Harjo, Joy. *The Spiral of Memory: Interviews*. Ann Arbor: University of Michigan Press, 1995. Harjo has a unique poetic voice that speaks of her experiences as Native American, woman, and Westerner in today's society. This book collects interviews with her over the years, covering her art, her origins, and the confrontation of Anglo and Native American civilizations.

Lincoln, Kenneth. *Sing with the Heart of a Bear: Fusions of Native and American Poetry, 1890-1999*. Berkeley: University of California Press, 1999. Lincoln examines contemporary poetry by way of ethnicity and gender. He tries to explain American as well as Native American literature, spirituality, and culture.

Lundquist, Suzanne Evertsen. *Native American Literatures: An Introduction*. New York: Continuum, 2004. An essential research tool for study of Native American literature. Includes not only a broad overview of the history and scope of Native American literature but also studies of individual authors and works. Includes excellent resources for further research.

Porter, Joy, and Kenneth M. Roemer, eds. *The Cambridge Companion to Native American Literature*. New York: Cambridge University Press, 2005. Contains seventeen scholarly essays on a wide range of subjects, including several that focus specifically on poetry and poets. Biobibliographies of forty authors. Time line and maps. An invaluable resource and guide.

Rader, Dean, and Janice Gould, eds. *Speak to Me Words: Essays on Contemporary American Indian Poetry*. Tucson: University of Arizona Press, 2003. A collection of critical essays on the genre. Includes Native American and nonnative authors, men and women, recognized experts and newcomers, using various critical and theoretical approaches. Subjects of the essays range from form and structures of poetry to self-definition or the identity of an entire community.

Ramsey, Jarold, and Lori Burlingame, eds. *In Beauty I Walk: The Literary Roots of Native American Writing*. Albuquerque: University of New Mexico Press, 2008. An anthology that places traditional oral selections beside modern works by Native Americans to demonstrate how present-day writers both use and reject the earlier tradition.

Rosen, Kenneth, ed. *Voices of the Rainbow: Contemporary Poetry by Native Americans*. New York: Arcade, 1993. Rosen has collected two hundred poems by twenty-one Native Americans, representing many tribes: Laguna, Sioux, Cheyenne, Pueblo, Chippewa, Oneida, Seneca/Seminole, Mohawk, and Blackfoot.

Rothberg, Jerome, ed. *Shaking the Pumpkin: Traditional Poetry of the Indian North Americas*. Rev. ed. Albuquerque: University of New Mexico Press, 1991. The author, who also has written on ethnopoetics, has assembled a large collection of poetry, exceeding four hundred pages. Selected poets include Leslie Marmon Silko.

Swann, Brian, ed. *Native American Songs and Poems: An Anthology*. New York: Dover, 1997. A good cross-section of Native American songs and poetry. The poems range from lullabies to works by contemporary modern authors, both male and female.

Wilson, Norma. *The Nature of Native American Poetry*. Albuquerque: University of New Mexico Press, 2000. A collection of appealing and accessible essays that introduce and celebrate the poetry of modern Native American writers. Wilson draws from contemporary criticism, tribal history and folklore, interviews with writers, and the poetry itself. She places Native American poetry in a global and historical context.

Helen Jaskoski; Gary Zacharias
Updated by Christina J. Moose

POLISH POETRY

Poland's acceptance of Christianity in its Western form in 966 resulted in the long-lasting domination of Latin as the language of written communication. It was three centuries later that Polish emerged as the language of literature. Paradoxically, the first known poem in Polish is, at the same time, the most accomplished literary product of the whole medieval period. "Bogurodzica" (Mother of God), an anonymous religious hymn from the thirteenth century preserved in a fifteenth century manuscript, consists of two stanzas with a highly complex parallel construction and sophisticated verse structure. Such a masterly piece could not have been created in a cultural vacuum; some tradition of oral poetry in Polish must have existed around that time, although nothing except "Bogurodzica" has been preserved in a written form.

Throughout the fourteenth and fifteenth centuries, Polish literature was characterized by the prevalence of religious poetry. The increasing participation of laypeople in religious life brought about the growth of popular devotional literature in the vernacular. Its lyric genre breaks down thematically into Lenten and Easter songs, Christmas carols, hymns to the Virgin Mary, and so on. While being, for the most part, adaptations from Latin, some of these poems manage to strike an original note. "Żale Matki Boskiej pod Krzyżem" (the lament of the Mother of God at the foot of the Cross), a first-person monologue, is distinguished by its individualized point of view and emotional intensity. The epic genre was poorly represented in Polish literature of this period. "Legenda o św. Aleksym" (legend of Saint Alexis), for example, is a typical verse hagiography, drawing on foreign sources and rather primitive in its form.

Polish secular poetry of the Middle Ages is less homogeneous. What has been preserved is a mosaic of poems written for various purposes and with various results. Some of them are merely mnemonic devices, while others are didactic or satiric; there are some shy attempts at erotic poetry as well. Perhaps the most interesting secular poem of the period is the fifteenth century "Rozmowa mistrza ze śmiercia" (conversation of a master with death); one of numerous variations on the medieval theme of *memento mori*, it stands out by virtue of its vivid imagery and macabre humor.

In its versification, Polish medieval poetry was apparently based on a system of relative syllabism, with lines equal to clauses and approximative rhymes. Judgments concerning the verse forms of this period, however, remain highly conjectural.

THE RENAISSANCE

Western European Humanism made its way into Poland as early as the second half of the fifteenth century, but it was only a hundred years later that the golden age of the Polish Renaissance came into full swing. Meanwhile, a few poets emerged who represent the period of transition.

BIERNAT OF LUBLIN

The first Polish poet whose biography is at least partly known is Biernat of Lublin (c. 1465-after 1529). *Raj duszny* (1513; paradise of the soul), his translation of a Latin prayer book, was thought until quite recently to be the first Polish book ever printed. His major poetic work, however, was *Zywot Ezopa Fryga* (c. 1522; the life of Aesop the Frygian). The first part of this work is a rhymed biography of the legendary Aesop; the second part presents a collection of fables supposedly told by him. The work expresses the philosophy of plebeian Humanism, but its style, versification, and humor are still of a distinctly medieval kind.

MIKOLAJ REJ

Another transitional figure, although much closer to the Renaissance mentality, was Mikolaj Rej (1505-1569), called, perhaps with some exaggeration, the father of Polish literature. A country squire with almost no formal education, he wrote prolifically all of his life and wrote exclusively in Polish. He therefore was not typical of the Renaissance epoch, which demanded from a writer equal fluency in Polish and Latin. Rej's stubborn defense of the vernacular was, however, also a result of the more general phenomenon of the awakening of national consciousness in the beginnings of the Renaissance. He was quite original in his appreciation of specifically Polish traits and ways of life. His poetry is mostly didactic, descriptive, or satiric, and it ranges from enormous versified treatises or dialogues to brief epigrams. As a poet, Rej undeniably lacks subtlety and artistic balance; his strengths are his passion for the particulars of life and his straightforward stylistic manner.

JAN KOCHANOWSKI

After all the shortcomings of his predecessors, the work of Jan Kochanowski (1530-1584) appears as a shining example of artistic perfection. He was a rare genius, not to be matched by any other poet of the Slavic world for the next two centuries. Kochanowski's work represents the Polish Renaissance in its most mature and refined form. A thoroughly educated Humanist, he was indebted to the classical heritage as well as to contemporary poetry of Italy and France, but he was able to give his writing a national specificity and personal tone. The bulk of his work is written in Polish, which he himself raised to the rank of a proficient literary language. His Polish output includes the collections *Fraszki* (1584; trifles), *Pieśni* (1586; songs), and *Treny* (1580; *Laments*, 1928); a masterly poetic adaptation of the Psalms, *Psalterz Dawidów* (1578); several epic poems; and a classical tragedy in verse, *Odprawa posłów greckich* (1578; *The Dismissal of the Grecian Envoys*, 1928). If the Anacreontic *Fraszki* and Horatian *Pieśni* present Kochanowski as a classical, well-balanced mind that enjoys the *aurea mediocritas* of everyday life, his *Laments* has a radically different tone. Written after the death of his young daughter, this sequence of funeral elegies presents a wide range of changing feelings, from utter despair and doubt to reconciliation with God. The poet's usually lucid and sedate style acquires an almost baroque complexity and tension.

Kochanowski's general influence on the subsequent phases of Polish poetry was enormous. Perhaps his most durable legacy was his contribution to the development of Polish versification. The radical change he carried out consisted of replacing the remnants of relative syllabism with a strictly syllabic system, with exact rhyme, stabilized caesura, and paroxytonic cadence. This rigor allowed him freedom to employ enjambments and thus make intonation and syntax in-

dependent of the verse structure. He was also able to introduce a bewildering variety of verse formats and stanza patterns. Despite the nineteenth century success of the more melodious syllabotonism, Kochanowski's syllabism remains one of the active verse systems of Polish poetry, and only since the beginnings of the twentieth century has it been rivaled seriously by tonism and free-verse systems.

MIKOLAJ SEP SZARZYŃSKI

A peculiar feature of Polish literary history is that its classical periods never last long. As early as the second half of the sixteenth century—that is, at the zenith of the Renaissance—new literary phenomena were foreshadowing the arrival of the Baroque. Oddly enough, Mikolaj Sep Szarzyński (1550-1581) was a full-fledged Baroque poet. His only collection, *Rytmy abo wiersze polskie* (published posthumously in 1601; Polish rhythms or verses), has been rediscovered and appreciated in recent decades, after centuries of oblivion. Szarzyński was a poet with a small output but endowed with extraordinary creative force. In particular, a handful of his metaphysical sonnets, which reveal his spiritual torment and religious crisis by means of tortuous syntax, violent enjambments, and oxymoronic imagery, bear comparison with the best of John Donne and George Herbert.

OTHER RENAISSANCE POETS

Compared with Kochanowski's perfection and Szarzyński's intensity, other poets of the Polish Renaissance seem definitely minor figures; however, some of them are not without significance. Sebastian Grabowiecki (1540-1607) was an author of quite refined devotional lyricism. Sebastian Fabian Klonowicz (1545-1602) wrote lengthy descriptive poems that abound with picturesque details. Szymon Szymonowicz (1558-1629) is best remembered as the author of the half-bucolic, half-realistic *Sielanki* (1614; idylls), a highly valuable contribution to the pastoral genre.

THE BAROQUE

After a brief, though brilliant, golden age in the Renaissance, Polish culture, prompted by the rapid progress of the Counter-Reformation, entered the prolonged era of the Baroque. In poetry, the new Baroque style soon evolved into two different manners, sociologically distinguished by the cultural horizons of royal or aristocratic court life, on one hand, and those of the petty gentry's manor life, on the other. While the former, more cosmopolitan, manner strongly resembled the Western European Baroque of Giambattista Marino and Luis de Góngora y Argote, the latter style, often called the Sarmatian Baroque, was much more local and conservative. Apart from these two trends within the vernacular, the tradition of classical poetry written in Latin was still cultivated. Maciej Kazimierz Sarbiewski (Mathias Casimirus Sarbievius; 1595-1640), who has been dubbed the "Polish Horace," achieved pan-European fame under the name of Casimire as an author of Latin odes as well as of the influential treatise *De perfecta poesi* (early seventeenth century).

Polish Marinism had its most illustrious representative in Jan Andrzej Morsztyn (1613-1693), who could also be compared with the English Cavalier poets. A courtier and statesman, in his opinions he was close to French libertinism, and his poetry shunned any didactic purpose. While considering writing a kind of entertainment, he nevertheless focused on the poetic analysis of the paradoxes of worldly happiness. The paradoxes of love are illustrated in Morsztyn's poetry by a wide variety of striking conceits, in which there is as much frivolity as metaphysical fear. The complex interplay of symmetries, oppositions, and contrasts makes many of his brief poems masterpieces of construction. Besides Morsztyn, the Polish line of wit was represented by, among others, his relative Zbigniew Morsztyn (1624-1698), author of erotic poetry as well as devotional "emblems," and Daniel Naborowski (1573-1640), author of dazzling poems close in style to Italian *concettismo*.

While the court poets excelled in brief lyric or epigrammatic forms, the powerful current of the Sarmatian Baroque was more diversified in this respect. Its choice of genres and styles ranged from pure, songlike lyrics to enormous epic poems. The lyric branch is best represented by Szymon Zimorowic (1608-1629), whose only book, *Roksolanki* (1654; Ruthenian girls), was published posthumously by his brother, Józef Bartlomiej Zimorowic (1597-1673), himself an interesting poet in the same vein. *Roksolanki* is an ingeniously composed sequence of songs or lyric monologues of country girls and boys, stylistically alluding to folk poetry and sounding the psychological mysteries of love with subtle simplicity. Kasper Miaskowski (1550-1622), on the other hand, was perhaps the most gifted representative of early Baroque poetry of nature; his *Zbiór rytmów* (1612; collected rhythms) added metaphysical depth to the traditional style of pastoral poetry.

What dominated, however, in the middle and late phases of Polish Baroque poetry were moralism, didacticism, satire, and a taste for historical epic. The historical epic was introduced in 1618 with a splendid adaptation of Torquato Tasso's *Gerusalemme liberata* (1581; *Jerusalem Delivered*, 1600) by Jan Kochanowski's nephew, Piotr Kochanowski. The poet who supremely exemplified all of these trends was Waclaw Potocki (1621-1696), a petty nobleman who, in the seclusion of his country manor, wrote an immense amount of verse, including the epic *Wojna chocimska* (1670, 1850; the war of Khotim) and the collections *Moralia* (1688) and *Ogród fraszek* (1907; a garden of trifles). Samuel Twardowski (1600-1661) was another poet of this type. In addition to writing yet another historical epic, the posthumously published *Wojna domowa* (1681; a civil war), he achieved some originality in his mythological tale in verse, *Dafnis drzewem bobkowym* (1638; Daphne transformed into a laurel tree), and in the poetic romance *Nadobna Paskwalina* (1655; the lovely Pasqualina). Krzysztof Opaliński (1609-1655), a magnate and statesman, was the most prominent representative of the satiric bent in Baroque poetry. Finally, Wespazjan Kochowski (1633-1700) was the central figure of the late Baroque; his collection of lyric poems and epigrams *Nieprózujace prózowanie* (1674; unleisurely leisure) surpasses the average production of those years in its technical finesse, and his long poem in biblical prose *Psalmodia polska* (1695; a Polish psalmody) is an early expression of messianic Polish historiosophy, full of powerful images and striking metaphors.

The so-called Saxonian Night, covering the first sixty years of the eighteenth century, marked a general decline in Polish culture. Polish poetry of this period, still dominated by the Sarmatian Baroque, was becoming monotonous in its shallow bigotry and its reliance

on worn-out conceits. The last great triumph of Baroque imagery and style—although a much belated
one—occurred around 1768, when the gentry uprising
called the Confederacy of Bar triggered an outburst of
anonymous poetic creativity. Some of the songs written at that time are gems of religious and patriotic
lyricism.

THE ENLIGHTENMENT

In the mid-1760's, new tendencies began to dominate the Polish cultural scene. Under the reign of the
last Polish king, Stanisław August Poniatowski (1732-
1798), the ideology of the Enlightenment rapidly gained
ground, coinciding with a renewed interest in Western
(especially French) cultural novelties. In poetry, the
last decades of the eighteenth century were marked by
another brief resurgence of neoclassicism. The purification of language (after the damage done by Baroque
writers with their habit of interpolating Latinisms into
their already ornate style) went hand in hand with a return to discipline and clarity in writing. Classical genres, including descriptive poems, mock epics, odes,
epistles, satires, fables, and epigrams, were revived
during this period.

BISHOP IGNACY KRASICKI

Among the circle of poets close to the royal court
and supporting the king's reformist policies, the most
outstanding was undoubtedly Bishop Ignacy Krasicki
(1735-1801). An extraordinarily gifted satirist, he made
a stir in 1778 by publishing anonymously his *Mona-
chomachia albo wojna mnichów* (monomachia, or the
war of the monks), a mock epic in ottava rima ridicul-
ing the obscurantism and indulgence of monks. As a satiric poet, he reached his climax in *Satyry* (satires published between 1779 and 1784), a series of penetrating
ironic observations of contemporary morals that succeeded in being didactic without an intrusive rhetoric.
Another of his masterpieces is the collection *Bajki i
przypowieści* (1779; fables and parables), later complemented by *Bajki nowe* (1802; new fables). Under
Krasicki's pen, the old genre of the animal fable acquired a new form, close to epigram and characterized
by conciseness. Krasicki's great virtues as a poet are his
ironic wit and stylistic precision. Despite his apparently
optimistic didacticism, his humor is often bitter and

disillusioned: He understood humanity too well to be
fooled by wishful thinking.

STANISŁAW TREMBECKI

A poet of almost equal stature was Stanisław Trembecki (1735-1812), another favorite of the enlightened
monarch. A libertine and courtier, he wrote with equal
ease political odes to the king and obscene, erotic poems. Trembecki's highest achievements, however, are
his Rococo Anacreontics and his descriptive poem
Sofjówka (Sophie's garden), which first appeared in a
periodical in 1806 and was published in book form in
1822. Trembecki also excelled in poetic fables, as a rule
more extensive and elaborate than the epigrammatic fables of Krasicki. In contrast to the latter's clarity and
moderation, Trembecki's style is expressive and colorful, always striving for emotional extremes; he remained as close to the Baroque as a poet of the Enlightenment could afford to be.

OTHER ENLIGHTENMENT POETS

Generally, though, the stylistic options of the Polish
Enlightenment were contained between a strict classicism and a pre-Romantic sentimentalism. The former is
exemplified by the work of Bishop Adam Stanisław
Naruszewicz (1733-1796); its belated extension can be
seen in the conservative and rigid stance of the so-
called Pseudoclassicists, including Kajetan Koźmian
(1771-1856) and Ludwik Osiński (1775-1838), during
the first decades of the nineteenth century. The trend of
sentimentalism, on the other hand, surfaced in lyric
songs and eclogues by Dionizy Kniaźnin (1750-1807)
and Franciszek Karpiński (1741-1825), who at their
best were able to produce fine examples of simplicity
and emotional directness. Another link between the
Enlightenment and Romanticism can be discerned in
the poetic work of the versatile writer Julian Ursyn
Niemcewicz (1757-1841): He was the first to popular-
ize the genre of the ballad through both his translations
and his original poetry.

ROMANTICISM

In Polish literary history, Romanticism is not simply another period. Its growth coincided with political
events that made literature, and particularly Romantic
poetry, the most powerful means of shaping the na-

tional mentality. One of the most conspicuous features of Polish Romanticism, however, is the enormous disparity between a few literary giants and all other poets of the period, as regards both their artistic innovation and their spiritual leadership. It is significant that the specifically Polish notion of the *wieszcz* (a "bard," but also a prophet) has been applied only to Adam Mickiewicz, Juliusz Słowacki, and Zygmunt Krasiński; twentieth century opinion has added Cyprian Kamil Norwid as the last of the great four. It is also significant that all four poets achieved their prominence in exile; their works, of unprecedented value to the spiritual life of the oppressed Polish nation, were written mostly in Paris.

Since 1795, the date of the final partition of Poland—when the Polish nation ceased to exist as an even nominally sovereign state and was divided among Russia, Prussia, and Austro-Hungary—the rhythm of Polish literary life has been defined, first and foremost, by the chronology of political events. Thus, the period of domination of great Romantic poetry is framed by the dates of two abortive insurrections against czarist Russia, in 1831 and 1863. The starting point of Polish Romanticism in a broader sense, however, is 1822, the year that saw publication of the first collection of poems by Mickiewicz.

ADAM MICKIEWICZ

Adam Mickiewicz (1798-1855) entered Polish literature as a young student at the University of Wilno and soon became the central figure within the rapidly emerging Romantic movement. His early work was still strongly influenced by the heritage of the Enlightenment; "Oda do młodości" ("Ode to Youth"), for example, is a peculiar combination of classical rhetoric and the new Storm and Stress ideology. Well read in Johann Wolfgang von Goethe, Friedrich Schiller, and Lord Byron, Mickiewicz developed his own Romantic style. His first volume, *Ballady i romanse* (1822; ballads and romances), was an audacious manifesto of a specifically Polish version of early Romanticism, in which references to native folklore provide ample means to introduce elements of fantasy and the supernatural and to express the "living truths" of emotions and sentiments. Mickiewicz's debut was hailed as a literary revolution by his own generation but was de-

spised by the "old ones," the rationalistic classicists. The ensuing strife between the Romantics and the classicists was fueled by Mickiewicz's subsequent publications during the 1820's. Two tales in verse, *Grażyna* (1823; English translation, 1940) and *Konrad Wallenrod* (1828; English translation, 1883), parts 2 and 4 of the poetic drama *Dziady* (1823; *Forefathers' Eve*, 1925), and the brilliant sequence of *Sonety krymskie* (1826; *Sonnets from the Crimea*, 1917) all offer an entirely new set of stylistic devices and ideological proposals. The stress falls on the Romantic notions of frenetic love, the tragic loneliness of the hero, and the value of individual sacrifice. While the diction of these works admits anticlassical regionalisms, colloquialisms, and exoticisms, the poet retains what he achieved in his classical training: conciseness, precision, and an infallible exactness in his choice of words and construction of metaphors.

Mickiewicz's leading role becomes apparent when contrasted with the emergence of other early Romantics. Antoni Malczewski (1793-1826) left behind only one work, though a highly valuable one: the Byronic tale in verse *Maria* (1826). Józef Bogdan Zaleski (1802-1866) was an author of serene, songlike lyrics alluding to the forms of folk poetry. Seweryn Goszczyński (1801-1876) appeared as an extreme example of political radicalism, which he professed particularly in the tale in verse *Zamek kaniowski* (1828; Kaniów Castle).

None of these poets achieved a position comparable to that of Mickiewicz. After the 1831 defeat of the November Insurrection, Mickiewicz became the uncrowned prince of Polish poets, many of whom settled in Paris as political refugees. He had already initiated, in *Konrad Wallenrod* and in some of the lyric poems of the late 1820's, a new thematic current in Romantic poetry: the theme of patriotic struggle and heroic sacrifice. After the shattering of the nation's hopes in 1831, Mickiewicz's patriotism acquired new, historiosophical and metaphysical dimensions, while in his poetic art he constantly sought new forms of expression. Part 3 of *Dziady* (1832; *Forefathers' Eve*, 1944-1946) offered a new vision of Poland's national destiny as well as a new step in the development of Romantic drama; the work is a masterpiece of innovative construction, style, and verse. Only two years later, Mickiewicz published a completely different book, yet another masterpiece, his greatest: *Pan Tadeusz: Czyli, Ostatni Zajazd na litwie historia Szlachecka zr. 1811 i 1812 we dwunastu ksiegach wierszem* (1834; *Pan Tadeusz: Or, The Last Foray in Lithuania, a Tale of Gentlefolk in 1811 and 1812, in Twelve Books in Verse*, 1917), a Homeric epic on the poet's homeland, the Polish-Lithuanian province at the time of Napoleonic wars, in which nostalgia and sorrow mix with warm humor and discreet irony. Thanks to both the subtlety of its narration (the interplay of the narrator's identification with and distance from the reality presented) and its stylistic richness, *Pan Tadeusz* remains to this day the crowning achievement of Polish epic poetry. After its publication, Mickiewicz, more and more absorbed in mystical soul-searching and political activity, lapsed into silence as a poet, interrupted only by a brief sequence of the so-called Lausanne poems (written in 1839), purely lyric in character and strikingly innovative in their use of indirect symbolic language.

JULIUSZ SŁOWACKI

Mickiewicz's authority as the primary poet of the Polish nation was never seriously challenged in his lifetime; his main rival, another exile, Juliusz Słowacki (1809-1849), was not appreciated by his contemporaries as he deserved to be, though his fame eclipsed Mickiewicz's for a time only a half century after the death of both men. Słowacki's voluminous output includes various genres, from lyric poems through poetic dramas to tales in verse and visionary epics. His plays are an extremely important contribution to Polish Romantic poetry as well as to the theater. Written mostly in verse, they experiment with both versification and dramatic construction; their settings are variously realistic, historical, fairy-tale-like or legendary, dreamlike or symbolic. In his poems, Słowacki was able to move freely from epic description to lyric digression and from complex stanza patterns to biblical prose. His long poem in ottava rima *Beniowski* (1841) is a magnificent example of the genre of "poem of digressions" and of Romantic irony, close in its style to Byron's *Don Juan* (1819-1824) and Alexander Pushkin's *Evgeny Onegin* (1825-1832, 1833; *Eugene Onegin*, 1881). The most impressive product of the last, "mystical" period in Słowacki's short life was an immense (even though

unfinished) poem, also in ottava rima, titled *Król-Duch* (1847; king-spirit), a mythological vision of Polish destiny shown through consecutive reincarnations of the nation's spirit. Słowacki's significance lies not only in his matchless technical virtuosity but also—and more important—in the fact that in his last phase, he was an early forerunner of Symbolism. Significantly, his fame grew rapidly in the 1890's and 1900's. His dazzling imagery and stylistic fireworks are in exact opposition to Mickiewicz's sparing and concrete manner; in fact, with all of his uniqueness taken into account, Słowacki can be considered the most typically Romantic of all Polish Romantic poets.

ZYGMUNT KRASIŃSKI

General critical opinion concerning the other two poets of the nineteenth century "great four" has dramatically changed in the twentieth century. Zygmunt Krasiński (1812-1859), for some time praised for his poetic genius, today is appreciated mostly as an author of fascinating letters and two political plays, the first of which, *Nie-boska komedia* (pr. 1835; *The Undivine Comedy*, 1924), written in 1833, is a prophetic analysis of revolution. With a perspicacious and sophisticated mind, Krasiński nevertheless lacked both Mickiewicz's poetic force and Słowacki's craftsmanship. His long poems *Przedświt* (1843; dawning) and *Psalmy przyszłości* (1845; psalms of the future), though interesting as expressions of his conservative historiosophy, have dated badly.

KAMIL NORWID

The posthumous career of the work of Cyprian Kamil Norwid (1821-1883) presents a stark contrast with Krasiński's diminishing popularity. Forgotten and isolated in his lifetime and discovered only several decades after his death, today he is considered the spiritual and artistic harbinger of modern Polish poetry. One generation younger than Mickiewicz, Norwid developed his art both under the influence of and as a polemic against Polish Romanticism. He replaced the prevalent Romantic attitude of nationalistic messianism with his original version of humanistic universalism: a concept of modern humanity as the heir to the great civilizations of the past. From this point of view, Norwid tried to analyze the most essential problems of history, politics, and culture. Although he employed a wide variety of genres and forms, he was certainly most successful in his brief lyric poems, distinguished by their highly intellectual content. In particular, his collection of one hundred such poems, *Vade-mecum* (written before 1866), offers an astonishingly modern model of poetry. The poems included are semantically dense, ambiguous, and often obscure; they replace an easy melodiousness with irregular verse in which rhythm and intonation adjust to the flow of thoughts. Norwid's poems can be analyzed as a constant dialogue with an implied reader who is forced to assume a much more active part in deciphering the poem's meanings than is usually required in Romantic poetry.

OTHER ROMANTIC POETS

In contrast to the achievement of the four great émigrés, the so-called "domestic" offshoot of Polish Romantic poetry was of rather inferior quality. Among the multitude of poets who wrote at that time, only a few names rise above the average. Kornel Ujejski (1823-1897) reached a large readership with his poems of patriotic lamentation. Ryszard Berwiński (1819-1879) was a bard of social revolution and an ironic observer of contemporary society. The strongest suit of Teofil Lenartowicz (1822-1893) was a lyric poetry imbued with stylistic references to folklore.

THE POST-ROMANTIC AND NEO-ROMANTIC PERIODS

The 1863 defeat of the January Uprising, another insurrection against the czarist oppressors, generated a distrust in Romantic ideology and particularly in Romantic poetry: The ensuing epoch of Positivism was definitely an antipoetic age. In literature, there was a general shift toward realistic and naturalistic fiction and drama. Only a few names of relative significance emerged in the field of poetry during this period. Adam Asnyk (1838-1897) owed his popularity to the post-Romantic conventions through which he expressed his anti-Romantic convictions. Maria Konopnicka (1842-1910) wrote in accordance with Positivism as far as its reformist tendency was concerned; her poetry of social criticism and defense of the oppressed is characterized by its skillful use of elements of folklore and its introduction of a speaker from the lower classes.

In the last decade of the nineteenth century, the "prosaic" epoch of Positivism gave way to another era of poetry. This new trend, variously called Young Poland, modernism, or neo-Romanticism, was strongly influenced by Western European Symbolism and the philosophy of Friedrich Nietzsche and Arthur Schopenhauer, but it also gave vent to specifically Polish doubts and perplexities. The Positivist program of social reform had evidently failed; it had been unable to find any cure for Poland's political enslavement. Thus, the end of the century marked the apogee of an ideological crisis: Literature was polarized between naturalistic objectivism in fiction and prosaic drama, and Symbolist or expressionist subjectivism in poetic drama and lyricism.

Perhaps the most typical representative of the decadent mood of the end of the century was Kazimierz Przerwa Tetmajer (1865-1940), who in his lyric poems published in the 1890's set up an emotional pattern for the whole generation of Young Poland—a norm of sensitivity consisting of pessimism, individualism, distrust of any dogma, and a despondency that easily turned into a cult of sensual pleasure. Other poets of this period underwent a more complicated development. Jan Kasprowicz (1860-1926), for example, started with naturalistic depictions of peasants' poverty and after intermediary stages of Symbolism and expressionism ended as a serene poet of reconciliation with God and with the world. What is most interesting in his work is his progress from a Promethean rebellion to a final Franciscan acceptance of Being; from the technical point of view, his late poems are an important contribution to tonism, a system of verse based on an equal number of stresses rather than syllables.

Stanisław Wyspiański (1869-1907), best known as a dramatist, was perhaps the most Romantic of all poets of Young Poland: He revived the genre of poetic drama and enriched it with Symbolist imagery. His visionary plays refer to both Polish history and contemporary events, mingling mythological or legendary figures with historical or present-day characters. Tadeusz Miciński (1873-1918), also an innovative (though less popular) playwright, wrote lyric poetry that anticipated expressionism; his only collection, *W mroku gwiazd* (in the darkness of stars), was published in 1902.

Leopold Staff (1878-1957) lived long enough to

participate in three consecutive literary epochs; within Young Poland, he represented the trend of Nietzscheanism, a trend opposing Decadence and favoring classical lucidity. In contrast to the majority of his poetic generation, he was aware of changing attitudes, and his model of poetry appealed to the tastes of the next generations. Indeed, his popularity has never diminished, and the last volume that he published, *Wiklina* (1954; osiers), amazingly modern in its style and versification, is undoubtedly his highest achievement.

The epoch of Young Poland abounded with poets, and its lyric style soon degenerated into worn-out conventions. Some of the second-rate poets, however, are a cut above the average. Antoni Lange (1861-1929) stands out as a Parnassian with exceptional technical abilities. Maria Komornicka (1876-1948) was also able to free herself from the prevailing stereotypes to create her individual, intensely Nietzschean verse; mental illness ended her writing career in 1907, although she lived for many years after that date.

BOŁESLAW LEŚMIAN

The greatest poet of Young Poland, however, emerged—quite paradoxically—when the epoch was already in decline. Bołeslaw Leśmian (1878-1937) published his first book in 1912, and his next two books appeared in 1920 and 1936. In other words, chronologically he belongs to the literary epoch that succeeded Young Poland. Nevertheless, he must be considered a belated Symbolist, and only the striking originality of his language obscures this genetic link. Leśmian's poetic style is utterly consistent with his philosophy. An enthusiast of Henri Bergson, he saw the world as a field of incessant conflict between inert matter and the creative force of spirit; the conflict cannot be resolved, and thus the world is always in the course of becoming. The task of poetry is to express this instability: Its rhythm should become the equivalent of the world's *élan vital*, and its imagery should fix the reflection of reality's metamorphoses. The poet should assume the cognitive stance of the primeval human, whose act of perception creates, as it were, the world perceived. Accordingly, Leśmian's poetry is distinguished by his astonishing variety of complex rhythms, his figures of speech that emphasize the mutual transformations of elements of reality, his frequent use of myth and folklore, and his

invention of new words (forming nouns out of verbs and verbs out of nouns, for example) in order to capture the flux of experience.

INDEPENDENT POLAND AND THE WAR YEARS

The twenty years of independent Poland (1918-1939) can be visualized as a gradual turn from light to darkness, from initial optimism and hope to final catastrophe. This change found its reflection in the evolution of poetry. The first decade of the interwar period was characterized by an explosion of new, mostly avant-garde programs and a multitude of poetic groups, periodicals, and even cabarets. Many of these initiatives were ephemeral, but some of them developed into influential schools and trends. As far as popularity was concerned, there was only one poetic school that managed to hold sway over public opinion for two decades, if not longer. Five poets who emerged as a group called Skamander—Julian Tuwim (1894-1953), Antoni Słonimski (1895-1976), Jan Lechoń (1899-1956), Jarosław Iwaszkiewicz (1894-1980), and Kazimierz Wierzyński (1894-1969)—owed their popularity to the fact that their poetry was original and innovative while also comprehensible.

Skamander's only program consisted of rejecting traditional concepts of poetry's "duties" and enjoying artistic freedom; accordingly, the group abandoned all neo-Romantic conventions and turned to contemporary reality and a refreshingly direct style. In fact, each of the five poets possessed a different personality, and the differences among them were to increase as their works progressed. Tuwim, perhaps the most talented of them all, was a master of verbal magic with an explosive lyric force. Słonimski's poetry was rationalistic, discursive, and rhetorical. Lechoń, obsessed with Polish history, made an interesting use of the Romantic tradition. Iwaszkiewicz, after his brief fascination with expressionism, chose aestheticism as his principal attitude. As for Wierzyński, his most impressive achievement is his postwar poetry written in exile and much modernized in form. Within the circle of Skamander's influence, some other poets followed their individual paths. Władysław Broniewski (1897-1962), a pro-Communist poet, managed to combine his radical ideology with close ties to the Polish Romantic tradition.

In her metaphorically concise poems, Maria Pawlikow-ska-Jarnorzewska (1894-1945) achieved a modern formulation of and a feminine perspective on the theme of love. Jerzy Liebert (1904-1931) was an original poet of religious experience.

While Skamander was dominating the poetic scene, more radical programs of new poetry were propounded by numerous avant-garde groups. The Polish Futurists, including Bruno Jasieński (1901-1939) and Aleksandr Wat (1900-1967), did not win a great following, but they prepared the ground for the program of the so-called Kraków Vanguard, the most outstanding representatives of which were Tadeusz Peiper (1891-1969) and Julian Przyboś (1901-1970). In contrast to the Futurists' anarchism, the Kraków Vanguard advocated constructivism and rigor based on metaphor and syntax. Their precise and consistent program had a great impact on the evolution of Polish poetry in the next decades, although as early as the 1930's it was quite clear that their poetry was unable to cope with the problems of twentieth century history. Among other avant-garde poets, Adam Ważyk (1905-1982) is worth mentioning as a representative of Surrealism, although his style changed radically in subsequent decades.

The 1930's, marked by intense economic, political, and ideological crisis, brought about the so-called Second Vanguard—a new generation of poets who prophesied the approaching global catastrophe. Konstanty Ildefons Galczyński (1905-1953), who later was to become one of the most popular Polish poets, did it by use of the grotesque and mockery. Józef Czechowicz (1903-1939), initially a highly accomplished poet of idyllic provincial landscapes, in his later poems expressed his fears using his own avant-garde technique of metaphorical condensation. Czesław Miłosz (1911-2004), one of the greatest Polish poets and the winner of the 1980 Nobel Prize in Literature, underwent a complicated evolution, from his prewar catastrophism to metaphysical lyricism.

The atrocities of World War II (1939-1945) confirmed the predictions and premonitions of catastrophist poetry, and the theme of "apocalypse come true" was central in the work of a new generation of poets, most of whom died young during the Nazi Occupation as underground fighters or soldiers in the Warsaw Up-

rising. Such was the fate of Krzysztof Kamil Baczyński (1921-1944), who left behind a brilliant collection of lyric poems, visionary and Symbolist in style.

POSTWAR POLAND

After World War II and the imposition of Communist rule on Poland, many poets worked in exile. Despite censorship, a great deal of émigré literature found its way into the country, and its popularity was remarkable, to mention only the examples of Miłosz, Wierzyński, and Wat. Those poets who remained in Poland or were repatriated faced a situation of more or less limited freedom of speech. In spite of that, postwar Polish poetry scored many artistic successes. The immediate postwar years brought about the debut of Tadeusz Różewicz (born 1921), who propounded a new, ascetic style devoid of metaphors and sparing in imagery. After a general decline of literature during the years of Stalinism, one of the first harbingers of the approaching "thaw" in cultural policy was the publication in 1955 of Adam Ważyk's "Poemat dla doroslych" ("Poem for Adults").

The year 1956 marked the beginning of a genuine eruption of new names, trends, and poetic programs. The poetry of the late 1950's and 1960's was characterized by the coexistence of a strong current of ironic moral reflection, as found in the works of Zbigniew Herbert (1924-1998), Wisława Szymborska (born 1923), and Wiktor Woroszylski (1927-1996), and an equally powerful trend of linguistic experimentation, as exemplified by Miron Białoszewski (1922-1983), Tymoteusz Karpowicz (1921-2005), and Witold Wirpsza (1918-1985). At the same time, poets such as Stanisław Grochowiak (1934-1976), Jerzy Harasymowicz (1933-1999), and Tadeusz Nowak (1930-1991) built their private worlds of imagination and fantasy. The school of neoclassicism and the "poetry of culture" is represented by, among others, Jarosław Marek Rymkiewicz (born 1935).

In the early 1970's, another generation of Polish poets came to the fore, combining the "moralistic" and "linguistic" tendencies in order to find a new language for antitotalitarian protest. Ryszard Krynicki (born 1943), Ewa Lipska (born 1945), Adam Zagajewski (born 1945), Julian Kornhauser (born 1946), and

Stanisław Barańczak (born 1946) are strong representatives of this trend, called the Generation of '68 or the New Wave. All trends in Polish poetry since World War II followed the vicissitudes of the socialist governments and looming presence of neighboring Soviet Union. Writers recognized by the state were guaranteed publication and a comfortable lifestyle. They also, however, agreed to write only what was acceptable to government censors. The underground writers were heard only as loudly as any current leadership allowed. Whether the objects of aggressive government crackdown or the minor concern of a government generally ignoring them, these writers were still reacting to government. They were not perceived as leaders in reform.

Most of the poetry created during these years was not considered truly Polish in character. It was all a reaction to an imposed and generally unpopular political structure. This structure fell apart in the 1980's. The decade began with the strong suppression of intellectual and artistic works. Thousands of journalists were suspended or forced to resign, publishers and writers' organizations were closed and disbanded, and authors and other intellectuals were arrested. The government relaxed its censorship by the mid-1980's, and underground publishing started to flourish. In 1988, Soviet president Mikhail Gorbachev declared that the Soviet Union would no long directly influence Polish politics. This statement effectively removed the yoke of censorship in Poland and the target or theme of writers for the past forty-five years.

END OF THE TWENTIETH CENTURY ONWARD

There seems little cohesion or uniformity in approach of the poets born after 1950. If there is a common thread, it seems to be a focus in the individual, the inner world, the self. This is in direct opposition to the committed poetry of the previous decades that spoke to and for the people. These newer voices include Marcin Baran (born 1963), Krzysztof Koehler (born 1963), Zbigniew Machej (born 1958), Jacek Podsiadlo (born 1964), Marcin Sendecki (born 1967), Jerzy Sosnowski (born 1962), Marcin Świetlicki (born 1961), and Robert Tekiel (born 1961).

The whole world then focused its attention on Polish poetry in 1996 when Szymborska was awarded the Nobel Prize in Literature. The choice seemed surprising at first; then more people read her poetry and discovered her wit, wisdom, irony, commitment to human issues, and complete mastery of the Polish poetic language. She well represented to the world a rich, deep, and still very dynamic poetic tradition.

BIBLIOGRAPHY

Barańczak, Stanisław, and Clare Cavanagh, eds. and trans. *Polish Poetry of the Last Two Decades of Communist Rule: Spoiling Cannibals' Fun*. Foreword by Helen Vendler. Evanston, Ill.: Northwestern University Press, 1991. Despite an oppressive government and a society permeated by despair, the twenty-nine poets represented in this collection created a poetic renaissance, especially in the lyric genre. An important anthology.

Carpenter, Bogdana, ed. *Monumenta Polonica: The First Four Centuries of Polish Poetry, a Bilingual Anthology*. Ann Arbor: Michigan Slavic Publications, 1989. Parallel English and Polish texts. Covers an extensive period of poetry. Bibliographical references.

Czerniawski, Adam, ed. *The Mature Laurel: Essays on Modern Polish Poetry*. Chester Springs, Pa.: Dufour Editions, 1991. Contains essays on poets, analyses of individual poems, and overview articles on history and theory. Appropriate for introductory readers of Polish poetry and scholars alike.

Eile, Stanisław. *Literature and Nationalism in Partitioned Poland, 1795-1918*. New York: St. Martin's Press, 2000. Published in association with the School of Slavonic and East European Studies at the University of London. Demonstrates how Romantic poetry contributed to the growth of nationalism in Poland and to the determination of the Poles to resist foreign rule.

Eile, Stanisław, and Ursula Phillips, eds. *New Perspectives in Twentieth-Century Polish Literature: Flight from Martyrology*. New York: Macmillan, 1992. The essays in this collection deal with fiction and drama as well as poetry. However, some of them discuss individual poets, while others consider more general topics, such as poets and politics or the new poetry emerging in the final decades of the twentieth century. Bibliography and index.

Grol, Regina, ed. *Ambers Aglow: An Anthology of Contemporary Polish Women's Poetry.* Austin, Tex.: Host, 1996. This important collection features the works of thirty women poets, presented in parallel English and Polish texts.

Hawkesworth, Celia, ed. *A History of Central European Women's Writing.* New York: Palgrave, 2001. Contains four essays on Polish women writers. Others deal with more general topics. Map, bibliography, and index.

Levine, Madeline G. *Contemporary Polish Poetry, 1925-1975.* Boston: Twayne, 1981. Part of Twayne's World Authors series. Examines fifty years of Polish poetry. Bibliography and index.

Mengham, Rod, et al., trans. *Altered State: The New Polish Poetry.* Ottawa, Ont.: Arc, 2003. Dual text translations of works by twenty-five Polish poets. Consists almost entirely of poems written after the end of communist rule.

Miłosz, Czesław. *The History of Polish Literature.* 2d ed. Berkeley: University of California Press, 1983. An updated version of the 1969 work, with an epilogue added by the author.

_____, ed. *Postwar Polish Poetry: An Anthology.* 3d ed. Berkeley: University of California Press, 1983. A collection of Polish poems, selected and edited by the 1980 Nobel laureate.

Tighe, Carl. *The Politics of Literature: Poland, 1945-1989.* Cardiff: University of Wales Press, 1999. With references to some two hundred writers, this volume demonstrates how postwar Polish literature was dominated by opposition to communism. Useful both as a political history and as a reference work.

Zagajewski, Adam, ed. *Polish Writers on Writing.* San Antonio, Tex.: Trinity University Press, 2007. A volume in the Writer's World series. Twenty-five prominent writers, including Nobel Prize winners Czesław Miłosz and Wisława Szymborska, comment on their art. Diary entries, letters, essays, and interviews are included.

Stanisław Barańczak

POSTCOLONIAL POETRY

As the British Empire spread to all corners of the world, so did the English language and literature. The empire faded after World War II, but what had become the international tongue and medium for creative writing survived and even prospered. English and its literature had long been enriched by speech and writing from Africa, the West Indies, Canada, India, Australia, and New Zealand. The dismantling of the Commonwealth neither subordinated nor silenced the distinctive voices that had arisen and that continue to arise. Traditionally, this body of fiction, drama, and poetry has been referred to as "Commonwealth literature" to distinguish it from English and American literatures. It is often still called Commonwealth literature for want of a better name, but as the old British Commonwealth recedes into history, so does a once-significant but now largely meaningless political term. These days, names such as "postcolonial literature," "world literature written in English," or "international literature in English" are more common. Some critics envision a time when all literature in English, including that of England and the United States, will blend into a single body, a time when no literary works will receive preference because of their national origins and all literature will be judged entirely on merit.

The circumstances in which poetry grew out of the one-time Commonwealth affected all aspects of the poetry's development. Such effects were felt in the poetry both of the "settler" countries—Australia, Canada, New Zealand, and South Africa—and that of the colonized areas—great parts of Africa, India, and the West Indies. The distinction between "settler" and "colonized" is simple: The settlers came to stay, taking over the land from those they considered primitives—the Aborigines in Australia, the First Nations in Canada, the Maoris in New Zealand, and the blacks in South Africa—and these peoples were variously ignored, enslaved, or exterminated. During the last few decades, the descendants of the dispossessed indigenous peoples have added their poetic voices to those of the settlers, who had through the years created their own exclusionary literature. The colonizers, on the other hand, went forth from England to rule and to exploit, not to settle; of course some did settle, but once the empire dissolved, their descendants left, unlike those in the settler countries. During the heyday of colonialism, the British set up schools for select groups of the natives they colonized; although those they educated in such places as Kenya, Nigeria, or India were intended to help rule their fellows, some became writers instead, thus giving Commonwealth poetry a third voice.

The writers in all three voices had available the centuries-old British literary tradition from which to draw forms, standards, and inspiration. Always, though, this fully developed text—a part of the colonial baggage—set up a creative tension that both benefited and hindered the poets.

SETTLER POETS

How were the settlers in Australia, South Africa, Canada, and New Zealand to express in poetry the peculiarities of a new land and the life there? Could English poetry alone serve as a model? The emu had replaced the skylark; the flamboyant blossoms of the frangipani had dimmed the daffodil and primrose. Colonial outposts like Cape Town or Sydney bore little resemblance to London. Makeshift towns or isolated homesteads on the bleak veld of South Africa or in the vast outback of Australia contrasted starkly with the villages, meadows, copses, and moors of England. As the settlers communicated less with their former home, even their language changed: New words came into usage to describe unfamiliar things, accepted grammar fell by the wayside, and indigenous expressions crept in. Neither could the heterogeneous and structured English society survive intact among those in the isolated pockets of the Empire; no matter how hard the settlers tried to preserve their traditions, they faced lives in altered societies where rules and conduct adjusted to circumstance.

Despite their circumstances, the poetic impulse loomed strong among the early settlers. Perhaps the writing of poetry served as a comfort, as a way to overcome loneliness and isolation, a way to grasp the radical changes the settlers experienced. For example, even though Australia's convict pioneers were not literate for the most part, they were the colony's first poets. Soon after their arrival in 1788, they altered familiar English and Irish ballads to express the despair and misery that marked their lives. Like the literate free settlers who followed them to Australia and like those who went to Canada, South Africa, and New Zealand, they drew from the established text, imitating it and adding a new dimension. In 1819, an Australian judge named Barron Field (1786-1846) published two poems in a booklet, *First Fruits of Australian Poetry* (1819), in which he claimed to be the colony's first poet: "I first adventure; follow me who list/ And be Australia's second harmonist." Traditional in form, these two poems—"The Kangaroo" and "Botany Bay Flowers"—are typical of much early settler poetry. While Field finds the unfamiliar flora and fauna intriguing, he neither captures it wholly in his imitation of English verse nor refrains from recording his amusement over such oddities.

On the other hand, an anonymous Canadian settler expresses greater appreciation for his new land in "The Lairds of Esquesing," which appeared in 1826. This poem celebrates "Canada's wild woody shore" and "The Oak and the Hemlock and Pine" as the means of a better life for those who "are still coming o'er;/ In hopes of a good situation." However, pride and delight in the potential exploitation of natural resources, not in their beauty, lies at the center of the poem. These examples—like the early poetry from New Zealand and South Africa—express not a national identity but rather a colonial mentality. Such was the case with the abundant verse that continued to be written well into the twentieth century. Some was brazenly nationalistic in its celebration of the heroic pioneers, those hardy individuals who conquered the land; although the pioneers have long been admired for destroying the forests or eroding the veld and killing the indigenous peoples, later generations have questioned whether these acts deserve epic status. Some records of pioneer exploits, usually too mundane for true heroic stature, have found posterity as folk verse, such as the work of Australia's Banjo Paterson (1864-1941). Much of the poetry was far removed in spirit from the place where it originated,

a pale imitation of distant literary fashions. For example, while there was no dearth of localized nature poetry, too often the poets saw the New World, the antipodes, or Africa through a Romantic sensibility they inherited from earlier English nature poetry. A true voice had not yet emerged, and for the most part, this poetry has been forgotten, deservedly so.

The established text continued both to bless and to debilitate, for that which came from England was considered the real literature and that written in the colonies a shadow of the original. Those who had never seen a daffodil or a skylark were strictly schooled in a poetry that celebrated such phenomena and were led to believe that the literature of their own country was second rate. After all, it was not until the 1950's that the national literatures entered into the school curriculum of the settler countries, which after World War II were at last breaking their ties with England. Further, as the political and economic influence of the United States spread during the postwar period, so did its literature, which had long before rebelled against the British tradition. The maturing of poetry in these countries, then, came about during the twentieth century and in particular after 1945.

ROY CAMPBELL

One exception is Roy Campbell (1901-1957), South Africa's major English-language poet. Born in Durban, South Africa, of British descent and schooled in English literature, Campbell broke away from his heritage. Revolted by South African racial attitudes, he became one of the country's first literary exiles and spent most of his life abroad, mainly in France, Spain, and Portugal. At times, he satirized South African settler society, as in the biting wit of a poem like "The Wayzgoose," whose opening stanza contains the lines: "Where having torn the land with shot and shell/ Our sturdy pioneers as farmers dwell,/ And twixt the hours of strenuous sleep, relax/ To shear the fleeces or to fleece the blacks." Campbell experienced a divided relationship with his native land, calling it "hated and adored" in his poem "Rounding the Cape." This dichotomy continues to haunt South African writers and consequently dominates much of the country's literature. Campbell, a major lyric poet and one of the first Commonwealth writers to attain an overseas reputation, also wrote about his homeland with fervor and captured its essence in poems like "The Zebras" and "Zulu Girl."

JUDITH WRIGHT

Another poet of international standing is the Australian writer Judith Wright (1915-2000), who discovered her homeland as a metaphorical entity from which she could draw meaning and through extending the metaphor express that meaning to others. For Wright, nature serves as a bridge to universal understanding, and the landscape she explores to attain this knowledge is purely Australian; she approaches nature with a sensibility untainted by the inherited text of English literature. Her first book of poems, *The Moving Image*, appeared in 1946. One of her major themes is the relationship between humankind and nature, which led her to become a public figure fighting to protect the environment: "a landscape that the town creeps over;/ a landscape safe with bitumen and banks," she laments in one of her poems, "Country Town." Some critics have observed that Wright's later poetry suffered from her political involvement with environmental issues. However this work might be judged, Wright helped to show the generation of poets who followed how they could be Australian without being provincial, how they could express an Australian sensibility without cringing, and how they could examine the landscape honestly.

Wright is also the first poet of Anglo-Saxon origin to treat the Australian Aborigine in an understanding way. One of the best of these poems is "Bora Ring," in which she mourns the loss of the ancient rites of those who inhabited the country for forty thousand years before the white man came: "The song is gone; the dance/ is secret with the dancers in the earth,/ the ritual useless, and the tribal story/ lost in an alien tale."

A. D. HOPE

A. D. Hope (1907-2000), the third poet from a settler country who gained an international reputation, was Australian as well. However, he made no effort to explore the metaphysical dimension of his native land as a basis for poetry; instead he followed the dictates of eighteenth century neoclassicism. Damning free verse, modernism, and lyricism, Hope wrote in a highly structured, witty, cosmopolitan way. For him, the inherited text was not to be discarded but to be used and improved upon. He rarely mentioned Australia, for he felt

more at home in Greece than he did in a place where, as he wrote in his poem "Australia," "second-hand Europeans pullulate/ Timidly on the edge of alien shores."

LES A. MURRAY

The Australian poet Les A. Murray (born 1938) gained recognition around the world, receiving numerous international awards and regularly publishing overseas. In 2000, a collection of his poems called *Learning Human: Selected Poems* appeared in New York. His poetry, noted for its verbal intensity and lyrical qualities, is undergirded by conservative political and religious views. A dichotomy marks his work. On one hand, it celebrates the strength and character of ordinary people and assumes an anti-intellectual pose. On the other, though, it is extremely erudite in its references and allusions.

AL PURDY AND MARGARET ATWOOD

Canada and New Zealand have strong poetic traditions, and both have many poets widely admired in their own countries, but who have not yet achieved the stature of Campbell, Wright, Hope, or Murray. Contemporary Canadian poets have moved far from the anonymous nineteenth century versifier who exulted in the pioneers' despoilment of the land. One of Canada's best-known poets, Al Purdy (1918-2000), for example, sees the necessity of reinventing a poetic tradition divorced from the colonial past, a tradition that takes into account Canada's geographical vastness, a primary theme in his own work. While Margaret Atwood (born 1939) has established a worldwide reputation as Canada's leading fiction writer, her considerable achievement as a poet is little recognized outside Canada.

THREE NEW ZEALANDERS

New Zealand, too, has produced a wide array of poets, the best-known being James K. Baxter (1926-1972). An old-fashioned poet by some standards, Baxter gained his popularity and lasting fame through a rare ability to meld language and location, for his was truly a national voice that spoke apart from the established British text. The far more sophisticated work of another New Zealander, Allen Curnow (1911-2001), is also highly regarded, for both its rich language and its handling of the metaphysical aspects of the remote country; for instance, in "House and Land," he speaks of the "great gloom" that "Stands in a land of settlers/ With never a soul at home." A New Zealand poet who has received attention overseas is Bill Manhire (born 1946). His poetry is simple and direct yet sophisticated and dense in its suggestiveness. It takes varied forms, covers a wide variety of subjects, and draws its material both from his native country and from places abroad.

INDIGENOUS POETS IN SETTLER COUNTRIES

Silent, or silenced, for the two hundred or so years since whites invaded their lands, the indigenous people of the settler countries—Australia, South Africa, Canada, and New Zealand—have added their voices to Commonwealth poetry. They are the victims of a secondary colonialism, for they have long been subjected and in the past often murdered by the settlers who saw them as one more pest on the landscape. Also secondary to the indigenes is the English language and literature, which was forced onto them for survival on the fringes of the white world. Beset by a borrowed written text and an oral literature that has eroded during two centuries of assimilation, the indigenous writers face peculiar problems as they set out to create a tradition that is not a thirdhand version of the British text. They need to determine whether they should write in the conqueror's language or their own languages, which sometimes have been corrupted or lost. They must decide whether to use standard English or the creolized language that many indigenes speak as a result of poor education and segregation. Other challenges include how to incorporate the remnants of their oral traditions and how to reach the largest audience.

The question of audience often seems the most important, for much of the poetry protests the second-class citizenship to which the indigenes have been relegated. At first, the main audience for such writing was white liberals, so English became the mandatory language. In the 1970's, though, the poetry began to play a more direct role in the lives of those it talked about, as the land-rights campaigns and the consciousness movement gained momentum, inspired in part by the Civil Rights movement in the United States. Because English stood as the common language among the indigenes, most of the writing was of necessity done in the borrowed language.

KATH WALKER

One of the first such voices to be heard was that of Kath Walker (1920-1993), an Australian Aborigine later known by her tribal name, Oodgeroo Noonuccal. In 1964, she published the volume of poetry *We Are Going*, and in "Aboriginal Charter of Rights," she asked, "Must we native Old Australians/ In our own land rank as aliens?" Widely admired by black Australians as well as by their oppressed fellows in other settler countries, Oodgeroo's poetry helped awaken these long-silent people. White readers also discovered her work, which made them realize that something new was afoot. The poems in *We Are Going* now seem tame and have in later years been called too conciliatory by some activist Aborigines, who have taken a harsher stance toward the white world in their poetry. Later Aborigine poets such as Lionel Fogarty (born 1958), Archie Weller (born 1957), and Kevin Gilbert (1933-1993) take a stronger approach in taking up the Aborig-

Australian Aborigine poet Kath Walker. (©Oliver Strewe/CORBIS)

ine cause. In their work and that of some emerging poets, the protest rings loud and the anger erupts. Often, though, a comic strain runs through the poems and makes them even more immediate. Also, these poets tend to mix aboriginal words and slang terms with standard English, which is an effective technique.

SOUTH AFRICAN POETS

The South African poet and novelist Dennis Brutus (1924-2009) was another early and widely acclaimed writer of protest poetry. In particular, his poems from prison, *Letters to Martha* (1968), describe vividly the abuse he and other political prisoners suffered. In "This Sun on this Rubble," he writes: "Under jackboots our bones and spirits crunch/ forced into sweat-tear-sodden slush/ —now glow-lipped by this sudden touch." Other black South African poets include Oswald Mbuyiseni Mtshali (born 1940), who published *Sounds of a Cowhide Drum* in 1971, and Mongane Wally Serote (born 1944), who, in "Ofay-Watcher Looks Back," observes that "jails are becoming necessary homes for people." Although it is too soon to make judgments or to name major poets, the post-apartheid era in South Africa has unleashed a vast amount of poetry by those formerly oppressed by the political system. For one thing, publishing opportunities and financial support have become more available. This work addresses the triumph over apartheid as well as its lingering effects, taking up the challenges, problems, and disappointments facing the majority native population after a century of submission.

MAORI POETS

New Zealand poets Rosemary Kohu (born 1947), Robert DeRoo (born 1950), and Hone Tuwhare (1922-2008) express in their work what it is like to be a Maori among the Pakehas—the Maori word for the Anglo-Saxon settlers. In "Taken," for example, Kohu recalls how as a child she was placed in the Bethlehem Native School, which methodically stripped away her heritage so she might become a "Pakeha-thinking Maori." Between stanzas of the poem appears the refrain "'To get on in this world you must be Pakeha.'" In "Aotearoa/ New Zealand/Godzone?," DeRoo speaks to the land, calling it "Aotearoa," its name before the colonial

"New Zealand" and the affectionate "Godzone" were affixed. He sees history as "conquest," in which "we claw each other for rights" to the land, then concludes that as an inhabitant of Aotearoa he can claim no single piece of the land but must embrace it all, telling Aotearoa that "my mind's birth-knot ties me irrevocably to you." Another Maori, Tuwhare is one of New Zealand's most popular poets. Neither didactic nor angry, his work is full of warmth and wit. Still, he speaks strongly for his community and its marginal place in New Zealand society.

CANADIAN INDIGENOUS POETRY

The work of the early Canadian activist-poet Duke Redbird (born 1939) condemns white society for its insensitive treatment of the indigenous peoples. "I Am the Redman," one of his best-known poems, became a rallying cry in the 1970's for the long-silent First Nations. Another native poet, Rita Joe (1932-2007), articulates her people's plight in a more conciliatory fashion—reminiscent of Oodgeroo in some ways—saying, for example, in one of her untitled poems published in *Poems of Rita Joe* (1978), "Pray/ meet me halfway—/ I am today's Indian." Other poets in this group include Chief Dan George (1899-1981), Daniel David Moses (born 1952), and George Kenny (born 1951).

COMBINING TRADITIONS

It would be misleading, though, to leave the impression that indigenous poetry constitutes nothing more than protest. As the years have passed, some rights have been gained and certainly consciousness has been raised, and many indigenous poets have moved toward familiar topics of poetry: love, home, nature, and spiritual quest. They have also combined with English-language forms their oral heritage, which has been retrieved through great effort. These writers are thus in the process of establishing a poetic tradition that echoes the borrowed literature and at the same time imbues it with their own ancient text.

One of the writers who has combined the two texts most impressively is the Australian poet Mudrooroo Narogin (born 1939), who published as Colin Johnson before taking a tribal name. His poetry volume *Dal-*

wurra (1988) records the travels of the Black Bittern, a totemic bird from Aborigine mythology. Like the poet himself, this bird sets out on a spiritual quest, visiting Singapore, India, the United Kingdom, and other parts of Asia before returning to his native Australia. In the introduction to *Dalwurra*, Mudrooroo describes the work as a way of showing how ancient Aborigine song cycles can serve as the framework for poems in English, adding that by using such traditional materials, the poet is to some degree disciplined by them.

The highly original poetry of Mudrooroo, of such Maori writers as Keri Hulme, born 1947 (who is better known abroad for her novel *The Bone People*, 1983, than for her poetry), and of emergent South African and Canadian poets promises that this new voice in Commonwealth poetry will prevail.

COLONIAL AND POSTCOLONIAL POETS

The most important poet of the colonial and postcolonial poets of India, Africa, and the West Indies, Derek Walcott (born 1930), is of African descent but was born and grew up in the West Indies when his remote Caribbean island still formed part of the British Empire. In "A Far Cry from Africa," he speaks of "the English tongue I love," but then asks a question common to many postcolonial poets who are not Anglo-Saxon but whose heritage and language is largely English: "Where shall I turn, divided to the vein?" While the West Indies have produced a number of poets, Walcott overshadows the others and to a great degree represents international poetry in English at its very best. He received the Nobel Prize in Literature in 1992. Walcott has incorporated his native Caribbean into a metaphor of universal proportions. Although some of his work takes up other locales and subjects, his best poetry returns to the land of his birth, with all its seductive beauty and internal decay.

Like Walcott, many of the postcolonial writers spent their first years as colonials, then at maturity found themselves in young nations set free from the imperial fetters of the past. Were they at that point to continue writing in English, thus building a national literary tradition based on the language and text of the departed conquerors? Should they not turn their backs on the English tongue they loved and write in the native languages of, say, Kenya, Nigeria, or India? By writing in English were they not pandering to the Western world rather than speaking to their own people, thereby creating what some have called "tourist literature"? While these questions have been debated by critics and writers in the half century since the era of independence, an English-language literature has continued to develop in Africa, India, and the West Indies. "Develop" carries significance: What has emerged in all the genres is not a postcolonial facsimile but a sturdy hybrid, which grows out of what West Indian novelist Wilson Harris (born 1921) calls "the universal imagination," be its source African, ancient Greek or Roman, British, European, or American; its mythology Hindu, Buddhist, Muslim, or Christian; its forms expressionistic, romantic, neoclassic, or indigenous.

SAROJINI NAIDU

The first major poet from India, Sarojini Naidu (1879-1961), long preceded independence. Born into an Anglicized Indian family at the height of the British Raj and educated in England, Naidu published her first book of poems in English, *The Golden Threshold*, in London in 1905 and received immediate recognition at home and abroad. She published three more books of poems that still hold charm—and immense promise—with their curious blend of Romantic and Victorian forms with Indian imagery and subject matter. Her poetry reveals a passionate love for India along with an Eastern preoccupation with death and immortality, as in "Imperial Delhi," which celebrates the ancient city of so many past glories: "But thou dost still immutably remain/ Unbroken symbol of proud histories,/ Unageing priestess of old mysteries/ Before whose shrine the spells of Death are vain." Naidu gave up her poetic career in "the English tongue" she loved to join Mahatma Gandhi's freedom movement and became one of Gandhi's closest associates throughout India's struggle for independence, which was finally gained in 1947. Had she been born later her story might have been different.

KAMALA DAS

In postcolonial India, one of the major poets is also a woman, Kamala Das (1934-2009). Her work, infinitely more modern in form, sophisticated in tone, and confessional in nature, still brings to mind Naidu's poetry as it blends Indian imagery, Western forms, and the universal concerns of love, passion, alienation, spirituality, and death. Although Das wrote in both the Indian language Malayalam and in English, she describes language in her poem "An Introduction" as nothing more than a tool for expression, a way of communicating what is said in the other language of nature and experience, which she calls "the deaf blind speech/ Of trees in storm or of monsoon clouds or of rain or the/ Incoherent mutterings of the blazing/ Funeral pyre." While the imagery is purely Indian, the idea it expresses reaches far beyond its source. Das validates her use of English by divorcing language from superficial nationalism and seeing it as just one form of human expression, which she calls in the same poem "the speech of mind that is/ Here."

NISSIM EZEKIEL

Another important Indian poet in English, Nissim Ezekiel (1924-2004), is considered a pioneer figure who introduced European expressionistic forms into Indian poetry but at the same time diffused what he borrowed to express a purely Indian sensibility. His often-experimental work encompasses a wide range: Some of it is highly personal in its revelation of the inner experience, as in "Two Images," and some in its frank treatment of sexuality, as in "Nudes"—two of his best-known poems. In "Poster Poems," he creates collages of the subcontinent's variegated human landscape. Some Indian critics, however, have found Ezekiel's work—and that of Das as well—too Western in orientation, objecting, for instance, to the use of Christian imagery; these poets and others writing in English should, the critics say, rely more heavily on Indian mythology, history, and literature, even if their language is non-Indian.

AN AFRICAN APPROACH

To a great extent, contemporary African poets have been more faithful than their sometimes all-too-literary Indian counterparts at integrating the African languages and heritage into English poetry. Many African poets write first in an African language and then render their work into English, often retaining many of the Af-

rican words. Some write in pidgin to reproduce the flavor that English has acquired in Africa. Others attempt to evoke, through verbal effects, traditional drum or flute poetry, or the chanted verses that are a part of tribal ceremonies. A single poem may refer to Christian mythology alongside allusions to African religion, or may contain lines from Ezra Pound or echo the rhythms of Gerard Manley Hopkins while focusing on a purely African subject. The Western hero Odysseus might be mentioned in the same breath as Chaka, the legendary African warrior.

The colonial African poets concentrated on subject matter, often protest, and let technique take care of itself, usually adhering to the forms and diction set by the British text. In contrast, postcolonial writers have exercised admirable craft in their work; from a technical standpoint, they do not write in a vacuum but show a keen awareness of the current trends in English-language poetry. Of course, many were educated abroad, in England, Europe, or the United States. Still, they do not sacrifice their Africanness in order to be fashionable or acceptable on the international scene. Finally, African writers, whatever their genre, have never indulged in art for art's sake, but see a high seriousness and purpose in what they do. The Somali novelist Nuruddin Farah (born 1945) expresses this intent forcefully in his 1981 address "Do Fences Have Sides?": "The writer in Africa and the Third World countries is looked upon as the contributor to and/or creator/shaper of the nation's enlightened opinion . . . he is, to a great number of people, the light whose beams guide the ark to safety."

WOLE SOYINKA

Certainly the approach to literature espoused by the Nigerian writer Wole Soyinka (born 1934) exemplifies Farah's statement. Soyinka, who received the Nobel Prize in 1986, is better known for his poetic drama than for his separate poems, even though he has excelled in the latter form, as well as in fiction and the essay. Soyinka's work is sometimes described as creatively eclectic; a single play or poem may bring together such disparate elements as African purification ceremonies, the rhythms of Shakespearean verse, folk narrative of the Yoruba people (Soyinka's tribal identity), and the dramatic techniques of Bertolt Brecht. His work represents brilliantly the subtle interaction that takes place when a writer borrows from and responds to a wide variety of texts. While nationalist critics and theorists in Africa and elsewhere may denounce such interdependence and call it artistic neocolonialism, the artists apparently—and fortunately—realize that they do not create within set boundaries.

CHRISTOPHER OKIGBO

Another such poet is Christopher Okigbo (1932-1967), who was born in Nigeria and was killed in the Biafran War. Lyrical, cryptic, intense, and frequently obscure, his highly personal work blends the sounds of African music and the performance of ancient ritual with Western artistic and literary elements. Okigbo is usually considered the most modern of the African poets, and the fusion of sound and symbol makes his work extremely difficult—at times incomprehensible—on an intellectual level, but it is always resonant and exciting.

OKOT P'BITEK

Okot p'Bitek (1931-1982) was born in Uganda but spent the last decade of his life in Kenya after his criticism of the Ugandan government made him persona non grata in his homeland. Trained as an anthropologist, p'Bitek received international attention when his four "Songs" were published, the first in 1961, the last in 1971. The overriding theme of the "Songs"—actually dramatic monologues in which various Africans speak—is the conflict between Western influence and African ways. For example, in the *Song of Lawino* (1966), the speaker laments her husband's desertion of her, complaining that the "manhood" of all the young African men "was finished/ In the class-rooms,/ Their testicles/ Were smashed/ With large books!" Witty, at times satirical toward both African and Western ways, the "Songs" record in addition to the lament of the African woman the observations and sometimes the desperation of a Europeanized African man, a prisoner, and a prostitute. The poems serve to supplement anthropologist p'Bitek's scholarly writing on African culture.

Along with their counterparts in India and the West Indies, the Africans join the settler poets and emergent indigenous writers to lend contemporary poetry in English voices that are unmistakably international.

BIBLIOGRAPHY

Bery, Ashok. *Cultural Translation and Postcolonial Poetry*. New York: Palgrave Macmillan, 2007. Included are critical essays on Judith Wright, Les A. Murray, Louis MacNeice, Seamus Heaney, A. K. Ramanujan, and Derek Walcott.

Coplan, David B. *In the Time of Cannibals: The Word Music of South Africa's Basotho Migrants*. Chicago: University of Chicago Press, 1994. History and critical analysis of Sotho music and poetry. Bibliography and index.

Keown, Michelle. *Pacific Islands Writing: The Postcolonial Literatures of Aotearoa/New Zealand and Oceania*. New York: Oxford University Press, 2007. The first book of its kind, this volume combines an introduction to the literatures of the region with specific analyses of major authors. Though the volume emphasizes literature in English, francophone and hispanophone writing are also discussed.

Kleinert, Sylvia, and Margo Neale, eds. *The Oxford Companion to Aboriginal Art and Culture*. New York: Oxford University Press, 2000. Contains a wealth of information, including comments on myth, ritual, and performance poetry.

Newell, Stephanie. *West African Literatures: Ways of Reading*. New York: Oxford University Press, 2006. Newell presents various approaches to literature and differing views on colonialism.

Patke, Rajeev S. *Postcolonial Poetry in English*. New York: Oxford University Press, 2006. Includes chapters on South Asia and Southeast Asia, the Caribbean, and black Africa, as well as the settler countries.

Ramazani, Jahan. *The Hybrid Muse: Postcolonial Poetry in English*. Chicago: University of Chicago Press, 2001. Discusses the cultural environment, as well as the artistry, of William Butler Yeats, Derek Walcott, A. K. Ramanujan, Louise Bennett, and Okot p'Bitek. Extensive bibliography and index.

Rymhs, Deena. *From the Iron House: Imprisonment in First Nations Writing*. Waterloo, Ont.: Wilfrid Laurier University Press, 2008. A volume in the Aboriginal Studies series. The chapter "Hated Structures and Lost Talk: Making Poetry Bear the Burden" is of particular interest.

Schürmann-Zeggel, Heinz. *Black Australian Literature: A Bibliography of Fiction, Poetry, Drama, Oral Traditions, and Non-Fiction, Including Critical Commentary, 1900-1991*. Bern, Switzerland: Peter Lang, 1997. Focuses on Australian Aborigines and Torres Strait islanders. An indispensable reference work for students of postcolonial literature.

Smith, Rowland, ed. *Postcolonizing the Commonwealth: Studies in Literature and Culture*. Waterloo, Ont.: Wilfrid Laurier University Press, 2000. Wide-ranging essays on various subjects, including J. Edward Chamberlain's "Cowboy Songs, Indian Speeches, and the Language of Poetry." Bibliographical references and index.

Robert L. Ross
Updated by Ross

RUSSIAN POETRY

For Russians, Aleksandr Solzhenitsyn says, "Poetry is born from the torment of the soul." Russia is a vast land, bordered on the north and south by the Baltic and the Black Seas, on the west by the Carpathian Mountains, and on the east by the mighty Volga River. In the thousand-year history of Russian literature, no natural barrier has preserved the Russian people from the agony of invasion, and Russian poetry has become unbreakably forged to their historical suffering.

THE POETRY OF RUSSIA'S YOUTH

The earliest ancestors of the modern Russians, the agricultural East Slavs, settled the inland plateau of the thirteen-hundred-mile Dnieper River and were preyed on during the ninth century by the Varangians, piratical Scandinavian merchants who founded petty principalities around Kiev. Under Grand Prince Vladimir of Kiev, their loose confederation was converted to Byzantine Christianity in 988 C.E., an immense religiocultural invasion that consolidated its position in Russia by introducing the Old Church Slavonic alphabet based on the spoken dialect, importing Byzantine Greek forms as literary models, and assimilating native pagan elements into religious ritual. Although Old Church Slavonic served as the chief vehicle of Russian literature from the eleventh to the eighteenth centuries, it choked off exposure to the classical Humanistic heritage of the West and rigidly identified church with state, fortifying the autocracy of Russian rulers.

Russia's earliest poetic form was the vernacular and formulaic *bylina* (plural *byliny*; literally, things-that-have-been). These oral epics celebrated mythological figures and, more frequently, human heroes in groupings that resembled the Arthurian cycles. In the Kievan *byliny* cycle centered on Grand Prince Vladimir, the hero Ilya becomes "a symbol of the self-consciousness of the people," according to Felix J. Oinas in *Heroic Epic and Saga* (1978). Novgorod, a northern city belonging to the Hanseatic League, had a *byliny* cycle whose central figure was Aleksandr Nevsky, prince and saint, who repelled the Livonian and Teutonic knights. The Galician-Volhynian *byliny* cycle records the strife between this area and its western neighbors in the thirteenth and fourteenth centuries. As Oinas remarks, the *byliny* of patriarchal Russia "captivated and thrilled people of all walks of life until the nineteenth century," inspiring later poets with traditional Russian ideals.

During the twelfth century, the disintegration of feudal Russia set the bitter groundwork for the Mongol invasion of 1237 to 1240 and the imposition of the "Tartar yoke." *Slovo o polku Igoreve* (c. 1187; *The Tale of the Armament of Igor*, 1915) is Russia's first written poetic achievement, a stirring blend of the aristocratic warrior spirit and a call to self-sacrifice in defense of the Land of Rus. The poem poignantly and accurately predicts the great defeat to come: "O, how the Russian land moans, remembering her early years and princes!/ . . . in discord their pennons flutter apart." Based on the Novgorod Prince Igor's unsuccessful attempt in 1185 to dislodge Turkish Polovtsian usurpers from the lands near the Don, and startlingly modern in its complex imagery, allusion, and symbolism, *The Tale of the Armament of Igor* has sometimes been considered an imposture since its discovery in the early 1790's. Alexander Pushkin claimed, however, that not enough poetry existed in the eighteenth century for anyone then to have written it, and more recent scholars concur.

Until 1480, the Mongol tribute was paid by a Russia brutally severed from the West and struggling to unite itself sufficiently to cast off the hated Tartar yoke. Little national strength was left for poetry. Looking back from 1827, the religious philosopher Pyotr Chaadayev observed, "At first, brutal barbarism, then crude superstition, then fierce and humiliating bondage whose spirit was passed on to our own sovereigns—such is the history of our youth."

FROM DARK AGE TO GOLDEN AGE

Kiev was destroyed in Russia's literary Dark Age under the Tartars, and Russian culture was dominated by the Grand Duchy of Moscow, whose ruler Dmitri won a victory over the Tartars at Kulikovo, memorialized in the fifteenth century Cossack epic *Zadónščina* (beyond the river Don). Ivan II at last drove the Tartars from a unified Russia in 1480, less than a generation after the Turkish conquest of Constantinople, and Moscow became the "third Rome." Imperial power was inseparable from Orthodox belief, and Ivan II, wed to a Byzantine princess, regarded himself as the sole genuine defender of the Orthodox faith. His grandson and namesake, Ivan IV, popularly known in the West as Ivan the Terrible (more accurately, the Awesome), a talented political polemicist, practiced heinous excesses in the name of personal absolutism. After Ivan murdered his oldest son, his line died out, and for the next generation civil disorder was exacerbated by crop failures, famine, and plague. Finally, in 1613, delegates from all the Russias elected Mikhail, the first of the Romanov czars.

During the post-Ivan Time of Troubles, literature in Russia was confined to Old Church Slavonic, though the people clung to folktales and Russianized Western romances. Under the first Romanovs, every Western form of literature except theology began to be translated and widely promulgated with the advent of Russian printing in 1564. In 1678, Simeon Polotsky, tutor to Czar Alexei's children, introduced a syllabic verse system, solemn and even pompous, that dominated Russian poetry for a century.

Westernization accelerated under Peter the Great, who during his reign from 1682 to 1725 reformed every aspect of Russian civilization. The czar personally directed this mammoth invasion of Western thought, but he enforced its adoption by ruthless, even barbaric means. Peter's unprecedented debasement of the Church removed schools and literature from religious control, and from 1708, all nonreligious texts were published in a simplified Russian alphabet rather than in Old Church Slavonic. West Russian syllabic verse, originally panegyric or didactic, became fashionable among Peter's courtiers as an instrument of amatory and pastoral poetry, in imitation of French and German models. Peter's reformations were implemented at enormous cultural cost. The secularization of literature contributed to the dangerous rift opening between the general population and Peter's sophisticated nobility, who largely abandoned the language and the folklore of the exploited populace.

In the thirty-seven years of political upheaval that followed Peter's death in 1725, the first four greats of Russian literature imposed French classical standards on Peter's simplified Russian language. All writers imported Western literary forms and theories while employing at the same time traditional Russian materials.

Prince Antioch Kantemir (1708-1744) is widely considered the first Russian writer to "blend life and poetry in his works." Kantemir served as Russian ambassador to London and Paris, and as a confirmed neoclassicist concurred with Nicolas Boileau-Despréaux that the highest of literary forms were the ode and the satire, which he used to attack reactionary Russian political and social elements. Kantemir's language is realistic, but his satires are framed in the imported syllabic verse dependent on fixed accents, a form of versification unnatural to the Russian language. Kantemir's less talented and nonnoble contemporary Vasily Trediakovsky (1703-1769) freed Russian poetry from these unnatural constraints by introducing a syllabo-tonic system based on equal bisyllabic metrical feet, a rhythm found in the Russian popular ballad.

Mikhail Lomonosov (1711-1765), a peasant poet, achieved scientific fame abroad and returned to found the University of Moscow in 1756. Lomonosov's *Pismo o pravilakh rossiyskogo stikhotvorstva* (1739; letter concerning the rules of Russian prosody) set stylistic criteria for poetry: a "Noble Style," employing Old Church Slavonic elements, used for heroic poetry and tragedy; a "Middle Style," for ordinary drama; and a colloquial "Low Style," for correspondence, farce, and everyday usage. Lomonosov's syllabotonic odes exhibit conventional patriotic themes, but as Marc Slonim has noted, Lomonosov's meditations are "still living poetry." With Lomonosov, the aristocratic poet Aleksandr Petrovich Sumarokov (1718-1777) established the principles of Boileau and Voltaire as paramount in Russian letters.

Russia's most famous empress, Catherine the Great, who ruled from 1762 to 1796, ranked herself with Peter the Great and consciously patterned her dazzling reign upon his. After the abortive Cossack uprising (1773-1775) under Emelian Pugachev and the sobering example of the French Revolution in 1789, Catherine tempered enlightenment with political conservatism. She extended education into the middle class and encouraged a fivefold increase in published translations from the major European languages. She also imported many foreign artists and sponsored secular music.

Catherine, who wrote widely herself, indelibly marked Russian literature by naming Gavrila Derzhavin (1743-1816) as her poet laureate. Nikolai Gogol called Derzhavin "the poet of greatness" who dominated Russian literature for more than thirty years. Alexander Pushkin (1799-1837), however, accused Derzhavin of thinking "in Tartar," a pungent assessment of Derzhavin's sacrifice of Russian syntax in favor of voicing his deistic and epicurean love of the sublime. Derzhavin's stylistic duality presaged the dismemberment of the Russian classical order; he pioneered Russian civic poetry, which burgeoned in the nineteenth century with Kondraty Rylevyev and Nikolai Nekrasov, and he left a sensually concrete language to the flamboyant oratorical poets of the twentieth century, his legacy as well to his immediate followers, who taught Pushkin.

The harsh fate of the prose writer Aleksandr Radishchev (1749-1802), however, indicates that Catherine did not practice what her humanistic love of letters preached. On calling for the empress to amend Russian social sins, especially serfdom, Radishchev was exiled to Siberia and later committed suicide. Despite heavy risks in a censored land, Radishchev, whom Pushkin called the "foe of slavery," was widely read by youthful poets well into the nineteenth century.

By 1800, historical research in Russia was uncovering folk literature, and young Russian poets were intensely discussing the unification of aesthetic principle with cultural heritage. Though rapidly Westernized under Peter and then Catherine, Russian literature now was straitjacketed by state, not Church, censorship, and the democratic ideals that emanated from the West were difficult to implement in Russian poetry. Into this complex literary milieu loomed the shadow of yet another invader: Napoleon Bonaparte.

Prior to the disastrous Napoleonic invasion in 1812, the country had passed through the lunatic reign of Catherine's son, Paul I, who despised revolutionary ideas and attempted to beat them out of his people. Af-

ter Paul was strangled in 1801 with the scarf of a palace guards officer, Paul's son Alexander I, whom Napoleon called "the cunning Byzantine," liberalized government, education, and literature, and writers began to hope for emancipation from the state.

Just as the novelist and historian Nikolai Karamzin had begun to use sentimentalism in prose, launching the pre-Romantic movement in Russian literature between 1791 and 1802, the poet and translator Vasily Zhukovsky (1783-1852) sounded the first poetic notes of the Golden Age. Zhukovsky believed that "translators of prose are the slaves of their original text, whereas the translators of the poets are the rivals of the poets themselves." Zhukovsky thus established a tradition that has ensured the excellence of Russia's poetic translations, such as the Russian *Iliad* of Zhukovsky's contemporary, Nikolai Gnedich (1784-1833), described by Slonim as "probably the best in the world." Zhukovsky's original poetry is highly subjective. He identified poetry with his virtue, and his lyric melancholy caused one of his contemporaries to observe, "Happiness would break his lyre's most beautiful string!" Later, under the influence of German Romantics such as Friedrich von Schlegel, Zhukovsky celebrated human sentiment in melodic diction and transitory impressions that introduced the enchantment of Romantic idealism to Russian verse. The young Pushkin praised Zhukovsky's captivating sweetness, and twentieth century Symbolists such as Aleksandr Blok revered Zhukovsky as their predecessor.

At the same time, however, bureaucratic Russian conservatives were furiously striving to preserve the Noble Style in Russian poetry and stamp out all vestiges of "that vile and foul word—Revolution!" As Slonim has noted, "A literary problem was, as is always the case in Russia, assuming the character of an ideological clash." Complicating the literary scene, the profound strain of classicism so eloquently displayed in Gnedich's *Iliad* dominated the poetry of Konstantin Batiushkov (1787-1855), who called himself "The bard of earthly happiness." Batiushkov was a modernist in form and diction, but he reveled in the mere joy of being, claiming that perfect happiness is attainable only by youth, physically capable of experiencing the heights of ecstasy. Batiushkov's delicate Latinate sweetness inflamed the youthful Pushkin, who rejoiced at his mingling of classical themes with sensual delights.

Pushkin's early poetic mentors, Zhukovsky and Batiushkov, soon fell from Russia's literary firmament—Zhukovsky abandoning poetry for the court of Alexander I, and Batiushkov, his closest friend, dying mad after serving as a Russian officer between 1812 and 1815. This period was marked by an internal struggle between Russia's conservatives, allied against the "infernal sophistication of French enlightenment," and the liberals, who believed that the victory against Napoleon had been won by the Russian people, not their leaders.

ALEXANDER PUSHKIN

Growing up during this crisis, Pushkin became, as Thaïs Lindstrom says, the Russians' "comrade in life . . . whose stanzas, recited with universal familiarity and pleasure, crystallize Russian life in the language of the people." Pushkin took pride in both his ancient Russian aristocratic family and his descent from "Peter the Great's negro," the Abyssianian engineer General Abram Hannibal. Pushkin's earliest poems date from 1811, and while he was still attending the new lyceum

Alexander Pushkin (Library of Congress)

in Tsarskoe Selo, the established poets Zhukovsky and Batiushkov came to consider him their poetic equal. Pushkin steeped himself in Russian and French literature, and at his lyceum graduation in 1817, he swept into the glittering debauchery of St. Petersburg, savoring wine, women, gambling, and dueling.

Because Alexander I had outgrown his youthful liberalism even before 1812, the Russian Army, sadly not for the last time, had been greeted by brutal government police as it returned victorious from the West in 1815. After the czar had become hypnotized by "exalted prophetesses," the uneducated General Arakcheyev, whom Pushkin called a "brutal and treacherous hangman of freedom," dominated Russia for a period characterized, in Alexander Herzen's words, by "servility, coercion, injustice everywhere . . . serfdom solid as a rock, military despotism, silence and whips."

Russia's youth, many of whom had been exposed to Western revolutionary ideals during the Napoleonic Wars, responded with what Slonim describes as "a revolt of words in a country where silence was compulsory." In 1817, a group of young Imperial Guards officers formed a secret Union of Salvation, the True Sons of the Fatherland. Their efforts culminated eight years later, on December 14, 1825, in the ill-fated Decembrist uprising. "Even if we fail," wrote the poet Kondraty Ryleyev, "our failure will serve as a lesson for others."

Remembering the Decembrists, Herzen recalled, "The cannons on Senate Place awakened a whole generation." Pushkin and his contemporaries were secretly familiar with the long historical poems of Ryleyev (1795-1826), who sacrificed family and life to the Decembrist cause. Ryleyev cited the democratic ideals of the Cossacks and the ancient Slavs, writing, "I know that death awaits those who are the first to fight the despots, yet self sacrifice is the price of freedom."

Such youthful idealism permeates *Ruslan i Lyudmila* (1820; *Ruslan and Liudmila*, 1936), Pushkin's first long poem, a romantic epic written under the sign of Byron. It captivated an immense audience, and Pushkin received a portrait of Zhukovsky inscribed, "To a victorious pupil from a vanquished master." Alexander I was less enthused about Pushkin's revolutionary epigrams, however, and the poet was exiled to the South for four years, a period inspiring his Caucasian verse tales. In these works, Pushkin moved from the stereotyped Byronic hero to a three-dimensional protagonist, the conception of which formed the nucleus of his monumental novel in verse, *Evgeny Onegin* (1825-1832, 1833; *Eugene Onegin*, 1881), begun in 1823.

After an unfortunate love affair that resulted in his expulsion from the Russian Civil Service, Pushkin spent a period under house arrest at his mother's estate, Mikhailovskoe. During this time he fell under the spell of William Shakespeare, after whose chronicle plays Pushkin patterned his *Boris Godunov* (1831; English translation, 1918), a towering attempt to banish French classicism from Russian literature. Lindstrom believes that *Boris Godunov* "recognizes and stresses the power of a faceless, formless mass of common people to alter the course of history."

Even Pushkin, a most uncommon man, found himself restricted severely by the Russian government. His poems had been found in the Decembrists' possession, and although he was allowed to live in Moscow again in 1826, censors reviewed all of his work before publication and secret police constantly monitored his words and actions. He continued work on *Eugene Onegin*, completing it in 1833. Regarded as his masterpiece, it is widely considered to be the greatest single work in Russian poetry, and generations of Russians have memorized passages from it.

Pushkin became infatuated with sixteen-year-old Natalie Goncharova and married her in 1831, after which he was constantly short of money. Their opulent St. Petersburg lifestyle detracted seriously from his writing, but Pushkin still produced remarkable lyric poetry and prose novellas in his last period, as well as the great dramatic poem *Medniy vsadnik* (1841; *The Bronze Horseman*, 1936), in which he accurately predicted Russia's eventual enslavement by totalitarianism. He died in a duel involving his lovely but vapid wife.

Pushkin's works, which Russians claim to be untranslatable, have influenced all the Russian arts—music, ballet, sculpture, and painting. Pushkin left Russian literature its modern language, a profound fusion of popular idiom and elegant expression that sublimely

weds sound to meaning. He bequeathed to world literature one of its most magnificent apologiae for the dignity of humanity, making poetry a living instrument of humanistic values. Gogol called him "an astounding and perhaps a unique phenomenon of the Russian spirit," embodying "what the Russian may become two hundred years hence." Pushkin's most fitting memorial, however, appears in his own rendition of Horace's "Exegi monumentum":

> I shall long be loved by the people
> Because I awakened their goodness with my lyre
> And in my cruel country celebrated freedom
> And appealed for mercy for the downtrodden.

For the multitude of other brilliant writers of Russia's Golden Age, Pushkin's creativity was, in Gogol's metaphor, "a fire tossed out of the sky, from which lesser poets of his day, like candles, become alight."

OTHER GOLDEN AGE POETS

Evgeny Baratynsky (1800-1844), an intellectual and classicist, lacked Pushkin's *sprezzatura*, that attribute of genius which makes the most difficult achievement appear effortless. A poet with a strong metaphysical bent, Baratynsky decried the decay of human vitality that accompanies industrialism. Nikolai Yazykov (1803-1846) contributed intoxicating rhythms to traditional Russian poetic recitation. Alexei Koltsov (1809-1842) based his Burnsian lyrics on Russian folk life, while more progressive poets of the 1830's, notably Aleksandr Poleshayev (1805-1848) and Prince Aleksandr Odoyevsky (1802-1839), rejected Pushkin's classicism completely and stressed the emotional impact of poetry. Odoyevsky, who died as a private soldier in the Caucasus, is chiefly remembered because Mikhail Lermontov, the most widely recognized heir to Pushkin, wrote an elegy for Odoyevsky that is often cited as the most beautiful in the Russian language.

MIKHAIL LERMONTOV

A Eugene Onegin with a touch of the demon, Mikhail Lermontov (1814-1841) was demoted and exiled in 1837 for circulating manuscript copies of a poem on Pushkin's death, attacking "base lovers of corruption" who dared to "strangle freedom, genius, glory, and hide within the shelter of the law." Lermontov had an unhappy early life. His mother had died young, and he was separated from his father by his wealthy grandmother, an unhealthy situation reflected in several of his poems. A precociously talented child, Lermontov matured into an unappealing young man who admired Lord Byron deeply, seeing in the English poet a reflection of his own passionate revolt and *Weltschmerz*. Lermontov nevertheless realized their essential difference: "No. I am not Byron; like him I am a persecuted wanderer, but mine is a Russian soul."

While attending Moscow University, Lermontov was influenced deeply by secretly obtained works of the revolutionary Decembrist Ryleyev. At that time, Lermontov wrote an uncanny prediction of Russia's future: "The dark day of Russia will come when the crown of the Czars will fall, when the mob, oblivious of its former allegiance, will spread death and blood far and wide." Such musings continued to obsess him even after he joined the Imperial Guard Hussars in 1832, though he abandoned himself to the dissipation of St. Petersburg. Just as eagerly, he welcomed his exhausting, dangerous Caucasian exile, where he began his most successful novel, *Geroy nashego vremeni* (1840; *A Hero of Our Time*, 1854). Lermontov's patriotic historical epics, influenced by the contemporary popularity of *byliny* collections, and his romantic monologue "Mtsyri" ("The Novice"), the tale of a religious novice who prefers freedom to the futile safety of the monastery, were all written in the Caucasus.

Almost all of Lermontov's important poetry was produced in the last four years of his life. He was pardoned in 1839 and became a celebrity in St. Petersburg. The novelist Ivan Turgenev remarked, "There was something fatal and tragic about Lermontov . . . grim and evil force, passion, pensiveness, and disdain." Lermontov's fury at the vacuousness of society appears in biting satire, as in "Smert Poeta" ("The Death of a Poet"), where, Coriolanus-like, he spurns the mob, and the powerful "New Year's Night," where he contrasts his early vision, "the creation of my dream, with eyes full of an azure fire," with his present disillusionment. Again he was exiled, and after a brief fling in the capital, he wrote as he left for the South, "unwashed Russia, land of slaves, of slaveholders, of blue uniforms and of the people whom they rule." Not long after, Lermontov dueled with a fellow officer over a woman and was killed at the first shot.

Like Pushkin, Lermontov shed his romantic postures early and adopted a vivid realism. Lermontov's style, unlike Pushkin's chiseled classicism, resembles "verbal masses molten into indistinguishable concrete," according to D. S. Mirsky, who sees Lermontov's "Valerik," "a letter in verse," as "a link between *The Bronze Horseman* and the military scenes of *War and Peace*." Nicholas I is said to have commented on Lermontov's end, "A dog's death befits a dog," but later critics rank Lermontov as one of Russia's greatest poets. Lermontov gloried in his "proud enmity against God," as "the Cain of Russian letters," and a melancholy rebellion lies at the heart of his finest works. He wrote, "There are words whose sense is obscure or trivial—yet one cannot listen to them without tremor," a quality of poetic expression used by the Symbolists at the turn of the century.

Perhaps Lermontov's greatest work is his long narrative poem *Demon* (1841; *The Demon*, 1875), composed between 1829 and 1839; his appeal to his countrymen lies above all in his "strange love" for Russia, as seen in "My Native Land," a peculiarly Russian response to "the cold silence of her steppes, her poor villages, the songs and dances of her peasants." For outsiders, the enigmatic life and abrupt death of this talented and tormented young poet seem to sum up the brief glory and the eloquent sunset of Russia's poetry in the first half of its Golden Age.

SLAVOPHILES VERSUS WESTERNIZERS

Although the glow of Pushkin's literary gold, subtly blending Romantic and classic elements, lingered through the 1840's, prose realism soon became the literary ideal in the harsh atmosphere inflicted on Russia by Nicholas I, determined to stamp out revolutionary liberalism at home. Discipline worthy of Ivan the Terrible was imposed on the Russian army, whose common soldiers served twenty-five-year terms. The czar's secret police dominated the country's political life, while "censors were unleashed on Russian literature like a pack of bloodhounds," according to one contemporary.

Paradoxically, in the thirty years of Nicholas's rule, writers and philosophers flourished. Herzen wrote, "We devoted ourselves to science, philosophy, love, military art, mysticism, in order to forget the monstrous shallowness about us."

Pyotr Chaadayev, the religious philosopher who was the first Russian dissident to be forcibly confined in a madhouse, claimed in 1837, "There is something in our [Russian] blood that repels all true progress," and he defined the opposing positions in Russian thought that have persisted until the present. Slavophiles determined to expel all foreign ideologies and Westernizers such as Chaadayev, seeking Russia's salvation in imported liberalism, clashed in an atmosphere of ferocious governmental repression in a land that was 90 percent illiterate. Vissarion Belinsky (1811-1848), poor and desperately ill, became Russia's first and most influential literary critic, still cited today in the Soviet Union as "a great teacher." Belinsky called literature "the vital spring from which all human sentiments percolate into society," and he insisted that "he who deprives art of its rights to serve social interests debases the reader instead of elevating him."

Belinsky's fellow believer in Western ideals, Herzen, looked to Russia's "naturalness of peasant life" and "our remarkable ability to assimilate foreign ideas" for his country's rebirth. From his exile in Europe, Herzen propagandized against the czarist government, while Belinsky defended the Russian natural school of literature, whose chief concern was social problems and whose leading representative was Nikolai Gogol. Herzen and Belinsky initiated Russian Socialism, while Mikhail Bakunin, later Karl Marx's opponent in the First International, promulgated revolutionary anarchism.

As Turgenev, Fyodor Dostoevski, and Leo Tolstoy were shaping their immense contributions to the world's great fiction, creating amazingly diverse panoramas characterized by acute political, social, and psychological analysis, Russian poetry developed along two distinct paths. One group espoused art for art's sake as an escape from everyday Russian reality, submerging themselves in stylistic simplicity, folk emotionalism, and Belinsky's dictum that poetry was "thinking in images."

NIKOLAI NEKRASOV

In contrast, civic realism in poetry found its voice in the works of Nikolai Nekrasov (1821-1878). Nekrasov's father had turned him out of the house because of his obsessive desire to become a man of letters. "Famished every day for three years," he managed to become the foremost publisher of Russia's new realistic school of fiction. A contemporary remarked that if the ceiling collapsed on a soirée given by Nekrasov's mistress, "Most of Russian literature would have perished."

Nekrasov chose to "sing of your suffering, O my people" in intensely emotional language and innovative metrical usage. His most important work was a satiric epic, *Komúna Rusí žit' chorošó?* (1870-1874, 1879; *Who Can Be Happy and Free in Russia?*, 1917), which traces the wanderings of seven peasants through "wretched and abundant, oppressed and powerful, weak and mighty Mother Russia." His "Reflections Before a Mansion Doorway" observes unequivocally, "Where the people are, the moan is."

Because of Nekrasov's message and his immense popularity, the government allowed only one edition of his works during his life. He felt the disparity between his peasant sympathies and his wealthy position keenly, and he was large enough in spirit to recognize and encourage his talented contemporary Fyodor Tyutchev, who pursued pure art. Though Tyutchev was overshadowed during his lifetime by Nekrasov, the Symbolists of the Silver Age claimed Tyutchev as their spiritual ancestor.

FYODOR TYUTCHEV

Fyodor Tyutchev (1803-1873) was Tolstoy's favorite poet, and like the great novelist, Tyutchev was a fervent Slavophile who, despite his noble rank, wrote, "I love poetry and my country above all else in this world." While a diplomat in Germany, he was profoundly affected by the pessimistic philosophy of Arthur Schopenhauer, and Tyutchev's poetry shows the influence of a dualistic universe in which a Manichaean chaos and the "all-engulfing, all-pacifying abyss of the cosmos" dominate human existence. For Tyutchev, a Schopenhauerean affinity between love and death was inherent in human nature, a confirmation for Dostoevski, too, of dark tendencies he recognized in his own writing. Tyutchev's four hundred short poems range from a perverse joy in destruction to a sublime desire to be "diffused in the slumbering Universe." His oratorical fervor continued the tradition established by Derzhavin of public poetic performance, and Tyutchev was the "last great master of the High Style," in which Old Church Slavonic rhetoric is supreme. Marc Slonim calls Tyutchev, after Pushkin, Lermontov, and Nekrasov, "the fourth great leader of Russian poetry . . . the profound interpreter of cosmic mysteries."

TOWARD THE SILVER AGE

Except for Count Aleksei Konstantinovich Tolstoy (1817-1875), a popular neo-Romantic poet in the German vein who opposed civic poetry bitterly and sought to reestablish the old norms of art, the 1860's and 1870's were dominated in Russia by fine poetic translations, not native Russian poetry. The costly Crimean War (1854-1856), a shocking waste of Russian lives brought about by the neglect and shortcomings of Russian leadership, had drained the nation's spirit. Russian prestige suffered a mortal blow through the ill-advised conduct of this war, and Alexander II and his government reluctantly faced the necessity of domestic reform. After taking the throne in 1855, Alexander freed the forty million Russian serfs in 1861, two years before Abraham Lincoln's Emancipation Proclamation, but taxes and land payments created tensions that resulted in many peasant uprisings throughout 1862. "The plague of Russian life" had ended, though, and the *zemstvos*, new self-governing bodies, relieved enough of the pressure on Russia's lower classes to maintain the status quo until 1905.

After 1865, Alexander's policies became more conservative. He was stalked and at last assassinated in 1881, ironically on the same day he had granted the *zemstvos* a larger voice in government, as the liberal intelligentsia had urged. Alexander III, his son, threw all reform proposals to the bitter winds from Siberia, increasing police powers, tightening the noose of censorship, and persecuting religious minorities, especially the Jews. His creation of a police state at home, coupled with his expensive and unsuccessful foreign ventures in Europe and Central Asia, made his reign a dismal time for literature. The last vestiges of the Golden Age had faded, and the Silver Age was waiting to be born.

In the 1880's, drought and poor agricultural practices resulted in massive famines and epidemics throughout Russia. Capitalism was fortifying a formidable industrial expansion, but the lives of ordinary Russians became increasingly miserable. Political theorists envisioned a necessary alliance of the peasantry, the workers, and the intelligentsia, and a new form of Russian populism began to become part of the country's cultural atmosphere, tinged by more ideas from the West, the doctrines of Karl Marx.

The precise date of the beginning of modernism in Russian literature is uncertain. Some critics date the period from the publication in 1893 of Dmitri Merezhkovsky's lecture *O prichinakh upadka: o novykh techeniyakh sovremennoy russkoy lityeratury* (on the origins of the decline of Russian literature and on new currents in it), a theoretical work that announces the principles of Russian Symbolism. Others believe modernism began later, with the turn of the century or even with the 1905 Revolution, which Merezhkovsky and his wife, the poet Zinaida Gippius, supported. The Bolshevik Revolution of 1917, however, concluded the modernist period in Russia, just as it decisively ended the Russian monarchy forever.

In the 1890's, young Russian artists began to look inward, reassessing their values and redefining the function of the artist and his or her art. They became absorbed in the creative individualism evident in translations of the works of Friedrich Nietzsche, Stefan George, the English Pre-Raphaelites, and the French Symbolists, especially Charles Baudelaire. Merezhkovsky and others protested against the radical intellectuals who had been dominating Russia's literary life and pronounced a new cultural dogma involving Western-style humanism, Russian tradition, mysticism, intuition, mystery, and myth—a spiritual obbligato to the strange goings-on of Grigory Rasputin at the Imperial Court.

At first, the new writers were dismissed as Decadents, but their successors became the spokespersons for a remarkable explosion of Russian art and literature, a conscious transmutation of Pushkin's Golden Age later known as the Silver Age of Russian letters. More Russian philosophical works appeared between 1890 and 1910 than during the part of the nineteenth century up to that point, and an abundance of small literary magazines provided an outlet for poetry and criticism.

Until 1903, the Russian literary scene was dominated by the Decadents' reaction against realism. They were led by Valery Bryusov (1873-1924), sometimes called the Peter the Great of Russian literature. After translating Maurice Maeterlinck and Paul Verlaine at the age of fourteen, Bryusov "sought a new body for the new art" in synaesthesia, "the subtle ties between the shape and the scent of a flower." The keynote of the landmark anthology *Russkiye simvolisty* (1894) is the slogan, "The personality of the artist is the essence of art." In 1903, Bryusov and his mesmerized followers founded *Vesy* (first published in January, 1904), which became the most important Russian Decadent literary periodical and preached such Baudelairean themes as erotic nihilism and Arthur Rimbaud's *dérèglement des sens* ("disorder of the senses").

Konstantin Balmont (1867-1943), the other great Decadent, a public performer as Bryusov was not, became "the Poet" of turn-of-the-twentieth-century Russia. Balmont drew a large and mostly youthful following at his public recitations. He was a spontaneous poet whose first poetic credo, "Words are chameleons," developed into Nietzschean vehemence by 1903: "I want daggerlike words and lethal moans of death. . . . Who equals my might in song? No one—no one!"

"Moans of death" erupted throughout Russia with the disastrous Russo-Japanese War (1904-1905), followed by the 1905 Revolution, which started on "Bloody Sunday," January 22. The following October, after months of turmoil, Nicholas II granted some civil liberties and the democratic election of a duma (legislative assembly). The czar's manifesto split the revolutionaries into three major camps: the Octobrists, satisfied with the czar's action; the Constitutional Democrats, liberals who wanted far more power invested in the Duma; and the Social Democrats, who had organized a soviet (workers' council) at St. Petersburg and attempted to force additional reform by strike. The czar put them down, trying to stamp out the revolutionaries and limiting the power of the Duma in late 1905. Counterrevolutionary forces in the Second and Third Dumas (1906-1912) prevented any advancement of liberalism prior to World War I.

After 1903, the Decadent movement in literature had an older faction and a younger one, the original Decadents being more occupied with social and political themes and the new Symbolists turning to the neo-Romantic inspiration of Lermontov and Tyutchev. Most critics agree, however, that no stated doctrinal differences distinguished the two groups in the prewar period, and that they lived harmoniously with each other in Moscow and St. Petersburg.

A startling manifestation of the Decadent movement appears in the work of the Satanist poet-novelist Solugub (the pen name of Fyodor Teternikov, 1863-1927). He regarded modern humanity as a horde of living dead, and he believed a poet inhabited a shadowy limbo, where, sorcerer-like, he had to make himself the only credible god in a universe as evil as its creator. His nihilism is somewhat restrained in his lyrics, which he compares in "Amphora" to a fine vase carried so carefully that no drop of the venom it contains is spilled. In his later years, he abandoned poetry for a perverse fictional vision of human debasement.

An antidote to Solugub's horrid view of humankind was offered by the metaphysical *Weltbild* drawn from the cult of Dostoevski at the end of the nineteenth century. The diverse works of Merezhkovsky and of Vladimir Solovyov (1853-1900) depart from Decadent nihilism and seek individual concepts of "Godmanhood," an absolute achieved through Sophia, the incarnation of Divine Wisdom, the archetypal Eternal Feminine. The German Neoplatonic idealism that had fostered the creativity of Lermontov and Tyutchev influenced many of the Symbolist disciples of Solovyov, who accepted the notion of the poet's intermediation between God and humans, conveying to ordinary mortals his experience of the ideals of Truth and Beauty reflected in the principle of Sophia. Solovyov himself accepted Christ's incarnation as proof of humanity's redemption. He believed that despite all of history's evils, humanity will at last attain divinity, and his concept of the Divine Sophia appeared frequently in his own verse, although he occasionally treated the symbol lightly, as in his long poem *Tri svidaniya* (1898; three encounters). Solovyov hoped for the reunion of all Christian denominations, and during his last years, he preached salvation through collective effort. Solovyov's teachings indelibly marked the entire religious movement connected with Russian Symbolism.

Each of the Symbolist triumvirate, Vyacheslav Ivanov, Andrey Bely, and Aleksandr Blok, owed a profound spiritual and artistic debt to Solovyov's definition of poetry as the "incantatory magic of rhythmic speech, mediating between man and the world of divine things."

Ivanov (1866-1949) considered all of human culture the path to God, and he believed that artistic intuition grasped symbols in the ordinary world that reflect the "real" reality of God. Hence the artist, having been given greater gifts, has the responsibility to lead men to the Divine Presence.

Bely (the pen name of Boris Bugayev, 1880-1934), whose strong enthusiasms bordered on the pathological, incorporated Solovyov's doctrine of Divine Wisdom in his lyrics *Zoloto v lazuri* (1904; god in azure), but within a few years, he had become the leading Russian disciple of Rudolf Steiner's Anthroposophy. An important novelist as well as a poet, Bely embodied the mixture of mysticism, diabolism, and obsession with the special fate of Russia that was so characteristic of his time.

ALEKSANDR BLOK

Despite the considerable achievements of Ivanov and Bely, Aleksandr Blok (1880-1921) was the culminating figure of the Silver Age. His lyrics place him with Pushkin and Lermontov, and his ideals remain a rare blend of ecstasy and despair. The young Blok experienced a supernatural vision of a "beautiful lady from Beyond," the Solovyovian Sophia, who inspired more than 240 of his lyrics. In "Gorod" ("The City"), however, set in St. Petersburg's "artificial paradises," disillusionment shattered Blok's Romantic dreams, and in "Nezna Komka" ("The Stranger"), one of his most powerful poems, his ideal woman appeared as an expensive prostitute. Such blasphemous irony caused Blok's break with the Moscow Symbolists. After 1906, Blok continued to suffer from his irreconcilable inner conflict; he wrote, "I see too many things clearly, soberly," and he hurled himself into intense experiences, trying to reconcile art and morality at the same time that he was frantically avoiding confrontation with himself.

By 1909, he had become infatuated with his "beloved fatal country," and his lyric cycle "On the Battle of Kulikova Field" celebrates the fourteenth century victory of the Russians over the Tartars. Just prior to August, 1914, Blok predicted in poetry Russia's "road of the steppe and of shoreless grief," and following the 1917 Bolshevik Revolution, in a Rilkean "dictated" composition, Blok produced his masterpiece, *Dvenadtsat* (1918; *The Twelve*, 1920), a poetic vision of a revolution that would cleanse Russia and redeem its soul from its long agony. By 1921, however, representatives of every segment of Blok's postrevolutionary world, from Communist officials to his old intellectual friends, had ridiculed *The Twelve*, and Blok died convinced that "Vile, rotten Mother Russia has devoured me."

INNOKENTY ANNENSKY

Innokenty Annensky (1856-1909), the Russian poet who links the Decadents and the Symbolists, devoted fifteen years to translating the works of Euripides. Not surprisingly, his own themes were beauty, suffering, and death, the absolutes of a futile human existence that could be ennobled only through art and love. Annensky's finely honed meters and rhythmic effects influenced both the Symbolists and the Acmeists, the next major poetic group in Russia.

ACMEIST POETS

The Symbolists' nebulous Westernized ideals did not prevail for long against the literary realism being promoted by Maxim Gorky in the relatively stable bourgeois climate of Russia between 1910 and 1914. Acmeism was born in 1912, a movement primarily based in St. Petersburg and resembling the controlled, concrete Imagism of Ezra Pound and T. S. Eliot. The three major Acmeist poets, Nikolai Gumilyov, Anna Akhmatova, and Osip Mandelstam, despite significant differences in style and message, concurred that "we want to admire a rose because it is beautiful, and not because it is a symbol of mystical purity."

Nikolay Gumilyov (1886-1921), leader of the Acmeists, had a "bravura personality" that blossomed in physical danger and exotic landscapes. In his 1912 article "Acmeism and the Heritage of Symbolism," he stressed the Greek meaning of "acme" as "the point of highest achievement," as well as Théophile Gautier's rule, "The more dispassionate the material . . . the more beautiful will the work come out."

ANNA AKHMATOVA

Often likened to Rudyard Kipling's, Gumilyov's virile style could not have differed more strikingly from that of his wife for eight years, Anna Akhmatova (1889-1966). Akhmatova's earliest poetry, mostly small lyrics that sang of the woman's inevitably unhappy role in love, was extremely popular immediately upon publication, and her work has since completely overshadowed Gumilyov's. Even today Russian readers memorize Akhmatova's poetry, and she remains Russia's foremost woman poet, unforgettably uniting passion and asceticism. Periodically suppressed by the Soviets, Akhmatova's work has endured; among her greatest works is the cycle *Rekviem* (1963; *Requiem*, 1964), her lament for the victims of Joseph Stalin's purges.

INFLUENCE OF THE POLITICAL STATE

Russia's human losses in the twentieth century defy comprehension. The agony of World War I, closely followed by the February Democratic Revolution and the October Bolshevik Revolution, both in 1917, combined with the ravages of the civil war, cost millions of lives. Later, the famines, the collectivization of agriculture, and the purges of the 1930's established a dark backdrop for the staggering losses, estimated at twenty to twenty-five million lives, that the Soviet Union sustained during World War II.

The Bolshevik Revolution and the consequent establishment of the Soviet state enormously affected Russian literature, although seldom in Russia's history, if ever, has literature enjoyed the freedom of expression provided by Western democracies. In the Soviet era, works of prose and poetry have often been surreptitiously circulated in *samizdat* (editions) and clandestinely shipped abroad, to become *tamizdat* (literally, three-published) works in less restricted societies. The cost of the human devastation suffered by Russians during the century, however, is reflected in the estimates of those lost in Stalin's prison system, the "Gulag Archipelago," where hundreds of writers perished among countless numbers of their countrymen.

In response to the phenomenon of Soviet Communism, too, literature of the period after the 1917 Revolution evidenced two major tendencies. Those writers who remained within the Soviet Union and functioned within its intellectual and artistic borders often turned to apolitical themes or those acceptable to their government, in both cases revealing glimpses both accurate and distorted of life within their country; commentators such as Ronald Hingley observe that the distortions sometimes provide the truest insights. Writers who dissented from official Soviet positions eventually exported either their works or themselves, and from exile their writings occasionally found their way back to their native land, to circulate at considerable risk among readers of Russian *samizdat*.

Indeed, the tyranny of the Soviet state has produced three distinct "waves" of emigration. The first emigration, the largest of the three, took place during the decade following the 1917 Revolution. Among the many Russian poets who emigrated at this time, perhaps the foremost were Marina Tsvetayeva, who later returned to the Soviet Union, and Vladislav Khodasevich, who died in exile. The fate of Khodasevich (1886-1939) is particularly representative. Little read in the West, Khodasevich, like many émigrés, has suffered from what the critic and translator Simon Karlinsky calls the "Western self-censorship"—the conviction, inherited from the thirties, that a Russian writer who resides outside the Soviet Union cannot be of any interest to a Western reader. The second emigration, following World War II, brought to the West fewer writers of note, but the third wave, beginning in the 1970's and continuing to the present, has carried with it a host of brilliant writers, including Aleksandr Solzhenitsyn, Andrei Sinyavsky, and the poet Joseph Brodsky (1940-1996).

OSIP MANDELSTAM

Among the poets who have remained in the Soviet Union, the finest invariably have suffered persecution at the hands of the state. No loss to the world of poetry seems crueler than the death of Akhmatova's friend and fellow Acmeist Osip Mandelstam (1891-1938), who perished in a Far Eastern transit prison, bound for the mines of Kolyma beyond the Arctic Circle. Nadezhda Mandelstam retrospectively described her husband's spirit as endlessly *zhizneradostny*, which approximates the English phrase "rejoicing in life." Mandelstam never bowed to political pressures; he was an admirer of classicism in the oratorical style of Derzhavin and Tyutchev, a Jew more aware of Russian tradition than the Russians themselves were. "I am nobody's contemporary," he wrote, because as an inveterate Westernizer he yearned for world culture. His solemn and exquisitely crafted poems were his conscious effort to achieve "pure" poetry, often employing little-known historical detail and a "sprung" rhythm somewhat resembling Gerard Manley Hopkins's metrical experiments. Like Akhmatova, Mandelstam was forbidden to publish under Stalin, and his mental and physical health collapsed under torture. What sustained him so long as his frail constitution could endure was his concept of poetry as a moral obligation to his countrymen: "The people need poetry that will be their own secret/ to keep them safe forever. . . ."

FUTURIST POETS

The Acmeists' contemporaries, the Futurists, opposed literary and artistic tradition with a zeal that owed a considerable debt to Nietzsche. In 1912, their manifesto, "Poshchechina obshchestvennomu vkusu" ("A Slap in the Face of the Public Taste"), presented Russian readers with an extreme literary case of shocking the bourgeois. One of its authors, Vladimir Mayakovsky (1893-1930), described himself in his important poem *Oblako v shtanakh* (1915; *A Cloud in Pants*, 1965), as "the loudmouthed Zarathustra of our day," and his associate Velimir Khlebnikov (1895-1922), a linguistically experimental poet, rejected all emotional emphasis derived from previous ages from his powerful poems. Russia, he insisted, had "amplified the voice of the West as though transmitting the screams of a monster," and he explored new symbolic uses of language to rouse the world from its petrification.

Aleksei Kruchonykh (1886-1968) provided Futurism with its most famous poem, "Dyr bul shchyl" (1913), written in words that have "no definite meaning," that is, in *zaum* (transrational language), which he and Khlebnikov pioneered. *Zaum* is akin to abstractionism in art in that it is intended to have a direct evocative power without a specific, definable referent, and it was one of the most avant-garde innovations in Rus-

sian poetry. Kruchonykh wrote quite a number of usually short poems in *zaum* and published them in primitive-looking handmade manuscript booklets. The *zaum* "opera" *Pobeda nad solntsem* (pr. 1913; *Victory Over the Sun*, 1971), which in St. Petersburg rivaled the premiere of Igor Stravinsky's *Rite of Spring* in Paris of the same year, was one of the signal Russian avant-garde events of the age.

Although the Moscow group of Futurists was most prominent and inventive, the St. Petersburg group included Vasilisk (Vasily) Gnedov (1890-1978), who became famous as the author of "Poema kontsa" (1913, "Poem of the End"). This proto-minimalist poem consisted of a blank space on a page where a text was supposed to be. Gnedov performed it with a silent gesture to much acclaim.

Just after the Bolshevik Revolution, the Futurists dominated Soviet cultural life briefly, mainly through the achievements of the dynamic Mayakovsky, who, like Nietzsche, called forcefully for the destruction of the old world and the invention of a new one to supercede it.

The Russian Formalist critic Viktor Shklovsky, Mayakovsky's contemporary, claims that Mayakovsky's chief accomplishment was the broadening of verse semantics, building an oratorical language that changed the very syntax of the Russian language. Mayakovsky's ego and his anarchic inclination feasted on the Bolshevik Revolution, but in "Homeward" (composed in 1925) he wrote, "From poetry's skies I plunge into Communism." In 1930, openly critical of Soviet bureaucracy, Mayakovsky committed suicide, which he described as "my final performance." The Soviet Union has enshrined Mayakovsky with their supreme poets, praising his declaration of the artist's obligation to the state. Mayakovsky's savage individuality is said to have stamped poets as diverse as Brodsky, Yevgeny Yevtushenko, and Andrei Voznesensky.

FOLKLORE AND RUSSIAN HERITAGE

Diametrically opposed to Mayakovsky's idiosyncratic poetic style is that of Sergei Esenin (1896-1925), a "peasant poet" who harked back to Russia's traditional past, its rich folklore, and its Orthodox religion. Esenin, a poet from the people, founded the Imaginist school of poetry between 1914 and 1919. His personal excesses led to a self-image he described in *Ispoved' khuligana* (1921; *Confessions of a Hooligan*, 1973), and his unhappy marriages, first to the American dancer Isadora Duncan and then to Tolstoy's granddaughter Sofya, contributed to his final breakdown. He attempted to write political poetry on contemporary topics, but near the end of his life his work was filled with nostalgia for the past and sadness at the fate of his home village, and his later poems made him the voice of many of his countrymen in their disenchantment with Soviet policies. After his suicide in 1925, Esenin's work was out of favor with the Soviet government, but he has since been fully rehabilitated.

Sergei Esenin with American dancer Isadora Duncan. (Getty Images)

MARINA TSVETAYEVA

Something of Mayakovsky's originality and force and something of Esenin's tender devotion to his Russian heritage meet in Russia's *inneres Mädchen*, as Rainer Maria Rilke called Marina Tsvetayeva (1892-1941), Akhmatova's friend and only rival as Russia's most famous woman poet. At eighteen, Tsvetayeva described her poetry as "torn from me like droplets from a fountain . . . their themes made up of youth and death." She emigrated to Paris in 1921, outraged at events in Russia, but she and her family returned in 1939 on the eve of war. After her husband, a Soviet secret agent, was shot by the government as a traitor and one of her children was sent to a labor camp, Tsvetayeva hanged herself in 1941.

As a daughter of the Russian intelligentsia, she wrote for this audience. Her intricate romanticism, like Rilke's, verged on the mystical, and she shared with him, as his long 1926 poem to her reveals, an awareness of "the other world" and the possibility of a new myth that would lead humankind to a better future. Akhmatova hailed Tsvetayeva's creative vitality in one of her last poems, a tender memory of "A fresh, dark elder branch/ Like a letter from Marina." Tsvetayeva, like

Boris Pasternak, was one of the outstanding idealists in Russian poetry. Her impressionistic technique and elliptic imagery show evidence of Pasternak's influence, and she once remarked that he was the only poet among her contemporaries whom she considered her peer.

BORIS PASTERNAK

Boris Pasternak (1890-1960), child of a gifted musician and a famous painter, synthesized the classical tradition in Russian verse, the musical qualities of the Symbolists, and the near-telegraphic style of the mature Tsvetayeva. Pasternak wrote poetry early, at first attracted and soon repelled by the flamboyant Mayakovsky. Pasternak found his own voice in *Sestra moyazhizn* (1922; *My Sister, Life*, 1959), a collection that immediately established him as one of the leading poets of his generation.

In his autobiographical sketch *Okhrannaya gramota* (1931; *A Safe-Conduct*, 1949), Pasternak wrote, "Focused on a reality which feeling has displaced, art is a record of this displacement." A sense of the artist's isolation pervades Pasternak's life and work. As Max Hayward has suggested, Pasternak believed it essential "by responding submissively to high and lonely destiny . . . to contribute in some vital way to the life of the times." Already during World War I, Pasternak had pondered his "contribution," later to become his novel *Doktor Zhivago* (1957; *Doctor Zhivago*, 1958), the record of the Russian intelligentsia caught in the savagery of those revolutionary times. For writing the novel, Pasternak was expelled from the Soviet Writers' Union and forbidden to accept the 1958 Nobel Prize in Literature. The novel closes on "The Poems of Doctor Zhivago," in which Pasternak reaffirms the Christian sanctity of his poetic mission: "If Thou be willing, Abba, Father,/ Remove this cup from me."

ABSURDIST POETS

It was not until the 1980's that the Russian reading public became fully aware of the work of a small group of absurdist poets from the 1920's and 1930's who named themselves Oberiu (Association for Real Art), the existence of which was declared in a 1928 manifesto. The leading figures in the group were Daniil Kharms (Yuvachov; 1905-1942), Aleksandr Vvedensky (1904-1941), and Nikolai Zabolotsky (1903-1958), the primary drafter of the manifesto. Zabolotsky was able to publish one book of poems, *Stolbtsy* (1929, columns), but the other two were able to publish only a few individual poems and stories for children. Their work, which included plays and, in the case of Kharms, short prose sketches that have since become famous, involves totally unexpected, illogical, and sometimes tautological twists of action, imagery, and thought, such as "The sun shines in disarray,/ and the flowers fly in their beds" (Vvedensky) and "This is This./ That is That./ This is not That./ This is not not This./ The rest is either this or not this./ All is either that or not that" (Kharms). They reveal a philosophical depth beneath an absurd, often nightmarish surface. The group ran afoul of the Stalinist regime, and Kharms and Vvedensky both died in prison. Their work has come to be perceived as a major literary movement and the last gasp of the pre-revolutionary Russian literary avant-garde. It became extremely popular among young intellectuals.

POST-STALIN ERA

The cooperation between the Western Allies and the Soviet Union during World War II dissolved in Cold War tension during the 1950's, but after Stalin's death in 1953 a degree of artistic freedom was temporarily achieved by Russian writers. An amnesty decree a month after Stalin's death led to the release of prisoners who had survived the rigors of the gulag, and the Writers' Union restored the membership of Akhmatova in 1954. By 1955, the "thaw" had occasioned the posthumous rehabilitation of many writers who had died in the camps and prisons; this revisionist movement reached its peak with Nikita Khrushchev's famous speech at the Twentieth Party Congress in February, 1956, denouncing Stalin. Despite the suppression of *Doctor Zhivago*, the thaw lasted long enough to permit the publication of Solzhenitsyn's novel *Odin den Ivana Denisovicha* (1962; *One Day in the Life of Ivan Denisovich*, 1963), but soon thereafter Leonid Brezhnev ousted Khrushchev from power. After Brezhnev's accession in 1964, literature in the Soviet Union was subject to rigid Stalinist controls, and one after another, the most talented Russian writers emigrated to the West or were forcibly exiled.

Nevertheless, the Soviet Union continued to exhibit an immense thirst for poetry, attested by the immense popularity of such poets as Yevtushenko and Voznesensky. Both rose to prominence in the early 1960's as spokespeople for liberal forces during that time of the thaw.

YEVGENY YEVTUSHENKO

Yevgeny Yevtushenko (born 1933), as the first poet to enunciate the shift in mood in his country, gained considerable acclaim at home and abroad for his revelation of Soviet anti-Semitism in "Babii Yar" (1961) and the effects of Stalinism as a social force in "Nasledniki Stalina" (1962; "The Heirs of Stalin"). Yevtushenko has used his travels abroad in several volumes of his works, such as the poetic drama *Pod kozhey statuey sbobody* (1972; under the skin of the Statue of Liberty). Certain of his more personal poems are reminiscent of Esenin's candor and nostalgia, but Yevtushenko's "novella in verse," *Golub' v Sant'iago* (1978; *A Dove in Santiago*, 1982), a tale of a tormented young art student in Chile at the time of the Augusto Pinochet coup, reflects the tragedy of a talented individual who is caught between his politics and his art.

ANDREI VOZNESENSKY

Like Yevtushenko, Andrei Voznesensky (1933-2010) survived the artistic restrictions imposed first by Khrushchev in 1963 and subsequently by Brezhnev and his successors. Voznesensky's histrionic style of poetic delivery, modeled on Mayakovsky's, made him popular with large and youthful audiences, while American critics have praised his imagery and originality. One of his translators, W. H. Auden, has cited the broad range of Voznesensky's subject matter as evidence of his imaginative power. Although Voznesensky was the object of articles in the Soviet press accusing him of intelligibility and "supermodernism," he was able to continue publishing. He published a number of works after the breakup of the Soviet Union and organized provincial poetry festivals before his death in 2010.

POEMS "TO REMEMBER"

The stream of *samizdat* and *tamizdat* poetry that emerged from the Soviet Union bears the self-imposed charge: "to remember"—to memorialize the victims of Stalin's gulag, and to speak out against the punishment of dissenters in labor camps and psychiatric hospitals. Poets who dissented against the Soviet government had to choose between writing "for the desk drawer," exile, or death, as the fate of Yuri Galanskov (1939-1972) demonstrates. In 1956, when the Hungarian revolt was suppressed by the Soviets, Galanskov gathered a *samizdat* collection of protest poems. After he set forth his "Human Manifesto," "calling to Truth and Rebellion . . . a serf no more," Galanskov was held in a Soviet special psychiatric hospital; he later died in a labor camp for his role in the human rights movement within the Soviet Union. The themes of *samizdat* and *tamizdat* poetry reflect the mediocrity of everyday Soviet life, the horrors of war, and the martyrdom of earlier poets such as Tsvetayeva, who perished under Stalin. Occasionally, too, this clandestinely exported poetry is quietly illuminated by the folk values of Old Russia, as in Gelb Garbovsky's "To the Neva": "I will come back, no matter what, even if, when I do return, I'm dying."

JOSEPH BRODSKY

The most famous poet-exile was Joseph Brodsky (1940-1996), who felt himself to be a poet by the grace of God and therefore for whom no other social role was necessary. A native of Leningrad, in the late 1950's, he became associated with the circle of young poets around Akhmatova and was recognized by her as a sig-

nificant new talent. Though his poems were apolitical, his independence of mind caused him to be arrested in 1964 for "parasitism," that is, not having a legally approved job, and he was sentenced to five years of internal exile in the north. Released in a year, he was ultimately forced into exile in the United States, where he spent most of the rest of his life teaching, writing, and reciting his poetry, which he did with a unique intensity and melodiousness. In 1987, he won the Nobel Prize in Literature, and in 1991, he became the United States poet laureate, the first nonnative to be so honored. Although he did not complete high school, his poetry is characterized by the erudition of someone steeped in classical learning and world culture. It has a philosophical depth and complexity of imagery comparable to his favorite English Metaphysical poets and modernists such as T. S. Eliot and W. H. Auden. His verse forms are basically traditional, but within them he created an unusual degree of lyrical tension. His typical themes are loneliness and suffering, death and salvation, often ventriloquized through some famous historical or mythological figure in a moment of realization or crisis. Though he had the opportunity in the late twentieth century to visit and even return to Russia, he chose not to do so, but instead to die in exile and to be buried in Venice.

THE UNDERGROUND

Parallel to the public existence of poetry in the post-Stalin period represented on one hand by Yevtushenko and Voznesensky, and on the other by Galanskov and Brodsky, there was a more private, underground development that occurred in formal and informal poetry circles. Formal circles centered around officially sponsored clubs and seminars in which senior poets mentored younger aspiring poets. This was in part a subtle way for the authorities to keep an eye on the younger generation, but in the better groups, for example, those led by Mikhail Svetlov (1903-1964) and Kirill Kovaldzhi (born 1930), some talented poets did find useful mentoring and occasional outlets to publication. More important were the informal groups of the underground. One of the earliest of these, the Nebyvalisty (Unprecedentists, 1939-1940) headed by Nikolai Glazkov (1919-1979), who coined the term *samizdat*, actually began before the war at the Moscow Pedagogical Institute as a continuation of Futurism. Though the group soon dissolved, Glazkov, and for their part Kruchonykh and Pasternak, were able to serve as personal mentors to several generations of younger poets. SMOG (Youngest Society of Geniuses), also in Moscow but in the early 1960's, like the Nebyvalisty, was not noted for the innovativeness of its members' poetry, but rather for their unrestrained behavior. It did include one lyric genius in the mold of Yesenin, Leonid Gubanov (1946-1983). On the other hand, the Lianozovo school, which centered around the suburban Moscow barracks apartment of Evgeny Kropivnitsky (1893-1979), fostered poets of genuine originality and innovation. Among them were Vsevolod Nekrasov (Kholin; 1920-1999), Genrikh Sapgir (1928-1999), and even the scandalous Eduard Limonov (born 1943), all of whom emerged as major literary figures in the glasnost period. In Leningrad in the late 1950's, the Philological school, which included Vladimir Ufliand (1937-2007), Lev Losev (1937-2009), Aleksandr Kondratov (1937-1993), and Mikhail Yeryomin (born 1936), was one of the first such underground groups. A monumental contribution to an awareness of this period, especially in Leningrad, is Konstantin Kuzminsky's nine-volume *Blue Lagoon Anthology of Modern Russian Poetry* (1980-1986).

BARD POETRY

Along with the poetry underground there developed another trend that had its roots in popular and folk song, namely, the guitar poetry of the so-called bards. These poets chose to set their texts to melodies with simple guitar accompaniment and sing them in private gatherings and around campfires. The recognized founder of this trend was Bulat Okudzhava (1924-1997), who began to compose such songs immediately after World War II. With the advent of readily available tape recorders in the 1960's, Okudzhava's songs became well known and popular throughout the Soviet Union, despite the lack of official recordings. Other important figures in this genre were Aleksandr Galich (1918-1977), whose songs developed a social protest edge that resulted in his being exiled abroad, and Vladimir

Vysotsky (1938-1980), whose broad-ranging themes and personae made him immensely popular with all levels of Russian society, a popularity that only increased after his untimely death from heart failure. What distinguishes the work of the bards from popular song is the high quality of the poetic text itself, which can usually stand on its own as fine poetry, regardless of its musical aspects.

POETRY OF FREEDOM

With Gorbachev's accession to power in 1985 and his introduction of a policy of glasnost, official censorship began to be reduced. By 1989, it was virtually eliminated, producing an ever-increasing wave of poetry publications. Initially, much of this was past work that finally emerged from the underground to reach the general reading public. Soon new voices and new work by older generations began to flood the public sphere, creating an impression of postmodern Babel. Where earlier there had been only a handful of published poets worth reading, there now were dozens, if not hundreds, with a range of orientations and styles. Parallel with this was a sharp decline in popular interest in poetry. What had been a narrow and exciting passageway to freer speech was made to face competition from a deluge of popular entertainment and the unfettered news media. At the same time, however, poetry has enjoyed a major flowering. Attempts to categorize the new poetry into trends such as metametaphorism and conceptualism are useful to some extent but do not do justice either to the richness and complexity of the situation or to such unique major figures as Gennady Aygi (1934-2006), Viktor Sosnora (born 1936), Aleksandr Kushner (born 1936), Ry Nikonova (born 1942), Lev Rubinstein (born 1947), Ivan Zhdanov (born 1948), Olga Sedakova (born 1949), Nina Iskrenko (1951-1995), Timur Kibirov (born 1955), and Vitaly Kalpidi (born 1957), to name just a few. Moreover, with the freedom to travel, publish, and distribute books, the separation among Russian poets living throughout Russia and those living abroad has been eliminated. The landscape of modern Russian poetry more and more resembles that in the West.

BIBLIOGRAPHY

Blok, Aleksandr. *Us Four Plus Four: Eight Russian Poets Conversing*. New Orleans, La.: UNO Press, 2008. An extensive collection of poetry from eight important Russian poets. The poems are arranged as a conversation.

Bristol, Evelyn. *A History of Russian Poetry*. New York: Oxford University Press, 1991. Covers Russian literature from the tenth century to the 1970's, placing writers and literary movements in a historical context. Biographical essay and commentary on each poet.

Bunimovitch, Evgeny, ed., and J. Kates, trans. and ed. *Contemporary Russian Poetry: An Anthology*. Champaign: Dalkey Archive Press, University of Illinois, 2008. A bilingual collection, consisting of works of forty-four living Russian poets, all born after 1945, who were selected for inclusion by Bunimovitch, a prominent Moscow poet.

Cornwell, Neil, ed. *A Reference Guide to Russian Literature*. Chicago: Fitzroy Dearborn, 1998. Detailed entries on some 273 writers, each consisting of a brief biographical sketch, a list of major works, and a selected bibliography. There are also thirteen essays on general topics. Russian-English title index.

_____. *The Routledge Companion to Russian Literature*. New York : Routledge, 2001. A reliable and accessible volume that spans a thousand years of Russian literature with essays on diverse subjects, each by an recognized authority in his or her area. Ideal both for students and for general readers. Bibliography and index.

Kates, J., ed. *In the Grip of Strange Thoughts: Russian Poetry in a New Era*. Brookline, Mass.: Zephyr Press, 2000. A collection of 118 poems by thirty-two writers, including fourteen women. A bilingual edition. Introduction and afterword on translation by the editor. Foreword by Mikhail Aizenberg. Annotated. Index of titles and first lines. Bibliography.

Nabokov, Vladimir Vladimirovich, comp. and trans. *Verses and Versions: Three Centuries of Russian Poetry*. Edited by Brian Boyd and Stanislav Shvabrin. Orlando, Fla.: Harcourt, 2008. Nabokov's English translations of Russian poems, preserving the rhyme schemes of the originals and presented side-by-side with them. Introduction by Boyd. Also includes Nabokov's translations from French to English and his comments about translation. Index of poets, index of titles and first lines. An invaluable volume.

Polukhina, Valentina, and Daniel Weissbort, eds. *An Anthology of Contemporary Russian Women Poets*. Iowa City: University of Iowa Press, 2005. English translations of works by more than eighty poets, some well established and others still unknown outside of Russia. Preface by Stephanie Sandler, concluding comments by Dmitry Kuzmin and Elena Fanailova. Biographical notes, bibliography, and index.

Scherr, Barry P. *Russian Poetry: Meter, Rhythm, and Rhyme*. Berkeley: University of California Press, 1986. One of the best treatments of the principles of Russian versification.

Smith, Gerald S. *Songs to Seven Strings: Russian Guitar Poetry and Soviet "Mass Song."* Bloomington: Indiana University Press, 1984. The main general source in English for information on the "bards."

Wachtel, Michael. *The Cambridge Introduction to Russian Poetry*. New York: Cambridge University Press, 2004. Discusses such matters as versification, poetic language, and traditional genres, drawing illustrations from poems by major Russian writers of the last three centuries.

_____. *The Development of Russian Verse; Meter and Its Meanings*. New York: Cambridge University Press, 1999. The first full-length study of Russian verse, demonstrating the influence of earlier uses of form on later poets, as well as the integral relationship between form and content. The author illustrates his ideas with close readings of more than fifty poets. A major scholarly achievement.

Yevtushenko, Yevgeny, et al., eds. *Twentieth Century Russian Poetry: Silver and Steel, an Anthology*. New York: Anchor Books, 1994. A large, sometimes quirky and inaccurate, but useful anthology of translations.

Mitzi M. Brunsdale
Updated by Gerald Janecek

SCANDINAVIAN POETRY

The oldest evidence of lyric writing in the Nordic countries can be dated back to the introduction of the runic alphabet in the third century. Thousands of runic inscriptions—first carved in wood and on tools and later in stone as memorials—are preserved in Denmark, Norway, and especially Sweden; more than two thousand inscriptions dating from the eleventh century are known to exist in Sweden alone. These inscriptions, characteristically concise and laconic, provide invaluable insights into both personal destinies and events of national scope. Frequently, the inscriptions employ a stylized language using alliteration and poetic circumlocutions called *kenningar*. At times, these messages, which may consist of several hundred runic signs, incorporate phrases known from the common Germanic

Odin, the Norse god, is a revered figure in Eddic poetry.

literary tradition and regular stanzas known from the far more sophisticated—and better preserved—West Nordic Old Norse poetry.

EDDIC POETRY

In order to form a better understanding of Old Norse poetry, one must turn to this early Norwegian-Icelandic literature, divided into Eddic poetry and skaldic poetry. The anonymous Eddic poems have been preserved primarily in the Codex Regius manuscript from the latter part of the thirteenth century, the *Poetic Edda* (ninth to twelfth centuries; English translations 1923, 1928, 1962, 1997). A number of these texts are also quoted in Snorri Sturluson's (1179-1241) book on Nordic mythology and poetry, written about 1220—the *Prose Edda* (English translations, 1916, 1954, 1987). The written tradition does not go further back, but it is evident that many Eddic poems were for several centuries transmitted via the oral tradition. They take their topics from both Old Norse mythology and Germanic heroic legends, employing three metrical measures: *fornyrthislag* (epic measure), *málaháttr* (speech measure), and *ljothaháttr* (chant measure). All of these measures are based on old Germanic alliterative long line, and all of them tend to be stanzaic.

Codex Regius opens with *Völuspá* (c. 1000; *Völuspá: The Song of the Sybil*, 1968), a prophecy about the Creation as well as the end of the world and the rise of a new world order. While this mythical vision is cultic, forming a Nordic parallel to the biblical Genesis and Revelation, the following poem, *Hávamál* (ninth and tenth century; *The Sayings of the High One*, 1923), is an expression of worldly wisdom. The first stanza advocates caution and distrustfulness through the sayings of the god Odin, who expresses the essence of Viking philosophy in the following lines: "Cattle die,/ kinsmen die,/ one dies oneself also;/ but fame [reputation] alone/ will never die/ for him who gains good fame."

Among the gods of the Eddic poems, Odin is the most distinguished, but, as in the Homeric poems, the frailties of the gods are also exposed. In *Hárbarthsljóth* (*The Lay of Hárbarthr*), Odin is thus played off, with coarse humor, against the god Thor, and Thor becomes the main character in *Thrymskvitha* (*The Lay of Thrymr*), the most popular of all Eddic poems. It tells of the god's recovering his hammer from the giant Thymr, a high point of Old Norse poetry with its pithy portraits and agile narrative. No direct Germanic counterpart to the Eddic mythological poetry is known to exist. The heroic poems in Codex Regius, on the other hand, have parallels in the British *Widsith* (c. seventh century) and *Beowulf* (c. 1000) and the German *Hildebrandslied* (c. 800). The basic concept of this heroic poetry, as well as that of its mythological counterpart, is epic and dramatic. The worldview is tragic-heroic, and human action is governed by the dictates of honor and revenge. The major portion of the Eddic heroic poetry is connected with the Germanic hero Sigurthr (Siegfried) and the specifically Nordic Helgi Hundingsbani, who is made a half brother to Sigurthr. In a number of poems, partly linked together and supplemented by prose sections, Sigurthr's youth, the avenging of his father, his dragon slaying, his winning of the hoard, his flame-wall ride to release the sleeping Brynhildr, and finally his death are related. The characters confront one another in terse, stylized dialogues, and a light of tragic pathos and timeless idealism is cast on their lives of strong wills and emotions.

SKALDIC POETRY

The skaldic poems, on the other hand, generally have a more current atmosphere and are linked to certain situations in the named authors' own time. Certain poets, skalds, were even employed as official chroniclers at the courts in order to celebrate the kings and their deeds. This historical function of skaldic poetry explains why it is frequently quoted in the sagas, especially the kings' sagas of the thirteenth century; in fact, a considerable portion of this literature has survived only as such quotations. Skaldic poetry (a selection of which appears in English in *The Skalds*, 1945, 1968) is a unique Nordic genre. Like Eddic poetry, it is alliterative, but it follows far stricter metrical rules. The use of *kenningar* as ornamentation is likewise much more widespread and creates an immensely concentrated imagery difficult to interpret in its sophisticated appeal to the intellect rather than to the emotions.

The first-known skald was the ninth century Norwegian Bragi Boddason (Bragi the Old). In his writing, the metrics and diction of skaldic poetry are already fully developed. A culmination is reached by Eyvindr Skáldaspillir (c. 920-990), the last of the Norwegian court poets, with his memorial poem *Hákonarmál* (c. 960; *The Lay of Hákon*, 1936), which describes how Odin sends two of his Valkyries to the battlefield to fetch King Hákon to Valhalla. Gradually, the genre became exclusively Icelandic. Egill Skallagrímsson (c. 910-990), the most important poet in Old Norse literature, introduces an important formal feature, the end rhyme, in *Höfuthlausn* (948; *The Death Song of Egil the Son of Grim*, 1921), a poem that Egill composed to save his life when he was captured by his mortal enemy. Particularly renowned is Egill's lament *Sonatorrek* (961; *The Loss of My Sons*, 1924), the title of which alludes to Egill's loss of two sons, one by drowning, the other by sickness. Primarily, however, the work presents the poet's lament concerning his own helplessness and loneliness and a critical description of his relationship to the gods and to poetry itself. Here, for the first time in Nordic literature, one recognizes a distinctly subjective and independent artistic personality.

SACRED MEDIEVAL POETRY

With the final victory of Christianity in all the Nordic countries around 1100, the Latin alphabet was introduced, establishing a Church culture and didactic genres such as the sermon and the legend of saints, which, besides bodies of laws and chronicles, dominate the prose of the Middle Ages. A unique position was occupied by the Icelandic sagas, and it was Iceland that dominated the religious poetry of the period, as if the forms of the Eddic and skaldic poems were adapted to praise Christian martyrs and saintly kings. The most exquisite of these sacred poems written in the Old Norse tradition is the anonymous *Sólarljóth* (c. 1200; *The Lay of the Sun*, 1950). The meter is the *ljothaháttr*, or chant measure, and occurs also in *The Sayings of the High One*. Both works are didactic, with concrete illustrations of the ways of evil, and they advise how to avoid eternal damnation. *The Lay of the Sun* concludes in apocalyptic visions reminiscent of *Völuspá*, placing the former in the European context of Catholic visionary literature such as Dante's *La divina commedia* (c. 1320; *The Divine Comedy*, 1802). The most encompassing religious medieval poem in the vernacular, however, is the Icelandic *Lilja* (c. 1350; *The Lily*, 1870), a panorama of the entire history of the world from a Christian perspective, from Creation to Last Judgment; it comprises one hundred stanzas and is attributed to the monk Eysteinn Ásgrímsson (died 1361).

A distinct group within the sacred medieval poetry is formed by the *Mariaviser* (songs to Mary), the most typical examples of which were written by the Dane Per Raer Lille (c. 1450-1500). In his poems, the biblical imagery from the Song of Songs is merged with the courtly ideals of the troubadour poetry. The Virgin Mary is praised with romantic chivalrousness as the quintessence of everything worth worshiping.

MEDIEVAL BALLADS AND FOLK LITERATURE

During the late Middle Ages, from about 1350 to 1500, the literary dominance of the West Nordic countries—especially Iceland—sharply decreased, accompanied by the artistic decline of the most distinguished genre of this country, the saga. Shortly after 1200, the anonymous folk ballad, originating in France, emerged to become the most prominent genre of the period, especially in Denmark and Sweden.

Scandinavian ballads are traditionally classified according to their contents. "Knightly ballads," by far the largest group, depict the milieu and characters of the medieval aristocracy and usually focus on erotic conflicts. The "magic ballads" deal with supernatural beings and events—revenants, transformations, and runic spells—and are based partly on folk belief, partly on internationally known motifs. Characteristic of Norwegian tradition are a number of later "troll ballads" from the fourteenth and fifteenth centuries, based on Old Norse folklore but often rendered with elements of burlesque irony. Whereas the rare traces of Christianity seem only secondary in these ballads, the "religious ballads" are clearly of Catholic origin. Very few of them exist in Scandinavia. In Sweden, they center on Saint Stephen; in Norway, on Saint Olav. Unique is the Norwegian *Draumkvede* (n.d.; *The Dream Ballad*, 1946), an offshoot of European visionary literature. Characteristic of Danish balladry are the numerous

"historical ballads," frequently centered on characters known from national history. Some of the historical ballads have been dated to the eleventh century, whereas the seemingly older "heroic ballads," whose subjects find counterparts in Old Norse and Germanic legends, are relatively late, dating from the fourteenth century. The heroic ballads are less formulaic and less tightly structured than the knightly ballads, for example, as are the "novelistic ballads," another late type, a Scandinavian offshoot of the courtly Continental poetry such as that about Charlemagne, Tristan and Isolde, and Paris and Helen. The novelistic ballads were especially popular in the Faeroe Islands, where some of the versions reach a length of more than two hundred stanzas, embroidering the original plot. A final group of ballads, the "jocular ballads," frequently with a racy erotic point, does not share the formal or metrical uniformity of the other ballad categories. The age of these ballads is difficult to determine, and they seem to have their origin in the lower social strata from the close of the Middle Ages.

A main function of the ballad was to accompany the chain dances. When the Middle Ages drew to a close, this type of dance went out of fashion—except in the Faeroe Islands—and the ballad survived only as a means of vocal entertainment. The ballad was not a creation of ambitious troubadours following strict aesthetic rules but rather an art form with a functional purpose—thus the simplicity and flexibility of ballad forms and meters: couplets and quatrains, as in the British ballad, with a refrain. The stanzas are end-rhymed, but assonance is acceptable. The milieu of the ballad is that of the country gentry; the ideals, those of feudal society. Character delineation is formulaic: "so fair a maid," "my handsome lad," and so on. The psychology of the characters is not individualized or analyzed but projected with great artistic finesse through dialogue and action. Feelings are described in set phrases— "proud Adelus" or "with truth and modesty"—and the characters are presented in a limited number of situations, each of which is described identically: "There was brave Sir Nilus/ from home he rode away;/ he betrothed proud Hillelil,/ she was so fair a maid."

The ballad texts were created by individuals but were transmitted orally from one generation to another as part of a living, centuries-long tradition. The ballads, therefore, should not be regarded as historical relics; likewise, they cannot be read as valid mirrors of the period in which they were sung. They are not merely statements but also highly sophisticated interpretations of the human condition. It is this existential perspective that, in the last resort, gives the Nordic ballads their timeless value.

Of a totally different character is the rich Finnish literature of medieval origin, which was not recorded until the period of nationalistic Romanticism. In 1835, Elias Lönnrot (1802-1884) published the nonstrophic epic poem *Kalevala* (enlarged 1849 as *Uusi Kalevala*, English translation, 1888), containing songs dealing with heroic mythological persons and themes. In 1840, he also issued the extensive collection of lyric folk poetry *Kanteletar* (*The Kanteletar: Lyrics and Ballads After Oral Tradition*, 1992), which, together with *Kalevala*, constitutes the major national work in Finnish literature.

FOURTEENTH THROUGH SIXTEENTH CENTURIES

During the fourteenth century, a more epic type of poetry—probably developed from the folk ballad—emerged in Iceland, the *rímur*, which gradually turned into entire lengthy cycles, frequently versifications of earlier prose works such as Continental chivalric novels. The chivalric novel in verse was introduced in the other Nordic countries in the early fourteenth century with the three *Eufemia visur* (Eufemia lays), reworkings from French originals. A further step toward pure prose was taken with the Danish and Swedish rhyming chronicles from the fourteenth and fifteenth centuries, which relate the national history of the two royal houses but nevertheless are continuations of a Continental, particularly German, genre.

This connection became disrupted through the Lutheran Reformation of about 1530, which in its militant phase of consolidation focused on strictly didactic literature: Bible translations and prayer books. In Denmark, the Reformation was characterized by fierce polemics, pamphlets, and primitive, versified anti-Catholic satires after German models. In Finland, however, a stronger Humanistic tradition prevailed, whose major figure was the bishop Mikael Agricola (c. 1510-1557), who

translated parts of the Psalms of David. In 1583, Jacobus Finno (c. 1540-1588) published a hymnbook; of its approximately one hundred hymns, ten are his own and the rest are translations. The hymn became the predominant lyric genre of the sixteenth century. Significant was the publication in Denmark in 1569 of a hymnbook by Hans Thomissøn (1532-1573), which achieved official recognition. Not until Hans Christensen Sthen (1544-1610), however, did an original Danish, and Nordic, hymn writer come forth, who in his poems succeeded in combining the meters and tone of the popular song with a specifically Christian message.

SEVENTEENTH CENTURY

Strong theological orthodoxy suppressed free artistic expression during the sixteenth century. Not until the end of that century and the first half of the seventeenth century were the ideas of Humanism and the Renaissance fully accepted, encouraging the creation of a literature in the vernacular based on classical traditions of genre, style, and meter. Limitations on subject matter were abandoned, literature became increasingly secularized, and individual authors were free to be as subjective as they wished. They were encouraged to experiment with language and expression, and gradually a literature emerged for which figures of speech were as important as ideas, a characteristic feature of the concluding literary trend of the seventeenth century, the Baroque.

The most ambitious genre, the religious epic, was, via a French model, introduced in Denmark by Anders Arrebo (1587-1637) with his *Hexaemeron* (published posthumously in 1661), a didactic poem describing the six days of the Creation and employing details from Nordic nature and folk life. The style is stately and rhetorical and does not match in vivacity the second large epic of the century, by the Swede Georg Stiernhielm (1598-1672). Written in hexameter, the topic for the latter epic, *Hercules* (1658), is classical, incorporating the motif of Hercules at the crossroads between two ways of life, that of pleasure and that of virtue.

The first original Swedish lyric poet, with his roots in the popular-song tradition, was Lars Wivallius (1605-1669). His reputation is based on a number of short, subjective poems in which the poet, writing in prison, succeeds in expressing his deeply felt, stirring concepts of freedom. Wivallius's vivid appreciation of nature, coined in graceful stanzas, was new in Swedish literature. In his poetry, private complaints give way to a broad stream of images of the changing seasons, of the occupations of farmers and shepherds, and of the joy to be found in nature.

A similarly Bohemian character was Lasse Lucidor (1638-1674), whose songs and hymns point to the intense and antithetical stylistic ideals of Baroque literature. His works are concerned with the horror of death and sin, of Satan's power and God's wrath. In *It samtaal emellan Döden och en säker menniskia* (a conversation between Death and a confident man), a dialogue related to the medieval motif of the Dance of Death, Lucidor tells in tightly structured stanzas how the arrogant pleasure seeker gradually is driven to despair but in his moment of death invokes Divine Grace.

The culmination of the Swedish Baroque is the monumental burial poem by Gunno Dahlstierna (1661-1709), *Kunga skald* (1697; the king's poet), a lamentation in response to the death of King Charles XI, brimming with allegorical figures, sweeping historical overviews, and a detailed description of a voyage around the world. A brighter aspect of Baroque literature is represented by Johan Runius (1679-1713), the most eminent Swedish writer of occasional poetry. Despite personal disappointments, Runius emerged as a poet as naïvely pious as he was unrestrainedly merry, juxtaposing religious emotion and comic effects.

The poetry of both Dahlstierna and Runius has a strong pastoral element, already present in the writing of Wivallius—an element that finds a noteworthy representative in Denmark in Anders Bording (1619-1677). Most of his work consists of occasional poetry, but more valuable are his pastoral verses composed in a simple yet elegant syntax.

The pastoral genre finds another Danish representative in the clergyman Thomas Kingo (1634-1703), whose graceful poem *Chrysillis* consists of a glowing declaration of love for his wife, framed by descriptions of idyllic nature. In Kingo's hymns, Danish—and Nordic—Baroque reached its culmination. His devotional work in two parts, *Aandelige siunge-koor* (1674-

1681; spiritual chorus), was intended to oust foreign, especially German, hymnbooks. The fundamental feeling evinced by the work is fear of the power of sin and the fickleness of this world, expressed through powerful antithetical constructions in the speculative poems "Far, verden, farvel" (fare, world, farewell) and "Sorrig og glæde" (sorrow and joy). The battle within the soul and the troublesome path toward God are portrayed with intense insight. Kingo was rewarded for his achievements by being appointed as a bishop, and in 1689, he published a collection of hymns, *Vinter-Parten* (the winter part), intended to be the official Danish hymnal. Easter hymns are the highlight of the volume, evoking the Passion with unsurpassed intensity and lifelikeness and peaking in a grand celebration of the Resurrection.

Another characteristic Baroque genre was the topographic description. Arrebo's epic of the Creation was an early example of topographic interest, and Kingo himself wrote a number of topographic works, but the artistic summit of this genre was reached with the Norwegian clergyman Petter Dass's (1647-1707) ambitious presentation of the geography, fauna, and folk life of northern Norway, *Nordlands trompet* (1739; *The Trumpet of Nordland*, 1954). Based on Dass's own journeys and on oral and written sources, it is a realistic and humorous portrayal of everyday life in the seventeenth century.

EIGHTEENTH CENTURY

In a European perspective, the Nordic literatures of the Renaissance and the Baroque—with the sole exception of the Danish hymn writer Kingo—appear strikingly poor. Not until the beginning of the eighteenth century, when French classicism reached Scandinavia combined with the philosophical ideas of the Enlightenment, did a modern literature of lasting value emerge, centered on the Dano-Norwegian writer Ludvig Holberg (1684-1754) and the Swede Olaf von Dalin (1708-1763). Characteristically, Holberg's merits lie within drama, while Dalin, through his weekly periodical *Den swänska Argus* (1732-1734; the Swedish Argus), virtually established modern Swedish prose.

In counterbalance to the Enlightenment, however, a

lyric and sentimental undercurrent—often connected with pietistic religiosity—runs throughout the literature of the eighteenth century up to the pre-Romantic period of about 1770. It was in this pietistic milieu that the emotional and fervent hymns of the Danish clergyman Hans Adolph Brorson (1694-1764) emerged. In 1739, he collected a number of hymn translations as well as his own poems in a volume titled *Troens Rare Klenodie* (the rare jewel of faith), all of which are based on the contrast between earthly and heavenly existence. Humankind is seen as corrupt, and conversion is portrayed in scenes of rebirth through prayer and grace. Brorson's texts were intended primarily for household devotion. Many are composed in complex meters, following the contemporary rococo aria, and employ ingenious rhyme patterns, encore effects, and dialogue verse—features that are present to an even greater extent in Brorson's final collection, *Svane-Sang* (1765; swan song).

Light and graceful stanzas and melodious rhythms can also be found in the writing of Ambrosius Stub (1705-1758)—in his hymns as well as in his drinking songs and occasional poetry. His masterpiece, and the first poem in Danish literature to be based on a direct observation of nature, is *Den kiedsom Vinter gik sin Gang* (the tiresome winter went its course). It depicts, with a multitude of delicate details, a walk on a spring day, but the scenery is personalized, and the poem turns into a symbol of the course of life. One senses in each stanza the Divine Creator guiding everything for the best.

Related in its theme but executed with more ingenious rhetoric is the wedding poem *En Maji Dag* (1758; a May day), by the Norwegian Christian Braunmann Tullin (1728-1765). The poem is a glorification of the countryside as an idyllic antithesis to corrupt city life, and, as in Stub's poem, the attention is shifted from nature to its Creator—a clear reflection of Deistic theology, with its notion of God as the Creator of the best of all possible worlds. At the poem's conclusion, the newly married couple appear dressed as rococo shepherds. Tullin was inspired by the nature scenes of Alexander Pope and James Thomson (1700-1748) and by Jean-Jacques Rousseau's attacks on modern civilization. Tullin's final work, *Skabningens Yypperlighed*

(1764; on the excellency of Creation), on the other hand, is a didactic and religious poem, the sense of infinity and high-flown style of which were influenced by Edward Young's renowned poem *Night Thoughts* (1742-1744).

The deliberate refinement of literary language and the aesthetic taste in general, which the poetry of Brorson, Stub, and Tullin exemplifies, can also be found in Swedish literature. A pietistic tone first colored the poetry of the Finno-Swedish writer Jacob Frese (1690-1729), but the clear emergence of a more subjective and emotional writing took place later in the thin volume *Den sörgande turtur-dufwan* (1743; the grieving turtledove), by Hedvig Charlotta Nordenflycht (1718-1763). The collection consists of lamentations by the young widow, rendered in a soft-spoken melodious aria form, and points toward the 1750's, a decade stylistically dominated by a combination of French classicism and elegant rococo and influenced by the Rousseauistic longing for primitive nature and unrestrained emotional life.

Leading authors besides Nordenflycht were Gustaf Fredrik Gyllenborg and the Finnish-born Gustaf Philip Creutz. Gyllenborg (1731-1808) established himself as a moralist and satirist, fiercely attacking church and society. Creutz (1731-1785) is the author of the most valuable lyric work of the period, the elegantly written *Atis och Camilla* (1762; Atis and Camilla). A love story with a pastoral setting, it analyzes the awakening youthful passion in which the gods of antiquity constantly intervene.

The last third of the eighteenth century in Sweden was dominated by King Gustav III and his brilliant, French-oriented court. The prose of this period is mainly nonfictional and of only minor interest; poetry, drama, and opera are the predominant genres.

It is among the lyric poets that one finds the greatest Swedish writer of the century, the Bohemian Carl Michael Bellman (1740-1795). The writings of Bellman—he was himself a celebrated singer and musician—have their point of departure in the drinking song, its tempo and wit, but with an undertone of tragic compassion. Another characteristic element is Bellman's penchant for imitation and parody—particularly of figures from the Old Testament in songs such as

"Gubben Noah" (Old Man Noah) and "Joachim uti Babylon" (Joachim in Babylon).

Bellman's major works are the two song cycles *Fredmans epistlar* (1790; Fredman's epistles) and *Fredmans sânger* (1791; Fredman's songs; selections in English translation appeared in 1939 and later). They consist of songs about Fredman and his friends—drunkards, Bohemians, and prostitutes from the Stockholm tavern milieu—interspersed with impressionistic passages concerning the city and its surroundings. Despite all of its realistic elements, the milieu of these texts is basically mythic, depicting a group of good-humored sybarites, not distinctly individualized, living in joy and sorrow in a tragicomic universe created as a divine jest. The pleasures of the moment appear as the only and highest goal, but transitoriness and death are the somber backdrop for the turbulent events. Bellman's stanzas are technically brilliant in their language, rhyme, and rhythm; nothing is improvised, and each detail is carefully rendered. Performing his own songs, Bellman used partly popular tunes of the times and partly his own compositions, achieving an unsurpassed unity of text and music.

A stricter representative of the French classicist ideas of the Enlightenment is Johan Henrik Kellgren (1751-1795), who embraced the radical philosophy of Voltaire. After writing some portentous odes—some celebrating an Epicurean outlook, some displaying stoic resignation—Kellgren found his personal style in *Sinnenas förening* (1778; the union of senses) and *Mina löjen* (1778; my ridicules), philosophical poems written in flowing, conversational stanzas; the latter contains strong satirical attacks on the clergy, scholars, and writers but also a considerable amount of self-directed irony in the author's portrait of himself. A more serious counterpart to *Mina löjen* is *Våra villor* (1780; our illusions), a didactic poem about the question of truth and illusion, which was a burning problem for Kellgren as a skeptical representative of the Enlightenment. In his later years, Kellgren was influenced by pre-Romanticism. *Den nya skapelsen* (1790; the new creation) is a dithyrambic glorification of Eros and fantasy. The beloved becomes the archetype of beauty that vitalizes and inspires all nature, which until now has seemed dead to the poet. Kellgren continued his fight for spiritual liberty and reason with numerous biting aphorisms and two great comic poems: *Dumboms lefverne* (1791; life of Mr. Simpleton), a suite of pointed satirical texts defending common sense against a large variety of follies, and *Ljusets fiender* (1792; enemies of the light), an allegorical paean to the French Revolution.

Philosophically more moderate than Kellgren is Karl Gustaf af Leopold (1756-1829), whose best-known poems, particularly from the 1790's, are long, speculative texts bearing titles such as *Försynen* (1793; providence) and *Predikaren* (1794; the sermonizer) and composed in a perfected, classical ode style that lends to the poet's philosophy of resignation a striking, personal touch.

Contemporary satire together with a detailed realism finds a convincing representative in Anna Maria Lenngren (1754-1817), whose writings were not published until 1819, in *Skaldeförsök* (poetic attempts). In her works from the 1790's, Lenngren succeeds in combining French classicism with the more concrete realism of a later era. In the satires *Porträtterna* (1796; the portraits) and *Fröken Juliana* (1796; Miss Juliana), the pretentiousness and folly of the Swedish nobility are displayed with burlesque vigor. Lenngren's criticism is also aimed at the other social classes, and occasionally it develops into stirring and compassionate tragicomic portraits of drab destinies in an insensitive society.

The only significant and aggressive representative of an opposite trend is Thomas Thorild (1759-1808). *Passionerna* (1785; the passions), a didactic poem about divine power and harmony and a hymn to nature, invokes Ossian, William Shakespeare, and Friedrich Gottlieb Klopstock, the heroes of pre-Romanticism. The tone is passionate, the style high-flown and abrupt. Thorild's subsequent writings are uneven, but in his unrhymed, free verses he is able to express both the unique greatness and the passionate sufferings of the lonely genius, thus anticipating the hero worship of the nineteenth century.

Pointing directly toward Romanticism is the poem by Frans Mikael Franzén (1772-1847) titled *Människans anlete* (1793; the human face). It is a bright, multicolored lyric picture of the sixth day of Creation, when the splendor of newborn nature pales when confronted with man, who mirrors God himself. The Christian viewpoint is further emphasized in *Det nya Eden* (1795; the new paradise), in which Franzén, through an almost chaotic stream of images and visions, conjures up a paradisaical dream of the ascension of the soul.

In Denmark, the ideals of the Enlightenment and rationalism were expounded by a group of writers centered on the Norwegian poet and playwright Johan Herman Wessel (1742-1785), but completely without the force and talent found in Swedish literature.

JOHANNES EWALD

The highly emotional pre-Romanticism based on English and German models has its greatest Scandinavian representative in Johannes Ewald (1743-1781). Through the German poet Klopstock, who lived in Denmark from 1751 to 1770, Ewald became acquainted not only with Shakespeare and Ossian but also with Old Norse mythology. Less successful as a playwright, Ewald must be regarded as the greatest Danish lyric poet before the Romantic era. His greatness emerges in the ode *Rungsteds Lyksaligheder* (1775; the joys of Rungsted). Taking its point of departure in concrete descriptions of the locality, the poem rises to an enthusiastic glorification of God, of whom nature is not merely a reflection but an integral part.

Ewald also displayed a great talent as a writer of occasional poetry. Through a combination of sensitivity and strict adherence to structure, he was able to elevate this genre above similar contributions of the period. Particularly successful are his death poems, which focus on the pain and sorrow of the bereaved, as well as a number of poems to friends and benefactors. Ewald's last, pietistically inspired poetry is predominantly confessional. He describes humanity's—and his own—condition until he has placed his destiny in God's hands in *Til Sielen: En Ode* (1780; ode to the soul). The fallen soul is symbolized by the disobedient young eagle, which has fallen from its nest to the depths and helplessly strives toward the light until its mother comes to its rescue. It is in his individualism, his sensitive self-consciousness, that Ewald points beyond his own time. He focuses directly on the self, emphasizing the importance of the subjective experience in humanity's encounter with God Almighty. This experience is expressed with overwhelming poetic force that is kept in tight rein by strict artistic discipline.

JENS BAGGESEN

Another link between rationalism and Romanticism is seen in the works of Jens Baggesen (1764-1826). The spirit of the eighteenth century is embodied in a number of ironic and satiric epic poems published as *Comiske Fortællinger* (1785; humorous tales). In his principal work, the travelogue *Labyrinten* (1792-1793; the labyrinth), Baggesen, using Laurence Sterne and Rousseau as his models, is primarily concerned with his emotional reactions to the places and people he encounters. Baggesen also wrote a number of intimate love poems: Platonic yet sensuous in their view of love, occasionally marred by sentimentalism, these love poems belong to the Romantic era. Baggesen is a tragic figure in Scandinavian literature. Vacillating between two epochs, he was never fully accepted at home, and his attempt to establish a career in Germany was unsuccessful.

ROMANTICISM

The Romantic movement, which originated in Germany, was introduced in Scandinavia in 1803 through Adam Gottlob Oehlenschläger's (1779-1850) *Digte* (1803; poems). The first decades of the nineteenth century in Denmark and Sweden were dominated by the so-called universal Romanticism, which set forth the pantheistic theories of the divine spirit's manifestation in nature and history, to be realized through the intuition of the poetic genius.

Oehlenschläger's *Digte* and the succeeding collection in two volumes, *Poetiske Skrifter* (1805; poetic works) contain all the elements of Romanticism: mixed genres including lyric poetry and ballads in changing meters, epic cycles, and prose and drama, culminating in the fairy-tale play *Aladdin* (1805; English translations, 1857, 1968), a symbolic glorification of the power of the genius over chaos and evil. *Poetiske Skrifter* also contains a saga imitation that points to further development of Oehlenschläger's writings, and of Danish literature in general, toward a national and patriotic Romanticism with motifs drawn from Nordic mythology and history. In the works of Oehlenschläger, this school is represented in the collection

Nordiske Digte (1807; Nordic poems) and in a large number of plays, culminating in the masterful epic cycle *Helge* (1814). Superbly executed in a multitude of meters, it concludes with a verse drama that elevates the entire work to a tragic vision of humanity as a plaything of merciless fate.

Oehlenschläger was the forerunner of a whole generation of poets. The clergyman N. F. S. Grundtvig (1783-1872), in his *Nordens Mythologi* (1808; Nordic mythology), as well as in his collection of lyric dialogues *Optrin af Kiempelivets Undergang i Nord* (1809-1811; scenes from the decline of heroism in the North), interprets Old Norse mythology as a universal drama, a reflection of the continuous battle between spirit and matter. An existential crisis in 1810 led Grundtvig to convert to Christianity, and he began producing not only didactic and occasional poetry but also religious poems and hymns. In 1837, the first volume of his *Sang-Værk til den danske Kirke* (collection of songs for the Danish church) appeared; the entire five-volume work was completely published by 1880. Approximately half of these more than fourteen hundred biblical poems and hymns are reworkings of foreign models such as the Caedmon, Martin Luther, the Psalms of David, and so on. Grundtvig's own poems are connected either with the liturgical year, especially Easter and Pentecost (such as the magnificent "I al sin Glands nu straaler Solen"—in all its splendor the sun shines) or with the sacraments of baptism and the Eucharist. The fundamental contrast is not between sin and grace but between life and death, isolation and the fellowship of love with God and humanity. From this contrast stems the affirmation of life and the defiance of death in Grundtvig's universe. Although many of his hymns are linguistically unpolished, his best texts are characterized by concrete observations employing imagery inspired by the Bible and Old Norse mythology.

Grundtvig's most important fellow writer on the national front was B. S. Ingemann (1789-1862). Following Sir Walter Scott, Ingemann wrote several historical novels that, together with his poetry cycle *Holger Danske* (1837; Holger the Dane), belong to the heyday of Danish national Romanticism. Purely religious is his *Morgen- og Aftensange* (1839; morning and evening

songs), whose naïve nature scenes express not only a child's feeling of insecurity with God but also a cosmic sense of infinity.

In Swedish literature, a similar development can be followed from a metaphysically oriented philosophical system toward a plainer, historical literature. The major mouthpiece for the early universal Romanticism was the monthly journal *Phosphoros* (1810-1813), which was dominated by contributions from P. D. A. Atterbom (1790-1855). His poetry cycle *Blommorna* (1812; the flowers), rather than spontaneous nature impressions, is a series of lyric meditations on transitoriness and immortality, symbolizing various human temperaments and ways of existence. More significant are the two fairy-tale plays *Fågel Blå* (1814; bluebird) and *Lycksalighetens ö* (1824-1827; the island of bliss). The latter, in two parts, although not intended for performance, is a dramatic dialogue, sustained by a richness of lyric episodes that develop into a complex philosophical work related to Johann Wolfgang von Goethe's *Faust: Eine Tragödie* (pb. 1808, 1833; *The Tragedy of Faust*, 1823, 1838) and Oehlenschläger's *Aladdin*.

Pure poetry, on the other hand, is the natural means of expression for Erik Johan Stagnelius (1793-1823). He early acquired the style and meters of German Romanticism, the melodiousness, coloring, and evocative imagery of which he was to carry further than any other Scandinavian writer without ever becoming vague or rambling. Stagnelius's extraordinarily musical poetry is concrete and precise both visually and sensuously, conveying an artistic experience difficult to interpret fully. His major collection, *Liljor i Saron* (1821; lilies of Sharon), is based on two themes: erotic fantasies and the tragic concept of man's continuous suffering as the beloved remains unattainable forever. The tension between these themes runs throughout his oeuvre: He wrote a series of short poems that portray the sensual bliss of love in a pastoral setting, while other works express contempt for this world and a clear religious and ascetic mood. On the basis of his deeply rooted Christianity as well as his speculative Platonism and his belief in a spiritual fellowship, Stagnelius constructs a rich world of symbols in an almost inaccessible but nevertheless evocative language. After the publication of *Liljor i Saron*, Stagnelius abandoned the ideas that had sustained this highly wrought work, and, during the last years of his life, he experimented with various genres. In dramatic scenes colored by Gothic Romanticism, he portrayed negative, almost demoniac, aspects of earthly eroticism; he also wrote his most accomplished dramatic poem, *Bacchanterna* (1822; the Bacchants), which, in subject and style, shows the influence of Greek tragedy.

The strong interest in the Nordic past that early became a dominating force in Danish Romanticism was paralleled in Sweden by a preoccupation with national history. This so-called Gothic movement was partly caused by the anger at the loss of Finland to Russia in the war of 1808-1809. The leading figure of the movement was Erik Gustaf Geijer (1783-1847). In the poem *Manhem* (1811), Geijer presents the program in the rhetorical language of Gustavian classicism, yet using the favorite stanza of Romanticism, ottava rima. In *Den siste kämpen* (1811; the last warrior), he describes in passionate monologues the demise of pagan religion and life in Scandinavia. *Odalbonden* (1811; the free-holder) and *Vikingen* (1811; the Viking), on the other hand, are somewhat stereotyped and idealized portrait poems, although rendered in a lucid and clear language and brilliantly varied rhythms, which have made them perfect for recitation.

The greatest poet of Swedish Romanticism, connected with the Gothic movement but impossible to categorize, is Esaias Tegnér (1782-1846). Inspired by the loss of Finland, he wrote a long patriotic epic poem, *Svea* (1811; English translation, 1840), the main part of which is a eulogy of the nation's forefathers. For most of the poem, Tegnér uses the traditional Alexandrine meter, but he concludes with a dithyrambic section, an ecstatic vision of battle and victory in varied meters with an eruptive, pre-Romantic coloring. The poem *Jätten* (1813; the giant), a monumental symbolic picture of the evil forces in life, is based on an Old Norse motif, while *Sång till Solen* (1813; song to the sun) is colored by Platonic Romanticism in its broad perspective of cosmic desolation, yet allows for a possible reconciliation of good and evil. During the 1820's, Tegnér began to suffer mental depression. During this period, he created the hexametrical religious idyll *Nattvards-barnen* (1820; *The Children of the Lord's Supper*,

1841), the Byronic verse epic *Axel* (1822; English translation, 1838), and his famous *Frithiofs Saga* (1825; *Frithiof's Saga*, 1833). It is composed as an epic cycle, inspired by Oehlenschläger's *Helge*, and represents the culmination of national Romanticism in Sweden. The characters possess psychological credibility, and both the dramatic tension of the narrative and the vigor of its style give the cycle a timeless vitality.

At the close of the 1820's, the Romantic flight from external reality was being replaced by a down-to-earth bourgeois idyllic literature. Traditional love poetry flourished, but the ecstatic, Romantic worship of Eros as a divine force was much more subdued, as in the writings of the Danish poet Christian Winther (1796-1876). Here, however, an influence from the more complex and disharmonic authors Lord Byron and Heinrich Heine is also noticeable. The essence of Winther's elegant and firm mastery of meter and style can be found in his long epic poem with a medieval setting and adventurous episodes of love and hatred, *Hjortens Flugt* (1855; the flight of the hart), while the strength of fellow Dane Emil Aarestrup (1800-1856) lies in short, pointed erotic scenes.

A clear break with this aestheticism is represented by the ironic heroic epic *Adam Homo* (1842-1849; English translation, 1980), by the Dane Frederik Paludan-Müller (1809-1876). It tells of how its opportunistic hero rises from the parsonage of his childhood to the top of society, relating along the way his first erotic encounters in Copenhagen and his engagement to Alma, whom he abandons for the sake of his career. Adam has become corrupt and is in danger of losing his soul, but the unselfish love of Alma, whom he sees again on his deathbed, saves him from perdition. The conclusion takes the form of an apocalyptic poem, a Danish counterpart to Dante's *The Divine Comedy* and Goethe's *Faust*, equaling these great works in artistic quality.

The epic poems that Paludan-Müller wrote after *Adam Homo* took their motifs largely from either the Bible or Greek mythology, pointing to the fact that Old Norse topics by the mid-nineteenth century had played out their role not only in Danish but also in Scandinavian Romanticism. An exception is the epic poem *Kung Fjalar* (1844; *King Fjalar*, 1912), by the Finnish writer Johan Ludvig Runeberg (1804-1877). The destiny of the title character, a fictitious saga king, mirrors the clash between human will and the power of the gods. Also unique in their time were Runeberg's hexameter idylls, such as *Älgskyttarne* (1832; the elk hunters), while his two-part heroic cycle of poems, *Fännrik Ståls sägner* (1848-1860; *The Songs of Ensign Stål*, 1925, 1938), is yet another expression of national Romanticism, an idealization of Finnish feats during the 1808-1809 war against Russia.

An extreme example of the spiritualism found in universal Romanticism is present in the works of the Swede Carl Jonas Love Almqvist (1793-1866). From 1833 to 1851, he published *Törnrosens bok* (the book of the briar rose), a diverse mixture of novels and tales, plays and essays, lyric and epic poems. His novel *Det går an* (1839; *Sara Videbeck*, 1919, also as *Why Not!*, 1994), a discussion of marriage as an institution, bears the first signs of realistic description and factual treatment of everyday life that were to influence Swedish literature increasingly during the 1840's.

The poetry of the period, however, remained strongly idealistic. On the threshold to the epoch of realism and naturalism stands Carl Snoilsky (1841-1903). His collection *Dikter* (1869; poems), dominated by his impressions from travels to southern Europe, employs melodious rhythms and colorful scenes. Snoilsky focuses on contemporary life, and his endorsement of political freedom, in the form of a glorification of Italy's struggle for independence, is interwoven with the poet's strong affirmation of life. At the end of the 1870's, his poetry became more socially involved; a number of portraits and scenes, primarily from Swedish history, deal with the adversities and the poverty of the lower class, while others tackle then-current social issues.

Similar motifs also appear in Viktor Rydberg's (1828-1895) essentially philosophical poetry, published in the two collections *Dikter* (1882; poems) and *Nya dikter* (1891; new poems). Here, Christian ethics and speculative idealism clash with a vivid interest in the current social changes resulting from the industrialization of Swedish society. The discussion of materialism, modern natural science, and naturalism is, however, frequently placed in a historical or mythological setting and executed in a rhetorical, declamatory style.

While Denmark and Sweden, and to some degree Finland, turned during the 1830's and 1840's toward greater realism in literature, the Romantic movement did not reach Iceland and Norway until these decades. Both countries had come under Danish rule in 1387, and contact with European cultural life was not very extensive until the 1830's. The leading spokespersons for Icelandic Romanticism were the two poets Bjarni Thorarensen (1786-1841) and Jónas Hallgrímsson (1807-1845); the latter's lucid poems about the nature and history of Iceland made him the national poet. Both were deeply inspired by their country's medieval literature, the sagas and the Eddic poems.

HENRIK WERGELAND AND JOHAN SEBASTIAN WELHAVEN

The year 1814 brought political and economic independence to Norway, but until the mid-nineteenth century, intellectual life was predominantly determined by the political events of the period. Not until the works of Henrik Wergeland and Johan Sebastian Welhaven did the newer Norwegian literature become original.

The theory of an animated universe and of a world of spirit and power permeates the dramatic poem *Skabelsen, mennesket, og Messias* (1830; creation, man, and Messiah), the major work of Henrik Wergeland (1808-1845). In crude and often verbosely rendered scenes from world history, the poem depicts the battle between earthly and divine spirits, between suppression and freedom. Wergeland rejected any kind of retrospective Romanticism; in his view, it is the task of the writer to look ahead, to be the teacher of his people and a leader of ideas. This sense of mission became increasingly important to Wergeland, who was an active participant in Norwegian political life. *Digte* (1833; poems) glorifies liberty in a style more lucid and plainer than Wergeland's previous work. This trend toward a more concise form became more pronounced in the volume *Poesier* (1838; poems), which introduced a lyric phase that continued until Wergeland's death.

Unlike Wergeland, his opponent Welhaven (1807-1873) stressed solidarity with Danish culture. A fierce debate raged between the two poets throughout the 1830's. Welhaven's main contribution was the collection of polemical sonnets *Norges daemring* (1834; Norway's dawn), but his most valuable poetry, published in *Digte* (1839; poems), takes its motifs from a personal love experience and from Norway's nature and folk life. The essential element in Welhaven's nature poetry is not its descriptive detail but the sense of totality which is created by its rich tapestry of sound. Whereas Wergeland brought to Norwegian poetry linguistic imagination and a wealth of imagery, Welhaven emphasized musicality and sophisticated versification.

REALISM AND NATURALISM

The atmosphere of the 1850's and 1860's was the worst conceivable for poetry. It was a time of practical interests, of economic and industrial development. The old Romantics sought in idyllic fantasy an alternative to the era of industrialization or actively rebelled against the new spirit of the times. The younger ones—in Norway as well as in the other Nordic countries—had to wait for the emergence of the new ideas of realism and naturalism.

DENMARK

The definite breakthrough of the theories of realism and naturalism in Scandinavia during the 1870's, entailing radical biblical and social criticism, can primarily be attributed to the Danish critic Georg Brandes (1842-1927). The most popular genres of this new school were the drama and the novel. Only Denmark and Iceland possessed significant lyric poets; most of them, however, were also accomplished prose writers. In the early poetry of the Dane Jens Peter Jacobsen (1847-1885), such as the cycle *Gurresange* (1869; Gurre songs), medieval motifs are treated in a Romance-like mode. Jacobsen is fully original in his purely speculative poetry, such as the death poem "Saa standsed'—" (thus ended—) and in his so-called arabesques, a series of free images of a penetrating spiritual content shrouded in ornamental language and illuminated by intense sense impressions. Jacobsen was by nature a dreamer, and the struggle between dream and reality is a principal motif both in his novels and in his entire lyric production (which was not published until 1886), titled *Digte og Udkast* (poems and sketches).

The best known of the early poems by the other outstanding Danish lyrical writer of the period, Holger Drachmann (1846-1908), is the melodramatic "Engelske Socialister" (English socialists) in the volume *Digte* (1872; poems). It was the revolution in Brandes's message that inspired Drachmann in this and the next collection, *Dæmpede Melodier* (1875; muted melodies), both based on social questions and the struggle between the reactionary old and the victorious new. Besides politically radical lyric poems, one finds Bohemian songs in which Drachmann appears as a sailor, a peasant, or a vagabond without bourgeois inhibitions. One also encounters enchanting, intimate verses in which bright nights and the sea are images of freedom and of the poetic spirit, pointing beyond naturalism. The collections *Ungdom i Digt og Sang* (1879; youth in poem and song) and *Gamle Guder og nye* (1881; old gods and new) mark a turning point in Drachmann's development. In them, he praises domesticity instead of free love and returns to a patriotic, bourgeois poetry heralding such ideals as the sanctity of mother, child and home. By the late 1880's, however, these ideals were again replaced by a revolutionary spirit, as in the volume *Sangenes Bog* (1889; book of songs). Nevertheless, the playful tone, caused by a new love experience, is mixed with pain. Behind the hectic happiness lurks anxiety about approaching old age. Drachmann considered freedom and beauty the main ideas of his creative work. An incorrigible dreamer, he lived outside his time, but his significance for later Danish poetry is extraordinary, owing to the greatness of his exceptional artistic personality and the infinite wealth of rhythms and moods in his poetry.

ICELAND

A development away from propagandistic naturalism is also a major feature of Icelandic poetry of the period. The first collection of poems by Thorsteinn Erlingsson (1858-1914), *Thyrnar* (thorns), was not published until 1897. Besides bitter political and social satires, it contains a number of rather traditional patriotic poems and sensitive, melancholy love poetry, exquisite in form and language. Lyric beauty and social satire are combined in Erlingsson's major work, *Eithurinn* (1913; the oath), a cycle of narrative poems composed on a tragic love theme.

Hannes Hafstein's (1861-1922) poems did not appear in book form until 1893, in *Ýmisleg ljóthmæli* (various poems). As in the poetry of Drachmann and Heine, Hafstein's artistic models, nature and love motifs dominate, with no trace of naturalistic determinism but marked, rather, by optimism and virility.

SWEDEN

The only significant Swedish lyric poet of the period, which is otherwise totally dominated by the towering figure of August Strindberg (1849-1912), is Ola Hansson (1860-1925). In his youth, he wrote pale social propaganda poems, but in his second collection, *Notturno* (1885), he created a nature poetry influenced by the Dane J. P. Jacobsen, based on exact observation and permeated by a soft and musical tone. Later, Hansson embraced Friedrich Nietzsche's doctrine of the "superman"—a notion which was to exert a tremendous influence on Nordic literature.

NORWAY

In Norway, the same epoch was dominated by the playwrights Henrik Ibsen (1828-1906) and Bjørnstjerne Bjørnson (1832-1910), the latter also an acknowledged author of lyric poetry. In the monologue romance "Bergliot," from the volume *Digte og sange* (1870; *Poems and Songs*, 1915), his portrayal of Bergliot's mourning of her murdered husband and son penetrates deeply the psyche of a saga character; equally imposing is the epic poem *Arnljot Gelline* (1870; English translation, 1917). Bjørnson published only one poetry collection from 1870, which was expanded in later volumes. His lyricism took the form of poetry only under great pressure caused by specific situations. The style is elevated, influenced by Grundtvig, particularly in texts in the saga mold or when linked to historical situations.

The only other significant poetry of the time was written by Arne Garborg (1851-1924). After a number of naturalistic novels, his two poetry cycles *Haugtussa* (1895; the mound elf) and *I Helheim* (1901; in hell) mark a transition toward the main literary trends around 1900, neo-Romanticism and Symbolism. *Haugtussa* portrays, in musically expressive strophes, the visionary peasant girl Veslemøy and her struggle against the dark powers. The supernatural element is also a theme and starting point for the sequel *I Helheim*, in which Veslemøy is led in a dream vision through the realm of the dead, where everybody receives his or her deserved fate, modeled on Dante's *Inferno* and the medieval dream ballad.

TURN OF THE TWENTIETH CENTURY

The new movement of the 1890's rejected the ethical demand for truth that characterized naturalism and favored instead an aesthetic demand for beauty. Heroic deeds were admired at the expense of the practical, and against anti-religious rationalism there arose a new metaphysical and mystically colored religiosity. Nature and history became the favorite sources of inspiration, and lyric poetry, which had been almost totally neglected, flourished again in all five Nordic countries.

SWEDEN

In Sweden, the new aesthetic program was expressed in *Vallfart och vandringsår* (1888; pilgrimage and wander years), a glorification of the carefree life of the Orient, the first collection of Verner von Heidenstam (1859-1940). In Heidenstam's historical novels and stories, a humanistic view underlies the descriptions of heroic, national events, and that view blossoms in Heidenstam's last work, *Nya dikter* (1915; new poems). In short, well-formed strophes, he confesses to a transfigured, fervent belief in life and a melancholy resignation to death. The Romantic has become a classicist, like his models Goethe and the aforementioned Finnish writer Runeberg. In 1916, Heidenstam was honored with the Nobel Prize in Literature.

A greater lyric talent, indeed one of Sweden's greatest poets, is Gustaf Fröding (1860-1911). His humorous, witty pictures of peasant life in his native Värmland as portrayed in his first collection *Guitarr och dragharmonika* (1891; *Guitar and Concertina*, 1925) were entirely new to Swedish poetry and were received enthusiastically, whereas his melancholy, wistful poems were overlooked. In several of these poems, one senses that the author feels kinship with the disreputable and unhappy characters; Fröding's feeling of ineffectuality and failure pervades all of his poetry. Scenes from Värmland, many of them written in the local dialect, form the first part of the next volume, *Nya dikter* (1894; new poems). Here, too, Fröding portrays folk figures from the countryside, but his poems, in spite of their apparent objectivity, also have a personal flavor, which comes clearly to the fore in his nature poetry conveying subjective moods of *Weltschmerz*.

In 1894, Fröding was plunged into a severe emotional crisis characterized by crippling anxieties and hallucinations, which form the transition to the dream moods and visions of his most significant book, *Stänk och flikar* (1896; splashes and rags). The new elements in this volume are the boldly erotic poems, shattering self-accusations, and gripping personal confessions. In "Sagan om Gral" (the story of the Grail), Fröding attempts to present a mystical unity of the universe, in the symbol of the Grail. This motif, which he drew from Richard Wagner's operas, appears more clearly in *Gralstänk* (1898; sprinklings from the Grail). During the last years of his life, Fröding returned to realistic poems about the life and people in his home region. In these poems, one finds an astonishing variety of expression: humorous portraits of folk types, philosophical speculations and meditations, and, not least, subjective, impassioned nature poetry distinguished by its musical virtuosity.

Erik Axel Karlfeldt (1864-1931) also drew inspiration from his home province; his writing expresses a longing for a vanished idyll. He achieved his first real success with *Fridolins visor* (1898; Fridolin's songs), followed three years later by *Fridolins lustgård* (1901; Fridolin's garden of delight). In these two volumes, one encounters not only dancing and happiness but also disharmony and melancholy, which gives depth to Karlfeldt's Fridolin poems. He transforms old rural notions of natural events into animated natural mysticism and uses legends, folk piety, and superstition to create a rich world of symbols. During World War I, Karlfeldt wrote the volume *Flora och Bellona* (1918; Flora and Bellona), which contains his reactions to the social and political movements of the new century, especially his attacks on both communism and capitalism. In his last work, *Hösthorn* (1927; Autumn horn), Karlfeldt returned to Fridolin's world. The mood is still one of resignation, but it is mingled with humility and gratitude for life, together with a clear acceptance of Christianity. Especially significant are Karlfeldt's artistic mastery of form and his melodious language. In Karlfeldt's poetry, Swedish neo-Romanticism finds its perfect conclusion. In 1931, he was posthumously awarded the Nobel Prize in Literature.

DENMARK

Unlike their Swedish and Icelandic counterparts, the young poets in Denmark did not turn to the national past or peasant life but to the soul. The primary figures, Johannes Jørgensen and Sophus Claussen, had begun their careers in the 1880's and introduced a new epoch in Danish literature influenced by J. P. Jacobsen, Drachmann, Nietzsche, and the French poets Charles Baudelaire and Paul Verlaine.

Jørgensen (1866-1956) became the leading exponent and theoretician of Danish Symbolism. His spiritual struggle with naturalism led in *Bekendelse* (1894; confession) to a religious breakthrough; the title poem closes with the cry: "Eternity! I am in your hands." The early texts still bear traces of pantheism, but in the concluding poem, "Confiteor," Christianity is victorious. In the collections appearing just after the turn of the twentieth century, Jørgensen achieved a more concentrated form of expression and a simpler, image-free style, and in *Der er en Brønd, som rinder* (1920; the well that flows), his poetic art reached its zenith. Like that of the French Symbolist Verlaine, Jørgensen's poetry consists of simple meters and rhythmic forms in which ideas are conveyed solely by means of the intensity of the described feelings. After his conversion to Catholicism in 1896, Jørgensen achieved a place as an international author with travelogues and biographies of saints, but the hallmark of his writing is his unique lyricism, expressed in a plain, songlike style evocative of intimate moods.

The greatness of Claussen (1865-1931) as a poet was established with the two collections *Pileføjter* (1899; willow pipes) and *Djævlerier* (1904; diableries). They are broadly expressive, from the darkly macabre to the exuberant and enchanting. Claussen studied the French Symbolists and was the first Danish poet to follow their aesthetics consistently. Nevertheless, *Pileføjter* was primarily influenced by Heine and the Danish Romantic Emil Aarestrup. The volume closes with the symbolic travel sketch "Røg" (smoke), the major poem of this period. Claussen lets his thoughts and moods drift like changing clouds of smoke, which become symbols of his encounter with reality. *Djævlerier* displays Italian and French motifs. With Baudelaire as his model, Claussen was inspired to an artistic Satanism whose central erotic theme is woman as vampire. The volume treats larger sets of problems, however, paying particular attention to the plights and prospects of the artist.

In *Danske vers* (1912; Danish verses), Claussen focuses on his home province. Side by side with pantheistic hymns in praise of nature, there is again a preponderance of erotic poems, more profound and bold than before. In his last significant collection, *Heroica* (1925), Claussen reconciles contradictory aspects within himself: exuberance and passion versus mildness and friendliness. His writing is a defense of fantasy and beauty against the closed horizons of naturalism and materialism. Like the other Symbolists, he wants to express the inexpressible and to form all words and emotions into images of a truth that the reader can only intuit.

LYRIC REVIVAL IN NORWAY AND FINLAND

The most outstanding representatives in Norway of the neo-Romantic movement as a national art form were Hans E. Kinck (1865-1926) and Knut Hamsun (1859-1952), both prose writers of the highest quality. The lyric poet who best expressed the spiritual breakthrough and who came to typify the fin de siècle mood in Norwegian poetry was the pietistically reared Sigbjørn Obstfelder (1866-1900). His writing has its point of departure in his notion that he "seems to have come to the wrong planet" and conveys his longing for the eternal truth underlying the world of material appearances. His speculative poetry, *Digte* (1893; *Poems*, 1920), unrhymed prose poems often of extraordinary beauty, is, with its evocative form and mystical attitude, a characteristic example of the Symbolism of the 1890's, signifying a decisive break with naturalism.

In Finland, the lyric revival was much more extensive than in Norway. The young neo-Romantics found their motifs not only in Finnish history and folklore but also in tales from distant countries, antiquity, mythology, and the Bible. The most talented writer and the most productive of the generation—also writing plays and novels—was Eino Leino (1878-1926). A hike through eastern Finland in 1897 left a strong imprint on his poetry. In 1903, the first part of *Helkavirsiä* (*Whitsongs*, 1978) was published, followed in 1916 by the second part, a bold attempt to give the old *Kalevala* motifs a modern historical and symbolic interpretation in stylized language. Both a national and a purely cosmic view of life is expressed here, influenced by Theosophical ideas of reincarnation. The climax in Leino's

lyric period is reached with the two collections *Talvi-yö* (1905; winter night) and *Halla* (1908; frost). The first contains a suite of erotic and sensuous texts with Asian settings; the latter is dominated by depressive and melancholy moods. Leino's later works were first inspired by the Finnish Civil War of 1918 between socialist and nonsocialist forces, then by a faith in universal human values, which made the poet turn to myth and history. Leino brought about a radical renewal of Finnish poetry. His pantheistic religion and universal humanism originated in Scandinavian and German literature, but his country's mythology and folklore supplied the most valuable impulses.

The second important neo-Romantic poet, Otto Manninen (1872-1950), was a striking contrast to Leino—very sophisticated and not easily accessible. In his lifetime, he was not much read, but his poetry has become increasingly appreciated. Manninen created his own style by extracting from language the greatest possible degree of expressiveness and precision. His writing is never sentimental or tedious; he succeeds in balancing intellect and emotion. In the volumes *Säkeitä, I-II* (1905-1910; verses), *Virrantyven* (1925; still waters), and *Matkamies* (1938; the traveler), there are several poems representing traditional poetic genres: patriotic and historical poems, satires and humoresques. Manninen's best works are his subjective lyrics, which, without illusion and with occasional irony, revolve around the dominating forces of life, love and death, praising love's omnipotence even when love is hopeless.

A lyric revival also took place within Finno-Swedish literature around 1900. The two greatest poetic talents, though essentially different, were Bertel Gripenberg (1878-1947) and Arvid Mörne (1876-1946). In his first poems, Gripenberg praises the wonders of love and youth, but beginning with the collection *Svarta sonetter* (1908; black sonnets), his vitality became increasingly imbued with a tragic tinge. Feelings of defeat are most exquisitely expressed in *Aftnar i Tavastland* (1911; evenings in Tavastland); death is regarded as a welcome rest, a merciful end to a wasted life. Mörne manifested himself as a political writer with socialist sympathies in the collection *Ny tid* (1903; a new time). The volume *Döda år* (1910; dead years), however, can be read as an expression of his disappointment with the outcome of his political commitment. Mörne turned for solace to Finnish nature, which for him combined freedom and sanity with loneliness and fierceness. The language in his nature poetry is sensitive and varied, stringent and exact, thereby pointing to the lapidary, reflective poetry which is his greatest achievement—increasingly bitter in tone, marked by his isolation and his feeling of not being understood.

ICELANDIC NATIONALISM

In 1904, Iceland's struggle for independence was crowned with the establishment of home rule. The new nationalism brought a renewed interest in the old traditions: The languishing medieval *rímur* poetry enjoyed a revival, and a generation of conservative peasant writers came forward. The period's foremost poets, Stephan G. Stephansson (1853-1927) and Einar Benediktsson (1864-1940), are two of Iceland's greatest writers. Stephansson emigrated to the United States at the age of nineteen and later became a farmer in Alberta, Canada. Much of his most valuable poetry, written in Icelandic, is published in six collections, titled *Andvökur* (1909-1938; wakeful nights). Here, he praises his adopted country, drawing a series of magnificent pictures of the prairie and pioneer life and also of Iceland, to whose cultural heritage he is inextricably linked. As Stephansson grew older, he increasingly included incidents from the Eddic poems, sagas, and legends, and he interpreted these incidents in such a way that they took on a symbolic and universal significance. He always had his own time in mind, however, and he criticized violence and oppression sharply. He was a glowing pacifist, vehemently denouncing modern warfare.

Politically, Benediktsson belongs to the wing opposite from Stephansson. He published and edited the first Icelandic daily, *Dagskrá* (1896-1898), in which he introduced European Symbolism—demanding of the young writers a reverence for not only beauty, infinity, and eternity but also national greatness and history. As a poet, Benediktsson gradually created his own universe and style—exclusive and hence not readily accessible. In his poetry, published in such volumes as *Hrannir* (1913; waves) and *Hvammar* (1930; grass hollows), he is able to capture in one short text the essential

elements in the atmosphere of great cities, to describe with great suggestive power factories and gigantic machines. Cosmopolitan as he was, Benediktsson was nevertheless fundamentally nationalistic, delighted to be writing on Icelandic subjects. In all of his poems, he wrestles with the desperate problems of human existence: the ultimate meaning and goal of life. He is obsessed with a boundless pantheistic longing to perceive and understand the mysteries of the universe.

BEFORE WORLD WAR I

The period from 1900 to the beginning of World War I was marked by many conflicting trends. Still, one can speak of a general reaction in Nordic literature by young poets against the predominance of Symbolism and neo-Romanticism. The new poetry reacted primarily against the preoccupation with the self; it opened new thematic areas, such as the realities of industrial revolution and city life, and experimented with language.

SWEDEN

In Sweden, many of the younger authors began as neo-Romantics. The most significant among them had lost their faith in evolution but maintained their belief in determinism. The influence of the 1890's can be recognized in a mood of disillusionment and refined skepticism, as in the pessimistic poetry of Bo Bergman (1869-1967). His first collection bears the characteristic title *Marionetterna* (1903; the marionettes), corresponding to the author's conception of life as a fatalistic game. It contains satiric texts, influenced by Heine, and melancholy scenes from Stockholm, as well as tender love poems and melodious songs.

Nietzsche's views and the cult of beauty in the 1890's found an outstanding representative in Vilhelm Ekelund (1880-1949). His early poetry captures moods of anxious loneliness and impressions of nature, but in the volume *Melodier i skymning* (1902; melodies in twilight), his nature poems have lost their descriptive character and have become the expression of emotional states; in lyric ecstasy, the poet seeks to unite nature and eternity, which gives peace to his restless soul. Influenced by German classicism, Ekelund found in Greek antiquity a way out of his Romantic melancholy and his Symbolist dreamworld. This attempt led to a new intellectual and ethically oriented poetry in the volumes *Elegier* (1903; elegies) and *In candidum* (1905). Ekelund's inclination toward verbal conciseness and personal coloration of words developed over the years—for example, in *Concordia animi* (1942)—into a cryptic style that can be interpreted only with difficulty. Nevertheless, Ekelund exerted a great influence on the modernistic movements in Swedish and Finno-Swedish literature.

NORWAY

In Norway, drama moved into the background, whereas prose, with such major writers as Olav Duun (1876-1939) and Sigrid Undset (1882-1949), and poetry were dominant, reestablishing a link to the poetry of the 1890's. In the major work of Olav Aukrust (1883-1929), *Himmelvarden* (1916; cairn of heaven), religious, ethical, and national themes are in the forefront. There is no epic substance in the single poems; rather, they bear witness to the struggle of good and evil powers in the soul of the poet himself. Through powerful symbols, modeled on visionary medieval poetry, Aukrust depicts the battle between Christ and Satan, a battle that ends with divine victory and the salvation of the soul.

A completely opposite point of departure characterizes the impressionistic poems of Herman Wildenwey (1886-1959), praising summer, wine, and women. He seeks not the abstruse, but the cheerful and light, which are expressed in the charming rhythms and exquisite musicality of his language. The writing of Olaf Bull (1883-1933) lacks, to be sure, Wildenwey's elegance and carefree quality, but it offers far greater visual and symbol-creating power. Bull called himself a nomad, "shrouded in my coat, my home," and his life became the restless existence of a bohemian in Oslo, Copenhagen, and Paris; it was in Paris that he discovered his source of inspiration, Henri Bergson's philosophy and the literature of Symbolism. Homelessness and spiritual unrest were the decisive, tragic experiences of his life; in vain he longed to exchange oppressive loneliness for a sense of fellowship, to leave the world of dreams behind him in favor of reality. This painful longing manifests itself in *Nye digte* (1913; new poems) but also sets the serious undertone of Bull's erotic poems in the collection *Oinos og Eros* (1930; Oinos

and Eros), permeated by Bull's brooding spirit—in elegies about the brevity of life or in despairing accusations against God. Life and pain are fulfilled only in death and, as expressed in the volumes *Stjernerne* (1924; the stars) and *Metope* (1927), reality, created by observing objects, is transformed into a longing for eternity and ecstatic fantasy.

JOHANNES V. JENSEN

The lyric, introspective poetry of the 1890's was followed in Denmark around 1900 by a new realistic and rationalistic wave, differentiated from the naturalism of the 1870's and 1880's by a decidedly materialistic approach and occasionally by socialist ideas. The poetry of Jørgensen expressed the longing and yearning for eternity of a spiritual man; now the central writer was Johannes V. Jensen (1873-1950), who, influenced by the imperialistic writing of Rudyard Kipling, portrayed characters striving to realize an extroverted, pragmatic view of life. The predominant genre was the novel. Only in the works of Jensen, one of the literary pathfinders in twentieth century Denmark and honored in 1944 with the Nobel Prize, is there a well-developed and highly disciplined poetic sense. It is expressed both in his evocative lyric prose and in his poetry, collected in five volumes (1906-1937). The first collection, *Digte* (1906; poems), which contains all of his youthful poems, is a milestone in the development of modern Danish lyric poetry. The most significant as well as the most characteristic texts are the prose poems—linked in their imagery to modern technology and the metropolis. Here, Jensen expresses his firm belief in the joy of the present moment and his untrammeled longing for the distant and the past. After 1920, the traditional closed-verse form and the alliterative poem in the Old Norse style predominated. In classic calm and harmony, Jensen praises children, Danish nature, and woman as wife and mother. Whether Jensen employs the most elevated expression or the most intimate whisper, he succeeds as no other Danish poet in melding precise observation, vision, and reflection into a perfect artistic entity.

BETWEEN THE WORLD WARS

Although prose predominated in Sweden from 1900 to the 1930's, a younger generation of important poets stepped forward during and immediately after World War I. A long artistic development led Birger Sjöberg (1885-1929) to his first success, *Fridas bok* (1922; Frida's book). These graceful songs derive from his numerous imitations of Swedish poets Bellman and Fröding. The elegant form of the 1922 poems, set to music by Sjöberg himself, are in sharp contrast to the sentimental contents attributed to the half-educated singer of these songs. His love for the office girl Frida is expressed in images and words that naïvely exaggerate his admiration and parody his jealousy. However, the idyll of the volume is an illusion, although the large audience did not recognize it. In contrast, Sjöberg's next collection, *Kriser och kransar* (1926; crises and wreaths), surprised and shocked the public; he suddenly showed an entirely new face, tormented by anguish and suffering. The motifs are the same as before; only the perspective has changed. Using symbols that are not always easy to grasp, Sjöberg deals with the futility of existence and the impenetrability of death. Death is present not only as a threat but also as a liberator that opens religious perspectives. Attempting to clarify and solve this mystery, Sjöberg uses bold juxtapositions, personifications of abstract concepts, and a mixture of pure naturalism with the most tender lyricism. With his first book, Sjöberg renewed the Swedish song tradition; with his last, he introduced modernism into Swedish literature.

The central figure of the 1920's, Pär Lagerkvist (1891-1974), emerged as a lyricist in 1916 with a volume titled *Ångest* (anguish). The fear of death that had filled him as a child, the shattering experience of World War I, and a deep personal crisis had released in him a boundless feeling of anxiety. In Lagerkvist's work, everything is loneliness, eternity is empty, and God is silent. Lagerkvist's originality lies neither in his symbolic language nor in his vocabulary, but in his use of classically simple language to voice spontaneous, desperate moods, making him the first Swedish expressionist. Lagerkvist's longing to reconcile himself with life succeeded after the war and is expressed both in his prose works and in two poetry collections with the significant titles *Den lyckliges väg* (1921; the path of the happy one) and *Hjärtats sånger* (1926; songs of the heart). These poems, frequently using traditionally rhymed verse forms, express how Lagerkvist's experience of love changed his life and conquered the darkness of his youthful works. The international crises of the 1930's sharpened his will to fight for the humanistic cultural heritage mirrored especially in his prose, which in the following decades won for him international fame—and, in 1951, the Nobel Prize. His prose expresses his continuous search for truth, a search which also permeates his poetry collection *Aftonland* (1953; *Evening-Land*, 1975).

World War I and the following world crises proved that the old values were bankrupt. A sense of disillusionment, of the transitoriness of existence, and a strong apocalyptic atmosphere prevailed. Many authors expressed a feeling of homelessness, brooding over the meaning of life or seeking in new value systems a replacement for what they had lost. The most significant Swedish poets of this trend were Hjalmar Gullberg, Nils Ferlin, and Karin Boye.

HJALMAR GULLBERG

The poetry of Hjalmar Gullberg (1898-1961) is distinguished by its formal virtuosity, ranging from elegant, sharp epigrammatic verse through melodious songs to classical cantatas. A religious admixture is present in his early works, and in the collection *Att övervinna världen* (1937; to overcome the world), he shapes a tendency toward mysticism into purely Christian symbols. In the 1940's, Gullberg found himself in a creative crisis, which he did not overcome until 1952, when he published *Dödsmask och lustgård* (death mask and garden of pleasure). Influenced by foreign and Swedish modernistic poetry, he changed his imagery and abandoned his view of the poet as a prophet called by God. Gullberg's last collection, *Ögon, läppar* (1959; eyes, lips), synthesizes a formbound style and free associative verse. The texts contain variations on and summaries of previous themes: the vocation of the artist, the personal struggle with Christianity, suffering, and death.

NILS FERLIN

The period's pessimism is aptly represented by Nils Ferlin (1898-1961). His life and writing are an incarnation of the myth of the bohemian artist and are related to the writing of Bellman. His occupation as a revue and cabaret writer, which inspired his use of the refrain and his surprising rhymes, can be deduced from his first collection, *En döddansares visor* (1930; ballads of a dancer of death). A satirical note is added in *Goggles* (1938), in which another characteristic trait emerges: his deep sympathy with the misfits of society, often expressed through biblical imagery.

KARIN BOYE

A similar restlessness is present in the writing and life of Karin Boye (1900-1941), a life that ended in suicide. With religious earnestness and passionate tenacity, constantly driven to new horizons, she tested all the various messages of salvation of her time. She rebelled against the ecstatic Christianity of her youth; with the help of the heroic philosophy of Nietzsche, she sought to perfect her personality and to affirm even the darker side of life. This striving characterizes her poems during the 1920's, which are strongly influenced by Ekelund in their prophetic attitude, free rhythm, and choice of words. In *För trädets skull* (1935; for the sake of the tree), Boye attempted to unify her divided nature in verses alternating between moods of affirmation and despair.

PRIMITIVISM

Influenced by D. H. Lawrence, a group of Swedish authors called the Primitivists emerged toward the end of the 1920's. In 1929, they published an anthology of modernistic poetry titled *Fem unga* (five young ones), in which they differentiated themselves from earlier Swedish modernists by their worship of instinctual drives and by their strong interest in exotic themes and primitive peoples.

Closest to this program was Artur Lundkvist (1906-1991). Motifs from the big cities and life in the countryside characterize his collections *Glöd* (1928; glow) and *Naket liv* (1929; naked life), which display an ecstatic intoxication with life as well as confidence in the instincts of human beings. In Lundkvist's later volumes of prose poems from the 1930's, Romantic sensuousness yields to gloom. He is now seeking the world of myths, and in dark and suggestive visions, along the lines of French Symbolism, he tries to give expression to the unconscious life of the soul. In *Liv som gräs* (1954; life as grass) and *Vindrosor, moteld* (1955; wind roses, counterfire), however, he again turns toward an almost propagandistic reverence for sensuality. The poems are filled with Lundkvist's faith in the power of the primitive and the ability of poetry to change life. They represent a revolutionary criticism of sterile civilization as well as a search for fellowship. Around 1980, Lundkvist published a series of prose poems and finally, in 1984, a gripping account of his visions while lying in a coma after a heart attack, *Färdas i drömmen och föreställningen* (*Journeys in Dream and Imagination*, 1991).

HARRY MARTINSON

A more genuine poetic talent is Harry Martinson (1904-1978). In all of his works, including several novels, the human being stands at the center. This humanism is particularly noticeable in the poem cycle *Passad* (1945; trade winds), in which he creates a sweeping picture of the fundamental division of Western culture. Here, Ulysses is contrasted with Robinson Crusoe—that is, the humanist and poet is compared with the empiricist and scientist. The trade wind becomes a symbol of the goodwill that can find the way to unity, a way that leads to humankind itself. In the volumes *Cikada* (1953) and *Vagnen* (1960; the car), Martinson continues his protest against violence. In a series of artless nature poems and resigned meditations, he gives vent to his disgust with the modern world. In *Tuvor* (1973; tussocks), he protests the exploitation and destruction of nature; on a larger scale is the verse epic *Aniara: En revy om människan i tid och rum* (1956; *Aniara: A Review of Man in Time and Space*, 1963), a vision of humankind on its way out of this world into eternity. The spaceship "Aniara" is a symbol of human civilization; during its voyage through space, the course of humankind's cultures and religions is recapitulated and the songs of the earth become holy myths, until finally all is silent. The work is one of the central poetic accomplishments of the twentieth century, a pioneering effort that gained international attention, not the least as an opera set to music by Karl-Birger Blomdahl.

GUNNAR EKELÖF

The most prolific modernist of interwar Sweden was Gunnar Ekelöf (1907-1968). He never embraced the gospel of primitivism, and in the collection *Sent på jorden* (1932; late arrival on Earth, 1967), he broke radically with traditional form and syntax. In *Dedikation* (1934; dedication), the revolt against the common conception of reality has changed to a belief in the task of the poet as a seer and redeemer. The volume is permeated with sumptuous imagery and a suggestive, lyric rhythm, linking it to Swedish Romanticism and French Surrealism. In *Non serviam* (1945) and *Om hösten* (1951; in autumn), Ekelöf regards the self as a battlefield for contesting spiritual forces. He seeks the unity behind the conflicting elements of this world and elevates the border between life and death to a mystical experience of the dissolution of the self in the universe. *Strountes* (1955; nonsense) consists of a series of fragmentary, bagatelle-like poems, in which Ekelöf employs satire, parody, and wordplay to reflect on the nature of language and the emptiness of existence. *En Mölna-elegi* (1960; *A Mölna Elegy*, 1984) analyzes the fantasies of the self at the moment when the present is combined with the past in a free-flowing chain of associations—reminiscences, recollections, and visions—which lead to purification in a consuming song of fire.

Interested in Persian poetry since his student days, Ekelöf took several trips in the 1950's and 1960's to the Near East, the inspiration for the trilogy that concluded his career, beginning with *Dēwān över fursten av Emgión* (1965; Diwan over the prince of Emgión). Ekelöf was a learned poet. Like T. S. Eliot and Ezra Pound, he used cultural history as material, as a constantly active reality. The two primary sources of his style are music and mysticism. He was the first Swedish poet to attempt to carry the vocabulary of music directly over to the language of literature. His poems are never structurally complete, nor are they definite expressions of thoughts and feelings; rather, they are attempts to reconcile his never-ending battle with the problems of the self, reality, and death. Ekelöf is regarded by many as the most difficult and the greatest modern poet in the Nordic countries.

MODERNISM

After World War I, a modernist breakthrough occurred in Finno-Swedish literature—a modernism that remained something of an underground movement during the 1920's and was not manifest in the other Nordic countries. One must turn to the Anglo-American poets Eliot and Pound to find corresponding trends. The first and perhaps greatest of these modernist writers, Edith

Södergran (1892-1923), made her debut in 1916 with *Dikter* (*Poems*, 1980). Characteristic of this volume is a series of brief pictures of nature, but the landscape is a dream landscape in which the natural and spiritual are blended completely. Södergran's next collections were influenced by Nietzsche's philosophy of the superman, which mobilized her vitality and strength of will. Hymns to the beauty and richness of life alternate in these works. This exertion of strength led in 1920 to a crisis in which Södergran's materialistic worldview collapsed. She sought religious stability and finally found her way, through Rudolf Steiner's Anthroposophy, to the Christ of the Gospels, where she experienced peace. Against this background, her last, profound, and transfigured poems of the posthumous collection *Landet som icke är* (1925; the land which is not) constitute a personal preparation for death.

A striking aesthetic radicalism is represented by Elmer Diktonius (1896-1961), who, in his collections from the 1920's, rejected any aesthetic view of art. In *Stark men mörk* (1930; strong but dark), he experimented with a number of Dadaistic effects and simultaneously assumed a humanistic attitude in the face of threatening political catastrophies. In addition, social criticism is present in a number of his proletarian poems, together with a new positive attitude toward nature, influenced by Walt Whitman. In *Jordisk ömhet* (1938; earthly tenderness), the previously very aggressive poet unreservedly accepts the brighter aspects of life, employing biblical motifs and shaping his poems with broad, vigorous strokes, fascinated by the tiny miracles of nature which symbolize the eternal cycle of life and death. Diktonius's exuberant joy in life is sustained throughout his work, as the title of his last book, *Novembervår* (1952; November spring), indicates.

The most singular and radical of the modernists was Gunnar Björling (1887-1960). As he attempted to capture life's boundlessness, he began to realize the limited possibilities of language. He therefore constructed his own syntax, in which parts of sentences and suffixes were dropped. The method is fully developed in *Korset och löftet* (1925; the Cross and the promise), expressing in Björling's own words, "a universal Dada-individualism," which culminates in *Kiri-ra!* (1930). After the publication of *Solgrönt* (1933; sun green), nature became an increasingly important source of inspiration as Björling reacted against intellectualism, and his early nihilistic tendencies were replaced by mystical calmness. In the 1940's, Björling published seven collections, then, beginning in the early 1950's, one volume each year. A representative selection of these, *Du jord du dag* (you earth you day), was published in 1957. His poetry became increasingly laconic; his point of departure was the realization that words will never be able to render a complete picture of experience, a realization that is raised in his verse to a metaphysical level.

The poetry of Rabbe Enckell (1903-1974), one of the main theoreticians of Finno-Swedish modernism, differs from that of the other poets of the group in that it is neither visionary nor prophetic, neither violent nor ecstatic, but rather consists of delicate analyses of his feelings. Enckell mastered the art of the miniature in *Vårens cistern* (1931; spring's cistern) and *Tonbrädet* (1935; the sounding board). The latter volume displays a fascination with classical motifs, and simultaneously Enckell began to write a series of Greek-inspired verse dramas that illuminate the often tragic relationship between human beings and fate. Throughout the 1950's and up to the date of his last collection, *Flyende spegel* (1974; fleeing mirror), Enckell published a number of volumes in which he employed additional classical motifs in small lyrical portraits or in dialogues—meditative, refined poetry that complements the visionary, provocative, and philosophical elements of Finno-Swedish modernism with moderation and strong self-criticism.

THREE FINNS

The most remarkable of the poets writing in Finnish during the interwar period were Uuno Kailas, Aaro Hellaakoski, and P. Mustapää. The early collections of Kailas (1901-1933) bear witness to his knowledge of Baudelaire and expressionistic German poetry in their use of free verse and exotic imagery. Kailas employs Christian symbols, though he seldom speaks of the relationship of humankind to divinity; for him, the world is governed by blind fate. *Silmästä silmään* (1926; eye to eye) marks a transition in Kailas's art from free verse to more traditional forms and shows his progressive introversion. The tension he felt was primarily ethical, a

Christian dualism between spirit and matter, ideal and reality.

An ethical element also dominates the writing of Hellaakoski (1893-1952) but in a much less speculative way. In his debut work, *Runoja* (1916; poems), Hellaakoski portrays the poet's struggle to acquire an artistic means of expression. The important part played by the creative will is demonstrated in *Me kaksi* (1920; we two), as a dialogue between reason and heart. *Jääpeili* (1928; ice mirror), the only work of the 1920's that can be considered parallel to those by the Finno-Swedish modernists, is epoch-making because of its innovative meters and varied content. Hellaakoski's modernism was based on his interest in pictorial arts, especially cubism, and the influence of the French Surrealist poet Guillaume Apollinaire. The collection *Uusi runo* (1943; new poetry) initiated a period of brilliant creativity, culminating in *Sarjoja* (1952; series), which placed Hellaakoski among Finland's greatest postwar poets; its long, meditative verses are reminiscent of Rainer Maria Rilke's *Duineser Elegien* (1923; *Duino Elegies*, 1930) and T. S. Eliot's *Four Quartets* (1943).

In the work of Mustapää (the pseudonym of Martti Haavio, 1899-1973), Hellaakoski's influence is evident in the rejection of traditional formal patterns and the refusal to adopt the fashions of the 1920's. As an internationally renowned folklorist, Mustapää was well acquainted not only with the *Kalevala* tradition but also with newer ballads and broadsides, whose style he slightly parodied to create a naïve mode of expression. Not until after World War II, however, did Mustapää, in volumes such as *Linnustaja* (1952; the fowler) and *Tuuli Airistolta* (1969; the wind blows from Airisto), create the rhythmic and metaphoric effects that so clearly point to new literary developments. The poems are rhythmically light and rather singable, filled with highly sensuous imagery reminiscent of Ezra Pound.

LYRICISTS AND RADICALS IN NORWAY

The only great lyricist in Norway during the 1930's, Arnulf Øverland (1889-1968), certainly belongs to the generation of Wildenwey and Bull, but the decisive influences on his work were from a different era. For no other Norwegian author did World War I, and even more the postwar period, signify such a sharp separation of past from present. His youthful poetry from

1911 to 1915 did not arouse particular attention. Death and isolation were very significant themes, and it was clear that Øverland was picking up where the poetry of the 1890's left off. Beginning with the volume *Brød og vin* (1919; bread and wine), he occupied himself with his own time; the poetry of the self gave way to bloody scenes from the battlefield hospitals, the aesthetic egocentric had become a moralist and an indignant satirist. In the 1920's, Øverland adopted a socialist, even communist, point of view. His collection of profound intellectual poetry, *Berget det blå* (1927; blue mountain), portrays in biblical terms the slavery of humankind and the migration to the promised land of social solidarity.

With the outbreak of World War II, Øverland changed his attitude again. Abandoning his communist and anti-Christian activism, he worked to unite the Norwegian people. His poems of resistance—lyrics of peace—circulated secretly during the German occupation and were not printed until 1945, in the volume *Vi overlever alt* (we shall live through all). Øverland's last collections contain more complicated, metaphoric, intellectual poetry. *Den rykende tande* (1960; the smoldering wick) is in part a stocktaking of reality, seen with the clear vision of age. Old truths are shown in new light, with altered contours. Øverland's lyric accomplishment has often been compared with that of Heinrich Heine; Øverland himself never concealed that the German poet was his immediate model. Like Heine, he was no formal experimenter, no artistic innovator; his poetry, nevertheless, presents a wealth of nuances and simple greatness.

Radical socialism remained a trademark in the writing of the playwright, novelist, and poet Nordahl Grieg (1902-1943). In the volume *Norge i våre hjerter* (1929; Norway in our hearts), however, Grieg's radicalism was entirely overlooked by the public; only the declamatory, patriotic effects were noticed, which made Grieg more popular than any other Norwegian poet. After a two-year stay in Moscow, from 1932 to 1934, Grieg returned as a determined communist, and his criticism of capitalist society became increasingly sharper. During World War II, he served as a pilot in the British Royal Air Force and was shot down over Berlin, enhancing his reputation beyond what his talent really merits. His greatest artistic accomplishment during the war was his war poems, collected in a volume titled *Friheten* (1943; all that is mine demand). Here Grieg took the basic theme of *Norge i våre hjerter* and carried it further in poems that are among the most valuable that have been written about war and the homeland.

A NEW GENERATION OF DANES

Immediately after World War I, there emerged in Denmark a new generation of lyric poets affirming the glory of existence. As the creator of a new poetic mentality, the central figure is doubtless Emil Bønnelycke (1893-1953), with his glowing enthusiasm for the technology of the modern metropolis. As a poet, however, Tom Kristensen (1893-1974) is the most significant. He learned much from Bønnelycke, whose poetry served as the model for the Copenhagen scenery and language in Kristensen's early collections *Fribytterdrømme* (1920; pirate dreams) and *Mirakler* (1922; miracles). With a purely artistic attitude toward existence as the point of departure, Kristensen sought to re-create metropolitan life in a new poetic form. He transformed external reality into a festive orgy of screaming colors. This occurs not only when he loses himself in exotic fantasies but also when he describes the brutal beauty of a fight in a billiard hall in a proletarian part of Copenhagen. Just as the colors are appreciated for their own sake, so is the sound of the words exploited in a purely aesthetic manner, intensified in the poem "Itokih" almost to Dadaism. In the volume *Paafuglefjeren* (1922; the peacock feather), Kristensen employs material from a trip to China and Japan; he breaks with the expressionistic style and finds a controlled lyricism, saturated with color, that approaches impressionism. The external harmony, however, only increases the tension in the homeless soul of the poet. This restlessness grows in Kristensen's novels from the 1920's and 1930's into despair and a longing for self-destruction that makes him the most important Danish representative of the "lost generation."

As in Norway, the major Danish authors of the interwar period were prose writers either dealing with social and political issues or analyzing human destiny on an existential level. The period was also a high point in Danish drama, with Kjeld Abell (1901-1961) and Kaj Munk (1898-1944); from completely different political standpoints, they defended the humanistic values of Western civilization. Nevertheless, as a result of the great success of the expressionistic writers Bønnelycke and Kristensen, a new generation of poets stepped forth, attempting in various way to find their footing in a changed world.

PAUL LA COUR

Paul la Cour's (1902-1956) two main collections from the 1930's, *Dette er vort liv* (1936; this is our life) and *Alt kræver jeg* (1938; I demand all), are dominated by feelings of guilt about the fate of Europe as the poet discerns the power of his own ruthless instincts. Simultaneously, there is a growing belief in the necessity of change. The result of la Cour's search beyond the intellect is presented in his major work, *Fragmenter af en Dagbog* (1948; fragments of a diary), a mix of philosophical teaching, poetics, and poetry describing the meeting of the rational and irrational forces in art.

JENS AUGUST SCHADE

Jens August Schade (1903-1978), in his turn, captures the tension between the infinite and finite in numerous collections of Surrealistic poetry, already fully developed in his first book, *Den levende violin* (1926; the living violin). All of the later volumes, from *Hjerte-Bogen* (1930; the heart book) on, are characterized by daring and disrespectful love poems, erotic nature poetry, and cosmic fantasies. They are permeated by Schade's all-embracing sexual message—the closest Danish literature has ever come to the primitivism of D. H. Lawrence.

NIS PETERSEN

The most artistically convincing expression of the restlessness and the nihilism of the period, besides the poetry of Tom Kristensen, is found in the novels and poems of Nis Petersen (1897-1943). He made his debut as a lyricist with the collection *Nattens Pibere* (1926; *Whistlers in the Night*, 1983), in which these moods are apparent. His later volumes, such as *En drift vers* (1933; a drove of verse), convey a similar atmosphere of doubt and despair but change from the rhetorical style influenced by Kipling and Wilde to plain verse of great beauty. Icelandic poetry, which around 1900 had been largely traditional and Romantic, moved after 1920 toward greater realism, stylistic flexibility, and receptiveness to foreign influences. A cult of the self,

the present, and sexuality emerged, together with a greater political awareness.

ICELAND

The first poems by Stefán Sigurthsson (1887-1933), collected in *Söngvar förumannsins* (1918; the wanderer's song), became a literary event. More personal than any encountered before in Iceland, they are revelations of all aspects of the poet's emotional life. Sigurthsson's next book, *Othur einyrkjans* (1921; the song of the lonesome crofter), is colored by his life as a farmer. The poems are more earthy and objective, and the range of themes greater, as the poet turns to folklore and fairy tales for inspiration. A eulogy of Catholicism, to which Sigurthsson converted in 1923, is found in *Heilög kirkja* (1924; holy church), reminiscent of the sacred poetry of medieval Icelandic writers, masterful in metrical excellence and lyric sensitivity, which also characterizes his later collections of religious poetry.

Davíth Stefánsson (1895-1964) is more typical of the changing times—an exaggerated worship of life contrasted, in his debut poems of *Svartar fjathrir* (1919; black feathers), with a destructive world war and presented with a self-conscious air of libertinism. A trip to Italy provided new motifs for Stefánsson's later collections: Colorful descriptions of the social misery he observed abroad dramatically contrast with the splendor of historic monuments. In 1947, *Ný kvæthabók* (a new book of poems) appeared, containing his reactions to the war and expressing his disillusionment at the rearmament of the superpowers. The variety of his motifs and forms, his straightforward language, and the fact that his emotional life is the subject of many of his poems make Stefánsson one of the greatest renewers of Icelandic poetry.

This renewal was furthered by Tómas Guthmundsson (1901-1983), who consistently has combined neo-Romantic language with everyday speech. He appeared in 1933 as a mature artist with *Fagra veröld* (fair world), in which the busy life of the Icelandic capital, Reykjavík, becomes an important theme, the poet discovering there a new dimension of beauty. In both *Fagra veröld* and the next volume, *Stjörnur vorsins* (1940; stars of spring), his worship of beauty takes on a mystical dimension. *Fljótith helga* (1950; the holy river) was written during and after World War II and contains a number of polemical poems against Nazism. His most powerful works, however, are those in which he confronts the transitoriness of life, clothing his sense of resignation in linguistic and rhythmic splendor.

The nature poetry of Jóhannes úr Kötlum (pseudonym of Jóhannes B. Jónasson, 1899-1972) follows the national, Romantic tradition of Einar Benediktsson. Less poetic, but far more convincing, are his satires on corrupt capitalistic society and his preaching of a new social order in *Samt mun ég vaka* (1935; yet I will stay awake), marking his conversion to communism. *Hart erí heimi* (1939; world is in chaos) is largely concerned with the anti-democratic signs of the times and the threat of war. His poetry from the 1950's and 1960's is written in a similar pacifist mode, but whereas the style of Kötlum's earlier works is characterized by rich lyricism, in his later works, it became fragmented and rhetorical, mirroring the revolutionary author's bitterness in response to postwar developments.

POSTWAR DEVELOPMENTS

Following the brutality and destructiveness of World War II, the quest for a meaningful metaphysical and existential basis of life became a driving force in Nordic literature. Anxiety and a feeling of powerlessness became the central experience. The social function of literature was negated; any private experience of the world was considered narrow and devoid of value. Every line of a poem was supposed to express a universal feeling. To capture the all-embracing nature of consciousness, the poets of the 1940's employ a rich metaphorical language; thus, the poetic image, inspired by Eliot, Pound, and Stéphane Mallarmé, assumed a dominant position. The literature is not easily accessible, since it reflects a splintered and complex reality that can be rendered only in a fragmented syntax.

SWEDISH POSTWAR POETS

Although Sweden adopted a neutral posture during World War II, the war's brutality influenced a whole generation of writers and became their central problem; one could no longer rely on national, religious, or even humanistic values. The work of Erik Lindegren (1910-1968) is in many ways typical. In addition to the disillusioning experience of the time, there is a Romantic attitude, an imaginative component reminiscent of French

Surrealism and the Welsh poet Dylan Thomas. Lindegren's poetry is set in an abstract universe. He seeks above all to express an inner psychological reality in ecstatic rhetoric in his volume *Mannen utan väg* (1942; *The Man Without a Way*, 1969), the unsurpassed masterpiece of the 1940's. It consists of forty unrhymed, symmetrical poems, almost every line of which is saturated with dissonant imagery. This work had a great influence on younger writers, but none of them went as far as Lindegren. In his later collections, however, he turned again to more traditional forms. Even his pessimism abated gradually, especially in *Sviter* (1947; suites).

If Lindegren was the era's inspiring stylistic innovator, Karl Vennberg (1910-1995) was its critic and theoretician. His poetry is deliberately anti-Romantic and is linked to the concrete worldview of the natural sciences. He is a didactic poet who constantly occupies himself with the problems of intellectual life. His pessimism finds its most bitter expression in *Tideräkning* (1945; reckoning of time), turning against all forms of faith and all solutions. In a series of ironic and scornful verses, Vennberg emphasizes that all teachings of salvation are merely the expression of selfish interests. Nevertheless, Vennberg could not maintain his distrust. The next collection, *Fiskefärd* (1949; fishing trip), displays an almost idyllic mood of intimacy and warmth, which yields in the religious poems to a hope for salvation. Yet this cheerful tone is only an intermezzo. In the 1950's, Vennberg became involved in politics as an advocate of a neutral position between the two superpowers—a view entirely in accord with his own poetics. Personal feelings are given more space, and a feeling of resignation predominates. After a period of silence Vennberg returned to poetry in the 1970's and in 1987 published his last collection, *Längtan till Egypten* (longing for Egypt), an exquisitely executed farewell to life permeated with resignation as well as a longing for an unknown god.

A tone of sarcasm and desperation similar to that in Vennberg's early poetry characterizes the volume *Skriket och tystnaden* (1946; the scream and the silence), by Werner Aspenström (1918-1997). Vennberg's dry, conversational tone, however, was replaced by tighter form and more precise expression. This tendency, developed into a more intimate tone and a simpler style, influenced by legend and fairy tale, can be found in *Snölegend* (1949; snow legend) and *Litania* (1952). Aspenström's extraordinary linguistic precision remained intact throughout the 1960's and indeed reached new heights of virtuosity in the collections *Ordbok* (1976; dictionary), *Enskilt och allmänt* (1991; private and public), and *Ty* (1994; for).

The lyric poetry of the 1950's in Sweden was based on the poetics of the 1940's. The influence of Lindegren, in particular, is noteworthy. Symbols—either sophisticated or naïve—continued to play an important role, but the tone was less gloomy. Typical subjects were nature and love, portrayed in poetic and playful language. Accordingly, Pound succeeded Eliot as an important source of inspiration. The catastrophic atmosphere of the 1940's is still evident in the first collection of Lars Forssell (1928-2007), *Ryttaren* (1949; the rider), containing compact and hermetic poems about the transitoriness of life and the inevitability of death. Here, and even more in *Narren* (1952; the jester), Forssell's preference for employing masks and roles and for allowing various personas to act as his spokespersons is evident. This technique was to form the basis of his transition to successful dramatist. He published two translations of Pound's poems, and his own poetry is indeed related to Pound's cryptic work. In the mid-1960's, however, Forssell turned to the cabaretlike song with *Röster* (1964; voices) and a few years later to political poetry. This trend reached its zenith with *Oktoberdikter* (1971; October poems) and *Forsök* (1972; attempt), texts dealing with the Bolshevik revolution and the U.S. bombing of Hanoi, respectively. Subsequently, Forssell focused on more personal themes, and his collection *Förtroenden* (2000; confidences) is permeated with a tragic awareness of his own aging in a world of suffering and misery.

Among the most successful poetry collections of the 1950's are the slim and rather exclusive volumes by Tomas Tranströmer (born 1931). In *17 dikter* (1954; seventeen poems), he works primarily with impressions of nature around Stockholm, using many concrete details; the basic experience, however, is that of a cosmic power, a universal coherence, which occasionally takes on a religious dimension. Tranströmer becomes more concrete in *Klanger och spår* (1966;

sounds and tracks), which deals with current political topics. In *Mörkerseende* (1970; *Night Vision*, 1971), however, he deals less with ideological issues than with moral questions concerning the individual; his vague political commitment is transformed into a discussion of society's responsibilities toward the human being. He deals with the same theme in *Östersjöar* (1974; *Baltics*, 1975), a volume that embraces both spiritual reflections and historical and political perspectives on the Baltic Sea. Now an earlier mood of pessimism recedes in favor of a more optimistic viewpoint which in *Sanningsbarriären* (1978; *Truth Barriers*, 1980) turns into a clear affirmation of a supernatural world. With the volume *Samlade dikter, 1954-1996* (2001; collected poems, 1954-1996) Tranströmer has confirmed his position as one of the most prolific writers of twentieth century Scandinavian literature.

Tranströmer, whose poems are characterized through an almost explosive metaphoric vitality, belongs to the Symbolist school and has been criticized for his uncommitted attitude. Sandro Key-Åberg (1922-1991), on the other hand, definitely wishes to provoke the reader into opposing brutal reality. Throughout his works, a dominant theme is the pain of the fleeting moment—in the midst of life, we are embraced by death. This romantically shaded pessimism culminates in *Bittergök* (1954; bitter fool). In his later poetry collections, such as *En stordikt till dej* (1968; a great poem for you), Key-Åberg, without abandoning this dark vision, makes a passionate appeal to people's sense of responsibility.

DANISH POSTWAR POETS

Much of the prose after World War II in Danish literature is a direct continuation of the realistic traditions of the 1930's. It is in poetry that innovative and provocative ideas come forth. Some poets, such as Piet Hein (1905-1996), follow tradition, writing simple, rhymed verse. In Hein's twenty volumes of *Gruk* (1940-1963; as Kumbel Kumbell; *Grooks* (1966-1978), he is exceptionally skilful with the epigrammatic play of words and ideas.

The absence of cultural consensus after the war was to be reflected in literary style, and a recognition of the crisis permeates the writing of the most significant Danish poet of the 1940's, Ole Sarvig (1921-1981). In his cycle in six volumes appearing between 1943 and 1952, he renders in a modernistic and imagistic language, related to abstract painting, a grandiose portrayal of modern man in crisis at a cultural and historical turning point. The driving force of his poems is the search for resolution to this crisis. The central poems of *Grønne Digte* (1943; green poems) form a coherent metaphysics of history. The tone is often surprisingly harmonious, standing in absolute contrast to the mood of crisis in the volume *Jeghuset* (1944; the house of self), a crisis that is overcome in *Menneske* (1948; man). The decisive themes of the latter are the experience of God and of love between man and woman. The retrospective cycle *Forstadsdigte* (1974; suburban poems) marks a return to the theme of Sarvig's early work, the experience of Christ and love. This theme also permeates his brilliant prose works and reaches the zenith in his last book, a collection of hymns, *Salmer og begyndelser til 1980'erne* (1981; hymns and beginnings to the 1980's), establishing his position in Danish literature as its most outstanding representative of a metaphysical outlook.

Sarvig saw love and grace as a liberation from chaos. For Thorkild Bjørnvig (1918-2004), faith in poetry was the liberator. In his first collection, *Stjærnen bag Gavlen* (1947; the star behind the gable), Eros is the dominant theme. Bjørnvig depicts the metamorphosis of young love, expounding on his belief that everything is governed by the law of transformation. *Anubis* (1955) employs the same theme, but in it, Bjørnvig's diction had matured and taken on greater musicality and substance. In the 1970's, he turned to contemporary issues, and ecological problems dominate the volumes *Delfinen* (1975; the dolphin) and *Abeguder* (1981; ape gods). *Siv vand og måne* (1993; rush water and moon) marks a return to Bjørnvig's main themes: the glorification of art and love as humanity's redeeming forces and of nature as the point of departure for cosmic experiences.

Erik Knudsen (born 1922) began as a typical representative of the 1940's with the volume *Blomsten og sværdet* (1949; the flower and the sword), in which he expressed his deep anxiety and called for human fellowship. In his later collections from *Sensation og Stilhed* (1958; sensation and silence) and *Journal* (1963) to *Ord fra Humlebæk* (1986; words from Humlebaek), Knudsen presented his socialist ideas and his criticism of Western society and culture. He maintained this stance in a number of successful television plays. Knudsen has always used language as a tool for agitation. The volume *Vietnam* (1973), for example, was directed against the involvement of the United States in Asia and against capitalism in general.

NORWEGIAN POSTWAR POETS

In Norway, there was also a sudden shift to poetry after the war. However, while modernism had gained a foothold in Denmark in the work of Sarvig and Swedish writers had established contact with modern world literature through the metaphysical poetry of the 1940's, similar trends were barely present in Norway, and there was little experimentation. On the other hand, there had been trends toward renewal already in the 1930's. Like the Danish poets Bønnelycke and, earlier, Jensen, Rolf Jacobsen (1907-1994) attempted to incorporate all of modern civilization, technology, and urban life into a cluster of poetic themes in his collections *Jord og jern* (1933; earth and iron) and *Vrimmel* (1935; tumult). In later collections from *Stillheten efterpå* (1965; the silence afterward) and *Headlines* (1969) to his last work, *Nattåpent* (1985; open twenty-four hours), however, Jacobsen expresses in somber language a strong disgust with the results of the machine age. His field of associations became increasingly more complicated; he creates bold images which he permits to work without interpretation, his writing therefore emerging as a sophisticated Norwegian parallel to Pound's Imagism.

Pound, together with Eliot and William Butler Yeats, were the major models for Claes Gill (1910-1973). In his epoch-making collections *Fragment av et magisk liv* (1939; fragments of a magic life) and *Ord i jærn* (1942; words of iron), Gill not only breaks with traditional metrics but also frees himself from traditional syntax. The metaphors flow in free succession, guided only by his often paradoxical associations.

For a long time, Gill and Jacobsen were isolated phenomena. Not until 1947 did Tarjei Vesaas (1897-1970) publish his volume of poems *Leiken og lynet* (games and lightning), marking the beginning of postwar Norwegian modernism. Vesaas's style developed under the influence of Edith Södergran's poems in his three collections published in the period from 1949 to 1956, followed in 1970 by his last volume, *Liv ved straumen* (life by the river). By eliminating everything superfluous and leaving only words and metaphors that bear associations, Vesaas created in his best poems a uniquely suggestive tension. The central motifs are the same as in his novels: the metaphysical evil of the time, the powers within and outside the uprooted person of the twentieth century, and the fear of catastrophe.

In 1949, Paal Brekke (1923-1993) published a translation into Norwegian of Eliot's *The Waste Land* (1922) together with his own collection *Skyggefektning* (shadow fencing), in which he attempted to explain the contemporary world picture. The volume is characterized not only by free rhythms but also by bold syntactical tension and, above all, a sparse modernistic vocabulary. Brekke's intellectualism, schooled by Eliot and Pound and influenced by Finno-Swedish and modern Swedish literature, was rejected by the public. After the negative reception of *Skyggefektning*, Brekke turned to prose. In 1957, however, he published another volume of poetry, *Løft min krone, vind fra intet* (lift my crown, wind out of nothingness), which is thematically linked to the first collection but marked by an even stronger inner tension; its poems show that chaos and fragmentation increasingly dominate. *Det skjeve smil i rosa* (1965; the wry smile in pink) is permeated by the poet's feeling of anguish. The volume is a nightmare with elements of so-called concrete poetry, dealing with the surrogates of modern consumer society and the indifference of human beings who wallow in commercialism and sexuality in the face of possible extinction. Moralist sentiments also dominate the prose poems in *Granatmannen kommer* (1968; the grenade man is coming). Inspired by the newspaper headlines about murder, war, and sex as a substitute for that love in which only poets believe, Brekke employs a collage-like form to demonstrate the power of evil. In later collections, such as *Aftenen er stille* (1972; the evening is quiet), *Flimmer. Og strek* (1980; shimmering. and lines), and *Men barnet i meg spør* (1992; but the child in me asks), Brekke—in a more subdued, ironic manner—focuses on aienation and isolation in contemporary Norwegian welfare society.

FINNISH AND FINNO-SWEDISH POSTWAR POETS

For Finland, World War II was a total catastrophe. The Winter War against Russia lasted from 1939 to 1940 and was resumed from 1941 to 1944 with the support of Germany, which did not prevent Finland's defeat. During the war years, almost all literary activity ceased, and modernistic poetry did not gain a foothold in Finland until the 1950's. The poets now concentrated on ridding language of clichés and rhetoric in order to release rhythm and images and to make the diction more colloquial.

The lyric breakthrough occurred with the collection *Tämä matka* (1956; this journey), by Eeva-Liisa Manner (1921-1995), a severe critique of over-intellectualized modern civilization, which leads humanity to a state of isolation and alienation. The poet sees a way out of desolation in the pantheistic experience of the unity of all things. This insight gradually leads her to a meditative attitude colored by ancient Chinese philosophy. The sources of Manner's next collection, *Orfiset laulu* (1960; Orphic songs), a journey into the land of myth and the subconscious, include the Revelation of Saint John, medieval troubadour poetry, and astrology. In the 1960's, Manner showed a new awareness of social reality, as in *Kirjoitettu kivi* (1966; the written stone), and, as a result, her style became more proselike and colloquial. The volume *Kuolleet vedet* (1977; dead waters), however, marked a return to the mystical perspectives of Manner's early poetry, focusing on contemporary human estrangement from nature.

Paavo Haavikko (1931-2008), the second modernistic Finnish poet of stature in the 1950's, consolidated his position through linguistic virtuosity, surprising juxtapositions of metaphors, and intense rhythmic expressions. No one has written of the insecurity and relativism of human life more convincingly than Haavikko in his collections from the early 1950's. A social and political approach becomes clearer in the volume *Synnyinmaa* (1955; the fatherland), which anticipates the critical attitudes of the 1960's, as well as Haavikko's own later poetry, such as *Neljätoista hallisijaa* (1970; fourteen rulers), the unifying element of which is the poet's criticism of fascist ideology. On the other hand, in *Kaksikymmentä ja yksi* (1974; *One and Twenty*, 2007), Haavikko's inspiration is the old *Kalevala* poem, and he alternates between modernistic language and the technique of folk poetry. In the 1980's Haavikko began to cross the border between literary genres. Thus *Rauta-aika* (1982; *The Age of Iron*, 1982) is an interpretation of the *Kalevala* poem, accompanied by *Kullervon tarina* (1982; *Kullervo's Story*, 1989). In addition, Haavikko has written historical works, novels, and dramas. Not only is the multiplicity of genres and the diversity of his subject matter extraordinary, but also his oeuvre in general marks the most radical rupture with tradition in modern Finnish literature.

A similar position in Finno-Swedish literature is occupied by Bo Carpelan (born 1926), who is the first poet to go beyond the prewar traditions. In his early collections from the 1940's, Carpelan employs elements from Swedish poetry of that decade: denseness, heavy imagery, and philosophical pessimism. *Objekt för ord* (1954; objects for words) clearly marks a change in Carpelan's position. He begins to express more openness and confidence—reality regains its concreteness. Carpelan abandons the private sphere at the same time that his language becomes more concise, developing into a rare formal mastery in the volumes *Källan* (1973; the source) and *I de mörka rummen, i de ljusa* (1976; in the dark rooms, in the bright ones). The selection of poems in *Dikter från trettio år* (1980; poems from thirty years) can be considered the summation of a remarkable career. Later volumes primarily pay tribute to a number of writers to whom Carpelan felt related; in *År som löv* (1989; *Years Like Leaves*, 1993), he glorifies the great German poet Friedrich Hölderlin.

ICELANDIC POSTWAR POETS

After World War II, Icelandic writers became less insular. Although some of them produced conventional epics, others began experimenting with style and language. Despite the political optimism of 1944 resulting from Iceland's proclamation of total independence from Denmark, a pessimistic note is sounded among the young writers, inspired by the Swedish poetry of the 1940's and approaching an almost nihilistic feeling of despair, voiced in unconventional free verse and impenetrable imagery.

Steinn Steinarr (1908-1958) led the experimentation with abstract styles. His short, simple, and un-rhymed poems express a radical skepticism based on a feeling of isolation and loneliness and on the realization of the absurdity of human existence, as pronounced in the programmatic titles *Sporí sandi* (1940; tracks in the sand) and *Ferth án fyrirheits* (1942; journey without promise). These volumes were influenced by American poet Carl Sandburg, abstract painting, and Swedish modernism. These models also led Steinarr to a number of typographical experiments, resulting in his most avant-garde work, the cycle of poems *Tímmin og vatnith* (1948; *Time and Water*, 1972).

Iceland's most important postwar lyricist, Hannes Pétursson (born 1931), wrote traditional verse before he began to employ a more experimental method; the shift in style reflecting his growing sense of alienation, a feeling of universal transitoriness. In the volumes *Í sumardölum* (1959; in the summer valleys) and *Stund og stathir* (1962; time and places), the poet clearly states that his feeling of helplessness can be overcome only when he recaptures what is closest and most precious to him: the beauty of Iceland and his childhood memories. His book *Úr hugskoti* (1976; recollections), a collection of occasional poetry and essays, demonstrates how Pétursson's work has moved from the traditional to the innovative and back to the traditional, a movement back to a formal concern which finds an exquisite expression in the much later volumes *36 ljóth* (1983; thirty-six poems) and *Eldhylur* (1993).

NEW SIMPLICITY

Nordic literature became increasingly marked by a demand for political commitment, which reached its climax in the 1960's. In addition, the modern welfare state and growing materialism became the targets of sharp attacks, which were also aimed at the ivory-tower attitude, defended by some writers as the only means of artistic survival. One group of writers emerged whose work was experimental, dealing with the function of language from a philosophical point of view. This eventually developed into the so-called concrete literature, which looks on language as a social and political system. Another group chose stylistic simplicity, a neorealistic approach called the New Simplicity, which first appeared in Sweden around 1960.

It is poetry's role in the communication process that

has constantly been stressed by the most significant spokesperson of the New Simplicity, Göran Palm (born 1931). His first collection, *Hundens besök* (1961; the dog's visit), contains deliberately simple, often aphoristic poems, which primarily convey basic elements of reality; but in addition, it treats of human isolation in a world determined by social gulfs. In *Världen ser dig* (1964; the world sees you), Palm demands that the poet abandon the traditional, aesthetic role and concentrate on establishing communication. Around 1965, Palm turned to the essay and published a number of "debate books," but in 1971, he returned to poetry with the volume *Varför har nätterna inga namn?* (why do the nights have no name?), which, although a thematic continuation of *Världen ser dig*, transfers responsibility from the poet to the politically awakened human being. After many years of silence as a poet Palm returned with *Sverige en vintersaga* (1984-1997; Sweden: a winter's tale), a three-volume epic poem about his home country filled with sarcasm, polemics, and humor reminiscent of Heinrich Heine.

Björn Håkansson (born 1937) is also paradigmatic of the 1960's. The volume *Mot centrum* (1963; toward the center) is an exercise in the methods of the New Simplicity, employing colloquial language from advertisements and newspapers. Håkansson meets the challenge of a politically involved literature with several collections, such as *Fronter i tredje världskriget* (1975; fronts in World War III), nondogmatic formulations of his political creed. In *Tjänstemannens son* (1978; the son of a civil servant), Håkansson violently protests a welfare-state bureaucracy that denies the individual's moral responsibility.

Much more direct in his political message is Göran Sonnevi (born 1939). A basic element in his poetry is his concept of the "structures," representing the principles that deprive life of its spontaneity. Language is one of these structures, and its power over our thoughts is analyzed in *Inngrep—modeller* (1965; interventions—models). Sonnevi's emergence as a political writer was marked by the separately published poem "Om kriget i Vietnam" (about the war in Vietnam), from 1965. His revolutionary activism is apparent in the titles of works such as *Det måste gå* (1970; it has to work), which places Sonnevi beside Danish author Ivan Malinovski

as one of the most convincing political writers of postwar literature. *Det omöjliga* (1975; the impossible) and its sequel, *Språk; verktyg; eld* (1979; language; tools; fire), are Sonnevi's most significant collections from the 1970's. *Oavslutade dikter* (1987; unfinished poems) as well as *Klangernas bok* (1998; the book of sounds) demonstrate a much increased thematic and formal sophistication. A visionary, even metaphysical aspect has been added; the previous expansion of the universe is now accompanied by an expansion of the soul that is triggered by various encounters with death. Sonnevi must be regarded as one of the great Swedish poets of the twentieth century.

LANGUAGE EXAMINED

Preoccupation with the function of language led not only to a literature critical of society but also to a so-called concrete poetry, in which words are employed as concrete, malleable material, freed of meaning and intention. The letters are arranged in patterns, and the words are exploited as sounds. A pioneer of this is Carl Fredrik Reuterswärd (born 1934). In his collection *På samma gång* (1961; at the same time), the latter gives up syntax completely and arranges single words in a lyric verbal tapestry. Where Reuterswärd writes with the intention of provoking the reader, Bengt Emil Johnson (born 1936) attempts above all to communicate his artistic experiences. For that reason, he let his collection *Gubbdrunkning* (1965; old man's drowning) be accompanied by a phonograph record, in order to convey more vitally the printed word. With the poems in *Skuggsång* (1973; shadow song), Johnson emerges as an accessible nature poet, a direction he continues to exploit throughout the 1980's with an increased focus on existential themes as convincingly demonstrated in the pessimistic volumes *Lika* (1991; equal) and *Över Oxbrobäcken* (1996; over Oxbro stream), in which nature is seen as incomprehensible and death perhaps as the only comprehensible truth.

The linguistic trend is continued by Tobias Berggren (born 1940), who clearly attempts to release language from the mental associations that bind one to old patterns. In *Den främmande tryggheten* (1971; the strange security), he, like Sonnevi, speculates about the possibility of creating a new language capable of bringing about change—thereby combining a political and a Romantic attitude. The abstract, occasionally dry statements of this volume have completely disappeared in *Namn och grus* (1973; names and gravel), a major work of modern Swedish poetry in which the author's presence is intense. A journey through an inferno toward the light occurs in the volume *Resor i din tystnad* (1976; journeys in your silence), containing poems of extraordinary visionary beauty, a trait even more characteristic of the collections *Bergsmusik* (1978; mountain music) and *Threnos* (1981). The volume *Fält och legender* (1997; spheres and legends) both marks a return to the earlier discussion of the cognitive function of language and a metaphysical expansion of the poet's universe.

Surrealist influences

Similarly eclectic is the work of Gunnar Harding (born 1940), who in the preface to his collection *Poesi, 1967-73* (1973; poetry, 1967-1973) mentions jazz, painting, and French Surrealism as important influences. In addition, Harding stresses that his poetry is clearly visual, a characteristic which in his earlier work is linked to language, but which gradually becomes associated with typography. In later volumes, *Gasljus* (1983; gaslight) and *Stjärndykare* (1987; star divers), a search for an all-encompassing unity, which extinguishes any boundary between the private and public spheres, is noticeable. This trend reaches its zenith with *Salongstycken* (2001; parlor pieces), a collection of highly sophisticated, poetic speculations on topics such as art, infinity, love, and death.

Lars Norén (born 1944) also found inspiration in French Surrealism. His early writing culminates in the hectic, visionary collection *Stupor: Nobody Knows You When You're Down and Out* (1968), the last volume in a series of autobiographical works since 1965; the background is the poet's hospitalization for schizophrenia. In these volumes, Norén deliberately recreates the passive impulses, voices, and images that had penetrated the mental emptiness resulting from his psychic paralysis. In his later poetry, Norén attempts to avoid the private sphere, thereby turning his writing in a more conventional direction, but this change is also an indication that the previous chaos has been overcome. The longing for purity that permeates Norén's

works of the 1960's was realized, with strong religious overtones, in the volumes *Order* (1978) and *Hjärta i hjärta* (1980; heart in heart), whose linguistic brilliance is unequaled in Norén's generation. In the 1980's, Norén emerged as one of Scandinavia's most prolific playwrights, a position he maintained throughout the 1990's.

Like Norén, the prose writer and lyricist Lars Gustafsson (born 1936) cannot be placed in a specific literary category. His poetry collections from *Ballongfararna* (1962; the balloon travelers) to *Varma rum och kalla* (1972; *Warm Rooms and Cold*, 1975) contain primarily variations on the themes of his novels: the relationship between fiction and reality, art and life, past and future. Gustafsson's superb handling of language is evidenced by the volume of formally brilliant poetry, *Sonetter* (1977; sonnets). Feelings of angst and transitoriness run as a leitmotif through Gustafsson's later collections, such as *Fyra poeter* (1988; four poets) and *Variationer över ett tema av Silferstolpe* (1996; variations on a theme by Silferstolpe), confirming his position in Swedish literature as an accomplished classicist who succeeds in establishing total correspondence between form and content.

Feminism

During the early 1970's, a political radicalization took place in Sweden just as in the other Nordic countries. It was accompanied by a radical women's movement and, in literature, by a growing feminism. This trend was anticipated by Sonja Åkesson (1926-1977), whose autobiographical collection *Husfrid* (1962; domestic peace) deflates various romantic myths about relations between man and woman. Elisabet Hermodsson (born 1927) wrote *Disa Nilsons visor* (1974; the ballads of Disa Nilson) as a corrective to the more romantic collection of Birger Söberg, *Fridas bok* from 1922. Disa is much more spontaneous and self-assured, and a related motif inspired the poems in *Gör dig synlig* (1980; make yourself visible): how women have tended to see themselves through the eyes of men rather than defining themselves. Hermodsson's collection from 1985, *Stenar skärvor skikt av jord* (stones, shards, layers of soil), on the other hand, focuses entirely on ecological concerns.

The same distance to feminist themes is found in the poetry of Katarina Frostenson (born 1953). Her early collections, *Imellan* (1978; between), *Den andra* (1982; the other), and *I det gula* (1985; in the yellow) express in a series of rather fragmentary texts her strong criticism of linguistic abuse in contemporary society; in *Stränderna* (1989; seashores), this criticism develops into a general distrust in language as it fails to convey the mutability of today's world. More accessible are the texts in *Joner* (1991; ions), echoing well-known medieval ballads, folk songs, and church hymns.

POSTMODERNISM

This approach of borrowing from many different sources and styles is characteristic of the eclectic, postmodern approach to literature. The most accomplished representative of contemporary Swedish postmodernism is the novelist, filmmaker, playwright, and poet Steig Larsson (1954-2004), whose concept of reality initially is strictly defined by the fictional universe. In *Minuterna före blicken* (1981; the minutes before the look) and *Händ!* (1988; happen!), he even strips away any semantic content and simply records his observations without using imagery and other stylistic means. In his later poetry collections, such as *Uttal* (1992; pronunciation), Larsson expresses his inability to shape experience and impression in words, and his inability to shape reality artistically, which to him pertains to a general problem haunting humankind: how to orient oneself in time and space, how to create one's own identity. Nevertheless, in *Natta de mina* (1997; putting the family to bed), the writing process appears to be the only means to rope in and hold on to reality and thus offer a way out of this existential predicament. Amid strong subjectivity, a belief in possible values surfaces time and again, a belief paralleled with religious faith. This volume is both a crucial source for a more thorough understanding of Larsson's own authorship and a remarkable Scandinavian contribution to the discourse on the relationship between utterance and meaning, writing and cognition.

A metaphysical orientation, as exemplified in Larsson's later works, is characteristic of contemporary Swedish poetry. In Christine Falkenland's (born 1967) collection *Blodbok* (1995; book of blood), a woman's relation in love to a man is paralleled to her relation to God; Lotta Olsson (born 1973), in her twenty-two sonnets in *Skuggor och speglingar* (1994; shadows and reflections), depicts Persephone on her way to Hades to become the consort of the God of Death, and Kristian Lundberg (born 1966), in his collection of poems *Är och blir* (1996; being and becoming), employs a rather exalted, hymnic tone to express his struggling relationship with God.

The relationship between fiction and reality as dealt with in Swedish literature by Larsson and, before him, for instance, by Gustafsson, is also discussed in the works of Stein Mehren (born 1935), who, together with Olav H. Hauge and Georg Johannessen, is among the most gifted Norwegian poets of the 1960's. The relationship between words and experience, the recognition of the environment and the self, take on an imposing form in Mehren's collection *Aurora det niende mørke* (1969; Aurora the ninth darkness). The internal structure is a journey through language, various styles and forms of expression that mirror one another. Mehren's dominant position among modernist poets in Norway is confirmed by *Vintersolhverv* (1979; winter solstice), which expresses the author's opinion that poetry is the only medium through which one can take hold of reality—an opinion which is particularly evident in Mehren's novels from the 1970's. His later poetry collections *Corona: Formørkelsen og dens lys* (1986; Corona: the eclipse and its light) and *Det andre lyset* (1989; the other light) have become increasingly philosophical, dealing with pairs of opposites: light and darkness, presence and absence, love and isolation.

Olav H. Hauge (1908-1974) published his first work, a collection of introspective poetry titled *Glør i oska* (embers in the ashes), in 1946, but was not recognized until he published *På ørnetuva* (1961; on eagle mound), which is marked by a laconic style influenced by Ezra Pound and Japanese haiku. Hauge's symbolic use of nature almost disappears in *Dropar i austavind* (1966; drops in the eastern wind). Here, the objects stand alone and speak for themselves, and in the collection *Spør vinden* (1971; ask the wind), the harsh environment of the fjords and mountains finds an almost aphoristic expression. His *Dikt i samling* (1985; collected poems) confirms Hauge's position as one of the foremost modernists in postwar Norwegian poetry.

The work of Georg Johannesen (1931-2005) reveals a more outward-directed tendency, behind which one senses a moral, ideological worldview. He possessed a rich, metaphor-filled creative talent and wrote poetry of great complexity. Johannesen sensed that traditional modernistic language does not capture reality. The simple title of his first collection, *Dikt 1959* (1959; poems 1959), reflects his demand for a poetry without superfluous decoration, as exemplified in the two volumes *Ars moriendi* (1965; the art of dying well) and *Nye dikt* (1966; new poems). Here, as well as in Johannesen's works from the following decades, primarily essays and novels, the main purpose was to analyze critically contemporary society.

JAN ERIK VOLD AND THE PROFIL GROUP

Simultaneously with Johannesen's neorealistic poetry, the New Simplicity and concrete poetry gained a foothold in Norway. One of the most talented representatives of these new trends is Jan Erik Vold (born 1939). He is aware of his time and often excessively sensitive to its prevailing moods and various forms of artistic expression. He made his debut in 1965 with *Mellom speil og speil* (between mirror and mirror), which includes a number of figurative texts about the search for a reality that is nonexistent—the world consists of mirrors, of emptiness and deception. *Mor Godhjertas glade versjon. Ja* (1968; Mother Goodheart's happy version: yes), like Mehren's *Aurora*, is a labyrinthine journey through language and fantasy, from a convoluted linguistic system to a recognizable reality of the self. A deep mistrust of words, on the other hand, prevails in *Kykelipi* (1969; cock-a-diddle-dee) and increases in the volume *Spor, snø* (1970; tracks, snow), in which Vold attempts to re-create an atmosphere of emptiness and inconsistency in short poems inspired by Japanese haiku. This manifestation of the New Simplicity is offset by the linguistic virtuosity and burlesque imagination that pervades *Sirkel, sirkel* (1979; circle, circle), a volume based on impressions from a trip around the world, but is resumed in the collections *Sorgen. Sangen. Veien* (1987; the sorrow. the song. the road) and *Elg* (1989; moose), focusing on basic aspects and details of everyday life.

Vold was a leading figure in the group of writers who contributed to *Profil* (established in 1943), a journal originally attacking the psychological and aestheticizing trends in Norwegian postwar literature and, since the 1970's, the mouthpiece for Marxist literary theory. The central poet of this group is Tor Obrestad (born 1938), who, in *Den norske løve* (1970; the Norwegian lion) and *Stå saman* (1974; stand together), conveys a direct, revolutionary message aimed at both the United States and the North Atlantic Treaty Organization and at social domestic questions. Here, as well as in *Vinterdikt* (1979; winter poems), political propaganda frequently overwhelms aesthetic form. In *Misteltein* (1988; mistletoe), on the other hand, Obrestad reaches back to Old Norse myths for inspiration.

A number of other writers in the *Profil* group joined Vold in refusing to enter the political fight. The first poetry collection by Einar Økland (born 1940), *Ein gul dag* (1963; a yellow day), although somewhat private in theme, is pointed toward the simplicity and the commonplace that dominated the second half of the 1960's. The volume *Bronsehesten* (1975; the bronze horse) is completely devoid of ideological commitment; underlying the description of an apparently trite reality is an analysis of language, or rather poetry, as the only, if problematic, means of communication.

NORWAY: 1970'S

Norwegian poetry of the 1970's was not as significant as the prose written during that decade. Nevertheless, a number of lyricists emerged who contributed to the antidogmatic trend that distinguished the decade. Tove Lie (born 1942) consistently follows a symbolic, antimodernistic mode, expressed in the volumes *Lotus* (1972) and *Vi sprang ut av ild* (1979; we jumped from the fire). Árvid Torgeir Lie (born 1938) moved from nature poetry to political propaganda with his collection *Skrive og tenke* (1971; write and think), but his later volumes, such as *Sju svingar opp* (1976; seven sharp curves), employ increasingly subtle means of expression. More uncompromising is the straightforward, forceful poetry of Stig Holmås (born 1946) in the collections *Vi er mange* (1970; we are many) and *Tenke på i morgen* (1972; think of tomorrow), works that also display a redeeming sense of humor, being both sarcastic and compassionate. Paal-Helge Haugen (born 1945) shows a strong affinity for contemporary American poetry, some of which he has translated into Norwegian. He made his lyrical debut with *På botnen av ein mørk sommar* (1967; at the bottom of a dark summer), a fine example of the Swedish school of New Simplicity, with its simple and striking imagery taken from everyday life. In later volumes, such as *Fram i lyset, tydeleg* (1978; forward into the light, distinctly), this trend continues—with, however, an increased focus on ideological issues. The beginning social awareness of a boy and the ensuing personal conflicts form the theme of *Steingjerde* (1979; *Stone Fences*, 1986); the collection of experimenting prose poems, *dette hus* (1984; in this house), deals primarily with the relationship between nature and culture; and *Det overvintra lyset* (1985; hibernated light) highlights, in a prehistoric setting, the contrast of love and war. *Meditasjoner over Georges de la Tour* (1990; meditations on Georges de la Tour) offers subdued reflections inspired by the French painter of the title, focusing, like Mehren's later poems, on themes of darkness and light.

NORWAY: 1980'S AND BEYOND

Norwegian literature is dominated by a number of gifted playwrights such as Peder W. Cappelen (1931-1992) and Cecilie Løveid (born 1951) and prose writers such as Bjørg Vik (born 1935), Herbjørg Wassmo (born 1942), Kjartan Fløgstad (born 1944), and Jan Kjaerstad (born 1953). However, several of them began as poets, Løveid with *Most* (1972; juice), a love story in poetry and prose, Wassmo with *Vingeslag* (1976; beating wings) and *Flotid* (1977; high tide), and Fløgstad with *Valfart* (1968; pilgrimage), conveying sensitive experiences of nature and city life. Løveid has continued to experiment with mixing genres. Thus, *Sug* (1979; *Sea Swell*, 1986), combines prose and poetry to depict the protagonist's struggle for self-realization. It is in Løveid's generation in particular that one finds the most interesting lyrical poets of today: young women writers, such as Inger Elisabeth Hansen (born 1950), Eva Jensen (born 1955), and Cindy Haug (born 1956), focusing in a nondogmatic fashion on the themes of love and power, not so much on attempts at exerting power over others than at gaining control over one's own selfhood. The younger generation's Eirik Lodén (born 1976) and Alexander Rubio (born 1974), both representatives of a new, form-oriented trend, deliberately see themselves as parts of a classical tradition. Lodén, in *Preludium* (1993; prelude), with his strict use of rhyme and rhythm, is clearly inspired by the formal mastery of John Keats, William Blake, and William Wordsworth, whereas Rubio, in *Nylonroser* (1993; nylon roses), patterns his beauty-seeking poetry on works by Edgar Allan Poe and Isidore-Lucien Ducasse (whose pseudonym is Lautréamont), allowing, in his compassionate love poetry (and quite in line with a significant trend in contemporary Scandinavian literature), a distinct religious tone be heard.

FINLAND: 1960'S AND BEYOND

In Finland, the poetry of the 1960's developed toward a clear political commitment that eventually found expression in realistic, everyday poetry. The writings of Pentti Saarikoski (1937-1983) reflect the entire literary development of this and the following decade. Disorder and the threat of chaos are characteristic and crucial themes in the volume *Kuljen missä kuljen* (1965; I walk where I walk). Saarikoski's aversion to absolute views and ideological authoritarianism leads to resignation and to a number of miniature poems about happy and unhappy love in *En soisi sen päättyván* (1968; I wish it would not end). The private sphere becomes a major motif in the 1970's. In *Alue* (1973; territory), Saarikoski writes about his family, his farm, and its surroundings. This development is reflected linguistically in a change from aphoristic to more lyric diction. The tension between Saarikoski's skepticism—which in the collection *Tanssilattia vuorella* (1977; the dancing floor on the mountain) leads him to depict the contemporary world as a fossilized labyrinth—and his need to experience faith and life as meaningful make him the most agile of the postwar Finnish writers and perhaps the one with the widest scope, a characteristic confirmed by the posthumous collection *Hämärän tanssit* (1983; *Dancers of the Obscure*, 1987).

The work of Väinö Kirstinä (1936-2007), the second major Finnish lyric poet of the 1960's, was linguistically far more advanced than Saarikoski's. He made his debut in 1961 with *Lakeus* (the plain), which reverts to the imagery of the 1950's. In *Puhetta* (1963; talk), Kirstinä did a complete reversal, employing correct and incorrect quotations, far-fetched associations, and excerpts from the Helsinki telephone directory in Dadaist word series and sound combinations—expressions of the poet's determination not to stagnate in rigid attitudes. During the 1970's, Kirstinä seemed to have found a solution to his search in depictions of the secluded, idyllic life in nature, portrayed with desperate humor in *Talo maalla* (1969; a house in the country), a humor that emerges with increasing clarity as the poet's only weapon against a world so absurd that everyone must laugh in order to remain sane. Oriented toward French culture, Kirstinä become increasingly influenced by the Surrealism of, for instance, André Breton. Thus his pessimistic visions of the dead end of human civilization increasingly were permeated with dreamlike sequences, as in *Säännöstelty euthanasia* (1973; rationed euthanasia) and *Yötä, päivää* (1986; night, day), although executed with a certain macabre linguistic and metaphoric beauty.

A stronger political emphasis is found in the works of Jyrki Pellinen (born 1940). The prose poems in *Niin päinvastoin kuin kukaan* (1965; so on the contrary than nobody) are primarily labyrinthine incursions into the world of words, whereas the concise poems in *Tässä yhteiskunnassa on paha nukkua* (1966; you cannot sleep well in this society) are more traditional, with refined nature scenes and romantic melancholy. In his collections from the 1970's, Pellinen moved toward surreal romanticism and mysticism. This trend, which added to the diversified quality of his writing, led to the cyclic poem *Kertosäkeiden laulu* (1976; the song of refrains), which is a prolonged search for the self, a dialogue with the poet's mirror image. In later collections, such as *Huulilla kylmä tuuli* (1990; a cold wind on the lips), Pellinen increasingly deals with the creative act, the writing process itself, and thus contributes to a general trend toward metapoetry that is particularly evident in contemporary Danish literature.

The protest literature of the 1970's is represented in the writing of Kari Aronpuro (born 1940), who openly satirizes a number of political and social situations inside and outside Finland. More rewarding but less accessible are Aronpuro's collections from the following decade, *Merkillistä menoa* (1983; remarkable progress) and *Kirjaimet tulevat* (1986; the letters are coming), displaying his intellectual curiosity and obsession with cultural studies.

Finnish protest literature reached its culmination in the work of Matti Rossi (born 1934), whose first collection, *Näytelmän henkilöt* (1965; the characters of the play), contains the most artistically varied poems on the Vietnam War in Finnish literature; it was followed by additional volumes of political poetry, *Tilaisuus* (1967; the opportunity) and *Agitprop* (1972). In his poetry of the 1980's, Rossi, like Haavikko, turns to the *Kalevala* epic for further inspiration.

The wave of debate literature reached its crest around 1975. From then on, the young poets became occupied with a more intimate atmosphere, a care for detail and a predominant interest in nature, partly motivated by opposition to the materialism of the modern welfare state. Thus, when Tommy Tabermann (born 1947) in 1970 published his first volume, *Ruusuja Rosa Luxemburgille* (roses for Rosa Luxemburg), critics looking for dogmatic political verse were greatly disappointed. They found sensitive and romantic poetry about nature and young love, themes that Tabermann also treats with successful variation in *Kaipaus* (1976; yearning) and *Anna mina kumoan vielä tämän maljan* (1977; grant that I may still drink up this cup). Jarkko Laine (1947-2006) used the features of Western popular mass culture to attack the culture of the welfare society. The tone of his collections *Muovinen Buddha* (1967; the plastic Buddha) and *Viidenpennin Hamlet* (1976; five-penny Hamlet) is critical but balanced by a strong element of humor and the use of puns. In the following decades, Laine became a major Finnish representative of a neo-Romantic, nonpolitical trend in Scandinavian literature. A very talented nature poet, Risto Rasa (born 1954), concentrates in a seemingly naïve fashion on the little things and the ways of nature, which he considers essential components of human life, in his collection *Kulkurivarpunen* (1973; the vagabond sparrow).

This romantic trend was continued in the 1980's by Jukka Kemppinen (born 1944) but counterbalanced by writers such as Tiina Kaila (born 1951) and Kirsti

Simonsuuri (born 1945). Kemppinen adds a religious tone to his poems in *Linnusta länteen* (1985; west of the bird) and *Kiertävä kivi on kuolut* (1986; a rolling stone is dead), the latter volume also including prose poems, in which he depicts nature as a reflection of God. A totally different topic dominates the volume *Riitamaa* (1989; disputed land), a commemoration—with frequent references to the battlefields of World War I—of the fiftieth anniversary of Finland's Winter War against Soviet Russia. Kaila writes in the same intellectual tradition as the aforementioned Aaronpuro. Thus her debut collection, *Keskustelu hämärässä* (1975; dialogue in the twilight), contains a sophisticated dialogue with the writer Franz Kafka about the absurdity of existence, whereas in the cosmological texts of the later volumes, *Kala on meren kuva* (1983; the fish is the image of the sea) and *Valon nälkä* (1986; light hunger), a strong pantheistic religiosity dominates, focusing on the unity of the small detail and the infinite universe. Simonsuuri's poetry—from *Murattikaide* (1980; the ivy balustrade) to *Enkelten pysäkki* (1990; angel's bus stop)—has its foundation in European intellectual history and avoids reference to social issues or the period's feminist discourse.

FINNO-SWEDISH POETS: 1970'S AND BEYOND

Contemporary Finno-Swedish literature is more accessible than during previous decades. The modern writers desire to embrace all social, political, and psychological realities, as demonstrated by Claes Andersson (born 1937). In *Bli, tilsammans* (1971; become, together), he interweaves debate poems and poems of love and personal happiness, alternating subjectivity and external issues. By the end of the 1970's, Andersson's poetry had turned away from social and political questions, and in *Trädens sånger* (1979; the trees's songs) he approaches a pantheistic view of nature if not outright mysticism. While strictly personal matters relating to parents, family life, and cohabitation are analyzed in *Under* (1984; miracles) and *Huden där den är som tunnast* (1991; the skin where it is thinnest), the scope is widened in *Mina bästa dagar* (1987, my best days), a pessimistic vision of terror and world destruction.

A similar somber tone permeates Andersson's collection from 1997 *En lycklig mänska* (a happy human being), in which death hits the apparent idyll like lighting. However, in contrast to life's transitoriness, love and music (the poet himself is an accomplished pianist) stand out as dynamic and positive forces portrayed with such exquisite artistry that the volume confirms Andersson's position as the leading Finno-Swedish poet of his generation. On the other hand, the conflicts in love, married life, and work form the subjects of the prose poems by Märta Tikkanen (born 1935) in *Århundradets kärlekssaga* (1978; *The Love Story of the Century*, 1984), combining, as do her various prose works, warmth and pithiness in their penetrating portraits. The same combination is found in the volume *Mörkret som ger glädjen ljus* (1981; the darkness that gives happiness depth), which deals with her child's emotional illness.

A focus on provincial life, another example of the romantic trend toward the end of the twentieth century, is present in the poems of Lars Huldén (born 1926), a selection of which was published in 1976 as *Långdansen* (the long dance), followed by subtle contemplations on the changing seasons and the aging process in *Jag blir gammal, kära du* (1981; darling, I am growing old). Influenced by the dialect and folklore of his home region, Huldén depicts life, with liberating and unique humor, as a series of coincidences. The concept that death as well as redemption is part of this life becomes the point of departure for *Psalmer för trolösa kristna* (1991; hymns for faithless Christians).

With Huldén, Finno-Swedish literature distanced itself from the ideological concerns of former decades. In this respect, Huldén can be seen as a forerunner of poets such as Kjell Westö (born 1961), Diana Bredenberg (1963-2005), and Agneta Enckell (born 1957). Whereas Westö (also an accomplished prose writer) in *Epitaf over Mr. Nacht* (1988; epitaph on Mr. Nacht) draws on features from pop music and excels in wordplays and melodramatic role-playing, Bredenberg analyzed her own emotions and attitudes in *Hinna* (1989; membrane) and *Sekvens* (1991; sequence); in the latter volume, she also expressed an ecological concern about nature's destruction. Enckell employs the technique of the comic strip in *Rum: Berättelser* (1987; rooms: narratives), which is partly a symbolic journey through the underworld realm of the dead, revisited in *Falla (Eurydike)* (1991; the fall [Eurydice]). However, in this volume the poems are also about sexuality as well as the writing of poetry—a metapoetic topic found among contemporary writers in the other Scandinavian countries as well.

ICELAND: 1960'S AND BEYOND

In the 1960's, Iceland experienced a considerable upsurge of leftist literature, turning in particular against foreign political and economic influences. This critical tone was especially prevalent in prose, while poetry only gradually became politically committed and experimental. Nature is, as it always has been, a major motif in modern Icelandic poetry.

One of the most talented contemporary poets, Thorsteinn frá Hamri (pseudonym of Thorsteinn Jonsson; born 1938), has been able to join new and old both linguistically and philosophically in a flexible and rhythmic language. Thus, in his poems against the Vietnam War, political radicalism is combined with nationalistic pathos. Hamri's preoccupation with Iceland's history, literature, and folklore resulted in a number of optimistic and well-balanced collections during the 1960's, such as *Lífandi manna land* (1963; land of the living). His growing awareness that the Hermetic style of modernism had established a barrier to communication led in 1972 to the strongly pessimistic poems of *Vethrahjalmur* (sun rings), which constitute a dream about the possibilities of human fellowship, further explored in collections from the following decades, including *Ljóth og myndir* (1988; poems and pictures) and *Sæfarinn sofandi* (1992; the sleeping seafarer).

A more direct political consciousness is found in the work of Pétur Gunnarsson (born 1947), a typical representative of the postwar generation who stepped forward around 1975 and spoke for a political activism that appears most convincing when combined with a linguistic renewal. Gunnarsson's collection *Splunkunýr dagur* (1973; a brand-new day) is, indeed, based on the optimistic realization that the world is ever in flux, that life is a continuous process. After this collection, Gunnarsson wrote primarily prose fiction.

Sigurður Pálsson (born 1948) displays verve and freshness in common with Gunnarsson, and both employ obviously autobiographical material. In *Ljóth vega salt* (1975; poems on the seesaw), Pálsson presents a number of half-nostalgic, half-mocking scenes from his childhood in the countryside, his school years, and various jobs. He is not, however, narcissistic; rather, the description of his youth becomes the point of departure for his emotional and intellectual movement toward a new, far more complicated reality in later collections such as *Ljóth vega gerth* (1982; poems on the road building), *Ljóthlínudans* (1993; poems—tightrope walking), and *Einhver í dyrunum* (2000; somebody in the door).

The trend toward the more private sphere as well as a focus on the artistic and cognitive function of language is continued by a number of outstanding contemporary poets. Linda Vilhjálmsdóttir (born 1958) made her highly acclaimed debut in 1990 with *Bláthráthur* (hanging by a thread), a collection of highly introspective poetry as well as exquisite nature descriptions also to be found in her following works, such as *Klakabörnin* (1992; the children of ice). A more pronounced feminist orientation can be found in the poetry collections of Kristín Ómarsdóttir (born 1962), such as *Therna á gömlu veitingahúsi* (1993; waitress in an old tavern), characterized by sophisticated linguistic experimentation and significantly less dogmatic than the literature of the 1960's and 1970's. An even more pronounced playfulness with language and image concealing an in-depth exploration of personal, existential issues is found in the work of Bragi Ólafsson (born 1962), particularly his collections *Ansjósur* (1991; anchovies) and *Ytri höfnin* (1993; the outer port)—here often combined with historical features.

A historical perspective is also found in the poetry of Sjón (pseudonym of Sigurjón Birgir Sigurðsson; born 1962). His first three collections were reprinted in the volume *Drengurinn meth röntgenaugun* (1986; the boy with the X-ray eyes), containing texts that combine the surreal with aspects of Icelandic experience and literary heritage. A similar combination can be found in the volume *Ég man ekki eitthvath í skýin* (1991; I remember something in the clouds). Likewise remarkable is the poetry of Ísak Harðarson (born 1956) with highly acclaimed collections such as *Slý* (1985; slime) and *Hvítur ísbjörn* (1995; white polar bear), and Sigfús Bjartmarsson (born 1955). In volumes such as *Hlýja skugganna* (1985; the heat of the shadows) and *Án fjathra* (1989; without feathers), Bjartmarsson emerges as the Icelandic poet who demonstrated the most advanced command of language and imagery at the beginning of the new millennium. His choice of foreign countries and cultures as topics is exceptional and innovative, primarily in *Zombí* (1992), a geographical expansion that is still rather unusual in Icelandic poetry.

DENMARK: 1960'S AND BEYOND

The lyrical blossoming of Danish literature during the 1960's is largely attributable to Klaus Rifbjerg (born 1931), the most productive and versatile Danish postwar author, whose more than one hundred titles include not only poetry but also prose, drama, film scripts, and reviews. Rifbjerg's breakthrough collection, *Konfrontation* (1960; confrontation), presents conflicts drawn from everyday experience, whereas an ecstatic element appears in his long poem *Camouflage* (1961), an attempt to conquer reality through a journey into the unconscious, back to myths and memories. The technique is strictly associative. Rifbjerg plays with words, using them in surprising combinations and fragmented syntax. This method of confrontation is modified in his later poetry but appears again in *Mytologi* (1970; mythology). These poems are based on a direct encounter of classical myth with modern conditions. Another reaction against the lyric style introduced in *Konfrontation* is *Amagerdigte* (1965; Amager poems). Here Rifbjerg's style is sober and matter-of-fact, inspired by the Swedish New Simplicity. The volume *Ved stranden* (1976; at the beach) resumes the uninhibited flight of fancy characteristic of the earlier works but in a more serene tone and with a new, original attitude of confrontation with nature, which is continued in the volumes *Det svävende trä* (1984; the floating tree) and *Septembersang* (1988; September song). In Rifbjerg's later volumes, from *Bjerget i himlen* (1991; the mountain in heaven) to *Terrains vague* (1998), he returns to the spunky tone of his earliest collections, blended with personal observations about human folly and the poet's own aging process. These are works that confirm Rifbjerg's position in Danish iterature not only as the most productive but also as one of the most accomplished post-World War II lyrical poets.

In 1960, Jess Ørnsbo (born 1932) made his debut with *Digte* (poems), imbued with a sense of social involvement which is new to modernism. The point of departure is a worker's district in Copenhagen, but the locale is subordinated in a series of confrontations with the malice of modern urban existence. Ørnsbo's baroque metaphors are developed further in *Myter* (1964; myths), an attempt to expand the choice of motifs to include the subconscious. The decisive themes are alienation, aggression, and death, described with piercing verbal effects. In *Mobiliseringer* (1978; mobilizations), Ørnsbo's social criticism is given political overtones in a bitter diagnosis of a society in the process of dissolution. This indignation reaches new heights in his later collections *Hjertets søle* (1984; slush of the heart) and *Tidebog* (1997; book of hours).

For Ivan Malinowski (1926-1989) the technique of confrontation also is a basic principle, a formal expression of his experience of the senselessness of existence. In *Romerske bassiner* (1963; Roman basins), a collection of catalog-like prose poems, objects are juxtaposed in an attempt to paint a pathological picture of modern civilization, while *Poetomatic* (1965) alternates between nihilism and hope in a series of pithy, concentrated aphorisms. Malinowski's socialist position emerges more clearly in *Leve som var der en fremtid og et håb* (1968; living as if there were a future and hope), in which there rises, above the zero point of absurdity, an imperishable will to live, leading the poet to a socialist political involvement. This theme is developed further in *Kritik af tavsheden* (1974; *Critique of Silence*, 1977) which, in addition, deals with the indoctrinating function of language. In Malinowski's most important collections from the 1980's, *Vinterens hjerte* (1980; the heart of winter) and *Vinden i verden* (1988; the wind in the world), he resumes his criticism of capitalism, but the social questions are now placed in the much larger context of nature and universe, distinctly expressing the longing for harmony and totality that has been the driving force behind his work.

Jørgen Sonne (born 1925), on the other hand, alludes constantly in his poems to distant times and foreign cultures. His first three collections, from 1950 to 1952, are still marked by the postwar period's spiritual crisis and search for meaning. These works can be seen as talented introductions to *Krese* (1963; cycles), one of the most mature works of the 1960's. The latter is an attempt to regain the primitive quality and richness of childhood feelings through intellectual introspection, an attempt to recognize the coherence of all things, which is also the theme of *Huset* (1976; the house). Here, Sonne combines observations, reflections, and visions in a long associative journey into fantasy, memory, and history, using a strictly imagistic technique. The poems in *Nærvær: Suite på rejsen* (1980; presence: suite on the journey), on the other hand, are based on concrete travel experiences; *Nul* (1987; zero) is an attempt to conjure moods of universal harmony. Here, and particularly in later volumes, such as *Have* (1992; garden), Sonne approaches a succinct, even aphoristic mode of expression.

The associative technique is developed to full mastery in the debut poems of Jørgen Gustava Brandt (1929-2006), *Korn i Pelegs mark* (1949; grain in Peleg's field), in which the poet constantly refers to the Old Testament, to Oriental mysticism, and to the poetry of Dylan Thomas. The formally skillful but somewhat impersonal collections of the 1950's are succeeded in 1960 by *Fragment af imorgen* (fragment of tomorrow). Narcissism is replaced by a perception that harmonizes the inner and outer worlds. Brandt's poems are often formed of tireless descriptions of an object, the details of which create the poetic image. The poems in *Ateliers* (1967) are characterized by myths and religious symbols. In *Her omkring* (1974; around here), Brandt uses such symbols to express his longing for a mystical rest in existence. A similar reflective mood, but now accompanied by a direct religious confession, dominates Brandt's numerous succeeding collections, such as *Giv dagen dit lys* (1986; give the day your light), with a subtitle meaning "church hymns," and *Ansigt til ansigt* (1996; face to face).

In Denmark, as in Sweden, there also arose around 1965 a tendency toward the concrete, in which words, functioning as signs, have intrinsic value. In poetry, it is present in Malinowski's *Romerske bassiner*, in Benny Andersen's easily accessible writing, and, to an even greater extent, in the esoteric works of Per Højholt (1928-2004). *Den indre bowlerhat* (1964; the inner bowler hat), by Andersen (born 1929), employs a witty, elegant form, in which the ambiguities of language create surprising and unexpected connections, seen in the light of social attitudes. Andersen cultivates the portrait poem, in which he depicts the alienated human being, generally by means of a monologue, as in his best-selling work *Svantes viser* (1972; Svante's songs), for which Andersen wrote the music as well. After publishing collections of poems dealing with private or political issues, Andersen returned in *Under begge øjne* (1978; under both eyes) to purely existential questions, which are also dealt with in the volumes *Andre sider* (1987; other sides) and *Skynd dig langsomt* (1998; hurry slowly), both concluding with the acknowledgment that close human contact is the only way to achieve lasting happiness.

The perception of language as a means of cognition is the dominant idea in the work of Højholt. He experiments with different types of language: quotations, technical jargon, neologisms, and clichés. Paper and type are used as artistic materials, a cultivation of formal elements which in *Punkter* (1971; points) transforms the language into mere signs and closed symbols. In a series of small, numbered collections with the common title *Praksis* (1977-1996; praxis), Højholt continues his linguistic experimentations.

The high point of this tendency is reached in *Det* (1969; it), by Inger Christensen (1935-2009). This work is composed strictly symmetrically and exhibits a flowing verbal creativity in rhymed strophes, prose, and song lyrics. Between language and experience an infinite chasm exists; only the self associates words with objects and makes possible a movement from chaos to order, a movement which is mirrored in the text. The interaction between the creator and the created continued to fascinate Christensen. After a decade of silence, she returned with *Brev i april* (1979; letters in April) and *Alfabet* (1981; alphabet), both highly sophisticated linguistic experiments, the latter concluding with a pessimistic apocalyptic scene. Yet, since words are needed to describe annihilation, there is still something of substance left, and on this basis Christensen built a vision of love, femininity, and nature. Again, after a long interval during which she published several prose works, she returned in 1991 with the collection *Sommerfugledalen* (the butterfly valley), an exquisite sonnet cycle that confirmed her position as one of Denmark's most accomplished modern poets.

Another of Denmark's best modern poets is Henrik Nordbrandt (born 1945), who, however, is much more accessible, expressing a neo-Romantic current in contemporary Danish literature. Whereas nature—Nordbrandt's favorite setting until 1998, when he moved to Spain, has been Asia Minor—and seasonal changes permeate the earlier volumes, love becomes increasingly important in the collections *Glas* (1976; glass) and *Guds hus* (1977; *God's House*, 1979). Both contain sensitive and philosophical poetry of great diversity. The metaphysical element found in the latter volume increases in Nordbrandt's books of the 1980's, of which *84 digte* (1984; 84 poems) must be considered a principal work of the decade, with its reflections on life and art as well as on the paradox that only through absence can the presence manifest itself. *Glemmesteder* (1991; places of oblivion) is characterized by accomplished formal experimentation, whereas a less polished existential approach is taken with *Ormene ved himlens port* (1995; the worms at heaven's gate), written on the occasion of a friend's death. In *Drømmebroer* (1998; bridges of dreams), for the first time, a Danish setting predominates.

Social and political engagement, absent from Nordbrandt's oeuvre, dominates the early collections of Marianne Larsen (born 1951), such as *Billedtekster* (1974; captions) and *Det må siges enkelt* (1976; it must be said simply). In a lucid and powerful manner, she covers issues of sexual politics, class struggle, and imperialism. A recurring theme is the inability of humans to express themselves, which is especially typical of oppressed and socially powerless groups. In later collections, Larsen tried to reconcile the private self with the outer world and found consolation and joy in everyday occurrences. *I en venten hvid som sne* (1996; in a waiting white as snow) and *Lille dansk sindsjournal* (1998; small Danish mind journal) analyze the poet's creative process and mildly satirize Denmark's welfare society.

Søren Ulrik Thomsen (born 1956)—from his first poetry collection, *City Slang* (1981), followed by additional four volumes, from which *Nye digte* (1987; new poems) and *Hjemfalden* (1991; become liable) stand out for their intellectual and formal sophistication—rejected any ideological function of literature. For Thomsen, art—poetry—can be created only when it relates to death, to the unknown and the mysterious. Thomsen's *Mit lys brænder* (1984; my light burns), in which he stresses the importance of artistic form as the only way of capturing the elusive, had an enormous impact on the young, individualistic Danish poets of the 1980's and 1990's.

Klaus Høeck (born 1938) wrote the 608-page collection *Hjem* (1985; home) in an attempt at encompassing the Creator, and the cultlike frontrunner Michael Strunge (1958-1986) recorded in *Skrigerne!* (1980; the screamers) with extreme sensitivity his collision with the world of the media, technology, and pop culture. After a collection of exquisite love poetry, *Væbnet med vinger* (1984; armed with wings), Strunge was afflicted by angst and severe depressions, analyzed in *Verdenssøn* (1985; son of the world), which led to his suicide the following year.

The more contemplative line drawn by Nordbrandt is followed up by Bo Green Jensen (born 1955), whose poetry cycle in seven volumes, *Rosens veje* (1980-1986; the roads of the rose), is an attempt to establish coherence in a fragmented postmodern world. Niels Frank (born 1963) produced the collection *Genfortryllelsen* (1988; the reenchantment), which describes a journey through loneliness to the regenerative sphere of love. Also Pia Tafdrup (born 1952), since her debut in 1981 with *Når der går hul på en engel* (when an angel is punctured), has tried using images of exquisite sensual beauty to establish coherence and unity, in her case, among erotic experiences, impressions of nature, and an awareness of the necessity to capture all aspects of life. The metaphysical orientation, so characteristic of Tafdrup's generation, finds expression in her ninth collection, *Dronningeporten* (1998; the queen's gate), an attempt to interpret the microcosm as well as the macrocosm of human existence.

These contemporary Danish poets, together with their colleagues in the other Nordic countries, exemplify how Scandinavian poetry is in a constant process of new departures and change. They hold forth the promise that the talent and versatility found in today's Scandinavian literature will also characterize future artistic developments.

BIBLIOGRAPHY

McTurk, Rory, ed. *A Companion to Old Norse-Icelandic Literature and Culture*. Malden, Mass.: Blackwell, 2005. Essays on a wide variety of subjects, including Christian poetry, Icelandic sagas, Eddic and skaldic poetry, secular poetry, and the roles of women in Old Norse poetry and sagas. Also sums up past scholarship and present-day scholarly controversies. Maps, bibliography and index. An invaluable resource.

Naess, Harald S., ed. *A History of Norwegian Literature*. Vol. 2 in *A History of Scandinavian Literatures*, edited by Sven H. Rossel. Lincoln: University of Nebraska Press, 1993. Provides a basic history of literature, including poetry, in Norway. Contains index and extensive bibliography focusing on secondary sources in English.

Neijman, Daisy, ed. *A History of Icelandic Literature*. Vol. 5 in *A History of Scandinavian Literatures*, edited by Sven H. Rossel. Lincoln: University of Nebraska Press, 2006. A basic history of literature, including poetry, in Iceland. Contains index and extensive bibliography focusing on secondary sources in English.

O'Donoghue, Heather. *Old Norse-Icelandic Literature: A Short Introduction*. Malden, Mass.: Blackwell, 2004. A good source of information about such subjects as family sagas, mythological poems, Eddic verse, and skaldic poetry. Also points out influences on later poets. Glossary and chronology are included, along with maps, bibliography, and index.

Page, Edita, ed. *The Baltic Quintet: Poems from Estonia, Finland, Latvia, Lithuania, and Sweden*. Hamilton, Ont.: Wolsak and Wynn, 2008. English translations of poems by twenty outstanding writers.

Rossel, Sven H., ed. *A History of Danish Literature*. Vol. 1 in *A History of Scandinavian Literatures*, edited by Rossel. Lincoln: University of Nebraska Press, 1992. A general examination of the history of Danish literature, including poetry. Contains index and extensive bibliography focusing on secondary sources in English.

Schoolfield, George C., ed. *A History of Finland's Literature*. Vol. 4 in *A History of Scandinavian Literatures*, edited by Sven H. Rossel. Lincoln: University of Nebraska Press, 1998. Covers both the Finnish and the Swedish traditions in Finland. Contains index and extensive bibliography focusing on secondary sources in English.

Simonsuuri, Kirsti, ed. and trans. *Enchanting Beasts: An Anthology of Modern Women Poets of Finland*. London: Forest Books, 1990. An extensive collection. Includes poems on a variety of themes, some of them originally written in Swedish and others in Finnish.

Sjåvik, Jan. *Historical Dictionary of Scandinavian Literature and Theater*. Lanham, Md.: Scarecrow Press, 2006. Biographical and bibliographical information. A useful reference work.

Sumari, Anni, and Nicolaj Stochholm, eds. *The Other Side of Landscape: An Anthology of Contemporary Nordic Poetry*. New York: Slope Editions, 2006. This collection of poems by seventeen poets born after 1962 demonstrates the vigor and the variety of contemporary Scandinavian poetry.

Warme, Lars G., ed. *A History of Swedish Literature*. Vol. 3 in *A History of Scandinavian Literatures*, edited by Sven H. Rossel. Lincoln: University of Nebraska Press, 1996. A general history of literature, including poetry, in Sweden. Contains index and extensive bibliography focusing on secondary sources in English.

Zuck, Virpi, ed. *Dictionary of Scandinavian Literature*. Westport, Conn.: Greenwood Press, 1990. A reference work with brief presentations and precise characteristics. With bibliography and index.

Sven H. Rossel
Updated by Rossel

Serbian Poetry

Like all other South Slavic literatures, Serbian literature began after the Serbs were converted to Christianity around 873, having migrated from somewhere in Eastern Europe, from the sixth century on, to their present territory on the Balkan Peninsula. A special alphabet had to be devised for that purpose. There is no doubt that the Serbs had brought along their oral poetry and that they composed poems in praise of the newly adopted religion, but manuscripts from before the twelfth century were not preserved. There were also folk poems imitative of chansons de geste, which were sung by the singers accompanying the crusaders of the First Crusade (1096-1097) passing through the Serbian lands along the southern Adriatic Coast (Duclea). These poems were preserved in a manuscript titled "Kraljevstvo Slovena" (twelfth century; the kingdom of the Slavs) by Dukljanin of Bar.

Early poetry

Among the earliest extant Serbian poems are church songs commissioned and often composed by Saint Sava (1175-1235), the founder of the Serbian Orthodox Church and of Serbian literature. These poems were patterned after Byzantine church songs, but there were also original Slavic songs among them. As the Serbian state grew in size and strength, more poetry was written, mostly in the form of *pohvale* (encomiums) to national and church leaders. In addition, in the famous biographies of Serbian kings and archbishops, as well as in historical writings, there are passages so strikingly lyrical and rhetorical that some scholars now treat them as poems. "Slovo ljubve" (c. fifteenth century; a song of love), by Stephan Lazarević, and "Pohvala Knezu Lazaru" (1402; the encomium to Prince Lazar) are good examples of this kind of poetic literature. "Slovo ljubve" is written in a rather intricate form of acrostic, indicating that the poet drew on a sophisticated literary tradition.

With the advance of the Ottoman army into the Balkans and the gradual loss of Serbian independence, beginning with the Battle of Kosovo (1389) and ending with the fall of the last piece of Serbian territory (1459), Serbian literature entered a period of eclipse that would last almost until the eighteenth century. During this period, written literature was very difficult to maintain. Books were written exclusively by monks in secluded monasteries, aided by numerous intellectuals and writers from other countries who were fleeing the Turks. Among these writers, Dimitrije Kantakuzin (c. 1410-1474) and Pajsije (1550?-1647) stand out with their spiritually suffused poems.

Folk literature

The demise of written literature was more than offset by abundant folk literature in oral form—lyric and epic poetry, folktales, fairy tales, proverbs, riddles, and so on—and this folk tradition exercised a powerful influence on Serbian poets down to the present day. Indeed, when Vuk Stefanović Karadžić (1787-1864) collected, classified, and published a rich variety of Serbian folk literature in the first half of the nineteenth century, it was praised by such writers as Johann Gottfried Herder, the Brothers Grimm, Johann Wolfgang von Goethe, Sir Walter Scott, Prosper Mérimée, Alexander Pushkin, and Adam Mickiewicz, and it inspired them to translate many poems and stories.

Serbian folk poetry consists of both lyric and epic poems. Lyric, or "women's poems," as Karadžić termed them, depict every phase of life: worship, work, play, customs, friendship, and, above all, love. Many poems have mythological elements, some of them showing kinship with the folk literature of other peoples in Europe and Asia, hinting at a common ancestry. These lyric poems are in various meters and verse forms and are often accompanied by a tune to be sung by a woman or an ensemble of women. As the poems were passed on from generation to generation, their linguistic form changed accordingly. They were recorded by Karadžić in a language that differs little from present-day Serbo-Croatian, indicating that they were probably the first literary works to be composed in the vernacular.

The epic poems of the folk tradition are on a much higher artistic level. For the most part, they deal with historical events, though often they transform history into legend. Divided chronologically into cycles, they follow the rise and fall of the medieval Serbian Empire, its glory and the subsequent misery under the Ottoman rule. Two cycles stand out: the cycle about the feats of the Nemanjić Dynasty from the twelfth to the fifteenth centuries, culminating in the tragic but glorious defeat at Kosovo, and the cycle of poems about the legendary hero of the Serbs, Kraljević Marko (Prince Marko). Like the lyric folk poetry, these epics reflect the national philosophy of the Serbs, their understanding of life as a constant struggle between good and evil, and their willingness to choose death rather than succumb to the forces of evil. It is the ethical value of these poems that sets them above others of a similar kind. Their artistic value is also considerable. Almost all of them are composed in a decasyllabic meter (resembling a trochaic pentameter), with a regular caesura after the fourth syllable. They are concise and straightforward, overflowing with formulaic patterns, striking metaphors, and images, and told in a highly poetic language. They were sung by a male singer called a *gouslar* (a few of these skilled oral poets are still active today), accompanied by a one-string bow instrument, the *gousle*. Since these poems have been handed down orally for generations, their original authors will never be known. For that reason, among others, Serbian folk poetry is revered as a national treasure.

SERBIAN DIASPORA

The long occupation by the Turks, lasting in one form or another from the end of the fourteenth to the beginning of the twentieth century, forced many Serbs to migrate north, into Austro-Hungarian territories north of the Sava River and in the Danube region called Voyvodina, where they were well received in the hope of stemming the Ottoman tide. They brought along their religion and cultural heritage, which they endeavored to advance under the auspices of the enlightened absolutist rulers of the Austrian Empire. When Austrian rule seemed to threaten the national identity of the Serbs, they turned toward the Russians for help. As a result, at the end of the seventeenth and into the eighteenth century, a new, hybrid language came into use, the so-called Russo-Slavic, employed by most Serbian

poets of the time. Outstanding among these were Gavrilo Stefanović Venclović (died 1746?) and Zaharije Orfelin (1726-1785). It is significant that they strongly advocated the use of a language comprehensible to the people and themselves wrote poems in a vernacular.

By the end of the eighteenth century, after a prolonged exposure to Western influence, Serbian poets wrote more and more in the spirit of the Enlightenment. The Russo-Slavic language gave way to a more comprehensible Slavo-Serbian, only to be supplanted by a full-fledged vernacular about the middle of the nineteenth century. Serbian poets displayed an ever-increasing erudition and familiarity with contemporary currents in world poetry, abandoning the provincial outlook of a confined culture. Their poetry became philosophical and contemplative, couched in higher, solemn, dignified tones. In line with Enlightenment trends, Serbian poetry in this period was highly didactic; it also reflected the influence of neoclassicism, as exemplified by the leading poet of the period, Lukijan Mušicki (1777-1837).

NATIONALISM AND ROMANTICISM

A reawakening of national awareness among the Voyvodina Serbs was spurred by uprisings in Serbia proper against the centuries-old Turkish rule. This patriotic enthusiasm, coupled with the revolutionary reform of the written language carried out by Karadžić in the first half of the nineteenth century on the principle "Write as you speak," led to a nationwide renaissance. It first manifested itself during the transitional period leading toward Romanticism.

The leading proponent of this trend was Jovan Sterija Popović (1806-1856), a playwright and a novelist as well as a poet. His only collection of poetry, *Davorje* (1854; laments), showing a mixture of classicist, didactic, and Romantic features, laments the transience of life. Other transitional poets with an increasing inclination toward Romanticism were Sima Milutinović Sarajlija (1791-1847), Petar Petrović Njegoš (1813-1851), and Branko Radičević (1824-1853). Milutinović is more significant for his influence on other writers, especially Njegoš, than for his own works, but the few poems Milutinović wrote are distinguished by their pure lyricism and their unaffected celebration of earthly love. Both he and Njegoš drew heavily from folk poetry, which, owing to Karadzić's work, the rise of Romanticism, and the successful national revival, became the primary source of poetic inspiration. Njegoš wrote all of his works, including his plays, in verse. His short poems reveal a predilection for meditation, a willingness to try new forms, and a language close to that of the people, while his long epic poem, *Luča mikrokozma* (1845; the ray of microcosm), which resembles John Milton's *Paradise Lost* (1667, 1674), offers in poetic form the author's philosophical views on the origin of life and on the moral order of the universe. With this poem and the epic play in verse, *Gorski vijenac* (1847; *The Mountain Wreath*, 1930), Njegoš established himself as the greatest Serbian poet. Branko

Facsimile of the cover of Serbian poet Petar Petrović Njegoš's Gorski vijenac *(1847), an epic play in verse.*

Radičević was the first to employ successfully in lyric poetry the vernacular as advocated by Karadžić. His ebullience and his celebration of simple, earthly joys would have been inexpressible in the era of neoclassicism.

The Romantic spirit reached its zenith with a group of poets all of whom owed their inspiration, in one way or another, to Milutinović, Njegoš, and Radičević. Again, it was the poets from Voyvodina who set the tone, but, unlike those of the earlier generation, they fused the patriarchal heroism of Serbia proper and Montenegro with the fervor of the Voyvodina Serbs acquired during the Revolution of 1848, thus uniting the literatures of the north and the south. The verse of Djura Jakšić (1832-1878) illustrates more clearly than that of any other poet this revolutionary fervor. In his highly emotional patriotic poems, his fighting spirit and his indignation against all enemies of his people are combined with a yearning for freedom as promised by the revolutions in Europe around the middle of the nineteenth century. His unabashed love poems and his avowed taste for earthly pleasures make him one of the most emotional of Serbian poets.

Jovan Jovanović Zmaj (1833-1904) dealt with similar feelings in a much more subdued manner. A physician by profession, he was capable of greater understanding of human nature and of inexhaustible love for his fellow human beings. Often struck by tragedy in personal life, he gave his sorrows a highly poetic expression in *Djulići* (1864; rosebuds) and *Djulići uveoci* (1882; rosebuds withered). His sincere patriotism was matched by his boundless love for children.

Other Romantic poets were Jovan Ilić (1823-1901) and Laza Kostić (1841-1910). While Ilić was a popular, down-to-earth poet of love and passion, of freedom ad faith in the Serbian people, Kostić was a poet of lofty flights of the imagination. Combining metaphysical speculation with forceful love lyrics, Kostić was a bold innovator in metrics, thoroughly acquainted with other literatures (he translated William Shakespeare), especially with European Romanticism, and he developed a unique style of his own that often ignored traditional forms.

Romanticism in Serbian literature manifested itself best in lyric poetry. Thus, it was no wonder that poetry took a backseat when realistic tendencies began to assert themselves in the last third of the nineteenth century. Of all the poets in this period, only Vojislav Ilić (1862-1894) reached the level of his predecessors, and in some ways he surpassed them. The son of Jovan Ilić, Vojislav discarded early the Romantic spirit in which he had been reared and instead combined classical themes with a realistic depiction of nature and human relationships. His ability to create lasting images was complemented by the musicality of his verses and by his sensitive impressions of life around him. Vojislav Ilić's potential was cut short by untimely death, but not before he had effected in Serbian poetry a turn that most new poets would soon follow.

EARLY TWENTIETH CENTURY

That turn manifested itself at the end of the century, when three powerful poets—Aleksa Šantić (1868-1924), Jovan Dučić (1874?-1943), and Milan Rakić (1876-1938)—brought completely new tones to Serbian poetry. While Šantič was, to a large degree, still related to the preceding generation in his emotional inclinations and closeness to the native soil, he nevertheless showed in his love poems and poems on social themes a new awareness of problems besetting his fellow humans. His pure, sincere, and highly emotional lyrics were often set to music and are still very popular among common readers.

It was with Dučić and Rakić, however, that the new turn in Serbian poetry received its full impetus. Both educated in the West, they were inculcated with the fin de siècle spirit of the Symbolists and the Parnassians. Dučić used his erudition, refined taste, and aristocratic spirit to modernize Serbian poetry and free it from provincial confines. All traditional modes of expression were transformed into his peculiar idiom, primarily through new sensitivity, formalistic excellence, clarity, precision, elegance, musicality, and picturesque images. Though he paid lip service to the Decadence fashionable at the time, he was too much a poet of Mediterranean joie de vivre and of faith in life's ultimate meaning to allow his pessimism to become a driving force.

Not so with Rakić, who was unable to alleviate his constant pessimistic outlook on life, especially in matters of love and the meaning of life. His few poems, collected in a single volume, *Pesme* (1903; poems), reveal a deep-seated decadence and a firm belief that life inevitably brings decay and misery. This intellectual awareness of humanity's futility in trying to mitigate pain and misery was not a mere pose, and it is Rakić's conviction and sincerity that, together with artistic excellence, render his poems highly poignant and aesthetically satisfying.

Other poets of the first two decades of the twentieth century worth noting are Vladislav Petković Dis (1880-1917), Sima Pandurović (1883-1960), Milutin Bojić (1892-1917), and Veljko Petrović (1884-1967). They all wrote in the shadow of Dučić and Rakić, yet they all contributed to the broadening of horizons in Serbian poetry of their time.

INTERWAR PERIOD

Amid titanic struggles and profound changes in Serbia during and after World War I, Serbian poets changed with the times, bringing on yet another decisive break with the past, not only in poetry but also in other forms of literature. The entire period between the two world wars was marked by these fundamental changes. At first, a new generation of poets raised its voice against the horrors of war and clamored, often in vain, for humaneness and greater understanding. Dušan Vasiljev (1900-1924), Miloš Crnjanski (1893-1977), and Rastko Petrović (1898-1949), the leaders among the modernist poets, reflected the influence of the German expressionists. Toward the end of the 1920's, a group of poets, led by Dušan Matić (1898-1980), Marko Ristić (1902-1982), Oskar Davičo (1909-1989), and Aleksandar Vučo (1897-1985), introduced a form of Surrealism, to which they gave a peculiarly Serbian twist.

In the 1930's, a socially conscious poetry developed, dwelling on the pervasive social turbulence besetting the world in the decade prior to World War II. This pronounced politicization resulted in great commotion but not in great literature. During the war, the muses fell silent, as is often the case, nor were they articulate in the immediate postwar years, a period marked by profound political and social changes. It was only at the beginning of the 1950's that Serbian poetry experienced another renewal.

LATER TWENTIETH CENTURY ONWARD

To be sure, several major prewar poets continued to write after 1945. Some added relatively little to their opus, while others reached their full potential only after the war. Crnjanski published only one significant poetic work after the war, the long poem *Lament nad Beogradom* (1962; lament over Belgrade), continuing where he left off almost four decades earlier. If this late work was not innovative, however, it did add a reflective quality to the essentially elegiac movement of Crnjanski's poetry. Stanislav Vinaver (1891-1955), another prewar modernist, also published only one collection after the war, *Evropska noć* (1952; the European night), in which he confirmed his reputation as an interesting experimenter with language. Desanka Maksimović (1898-1993) wrote some of her best poetry after the war. Combining patriotic feelings with traditional lyricism and the apotheosis of nature, her poems in *Tražim pomilovanje* (1965; I seek mercy) are among the best in contemporary Serbian poetry.

Davičo also reached his full stature only after the war. In numerous collections, he exhibited his revolutionary spirit and his mastery of imagery and language. Unable or unwilling to compromise, he always went to the heart of the matter, carrying on polemics, attacking, changing positions, and often preaching. Above all, his strong sensual imagination, manifested in unexpected metaphors and paradoxical twists of language, makes Davičo one of the most gifted of contemporary poets.

Two other Surrealists wrote significant poetry after the war, Matić and Milan Dedinac (1902-1966). Matić influenced many younger poets with his contemplative, controlled poetry, which often has the fragmentary quality of journal entries. He was interested primarily in the essence of appearances, and his range is wide and rich in imaginative possibilities. The case of Dedinac is much simpler. After the turbulent Surrealist era, he combined, in his mature years, the old avant-garde spirit with an almost traditional lyricism.

In the first generation of postwar poets, Vasko Popa (1922-1991) and Miodrag Pavlović (born 1928) played a very important and influential role. All the complex problems of tradition and the manner in which this tradition is to be absorbed, can be seen through the two distinct approaches these poets have taken. The aim of both poets, broadly speaking, is to rediscover the authentic native poetic tradition, to make its imagination contemporary, and, at the same time, to make available the processes and laws of that discovery.

Popa is generally considered to have been the best contemporary Serbian poet. His intensely original poetry is the result of a close attention to the metaphorical and mythical overtones that one finds buried in idiomatic language: For Popa, the archetypal animistic imagination survived in contemporary idioms. Informed by Surrealism and folklore, his cycles of poems construct intricate and precise systems of symbols that are never merely arbitrary, however baffling they may appear at first glance. His poems, even when they refer to historical events, have a timeless quality. With each new cycle, it became apparent that his entire opus partook of one vast and original vision of humanity and the universe.

Pavlović began his career with preoccupations similar to those of Popa, but Pavlović's verse has gradually assumed a more historical orientation and a classical sense of form. Exploring the historical continuum which leads back to Byzantium and the ancient Slavs, Pavlović's method, in contrast to that of Popa, is highly intellectual. Pavlović is searching for the philosophical and religious legacy of Serbian culture. To understand the need for and the complexity of that search, one must remember that historically the development of Serbian culture has been interrupted by several "dark ages." Pavlović's search is not a matter of literary antiquarianism (for very little of the actual material of Serbian culture remains) but of an imaginative search for origins. At the same time, it cannot be denied that Pavlović taps the most ancient currents of Serbian poetry.

Ivan V. Lalić (1931-1996) also sought a living tradition, and he shared the intellectual and classical sensibility of Pavlović. What distinguishes his poetry from the latter's is his sensuousness, his lyric precision and immediacy, which render the poet visible in his poems. Lalić's historical vision always has at its center a contemporary individual, as a victim or simply as a witness. His genuine mastery of form and the beauty of his language must also be emphasized.

Similar characteristics can be seen in some other

Serbian poets of the same generation. The poetry of Jovan Hristić (1933-2002)—meditative, philosophical, and with an austere, almost classical rhetoric—has a cool elegance. Milorad Pavić (1929-2009) is closer to Popa, in that Pavić, too, has based his poetry on language, specifically the predominantly religious texts of seventeenth and eighteenth century Serbian literature. He approaches these texts with the eye of a Surrealist who dreams of being a mythmaker. His poems have the appearance of metaphorical tapestries. Ljubomir Simović (born 1935) is much more an instinctive poet, guided by an intimate, often confessional lyric sense. His poems combine simplicity of language with expressionistic imagery and a kind of Breughelian earthiness. The lyricism of Božidar Timotijević (1932-2001) is more traditional and subdued. The poet is always in the foreground, and it is his own life that is being explored. What is remarkable about all of these poets turned toward the various aspects of native tradition is that they are often the ones who are, from the point of view of prosody and imagery, the most experimental.

Stevan Raičković (1928-2007) represents the neo-Romantic wing in contemporary Serbian poetry. His books express his basic themes: nature as a source of perfection, and yearning for silence and solitude. Raičković's anxiety over humanity's disappearing ties with nature leads him at times into deep pessimism. Simplicity, directness, and a genuine lyric gift are his main traits. One of the most talented postwar Serbian poets, Branko Miljković (1934-1961), committed suicide and thus gave rise to a considerable legend. Influenced by French and Russian Symbolists as well as by the intellectual Surrealism of Yves Bonnefoy, Miljković's poetry abounds in epigrammatic utterances, unexpected metaphoric constructions, and philosophical questioning, resulting in a poetry of heightened lyricism. Each one of his poems has the intensity of a farewell note.

Miljković influenced many young poets. Borislav Radović (born 1935) owes a debt to him and to Matić. Radović is probably the most Hermetic poet of his generation. Beneath the prosiness of his lines, there is a powerful lyric pressure, and his poems open areas of language and style that are entirely new for Serbian poetry. Matija Bećković (born 1939) stands somewhat by

himself. His socially conscious poetry, his original and deliberate selection of antipoetic images, and his sense of humor establish his kinship with other Eastern European poets such as Miroslav Holub and Tadeusz Różewicz. The Villonesque emotional climate of Bećković's poems has had a great influence on younger Serbian poets and foreshadows an interesting new development in Serbian poetry.

Among the younger poets, there are many who are worth mentioning, especially Dragan Jovanovic Danilov (born 1960) and Milan Orlić (born 1962). Serbian poetry at the beginning of the twenty-first century continued in a state of growth, quantitatively if not qualitatively. There has never been a period in Serbian history that has witnessed such a proliferation of talent and poetic output. More important, young poets are completely open to the world, follow the development of poetry everywhere, are susceptible to cross-cultural influences, and regard themselves as true members of the world poetic community. At the same time, they are constantly searching for their roots and examining their poetic tradition, sometimes making discoveries in the most unexpected places. The language of present-day Serbian poetry has reached an unprecedented stage of development. There is also a tendency among young poets to close themselves hermetically and guard their isolation fiercely.

BIBLIOGRAPHY

Armstrong, Todd Patrick, ed. *Perspectives on Modern Central and East European Literature: Quests for Identity—Selected Papers from the Fifth World Congress of Central and East European Studies.* New York: Palgrave, 2001. A collection of essays, many on relevant general topics, such as the quest for identity and problems associated with censorship, as well as one entitled "The Poetic Messages of Serbian Women Writers in Diaspora."

Barac, Antun. *A History of Yugoslav Literature.* Ann Arbor, Mich.: Joint Committee on Eastern Europe Publication Series, 1973. A standard history of all Yugoslav literatures and poetry, including Serbian, by a leading literary scholar. Although somewhat outdated, it still provides reliable information, especially of the older periods.

Debeljak, Aleš. "Visions of Despair and Hope Against Hope: Poetry in Yugoslavia in the Eighties." *World Literature Today* 68, no. 3 (1992): 191-194. Debeljak looks at poetry from the former Yugoslavia, including Serbian poetry, on the eve of tumultuous events and changes in Yugoslavia in the 1990's. Poetry of the 1980's in some ways foreshadowed those events, giving vent to despair and forlorn hope.

Dragić Kijuk, Predrag R. *Medieval and Renaissance Serbian Poetry 1200-1700*. Belgrade: Relations, 1987. This anthology provides an extremely valuable and lengthy introduction by Kijuk, an eminent authority on the subject, about all aspects of this significant period in Serbian poetry.

Holton, Milne, and Vasa D. Mihailovich, eds. and trans. *Serbian Poetry from the Beginnings to the Present*. New Haven, Conn.: Yale Center for International and Area Studies, 1988. In this unique anthology, extensive introductions to the periods and individual poets offer not only a comprehensive overview of Serbian poetry but also succinct portraits of key poets.

_____. *Songs of the Serbian People: From the Collections of Vuk Karadžić*. Pittsburgh, Pa.: University of Pittsburgh Press, 1997. Contains both Serbian epic poetry and Serbo-Croatian folk songs.

Mikić, Radivoje. "On Significant Features of Modern Lyrical Speech." *Serbian Literary Quarterly* nos. 1/2 (1995): 349-360. The author endeavors to define and analyze the neo-Symbolist tendencies in contemporary Serbian poetry.

Petrov, Aleksandar. "In the Stream of Time: Contemporary Serbian Poetry." *Literary Quarterly* 1, no. 2 (1965): 58-69. A sophisticated analysis of modern Serbian poetry by a leading contemporary Serbian literary critic and historian. Petrov addresses the modernistic tendencies of Serbian poetry, highlighting its greatest achievements.

Simic, Charles, ed. and trans. *The Horse Has Six Legs: An Anthology of Serbian Poetry*. St. Paul, Minn.: Graywolf Press, 1992. Eighteen twentieth century poets whose work the editor-translator found especially memorable are represented in this collection. The work is arranged chronologically, according to the birth date of the poets.

Vasa D. Mihailovich

SLOVAK POETRY

Slovakia is the least known among the West Slavic group of nations: Poland, Bohemia, and Slovakia. That is also true of its poetry. The reasons are mainly historical. The Slovak nation dates its beginnings to the ninth century Great Moravian Empire that, in its flourishing under Svätopluk, included the territory of the former Czechoslovakia, southern Poland, parts of Austria, and most of Hungary. Attempts to Christianize this territory go back to the eighth century missions from the West, but it was in 863 that the apostles of the Slavs, Saints Cyril and Methodius, arrived from Constantinople with the Old Church Slavonic liturgy. In the tenth century, the Great Moravian Empire, after a period of decline, was defeated by the Magyars, and Slovakia became a part of the Kingdom of Hungary. Slovakia remained under Hungarian rule until 1918, when the new state of Czechoslovakia was established.

Slovak literature in general, and Slovak poetry in particular, reflect this tragic history. The lack of independence for more than a millennium forced Slovak poets, historians, and scientists to use other languages: Latin, Hungarian, German, and biblical Czech. While such literary works are usually mentioned in Slovak literary history, they are also claimed by others. There was, then, a long period when Slovak poets wrote their poetry predominantly in foreign languages: the Multilingual Period (tenth through sixteenth centuries). The Revival Period (1790-1863) saw a great flourishing of Slovak literature, especially of poetry. In the Period of Struggle (1863-1918), this revived literature met the challenge of Magyarization, the campaign by Hungarian authorities to stamp out the Slovak nationalist aspirations and to suppress the Slovak language. Large-scale emigration to the United States was one consequence of this harsh policy. The Modern Period (1918 to present) has been shaped by the increasing influence of foreign literary trends, by the ideological influence of the former Soviet Union, and by the resurgence of Catholic poetry.

MULTILINGUAL PERIOD (900-1790)

Slovak poetry did appear sporadically even in the multilingual context. Of crucial importance to Slovak poetry is the rich heritage of folk songs, some of which are of ancient origin. Also extant are a number of religious and historical songs; the latter describe military events resulting from Tatar (1241) and Turkish (sixteenth and seventeenth century) invasions of Slovakia. Descriptions of sackings of castles and fortresses predominate, as in *Muráó* (song about Murán castle) and *Modrý kameó* (song about Modrý Kameň castle), but there is also a more sophisticated poetry, based on the chivalrous epic, as in the ballad *Siládi a Hadmázi* (Siládi and Hadmázi), a tale of battle against the Turks. Most of these historical compositions are anonymous.

Of more importance are the religious songs. The popularity of this genre is attested by the approximately 150 editions of *Vithara sanctorum* (1636; the lyre of saintliness), a Protestant hymnal compiled by Juraj Tranovský (1591-1637). Among translations, this hymnal included Slovak songs still sung in Slovakia today. *Cithara sanctorum* was also tremendously influential as a manual of versification and therefore played an important role in the development of Slovak poetry. The establishment of the Jesuit University in Trnava further strengthened the use of Slovak for literary purposes; there Benedikt Szöllösi-Rybnický compiled a collection of songs, *Cantus catholici* (1655; Catholic hymnal), with more than two hundred songs in Slovak.

The Jesuit University of Trnava was not the first Slovak university; that honor goes to the Academia Istropolitana, founded in Bratislava in 1467, a center of Humanistic studies influenced by Western European Humanism. Slovaks who studied there published in Latin, but in Trnava, Slovak was encouraged and a number of historical, philosophical, and grammatical works appeared, supporting the national cause. Whether Protestant or Catholic, the poetry of the Baroque period was largely the work of priests. Indeed, a poet without a priestly vocation was a rarity; one such poet was Peter Benický (1603-1664), author of *Slovenské verše* (1652; Slovak poems).

A poet close to Benický and probably influenced by him was the Franciscan Hugolín Gavlovič (1712-1787), author of *Valaská šola* (1755; the shepherd's school), the most significant work of the Multilingual Period. A poem of some seventeen thousand lines, *Valaská škola* is divided into twenty-two cantos of fifty-nine "ideas" each, in three rhymed quatrains. The work is a compendium of genres: satire, fable, folk poetry, exemplum, and even social poetry.

A great disadvantage the poets of the period had to face was the absence of codified Slovak. Thus, some variety of Slovakized Czech was often used. Moreover, it was biblical Czech, derived from the standard Czech translation of the Bible, not the living, contemporary Czech language, which the Slovak poets used. In Slovakia, a variety of Slovak dialects vied for poets' attention. Of the three main dialect groups, Western, Central, and Eastern, Antonín Bernolák (1762-1813) championed the Western dialect in his pioneering *Grammatica slavica* (1790; Slovak grammar). It was not the best choice, but nevertheless Bernolák's work provided a basis for the systematic literary use of Slovak as an alternative to the artificial Slovakized Czech.

REVIVAL PERIOD (1790-1863)

Bernolák's Slovak was only a beginning, and there was quite a struggle ahead for the literary use of the Slovak language. Those who used Czech advanced the argument of unity to anyone suggesting the use of Slovak for literary purposes, while others would use Slovak, but not of Bernolák's variety—that is, they preferred another dialect. Thus, Jozef Ignác Bajza (1755-1836) published *Slovenské dvojnásobné epigramatá* (1794; Slovak double epigrams) in his own Slovak, using hexameter and pentameter in the first attempt to adapt classical prosody to Slovak poetry. Bajza's work was mercilessly criticized by Bernolák, and Bernolák's approach prevailed. An entire Bernolák movement appeared, first acting through the Learned Society, founded in 1792 and comprising some five hundred influential members throughout Slovakia. It is the Bernolák movement that must be credited with saving Slovakia from total assimilation. Bernolák also authored the monumental *Slovak-Czech-Latin-German-Hungarian Dictionary* (1825-1827), which runs to six volumes and more than five thousand pages.

After the generation of Bernolák and his followers, who prepared the soil with dictionaries and grammars,

a generation of talented poets appeared. Pavel Jozef Šafárik (1795-1861), the founder of Slavic studies, wrote a collection of poems, *Tatranská múza s lýrou slovanskou* (1814; the Muse of Tatras with a Slavic lyre), that includes poems about the legendary robber Jánošík (1688-1713), a Slovak Robin Hood. Šafárik also organized the systematic collection of folk songs and inspired Ján Kollár (1793-1852) to do the same. The latter thus produced *Národnie zpiewanky* (1834, 1835; folk songs). Šafárik also popularized Bernolák's notion concerning the unity of Slavs, later known as Pan-Slavism. Individual Slavic nations, according to this idea, were merely various tribes of Slavdom. Kollár wrote a great epic poem animated by Pan-Slavism: *Slávy dcera* (1824, 1832; the daughter of Slava).

An equally important poet of this period was Ján Hollý (1785-1849), author of historical epics and beautiful nature lyrics. His epic trilogy, *Svatopluk* (1833), *Cyrilometodiada* (1835), and *Sláv* (1839), is a triumph of classicism, a happy marriage of history, legend, myth, and religion.

The poems of Kollár and Hollý were used to build up national consciousness. The new generation of revivalists found their inspiration in poetry. The Romantic movement in Slovak poetry coincided with the revival movement: Both were nurtured by Slovak classicism, with its Pan-Slavic ideal. Literary magazines and almanacs (such as *Hronka*, *Tatranka*, *Plody*) appeared to help the movement along.

The greatest figure of the revival movement was Ľudovít Štúr (1815-1856). In 1843, he definitively solved the language problem by suggesting the Central Slovak dialect for the literary language. His suggestion was soon accepted, and today's Slovak is a modified form of Štúr's. Štúr published the first Slovak political newspaper, *Slovak National Newspaper*, with a literary supplement, *Orol Tatránski* (the eagle of Tatras). There, as well as in the almanac *Nitra*, Štúr's generation published the best poetry yet to appear in Slovakia. The remarkable group of poets associated with Štúr included Samo Chalúpka, Janko Král, Andrej Sládkovič, and Ján Botto. Štúr himself published a book of poetry, *Spevy a piesne* (1853; lyrics and songs).

Janko Král (1822-1876), more than any other Slovak poet, was the embodiment of Romanticism. His poetry, marked by strong balladic and folk elements, celebrates the outsider, the Romantic hero, and bristles with imagery derived from dreams and fairy tales, as in *Zakliata panna vo Váhu a divný Janko* (1844; the enchanted maiden in the river Váh and strange Janko). In the revolutionary year 1848, Král rushed to fight and, like Štúr and others, languished in disappointment over the failure of the revolution. The haunting, prophetic, and enchanting quality of Král's poetry is entirely his own.

Of the four great poets associated with Štúr, Andrej Sládkovič (1820-1872) has the distinction of having written the most beautiful and memorable poetry—poems that generations of students have memorized and loved. His *Marína* (1846) is a personification of the beauty of Slovakia and its language, as well as a deeply felt tribute to his beloved. His *Detvan* (1846), which tells of the freeing of a poor mountain boy from a certain punishment, is a parable of national liberation. Stylistically, Sládkovič's poetry is very original, and it exercised a significant influence on the next generation of poets.

Samo Chalúpka (1812-1883) and Ján Botto (1829-1881) are also numbered among the four great poets of the Štúr generation. Chalúpka, in *Spevy* (1868; songs), consciously revised the classical tradition of such heroic epics as Hollý's *Svatopluk*. Chalúpka's hero is anonymous or collective. Botto returned to the Jánošík epic with his *Smrt Jánošíková* (1862; the death of Jánošík), a work that is at once legendary, fantastic, exaggerated, and tragic. There is both grandeur and pathos here, as well as deeply satisfying beauty.

The beginning of the 1860's marked the end of Slovak Romanticism, although Slovakia's nationalistic ambitions had not been satisfied. A new period of reaction and national oppression was about to begin, coinciding with the advent of realistic conventions in prose and Symbolism in poetry.

PERIOD OF STRUGGLE (1863-1918)

In 1867, the political situation in Hungary (the northern part of which was Slovakia) radically changed for the worse: Minorities were held in disfavor, and Slovak nationalist aspirations were deemed treasonous.

The two leading poets of this period, particularly of the last two decades of the century, were Svetozár Hurban-Vajanský (1847-1916) and Pavol Országh-Hviezdoslav (1849-1921). Vajanský, the author of *Tatry a more* (1879; the Tatras and the sea) and two other collections, was a journalist, novelist, and critic, as well as a poet. His first book of poems was a breakthrough and gained for him a wide readership, but his attempt to write a novel in verse was abandoned in favor of prose writing. Vajanský, though very interesting, is overshadowed by Hviezdoslav. Hviezdoslav's best-known work is *Krvavé sonety* (1914; bloody sonnets), but this collection alone does not permit a fair assessment of his lifework. Indeed his oeuvre, which includes lyric and epic poetry as well as drama, is of such variety and richness that it has no equal in Slovak literature. Among his epics, *Hájniková žena* (1844-1886; gamekeeper's wife) should be mentioned, and among his dramas, *Herod i Herodias* (1909).

Ludmila Podjavorinská (1872-1951) was the first significant female Slovak poet. She painstakingly documents the clash of Romantic and realistic worldviews in works such as *Po bále* (1903; after the ball), while her *Balady* (1930) takes up allegorical, symbolic, and tragic themes close in spirit to the Romantic school.

Podjavorinská in one way and Hviezdoslav in another seem to be poets of transition, ushering in the new poetic sensibility in Slovak literature known as *Moderna*. The main representative of this movement was Ivan Krasko (1876-1958), author of two slender collections: *Nox et solitudo* (1909) and *Verše* (1912). Another *Moderna* poet of note was Vladimír Roy (1885-1936), who, influenced by the power of Krasko's art, took the modernizing tendency even further, into the modern period.

MODERN PERIOD

Out of the ashes of the Austro-Hungarian Empire at the end of the World War I, a new state appeared: Czechoslovakia. Slovak national life was strengthened, despite the fact that the new government continued the nineteenth century fiction of a Czechoslovak nation, instead of two distinct nations of Czechs and Slovaks. Thus, the Slovak nationalist movement persisted, and in 1939, a Slovak Republic was proclaimed under Nazi pressure and with a pro-Nazi government lasting until 1945, when the Czechoslovak Republic was reestablished. The communists took over the government through a coup in 1948, and only after the fall of communism in 1989 did the country manage to free itself of totalitarianism and become a democracy. In 1993, the Czech and Slovak Federation separated, and two states emerged: the Czech Republic and the Slovak Republic. This was an amicable divorce, arranged by the political elite.

Institutionally, Slovak culture received a tremendous boost with the reopening in 1919 of Matica Slovenská, a central cultural institution. Slovak schools were organized, from the elementary level to Comenius University, founded in 1919 in Bratislava with the help of Czech professors. Thus the obligatory instruction in Hungarian ended, and Slovak poetry ceased to be the sole repository of Slovak cultural, national, and linguistic aspirations.

Enthusiasm, a sense of a new beginning, a desire to catch up with the rest of Europe—such was the prevailing mood of the period between the wars. Slovak poets became aware of a variety of foreign literary movements from which they borrowed eclectically without committing themselves wholly to a single program. The only exception is Surrealism. From the mid-1930's to the mid-1940's, this movement united poets, artists, and critics in a spontaneous manifestation of creative and aesthetic unity reminiscent of the efforts of the revivalist generation of Štúr. The older, more conservative, but at the same time best forum for Slovak literature during this period was the literary magazine *Slovenské pohlǎdy* (Slovak views), founded in the nineteenth century (1846), Europe's oldest continuously published literary magazine.

Ján Smrek (1898-1982), the most popular and widely read Slovak poet of the twentieth century, began his career with an eclectic style influenced by French Symbolism and, to a lesser degree, Hungarian poetry. Soon, however, he formed his own vision: Sensuality, healthy eroticism, and the celebration of love and tenderness are his main characteristics, as in his *Básnik a žena* (1934; the poet and a woman). To these he added in later years melancholy reminiscences and the nostalgic celebration of women.

The career of this Dionysian poet was complemented by that of the Apollonian poet Emil Boleslav Lukáč (1900-1979). While in Smrek's works, from *Básnik a žena* to the nostalgic *Obraz sveta* (1953; image of the world), the reader encounters the world of the senses—of the individual appreciating the happiness, beauty, and love of women—in Lukáč one finds the opposite. Lukáč was tormented by his philosophical musings, from his first collection, *Spoved* (1922; confession), to his highly personal *O láske neláskavej* (1928; on unkind love) to his late *Óda na poslednú a prvú* (1967; ode to the last and the first of Eumenides).

The third and perhaps the most eminent of this generation was Valentín Beniak (1894-1973). From his first collection, *Tiahnime dalej oblaky* (1928; clouds, let's move on), to his magisterial epic trilogy *Žofia* (1941; Sophia), *Popolec* (1942; ashes), and *Igric* (1944; the minstrel), he experimented with language, style, and imagery, presenting a haunting, hallucinatory, and obsessively hypnotic vision of the world both distant and immediate, the world of war and love, of tormenting hopes and soul-searching. This fine Catholic poet was joined by an entire Catholic *Moderna* movement, including Pavol Gašparovic Hlbina (1908-1977) and Rudolf Dilong (1905-1986), a prolific and gifted author of mystical poetry who blended Fransiscan religiosity with Surrealist imagery, as in *Mladý svadobník* (1936; young member of the wedding party). They had many followers, particularly Mikuláš Šrinc (1914-1986) and Ján Silan (1914-1984).

The first important Surrealist work in Slovak poetry was *Utaté ruky* (1935; severed hands), by Rudolf Fábry (1915-1982). The most talented of the Slovak Surrealists proved to be Stefan Žáry (born 1918), whose *Pečat plných amfór* (1944; the seal of full amphoras) expresses the tragedy of uprooted modern humanity at the mercy of wars and ideologies and suffering from lack of love. Vladimír Reisel (1919-2007), Pavol Horov (1914-1975), and others also published fine Surrealist poetry, giving the movement a strong foundation. This potential could have resulted in a richer harvest had it not been for the official disbanding of the movement following the communist takeover after 1948.

The proletarian school of Slovak poets was influenced by the Czech poet Jiří Wolker (1900-1924) as much as by the socialist ideals and the Russian Revolution of 1917. The most talented of the group of the so-called *DAV* poets (named after their magazine) was Ladislav Novomeský (1904-1976), as his *Svätý za dedinou* (1935; a patron saint behind the village) shows.

Ludo Ondrejov (1901-1962) brought into his poems the untamed world of folk poetry, especially in his *Pijanské piesne* (1941; drinking songs). Folk poetry also influenced such poets as Andrej Plávka (1907-1982) and Ján Kostra (1910-1975).

The decade of the 1960's was a time of experimentation and of a departure from the sterile dictates of the Socialist Realism imported from the Soviet Union. A strong group of "concretist" poets, gathered under the leadership of Miroslav Válek (1927-1991), included such poets as Ján Ondruš (1932-1999), Ján Stacho (1936-1995), and Lubomír Feldek (born 1936), all of whom turned away from Socialist Realism toward the heritage of the Western avant-garde and modernism. Válek's collection of his four early collections, *Štyri knihy nepokoja* (1971; four books of unease) documents his search for an original voice, as well as the initial schematic beginnings to which he returns in his last period.

Beginning in the late 1950's, Milan Rúfus (1928-2009), the strongest Slovak voice of the second half of the twentieth century, began to be noticed. His most important work, collected in *Básne* (1972, revised 1975; poems), represents a different path from the one taken by the concretists. Rúfus is purposefully antimodern in the sense that it is not the avant-garde that inspires him, but rather his rural background, his family, and the Bible with its imagery. Rúfus has successfully integrated his religiosity in his work and managed to find a form acceptable to the authorities. After the fall of communism, the religious component of his work became even more pronounced.

Before the end of the century another movement of poets of different orientations appeared, the so-called lonely runners: Ivan Laucík (1944-2004), Peter Repka (born 1944), and particularly Ivan Štrpka (born 1944). Their roots are in the 1960's and in the protest against stale schematic poetry. A poet of Dionysian character

who experimented with language and celebrated the Western Slovak region of Záhorie with panache and genius as a counterpart to the lonely runners is Štefan Moravcík (born 1943). Moravcík chose the world of senses, of eroticism, and above all the world of nature over the world of the decaying order of the 1980's, beginning with his first collection, *Slávnosti baránkov* (1969; the feast of the lambs). His Záhorie is a refuge as well as a fount of inspiration for his playful linguistic experimentation. This tendency to excess continues with Ivan Kolenic (born 1965), whose stress on hedonism and intimate relationships is actually an attempt to build an autarchic world of the senses uncontaminated by ideology, as demonstrated in his *Prinesené búrkou* (1986; brought by the storm). Thus, the Modern Period demonstrates that Slovak poetry, which long served as a repository of a subjugated people's hopes and dreams, remains a vital force in the twenty-first century.

BIBLIOGRAPHY

Cincura, Andrew, comp. *An Anthology of Slovak Literature*. Riverside, Calif.: University Hardcovers, 1976. An extensive collection of works in various genres, including poetry.

Hawkesworth, Celia, ed. *A History of Central European Women's Writing*. New York: Palgrave, 2001. Contains a number of essays that focus specifically on Czech and Slovak women writers. Map, bibliography, and index.

Kirschbaum, J. M. *Slovak Language and Literature*. Winnipeg: Department of Slavic Studies, University of Manitoba, 1975. A volume in the Readings in Slavic Literature series. Illustrated. Bibliography and index.

Kovtun, George J. *Czech and Slovak Literature in English: A Bibliography*. 2d ed. Washington, D.C.: Library of Congress, 1988. A useful reference work.

Kramoris, Ivan Joseph, ed. *An Anthology of Slovak Poetry: A Selection of Lyric and Narrative Poems and Folk Ballads in Slovak and English*. Scranton, Ohio: Obrana Press, 1947. A varied collection of works in several genres.

Manning, Clarence A., ed. *An Anthology of Czechoslovak Poetry*. New York: Columbia University Press,

1929. The first volume in the Publications of the Institute of Czechoslavak Studies series.Includes both Bohemian and Slovak poetry.

Petro, Peter. *A History of Slovak Literature*. Montreal: McGill-Queen's University Press, 1995. A thoughtful work, combining history and literary criticism. Bibliographical references and index.

Smith, James Sutherland, Pavol Hudik, and Jan Bajanek, eds. *In Search of Beauty: An Anthology of Contemporary Slovak Poetry in English*. Translated by Jan Bajanek. Mundelein, Ill.: Bolchazy-Carducci, 2004. Thirty-eight members of the Slovak Writer's Society contributed to this collection of 177 poems. Includes works by Jan Bajanek, Dezider Banga, Rudolf Cizmarik, and Millan Ferko.

Peter Petro

SLOVENIAN POETRY

The Slovenes, of a small Slavic nation at the northwestern edge of the former Yugoslavia, have had a very unhappy history. One of the first among the Slavic peoples to have their own independent state (in the eighth century), they were the first to lose it (to Germanic tribes in the ninth century). They remained under German or Austrian domination until 1918—a period of almost a thousand years. It is not surprising that under such conditions Slovenian culture could not develop properly; indeed, it is a miracle that it survived. Like their South Slavic brethren, the Slovenes began their literature during their conversion to Christianity, in the ninth century, but the work among them of the disciples of the missionaries Saint Cyril and Saint Methodius was of such short duration that it left no lasting literary documents. Indeed, until the Reformation, very little Slovenian literature was preserved. Among the few pieces that have survived are church and ritual songs, troubadour lyrics, and folk poems, all of which are anonymous; most of them are translations, preserved only because they were interspersed in German texts.

EARLY POETRY

The Reformation in the sixteenth century produced some poetry, mostly connected with the Church. Indeed, for many centuries, the clergy alone sustained Slovenian culture. It was not until 1689 that the first Slovenian secular poem, by Jozef Zizenčeli, was recorded. It was only in the second half of the eighteenth century, under the enlightened absolutist rulers of Austria, that Slovenian literature began to develop. The poetry contained in three almanacs, the *Pisanice* (1779-1781), marked the first noteworthy attempt at genuine poetry in Slovenian. Although much of this poetry was highly derivative, it was written by Slovenes in their own language, which had been suppressed for centuries.

The first poet to write in the native tongue was Valentin Vodnik (1758-1819), usually considered to be the founder of Slovenian poetry. After unsure beginnings in *Pisanice*, he published two books of poetry, *Pesmi za pokušino* (1806; poetic attempts) and *Pesmi za brambovce* (1809; poems to the defenders). Vodnik discarded foreign models and took Slovenian folk poetry as the basis for his language, meter, and even subject matter. He greeted Napoleon's creation of Illyria, in which the western Southern Slavs were united for the first time since their common arrival in the Balkans. Enthusiastic about the opportunities for education and liberation of his people promised at the beginning of the nineteenth century, he encouraged his mostly peasant nation to work and fight for its betterment. After Napoleon's demise, Vodnik lost his position and soon died, but not before he had laid the foundations for Slovenian poetry, inspiring his followers to use the people's language. He also was a forerunner of the Slovenian Romantic movement, which would have been unthinkable without his contribution.

NINETEENTH CENTURY

Slovenia produced its greatest poet in France Prešeren (1800-1849), interestingly enough at about the same time as other Slavic literatures produced their greatest—Alexander Pushkin in Russia, Adam Mickiewicz in Poland, and Petar Petrović Njegoš in Montenegro, for example. The son of a peasant, Prešeren broke with many traditions: Instead of entering the priesthood, he studied law in Vienna; instead of writing religious and didactic literature, he expressed his own thoughts and feelings, particularly about love; instead of limiting himself to the narrow confines of a small nation, he employed classical, Renaissance, Romantic, and even Oriental forms and metrics and endeavored to write poetry at the world level. His *Sonetni venec* (1834; the wreath of sonnets) shows a remarkable maturity for a young poet from a hitherto unknown nation. Although the work deals primarily with his unhappy love affair and resulting suffering, it also declares, in an astonishingly developed Slovenian language, his love for, and faith in, his nation. It is this combination of the personal, the national, and the universal that lends Prešeren's poetry its power and poignancy. The epic poem *Krst pri Savici* (1836; the baptism on the Savica) underscores his preoccupation with the fate of his people, represented by a pagan leader who resists conversion to Christianity until his love for his betrothed leads him to it. It is generally thought that this epic signifies the poet's own defeat at the hands of many enemies (the foreign-dominated clergy and the narrow-minded, middle-class cultural officials). Prešeren's last book, *Poezije* (1847; poems), voices the pessimism that marked the last years of his life. The unity of form and subject matter in this work, the genuineness of the poet's feelings, the purity of his language, and the clarity of his ideas combine to distinguish this masterpiece, a work unequaled in Slovenian literature before or since.

Prešeren's achievements opened the gate for a number of excellent poets during the Romantic era. At the head of this group was Fran Levstik (1831-1887). Although not a poet of Prešeren's stature, he wrote sincere poetry about his personal misfortunes in love and in life generally, for he was often misunderstood and persecuted by conservative critics. Josip Stritar (1836-1923), also a son of a peasant family, fortunately did not have to spend most of his energy fighting the powers that be. Of a more practical nature, he spent his life educating his people and traveling in Europe. His main contribution lies in the field of literary education through critical writings. His predominantly pessimistic poetry is augmented by high artistry. Another Romantic poet, Simon Jenko (1835-1869), also wrote love poetry, severely criticized by the conservatives for its alleged eroticism. In addition, he wrote patriotic poems, one of which, "Naprej zastava slave" (onward, the banner of glory), became the Slovenian national anthem. Jenko's poetry is characterized by pure lyricism, youthful enthusiasm, kinship with folk lyrics, and closeness to nature, although his later verse is dominated by a melancholy realization of the transience of life. The last noteworthy Slovenian Romantic, Simon Gregorčič (1844-1906), followed more or less in the footsteps of others. He, too, sang of love and of the harsh lot of his people. Forced into the priesthood, he felt confined and unable to express himself freely except in his poetry, for which he was heavily criticized. The immediacy, freshness, and warmth of his poetry make him a very popular poet to this day.

By the closing decades of the nineteenth century, Romanticism in Slovenian literature had run its course, and a more realistic literature took its place, along with similar movements in the Serbian and Croatian literatures and under similar influences—French and Russian. Like the poetry of those other Slavic literatures, Slovenian poetry did not fare well in this period, with the exception of one poet worthy of note, Anton Aškerc (1856-1912). Another priest, author of numerous books of ballads and romances, of lyric and epic poems, Aškerc reflected in his poetry the changing spirit of the times. Instead of voicing private concerns in an overly subjective manner, as the previous generation had done, he raised his voice in support of social changes. Instead of sentimentality and passive pessimism, he called for a struggle against the enemies of his people, not necessarily always foreigners. In order to bolster his pleas and arguments, he borrowed motifs from Slovenian history as well as from that of other nations. He was and remains a very popular poet.

Modernism

At the turn of the century, Slovenian poetry, like that of other Slavic literatures, was transformed by a strong modernistic movement led by several strong personalities. The first of these, and perhaps the greatest writer in Slovenian literature, was Ivan Cankar (1876-1918). A great fiction writer and playwright, he made his debut with a book of poems, *Erotika* (1899; erotica). There is in these poems little of the fiery activism in the service of social justice that he would later espouse, yet they are indicative of his future development. They shocked the establishment by their boldness and directness, if not by their artistic quality.

Another modernist, Dragotin Kette (1876-1899), died too young to develop fully his poetic talent. In his only book of poetry, *Poezije* (1900; poems), he revealed himself as a genuine lyricist of an openhearted, direct, and cheerful disposition. His sonnets are proof of his knowledge of world literature and of his artistic promise. Josip Murn Aleksandrov (1879-1901) also died young (of the same disease and in the same room as Kette) and consequently never achieved his full potential. He began as a poet of the countryside idyll, but the premonition of death colored his outlook with premature melancholy. Most of his poems are impressionistic sketches that captivate the reader with their directness and genuine feeling.

By far the greatest modernist poet was Oton Župančič (1878-1949). He was born in a village but, through schooling and traveling, developed into a cosmopolitan intellectual and managed to be at home in both the city and the country. During his career of almost five decades, he assumed a wide variety of literary attitudes: The freewheeling modernist became a contemplative aesthete who measured every word and thought. His first book, *Čaša opojnosti* (1899; a cup of bliss), is marked by restlessness, decadent sensualism, and unbridled individualism, while his last, *Zimzelen pod snegom* (1945; evergreen under the snow), expresses his love and concern for his homeland during the struggle against the enemy in World War II. Between these two poles lies a steadily improving artistry that eventually made him the second-best Slovenian poet, after Prešeren.

Srečko Kosovel (1904-1926) is considered the best Slovenian poet of the interwar period. Like so many of his fellow writers, he died too young to achieve his full potential, but he succeeded in writing a number of powerful expressionistic poems in which he combined a total experience of life with a premonition of death, not only his own but also that of the European intellectual. Alojz Gradnik (1882-1967) was similarly preoccupied with death, but he also wrote about the power of love, about the love of his country, and about the meaning of life. Gradnik stands high among Slovenian poets of all time.

LATE TWENTIETH CENTURY ONWARD

The traumatic experiences of World War II and the ensuing years of difficult reconstruction left little room for the development of poetry, particularly because the older poets who had survived the war were not heard from again. It was left to the new generation to revive poetry, although not necessarily to continue prewar traditions. In a relatively short time, a number of new poets arrived on the scene. Of these, Matej Bor (pseudonym of Vladimir Pavšič; 1913-1993) won fame with his war poetry, in which he proved himself to be the most engaged of contemporary Slovenian poets. He

shows a similar attitude in later poems about heroes and the dangers of the atomic age. Edvard Kocbek (1904-1981) wrote sparingly, but his poems reveal a completely contemporary spirit which draws him closer to young poets such as Tomaž Šalamun (born 1941) than to older figures such as Bor. Kocbek's well-crafted poems, quiet in tone, cast an ironic eye on the world. His is not the irony of a man who feels superior to what he sees, but rather that of a man who is an endless victim, tied to the very thing he abhors.

Of the younger poets, Ciril Zlobec, Dane Zajc, Cene Vipotnik, and Gregor Strniša signal a decisive change. Zlobec (born 1924) began as a neo-Romantic, exploring the traditional themes of love and loss of childhood. Later, he turned to the problems of contemporary society and the individual. Zajc (1929-2005) similarly showed a strong individualistic attitude unhindered by the burden of war trauma. In that sense, his poetry broke with that of revolutionary Romanticism. Instead, one finds in his poetry Symbolist tendencies, and his subject matter is the loneliness and the resulting negation of humanity. Vipotnik (1914-1971), who made his debut rather late, was first influenced by the war but moved in his later works toward a more private, lyric poetry with love as its main focus. Strniša (1930-1987), a unique and highly articulate poet, developed an original and easily recognizable style. His reaction to the fear and alienation of modern humanity is expressed through elaborate historical allegories and dream sequences, cyclically arranged. Each cycle revolves around a central metaphor, the dialectic of which is then explored with economy and precision of expression. There is a desire here to mythologize, not too far removed in spirit from that of Serbian poet Vasko Popa.

Other significant poets writing in the 1980's and 1990's were Tone Pavček (born 1928), Kajetan Kovič (born 1931), Veno Taufer (born 1933), and Šalamun. In some respects, these were the most experimental poets writing in the former Yugoslavia. While Croatian and Serbian poets were often torn between their native tradition and the need "to make it new," these Slovenian poets seem to have completely committed themselves to discovering a modern style. Taufer and Šalamun are by far the most radical experimenters, and Taufer appears to be the more calculating of the two.

The strategies of his poems reveal a close knowledge of modern art and literature. Šalamun's poems, have an associative quality that gives the impression of automatic writing. What ties them together and gives them their inevitability is his keen sense of the organism of the poem with all of its verbal and lyric connotations. Consequently, the apparent chaos of Šalamun's poems is a ruse, a freeing agent, for his poems never fail to drive their meaning home. Šalamun and Taufer, with their creative freedom and adventurousness, initiated a new beginning for Slovenian poetry.

BIBLIOGRAPHY

Barac, Antun. *A History of Yugoslav Literature*. Ann Arbor, Mich.: Joint Committee on Eastern Europe Publication Series, 1973. A standard history of all Yugoslav literatures and poetry, including Slovenian, by a leading literary scholar. Although somewhat outdated, it still provides reliable information, especially about the older periods.

Biggins, Michael. "Slovenian Poetic Tradition and Edvard Kocbek." *Litterae Slovenicae* 33, no. 2 (1995): 9-18. Biggins looks at the Slovenian poetic traditions as embodied in the poetry of perhaps the greatest contemporary Slovenian poet, Edvard Kocbek.

Cesar, Ivan. "In the Beginning Was a Sign: Contemporary Slovene Poetry." *Slovene Studies* 7, nos. 1/2 (1985): 13-22. An expert survey of contemporary Slovene poetry.

Cooper, Henry R., ed. *A Bilingual Anthology of Slovene Literature*. Bloomington, Ind.: Slavica, 2003. Fascicle 1, in the Anthology of South Slavic Literatures series. Includes both short poems and excerpts from longer works.

Debeljak, Aleš. "Visions of Despair and Hope Against Hope: Poetry in Yugoslavia in the Eighties." *World Literature Today* 68, no. 3 (1992): 191-194. Debeljak looks at Yugoslav poetry, including Slovenian, on the eve of tumultuous events and changes in Yugoslavia in the 1990's. Poetry of the 1980's in some ways foreshadowed those events, giving vent to despair and forlorn hope.

Hawkesworth, Celia, ed. *A History of Central European Women's Writing*. New York: Palgrave, 2001. Includes general essays on women's literature in the region, as well as one focused specifically on Slovenian writers. Map, bibliography, and index.

Jurkovič, Tina, ed. *Contemporary Slovenian Literature in Translation*. Translated by Lili Potpara. Ljubljana, Slovenia: Študentska založba, 2002. A useful anthology. Includes biographical information and bibliographical references.

Mihalilovich, Vasa D., and Mateja Matejic. *A Comprehensive Bibliography of Yugoslav Literature in English, 1593-1980*. Columbus, Ohio: Slavica, 1984. The same writers produced supplements in 1989 (covering the years 1981-1985) and in 1992 (covering 1986-1990). These three volumes are indispensable reference works.

Mokrin-Pauer, Vida. *Six Slovenian Poets*. Translated by Ana Jeinika, edited by Brane Mozetič. Todmorden, Lancashine, England: Arc, 2006. The three poets selected for this anthology, who are all young writers at the beginning of their publishing careers, reflect recent, radical changes in Slovenian society. The Slovenian literary tradition and the poets' reactions to it are discussed in the introduction.

Ožbalt, Irma M. "Slovene Poetry in English: Challenges and Problems." *Acta Neophilologica* 27 (1994): 67-74. Ožbalt discusses the state of the translation of Slovenian poetry into English and achievements and problems connected with it.

Zawacki, Andrew, ed. *Afterwards: Slovenian Writing, 1945-1995*. Buffalo, N.Y.: White Pine Press, 1999. An extensive section of this volume is devoted to poetry, with an essay by the well-known poet Edvard Kocbek, followed by some seventy poems by various writers.

Vasa D. Mihailovich

Spanish Poetry to 1400

The development of Spanish poetry through the fourteenth century is a facet of what Ramón Menéndez Pidal, the preeminent Spanish medievalist, called *frutos tardios* (late fruits). Extant manuscripts from this period are few in number, and their condition is generally poor, but their literary quality is very high. Although this essay will focus on poetry written in Spanish, it is important to note that, during this rich period in the cultural history of Spain, significant poetry was written in other languages as well—notably the Arabic-Hebraic *jarchas*, the Galician *cantigas de amigo*, and Catalan lyric verse. Just as many consider modern Spain a quilt of five distinct national patterns (Galacian, Basque, Catalan, Andalusian, and Castilian), so medieval Spain was a mosaic of regional political entities—Asturian, Galician, Leonese, Castilian, Navarrese, Aragonese, and Catalonian, to name a few—as well as racial and religious patterns: Christian, Jewish, and Muslim.

Eighth through tenth centuries

The Moorish invasion of 711 and the virtual conquest of the Iberian Peninsula by the year 718 left the Hispano-Visigothic kingdom in disarray. Many of the conquered Visigoths were absorbed into Islamic culture (they became known as *mozarabes*), while others retreated into the protective mountain ranges of the northern Cantabrian coastline. From the latter came the Reconquest, a seven-century-long effort to recapture the Peninsula. Isolated pockets of resistance to Moorish domination grew into kingdoms with competing priorities and interests involving territory, preeminence of power, and collection of taxes as well as the cultural variables, such as language and literature, that made each of them distinct. Intriguingly, Galicia, Castile, León, Navarre, Aragon, and Catalonia all developed separate linguistic traditions, but only Galicia, Castile, and Catalonia produced literatures that have survived. While much medieval knowledge was hoarded and hidden to benefit a specific interest, language and literature were much more democratic; every bard, *juglar* or *jongleur*, needed to keep his material fresh, and the subsequent give-and-take of poetic style and vocabulary crossed from one language to another and from one culture to another. Medieval Spanish poetry is the product of these many influences.

The development of the Spanish language followed a path distinct from that of other languages of the Iberian Peninsula. With a tendency toward simplification of sounds and forms, Castilian standardized its grammar and vocabulary very early, making possible, for example, the reading of eleventh and twelfth century documents by an untrained twentieth century eye. (By comparison, the fourteenth century English of Geoffrey Chaucer's *The Canterbury Tales* [1387-1400] is resistant to the untrained modern reader.) The early formation of Spanish clearly had an effect on Spanish literature, as did the pioneer environment of its origin. Artificial attempts have been made to differentiate Castilian from Spanish. In the purest of senses, Castilian can be distinguished as a dialect with its marked peculiarities, but it exerted its dominion over an entire peninsula and subsequently, the New World, thereby becoming the language of Spain.

Eleventh century: Beginnings

The extraordinary and controversial beginning of Spanish verse must be assigned to the *kharjas*. Written in Arabic and Hebrew script—hence the controversy concerning their "Spanishness"—these refrains served as transitional passages between longer classical Arab stanzas known as *muwassahas*. When one transliterates *kharjas* into Roman characters and adds the missing vowels, the resulting text is clearly an archaic form of Spanish. Thus, according to Alan Deyermond, the refrain

> tnt' m'ry tnt' m'ry hbyb tnt'
> m'ry
> 'nfrmyrwn wlyws gyds(?) ydwln tn m'ly

becomes

Tant' amare, tant' amare habib, tant'
amare
enfermiron welyos nidios e dolen tan male.

My love is so great, my love is so great
Lover, my love is so great
My healthy eyes have sickened
And hurt so badly

In a 1948 article that constituted the first systematic study of the *kharjas*, S. M. Stern demonstrated that a Spanish vocabulary lies hidden in the Arabic and Hebrew script of these refrains. Stern's discovery revolutionized critical understanding of the origins of Spanish verse—and, indeed, of European lyric verse. Dámaso Alonso, the distinguished Spanish poet and critic, refers to these verses as the "early spring" of the European lyric, for they predate by a century the earliest poems written in Provence.

The content of the *kharjas* is almost invariably love-oriented. Like the example quoted above, many of these refrains express the pain of separation, the sense of hurt as a result of a lover's absence or infidelity; others employ "love" as a metaphor for the relationship between a poet and his patron. Since these verses were written as transitional passages between longer texts and rarely can stand on their own as expressions of a complete sentiment, their acceptance as the earliest form of the European lyric has been questioned. On the other hand, their beauty and compactness of expression reflect the existence of a tradition of popular song or cultured verse, or both, in the Spanish eleventh century.

TWELFTH CENTURY: TEXTUAL DESERT

Study of Spanish poetry in the twelfth century is hampered by a scarcity of texts. Despite the lack of texts, however, it is clear that lyric traditions were well established by the twelfth century. This is confirmed not only by the *kharjas* but also by two other verse forms which appeared in this century: the Galician-Portuguese *cantigas* and the Castilian *villancicos*. The *cantigas*, which have survived in three *cancioneros* (songbooks), of the fifteenth century, fall into three categories: a woman's lament for her lover (*cantigas de amigo*); a man's lament (*cantigas de amor*); and invective verse (*cantigas d'escarnho*). The similarity of content (lament for a lover) and speaker (a woman) between the *cantigas de amigo* and the *kharjas* suggests a connection, though none has been established.

Villancicos, multiverse refrains, repeated before and after every stanza, were not written down until the fifteenth century but are generally considered to date from the twelfth century. Their similarity to the *kharjas* is striking: They share a similar structure (refrain), content (lament for a lover), and speaker (a woman).

THIRTEENTH CENTURY: POETS AND MONKS

Thirteenth century Spanish poetry is notable for the genesis of native epic verse; unfortunately, scholars of the thirteenth century Spanish epic have barely five thousand lines of text with which to work, in comparison to the million lines of verse available to French medieval scholars. Adducing plot summaries in later chronicles, some critics postulate the existence of lost epics, while others suggest that many poems of epic nature were never written down because of their oral means of transmission. In any case, Spanish scholarship has been left with four national epic poems: *Cantar de mío Cid* (early thirteenth century; *Chronicle of the Cid*, 1846; better known as *Poem of the Cid*), *Las mocedades de Rodrigo* (fourteenth century), and *Cantar de Roncesvalles* (thirteenth century; *Song of Roland*), composed in traditional epic meter (assonant lines of fourteen to sixteen syllables), and *Poema de Fernán Gonzalez* (c. 1260), composed in *cuaderna vía*, a syllabic meter distinguished by its rigidity of form.

The single most important epic composition of the thirteenth century was *Poem of the Cid*. Like the other epics of its period, *Poem of the Cid* is the subject of ongoing critical debate concerning the nature of its composition. The so-called traditionalist critics argue that the Spanish epic originated in popular culture, in the songs of traveling entertainers or *juglares*. The most popular of these traditional songs, so the theory goes, were set down in manuscript and preserved for future generations. In contrast, the so-called individualist critics believe that the great epics of medieval Spain were the work of individual poets, shaped by individual genius. Finally, the oralist critics argue that the epics of this period were transmitted exclusively by oral performance and were not committed to writing until a later date.

A manuscript of *Poem of the Cid* does exist, yet a gap in the transcription of the date, "MCC VII," has convinced the traditionalists that the date of composition was actually 1307. The individualists see the gap as typical of scribal transcription and build an argument for a date of 1207. Traditionalists argue that Per Abad, the name appearing at the end of the manuscript, refers to a copyist, while the individualists suggest that he was the actual author of the epic. In *The Making of the "Poema de mío Cid"* (1983), a book C. C. Smith calls "bold," Smith affirms that his work

> . . . is the first in which the following proposition is argued: that the *Poema de mío Cid*, composed in or shortly before 1207, was the first epic to be composed in Castilian; that it was in consequence an innovatory and experimental work, in ways apparent in the surviving text; and that it did not depend on any precedents or existing tradition of epic verse in Castilian or other Peninsular language or dialect.

Smith goes on to assert that Per Abad was the actual author of the poem, not merely the copyist. Regardless of the exact method of composition of *Poem of the Cid*, however, it seems reasonable to assume that *juglares* sang verse narratives of this type, commemorating historical events and following a general, though loose, metric pattern.

Composed in traditional Spanish epic meter, *Poem of the Cid* is the story of a nobleman who is banished from the kingdom of Castile, survives the rigors of exile by defeating Moorish forces and fending off Christian encroachments on his territories, and finally achieves renown by conquering the Caliphate of Valencia. The work is divided into three *cantares*, or "tales," which highlight the rise and fall of the Cid's fortunes.

A powerful noble, the Cid is banished when King Alfonso VI of Castile heeds the insidious rumors of the Cid's enemies. Feudal relationships in the poem are not clear, and the reader is left with the impression that the two hundred men who join the Cid in exile do so of their own free will. The Cid leaves his wife, Jimena, and his

two daughters, Sol and Blanca, in the monastery of San Pedro de Cardeña for safekeeping.

The second division of the poem, the *Cantar de Bodas*, relates the Cid's triumph in his struggle to survive. Fighting Moor and Christian alike, he multiplies his fortune and his prestige. With the conquest of Valencia and the betrothal of his daughters to the sons of the Count de Carrión, a match specifically arranged by the King of Castile, it appears that the Cid's achievements are complete.

In a masterful juxtaposition of villainy and nobility, however, the third division of the poem, the *Cantar de Corpes*, plays havoc with the Cid's world prior to a resolution in the final verses. The engagement of the Cid's daughters to future counts is an extraordinary achievement, given his status as a middle-line noble, yet the *Cantar de Corpes* reveals the cowardice, egotism, and greed of the de Carrión brothers. The brothers, known as the Infantes, decide that their wives are not worthy of them; but they do not want to lose their dowries. Convincing the Cid that it is time to return to Carrión, the Infantes, once well away from Valencia, take their wives into a secluded glade, beat and strip them, and leave them to die. Fortunately, a retainer, disobeying the Infantes' orders to stay away from the area, rescues them.

The conclusion of the poem celebrates the triumph of civilizing order over brutality justified by birth. Instead of pursuing and punishing the Infantes, the Cid appeals to Alfonso VI, who by this time has come to consider the Cid an equal, to summon a convocation of nobles to judge his accusations against the Infantes. In the trial, the arrogant brothers are stripped of honor: First, the Cid demands that his swords be returned by the Infantes, then the dowry of his daughters; finally, the Cid accuses the brothers of *menos-valer*, or "less worthiness." The Infantes, enraged at this affront, call for a duel and subsequently lose to the Cid's champions. As the crowning glory to the Cid's success and the triumph of judicial process, emissaries from Navarre and Aragon appear, requesting the hands of the Cid's daughters for their kings.

Poem of the Cid is a monument to the individual whose dedication to right values is ultimately rewarded and whose salient qualities are protection of his family, generosity to all, religious devotion, and loyalty to the established order. The Cid's concern for his family is presented early in the poem as he leaves them in the care of the monks at San Pedro de Cardeña, promising to reward them richly. Parting causes such anguish in him that the poet observes that "parten unos d'otros como la uña de la carne" (they part like a fingernail pulling away from the skin).

The oldest manuscript of the poem signed by the enigmatic Per Abad is missing the first folio and two others within the work. The meter, as has been noted, is traditional to Spanish epics: mono-rhymic assonanced lines divided into half by a caesura and normally totaling fourteen syllables, though the irregularity of the meter, as shown in the third line of the following passage, is a puzzle to critics.

> Dezidle al Campeador, que en buen hora nasco,
> que destas siet sedmanas adobes con sos vassallos,
> vengam a Toledo, estol do de plazdo
> Por amor de mío Cid esta cort yo fago.

> Say to the Campeador he who was born in good hour
> to be ready with his vassals seven weeks from now
> and come to Toledo; that is the term I set for him
> Out of love for My Cid I call this court together.

The verse of *Poem of the Cid* is characterized by the oral qualities of the *mester de juglaría* (minstrel's meter, the meter of the *juglares*). It is instructive to compare this form with the *mester de clerecía* (clergy's meter), an almost exclusively thirteenth century verse form. While the *mester de juglaría* allows, along with its oral formulas, considerable freedom, resulting in verse with a tentative, experimental flavor, the *mester de clerecía* is highly formalized. The term *mester de clerecía* is often used interchangeably with the name of the meter in which verse so designated was generally written, *cuaderna vía*. A rigidly structured syllabic verse form, *cuaderna vía* is composed of four-line stanzas; each line must be fourteen syllables long, with a caesura exactly in the middle and a full rhyme of *aaaa*. The demanding rigidity of the form is evident in the following example, as presented by Germán Bleiberg (1915-1990), from the *Libro de Alexandre* (c. 1240; book of Alexander):

> Mester traigo fermoso, non es de juglaría
> mester es sin pecado ca es de clerecía
> fablar curso rimado por la cuaderna vía,
> a sílabas contadas que es de gran maestría

> A beautiful skill I bring, it is not of the singers:
> a skill without sin since it comes from churchmen.
> To follow a rhymed course using the four verse way
> by counted syllables that requires great mastery.

Another example of the *mester de clerecía* is a work in the hagiographic tradition, the *Vida de Santa María Egipcíaca* (thirteenth century; life of Saint Maria the Egyptian), but curiously enough, it is not composed in *cuaderna vía*. The poem is a rendition of the legend of an Egyptian prostitute who, after a lifetime of dissipation, converts to Christianity when two angels deny her entrance to the temple at Jerusalem. While artistically the poem does not represent a significant advance, the clear expression of the craft of the *mester de clerecía* makes worthwhile reading. The author was able to adapt a Latin source to Spanish in a learned yet popular style; numerous learned words are integrated into the text without disturbing the poet's rapport with his audience.

The first major poet to use *cuaderna vía* as a distinguishing characteristic of his work was Gonzalo de Berceo (c. 1190-after 1250), a secular priest. Born around the end of the twelfth century, his name probably reflects his birthplace, the village of Berceo in the province of La Rioja. Information about his death is equally sketchy, and internal evidence in his poetry suggests that he died after 1250.

Gonzalo de Berceo's work can be categorized into three groups: hagiographic poems commemorating the Spanish saints Millán, Domingo, and Oria; devotional poems dedicated to the Virgin Mary; and doctrinal works related to apocalyptic material and the symbolism of the Mass; in addition, three hymns are attributed to him. His best-known works, however, are his poems about the Virgin Mary, particularly the *Milagros de Nuestra Señora* (c. 1252; the miracles of Our Lady).

The relationship between man and the Virgin Mary in the *Milagros de Nuestra Señora* could be described as maternal vassalage. The theme of the work is not obscure; those who show devotion and loyalty to the Virgin Mary will be rewarded, saved from peril or death, and even have their souls rescued from Hell. The poem relates twenty-five miracles performed by the Virgin Mary, adapted from a Latin manuscript collection. The opening lines describe an allegorical *locus amoenus*. After calling on his "amigos e vasallos de Dios" ("friends and vassals of God") to listen, he writes:

> Yo maestro Gonçalvo de Verçeo nomnado
> Idendo en romeria caeçi en un prado
> Verde e bien sençido, de flores bien poblado,
> Logar cobdiçieduero pora omne cansado.

> I, master Gonzalo of Berceo by name
> While out walking I lay down in a field
> Green and lush, with abundant flowers
> A comforting place for a tired man.

The story of the second miracle presents a good example of Berceo's art. Presented in a simple, straightforward progression of events, the narrative deals with a monk who demonstrated his devotion to the Virgin Mary by kneeling in front of her statue and reciting an "Ave Maria" every time he passed. A demon, "a vicar of Beelzebub," corrupted him with lust at night, and the monk began to wander, though every time he passed the statue of the Virgin, he would kneel and pray. One night, after an escapade, he fell into a river and drowned.

At this point, the story becomes a metaphysical dispute between devils and angels for the wayward monk's soul. The Virgin Mary intervenes, citing his devotion to her statue, but she is challenged by the chief devil, who reminds her that dogma decrees that whatever state of grace exists at death determines a man's life after death. The Virgin refuses to argue and calls upon Jesus to resolve the problem; the solution is the revival of the monk, who dies much later after a long life of devotion to the Virgin.

Stylistically, Berceo's verse is measured, consistent, and reminiscent of several traits of the *mester de juglaría:* direct address, enjambment, and popular vocabulary. Indeed, the poem's diction is remarkably non-Latinate, even though the topic is religious; for example, Berceo uses the word *beneito*, a vulgarized form of *benedictino*, for the term "Benedictine."

Berceo's authorship has also been claimed for the *Libro de Alexandre*, a poem of 2,675 lines composed in *cuaderna vía* around 1240. The importance of the *Libro de Alexandre* cannot be dismissed; it is the longest epic poem of the thirteenth century, in addition to being the only survivor of Spanish verse epics about antiquity. Its artistic merit is substantial as well. In his 1934 edition, Raymond S. Willis notes that

> . . . the poem is not an artless assemblage, but a well contrived and coherent whole. The poetic gift and charm of its author, even though distorted by our present corrupt manuscripts, can be discerned as considerable. And, finally, this epic is a symposium of much of the erudition of the period and a mirror of contemporary life, thought, and language.

The *Libro de Alexandre* is a pageant of figures of antiquity across an epic stage. The poem begins with the birth and childhood of Alexander, with Aristotle playing a major role as adviser, councillor, and teacher. When his father, Philip, dies, Alexander's succession is challenged in Athens and Thebes, and, immediately after his coronation, he is forced to put down rebellions in those cities.

The core of the story is the conflict between Alexander and another great figure of antiquity, his rival Darius of Persia. Alexander's success in Macedonia and Greece moves him to challenge the persistent Persian threat, and he crosses the Hellespont to invade Asia Minor. The ensuing battles cast Alexander more and more in the role of a demigod. He creates the Twelve Peers, cuts the Gordian Knot, defeats Darius twice, captures Persepolis, and presides at Darius's funeral. The steady encroachment of the pathos of power on Alexander's character is developed in this central part of the epic, preparing the reader or listener for the conclusion.

Alexander cannot stop his conquests. Even though the pressure to return home is ever-growing, he alternately harangues and leads his men to defeat the Hyrcanians and the Scythians and to conquer the subcontinent of India. The element of fantasy also grows in the narrative: Alexander is visited by the Amazons; there is a detailed description of the wonders of the Orient (such as the flight of a griffon); and Alexander descends into the sea in a submarine-like vessel. Only metaphysical forces, Nature and Satan, can play a causative role in Alexander's death. The world has surrendered to him, but at the moment of his greatest achievement, he is poisoned by a trusted lieutenant, Jobas.

The interweaving of the fantastic, the allegorical, and the moral threads in the frame of the Alexander lore that had accumulated over the previous thousand years makes the *Libro de Alexandre* a notable monument in medieval Spanish verse for the modern scholar; indeed, its merits were recognized in its own day, for it is now accepted that the author of the *Poema de Fernán González* closely imitated the *Libro de Alexandre*.

The *Poema de Fernán González* (poem of Fernán González), written around 1260, is the second great epic of the thirteenth century. Though its topic is local—the deeds of a Castilian nobleman—and thus characteristic of the *mester de juglaría*, the poem is clearly a product of the *mester de clerecía* tradition. The meter is *cuaderna vía*, and the details of the story reveal a dependence on Latin historical sources, the poems of Berceo, and the *Libro de Alexandre*, all of which leads modern scholars to believe that a cleric was the author. Another clue to authorship, reinforcing the attribution to a churchman, is a mythical-biblical pattern that J. P. Keller, in his article, "The Structure of the *Poema de Fernán González*," classifies as "rise, treachery, and fall," though ultimately the hero achieves a state of prominence. Fernán González is present as a divinely chosen figure in the mold of biblical heroes.

The poem consists of three parts. The first sets the overall dimensions of the three significant episodes in Spanish history until that time: the Visigothic Empire, the Arab invasion, and the beginning of the Reconquest. The second and third parts reflect the rise of Castile: The small, frontier region gains prominence with the victories over the Moors won by its heroic leader, Fernán González, who subsequently is seated in the *cortes* (parliament) of the kingdom of León. Ambushed and imprisoned by Leonese jealous of his success, he escapes to lead the Castilians to independence from León and supremacy over the kingdom of Navarre.

In contrast to the pragmatic religious devotion of the Cid, Fernán González is carefully characterized as a God-chosen leader who reciprocates with Christlike behavior. He prays continuously, has dreams in which spirits visit, and hears voices of saints during battle that tell him how to direct his troops, and he encourages his men with the promise that those who die on the battlefield will rejoice with him in paradise.

The anonymous *Libro de Apolonio* (book of Apolonio, c. 1240) and the *Castigos y ejemplos de Catón* (the punishments and examples of Catón, c. 1280) are two other significant verse compositions. The first descends from the tradition of late classical Greek romance, full of plot mechanisms turning on storms, pirates, separations, misfortunes, and, finally, a happy ending in which virtue and trust in God are rewarded. The second is notable for its popularity in the sixteenth century but is distinct from other poems of the *cuaderna vía* style. It has no story line and is more similar to wisdom literature than to the hagiography and classical and historical epics typical of the *mester de clerecía*.

Fourteenth century: Diversification

In his classic study, *European Literature and the Latin Middle Ages* (1953), Ernst Curtius describes the impact of the *Libro de buen amor* (c. 1330; *The Book of Good Love*, 1933), the most poetically and artistically diverse composition of the Spanish Middle Ages:

> Then about 1330 Juan Ruiz (1283?-1350?) makes a bold innovation with his *Libro de buen amor*. He imports Ovid's eroticism and its medieval derivatives. To a free rendition of the *Ars amandi* . . . he added a recasting of the extremely popular medieval comedy *Pamphilus de amore*, which in turn goes back to an elegy of Ovid's (*Amores* I, 8). . . . There are critics who rank the *Libro de buen amor*, the *Celestina*, and *Don Quijote* together as the three peaks of Spanish literature.

Curtius's description, though, is only the half of it. As a peak, *The Book of Good Love* has yet to be scaled. Its structural diversity, thematic multiplicity, and rich characterization make it one of the most intriguing works of European literature.

The author, like the work itself, is a mystery. Little is known about Juan Ruiz, the archpriest of Hita, a small town north of Madrid. This lack of biographical data has given rise to the notion that perhaps "Juan Ruiz" was not the actual author but rather a persona through which the author represented himself.

In the poem, there are tidbits of biographical information about Juan Ruiz, such as a plea for mercy in response to an unjust incarceration and constant reminders that he has not been a very successful lover. Critics have sought to extrapolate information about the author from his work. They have concluded, for example, that he was almost certainly a priest, since he reveals great familiarity with ecclesiastical terminology; indeed, it is likely that he was an archpriest—that is, a priest with administrative responsibility over several dioceses. His education, however, was not confined to scripture and religious literature: He paraphrased the *Pamphilus de amore* (twelfth century), a medieval Latin love farce, and composed his verse in a variety of meters.

The Book of Good Love is a tour de force. Opening with an invocation to God or the Virgin Mary, the poet pleads for help in his present trouble, which seems to be an imprisonment. A sermon, based on the scripture "I will give understanding" (Psalms 31:8), states the purpose of the work, ostensibly to instruct the audience in the forms of "bad" (that is, sexual) love in order that they might avoid it and practice "good" love—that is, the love of God. This is followed by a series of *loores* (praises) extolling the virtue and power of the Virgin Mary. Scattered throughout are fables, illustrating a moral through tales of animals characterized as humans, and fabliaux, often of a ribald nature. The poet then begins his autobiography and follows it with a *cazurro* verse, a coarse, often humorous love story—though in this case, Juan Ruiz flirts with sacrilege as he compares forlorn lovers with the Crucifixion of Christ. A panegyric arguing that love changes men completely leads into a vision, an allegorical narrative of the poet's three-time failure at seduction.

After his failures, a debate ensues between the poet and Don Amor (Sir Love) concerning the joys and dangers of love; this is followed by invective verse condemning love. A scriptural parody, based on sexual allusions in the canonical hours, is concluded by an Ovidian *ars amandi*.

The source of the longest verse narrative in *The Book of Good Love* is the *Pamphilus de amore*, a popular twelfth century Latin comedy. Notable is the poet's introduction of the character Trotaconventos, an old go-between destined to become a type in Spanish literature. Her intervention into his love life does not provide satisfactory results, and the poet, in a counsel, warns women about the wickedness of love and suggests that men not use negative epithets for their go-betweens. He finishes the section with an enumeration of the various comments gentlemen have been known to make.

The *cantigas de serrana* are bawdy verses telling how mountain women jump unsuspecting travelers, such as the poet; these verses are followed by a collection of devotional poems concerning the Passion of Christ. Another baffling shift in tone follows, as the poet introduces a satirical mock-epic contest between Don Carnal (Lord Flesh) and Doña Cuaresma (Lady Lent), terminating in the triumphal procession of Don Carnal's forces.

A "book of hours" with allegorized seasons of the year prepares the reader for an extended reappearance of Trotaconventos, the procuress, who attempts (unsuccessfully) to woo a nun for the poet. Her rhetorical portrait of the nun provides an intriguing insight into the concept of beauty in the Spanish Middle Ages. When Trotaconventos dies, the poet delivers an impassioned lament and subsequently writes her epitaph.

Juan Ruiz's irreverence resurfaces in a mock sermon on the virtues of little women, and the poem concludes with a summation in which the poet suggests how his work should be understood. A postscript follows with a collection of *cantares de ciegos* (beggars' songs), a complaint, and goliardic verses attacking the Church.

The metric patterns in *The Book of Good Love* reveal a conscious manipulation of verse length to combat monotony and to enhance the content. While most of the narrative sections of the poem are in *cuaderna vía*, the poet often shifts between lines of fourteen and sixteen syllables. The rhyme is virtually perfect. The lyric sections of the poem present a dazzling array of verse forms, ranging from the *zéjel* (a Moorish composition with stanzas and a refrain) to the *pie quebrado*, in which four-syllable lines and eight-syllable lines are used in a single stanza.

The diversification of Spanish verse in the fourteenth century continued with the appearance of lyric poetry. Setting aside the disputed nature of the *kharjas*,

Rafael Lapesa, the noted Spanish critic and linguist, suggests that lyric verse of a learned nature did not appear until 1300, with the composition of the *Razón de amor*. This earliest extant lyric poem survives in a confusing manuscript in which the first part narrates the visitation of a young man in a *locus amoenus* by a young woman who has prepared a glass of wine and another of water for them. Their lyric conversation is reminiscent of the *cantigas de amor* and *cantigas de amigo*, in which the lovers complain about love. Suddenly, the young woman leaves, and a white dove appears, spilling the vessel of water into the wine. The rest of the poem, called the "Denuestos del agua y del vino," is of the debate genre: The personified wine and water argue their respective strengths and defects; for water, wine is too sentimental; for wine, the water is too coldly rational. In *A Literary History of Spain: The Middle Ages* (1971), Alan Deyermond accurately sums up the *Razón de amor* as "the best and most puzzling" of poems. The dramatic change midway through the poem has generated considerable critical debate, some scholars arguing that the work is in fact a single poem while others contend that it comprises two distinct poems rudely joined.

It is appropriate that a survey of Spanish verse through the fourteenth century should end on the note with which it began: the dichotomy between popular and learned verse. The early contrast between the *mester de juglaría* and the *mester de clerecía* repeats itself at the end of the Middle Ages. There are, on the one hand, the predecessors of the popular *romanceros* (collections devoted exclusively to romances or ballads), and, on the other, the philosophical verse of Rabbi Sem Tob and the early Spanish Humanism reflected in Pero López de Ayala.

The diversity of medieval Spanish literature is exemplified by the *Proverbios morales* (fourteenth century) of Rabbi Sem Tov (or Santob), born in Carrión de los Condes around 1290. The distinguished Spanish historian Claudio Sánchez Albornoz referred to Sem Tob as the first Spanish intellectual. The *Proverbios morales* entries are almost exclusively composed in Alexandrine verse and—oddly, for a medieval composition—contain virtually no exempla relating the content to everyday life. The poet is a philosopher, observing life through the prism of classical and Hebraic thought, never losing sight of the reality of being a Jew in an ever-hostile environment. His poetry is a celebration of learning and knowledge, tempered with the reservations of a skeptic.

Spanish Humanism begins with Pedro López de Ayala, courtier, knight, and man of letters. As an adult, he lived through the cataclysms of fourteenth century Spain: the plague, the Trastámaran usurpation of the Castilian throne, international wars, and the Great Schism of the Roman Catholic Church. As a man of letters, he translated or was connected with the translations into Spanish of works by Livy, Boethius, Gregory the Great, and Giovanni Boccaccio. His great poetic work, the *Rimado de palaçio* (fourteenth century), stands alongside his chronicle of the reign of Peter I of Castile as a significant contribution to Spanish literature.

The *Rimado de palacio*, an extensive poem of 8,200 lines composed over several years, provides a serious counterpoint to the frivolity of Juan Ruiz's *The Book of Good Love*. The poem is divided into three sections. The first is a scathing satire of the secular and ecclesiastical society of the day. The second part is composed of lyric *loores* and prayers to the virgins of Monserrat, Guadalupe, and Rocamador and to other religious icons, invoking their favors. It is believed that this portion was written during an imprisonment, while the third and final part was set down in the last years of Ayala's life. This last section is a compendium of religious and ethical reflections based on the Book of Job and Saint Gregory's *Moralia* (c. 6 C.E.).

In contrast to the learned verse of Ayala and Sem Tob, the late fourteenth century saw the first appearance of the *romanceros*, or romances. It is generally accepted that the composition of these popular ballads began as the longer epic poems (their probable source) were forgotten or lost their relevance. The romances are written in the same sixteen-syllable assonant line that characterizes Spanish epic verse and are generally categorized as historical (based on a recent event), literary (derived from a previous chronicle or epic), or adventurous (a miscellaneous grouping of diverse themes such as love, revenge, mystery, or simply adventure).

The quilt of Spanish culture is at once a social, political, religious, and literary phenomenon. The interplay between learned and popular, Galician and Castilian, Moor, Jew, and Christian created a poetic tradition as multifaceted as any found in Western Europe, a tradition enriched and deepened by its diversity.

BIBLIOGRAPHY

Florit, Eugenio. *Introduction to Spanish Poetry.* Mineola, N.Y.: Dover, 1991. Offers works ranging from the twelfth century *Poema de mío Cid* to twentieth century poets. Full Spanish texts with expert literal English translations on facing pages. Also contains a wealth of biographical information and critical commentary. Illustrated.

Gies, David T., ed. *The Cambridge History of Spanish Literature.* New York: Cambridge University Press, 2009. A comprehensive English-language work, prepared by Gies in collaboration with forty-six other eminent scholars. Includes chronology and index.

Merwin, W. S., ed. and trans. *Spanish Ballads.* Port Townsend, Wash.: Copper Canyon Press, 2008. A reissue of the volume first published in 1961, early in the career of the translator, who became one of America's most admired poets. Includes ballads from the late Middle Ages to the twentieth century, arranged by type and in chronological order.

Schippers, Arie. *Spanish Hebrew Literature and the Arab Literary Tradition: Arabic Themes in Hebrew Andalusian Poetry.* New York: Brill Academic, 1993. An introduction to the Arabic poetry of eleventh century Muslim Spain and to the major Hebrew poets of the same period. Demonstrates how Arabic themes appear in Hebrew Andalusian poetry.

Simpson, Lesley B., trans. *The Poem of the Cid.* 2d ed. Berkeley: University of California Press, 2007. A classic translation of the great Spanish epic.

Smith, Colin C. *The Making of the "Poema de mío Cid."* New York: Cambridge University Press, 1983. The well-known scholar and editor of the Collins English-Spanish dictionaries traces the development of the Spanish epic. Bibliography, index.

_____, ed. *Spanish Ballads.* 2d ed. London: Bristol Classical Press, 1996. Originally published in 1964, this collection is accompanied by a useful introduction and notes by Smith.

Walters, Gareth. *The Cambridge Introduction to Spanish Poetry.* New York: Cambridge University Press, 2003. Bilingual edition. A survey of Iberian and Latin American writing from the Middle Ages to the present. Conveniently arranged by genres and themes. Bibliography and index.

John Richard Law

Spanish Poetry Since 1400

During the fifteenth century, Spain's mercurial transformation into a world power was the direct result of having achieved national unification (1492)—a reality that took more than seven centuries of armed conflict between the various Christian principalities scattered throughout the northern half of the Iberian Peninsula and the powerful Muslim caliphates that dominated virtually all of Spain for several centuries following the Moors' initial invasion in 711. As Spain found itself emerging into a modern state whose strong central government was busy removing the last medieval vestiges from its newly created empire (thus ushering in an era of unsurpassed economic prosperity), so, too, in the field of art and literature, a new awareness of the ancient Greek and Latin masters was taking root.

Fifteenth and sixteenth centuries

The two men most responsible for introducing Spain to a new spirit of Humanism via Greek, Latin, and Italian literary traditions were Juan Boscán (c. 1490-1542) and Garcilaso de la Vega (1501-1536).

Whereas 1492 marked the political birth of modern Spain, the year 1543 may be said to have marked Spain's cultural rebirth into the Humanistic tradition that had been eclipsed until its rediscovery a century earlier by the great fifteenth century Italian poets. With the publication of *Las obras de Boscán y algunas de Garcilasso de la Vega repartidas en quatro libros* (1543; the works of Boscán and some of Garcilaso de la Vega), a wholly new poetic vision was introduced into Spanish literature. To appreciate the magnitude of change that Boscán and Garcilaso brought to sixteenth century Spanish poetry, both in its form and in its content, one must recall the tradition from which their revolutionary poetics were born.

Not until the fifteenth century did the Spanish literary lyric first appear as an independent written work of art. Prior to that time, Castilian verse was dominated, for the most part, by the fourteenth century romance (ballad) and the thirteenth century *villancico*. While traveling troubadours sang of the joys and woes associated with courtly love, clerics were creating their own

tradition, focused on more spiritual themes, such as the many miracles of the Blessed Virgin. In 1445, the first important collection of Castilian verse was published, the *Cancionero de Baena* (songbook of Baena). Here were recorded numerous *canciones de amor* (love songs) which echoed the earlier ballads in both theme and form.

Two exceptions to these traditions were the marquis of Santillana and Juan de Mena. They transcended the traditional compositions that were recorded in the *Cancionero general* (1511; general songbook), a collection of fifteenth century verse filled with *villancicos* and ballads that reflected the love songs of the earlier troubadour tradition. Santillana is credited with the first sonnets written in a language other than Italian, while Mena's allegorical and philosophical poems are sprinkled with frequent classical allusions and a Latinized vocabulary.

The poetic revolution that was to characterize sixteenth century Spain, however, did not truly begin until 1526, when the Spanish poet Boscán met with the Venetian ambassador to the court of Charles V, Andreas Navagero. It was at this time that Boscán was first introduced to the new Italianate forms with their classical focus on humans and nature. Although it would be another seventeen years before Navagero's revolutionary seeds would bear Spanish fruit, the poetic manifesto contained within *Las obras de Boscán y algunas de Garcilasso de la Vega repartidas en quatro libros* heralded a radical change in the exterior form of poetic expression and promised a vibrantly new vision of humankind.

Boscán found that the Italian hendecasyllable created a cadence much less emphatic than that of the traditional Castilian octosyllable, allowing the poet to express subtleties of rhythm and rhyme previously unattainable. The flexibility afforded by this new meter complemented the new aesthetic sensibility that Boscán and Garcilaso brought to Castilian verse. For example, in Boscán's *Canzoniere* (songbook), which consists of ninety love sonnets and ten *canzones* (songs), the theme of human love is explored in all its splendor. Unchecked by reason, it is a passion fraught with pain and suffering; when properly expressed, this same love brings peace and joy to the human spirit.

Garcilaso, too, reflects this newfound faith in humanity's ultimate worth and goodness. Innovative in form (he introduced into Spanish verse, among other meters, the five-line stanza known as the *lira*), his poetry evokes a landscape whose sensuously bucolic images and mythological allusions have forever changed the course of Spanish poetry. Indeed, Garcilaso might be considered the cornerstone on which modern Spanish verse has been built.

Following Garcilaso's lead, two schools of Castilian poets developed—one centered in Salamanca, and the other in Seville. Whereas the Salamancan group (known as El Broncense), headed by Francisco Sánchez, was known for moralistic and philosophical perspectives exemplified in the work of its most renowned poet, Luis de León, the Sevillan poets, whose outstanding figure was Fernando de Herrera, were known for their sensuous musicality and erudite knowledge of classical mythology. Both groups put unwavering faith in Aristotelian poetics: Art was to imitate nature, not the ephemeral happenings associated with the senses but the ideals and principles that lay hidden beneath the surface. Masters such as Horace, Vergil, and Petrarch served as models for the expression of universal themes.

Distinct from the schools of Salamanca and Seville but of equal quality was a specialized tradition, that of mystical verse. The Carmelite monk Saint John of the Cross (1542-1591) represents the zenith of this uniquely Spanish poetic expression. In his masterpiece, *Cántico espiritual* (c. 1577-1586; *A Spiritual Canticle of the Soul*, 1864, 1909), based on the Bible's Song of Solomon, he expressed with erotic intensity the soul's passionate quest for God. One can detect in the sensuous pastoral imagery produced by Saint John of the Cross the presence of Garcilaso's eclogues: Even the most religious of poets found himself enveloped within the growing Humanism of the Renaissance spirit.

The Renaissance not only reawakened an interest in classical mythology but also engendered a renewed sense of national identity. Unlike its neighbors to the west, Spain did not produce an epic comparable to Portugal's *Os Lusíadas* (1572; *The Lusiads*, 1655), by Luís de Camões. One of Spain's native sons, however, did record the heroic events involving the conquest of Chile. Alonso de Ercilla's *La Araucana* (1569-1590; English translation, 1945) sings the praises of both the conqueror and the vanquished. His vivid account of the heroic deeds accomplished by his Spanish comrades and the valiant defense of the proud Araucanian people places Ercilla y Zúñiga's poem alongside the other great epics of Western civilization.

SEVENTEENTH CENTURY

During the seventeenth century, as Spain's political and economic prowess began to show the first signs of vulnerability, the stylistic innovations first introduced into Spanish literature by Boscán and Garcilaso were embellished and brought to their ultimate poetic fruition—to the point of excess. The simplicity and clarity

Garcilaso de la Vega (©CORBIS)

of the Renaissance gradually gave way to the complexity and obscurity of the Baroque.

Encouraged by literary academies and an ever-increasing number of literary competitions, poets began to create newer and more unusual images, to experiment with traditional word order, and to search for subtler allusions. In particular, two main currents came to dominate seventeenth century poetic expression: *culteranismo* and *conceptismo*. The former is characterized by its emphasis on ornate and complex images, its revolutionary syntax, and its obscure mythological allusions; the latter is characterized by its intellectual and philosophical sophistication. The many puns and double entendres which one encounters in this poetry reveal the *conceptistas'* fundamental cynicism and disillusionment with life. For the *culteranistas*, beauty was to be found in the most complex of metaphors, whereas for the *conceptistas* truth was to be expressed in satire and wit.

Of the many poets associated with these two literary tendencies, four overshadow the others because of the quality and depth of their work. The driving force behind the *culterano* style of poetry was Luis de Góngora y Argote (1561-1627); his very name has become synonymous with intricately complex metaphors and tantalizingly obscure images. Góngora's influence on seventeenth century Spanish verse was monumental; like Garcilaso de la Vega a century earlier, Góngora was imitated by virtually all of his fellow poets, even those who were most vocal in their criticism of his stylistic intricacies.

Although the term Gongorism is frequently used today to describe a type of poetry characterized by excessive ornamentation and artificially complex syntax, Góngora himself was not guilty of such literary failings. The negative connotations associated with his name more accurately describe the many less gifted poets who attempted to emulate the master's unique gift for expressing beauty in startling metaphors that both dazzled and amazed the sensitive reader. His ability to juxtapose vibrant, concrete images in a world of poetic illusion makes his verse the high point of the Spanish Baroque.

In his two masterpieces, *Fábula de Polifemo y Galatea* (wr. 1613, pb. 1627; *Fable of Polyphemus and Galatea*, 1961) and *Soledades* (wr. 1613, pb. 1627; *The Solitudes*, 1964)—a projected series of four poems only one of which, written in 1613, was completed—Góngora contrasted human mutability with nature's lasting beauty and grandeur. His fable about Polyphemus and Galatea is based on a story found in Ovid's *Metamorphoses* (c. 8 C.E.; English translation, 1567), which recounts the love affair between Acis and Galatea. Acis is eventually killed by the jealous Cyclops, Polyphemus, but, through the intercession of the gods, the slain Acis is transformed into a stream. Góngora's version, although true to the original, is much more a celebration of nature's inherent dynamism and beauty than is Ovid's.

Góngora intended to write four *Solitudes* but died before completing his second. The first one describes a love-smitten youth, who, as he travels through the countryside, comes upon a pastoral wedding celebration. In the fragmentary second poem of the series, the young man is seen visiting with a seafaring family. Although their plot is a simple one, *The Solitudes* are rich in subtle allusions and bewildering syntax, which, once properly contemplated, lead the reader to a greater sense of nature's overpowering majesty.

If Góngora is remembered today because of the sheer perfection of his poetic technique, Lope de Vega Carpio (1562-1635) is remembered for his prodigious creative output. The great lyrical playwright of Spain's Golden Age, he also managed to compose more than sixteen hundred sonnets, several literary epics, ballads, and several volumes of miscellaneous verse. Vega Carpio's poetry is not as polished as Góngora's refined verse, but what it lacks in erudition and technical skill, it more than adequately possesses in spontaneity and flowing grace.

Still further removed from the ornate images of *culteranismo* was the epigrammatic style of Francisco Gómez de Quevedo y Villegas (1580-1645). Indeed, Quevedo was one of Góngora's most caustic critics. Unlike his rival, who tried to capture in words the beauty and dynamism of nature, Quevedo was fascinated by humanity's ugliness and corruption. Rejecting the sensuous style of the *culteranistas*, he preferred a more austere and elliptical mode of expression, filled with tersely worded puns, that reflected his cynical view of life. The satirical observations and witty wordplay that characterize his poetry exemplify the mode of poetic expression known as *conceptismo*. Quevedo's stoicism led him to employ poetry as an effective way to teach his fellow man about the ugly reality of life. If there is one principal theme running through Quevedo's poetry, it is *disengaño* (disillusionment): a total disenchantment with the things of this world.

Ironically, the poet who encompassed most fully the complexity and obscurity of seventeenth century Spanish verse did not live in Spain, but in New Spain (Mexico). Her name was Sor Juana Inés de la Cruz (1651-1695). In a society that favored men, Sor Juana was regarded as one of the New World's finest examples of seventeenth century Humanism. She explored the wonders of science, the mysteries of philosophy, and the marvels of art and literature. Nevertheless, she saw the highest achievements of Renaissance Humanism as ultimately futile. In her major poem, "Primer sueño" (first dream), she expressed, in true *culterano* style, the human mind's inability to grasp life's purpose by means of purely intellectual or aesthetic activity. Ultimately, for Sor Juana, the things of this world led to disillusionment. What began in the sixteenth century as a optimistic quest for truth and beauty, ended, at the close of the seventeenth century, with man's faith in himself deeply shaken if not shattered.

EIGHTEENTH CENTURY

As the eighteenth century approached, Spanish poetry, like the other major literary genres of the time, was in a state of decline. Poets, for the most part, attempted to imitate dominant styles of the seventeenth century. Just as political decline ultimately led to a change of royal families (the House of Bourbon inherited the Spanish throne in 1700), so, too, the decadence to which Spanish literature had fallen led to serious attempts at literary reform. For example, in 1713, the Royal Academy was founded with the responsibility of protecting and guiding the Spanish language, and was commissioned to produce an authoritative dictionary and grammar.

In 1732, there appeared a journal titled *Diario de los literatos de España* (diary of the writers of Spain),

which, until its demise in 1742, attempted to review and to evaluate the literary merit of all the books being printed in Spain at that time. In one of its last editions, it published a work titled *Sátira contra los malos escritores de este siglo* (satire against the poor writers of this century), which condemned the Baroque excesses associated with the poetry of the day. The inclusion of French terms in this critical diatribe suggests a knowledge of the French neoclassical critic, Nicolas Boileau-Despréaux.

The most significant evidence of literary reform, however, appeared in 1737 with the publication of Ignacio de Luzán's *La poética o reglas de la poesía* (poetics or rules of poetry). In it are criticized the inordinate use of artificially contrived metaphors, unnecessarily complex syntax, and unusually difficult puns characteristic of many contemporary poets. Rejecting the sophisticated cynicism of Gabriel Alvarez de Toledo (1662-1714) and the bitterly satirical language of Diego de Torres Villarroel (1694-1770), Luzán advocated a clear and concise language. Literature, besides pleasing and entertaining the reader, should instruct him. Above all, a literary work should exhibit good taste. Exaggeration, either in form or in content, was to be avoided, since order and symmetry best reflected the natural harmony existing within the universe.

Luzán's poetics, like those of his French counterpart, Boileau, were an attempt to return to the clear and measured writing which had characterized the ancient Greek and Latin poets. Whereas France looked more toward classical antiquity for its models, Spain rediscovered its own classical writers such as Garcilaso de la Vega and Luis de León.

The neoclassical reformation championed by Luzán did not begin to bear fruit until the second half of the eighteenth century. Of the many poets who followed the dictates of neoclassical good taste, Nicolás Fernández de Moratín Leandro Fernández de Moratín (1737-1780) was the most respected and influential. Known primarily for his innovative ideas and techniques in the field of drama, Moratín was a key figure in the popularization of Luzán's poetic theory. Moratín formed a group of writers known as the Tertulia de la fonda de San Sebastián, among whom were such leading literary figures as José Cadalso and Tomás de Iriarte.

From their literary soirées came some of the most important critical essays in support of the neoclassical style of writing.

Perhaps the most appropriate genre for expressing the neoclassical ideal of instructing while entertaining was the fable. At any rate, the second half of the eighteenth century saw the publication of two collections of fables, the second of which was a direct defense of Luzán's poetics. From 1781 to 1784, Félix María de Samaniego (1745-1801) published his *Fábulas morales* (moral fables), in which he imitated both classical and modern fabulists. In 1782, Tomás de Iriarte published his highly original *Fábulas literarias* (literary fables), in which he expressed his ideas on literature. In his fables focusing on poetry, he satirized those poets who disregarded the neoclassical call for clarity, order, and balance.

The eighteenth century neoclassical emphasis on order and sobriety clearly reflected the spirit of the times. The political and civil reforms instituted by the newly installed House of Bourbon established an atmosphere of well-being throughout the country. In particular, the highly progressive reign of Charles III (1759-1788), whose economic and social reforms helped instill within the Spanish people a newfound feeling of prosperity and stability based on intelligent planning and careful implementation of programs, supported the neoclassicists' demand for clear and orderly writing. Poetry, it was thought, like all meaningful elements of society, should not only amuse and distract but also provide the utilitarian function of instructing its citizenry. To the neoclassicists' chagrin, however, Charles III's well-ordered society soon found itself beset once again by turmoil and confusion. As the eighteenth century came to a close, the winds of change began to blow from within and without the Spanish borders, giving birth to a new literary mentality.

NINETEENTH CENTURY

The first two decades of the nineteenth century saw the total collapse of Spain's traditional political system, which is perhaps best described as a form of enlightened despotism. There followed an onslaught of radical political and social changes that combined to undermine the many years of apparent prosperity and stability associated with eighteenth century Bourbon Spain.

In 1807, heeding the unwise advice of his prime minister, Manuel de Godoy, Bourbon monarch Charles IV allowed Napoleon's forces to enter Spain (Napoleon's ostensible target was Portugal). Six years of foreign rule and a brutalizing civilian-led revolution followed Napoleon's entry into Spain. Once having ousted the foreign monarch (Joseph Bonaparte) and having restored the legitimate Bourbon heir (Ferdinand VII) to the Spanish throne, Spain experienced even greater political turmoil. Ferdinand ruled with the absolutism of his predecessors but lacked their vision and dedication. The liberal revolutionary groups that had fought so valiantly for restoration felt betrayed by their conservative monarch. After six years of absolutist rule, a coup d'état in 1820 ushered in three years of liberal reforms. With France's help, Ferdinand managed to regain his throne and ruled uncompromisingly until his death in 1833. After his death, although the pendulum was to swing in favor of the liberals, Spain suffered no less than three civil wars (the Carlist Wars) over royal succession. What was once a well-organized and well-integrated society soon found itself polarized into opposing camps: *afrancesados* (French supporters) versus those in favor of restoration, absolutists versus constitutionalists, conservatives versus liberals. The resulting chaos found its intellectual and aesthetic expression in the Romantic movement, which reflected both in its form and in its content the turbulent reality of early nineteenth century Spain.

In the field of Spanish poetry, two men in particular foreshadowed the literary revolution of the nineteenth century. Manuel José Quintana (1772-1857) and Juan Nicasio Gallego (1777-1853), although trained in the rigors of neoclassicism, infused new vigor into their verse by unabashedly singing the praises of their homeland. Quintana, in his "A España" ("Ode to Spain"), and Gallego, in his "Al dos de Mayo" (to the second of May), took the first steps in the transition from a poetics dominated by reason to one that was primarily an expression of deep emotion.

Not until Ferdinand VII's death, however, did Spanish poetry begin to free itself in earnest from the artificial bonds imposed on it by the neoclassical demand for moderation in the name of good taste. With Isabel II's accession to the throne in 1833, many of the liberals who were formerly living in exile in England, France, and Germany returned to Spain, bringing with them a radically uninhibited style of poetry.

Nineteenth century Romanticism was unquestionably a love affair with freedom. It was a direct response to and rejection of the literary norms of the day. Like most reactions, however, it frequently defined itself in terms of what it rejected. Since eighteenth century neoclassicism produced a poetry refined by reason, Romanticism strived to express a poetry unshackled by reason's tyranny. In its place, the Romantics exalted human feelings, emotions, instincts, intuition, and imagination—all of those qualities that had waited so long to be liberated. The freedom of the Romantics, therefore, was a freedom from the established rules of society, be they political, social, or aesthetic. Like Ferdinand VII's political tyranny, which ultimately coerced the majority of liberals to search for a means of escape via self-imposed exile, so, too, reason's tyranny over free poetic expression ultimately led the young Romantics to seek refuge by escaping into private worlds, unencumbered by the demands and responsibilities that society exacts from its members.

Although the Romantic movement, which dominated the first half of the nineteenth century in Spain, produced many fine poets, three are of major literary importance: Ángel de Saavedra (better known by his title, Duque de Rivas, 1791-1865), José de Espronceda (1803-1842), and José Zorrilla y Moral (1817-1893). These three men revolutionized both the form and content of nineteenth century Spanish poetry.

Ángel de Saavedra, in his *Romances históricos* (1841; historical ballads), turned the focus of Spanish verse from the ancient Greek and Latin myths to Spain's own heroic past. Rejecting the artificial syntax and latinized vocabulary of previous generations, he captured his country's customs in a lively language that complemented its exciting history.

Accompanying their interest in Spain's glorious past was the Romantics' fondness for expressing intimately personal feelings. One of Spain's greatest lyric poets, José de Espronceda expressed more vividly than most his deepest emotions. One notes immediately, both in his disregard for traditional forms and in his rebellious themes and motifs, his unbounded love of freedom and spontaneity. Five poems in particular manifest his almost adolescent contempt for any form of coercion. In his "Canción del pirata" ("Song of the Pirate"), "Canto del cosaco" (cossack's song), "El mendigo" ("The Beggar"), "El reo de muerte" ("The Condemned to Die"), and "El Verdugo" ("The Headsman"), he expressed a deep desire to be freed from society's dominion over the individual. In his later work, "A Jarifa en una orgía" ("To Harifa, in an Orgy"), one of the most pessimistic poems ever composed in the Spanish language, he views death as the only path to freedom.

From Zorrilla, known today principally for his dramatic reworking of Tirso de Molina's *El burlador de Sevilla* (1630; *The Trickster of Seville*, 1923), titled *Don Juan Tenorio* (1844; English translation, 1944), Spain received not only some of its most beautiful lyric poetry but also a series of legends that recorded many of the memorable deeds associated with Spain's colorful and turbulent past.

As the political turmoil of the first half of the nineteenth century gradually subsided and Spanish society once again began to experience relative stability, poetic expression showed signs of losing much of its revolutionary fervor. During the latter half of the nineteenth century, poetry became less lyrical as it attempted to involve itself with philosophical, political, and social questions being discussed in the novel, the recently rediscovered genre whose popularity was rapidly increasing. In an effort to be more relevant, poets such as Ramón de Campoamor (1817-1901) and Gaspar Núñez de Arce (1832-1903) began to focus on philosophical and social issues.

Two notable exceptions to that trend were the Andalusian poet Gustavo Adolfo Bécquer (1836-1870) and the Galician poet Rosalía de Castro (1837-1885). In many ways, their delicate lyricism bridged the high-spirited and spontaneous verse of Romanticism with the subtler subjectivism associated with Symbolism and the measured plasticity of Parnassianism.

In particular, Bécquer might be considered the culmination of the Romantic movement, inasmuch as his *Rimas* (1871; *Poems*, 1891; better known as *The Rhymes*, 1898) expressed the most intimate of feelings. In a sense, Bécquer's verse is Romanticism come of age. Whereas Espronceda's raison d'être as a poet lay in his puerile attempt to escape the harsher realities of life by vicariously experiencing, through his verse, the imagined lives of such exotic personalities as a gun-toting pirate, an arrogant beggar, and a defiant prisoner, Bécquer drew from the springs of his own soul to express a precise, melodic language that ultimately transcended words—Beauty, Love, Poetic Creation. With delicate nuances of light and color, sound and rhythm, he created some of the most beautiful images in Spanish poetry.

TWENTIETH CENTURY: 1898-1936

European Romanticism during the latter part of the nineteenth century had been dominated by Bécquer. During his reign, Romanticism attained a particularly Spanish style. Current European literary trends, including French liberalism, had influenced Spanish Romantic poets. Bécquer's style eventually gave way to *costumbrismo*, the depiction of customs and manners, and realism replaced Romanticism as prose began to become the dominant form. Realism characterized Spanish prose fiction during the early twentieth century.

The literary movements of the *fin de siglo* passage from the nineteenth to the twentieth century were marked by political, philosophical, and artistic turbulence. In 1898, Spain lost its last colonies. Since the seventeenth century, Spain's expansionism had been in decline. The *generación del 98*, or Generation of '98, rose as both a literary and a philosophical movement of writers who referred to 1898 as a turning point in Spanish society. They searched for causes of its decline and ways to regain their nation's past glories. Together, the Generation of '98 and the *generación del 27*, or Generation of '27, created a kind of Silver Age that approached the literary and artistic excellence of the masters of the Spanish Golden Age. This era of literary brilliance and prolific creative activity reigned until 1936, stifled by the onset of the Spanish Civil War.

Literary influences shifted from *costumbrismo* and

realism to *Modernismo*, similar to French Symbolism, and artistic and musical impressionism. A group of young writers at the turn of the century proclaimed a moral and cultural rebirth for their defeated homeland. Through studying the simplicity and austerity of Castilian life, these writers found the essence of Spain. They sought to portray it through a direct and compact style. The literary association rejected most European literary and aesthetic trends, but embraced political liberalism.

The Basque poet and prose writer Miguel de Unamuno y Jugo (1864-1936) anticipated the essential themes of existentialism. Unamuno believed that the personal aspects of history were eternal because they sustain the temporal events of public history. This concept of *intrahistoria* permeates his poems. Their symbolic elements acquire universal relevance as they relate to the Spanish experience between 1898 and 1936. After a spiritual crisis reflected in *En torno al casticismo* (1902), Unamuno sought to identify a popular protagonist. This "intrahistorical" way of life defined the Spanish spirit for his literary as well as spiritual generation.

Azorín (José Martínez Ruiz, 1873-1967) coined the phrase *generación del 98*. In his overriding goal to define the eternal qualities of Spanish life, he depicted the Castilian people and countryside with impressionistic sensitivity that captured the beauty of ordinary life. His poetry acquired an original musicality rooted in folk songs. His poetry's lyrical quality results from an adept application of rhyme and meter. Azorín is best known for his novels, but he promoted the works of poets whose idealism rebelled against bourgeois styles and themes.

Antonio Machado (1875-1939) founded modern Spanish poetry by blending symbolism with profound meditations on time and place and concern for the nation's future. His original voice paved the way for the poets of the Generation of '27 to experiment with rhyme and meter in order to express their particular voice. His poems are lucid meditations that evoke a harsh yet sharply defined Spanish landscape. *Campos de Castilla* (1912; *The Castilian Camp*, 1982) was inspired by his wife. The transition from lyricism to reflection is evident in the 1924 publication of *Nuevas canciones* (new songs), which followed *Soledades, galerías, y otros poemas* (1907; *Solitudes, Galleries, and Other Poems*, 1987). Together, they paint the Castilian landscape with clarity and sonority. He also wrote plays and translated French literature with his brother, the poet Manuel Machado (1874-1947). Tragedy marked his later works: Machado's wife died after five years of marriage from a sudden illness. Antonio died in 1939 while fleeing from the Spanish Civil War with his brother and mother, all exiled loyalists and victims of the national tragedy.

Juan Ramón Jiménez (1881-1958) wrote symbolic poetry. Over time, he developed an abstract and complex lyricism. He expanded the limits of language to convey truth through nature's images. A later stage of his work evidences his images whittled away to their essence. In *Platero y yo* (*Platero and I*, 1956), published to popular acclaim in 1914, a young poet is followed by a donkey during his reveries and idyllic journeys. Other works demonstrate the transformation and maturity of his style and structure. *Eternidades* in 1918 and *Belleza* in 1923 contemplated the changing face of beauty. He did not publish new works until the outbreak of the Spanish Civil War, when General Francisco Franco sent him to the United States as a cultural attaché. He taught at the University of Maryland and University of Puerto Rico until his wife's death in 1956, soon after he had won the Nobel Prize. His last major work, *Dios deseando y deseante* (1964), identifies with a universal consciousness that seeks beauty in nature.

The Generation of '98 initiated a cultural revival, an ongoing literary movement that gained momentum as it was energized by the new wave of writers after 1927 until the outbreak of civil war in 1936. As literary revisionists, they were responsible for the renewal of Spanish themes and traditions as they exposed their nation to European modernity.

The transition to the twentieth century inevitably led to European cultural influences, despite Iberian isolationism. José Ortega y Gasset (1883-1955) criticized the "Europeanization" of Spain with a landmark essay, *La deshumanización del arte* (1925; *The Dehumanization of Art*, 1948), which criticizes literary realism. According to Ortega y Gasset, the Industrial Revolution of the early nineteenth century led to the confusion of life with art so that art represented reality. Through the method of dehumanization, the narrative and descriptive elements of literature are removed and devalued. This approached the avant-garde European movements such as Futurism, creating a marginal literature that gained popularity during the first decades of the twentieth century. Spanish translations of works by James Joyce, Maxim Gorky, André Gide, and Marcel Proust were popular.

The tercentenary of the death of the Golden Age master poet Góngora began a new poetic age. Literary as well as artistic genius coincided in Madrid during the second decade of the new era. The surrealist Catalonian artist Salvador Dalí (1904-1989) lived and worked with Zaragozan Luis Buñuel (1900-1983) and Federico García Lorca in the Residencia de Estudiantes (student residence) area in Madrid. The intellectual atmosphere was fed by the creative geniuses of several more residents in this neighborhood. The group of poets known as the Generation of '27 was founded in this creative community. Not since the seventeenth century's Golden Age had such a preeminent group of poets come together. Jorge Guillén (1893-1984), García Lorca (1898-1936), Pedro Salinas (1891-1951), Rafael Alberti (1902-1999), Vicente Aleixandre (1898-1984), Dámaso Alonso (1898-1990), Luis Cernuda (1902-1963), and Gerardo Diego (1896-1987) were among the major poets.

Several literary movements characterized this generation. The European avant-garde and cinematographic realism inspired them stylistically. French Symbolism and Eastern European Dadaism influenced their approaches to art and its role in society. The concept of art for art's sake gained acceptance. As a result, art was dehumanized. The role of the symbol or metaphor was not transcendent, but ephemeral. The metaphor was elevated to serve a central temporal function in poetry. This symbolic impact had political implications. During the first phase of the movement, from 1920 to 1927, the poets distinguished themselves from their predecessors with their new poetic vision. During the second phase, from 1927 to 1936, their poems were politically motivated. The creation of the Second Republic and weakening of the bourgeoisie inspired them politically to envision a societal and aesthetic revolution in which art was the patrimony of the people.

The most emblematic poet and dramatist with enduring international prominence is García Lorca. From 1919 until his death, García Lorca devoted himself to creative activity in the Residencia de Estudiantes. *Flamenco andaluz* and the Gypsy culture influenced his poetry. His publication of *Romancero gitano, 1924-1927* (1928; *The Gypsy Ballads of García Lorca*, 1951, 1953) gained for him international fame. A few years later he visited New York and related the similarities between the spirituals of Harlem and the *cante jondo*, or deep song of the Gypsy culture. The collections *Poema del cante jondo* (1931; *Poem of the Gypsy Seguidilla*, 1967) and *Poeta en Nueva York* (1940; *Poet in New York*, 1940, 1955) resulted from his American experience. He established the theater company La Barraca, which toured throughout Spain. At the outbreak of the Spanish Civil War, Franquista soldiers tortured and murdered García Lorca soon after assassinating his brother-in-law, the mayor of Granada. His poems and plays were burned and banned until the end of Franco's reign.

The Spanish Civil War destroyed many of these poets' utopian dreams as well as their lives. García Lorca's assassination by the Franquistas came to symbolize the destruction of the creative hopes of the nation. Alberti, Cernuda, Salinas, Guillén, Rosa Chacel, and María Zambrano were forced into exile. The nation torn apart by Franco's brutal and intolerant fascist regime was gradually regenerated after almost fifty years of *franquismo*. Despite the domestic tragedies, the nation's banished intellectuals were extraordinarily prolific in exile.

Vicente Aleixandre, winner of the Nobel Prize in 1977, was the lone member of the Generation of '27 to remain in Spain during *franquismo*. He served as mentor and spiritual guide for the succeeding postwar generation. In 1933, he won Spain's national prize for literature. His greatest work, which led to his nomination for the Nobel Prize, was *Sombra del paraíso* (1944; *Shadow of Paradise*, 1987). Aleixandre's imagery of human pain and horror contrasts with that of the immutable power and harsh reality of nature. Loss, sorrow, and despair characterize this stage of poetic production.

Without overtly political imagery, the Spanish Civil War experience was acutely portrayed. Aleixandre's later works revealed elements of Surrealism. This technique enabled him to escape from the desolation of a paradise lost and envision a peaceful and whole Spain.

Alonso developed the concept of "poetry for the people." He communicated with the reader by abandoning the ivory tower and humanizing his poetry. Alonso used free verse, lexical variation, and rationalism that countered the trend toward Surrealist poetry. His major works include *Poemas puros: Poemillas de la ciudad* (1921) influenced by the work of Jiménez and Machado, and *Hijos de la ira* (1944), an intellectual inquiry into the role of humans in society and into their relationship to God. In his final work, *Duda de amor sobre el Ser Supremo* (1985), Alonso reflects upon his imminent death and the eternal nature of the soul.

The poetry of Salinas can be divided into three stages. His early work includes *Presagios* (1923), influenced by Jiménez. *Fábula y signo* (1931) begins the reference to the "beloved" in order to continue a quest toward attaining higher goals through his poetic voice. His second phase is characterized by love poetry: *La voz a tí debida* (1933; *My Voice Because of You*, 1976) and *Razón de amor* (1936), in which love is reinvented. The concept of "I" and "you" is redefined by the interplay of words. For Salinas, to love was to live within each other. During the third stage of his poetic evolution, Salinas was concerned with the role of the poet and the philosophical search for permanence through art. In *El contemplado* (1946; *The Sea of San Juan: A Contemplation*, 1950), he contemplated the sea through a series of philosophical reflections. In *Todo más claro y otros poemas* (1949), Salinas conducted a dialogue with nature and, in "Cero," contemplated the horrors of human nature.

Guillén wrote a series of poetry in five sections collected over thirty years as *Cántico: Fe de vida* (1928, 1936, 1945, 1950; *Canticle*, 1997). The series reflects his faith in a life centered in nature. *Clamor: Tiempo de historia* (1957-1963; includes *Maremágnum*, 1957; *Que van a dar en el mar*, 1960; and *A la altura de las circunstancias*, 1963), translated in 1997 as *Clamor*, reflects on human history and the fall of humanity into chaos. *Homenaje* (1967; *Homage*, 1997) reflects on the generous nature of art to forgive and eventually conquer human frailties.

The poetry of Cernuda serves as a biography of his lifelong spiritual journey. In *Perfil del aire* (1927) he follows the model of Bécquer as he expresses internal and external realities. *Un río, un amor* (1929) displays Surrealist characteristics, and here he laments the absence of love. The pessimistic tone of *Donde habite el olvido* (1934) reflects the predominant theme, the death of love. Cernuda's *Invocaciones* (1935) seeks to evade reality; here the poet's pessimism leads him to fall into the depths of despair.

Diego developed his own style of creationist poetry. Creationist techniques dominate in *Imagen* (1922). He won the Premio Nacional de Literatura after publishing *Versos humanos* (1925; human verses). In honor of his poetic icon Góngora, Diego published *Antología poética en honor de Góngora* (1927). Góngora's influence is evident in Diego's postwar work *Alondra de verdad* (1941; lark of truth). These later sonnets paid homage to their Golden Age models as they followed traditional patterns of rhyme and meter rather than the creationist forms and syntax of Diego's early poems.

MID-TWENTIETH CENTURY ONWARD

Miguel Hernández (1910-1942) represents the transition from the Generation of '27 to the succeeding generation. His poetry was influenced by the Golden Age genius Góngora. Henández blended formal structure with surreal imagery. He befriended García Lorca, Aleixandre, and the Chilean poet Pablo Neruda, among others. After serving with the losing army of the Republicanos during the Spanish Civil War, Hernández fled to Portugal. He was captured and imprisoned until his death. When offered his freedom only if he would be exiled forever from Spain, Hernández refused. His most original poetry, written while in prison, reveals unwavering compassion and faith in the human spirit. It was published posthumously as *Cancionero y romancero de ausencias* (1958; *Songbook of Absences*, 1972).

Writers within Spain during *franquismo* either went along with Franco's political policies or devoted their creative energy to resistance. Luis Rosales (1910-1992) and Leopoldo Panero (1909-1962) wrote insular poetry with aesthetic objectives. Blas de Otero (1916-1979), Gabriel Celaya (1911-1991), and José Hierro (born 1922) were influenced by Social Realism.

Salvador Espriu (1910-1992) was stylistically influenced by the avant-garde in his prose poems characterized by nationalist themes. The group of *Novísimos* ("very recent ones") experimented with avant-garde poetry and developed a particular style. This regional literary and philosophical movement was led by José María Castellet, a Catalonian critic. The *Novísimo* phenomenon represents the politicized literary milieu of the postwar generation. Major poets were Catalonian Socialists who considered Barcelona the center of avant-garde creativity. The Editorial Seix Barral supported their efforts by publishing and distributing their poetry and prose.

Spain lacks a literary tradition for women writers. Some twentieth century women poets and prose writers have distinguished themselves, despite the success of their male counterparts. The philosopher, essayist, and poet María Zambrano (1904-1991) and novelist and poet Rosa Chacel (1898-1994) have distinguished themselves among their male literary peers with many national honors.

The women writers during the Republic include Chacel and Mercè Rodoreda (born 1908). Women who wrote during *franquismo* include Carmen Laforet (born 1921), Ana María Matute (born 1926), Elena Quiroga (1921-1995), and Carmen Martín Gaite (born 1925). In her essay "Hipótesis sobre una escritura diferente" (hypothesis about a different writing), Marta Traba finds a textual difference between the works of male and female writers. She finds that feminine poetics link images rather than endow them with symbolic value. Their poetry is more concerned with explanations rather than with interpretations of the universe. Feminine text depends on the impetus of detail to convey meaning. Another feminist critic, Carme Riera, finds stylistic and thematic tendencies in feminine writing. The interplay between subject and object, syntactic repetition, greater lexical variance, and thematic commonalities is addressed by female poets.

Since 1979, the definitive end of the Franco era, poetry production has been more identified with cultural and linguistic groups than by nationalist interests. Catalonia, Galicia, and the Basque provinces have created poetry with regional rather than centralized national identities.

BIBLIOGRAPHY

Bellver, Catherine G. *Absence and Presence: Spanish Women Poets of the Twenties and Thirties*. Lewisburg, Pa.: Bucknell University Press, 2001. The reception of major women poets of Spain is examined from a feminist perspective. The work and literary status of Concha Méndez, Josefina de la Torre, Rosa Chacel, Carmen Conde, Ernestina de Champourcin, Blanca Andréu, and others are analyzed within their social and historical contexts.

Davis, Elizabeth B. *Myth and Identity in the Epic of Imperial Spain*. Columbia: University of Missouri Press, 2000. Davis discusses the cultural role of the epic poem during the era of Spanish Imperialism. The political implications of the genre as well as the transition into the Baroque literary styles and cultural values are explored.

Flitter, Derek. *Spanish Romantic Literary Theory and Criticism*. New York: Cambridge University Press, 1992. Uses detailed summaries of articles by nineteenth century critics to prove that Spanish Romantic writers were inspired by traditional, Christian elements in German Romantic thought.

Florit, Eugenio, ed. *Introduction to Spanish Poetry*. New York: Dover, 1991. Contains thirty-seven poems in Spanish with English translation on facing pages, along with biographical and critical commentary. Illustrated.

Fox, Gwyn. *Subtle Subversions: Reading Golden Age Sonnets by Iberian Women*. Washington, D.C.: Catholic University of America Press, 2008. In their sonnets, five seventeenth century women in Spain and Portugal were able to voice their feelings about the patriarchal system that denied them education and the most basic rights.

Gies, David T., ed. *The Cambridge History of Spanish Literature*. New York: Cambridge University Press, 2009. A comprehensive English-language work, prepared by Gies in collaboration with forty-six other eminent scholars. Includes chronology and index.

Glendinning, Nigel. "The Eighteenth Century." In *A Literary History of Spain*. New York: Barnes & Noble, 1972. Discusses the eighteenth century and literature in Spain at length; includes information on poetry.

Griffin, Nigel, et al., eds. *The Spanish Ballad in the Golden Age: Essays for David Pattison*. Rochester, N.Y.: Tamesis, 2008. Nine poems are analyzed in detail in order to demonstrate how a knowledge of contemporary references and allusions aids in understanding such works.

Mudrovic, W. Michael. *Mirror, Mirror on the Page: Identity and Subjectivity in Spanish Women's Poetry, 1975-2000*. Bethlehem, Pa.: Lehigh University Press, 2009. Analyses of eight poems by Spanish women, showing how each writer identifies with and differs from a female figure in the text. A revealing study, focusing as it does on works produced in the new, democratic era that followed the fall of Franco.

St. Martin, Hardie, ed. *Roots and Wings: Poetry from Spain, 1900-1975*. Buffalo, N.Y.: White Pine Press, 2004. A reissue of a landmark bilingual anthology, containing works by thirty major Spanish poets, translated by highly acclaimed American poets.

Soufas, C. Christopher. *The Subject in Question: Early Contemporary Spanish Literature and Modernism*. Washington, D.C.: Catholic University of America Press, 2007. The first systematic study of Spanish modernism, arguing that Spanish thinkers had adopted modernist theories long before the movement reached the rest of Europe. The poetry of Jorge Guillén, Vicente Aleixandre, Luis Cernuda, and Rafael Alberti is discussed at length.

Walters, Gareth. *The Cambridge Introduction to Spanish Poetry*. New York: Cambridge University Press, 2003. Bilingual edition. A survey of Iberian and Latin American writing from the Middle Ages to the present. Conveniently arranged by genres and themes. Bibliography and index.

West-Settle, Cecile, and Sylvia Sherno, eds. *Contemporary Spanish Poetry: The Word and the World*. Madison, N.J.: Fairleigh Dickinson University

Press, 2005. A collection of essays on the theory and practice of various contemporary poets. Bibliographical references and index.

Wilcox, John. *Women Poets of Spain, 1860-1990: Toward a Gynocentric Vision*. Urbana: University of Illinois Press, 1997. This study focuses on often-overlooked women poets who have contributed to literary movements as well as developed original poetic voices. Poets include Rosalía de Castro, Francisca Aguirre, Carmen Conde, and Clara Janés. Contemporary poets include Amparo Amorós, Ana Rosetti, and Blanca Andréu.

Richard Keenan
Updated by Carole A. Champagne

TIBETAN POETRY

Tibetans refer to their country as the "Land of Snows," and this name accurately conveys the remoteness, mystery, and beauty of the land that contains the world's highest mountain, Everest (or "Goddess Mother of the Snows" in Tibetan). Tibet continues to be, even in the twenty-first century, nearly geographically and politically isolated. Tibet, an autonomous region of the People's Republic of China, covers an area of approximately 500,000 square miles. By contrast, historical Tibet—the region over which the cultural, religious, and frequently political influence of Tibet extended—encompassed roughly double that area and included all the highland plateaus between the Himalayan mountain range in the south and the Altyn Tagh and Kunlun ranges in the north.

The Tibetan Empire was established prior to the seventh century C.E., and recorded Tibetan history begins with the reign of Srong-brtsan sgam-po, who ruled Tibet from 620 to 649. Through its military campaigns, Tibet came into contact with a number of civilizations which had an immediate and profound influence on Tibetan culture. The religions and cultures of Iran, Gilgit, Kashmir, Turfan, Khotan, China, and, perhaps most important, the Buddhist kingdoms of northern India, all had an impact on the development of Tibetan civilization.

Tibetans attribute the invention of their alphabet to Thonmi Sambhota, a minister of Srong-brtsan sgam-po. The king first sent a group of Tibetans to India to study Indian alphabets to develop an alphabet suited to the Tibetan language, but this group met with failure. Srong-brtsan sgam-po then sent Thonmi to India. Thonmi's success is attested by the epithet "Sam-bho-ta" ("Excellent Tibetan"), given him by his Indian teachers, and by the attribution to his authorship of eight books, only two of which are extant, on the subject of Tibetan grammar and scripts.

The Tibetan language, part of the Sino-Tibetan language family, is a monosyllabic language with no inflection of verbs or nouns. The alphabet that Thonmi devised for Tibetan includes thirty consonants and four vowels and is written from left to right. Thonmi

adapted his alphabet from a Kashmiri model and fashioned two styles of script: The *dbu-can* (literally, "having a head") script is most frequently used in printed books, while the cursive script, *dbu-med* (literally, "without a head"), is used in documents, letters, and some books. Later, a more stylized cursive called *khyug-yig* (literally, "running script"), was developed and used for correspondence as well as for official documents.

The format of Tibetan books also followed an Indian model, the *pothi*: Tibetan books were printed on oblong pages and kept unbound between two wooden covers, which were frequently decorated with carvings or with polychrome paintings. Tibetan manuscripts were frequently adorned with illuminations of the Buddha or of various religious teachers, done in gouache; these manuscripts were often written in an ink made of ground gold or silver. Tibetan printed books were produced by means of hand-carved printing blocks or, less frequently, metal plates. Because an individual block or plate was required for each page of a work, the expense of producing a Tibetan book was considerable, and vast warehouses were required for the storage of printing blocks. The religious nature of Tibetan literature, however, transformed the labor and expense of book printing into an act of religious devotion. The colophons of Tibetan books customarily record the names of carvers, artists, editors, and patrons whose dedicated labor and financial support made the production of such books possible and gained spiritual merit for the participating individuals.

The actual printing of Tibetan books was supervised by the monasteries which owned the appropriate printing blocks, and it was customary for books to be printed only on demand. The customer generally was responsible for providing the necessary paper and was naturally expected to compensate the monastery for the labor involved in printing and, just as important, checking the finished edition for completeness and legibility. The paper of Tibetan books is frequently toxic, a result of the use of poisonous plants, notably several species of daphne, in its production, and of the practice of adding arsenic to the paper to discourage its destruction by insects. Extant catalogs (*kar-chag*) of many monastic printing houses are of enormous value in the study of Tibetan literary history. Manuscripts, particularly those with ornamental writing and illuminations, were produced up to the present century and were particularly favored by wealthy, if only marginally literate, patrons. Such manuscripts were most frequently copies of various editions of well-known Buddhist works, such as the *Prajnyaparamita* (perfection of wisdom), and were usually consigned to the altar of a wealthy individual to serve as an object of veneration, to be read only when a visiting monk was commissioned to read or chant the text.

RELIGION AND TIBETAN LITERATURE

Although Tibet enjoys a rich tradition of folk literature, the bulk of Tibetan literature is religious, representing the country's two major religions, Buddhism and Bonpo, the latter a pre-Buddhist Tibetan religion incorporating some elements of indigenous folk beliefs as well as influences from the religions of other countries, such as Iran. A significant amount of Buddhist literature consists of translations from the Indian Buddhist canon. The Tibetan *bKa'-'gyur* (also known as *Kanjur*), which is considered to contain the actual teachings of the Buddha, consists of 108 volumes, while the *bsTan-'gyur* (also known as *Tanjur*), which contains the orthodox textual exegesis of the *bKa'-'gyur*, contains 225 volumes.

The indigenous religious literature of Tibet is immeasurably vast and rich, including works which deal not only with religion and philosophy but also with history, medicine, science, grammar, astrology, divination, and the techniques of crafts, such as painting and the casting of bronze images. The collected works (*gsung-'bum*) of many important Tibetan religious figures are, in fact, encyclopedic in their contents and contain, in addition to learned discourses on the topics mentioned, a wealth of information in the form of correspondence and private biographical writings.

Tibetan literature abounds with a variety of minor religious genres that parallel those of medieval Europe, such as the hagiography, the pilgrimage guide, the exemplum, and the mystical visionary account. The *'das-log* genre, which deals specifically with visionary accounts of the journey to the underworld, is particularly rich in its correspondences, not only to similar visionary literature in the writings of medieval Christian saints but also to similar themes in many epic and folk traditions throughout the world.

The influence of earlier literary and oral traditions is often evident in Tibetan literature, particularly in the hagiographic literature. In addition to containing motifs and themes which clearly derive from a folk tradition, such works sometimes alternate passages of prose and verse, in which religious teachings are presented in the form of didactic poetry. The *Hundred-Thousand Songs* of the Tibetan poet and saint Milarepa (1040-1123) is the best-known example of such a work.

The provenance of many early Tibetan religious works, particularly those of the Buddhist *rNying-ma* (old ones) school and many works in the Bonpo tradition, is obscure. An entire genre called *gTer-ma* ("treasure") is purported to be the work of various historical (and sometimes mythical) religious personages and to have been unearthed by later religious masters called *gTer-bston* ("revealers of treasure"). The *Bar-do thos-sgrol* (book that grants liberation in the place between death and rebirth merely by its hearing, commonly called *The Tibetan Book of the Dead* in Western translations) is such a work and is attributed to the eighth century Indian Tantric master Padmasambhava, who is venerated as one of the two major founders of Tibetan Buddhism.

The Tibetan Book of the Dead is perhaps the best-known Tibetan work in the West, although it is far from representative of the many genres and schools of Tibetan literature. The book contains teachings that guide the deceased person through the transitory illusions that appear after death. These illusions serve to confirm the individual's belief in the existence of his or her individual ego, binding the individual to the cycle of death, rebirth, and suffering, which, in the Buddhist view, prevents one's entry into the state of nirvana. In *The Tibetan Book of the Dead*, poetic prayers alternate with admonitions and instructions in prose, both couched in an archaic style. Despite the book's title, which seems to guarantee its efficacy if it is simply read to the deceased, most Tibetan religious teachers insist that its contents must be internalized over years of serious study, so that one's responses to the illusions of *The Tibetan Book of the Dead* are both spontaneous and deliberate.

Since *The Tibetan Book of the Dead* contains several references to deities that may be of Bonpo origin, it is frequently supposed that much early Tibetan Buddhist literature, particularly of the rNying-ma sect, is suffused with non-Buddhist (that is, Bonpo, animist, or even shamanistic) ideas. This view does little justice to the seriousness with which the Tibetans translated Indian Buddhist works and ignores the system through which teams of highly educated monks proofread editions of religious works prior to their publication. Although Buddhist teachers were willing to accommodate the indigenous Tibetan deities, who were converted to the status of "Protectors of the [Buddhist] Religion" by Padmasambhava and other religious masters, the correct doctrinal content of Buddhist literary works was scrupulously maintained. Thus, the view that Tibetan Buddhism represents an unorthodox version of Buddhism (often labeled "Lamaism") is inaccurate and misleading.

It is evident that many of the similarities of Bonpo and Buddhist literature derive from a Bonpo imitation of the script, style, and genres of Buddhist literature brought to Tibet from India. Although the Bonpo religion had a rich tradition of its own, the existence of a Bonpo literature before the advent of Buddhism in Tibet is doubtful. The Bonpo possess several of their own specialized scripts, but the majority of these scripts clearly derive from the cursive Tibetan alphabet. The language of these texts is exceedingly complex, partly because of the custom of writing in an abbreviated form (in which several letters of certain words may be omitted) and partly because the vocabulary of Bonpo writings contains words of Zhang-zhung, rather than Tibetan, origin. Zhang-zhung was an area that lay to the west of Tibet in the Himalayas; it was at one time an independent country with its own language, and it was there that gShen-rab, the founder of the Bonpo religion, is believed to have lived. When the area was incorporated into the Tibetan state in the late eighth century, the language and script of the Tibetan Empire were

adopted. The writings of the Bonpo religion, which flourished in Zhang-zhung, were thus translated into Tibetan and naturally followed the stylistic pattern of Buddhist writings. The Bonpo possess an extensive literature, including their own versions of the *bKa'-'gyur* and *bsTan-'gyur*.

The first period of Buddhist development in Tibet, initiated by its establishment as the state religion in 779, lasted until the reign of Glang-dar-ma, who ruled Tibet from 838 to 842 and who restored Bonpo as the official state religion. This period signaled the decline of Tibet as an imperial power in Inner Asia and witnessed the persecution of Buddhists and the return to a state of feudal anarchy. The establishment of the state of Gu-ge in western Tibet in the late ninth century marked a return to both political stability and Buddhism. This period is known as the "second introduction" of Buddhism to Tibet, and the vital link with Indian Buddhist teachers and monasteries played a central role. Countless Tibetans made the rigorous and expensive journey to India to learn Buddhist doctrine directly from eminent Indian Buddhist masters, and on their return to Tibet, many of these individuals naturally attracted their own disciples. The groups that formed in this manner developed their own particular literatures and liturgies. Each was Buddhist, but each had a peculiar identity shaped by the characteristics of its founder.

In this fashion, a number of Buddhist schools developed in Tibet: The bKa'-rgyud-pa school was founded by Mar-pa (1012-1096); the Sa-skya-pa school was founded by 'Khon-dkon-mchog rGyal-po in 1073; and so on. Several of these schools played a major role in both the internal and the external politics of Tibet. In the thirteenth century, the Sa-skya-pa school had a central role in Tibet's relations with the Mongol Empire, and in 1642, the control of secular power in the Tibetan state was transferred to a religious leader, the Dalai Lama (a Mongolian epithet meaning "Religious Teacher [whose knowledge is as vast as the] Ocean"). Thereafter, ecclesiastical rule (often, and inexactly, called a "theocracy") was to continue in Tibet until the Fourteenth Dalai Lama's flight from Tibet to India during the Chinese annexation of Tibet in 1959.

PRE-BUDDHIST FOLK LITERATURE

Both the Tibetan Buddhists and the Bonpo distinguish the period preceding the Tibetan imperial period as the time in which the *mi-chos* (religion of humans) flourished, in contrast to the later period in which Buddhism and Bonpo, which share the common label of *lha-chos* (divine religion), came to Tibet. The literature of this period consisted mainly of two genres: the *lde'u*, or riddle and the *sgrung* (sometimes called *sgrung-gtam*), a narrative legend or fable.

These early works dealt chiefly with creation legends and traditional codes of behavior. The *lde'u* are essentially proverbs that carry a moral message, while the *sgrung* are tales composed by storytellers and based on the earliest myths and legends of the Tibetan people. The language of these works is frequently complex, and the abundance of often obscure metaphors increases the difficulty of understanding such texts. Nevertheless, these texts are of great interest, since they represent an archaic body of writings which obviously had a basis in an oral tradition.

Some of the most striking examples of such literature are found in the ancient literary fragments unearthed at Dunhuang, an oasis city in the western part of the Chinese province of Gansu. Here, an ancient library was sealed up in the early part of the eleventh century, escaping discovery until the early part of the twentieth century. A collection of approximately eight hundred manuscripts was obtained from this site by the famous explorer Sir Marc Aurel Stein, and a selection of these manuscripts is available in English translation with extensive introductions and notes in F. W. Thomas's *Ancient Folk-Literature from North-Eastern Tibet* (1957).

The collection edited by Thomas includes writings in both prose and verse, the latter generally favoring dactylic meter. These texts include several tales of a mythical nature. One tale tells of humankind's fall from an earlier golden age to an "Age of Debts and Taxes," which was brought on by the return to the sky of a lineage of divine kings. Another tale repeats the theme of the decline of a golden age, during which all creatures lived in harmony, and the subsequent dark age, brought on by the influences of evil demons and ill luck, during which the horse became separated from its wild relative, the *kiang* (a species of wild ass) and fell under the subjugation of humans. Other texts contain long lists of proverbs or manuals devoted to the methods of *mo* divination. These writings display a vigorous style with frequent repetitions and parallelism, derivative of earlier oral sources, and extensive onomatopoeia. The overall tone of these works is decidedly pessimistic, and the theme of social decline that pervades them is reminiscent of similar complaints found in the authors of classical antiquity in the West.

THE GE-SAR EPIC

The Ge-sar epic is the most important epic cycle in Inner Asia, and versions of it are found in all the major areas of Tibet and Mongolia, as well as in areas occupied by various Turkic tribes and in areas bordering the Himalayas, such as Sikkim and Hunza. The epic alternates brief prose passages with longer poetic sections, which are sung by an epic bard in a variety of melodies; each melody implies a particular mood or tone and is selected by the bard to suit each poetic passage. The first written version of the Ge-sar epic dates from approximately the fifteenth century, but the earlier existence of the epic cycle is attested by references in eleventh century texts, and it is certain that portions of the epic existed in the oral literature of Inner Asia for centuries before that date.

Ge-sar's name derives from the Byzantine word for emperor, *kaisar*, a cognate of the Latin *caesar* and the German *Kaiser*, and early texts connect his name with the place-name Phrom (Rome, meaning, in this context, Byzantium). Despite this unexplained connection with Byzantium, the hero of the Tibetan epic is identified as the ruler of a land called Gling, a kingdom which once existed in an area of Tibet that later became part of the provinces of Kham and Amdo. It has been pointed out by Rolf A. Stein in *Tibetan Civilization* (1972), however, that the term *Gling* is to be considered an abbreviation for the phrase *'dzam-bu-gling*, a Tibetan term referring to the world continent of Jambudvipa; thus, the epithet *Gling* may be taken to mean that Ge-sar is the ruler of the entire world, not merely of a particular Tibetan kingdom.

There are many versions of the Ge-sar epic in Tibet, with many episodes devoted to his conquest of various countries, including China, Iran, Kashmir, and the Na-khi region of Yunnan. Several versions of the epic even include an episode in which Ge-sar descends to Hell and conquers the Lord of the Underworld; this episode is of particular interest to the comparative study of the epic in Asia and the West, since a majority of epics, including *The Epic of Gilgamesh* (c. 2000 B.C.E., *Gilgamesh Epic*, 1917), Homer's *Odyssey* (c. 725 B.C.E.; English translation, 1614), and several versions of the romances of Alexander the Great, feature an underworld journey. The Ge-sar epic invariably begins in a heavenly realm. There, a group of gods decide that it is necessary to send a divine leader to humankind, and they convince one of their number to be born as a man. After a miraculous birth and several attempts on his life by his uncle, the child who is to become Ge-sar retreats with his mother to a desert. By the use of magically produced illusions, Ge-sar convinces the tribal leaders—particularly his uncle—to take part in a horse race that will determine the leadership of the empire. Ge-sar naturally triumphs and goes on to lead his people to victory over all the countries of the world.

The religion of the Ge-sar epic belongs to the *mi-chos* tradition, although the epic has exerted an influence on later Bonpo and Buddhist works. The Ge-sar epic is still sung by epic bards and may take days or weeks to complete. The propagation of the Ge-sar epic is generally not encouraged by Tibetan Buddhist schools, although some versions of the epic have been recast in the Buddhist mold and maintain that Ge-sar was sent to Earth to protect the Buddhist religion from its enemies. Ge-sar is nevertheless an important popular hero in Tibet, and, like many folk heroes such as King Arthur in Britain and Frederick I in Germany, is connected with an apocalyptic *cultus* which maintains that Ge-sar will one day lead his people in a final battle against the evil forces of the world.

TIBETAN FOLK POETRY

Several distinct genres of folk poetry and songs exist in Tibet and are still performed at special times of the year, such as at the time of planting or harvesting crops, at the celebration of the new year, and at marriages and other special occasions. Popular songs and poems are generally termed *glu* or *glu-bzhas* and are distinguished from poems found in religious writings, which are most often called *mgur* or *dbyangs*.

Gral-glu (row songs) are chanted by groups of singers arranged in rows; their texts consist mainly of sayings whose recitation brings good luck, and they are therefore most frequently sung at weddings or at new year's festivals. *Chang-glu* (beer songs) are poems composed during drinking parties, while *sgor-bzhas* (circle songs) are sung by groups of men and women who hold hands in a circle and move to the left and right as they chant. *Bzhas-chen* (great songs) are long poems chanted at harvest celebrations.

POETRY IN INDIGENOUS BUDDHIST LITERATURE

When Tibetan Buddhists engaged in an organized and meticulous campaign of translating the corpus of Indian Buddhist literature, the sophisticated metrical patterns of Indian literature became the models for Tibetan Buddhist poetry; the Tantric songs, called *doha*, of Indian Buddhist mystic poets such as Kanha and Saraha also exerted an influence on Tibetan poetry. The dactyl, which had been the dominant meter in the early Tibetan poetry of the Dunhuang documents, was supplanted by the trochee, which became the dominant form not only in most religious poetry but also in many varieties of secular songs.

Poems containing maxims and proverbs, which have been found in the earliest Tibetan documents excavated at Dunhuang, also found popularity in the writings of Tibetan Buddhist authors. The *Subhasitaratnanidhi*, composed by the eminent Tibetan master Sa-skya Pandita (1182-1251), is an excellent example. The work contains more than 450 four-line poems of an aphoristic nature; its popularity was so great that it was widely circulated in Mongolia as well as in Tibet.

Tibetan exegeses of Tantric Buddhist texts often contain verses which exactly duplicate the Indian *doha*. In a treatise dealing with the *Cakrasamvaratantra*, the Tibetan Sa-skya-pa master Sa-chen Kun-dga'-snying-po relates the legendary biography of the Indian teacher Kanha, a renowned master of the *doha*, by interweaving the narrative of his hagiography with Tibetan *doha* verses composed by Kun-dga'-snying-po. The alternation of prose and verse is a characteristic of much Tibetan literature; perhaps the finest example of this alternating structure of prose and verse is found in the *Biography* and *Hundred-Thousand Songs* composed by the Tibetan poet and Buddhist saint Milarepa.

MILAREPA

Milarepa's *Biography* and *Hundred-Thousand Songs* (here, "hundred-thousand" is to be construed as meaning "many" and is not to be taken literally) are perhaps the most widely read books among literate Tibetan laymen and monks alike. Although Milarepa is venerated as one of the founders of the bKa'-rgyud-pa school in Tibet, his works are read by members of all Tibetan religious schools, and literary references to his writings are to be found in the literature of all Tibetan Buddhist sects. The best-known editions of the *Biography* and *Hundred-Thousand Songs* are those compiled by gTsang-smyon He-ru-ka (literally, the mad yogin of gTsang) in 1488, but other editions are known to exist; an especially important edition of the *Hundred-Thousand Songs*, compiled by Rang-byung rDo-rje (1284-1339), the Third Black Hat Karmapa, contains nearly twice as much material as is found in the gTsang-smyon version and was reprinted in 1978.

Milarepa's *Biography* begins with the story of the hero's childhood; in the manner of many Inner Asian folktales and epics, such as the Ge-sar epic and the *Secret History of the Mongols*, the death of Milarepa's father precipitates a period of degradation and poverty for his family that must be avenged by the son. Milarepa's aunt and uncle, who are named as custodians of the father's legacy, treat Mi-la, his mother, and his sister as virtual slaves, and the mother urges Mi-la to learn black magic to effect vengeance. Mi-la travels to study with several sorcerers, and his personal qualities of perseverance and obedience become evident. After acquiring the necessary magical powers, Mi-la avenges the greed of his aunt and uncle by sending a powerful magical assault on their eldest son's wedding feast, destroying his relatives' property and killing all of their guests. His mother is momentarily satisfied but soon informs her son that the villagers are planning to punish her for this destruction. Mi-la responds by sending a hailstorm to devastate the village's crops and thus complete his campaign of vengeance.

Far from resulting in satisfaction, these deeds trouble Milarepa's conscience and lead to an awareness of the karmic consequences that will follow Mi-la for countless future lives. Mi-la then decides to follow the Buddhist path of salvation with the same dedication he showed in his previous studies of black magic. He eventually encounters his religious teacher (*bla-ma* or lama), Mar-pa, whose rigorous and often brutal treatment of Mi-la fills the next section of the *Biography*. Milarepa's determination is rewarded when Mar-pa initiates him as his foremost disciple, and the final third of the *Biography* is an account of Milarepa's experiences as a Buddhist master who leads his own disciples toward the path of enlightenment.

The *Biography* and the *Hundred-Thousand Songs* both consist of prose passages interwoven with Milarepa's religious poems, fashioned after the mystic poems of the Indian *doha* tradition. Milarepa's works achieve a unique beauty, combining the clarity of Buddhist teachings with a distinctly Tibetan appreciation for the beauty of nature (generally perceived as an illusion in conventional Buddhist literature) and for the customs, occupations, and tastes of the Tibetan people. For this reason, Mi-la occupies a central position in Tibetan literature and especially Tibetan poetry; his influence and popularity have been both pervasive and constant in the history of Tibetan literature, art, and drama.

THE SIXTH DALAI LAMA

"The Love Songs of the Sixth Dalai Lama" (Tsang-yang Gyatso; 1683-1706), translated in 1930 in the *Academia Sinica Monograph*, are a collection of four-line poems that resemble the most common form of the Tibetan folk poem, the *gtang-thung bzhad* ("short song"). This collection contains approximately sixty songs, written in a deceptively simple language. The Sixth Dalai Lama was reputed to be a libertine who frequently left the cloister of his palace, the Potala, in disguise to visit a variety of lovers in Lhasa and to enjoy the local taverns. Such behavior was contrary to the vows of all Buddhist monks, and the Dalai Lama's reputation became the pretext for an invasion of Lhasa by the Khoshot Mongols, who sought to gain control of Tibet. The Dalai Lama was replaced by a monk chosen by the Khoshot leader Lha-bzang and died in captivity.

Despite the seemingly unorthodox behavior of the Sixth Dalai Lama, Tibetans refused to recognize the Khoshot pretender and even today consider Tsangyang Gyatso to have been the legitimate Dalai Lama. It has been suggested that his poetry is, in fact, metaphorical and that the poems should be viewed within the context of Tantric Buddhism rather than as evidence of actual romantic adventures. The question of whether the Sixth Dalai Lama remained true to his monastic vows, however, remains secondary to the beauty of his poems, which may be appreciated for their imagery and language in any case. Several of his poems are remarkably similar to a medieval European form, the aubade, in which lovers are parted by the calls of a town watchman which signal the coming of a new day.

MODERN SECULAR POETRY

In addition to the *gtang-thung bzhad*, which is the most frequent model for secular poetry, a poetic form favored by educated Tibetans in the past several centuries is the *ka-bzhas*. This poetic form derives its name from the letter *ka*, the first letter of the Tibetan alphabet, and uses the thirty consonants of the Tibetan alphabet as the initial letters, in alphabetical order, of a thirty-line poem. The *ka-bzhas* is often employed in love poems and is also used as an elegant form for correspondence.

WRITERS IN EXILE

During the early years, most of the Tibetan exiles producing literary works were monastic scholars, and if they wrote poetry, it was incorporated in religious texts. The generations that followed were unlikely to know the Tibetan language, for whether they lived in India, in the United States, or elsewhere, they used English in daily life. However, in the 1980's, after the Chinese government relaxed its policy on border crossings, young Tibetans began to arrive in India. Among them were a few who were both fluent in their native language and passionate about literature. In 1990, four of them founded the magazine *Ljang gzhon* (young shoots), whose purpose was to publish literary works written in Tibetan. Other similar publications followed,

making it possible for an international literary community to develop. In 1995, the first conference of Tibetan writers was held, with some sixty people in attendance, some of them from as far away as Switzerland and the United States. That same year, several Tibetan anthologies were published.

When four volumes of poems by Hortsang Jigme appeared in 1994, it was the first time in Tibetan history that such a collection had been produced by a layperson, instead of a religious figure, such as a lama. Almost immediately, a number of other collections by lay poets were published, several of them by women writers who had recently escaped from Tibet. Thus literary works by women were accepted into the Tibetan canon. By the beginning of the twenty-first century, though each generation of Tibetans living under Chinese rule was becoming less Tibetan and more Chinese, Tibetans in exile were preserving their language and their culture, and many of the heroes and heroines of this effort were the writers who fled from their native country in order to live in freedom.

BIBLIOGRAPHY

Bosson, James E. *A Treasury of Aphoristic Jewels: The Subhasitaratnanidhi of Sa Skya Pandita in Tibetan and Mongolian*. London: Routledge Curzon, 1997. A collection of 457 quatrains, divided into three sections, Tibetan texts, Mongolian texts, and translations. Excellent introduction, notes, glossary, and bibliography.

Cabezon, Jose I., and Roger R. Jackson. *Tibetan Literature: Studies in Genre*. Ithaca, N.Y.: Snow Lion, 1995. Survey of poetry, novels, biographies, histories, and other writings that span thirteen hundred years.

Coleman, Graham, ed., with Thupten Jinpa. *The Tibetan Book of the Dead*. Composed by Padmasambhava. Translated by Gyurme Dorje. London: Penguin Books, 2005. The great Buddhist work about after-death experiences. Includes an introductory commentary by His Holiness the Dalai Lama. Illustrated. Appendixes, glossary, notes, bibliographical references, and index.

David-Neel, Alexandra, and the Lama Yongden. *The Superhuman Life of Gesar of Ling*. Reprint. Whitefish, Mont.: Kessinger, 2004. A version of the famous Central Asian epic, based on notes the author took at oral recitations.

Evans-Wentz, W. Y. *Tibet's Great Yogi Milarepa*. 3d ed. New York: Oxford University Press, 2000. A new edition of a classic biography of Milarepa, with the original annotations by Evans-Wentz and a new foreword by Donald S. Lopez, Jr.

Hartley, Lauran R., and Patricia Schiaffini-Vedani, eds. *Modern Tibetan Literature and Social Change*. Durham, N.C.: Duke University Press, 2008. Foreword by Matthew T. Kapstein. A volume of essays that has been acclaimed as the first systematic overview of modern Tibetan literature. Appendixes include glossaries of Tibetan spellings and of Chinese terms and a list of contemporary Tibetan literary works in translation. Index.

Jinpa, Thupten, and Jas Elsner. *Songs of Spiritual Experience: Tibetan Buddhist Poems of Insight and Awakening*. Boston: Shambhala, 2000. Fifty-two newly translated works ranging from the eleventh to the twentieth century. Includes helpful introduction and glossary-commentary.

Milarepa, Jetsun. *Drinking the Mountain Stream: Songs of Tibet's Beloved Saint, Milarepa*. Rev. ed. Translated by Lama Kunga Rinpoche and Brian Cutilla. Boston: Wisdom, 1995. Buddhist songs about meditation and liberation. Introductory material explains Buddhist theory and practice, describes Milarepa's world, and comments on his style. Illustrated. Notes and glossary.

Schaeffer, Kurtis R. *The Culture of the Book in Tibet*. New York: Columbia University Press, 2009. Traces the influence of printed works on Tibetan history and culture from the fourteenth century to the eighteenth. Bibliography and index.

_____. *Dreaming the Great Brahmin: Tibetan Traditions of the Buddhist Poet-Saint Saraha*. New York: Oxford University Press, 2005. Explains how such figures as the legendary, mystical poet Saraha were transformed over time and places him and the songs attributed to him within the context of Tibetan literature.

Tucci, Giuseppe. *Tibetan Folk Songs from Gyantse and Western Tibet*. 2d ed. Ascona, Switzerland: Artibus Asiae, 1966. Includes two appendixes by Namkhai Norbu and biographical footnotes.

Zeitlin, Ida. *Gessar Khan: The Legend of Tibet*. 1927. Reprint. Varanasi, India: Pilgrims Publishing, 1998. Chiefly based on the German version of the Mongolian text, edited by Isaac Jakob Schmidt and published in St. Petersburg, Russia, 1839, under the title *Die Thaten Bogda Gesser Chans*. Illustrated by Theodore Nadejen.

Paul A. Draghi
Updated by Rosemary M. Canfield Reisman

LITERARY MOVEMENTS

METAPHYSICAL POETS

In the eighteenth century, the term "Metaphysical poets" was coined to refer to certain writers, primarily of religious verse, of the late sixteenth and early seventeenth centuries who shared similar characteristics. Although scholars have suggested many alternative names (Louis Martz called their works the poetry of meditation, and Mario DiCesare's anthology spoke simply of seventeenth century religious poets), the term "Metaphysical poets" remained useful to literary historians for more than two hundred years.

The Metaphysicals were never a self-conscious group, for the most part having limited or no contact with one another—even though the literary world of London at the time was quite small. The list of who is considered a Metaphysical poet has fluctuated through changes in fashion and, of course, in the very definition of Metaphysical verse. Prominent names in most discussions of Metaphysical poetry include John Donne (1572-1631), George Herbert (1593-1633), Andrew Marvell (1621-1678), Thomas Traherne (c. 1637-1674), Henry Vaughan (1622-1695), Richard Crashaw (c. 1612-1649), Robert Southwell (c. 1561-1595), Abraham Cowley (1618-1667), Sir William Davenant (1606-1668), Sir John Suckling (1609-1642), and Thomas Carew (1594-1640). American critic Louis Martz has recognized two early American poets, Anne Bradstreet (1612?-1672) and Edward Taylor (c. 1645-1729), as sharing many characteristics with these English poets.

Lists of those characteristics vary, but the primary quality critics have found in the works of these poets is reflected by their epithet, "metaphysical." The poetry is often built around metaphysical speculation, usually of a formal, scholastic type ("scholastic" in the seventeenth century sense, referring to the "schools" of thought at the University of Paris, predominantly those of Saint Thomas Aquinas and Saint Bonaventure). Because scholastic thought is primarily theological, the poems are often religious in nature. However, equally common is a conflation of the religious and the erotic reminiscent of the troubadour poets. In Herbert, this combination became a self-conscious "war on poetry," declared in a 1610 letter to his mother (first published

by Izaak Walton in 1670). Herbert employed what the German poets of his time called *kontrafaktur*, inverting the clichés of secular love poetry to express the higher love of Jesus Christ. At the other extreme may be the love poetry of Donne, who risks what may seem blasphemy in using religious language to describe the speaker's quite human love, in poems such as "The Canonization" and "The Relic," wherein the speaker imagines himself and his beloved as "saints of love" venerated by the church and its faithful.

Intellectual speculation in these poems, however, is not limited to metaphysics or theology, but extends to all learning of the day, including new scientific ideas and geometrical analysis. In "The Definition of Love," for instance, Marvell used cartographic experiments in representing the sphere of the earth in two-dimensional drawings (the planisphere) as a metaphor for confining something as multidimensional as love within the "flat" boundaries of a definition. Such intricate and sometimes counterintuitive analogies, known as metaphysical conceits, were themselves a typical element of these poems, and a major source of the disfavor the Metaphysical poets met from the time Samuel Johnson coined the term "Metaphysical poet" in 1781 until T. S. Eliot's influential review in 1921 of Sir Herbert Grierson's *Metaphysical Lyrics and Poems of the Seventeenth Century: Donne to Butler* (1921).

HISTORY OF THE CONCEPT

Although the specific designation "Metaphysical poet" was not used until 1781, the adjective "metaphysical" was applied to the works of these poets in their own time. The Scots poet William Drummond of Hawthornden spoke of a tribe of writers in his day filling poems with "metaphysical *Ideas* and *Scholastic Quiddities*." In 1693, the most influential of restoration critics, John Dryden, scorned the verse of Donne because in it he "affects the metaphysics." In the early eighteenth century, Alexander Pope identifies Cowley (and, parenthetically, Davenant) as a poet who "borrowed his metaphysical style from Donne." In fact, it was in the context of Cowley, and not of Donne, that

Johnson invented the term "Metaphysical poet." In his essay on Cowley in *Lives of the Poets* (1779-1781), Johnson wrote "About the beginning of the seventeenth century appeared a race of writers that may be termed *metaphysical poets*."

For about a century and a half, Metaphysical poetry fell out of favor, although the Romantics, especially Samuel Taylor Coleridge, expressed a liking for them. It remained for Grierson's work (and Eliot's famous review of it) to revive an interest in these poets—and to provide at least one theory of why they had been ignored for so long. In his introduction, Grierson, after listing what he considers the major hallmarks of the Metaphysical poets, ends with the most important: "above all the peculiar blend of passion and thought, feeling and ratiocination which is their greatest achievement." This "passionate thinking" as Grierson put it, was the hint that led Eliot to theorize that Dryden's generation lost or turned against that ability to feel thought. Eliot's catch-phrase for the theory was "dissociation of sensibility."

Eliot's theory—and it was never presented as more than a theory, a convenient story explaining the fall of the Metaphysicals from popularity—was simply this: "In the seventeenth century a dissociation of sensibility set in, from which we have never recovered." Donne and his generation, according to the theory, were able to "feel their thought as immediately as the odor of a rose." After Dryden, this was no longer possible. Hence Johnson's criticism of the Metaphysicals, occurring after the supposed disintegration of thought and feeling, was understandably negative.

Eliot's theory was never universally adapted; indeed, Eliot himself seemed to turn from it a decade later in the 1931 essay "Donne in Our Time," in which he asserts that Donne himself showed the split between thought and feeling. In his 1951 volume, *The Monarch of Wit*, J. B. Leishman systematically demolishes the theory with counterexamples. Nevertheless, the notion that the generation between World Wars I and II resonated with that of Donne allowed a resurgence of interest in Metaphysical poetry that continued into the twenty-first century.

CHARACTERISTICS

The criteria by which Johnson faulted Cowley and his "race" of Metaphysicals became standard hall-

marks of their poetry: (1) ostentatious learning; (2) metrical irregularity; (3) "metaphysical wit," defined as novel connections in image and metaphor; (4) unusual diction; and (5) using "courtship without fondness" in their love poetry. Each of these supposed poetic vices have been considered virtues by critics who revived interest in Metaphysical poetry in the 1920's.

The first quibble, "showy" erudition, depends on the reader's judgment of the poet's motive. When Cowley likens human judgment to a telescope or "multiplying glass" in his "Ode of Wit" (1668), detractors such as Johnson might think he is either parading his learning or trying to be up-to-date. However, more sympathetic readers may read that as just being playful, or simply choosing the most effective analogy.

The second charge, roughness of poetic rhythm, can likewise be met by inquiring how the poets actually read their verse. In the early nineteenth century, poet and critic Coleridge observed that ignoring function words, such as prepositions, articles, and conjunctions, will usually smooth out the most seemingly irregular of Donne's verses. Nevertheless, many a reader has found Donne's rhythms—and those of his fellow Metaphysicals—quite awkward. Donne's contemporary Ben Jonson even quipped that Donne's looseness of accent was a hanging offense.

The third, an accusation of seeking novelty rather than appropriateness in metaphor, is virtually a repetition of the complaint that Metaphysical poets show off their learning. Johnson, with justice, observed that the Metaphysical notion of wit, which Johnson supposed was seeking to surprise the reader with something unthought of, was directly opposed to the reigning notion of wit best described by Pope in *An Essay on Criticism* (1711) as "what oft was thought, but ne'er so well expressed." The Metaphysical notion of avoiding the too-obvious analogy has at least as ancient a pedigree as Pope's neoclassic one, however, as the pre-Socratic philosopher Heraclitus taught that hidden connections are better than the obvious ones.

The quibble over diction, the fourth point, is simply a matter of taste. Metaphysical poets wanted their poetry to echo the rhythms of conversation rather than art, and so their lyrics often open abruptly with colloquial exclamations: "I struck the board, and cry'd, No more"

(Herbert, "The Collar"); "Goe! Hunt the whiter Ermine!" (Davenant, "For the Lady Olivia Porter"); "Out upon it, I have lov'd" (Suckling, "Song"). "Rough" words such as Donne's "snorted" (snored) for "slumbered" in "The Good Morrow" were not considered poetic enough for neoclassic writers.

The last point, a supposed confusion of love and intellect, is implicit in Dryden's initial comments on Donne, in effect accusing him of creating poetic lovers who attempt to reason women into love with them, instead of wooing. One answer to this charge is Eliot's concept of the dissociation of sensibility.

METAPHYSICAL CONCEITS

What Johnson called metaphysical wit is most characteristically expressed in the form of the metaphysical conceit. In modern usage, the literary term "conceit" generally refers to an extended comparison, though as Joseph Anthony Mazzeo pointed out, the word "conceit" could be used in the seventeenth century as a simple synonym for "metaphor." Typical conceits before the Metaphysicals treated clichéd comparisons, such as love as a storm at sea in Rima 189 of Petrarch (1304-1374). The specific poem was well known in the sixteenth century through translations by Sir Thomas Wyatt and Edmund Spenser.

Such a comparison stated baldly or succinctly would just be a simile, "love is like a storm at sea," or, if expressed more directly a metaphor, "love is a storm at sea." However, Petrarch's figure becomes a conceit by expanding the comparison and multiplying details: the lover's sighs are the winds, his tears the rain, the lady's scorn for him the dark clouds, and so on. Petrarch's conceit is not, however, metaphysical. The conceits of the Metaphysical poets differ from the conceits of Petrarch and his many English imitators of the sixteenth century by doing just what Johnson scorned: making comparisons that were novel rather than traditional.

The most-discussed metaphysical conceit, Donne's comparison in "A Valediction: Forbidding Mourning" of a loving husband and wife as two legs of a compass, is a convenient example. The speaker of the poem is a husband chafing under the necessity of leaving his wife behind as he goes off on business. (Donne's friend and biographer, Walton, asserted that the poem was written by Donne to his wife on setting off to France in 1610.) In urging his wife not to mourn, the speaker reminds her that they are one, so that they can never be truly separated even if one should leave the other. Or if one insists on seeing husband and wife as two only in a limited sense, he says, turning to the famous conceit: "If they be two, they are two so/ As stiff twin compasses are two:/ Thy soul, the fixed foot, makes no show/ To move, but doth, if the other do . . . ." Donne does not stop there, and it is his elaboration which makes the analogy typically metaphysical. As Donne works through the analogy, he proves its aptness by making all of his observations on the compass apply equally well to the husband and wife. She is the "fixed foot," while he is the one that moves; yet the farther he is from her, the more she "leans and hearkens after" him—and indeed, the farther the moving foot of a compass goes, the more the fixed foot leans. When the moving foot is brought back to the fixed foot, the fixed foot "grows erect"—and of course the husband's return would cause the wife to rise from her seat. Finally, the poet observes, the only way a compass can make a perfect circle is if the fixed foot remains fixed. Similarly, the wife, by being steadfast, brings the husband home. "Thy firmness makes my circle just."

UNIVERSAL ANALOGY

Whether or not Johnson was right in attributing the elaborateness of such Metaphysical images to a lust for novelty depends on how apt the reader finds the analogy. Johnson thought the typical Metaphysical image to be not at all apt. In Metaphysical poetry, he asserted, "the most heterogeneous ideas are yoked by violence together." How "natural" a comparison seems to the reader may be a function of the reader's culture, poetic tradition, and to some extent, mere taste. For example, the well-known hardness of flint, yielding to no other substance, sprang easily to Petrarch's mind when describing the unyielding heart of the beloved, deaf to the lover's pleas. So the Petrarchan cliché of the "flint-hearted lady" seemed "natural" to Renaissance poets and readers, no less poetic for being conventional.

In the sixteenth century, however, arose an anti-Petrarchan sentiment that was tired of clichés. Parodies of Petrarch's comparisons ridiculed their conventionality. William Shakespeare's sonnet 130 meets the traditional lover's hyperbole of his beloved's eyes being brighter than the sun with "My mistress' eyes are nothing like the sun," and goes on to offer similar reductive satire of other stock images. Donne's elegy "The Comparison" presents typical analogies for his beloved, inverts them into disgusting images for someone else's beloved, and concludes, "She, and comparisons, are odious."

Johnson apparently assumed that all metaphysical conceits were similar inversions of tradition in search of novelty, but there is another possibility that critics have explored since the middle of the twentieth century. Roughly the same time as Metaphysical poetry was gaining popularity, a Platonic idea known as universal analogy was also being revived. Giordano Bruno argued in *De gli eroici furori* (1585, "on heroic madness") that, far from being attempts to yoke disparate ideas, metaphysical conceits (*concetti*) stem from the poet's recognition of a hidden kinship in the nature of things, not immediately recognized in surface appearances. That doctrine, known to later philosophers and divines as a theory of "correspondences," was known in the seventeenth century as "universal analogy."

In a series of articles in the early 1950's, Mazzeo presented the doctrine of universal analogy, especially in Bruno's formulation, as a poetic that explains Metaphysical poetry better than any of the then-current theories. Whether the Metaphysical poets were adherents of this philosophy, or even conscious of it, its very existence offers an alternative possibility to the unflattering notion that these poets simply wanted to try analogies that had not been used before or to see how far they could stretch a patently absurd comparison. Readers need not see them, as Johnson apparently did, as overgrown adolescents trying to shock their readers.

MARINISMO AND GONGORISMO

While Metaphysical poets were identified as a type in the English-language tradition, the phenomenon of highly conceited poetry merging thought and feeling was a widely European development in the late sixteenth and early seventeenth century. In Italy, Giambattista Marino (1569-1625) was famous, and widely imitated, for his reversal of Petrarchan conventions in love poems collected in *Le rime* (1602; *Steps to the Temple*, canto 1 only, 1646) and *La Lira* (1615). Ma-

rino and his father, a Neapolitan lawyer, became part of the literary circle of Giambattista Della Porta, where Marino encountered the philosophy of Giordano Bruno. The result was a series of lyrics that produced poetry criticized for seeking novelty, not only in its comparisons but also in its subject matter and diction. Marino was exploring metaphysical *concetti* independently of early English Metaphysicals such as Donne, though he directly influenced a second English generation, particularly Crashaw, who translated Marino's verse. By 1627, Marino's imitators in Italy were called *i Marinisti*, "the Marinists," and the Italian equivalent of Metaphysical poetry was *Marinismo* or *secentismo* (seventeenth-century-ism).

In Spain, the poetry of Luis de Góngora y Argote gave the name of Gongorism to the metaphysical style in Spanish poetry. Gonogora's opponents called this style *culteranismo*, combining the words *culto* ("cultivated," which sounds flattering, but implies an overworking of the material) and *luteranismo* ("Lutheranism," which implies a heresy against poetry).

STRONG LINES

One quality celebrated (or condemned) in the poetry of both Marino and Gongora was also identified in the English Metaphysicals by their contemporaries, who did not use the term "metaphysical." Helen Gardner opens her influential introduction to her anthology of the Metaphysicals with a discussion of this quality under the name of "strong lines." Lines of poetry were considered "strong" if they were concise, packing a great deal of meaning into few words, which at the same time made them difficult to interpret.

Identifying the Metaphysical poets as purveyors of strong lines presents a paradox, since the metaphysical conceit is characterized by elaboration—tracing down every nuance of a comparison—and the strong, or "masculine," style is characterized by epigrammatic, elliptical conciseness. Mario Praz met this criticism by theorizing that the Metaphysical style began as a sort of offshoot of the vogue for emblems, allegorical pictures of abstract concepts accompanied by epigrams defining that concept. Praz's theory depends rather heavily on not making fine distinctions between several types of seventeenth century verse and is no longer widely held.

DOCTRINE IN METAPHYSICAL VERSE

With the notion that the Metaphysical poets read their learning into their poetry came the obvious question (though it was not apparently obvious until the 1970's): If the thought in the devotional lyrics of the Metaphysical poets is theological, then what is the relation of doctrine to the poems? Can the reader determine the denominational drift of the poet's Christianity from the poems? In the 1950's, critic Martz discovered a curious phenomenon: Though largely Anglican, the Metaphysical poets were, Martz was convinced, influenced by Catholic devotional manuals from the continent.

Then a series of critics, starting with William Halewood in *The Poetry of Grace* (1970), began to assert the existence of what by the end of the decade became known by Barbara Lewalski's term, "Protestant poetics," in these poets. Whether a particular poet leaned more toward Calvinism or Anglican orthodoxy (other than the two Roman Catholic poets in the group, Crashaw and Southwell), this theory maintained, their sensibilities were decidedly Protestant, not informed by Ignatian guides to meditation as Martz suggested. However, in *The Emotive Image* (1983), Anthony Raspa posited a "Jesuit poetics" in English poetry of the seventeenth century, and in *Doctrine and Devotion in Seventeenth Century Poetry* (2000), R. V. Young demonstrated that most of the supposedly Protestant elements of this poetry were common in Catholic thought and doctrine as well.

Paradoxically—and the Metaphysical poets loved paradox—this critical attention to theological subtleties long since forgotten or ignored by English-speaking culture at large has helped to keep the Metaphysical poets not only relevant but also vital to twenty-first century literary discourse. Terms such as "provenient grace," which had not been a part of ecumenical dialogue between Catholic and Protestant theologians for centuries, became vital to arguments for or against the notion of Protestant poetics in the twenty-first century. Nor are these theological discussions peripheral, for most participants in the controversy assume that whatever theology informs the poetry is crucial to reading and interpreting it.

The relevance of the Metaphysical poets to modern readers is not limited to their religious verse, however. The Donne revival that led to a rekindling of interest in all Metaphysical poets in the 1920's was feared in the decades immediately following to be a mere vogue. C. S. Lewis opened a 1938 essay on Donne's love poetry by citing E. E. Kellett's *Whirligig of Taste* (1929) as a convenient emblem for the shifting views toward the Metaphysicals: Scorned by Victorians, lionized by the Jazz Age, perhaps the revival was merely a phase, to be replaced by another hibernation. That has not happened, however. The metaphysical poets show no sign of being dislodged from the curriculum of English poetry in the early twenty-first century.

BIBLIOGRAPHY

Dickson, Donald R. *John Donne's Poetry*. New York: W. W. Norton, 2007. Though this edition treats only Donne, the critical essays are excellent overviews of critical controversies on metaphysical poetry.

Gardner, Helen. *The Metaphysical Poets*. New York: Oxford University Press, 1961. A revision of the 1957 Penguin anthology, correcting the text of Donne's poems and reprinting Gardner's now-classic essay on metaphysical poetry as an introduction.

Grierson, Sir Herbert J. C. *Metaphysical Lyrics and Poems of the Seventeenth Century*. Oxford, England: Clarendon Press, 1921. The standard anthology that almost singlehandedly revived interest in Metaphysical poetry, with a perceptive and influential introduction.

Mazzeo, Joseph. *Renaissance and Seventeenth-Century Studies*. New York: Columbia University Press, 1964. This collection includes Mazzeo's discussion of "universal analogy" in Metaphysical poetry, a more accessible version than in his earlier scholarly articles.

Young, R. V. *Doctrine and Devotion in Seventeenth-Century Poetry: Studies in Donne, Herbert, Crashaw, and Vaughan*. Cambridge, England: D. S. Brewer, 2000. A detailed study of how these four Metaphysical poets (and others) interrelated theological thought and religious feeling.

John R. Holmes

RESTORATION POETRY

The Restoration period (1660-1700) takes its name from the return of Charles II to the throne of Great Britain after that nation's experiment with republican government. As an indication of the illegitimacy of the Commonwealth, Charles II's reign was dated from 1649, when his father, Charles I, was executed, rather than 1660, the year he assumed power. Just as official records recognize no break between reigns, so poetry in the latter part of the seventeenth century is in many ways continuous with what preceded it. Jacobean and Caroline poets such as Ben Jonson (1573-1637), Robert Herrick (1591-1674), and Sir John Suckling (1609-1642) remained influential. The two most important Restoration poets, John Dryden (1631-1700) and John Milton (1608-1674), began their careers before 1660. While the Metaphysical impulse of John Donne and George Herbert was largely spent by the time Charles II came to the throne, the Greco-Roman classics still served as models and ideals. Milton's *Paradise Lost* (1667, 1674) is Vergilian, and Dryden's satires owe much to Juvenal, some of whose works Dryden translated. Nonetheless, during the forty years of the Restoration period, new verse forms emerged, older genres flourished and changed, and writers penned some of the greatest English poems ever written.

THE LYRIC

Print culture had not yet developed, as it would in the next century, to the point where it would allow a writer to earn a living by his or, less frequently, her pen. Indeed, in 1660, print was still regarded as less prestigious than manuscript, the form in which poetry largely circulated. The poems of Andrew Marvell (1621-1678) were not published in book form until 1681, three years after his death. Most of the poetry of the John Wilmot, earl of Rochester (1647-1680), was not printed until after his death in 1680. The same is true for the works of Katherine Philips (1632-1664) and Anne Killigrew (1660-1685). The profession of letters remained much as it had been in the time of Augustus Caesar, when writers hoped that their work would secure them patronage.

In this literary environment, the aristocracy and gentry had the advantage not only of education but also of the leisure to compose. Alexander Pope (1688-1744) characterized the poets of the Restoration as "the mob of gentlemen who wrote with ease." A coterie of fourteen of these men close to Charles II contributed significantly to the poetic output of the period, writing more than five hundred songs, satires, prologues, and other occasional verse. Following Roman and Cavalier models, they addressed love poems to Phyllis, Chloris, Aurelia, Celia, Corinna, Daphne, Sylvia, Urania, and other such pastoral names, behind which may or may not have lurked real women. In 1671, Charles Sackville, earl of Dorset (1638-1706), one of these court wits, complained, "Methinks the poor town has been troubled too long,/ With Phillis and Chloris in every song." Sackville devoted his verses here to the praises of Bess Morris, a well-known prostitute.

Sackville's mocking of the pastoral mode was characteristic of the age. Some Restoration lyrics adopt the conventions of eternal vows of love and praise of the lady's mind rather than her body. Examples include "Love's Slavery," by John Sheffield, the earl of Mulgrave (1648-1721); "I cannot change, as others do," by Sir Carr Scroope (1649-1680); and "Fear not, my Dear, a Flame can never die," by Sir Charles Sedley (1639-1701). Most, however, advocate the carpe diem philosophy that reflects the attitude of Hobbesian materialism, the age's licentiousness, and the literary heritage of the Cavalier poets. Written in ballad form or iambic tetrameter couplets, the poems reject the pastoral ideal that dates back to Theocritus and Vergil in favor of more realistic portraits of country life and sex. The title of the earl of Rochester's "Fair Chloris in a pigsty lay" (1680) indicates the tone that court wits, urban and urbane, took toward the rural. These works similarly reject the sexual innocence of the women presented. Chloris at the end of Rochester's poem is "innocent and pleased" not because she has refused sex but because she has gratified herself. This or another Chloris in another Rochester poem begins "full of harmless thought" and concludes by having sex with a passing shepherd. The Phyllis of Rochester's "Mock Song" (1680) declares herself natural, just like the nymphs of Arcadia, but in her case, being natural means, as it did for Restoration wits, having sex with lots of people. "'Can I,' said she, 'with nature strive?/ Alas I am, alas I am a whore!'"

Restoration lyrics praise the woman (and the man) who is not coy, and offer arguments against delaying sexual pleasure. Rochester, in "Fling this useless Book away" (1697), asks how Phyllis can hope for divine mercy unless she helps "poor mortals in despair" by sleeping with them. In "The Advice" (1672), Rochester urges, "Submit, then, Celia, ere you be reduced,/ For rebels, vanquished once, are vilely used." Rochester's "Phyllis, be gentler, I advise" (1680) warns that if the lady remains chaste, she will "Die with the scandal of a whore/ And never know the joy."

In "Out upon it!" (1659), Suckling's speaker announces that he has loved three whole days, and he may love another three if the weather holds. Restoration wits cannot promise that much constancy. "If I, by miracle, can be/ This livelong Minute true to thee,/ 'Tis all that Heaven allows," Rochester writes in "Love and Life" (1677). The title of his "Against Constancy" (1676) summarizes the attitude of that piece and many others. In "Persuasion to Love," Sir George Etherege (c. 1635-1691) acknowledges, "It may be we within this hour/ May lose those joys we now do taste." As these examples show, the Restoration lyric is polished, witty, and realistic.

SATIRE

The period from 1660 to 1798, sometimes extended to 1832, known as the long eighteenth century, is the age of satire. The genre traces its roots at least as far back as the fifth century B.C.E. comic playwright Aristophanes, although the models for Restoration writers are primarily the Augustan Horace and the early second century C.E. Juvenal. English precedents include the sixteenth century John Skelton, John Marston, and Thomas Nashe. After 1660, however, the popularity of this literary form soared. Coffeehouses, the first of which opened in London in 1652, provided a venue for the circulation of personal lampoons and more general attacks. The rise of the political parties Whigs and To-

ries in about 1680 prompted partisan poetical broadsides and pamphlets, which could easily be rushed into print to meet the demands of the moment. In 1679, the Licensing Act temporarily lapsed, making satire safer. Even after the law was renewed in 1685, it was less strict, and the number of master printers in London was no longer limited. The act expired in 1695, not to be renewed. Satire in the Restoration was popular culture, not necessarily high art, although it might rise to that level in the hands of a writer such as Dryden. It focused on individuals and current affairs, doing what Samuel Johnson (1709-1784) referred to as "paying court to temporary prejudices" in *Life of Cowley* (1779). The aim of such works was as much to display the wit of the writer as to point out the perfidy of the person or cause attacked.

Court ladies provided targets for often-anonymous lampoons. The anonymous "A Panegyric on Nelly" (1681) is, despite its title, an attack on royal mistress Nell Gwyn. So is Etherege's "Madame Nelly's Complaint" (c. 1682). "Lais Senior: A Pindarick" and "A Satyr which the king took out of his Pocket" both criticize the duchess of Cleveland, another of Charles II's lovers. One of Rochester's songs begins, "Quoth the Duchess of Cleveland to counselor Knight,/ 'I'd fain have a prick, knew I how to come by't'" (1680). "The Royal Buss" is directed against the duchess of Portsmouth, yet another royal lover. "Portsmouth's Looking Glass" (c. 1679) portrays the duchess of Portland as the true ruler of England. "A Faithful catalogue of our Most Eminent Ninnies" (1683) assails both the duchess of Cleveland and the duchess of Portland, as does the earl of Mulgrave's "Essay on Satyr" (pr. 1721).

Writers did not spare each other. Rochester's "An Allusion to Horace" (1675) catalogues the faults of the leading authors of the period, particularly Dryden, although it praises Rochester's friends. In his "Preface to *All for Love*" (1678), Dryden responded by claiming that "An Allusion" was the work of a hack pretending to be Rochester. Sackville's "The Duel" (1687) takes as its target the two minor poets Philip, Lord Wharton, and Robert Wolseley. After Edward Howard published *The British Princes* (1669), he became the subject of at least eight lampoons by various court wits. Rochester and Scroope exchanged a series of verse attacks. Rochester and Etherege also undertook a verse battle with the earl of Mulgrave, whom they designated as Bajazet for his promiscuity, a name that stuck. Rochester also satirized him as "My Lord All-Pride" (1679).

One of the best contributions to the poetomachia of the period is Dryden's *Mac Flecknoe: Or, A Satyre upon the True-Blew-Protestant Poet, T. S.* (1682), directed against Thomas Shadwell. In this 217-line mock-heroic poem in iambic pentameter, Dryden presents Shadwell as heir to the throne of dullness that had been held by the Irish author Richard Flecknoe (d. 1678). Dryden's poem abounds in literary allusions to the classics, the Bible, Milton's *Paradise Lost*, and Shadwell's own works. Shadwell promises to support dullness and to make no treaty with sense or wit.

This poem was published without Dryden's permission in an effort to capitalize not on a literary but on a political controversy. Charles II had no legitimate offspring to inherit the throne, making his Roman Catholic brother James, duke of York, his heir. Some Protestants wanted Charles to legitimize James, duke of Monmouth, the king's illegitimate son, whom Charles II liked but was not prepared to name as his successor. Parliament twice voted to exclude James from the throne; twice the king rejected this measure. Leading the opposition to James were the Whig earl of Shaftesbury and the duke of Buckingham. In 1681, Charles II imprisoned Shaftesbury in the Tower of London and charged him with treason. The case came before a grand jury in November, 1681. To influence the decision, Dryden anonymously published *Absalom and Achitophel* (1681, 1682), a skillful blending of the heroic and the satiric in skillfully modulated iambic pentameter rhymed couplets.

Dryden had to tread carefully, since the king loved Monmouth, and the political crisis was not yet resolved. He therefore imagined that David/Charles II ends the rebellion before it begins, so that, unlike in the biblical story, no fighting occurs and Absalom survives. Lacking action, the poem derives its energy from a series of brilliant character sketches in which the leading political figures of 1681 are thinly veiled as David's contemporaries. Shaftesbury is Achitophel; Buckingham appears as Zimri; Titus Oates, who invented the Popish Plot, is Corah; the duke of Ormond, supporter of

the king, is Barzillai. Dryden acknowledged the virtues of his opponents. Achitophel is "Sagacious, bold, and turbulent of wit." This sketch includes the well-known line, "Great wits are sure to madness near allied," an example of the aphoristic quality of Dryden's verse. Monmouth is "Unblamed of life (ambition set aside),/ Not stained with cruelty, nor puffed with pride."

After a grand jury acquitted Shaftesbury in November, 1681, his supporters produced a medal to celebrate his release. Dryden again criticized Shaftesbury in *The Medall: A Satyre Against Sedition* (1682), and Shadwell, a leading Whig poet, retorted with *The Medal of John Bayes* (1682), the "Bayes" a reference to Dryden's post as poet laureate. This poetic feud encouraged a printer to release *Mac Flecknoe*. Another political poem of the period, the Sackville's "Opinion of the Whigs and Tories," criticizes both the Whig duke of Monmouth and the Tory duke of York. Henry Savile's "Advice to a Painter to draw the Duke by" (wr. 1673) condemns the duke of York's Catholicism. Rochester's song about the duchess of Cleveland ends by mocking the prominent courtiers John Churchill and Henry Jermyn.

Although much Restoration satire is directed against individuals, some was more general. The most popular example of such writing is *Hudibras* (1663, 1664, 1678), by Samuel Butler (1612-1680). The poem is written in iambic tetrameter couplets. The jog-trot rhythm and frequent double rhymes contribute to the humor: "Twice I/vici," "ecclesiastic/a stick," "duty/show tie," "discourse/whiskers," and "or drunk/for Punk." Butler claimed that only the poem's eponymous Presbyterian hero and his partner, the Independent (Congregationalist) Ralph, were based on real people. The Puritan Sir Samuel Luke has been a popular choice for the model of Hudibras, though John Wilders in his 1967 Clarendon Press edition of the work questions this choice.

Butler began writing his poem toward the end of the Interregnum and starts the action in 1647-1648. Published in the early years of the Restoration, the work owes much of its popularity to its ridicule of the defeated Puritans. Butler's mock-epic uses the opposite method from Dryden's *Mac Flecknoe*. Whereas Dryden elevates the low to make it absurd, Butler debases the heroic, taking as his model Miguel de Cervantes's *El ingenioso hidalgo don Quixote de la Mancha* (1605, 1615; *The History of the Valorous and Wittie Knight-Errant, Don Quixote of the Mancha*, 1612-1620; better known as *Don Quixote de la Mancha*). Hudibras's great battle in part 1 is fought against a bear-baiting crowd, and the knight is defeated by Trulla, a woman whose name aptly describes her. Characters include a bearward, butcher, tinker, cobbler, and clown rather than the nobles of true epic. Hudibras's durance vile (imprisonment) involves being placed in the stocks, the punishment for lower-class criminals. Hudibras and Ralph appear as hypocritical and violent; their words and actions undercut their pious protestations.

Butler's targets transcend the political and religious controversies of the Commonwealth. He mocks lawyers, pedantry (Hudibras has acquired so much learning that he has become a fool), and pretensions of all sorts, including what Butler saw as the absurdities of the new science and the Royal Society. In the third canto of part 2, Hudibras and Ralph visit the astronomer-astrologer Sidrophel. Through his telescope, Sidrophel sees a kite, which he first mistakes for a comet and then for the planet Saturn. Butler returned to this theme in "The Elephant in the Moon" (pr. 1759), in which another astronomer thinks he sees this giant mammal when in fact he is looking at a mouse that has crept into his tube. Other poems on this subject include Bulter's "Satyr upon the Royal Society" and "Satyr upon the Imperfection and Abuse of Learning." Butler held no brief for those who had supplanted the Puritans, writing a "Satyr upon the licentious age of Charles the 2d." The earl of Rochester also penned general satires, including "A Satyr against Reason and Mankind" (1679) and "Upon Nothing" (1679).

EPICS

The greatest poem written in the Restoration period is Milton's *Paradise Lost*, which can rival the finest work of any era. Unlike so much of the poetry of the period, Milton's epic rejects the heroic couplet, so named because of its frequent use in the heroic tragedies of the time. In a note prefixed to *Paradise Lost*, Milton observed that Homer and Vergil shunned rhyme, which, he claimed, had been introduced "to set off wretched matter and lame metre." He linked unrhymed verse to "ancient liberty" and rhyme to "troublesome and modern bondage," indicating that his choice of blank verse was political as well as aesthetic. His line is typically iambic pentameter, though he sometimes adds an extra syllable. For further variety, he introduces the occasional trochee or anapest and varies the placement of the caesura, the mid-line pause. To elevate his diction, he uses Latinate syntax and language, such as "arborous," "concoctive," "conflagrant," "myrrhine," "plenipotent."

Milton had long been contemplating an epic, but the English Civil War and Commonwealth drew him into public affairs. Ironically, only the defeat of his political hopes provided him the leisure to make his greatest contribution to his country. Political defeat also provided him with his subject. F. J. C. Hearnshaw wrote in *English History in Contemporary Poetry* (1912), "*Paradise Lost* is not only the epic of the Fall of Man, it is also the epic of the ruin of the cause of the Commonwealth."

Milton's epic can be read as an allegory of the failed Puritan revolution, with Satan and his forces as the republicans and God as the ultimately triumphant Stuarts. However, the focus of the poem is on the human, as the first line announces. The Puritan experiment failed not because the Roundheads were impious in rejecting God's anointed king or because, like Satan, they were too weak to prevail. The revolution failed because the English, like Adam and Eve, were seduced by evil counsel and by their desire for autonomy rather than obedience. At the end of book 9, Adam and Eve "in mutual accusation spent/ The fruitless hours," a tragic version of the absurd debates between Butler's Hudibras and Ralph but equally representative of the failure of the various republican factions to concur. The separation of Adam and Eve at the beginning of book 9 provides the opportunity for Satan to seduce Eve and thereby cause Adam's fall as well.

Human error led to the loss of Eden. *Paradise Lost* concludes with the theological consolation that in time Christ will defeat Satan. It thus also holds out the possibility of political redemption. Milton had not surrendered his republicanism. Until the final triumph, Adam and Eve and the seventeenth century English could create their own Eden through love. In its final books, *Paradise Lost* turns away from the public to the private sphere, where Adam and Eve can build a paradise for themselves. Like Vergil's *Aeneid* (c. 29-19 B.C.E.; English translation, 1553), whose hero serves as Milton's chief classical model for Adam, Eve, and Christ, *Paradise Lost* values endurance and suffering over great actions; the greatest triumph is over oneself.

Paradise Regained (1671) picks up this theme. This poem, too, offers hope for a new political Eden: "Soon we shall see our hope, our joy return." Again, the work emphasizes obedience, patience, and fortitude in suffering. *Paradise Regained* lacks the drama of *Paradise Lost* because Satan has no chance against Christ, the poem's hero not as warrior but as patient sufferer. Glory comes "By deeds of peace, by wisdom eminent,/ By patience, temperance." This is the role that English men and women need to assume until the second coming of the English republic.

WOMEN

The Ladies' Calling (1673), attributed to Richard Allestree, lists women's accomplishments, beginning with "ornamental improvements which become their quality as Writing, Needle works, Languages, Music or the like." Pope's "mob of gentlemen who wrote with ease" was matched by a fair number of women writers, including the first to earn a living by her quill, Aphra Behn (1640-1689), though her income derives mainly from her plays rather than her poetry. Like their male counterparts, most women circulated their verse in manuscript. Dorothy Osborne, herself an intelligent and articulate women, wrote in 1653 that Margaret Cavendish, duchess of Newcastle (1623-1673), must be "a little distracted" to have her books of poetry printed. Popular female genres were elegies for dead children, husbands, and friends. Women about to die or give birth, then an often-fatal procedure, wrote verse farewells to their husbands. Though much female poetry of the period is religious, secular love was also a common theme.

Behn, who is buried in Westminster Abbey, produced a body of work representative of the poetry of the period. She imitated classical writers, as in "A Paraphrase on Oenone to Paris" (1680), based on Ovid's *Heroides* (before 8 C.E.; English translation, 1567). She also produced an imitation of Horace's Ode 1.5, but whereas the original is addressed to a woman, Behn urges a man not to be so seductive. Behn's "The Disappointment" was included with the earl of Rochester's poems in the 1680 collection of his work. The poem resembles Rochester's "The Imperfect Enjoyment," which also appears in that volume. Both deal with premature ejaculation, but whereas Rochester focuses on the man's feelings, Behn examines the woman's. In "To Alexis in Answer to his Poem against Fruition: Ode" (1684), Behn again explores female attitudes toward love and sex.

The wife of James II, Mary of Modena, attracted a coterie of intelligent, witty women that corresponds to the court wits around Charles II. Among them was the talented Killigrew, a skillful painter and poet. Her *Poems* (1686) includes thirty pieces, including "On a Picture Painted by her self . . ." She adopts the pastoral convention by depicting chaste nymphs, but then introduces a realistic note at the end of the work by noting that such women exist only in literature.

Another important female poet of the age was Philips, known as the matchless Orinda. A possibly unauthorized edition of her poems appeared in 1664; other editions followed in 1669, 1678, and 1710. She celebrates platonic friendship among women and also used her work to comment on current events. Writing as Galesia, the female form of Galaesus, son of Apollo, Jane Barker (1652-1732) published more than fifty poems in part 1 of *Poetical Recreations* (1688). She also wrote religious verse under the name Fidelia.

LEGACY

Though best remembered for its witty comedies, the Restoration produced a substantial body of enduring poetry, including Milton's epics and Dryden's satires, translations, and odes for Saint Cecilia's day, in which language imitates musical instruments. The second of these poems, "Alexander's Feast," was set to music by Georg Handel. The period purified the iambic pentameter couplet, but it also popularized blank verse, not only because of Milton but also through the blank-verse tragedies of Dryden and others. Its satires and classical imitations and translations inspired the leading poets on the eighteenth century: Pope, Johnson, and Jonathan Swift. The period also saw the entrance of women into the literary marketplace, a movement that would subsequently accelerate. In his *Life of Dryden* (1781), Johnson wrote, "What was said of Rome, adorned by Augustus, may be applied by an easy metaphor to English poetry embellished by Dryden, *lateritiam invenit, marmoream reliquit*, he found it brick, and he left it marble." This assessment might aptly be extended to the contribution of all Restoration poets to the edifice of English verse.

BIBLIOGRAPHY

Jack, Ian. *Augustan Satire: Intention and Idiom in English Poetry, 1660-1750*. Oxford, England: Clarendon Press, 1952. Includes chapters on *Hudibras*, *Mac Flecknoe*, and *Absalom and Achitophel*.

Miner, Earl. *The Restoration Mode from Milton to Dryden*. Princeton, N.J.: Princeton University Press, 1974. A survey of the period's poetry; emphasizes the contributions of Samuel Butler, John Milton, and John Dryden.

Parfitt, George. *English Poetry of the Seventeenth Century*. London: Longman, 1985. The poems in this anthology are arranged by genre, such as the lyric and epic, and span the entire century.

Prescott, Sarah, and David E. Shuttleton, eds. *Women and Poetry, 1660-1750*. New York: Palgrave Macmillan, 2003. Part 1 provides essays on such individual poets as Aphra Behn and Anne Killigrew. Part 2 deals with the social, economic, and literary contexts in which women wrote, and part 3 looks at literary models, political concerns, and working-class female poets.

Wilson, John Harold. *The Court Wits of the Restoration*. Princeton, N.J.: Princeton University Press, 1948. A study of the work of Pope's "mob of gentlemen who wrote with ease," with chapters on their contributions to lyric poetry, satire, and drama.

Joseph Rosenblum

ROMANTIC POETS

Between 1780 and 1830, British poetry took a radically new turn. This is commonly known as the Romantic Revolution. It is best to see this change as part of a much wider movement across all the arts and covering much of Western Europe and the United States, the earliest manifestations perhaps going back as far as 1740, and continuing right into the twentieth century. Generically, this very wide-embracing movement is known as Romanticism.

Between 1780 and 1830, there were parallel radical and even revolutionary movements to this cultural and artistic one, including the American and French Revolutions. There were also revolutions in agriculture, which in Britain changed the face of the landscape and the lifestyle of its inhabitants. Even more profound was the Industrial Revolution, which began in Britain, with its rapid urbanization and concomitant social problems. Industrialization was then followed by colonization throughout the nineteenth century, and a vast increase in wealth. Writers such as C. S. Lewis have claimed that this machine age was the biggest cultural shift since medieval times. The links between the Romantic Revolution and these other revolutionary developments are complex and widely debated, but lie outside the focus of this discussion.

ROMANTICISM DEFINED

The related terms "Romantic," "Romance," and "Romanticism" are often used very loosely, and need some definition. First, the terms are used with a capital letter, to distinguish them from "romance" and "romantic," terms that are usually applied to love stories or erotically heightened situations. Although Romances often contain a love interest, that is not what defines them. Likewise, Romantic poets deal with the whole gamut of human experience, not just love affairs or the experience of being in love.

The British Romantic poets of this period never used the term "Romantics" to describe themselves. It was the next generation, the Victorians, who applied the term to them. They used, in certain situations, the term "Romance," to designate a certain traditional genre of literature that can be traced back to medieval times. This genre deals with tales of wonder and adventure, often involving the marvellous and the supernatural. It can be written as either prose fiction or as verse. Samuel Taylor Coleridge (1772-1834) wrote his famous poem *The Rime of the Ancient Mariner* (1798) as such a Romance, part of a long tradition of magical voyages.

However, it is best to set this genre aside in thinking of the terms "Romantic" and "Romanticism." Although generalizations are difficult, the best way to come to an understanding of the terms is by seeing how Romanticism differs from the cultural movement against which it reacted in the first place, and the cultural movement that succeeded it, in which contemporary poetry finds its place.

ROMANTIC VS. CLASSICAL

The cultural movement that preceded Romanticism is known by a variety of names. At its widest, it can be called the Enlightenment, which can be seen as an artistic, philosophical, and scientific movement that privileges the human reason, seeing humankind as self-sufficient in its ability to discover truth of whatever sort. The supernatural is either banished altogether as "superstition" or put into the background as no longer necessary. Thus, Christianity became Deism or atheism. Excessive shows of emotion were seen as antirational and to be suppressed. Intuition, the feminine, and the spiritual were demoted to the second rank of worthwhileness in human study and endeavor.

In terms of literature, the expression of this cultural movement was usually termed classical or neoclassical, since its models went back to Greek and Roman literature. The study of Roman and Greek language, culture, and literature has always been known as studying the classics. In the history of English literature, sometimes the term "Augustan" is used to denote the particular period of the Roman emperor Augustus as the peak of classical civilization.

Romanticism, by contrast, sought to privilege the imaginative and the intuitive as ways to truth. The term "imaginative truth" was coined, and this truth was claimed to be of equal worth to scientific and philosophical truth, or even higher. Poets were seen as truth tellers and prophets to their generation, often taking on a quasi-religious role as members of a new priesthood. Percy Bysshe Shelley (1792-1822) and other anti-Christian Romantics in fact claimed poetry had taken over religion, as did the Victorian Romantic, Matthew Arnold (1822-1888).

This does not mean that all Romantic poets were antireligious or antiscientific, but rather that they downgraded the rational and the logical and valued the intuitive. One manifestation of this was the trust in childhood states of being, of "innocence" as being a form of truth. This goes back to the Greek philosopher, Plato, who held that the human soul comes straight from heaven, entering a baby uncorrupted. Thus, young children are naturally nearer to heaven in their innocence. "Now We Are Seven" and "Ode: Intimations of Immortality from Recollections of Early Childhood," by William Wordsworth (1770-1850) are excellent examples of this, as are the poems in *Songs of Innocence* (1789), by William Blake (1757-1827). By contrast, the Enlightenment philosopher John Locke believed children to be born with nothing, to be "blank slates," and orthodox Christianity believed children to be born already "fallen" and corrupt.

Generally Romantic poets were Platonists, following a long tradition in English poetry that includes the late Elizabethan poet Edmund Spenser, the seventeenth century poet John Milton, and the mystics Henry Vaughan and Thomas Traherne. Classicism tends to build on the thinking of the other great Greek thinker, Aristotle. This Platonism was reinforced by the writings of the eighteenth century French philosopher Jean-Jacques Rousseau, who might well be called the philosopher of childhood. He saw the perfect education as preventing the child's soul from becoming corrupted, which is essentially by contact with society. The ideal education is homeschooling in a country milieu, in nature, a schooling which, by chance, Wordsworth enjoyed in the Lake District of northern England. Rousseau also suggested that in society, the city was more corrupt than the country. This was at odds with neoclassicism, which was basically an urban culture.

The Romantics tended to privilege country people, folkways, and primitivism in general as being less corrupt. This led to an interest in remote cultures and poetry.

Neoclassical theory had emphasized the need for a "poetic diction" distinct from everyday speech. In reaction, Wordsworth proposed a vocabulary and speech of ordinary people. He had in mind particularly the speech of the independent small farmers of his native Lake District, who, like their counterparts in Scotland, would have had some education and an oral tradition. This particular part of the Romantic agenda was never fulfilled, and it was left to modernism to embrace demotic speech and ordinary speech rhythms.

ROMANTICISM VS MODERNISM

Generally, the Romantic poets kept to traditional and classical verse forms and genres. Thus, they used sonnets, lyrical verse, odes, epic forms, and especially blank verse and rhymed heroic couplets. They tended to revert to classical imagery, although their concept of Greek and Roman myths was of something dynamic and truth bearing rather than merely ornamental, as it had become in later neoclassical poetry. John Keats (1795-1821) and Shelley, for example, were both fascinated with Greek mythology.

By contrast, twentieth century modernism completed the revolution in speech rhythms and freer verse forms. In modernism, imagery also broke away from either nature imagery or classical mythology. Although Romantic poetry had at first sought engagement with the more sordid aspects of reality, as in Blake's *Songs of Experience*, it quickly withdrew from this, and it was left to modernist poets to reengage with urban, ugly, and sordid scenes and experiences. Romanticism sought to see itself as "uplifting" in its idealism and views on the perfectability of human beings.

In political dimensions, Romantic poets had embraced revolutionary and radical stances. To some extent, these were actually born out of the Enlightenment, with its stress on the dignity of humankind and concepts of human rights. Wordsworth totally embraced the French Revolution at first, as he recounts in his autobiographical long poem *The Prelude: Or, The Growth of a Poet's Mind* (1850). Shelley and George

Gordon, Lord Byron (1788-1824) supported Greek freedom from the Turks.

After the excesses of the French Revolution, the older generation of Romantic poets became conservative, although Wordsworth never lost certain radical views. However, the younger generation of Romantic poets, as Keats, Shelley, Lord Byron, and Leigh Hunt (1784-1859), held the faith and either went into exile or finished up in prison on sedition charges. Nevertheless, it was left to modernist poets to reengage with radical politics, although the record here has been as patchy as with the Romantics.

EARLY MOVES

Romantic poetry did not suddenly arrive in Britain with the publication of Blake's *Songs of Innocence* or Wordsworth and Coleridge's joint venture, the *Lyrical Ballads* (1798). There had been a growing interest in different types of poetry to do with three topics: nature, heightened feelings, and primitive cultures.

There had been a long tradition of nature poetry in British poetry, some of it in the classical pastoral tradition, but some of it involving more of a nature mysticism, as in the poetry of Vaughan. In the eighteenth century, there was a growing interest in cultivating nature as well as the well-designed garden. *The Seasons* (1730), a long blank-verse poem by James Thompson (1700-1748), marks a high point of such interest.

An example of the poetry of heightened feelings can be seen in the very popular *The Complaint: Or, Night-Thoughts on Life, Death, and Immortality* (1742-1744; commonly known as *Night-Thoughts*), by Edward Young (1683-1748). These were meditations on death and mutability set in a graveyard. Such meditations were to provoke sensations of fear, dread, and also the sublime. There was, in fact, an intense discussion as to the nature of sublimity and how it might be expressed in art and poetry. This ran parallel to discussion on the nature of beauty. Both were conducted in a neoclassical setting but proved central to Romantic poetry.

There was also a growing interest in primitive, especially Celtic, cultures. When a long poem by the Scottish poet and antiquarian James Macpherson (1736-1796), entitled *Ossian*, based on the adventures of

Oisín, a legendary Celtic hero, purportedly translated from the ancient Gaelic, was published in 1761, it took the country by storm. The staunch neoclassical poet and critic Samuel Johnson (1709-1784) denounced it as a forgery, and Macpherson was challenged to produce the original documents. A huge furor ensued, giving the poem further publicity. The incident shows the craving for such primitive lost literature. The poem was translated and influenced early German Romanticism, the Storm and Stress movement, as well as German Romantic music. Felix Mendelssohn's *Fingal's Cave* is directly inspired by *Ossian*.

Also catering to this desire were the forgeries by Thomas Chatterton (1752-1770), beginning with a fabricated history of the old Bristol Bridge in 1768 and including *Poems Supposed to Have Been Written at Bristol, by Thomas Rowley, and Others in the Fifteenth Century*, edited by Thomas Tyrwhitt and published in 1777, after Chatterton's death. Even Johnson was impressed by this sixteen-year-old's gifts. Tragically, Chatterton, "the marvellous boy" as the Romantics called him, committed suicide at the age of seventeen, the first in a long list of early deaths that somehow have come to typify the Romantic poet.

WORDSWORTH AND NATURE POETRY

Wordsworth is probably the best-known British Romantic poet. For much of Wordsworth's own lifetime, he had only a small, if admiring, audience. His poetry was eclipsed by that of Sir Walter Scott (1771-1832) and that of Lord Byron in popularity and sales, and he was dependent on gifts, bequests, and government appointments. It took him until 1830, with the help of Coleridge, to gain sufficient recognition to be seen as a major poet, and it was not until nearly before his death, that he received general recognition in his appointment as poet laureate by Queen Victoria's request.

At first, Wordsworth's poetry offended literary taste by seeming too ordinary, even too childish. The *Lyrical Ballads* was a collection of ballad-type poems about country folk who often had suffered some misfortune and it used deliberately simplistic language. Some characters are decrepit, and some are mentally retarded or unbalanced. However, they are survivors and are meant to show how those living close to nature

Among the Romantic poets depicted in this 1815 engraving are William Wordsworth, Robert Southey, Samuel Taylor Coleridge, and Lord Byron. (The Granger Collection, New York)

can have moral courage in the face of the worst circumstances.

One poem in *Lyrical Ballads*, which Wordsworth added to the collection at the last moment, was completely different: "Lines Composed a Few Miles Above Tintern Abbey." It spoke of mystical experiences, epiphanies of nature, and the belief that there was a divine spirit working in and through nature. Through memory and meditation, the perceptive receiver would become a better, more moral person. This statement lies at the heart of Wordsworth's Romanticism.

The immediate impact of such beliefs was to replace the static Enlightenment concept of Creation, an ordered, even mechanistic creation of a distant God with a concept of nature as divine force. At times, Wordsworth is explicitly pantheistic, although in midlife he became more orthodoxly Christian. However, this dynamic view of nature has stayed within Western culture. This must be considered the beginning of nature poetry as it is now understood.

Even in his own day, Wordsworth succeeded in

opening up the Lake District as a tourist destination, just as the Scottish Highlands were also being opened up by the Scottish Romantics. Of these, the most significant was Robert Burns (1759-1796), who has come to be regarded as Scotland's national poet. From very humble origins, he devised a poetry using local Scottish dialect that was often humorous and often satirical. He also wrote many poems of great lyric beauty or national fervor, such as "Scots, Wha Hae wi' Wallace Bled." His first volume of poetry was published in 1786, with his famous "Tam O'Shanter" coming out in 1792.

Other Scottish Romantics are Scott, whose major works include *Minstrelsy of the Scottish Border* (1802-1803) and *The Lay of the Last Minstrel* (1805), and James Hogg, the "Shepherd of Ettrick" (1770-1835). Both these men knew Wordsworth, having collected traditional ballads of the border area between England and Scotland. Scott's poetry and novels became popular throughout Europe. His *The Lady of the Lake* (1810), with its typical medieval setting, became the direct inspiration for Keats's *Eve of St. Agnes* (1820).

COLERIDGE AND THE SUPERNATURAL

When Wordsworth and Coleridge collaborated on the *Lyrical Ballads*, Coleridge's task was to write tales of the supernatural. This built on an already existing audience for the gothic, stemming partially from *Night-Thoughts*. Coleridge's major contribution was *The Rime of the Ancient Mariner*, which subsequently became one of the most famous long poems in the English language. Again the theme is nature, but this time, nature as a retributive force if it is wantonly destroyed.

Coleridge wrote other mystical poems, including "Kubla Khan" (1816), which was probably written under the influence of opium. He also wrote a number of poems exploring the state of melancholy, a state that has a long history in English literature, from William Shakespeare's melancholic *Hamlet, Prince of Denmark* (pr. c. 1600-1601) to Robert Burton's *Anatomy of Melancholy* (1621). This state is often associated with the Romantic poets, perhaps through the famous novel *Die Leiden des jungen Werthers* (1774; *The Sorrows of Young Werther*, 1779) of the German poet Johann Wolfgang von Goethe (1749-1832) and perhaps through Keats's "Ode on Melancholy" or "Ode to a Nightingale." Such states are often near suicidal, and their exploration was part of the growing interest in extreme states of being in which perceptions are altered. One of Wordsworth's admirers, Thomas de Quincey, wrote *Confessions of an English Opium-Eater* (1821) which examined altered states of consciousness and became a massive best seller.

Later criticism has linked Coleridge's interest in the supernatural with subconscious states of being. However, Coleridge was a Unitarian and later spoke up in defense of Christianity. Rather than developing as a poet, Coleridge became a spokesperson for Romanticism, and in his *Biographia Literaria* (1817) throws out vital clues as to the early thinking of the British Romantic poets, as did Wordsworth's preface to the second edition of the *Lyrical Ballads* (1800). Other Romantics who wrote or lectured to promote Romanticism were Hunt, William Hazlitt (1778-1830), and Charles Lamb (1775-1834).

KEATS AND SHELLEY

Sometimes the British Romantic poets are divided into the older generation of Blake, Wordsworth, and Coleridge and the younger generation of Byron, Shelley and Keats. While the older generation lived long, the second generation died young, in fact before the first generation. The period in which the two generations coincided, 1810-1820, is one of the most productive periods in the whole of British poetry.

The usefulness of setting the younger Romantics apart is that they can be differentiated by some distinctive developments, especially in terms of using classical mythology for inspiration and subject matter. This is nowhere better seen than in the attempt to write an epic poem. Wordsworth's great unfinished epic, *The Recluse* (1888), was to be set domestically in the Lake District and be a meditative poem about the getting of wisdom through nature. What was published in 1888 was a manuscript left at Wordsworth's death, containing the first book of the first part of the epic poem, which was to have three parts and to contain *The Prelude* as an introduction. *The Prelude* is an epic account of Wordsworth's own poetic formation through epiphanies in nature, education, and the experience of living through the French Revolution. Keats called the type of writing the "egotistical sublime." It is the poet as the subject of his own epic statement.

By contrast, Keats and Shelley attempted to rewrite John Milton's great Christian epic, *Paradise Lost* (1667, 1674), using classical mythology. Keats and Shelley were both atheists and so wanted to reconstruct an epic subject in non-Christian terms. Keats tried with *Hyperion: A Fragment* (1820), which he gave up as "too Miltonic." He tried again with *The Fall of Hyperion: A Dream* (1856), but failing health precluded its completion. The topic was the revolution of the Olympian gods over the older Saturnian ones. Shelley's attempt was more successful. *Prometheus Unbound: A Lyrical Drama in Four Acts* (pb. 1820) takes the myth of Prometheus, the bringer of civilization to humanity in the face of the gods, as a statement about throwing off religious beliefs and embracing a new spirit of liberty.

Both poets wrote other longer mythological poems, but are better remembered for shorter, more lyric pieces, such as Keats's odes and his sonnets, and Shelley's "Ode to the West Wind" and *Adonais: An Elegy* on the Death of John Keats (1821), his very fine tribute to Keats, who died a year before he did.

BLAKE, BYRON, AND OTHERS

Both Blake and Lord Byron stand slightly apart from the other Romantic poets. Both were highly eccentric, but that is not relevant. Although Blake's earliest poetry predates *Lyrical Ballads* by a decade, it was self-published and not widely known until the first decade of the nineteenth century. As such, it had no real appreciable influence on the other poets. Apart from the very simply written ballads of *Songs of Innocence and Experience* (1794), most of his other poems are long, some of epic proportions, after his hero, Milton. Many are highly symbolic and set out Blake's own mystic theology, based on his version of Neoplatonic Christianity.

Byron's eccentricity was to do with self-image. Byronism threatened to take over Romanticism at one stage, so popular were his autobiographical heroes in their mock-epic quests for self-discovery or adventure, described in *Childe Harold's Pilgrimage* (1812-1818, 1819) and *Don Juan* (1819-1824, 1826). It can be questioned whether Byron was a Romantic at all. His verse forms are more typically Augustan, as is his mockheroic satire, and he quite scathingly attacks certain minor Romantic poets, such as Robert Southey (1774-1843).

However, like Shelley, Byron was a revolutionary and an exile, adding to the picture of the Romantic poet as exile or wanderer, ever restless. It could be argued that he developed, with Shelley, what might be called Mediterranean Romanticism, which was carried on by Victorian poet Robert Browning; his wife, Elizabeth Barrett Browning; and a host of painters.

Other forms of Romanticism also developed. Oriental Romanticism became as interesting as Celtic Romanticism. *Lalla Rookh* (1817), a long poem by Thomas Moore (1779-1852), represents a first step in the newly developing colonial literature of the nineteenth century. Moore was an Irishman, and he exploited Irish folksong, as Hogg (*Scottish Pastorals*, 1801; *The Mountain Bard*, 1807), and Scott had done for Scottish folk songs.

Less well-known poets wrote of the English countryside, such as George Crabbe (1754-1832), whose *The Borough: A Poem, in Twenty-four Letters* (1810) inspired Benjamin Britten's most famous opera, *Peter Grimes* (pr. 1945), and John Clare (1793-1864), whose *The Village Minstrel, and Other Poems* appeared in 1821.

WOMEN WRITERS

Efforts have been made to set up a school of female Romantic poets. Volumes such as Jennifer Breen's *Women Romantic Poets, 1785-1832: An Anthology* (1992) are typical of this enterprise. Certainly, there were a great many women poets of the period, including some quite famous writers such as Hannah Moore, the social reformer. However, whether these writers were really Romantic, or whether they have been suppressed in a male-dominated canon is open to debate.

Wordsworth's sister, Dorothy Wordsworth (1771-1855), might seem an obvious candidate, as her brother actually published some of her poems in his collections. Her *Grasmere Journals* has become rightly famous as an important Romantic document, although it was not published until 1987, but her other poetry, much like that of many of the other women, is somewhat domestic.

Considering the fact that female novelists, such as Fanny Burney and Jane Austen, had no difficulty winning recognition, if not immediately, then not too long after their deaths, then it is difficult to substantiate a male plot of suppression against female poets. However, barring discovery of a yet-unknown female Romantic poet, it seems best to conclude that the great female Romantic poets appeared a generation later, with the emergence of Emily Brontë, to be followed by Emily Dickinson, Elizabeth Barrett Browning, and Christina Rossetti.

LEGACY

Romanticism between 1780-1830 was not confined to Britain or even to literature. German Romanticism pre-dates it, having occurred in the Storm and Stress period, which included the early Goethe, and Romantic artists John Constable and William Turner revolutionized British painting as much as the poets did poetry.

In Victorian times, Byron and Scott reigned supreme in popular taste, with a solid recognition of Wordsworth, Coleridge, and Shelley. Keats needed some rehabilitation, as did Blake. Tennyson and Browning took various aspects of Romanticism and worked within that, as did other Victorian poets.

The Georgian poets of the first decade of the twentieth century represent a last sentimental flowing of Romanticism before modernism captured the center ground of British poetry. The one colossus representing "the last of the Romantics" was the Irishman, William Butler Yeats, who developed Romantic poetry in significant new ways and made it workable for twentieth century poets.

BIBLIOGRAPHY

Abrams M. H. *Natural Supernaturalism: Tradition and Revolution in Romantic Literature*. New York: W. W. Norton, 1971. A groundbreaking study of the Romantic revolution set against its critical fortunes.

Butler, Marilyn. *Romantics, Rebels, and Reactionaries: English Literature and Its Background, 1760-1830*. New York: Oxford University Press, 1981. Attempts to account for the rise of Romanticism in the light of its historical and cultural context.

McLane, Maureen N., and James Chandler, eds. *The Cambridge Companion to British Romantic Poetry*. New York: Cambridge University Press, 2008. This volume is part of the Cambridge Companions to Literature series, with specially commissioned essays on a wide range of topics and authors.

O'Neill, Michael, ed. *Literature of the Romantic Period: A Bibliographical Guide*. New York: Oxford University Press, 1998. The definitive bibliographical guide to the period.

Wu, Duncan. *Romantic Poetry*. New York: Wiley-Blackwell, 2002. Perhaps the best introductory guide to Romantic poetry, giving full extracts from the major poets and an overview of Romantic poetry.

David Barratt

FIRESIDE POETS

In the nineteenth century, American families would gather around the fireside to listen as a family member read. Among the works selected were the poems of several American poets who had gained critical respectability and popularity that rivaled that of their British counterparts. The poems of these New England poets—Henry Wadsworth Longfellow, James Russell Lowell, John Greenleaf Whittier, Oliver Wendell Holmes, and William Cullen Bryant—were included in textbooks, and their portraits often adorned schoolroom walls. Therefore, this group is called Fireside or Schoolroom poets.

The Fireside poets shared several characteristics. From youth they displayed language skills. Although their families envisioned legal careers for them, they chose to become magazine editors and contributors, preachers, or college professors. Their interests were literature and education, which for them were closely related. Most wrote about American politics and New England landscapes. They publicly opposed slavery. Some, such as Longfellow, presented Native Americans sympathetically. Generally their poems were highly didactic, emphasizing conventional nineteenth century values: duty, honor, personal responsibility, and hard work. A staple of textbooks, these poems were memorized by generations of schoolchildren.

Several Fireside poets translated the classics, providing many students an introduction to classical mythology and Renaissance literature. These poets used conventional meter and primarily end-rhyme. Most eventually developed friendships with contemporary English poets. Modern critics fault the Fireside poets for their failure to experiment with innovative metrical forms, their conventional ideas, and their excessive sentimentality, but the Fireside poets regarded themselves as the voice of the average American. Literary historians have examined the Fireside poets primarily as nineteenth century cultural icons.

HENRY WADSWORTH LONGFELLOW

The most consistently popular Fireside poet is Henry Wadsworth Longfellow (1807-1882), the only American poet with a bust in the Poets' Corner in West-minster Abbey. On his final visit to England (1868-1869), he received honorary degrees from Oxford and Cambridge Universities; he was also received by Queen Victoria and the prince of Wales.

In the early 1800's, when Longfellow was born, few people believed that an American writer could be successful, because neither English nor American critics and readers respected American writers. Stephen Longfellow wanted his son to follow his example and become a successful lawyer; however, Longfellow's mother, Zilpah Wadsworth Longfellow, herself a writer, encouraged her son's sensitive side.

Reluctant to study law, Longfellow explored other careers. His first choice was writing; he published several poems in local gazettes but quickly realized that an academic career offered financial security unavailable to poets or journalists. After his graduation from Bowdoin College in 1829, the trustees offered him a professorship of modern languages—provided he travel to Europe and become fluent in Romance languages. Longfellow decided to add proficiency in German.

At Bowdoin, Longfellow modernized foreign language instruction, replacing rote exercises with conversational approaches. Not completely happy there, he eagerly accepted an offer to become Smith Professor of Modern Languages at Harvard University in 1837, first traveling to Europe, this time to acquaint himself with Scandinavian languages and literature, for which he discovered a real affinity. On each trip, Longfellow developed personal friendships with writers.

Longfellow had a gift for intellectual friendships. After retirement from Harvard in 1854, he maintained contact with his academic colleagues and fellow poets. In 1855, a group of American writers calling themselves the Saturday Club began meeting monthly. In 1857, Longfellow joined other *Atlantic Monthly* contributors in founding the Atlantic Club.

Longfellow's popularity was established with the 1847 publication of *Evangeline*, a long poem in dactylic hexameter. Although it seems excessively sentimental to most twenty-first century readers, this narrative poem about the separation of lovers when the Acadians were exiled to Louisiana immediately appealed to readers in the United States and Europe and retained its popularity well into the twentieth century. Almost as popular was *The Song of Hiawatha* (1855), which Longfellow intended as the Native American equivalent of Scandinavian epics. Portrayed as honorable and noble, Hiawatha was doomed to defeat by manifest destiny. Longfellow focused on New England history in *The Courtship of Miles Standish, and Other Poems* (1858), source of the familiar admonition that John Alden speak for himself. In *Tales of a Wayside Inn* (1863), Longfellow imitated the narrative structure of Geoffrey Chaucer's *The Canterbury Tales* (1387-1400) and Giovanni Boccaccio's *Decameron: O, Prencipe Galetto* (1349-1351; *The Decameron*, 1620). Several poems dealt with New England subjects, but most reflected his European travels. In *The New England Tragedies* (1968), Longfellow compared the careers of rebellious colonial figures John Endicott and Giles Corey. Longfellow's *The Divine Tragedy* (1971), his meditation on the passion of Christ, confused some readers, and his later volumes did not sell as well as earlier ones had. Nevertheless, Longfellow remained the quintessentially American poet, respected by fellow poets such as Walt Whitman and critics such as Edgar Allan Poe.

Although Longfellow experienced his share of personal tragedy, his poems generally dealt with historical events or sentimental portraits of family life (as in the popular "The Children's Hour") and were almost never confessional; one exception is the posthumously published "The Cross of Snow," which chronicled his grief at the death of his second wife, Frances Appleton. Longfellow's solace was his work. When his first wife, Mary Potter, suffered a miscarriage and died, he immersed himself in the study of German literature. When his second wife died in a fire, he turned to his blank-verse translation of Dante's *La divina commedia* (c. 1320; *The Divine Comedy*, 1802). While translating this epic, Longfellow met weekly with the Dante Club, other poets working on their own translations. Again, Longfellow's metrical and linguistic skills served him well; his translation of Dante is still considered one of the best.

Longfellow and his second wife, Frances, were the parents of six children (Charles, Ernest, Fanny, Alice, Edith, and Anne Allegra), and when Longfellow died of phlebitis a few days after his seventy-fifth birthday, he left them an estate of $356,320—a remarkable sum for a nineteenth century writer. His poems had been translated into twenty-four languages, and he had proven one could become a successful American writer.

JAMES RUSSELL LOWELL

James Russell Lowell (1819-1891) never achieved the general popularity of his friend Longfellow; Lowell is remembered less for his poetry than for his essays, his diplomatic service, and his founding editorship of *The Atlantic Monthly*.

Lowell was the son of the Reverend Charles Russell Lowell and Harriet Brackett Spence, both descendants of prominent New England families. Lowell graduated from Harvard College in 1838 and Harvard Law School in 1840, but quickly decided on a literary career. Influenced by Maria White (whom he married in 1844), Lowell published a poetry collection, *A Year's Life* (1841), which was neither a commercial nor a critical success. Reviewers pointed out the flaws that would plague Lowell throughout his career: technical infelicities, metrical irregularities, extreme didacticism, and obscure allusions.

In 1848, Lowell published the three works for which he is most remembered: *The Biglow Papers*, *A Fable for Critics*, and *The Vision of Sir Launfal*. An instant popular success, *The Biglow Papers* uses a prose framework to present dialect verses of Yankee farmer Hosea Biglow, who opposes the Mexican War. *The Biglow Papers* remained so popular that Lowell issued *The Biglow Papers: Second Series* (1867), this time dealing with the American Civil War. *A Fable for Critics*, published anonymously, is a humorous appraisal of Longfellow's literary contemporaries. Lowell's critical acumen, as evidenced in this work, is still much admired. Less enduringly successful was *The Vision of Sir Launfal*, a conventional, didactic, and sentimental account of an Arthurian knight's Grail quest. Though Lowell published several additional volumes of poetry, none was as successful as these.

After Maria's death in 1853, Lowell subordinated

poetry to teaching, replacing Longfellow as Smith Professor of Modern Languages at Harvard in 1855. He served as the first editor of *The Atlantic Monthly* (1857-1861) and influenced the careers of many American writers. Lowell's reputation as writer and reformer led eventually to his appointment as minister to Spain (1877-1880) and England (1880-1885). He was elected to membership in the Spanish Academy (1878) and awarded honorary degrees from Oxford and Cambridge (1885).

In 1857, Lowell married Frances Dunlap, originally governess for his sole surviving child, Mabel. After her death in 1885, Lowell returned to his family's estate, remaining there until his death in 1891. His reputation rests on his critical astuteness, his effective and accurate use of Yankee dialect, and his contributions as editor of *The Atlantic Monthly*; his poetry is rarely read.

JOHN GREENLEAF WHITTIER

Directly influenced by Longfellow's successful career was John Greenleaf Whittier (1807-1892), whose ambition to become the poetic voice of New England was inspired by Longfellow's "A Psalm of Life," just as his introduction to the Scottish poet Robert Burns had awakened his appreciation for his natural surroundings.

Whittier's devout Quaker parents—John Whittier and Abigail Hussey Whittier—were farmers in Haverhill, Massachusetts, where their second child, John Greenleaf, was born in 1807. The Whittiers were neither rich nor poor, but the family library was reasonably varied. Whittier's father opposed his son's continued education as impractical. When Whittier's sister, Mary, sent one of his poems anonymously to William Lloyd Garrison, the abolitionist editor persuaded the Whittiers to allow their son to attend Haverhill Academy for two terms, though he had to earn his own way.

After Whittier left Haverhill

Academy, his formal education ended, although his practical education continued, as he edited several New England gazettes, including the pro-Whig *American Manufacturer* (Boston, 1828), *Haverhill Gazette* (1830 and again in 1836), the *New England Weekly Review* (Hartford, 1830), and *National Era* (Washington, 1845).

Increasingly Whittier became an abolition movement propagandist, writing several abolitionist poems. "Massachusetts to Virginia" (1843) is his response to the Fugitive Slave Law. "Song of Slaves in the Desert" (1847) translates laments of a coffle of slaves being transported for sale. "Letter from a Missionary of the Methodist Episcopal Church South, in Kansas to a Distinguished Politician" (1854) describes the abolitionist struggle in Kansas. "Laus Deo" (1865) reflects Whittier's reaction to the ratification of the Thirteen Amendment; although Whittier expresses his delight, he warns that slavery's problems have not been alleviated.

More famous is "Ichabod" (1850), Whittier's denunciation of Daniel Webster for supporting the Missouri Compromise. With sorrow and disappointment rather than anger, Whittier laments the departed honor and glory of the man he once idolized. In contrast,

American students studying the works of Fireside poet John Greenleaf Whittier, circa 1899.
(Getty Images)

"Barbara Frietchie" (1863) and "Abraham Davenport" (1866) portray heroes who steadfastly maintain their principles. Barbara Frietchie is an older woman who refuses to lower her flag when the Confederates take control of her hometown. When a solar eclipse convinces the other Connecticut legislators that Judgment Day has arrived, Abraham Davenport insists on continuing to do his duty, ordering candles to combat the darkness. Less admirable is the subject of "Skipper Ireson's Ride" (1857), a merciless sea captain whose cruelty finally drives the women of Marblehead to tar and feather him. The strength of this poem is Whittier's use of dialect in a refrain chanted by the women.

Whittier's greatest popularity came from his portraits of Yankee farm life. In his first poetry collection, *Legends of New-England* (1831), Whittier described his boyhood memories. In "Telling the Bees" (1858), the first-person narrator learns of his beloved's death when he sees a servant draping the hives with black ribbons. Failed love is also the subject of "Maud Muller" (1854), whose central characters admire each other from a distance but fail to make any romantic overtures because they belong to different social classes. For the rest of their lives, they think about what might have been. The sentimentality of these poems appealed to nineteenth century readers, but most modern readers prefer less sentimental poems.

Snow-Bound: A Winter Idyl (1866) was Whittier's tribute to his family, most of whom had died by the time the work was published. Whittier describes a winter storm that isolates a farm family for a week. To combat the sinister force of the storm, the family (a father and mother, their son and two daughters, a bachelor uncle, and an unmarried aunt) sit around the fire, exchanging stories of colonial days and the Revolution, observations about nature, and memories of their youth. To a country still predominantly rural but beginning to experience the effects of industrialization, this narrative poem presented a nostalgic look at the life they remembered or wished they had experienced. After the publication of *Snow-Bound*, Whittier suddenly became affluent, and his popularity continued for many years after his death in 1892 in Hampton Falls, New Hampshire. He was buried in the cemetery at Amesbury, with the family he had immortalized.

WILLIAM CULLEN BRYANT

Though often grouped with the Fireside poets whom he rivaled in popularity, William Cullen Bryant (1794-1878) was more closely associated with the Knickerbocker writers (such as Washington Irving and James Fenimore Cooper), as he spent most of his life as a New York City journalist. Though he was widely admired as a poetic prodigy in his own era, his reputation now rests on only a few nature poems; however, he is still respected for his long editorship of the *New York Evening Post*, where he advocated a variety of reforms.

Born in Cummington, Massachusetts, Bryant was the son of Peter Bryant (a physician) and Sarah Snell Bryant, both of whom were descended from old New England families. A sickly child, Bryant was allowed to roam the woods near his western Massachusetts home, where he developed an enduring love for nature. When Bryant was thirteen, his father helped him publish "The Embargo" (1808), an anti-Jeffersonian satire, in which the young poet echos his parents' Calvinistic religion and Federalist politics. This poem established him as a prodigy. In 1817, the publication of "Thanatopsis" confirmed his virtuosity, and in 1821, he published his first collection, *Poems*.

Still not regarding poetry as his vocation, Bryant attended Williams College (1810-1811), then studied law, being admitted to the bar in 1815. After practicing law for several years, he turned to writing for magazines. He moved to New York to pursue a journalism career in 1825, and he became an assistant editor at the *New York Evening Post* in 1826. In 1826, he was promoted to editor, a position he retained for fifty years. Philosophically, he abandoned conservative religion and politics, eventually becoming a founder of the Republican Party.

Bryant's home life was apparently happy. In 1821, he married Francis Fairchild; though she became an invalid, he devotedly cared for her. Daughters Frances and Julia were born in 1822 and 1832. In 1844, Bryant purchased a home on Long Island, in an area still somewhat rural. Though his wife died in 1866, Bryant remained physically and intellectually active until a fall in May, 1878, which led to a stroke and ultimately to his death on June 12, 1878. He willed his papers to the New York Public Library.

Among nineteenth century readers, Bryant's popularity rivaled that of Longfellow. Especially popular in textbooks was the 1821 revision of "Thanatopsis," with sixteen and a half additional lines modifying the poem's original stoicism and establishing nature as consoler of humankind. Also frequently anthologized was "To a Waterfowl," composed in December, 1815. In this poem, somewhat depressed about his future, Bryant sees a lone waterfowl and remembers that Providence guides all creatures. Bryant also appealed to his readers when he praised forests as God's first temples in "A Forest Hymn" (1825). "The Yellow Violet" (1814) didactically warns readers against forgetting early, simple flowers; "The Fringed Gentian" (1829) praises the last flower of the season. More sentimental is "The Death of the Flowers" (1825), in which Bryant parallels the death of flowers in the fall and the untimely death of a favorite sister. "The Two Graves" (1826), a further meditation on the destination of the soul, insists that the dead would choose to remain in familiar places until Resurrection day.

Modern readers find Bryant's journalism more impressive than his poetry, which is generally considered too abstract and didactic, with language and meter subordinated to theme. Nevertheless, Bryant is considered important for establishing American poetry as a significant genre; in 1986, Fordham University published *Under Open Sky: Poets on William Cullen Bryant* (edited by John DePol and Norbert Kropt), contemporary poets' analysis of Bryant's place in American poetry.

OLIVER WENDELL HOLMES

Oliver Wendell Holmes (1809-1894) wrote in a number of genres besides poetry, producing novels such as *Elsie Venner* (1861) and *The Guardian Angel* (1867); collections of essays, including *The Autocrat of the Breakfast-Table* (1858), *The Professor at the Breakfast-Table* (1860), and *The Poet at the Breakfast-Table* (1872); biographies; and essays on medicine.

Holmes was born in Cambridge, Massachusetts, to Abiel Holmes, a Congregational minister, and Sarah Wendell, a descendant of the poet Anne Bradstreet. Early in his life, Holmes developed an interest in natural science, which was augmented by an interest in poetry. He was named class poet when he graduated from Harvard University in 1829 and received an M.D. from

Harvard in 1836. He became a physician, research scientist, and teacher, serving as professor of anatomy at Dartmouth College (1839-1840) and the Parkman Professor of Anatomy and Physiology at the Harvard Medical School (1847-1882).

In 1830, he wrote "Old Ironsides" in response to reports that the U.S.S. *Constitution* was to be demolished. The publication of the poem in the Boston *Daily Advertiser* helped save the frigate and brought Holmes to national prominence as a poet. That same year, Holmes published "The Last Leaf," a poem in honor of Major Thomas Melville, which was praised by critic Poe and memorized by Abraham Lincoln. His first poetry collection, *Poems*, appeared in 1836. In 1831 and 1832, two essays entitled "The Autocrat of the Breakfast-Table" were published in the *New England Magazine*. In 1857, he published a series of Autocrat essays in the newly created *The Atlantic Monthly* that were later collected and published as *The Autocrat of the Breakfast-Table*. Two of his well-known poems, "The Deacon's Masterpiece: Or, The Wonderful 'One-Hoss Shay'" and "The Chambered Nautilus," first appeared in an Autocrat essay. "The Deacon's Masterpriece" has generated some controversy in regard to how it is to be interpreted, but it can be enjoyed for its use of New England dialect and humor. In "The Chambered Nautilus," Holmes describes the growth of the nautilus, a sea creature that lives inside a shell to which it continually adds new chambers. He compares it to the need for humans to develop and progress.

Holmes was immensely popular during his lifetime, but like most of the Fireside poets, his popularity and critical acclaim have diminished. Many of his poems were occasional poems, and their relevance and appeal has faded. However, several of his poems are still anthologized and appreciated.

BIBLIOGRAPHY

Boswell, Jeanetta. *The Schoolroom Poets: A Bibliography of Bryant, Holmes, Longfellow, Lowell, and Whittier, with Selective Annotation*. Metuchen, N.J.: Scarecrow Press, 1983. A basic bibliography of a number of the Fireside poets.

Calhoun, Charles C. *Longfellow: A Rediscovered Life*. Boston: Beacon Press, 2004. Calls Longfellow an influential poet and educator who introduced Americans to much of European culture, popularized Native American folklore, and criticized the Puritan focus on material success.

Justus, James J. "Fireside Poets: Hearthside Values and the Language of Care." In *Nineteenth-Century American Poetry*, edited by A. Robert Lee. London: Barnes & Noble, 1985. This essay looks at the group known as Fireside poets, noting their values and how they were reflected in the poetry.

Lowell, James Russell. *The Poetical Works of James Russell Lowell*. Eastbourne, East Sussex, England: Gardners Books, 2007. Reprint of a classic collection of Lowell's poetry.

Muller, Gilbert H. *William Cullen Bryant: Author of America*. Albany: State University of New York Press, 2008. This biography details Bryant's life and regards him to be an important American literary voice.

Parini, Jay, ed. *The Oxford Encyclopedia of American Literature*. New York: Oxford University Press, 2004. Contains a chapter on the Fireside poets, looking at their early importance and legacy.

Pickard, Samuel Thomas. *Life and Letters of John Greenleaf Whittier*. Vol. 1. Honolulu, Hawaii: University Press of the Pacific, 2005. This biography of Whittier, a Fireside poet, covers his life and works.

Sorby, Angela. *Schoolroom Poets: Childhood, Performance, and the Place of American Poetry, 1865-1917*. Durham: University of New Hampshire Press, 2005. Examines a time when poetry was part of middle-class life and popular poems were recited and learned by children. Examines several poets and numerous poems.

_____. "Teaching the Schoolroom Poets." In *Teaching Nineteenth-Century American Poetry*, edited by Paula Bennett, Karen L. Kilcup, and Philipp Schweighauser. New York: Modern Language Association of America, 2007. Contains information on the Fireside poets and how to make them relevant to modern students.

Charmaine Allmon Mosby

FRENCH SYMBOLISTS

During the first half of the nineteenth century, poetry in France was dominated by Romanticism, which had broken the rules of classicism and had opened the way for freedom of poetic creation. Poetry had become emotive and descriptive; the poet had been recognized as an isolated individual alienated from society by his genius. Materialistic bourgeois society had been rejected by the poets. As the century progressed, French poetry evolved into three main schools or styles: Parnassianism, Decadence, and Symbolism. The Parnassians took as their credo the art-for-art's-sake theory of poetry put forth by Théophile Gautier, in which form mattered more than idea. Purity of form and emotional detachment permeated the Parnassians' works, which treated subjects from antiquity or described exotic places. The Decadents exploited the darker traditions of Romanticism and showed a preference for morbid and erotic subjects. The extreme dislike of the bourgeoisie and the pleasure in shocking them, the idea of the poet as alienated from society, and the preoccupation with death were major elements of their poetry. They regularly used opium, hashish, and absinthe to find an inscrutable truth beyond reality. The Symbolists rejected sentimental effusion of emotion over nature and did not accept this world as the true reality. Their poems expressed states of mind, moods, and sensations evoking inner experiences and communication with a transcendental other world. The musicality of the verse became an extremely important element of their poetry. Much of the poetry of the nineteenth century, especially that of Charles Baudelaire and Arthur Rimbaud, combined characteristics of Decadence and Symbolism.

Although elements of Symbolism can be found in French poetry as early as the 1850's, the Symbolist movement was not founded until the last decades of the century. On September 18, 1886, Jean Moréas (1856-1910) published the *Manifeste du symbolisme* (the Symbolist manifesto) in *Le Figaro*. Moréas was actually the first to refer to the poets using symbolism as Symbolists and to a Symbolist movement. The manifesto declared Symbolism to be the major school of French poetry and distinguished Symbolism from Decadence. Because the Decadents treated morbid or erotic subjects in their works and used hallucinatory drugs to achieve states of heightened consciousness, they were considered amoral. Critics and the general public often referred to both Symbolist and Decadent writers as Decadents, and Moréas and his fellow poets wished to avoid being called Decadents, although some of the earlier poets such as Gautier and Baudelaire, whom they admired and whose poetics had strong influences on their work, had taken pride in being considered Decadents. In addition to distinguishing the Symbolists from the Decadents, Moréas defended Symbolism as the superior literary form and severely criticized not only Parnassian poetry but also the realism and naturalism prevalent in the plays and novels of the period.

SYMBOLISM AS A LITERARY MOVEMENT

In 1885, Gabriel Vicaire and Henri Beauclaire had published a scathing satire of symbolism, *Les Déliquescences d'Adoré Floupette* (the corruption of Adoré Floupette). At first, the satire was viewed by the public as an actual Symbolist work. Then, when the truth was known, the work actually benefited the symbolists as it stimulated the public's interest in their work. Several journals and reviews devoted to Symbolism were founded during the late 1880's. Gustave Kahn published *La Vogue*; he was the first to publish works of Rimbaud and Stéphane Mallarmé. Kahn, Paul Adam, and Moréas founded *Le Symboliste*. In 1889, Alfred Valette and his wife, Marguerite Eymery (known as Rachilde), founded Symbolism's most important journal, *Le Mercure de France*. They also held a salon at which the Symbolists gathered to discuss their poetry and literary theory. While Mallarmé never presented himself as the leader of the Symbolist Movement, he is often considered as such because of the *mardis* (Tuesdays) when he hosted writers for literary discussions. He also acted as mentor to a number of young writers. One of these younger poets was Paul Valéry, who carried Symbolism into the twentieth century with his poems *La Jeune Parque* (1917; *The Youngest of the Fates*, 1947; also known as *The Young Fate*) and "Le Cimetière marin" (1920; "The Graveyard by the Sea").

The Symbolist movement was at its peak from 1886 to 1892, and was largely over by 1905. Among the Symbolists were anarchists or supporters of the anarchist cause. When the anarchists adopted violent tactics (an anarchist threw a bomb into the French chamber of deputies in 1893), the popularity of the Symbolists suffered. After the turn of the century, Symbolism had become the established literary form against which new young writers were reacting, by either pushing its limits farther as in Surrealism or returning to older forms.

Symbolist poets Paul Verlaine, left, and Jean Moréas, depicted in a poster for an art exhibition in 1894. (The Granger Collection, New York)

THE POETS AND THEIR DOCTRINE

The major poets involved in the movement were Moréas, Kahn (who wrote free verse), Henri Régnier, Jules Laforgue, Emile Verharen, and René Ghil (who wrote purely Symbolist poetry). In 1891, however, Moréas abandoned Symbolism, returned to the poetic style of the Renaissance, and founded the École Romane. When Moréas left the movement, Remy de Gourmont, one of the editors of the *Le Mercure de France*, became the most enthusiastic advocate of Symbolism. Gourmont not only was a critic but also wrote in all literary genres and even created book designs and typography based on Symbolist theories. However, most of these poets were practitioners rather than creators of symbolist poetical theory. Symbolism as poetry and theory was developed in the works of Mallarmé, Verlaine, Rimbaud, Baudelaire, and Tristan Corbière, five of the poets praised in Verlaine's *Poètes maudits* (1884; *The Cursed Poets*, 2003).

The poetry of the Symbolists did not present concrete realistic images and did not actually set forth ideas; instead it sought to convey nuances of feeling, states of mind, and the invisible world. It also suggested a connection between the world that is visible to the human eye and the invisible world that the Symbolists believed to be the real world. The qualities most appreciated in Symbolism were the poetry's musicality, nuances, vagueness, and lightness. Meaning gave way to lyricism, and Symbolist poetry became poetry in its purest sense as it evolved into rhythm and sound.

CHARLES BAUDELAIRE

Les Fleurs du mal (1857, 1861, 1868; *Flowers of Evil*, 1931), especially the poem "Correspondances" ("Correspondences"), by Charles Baudelaire (1821-1867), is the work to which Symbolism traces its origins. Baudelaire envisioned an invisible world beyond the one that appeared to the human eye. For him, everything he perceived was a portal to the invisible world, to the beyond. His senses, imagination, and intelligence—all superior in a poet—enabled him to unlock this invisible world and lead his readers and listeners into this world. The poem had to be heard, because for Baudelaire, the sound, the combination of syllables, alliterations, rhymes, and rhythms were as important, or more important, than the sense of the words of the poem.

In "Correspondences," Baudelaire reveals that, for the most part, humans move through life without ever becoming aware of the real invisible world. Preoccupied by daily concerns and ambitions, people move within the temple of living pillars, which is nature, without ever hearing the words uttered. People are totally unaware of the symbols that observe all human activity with a friendly gaze. The last three stanzas of the poem present examples of the phenomenon of synesthesia, the correspondence of human sense perceptions. Baudelaire believed that the sensations received through the different senses interact, that a visual perception could trigger an olfactory or tactile perception or recall a memory of such a sense perception. In the second stanza, he describes echoes that are merged into each other far away in the world beyond the visible world and present themselves in the visible world as perfumes, colors, and sounds reaching humans through the olfactory, visual, and auditory senses. In the third stanza, he uses images in which the sense impressions of the perfumes transform and result in unexpected stimulation of the senses. The first image is tactile as the perfumes are compared to children's flesh. The second is auditory, for these perfumes are as sweet as oboes; the third is visual, as the perfumes possess the greenness of prairies. The final verse of the stanza invokes other perfumes that are corrupted, rich, and triumphant; the image once again unites the sensatory reactions in a vague confusion. In the final stanza, Baudelaire reiterates the power or capacity of these elements to transport the soul as well as the senses into the invisible world of the spirit.

This invisible world that comforts the soul and transcends the misery of the materialistic world appears in many of Baudelaire's poems. In "Elévation" ("Elevation"), he advises his spirit to leave the unhealthy reality of the visible world and to fly off to the other realm, where it can purify itself and drink the clear liquid fire. He celebrates the individual who can reach behind or beyond the boredom and misery of existence to the realm where serenity and light are found. Baudelaire speaks of the joy of those who can understand the language of flowers and mute things. The poem builds on

the same theme as that of "Correspondences" and adds the theme of the voyage of the spirit. In the poem "Le Voyage" ("The Trip"), Baudelaire again treats this theme. The poem begins with a description of travel that is familiar; it is a sea voyage. At first, the travelers are homesick, but soon the effect of the sea on their senses washes away all thoughts of the life they have left. In the next stanza, Baudelaire shifts from this description of everyday travel to the experiences of travelers who, like balloons, take flight for unknown sensations and pleasures beyond earthly human knowledge. Their voyage transports them away from the everyday material reality and into the ethereal other existence.

In his poems about cats, Baudelaire celebrates his concepts of mystery and of the *au-délà*, the realm beyond this world where all is comfort, solace, and pleasure. In "Le Chat" ("The Cat"), the cat is both in his apartment and in his spirit (mind and soul). The voice of the cat carries him into the invisible world. The smell and feel of the cat's fur transport him. When he looks into the cat's eyes and then into himself with his mind's eye, he sees within his mind the cat's eyes, because there is a mysterious union, transference, and correspondence that transports the poet beyond his miseries and suffering.

Baudelaire's poetry is vastly different in its entirety from that of the Symbolist movement at the end of the century. Baudelaire's poetry is the poetry of Decadence and of the agony over the attraction to evil, yet it is also the quest for that which is beyond the misery, sufferings, and impossibility of the visible world. While Baudelaire is much more, he is the "first" Symbolist.

ARTHUR RIMBAUD

Influenced by Baudelaire, Arthur Rimbaud (1854-1891) envisioned the poet as a seer. He believed that it was necessary to achieve a deranged state of the senses and the mind to see into the hidden, inscrutable other existence where true reality could be found. He achieved this state by the use of drugs, particularly hashish. The Symbolist aspects of his poetry are found in his unconventional images, his suggestions of elsewhere, and the freedom and fluidity of his verse. "Le Bateau ivre" ("The Drunken Boat") is his best-known poem and is the poem that had the greatest influence on the Symbolist movement. Rimbaud's "The Drunken Boat" was not published until 1883 when it appeared in the periodical *Lutèce*. He had, however, written it some time before his arrival in Paris in September of 1871. The poem, which reflects Rimbaud's familiarity with many works about the sea and exotic places and their inhabitants, both human and animal, brings to mind Baudelaire's "The Trip." However, Rimbaud's poem is in no way an imitation of Baudelaire's poem. The voyage becomes more vast, more exhilarated, and more intense as Rimbaud continually juxtaposes images drawn from the world of material reality with those of the imagination, of the other existence seen once the senses and the intellect have been altered.

Rimbaud's entire poem is filled with mystery as it refuses to permit its reader or listener to understand or to definitively identify the "I" of the poem. The "I" implies the boat itself, which sails without guides, but it also suggests a person sailing on the aimless boat, and this image then slides into that of an imaginary voyage of the mind. Rimbaud enforces this vacillation of meaning by including concrete, real images and places such as European merchant ships, "redskins" and panthers, intermingled with images of unchained islands, of the "I" lighter than a cork dancing, and of the "I" bathed in the poem of the ocean. Rimbaud also alters his syntax so that it multiplies and confuses meaning. Consequently, the poem can be read from a point of view that rearranges the words and makes everyday sense out of what it says. However, if readers suspend their intellect and free their understanding so that they can accept word combinations as they come, the so-called sense or meaning of the poem constantly changes and reproduces the image of the boat traveling unguided down the rivers and across the seas. The poem becomes the mind's voyage into the transcendental otherworld. Rimbaud's "The Drunken Boat" was a rich source of symbols and images for the Symbolists.

PAUL VERLAINE

Paul Verlaine (1844-1896), like Mallarmé, influenced the Symbolists most in his insistence on the musicality of poetry. Verlaine's "L'Art poétique," written in 1882 and published in *Jadis et naguère* (1884), was taken by the poets of the Symbolist move-

ment as a set of standards for their poetic creation. In his poem, he emphasized that before everything else, the verses and language of a poem must create music. His own poems attest to the value of this characteristic in poetry. Verlaine then proceeds to explain how to write poetry that is music. He recommends an uneven rhythm created by verses having a uneven number of syllables. Word choice is critical. He recommends joining together precise words and vague words. The poem then must be filled out with subtle nuances. Verlaine also admonishes the poet to avoid clever wit, cruel sarcasm, and dissolute and common images. Verlaine's influence led the Symbolists away from the Decadent aspect of the poetry of Baudelaire and Rimbaud. His influence also directed them toward a poetry that was less and less concerned with meaning and was directed toward a pure lyricism as poetry became music in words.

Verlaine's other major contribution to the development of Symbolist poetry was his book *The Cursed Poets*, published by Vanier in 1884. In the text, Verlaine celebrated eight poets who were accursed by the sorrows of their lives and their alienation by a society that failed to appreciate their genius. The poets whom he declared absolute poets because of their imagination and their expression were Baudelaire, Rimbaud, Corbière, Gérard de Nerval, Marceline Desbordes-Valmore, Villiers de l'Isle-Adam, Mallarmé, and himself under the anagram of Pauvre Lelian. He included poems of each of the poets and a critique of the poems and called attention to their work.

TRISTAN CORBIÈRE

While seven of the poets were well known in poetic circles, Tristan Corbière (1845-1875) had received little attention. Afflicted with rheumatoid arthritis and tuberculosis, Corbière had spent the majority of his life at Roscoff in Bretagne. Corbière had written and published *Les Amours jaunes* (1873; *These Jaundiced Loves*, 1995), a book of Decadent and Symbolist poems, before his death in 1875. Corbière was a master of wordplay, of exploiting the musical quality of language, of creating startling images, and of evoking the invisible otherworld. Through Verlaine, Corbière's poetry influenced the development of the Symbolist movement.

STÉPHANE MALLARMÉ

Stéphane Mallarmé (1842-1898) was recognized as the leader of the Symbolist movement in the 1890's both for his poetic theory and for his poetic production. Mallarmé sought to create in his poetry the essence of perfect form, which he believed was contained in the nothingness that he envisioned beyond the reality of this world. He strived to write pure poetry that would be free of all conventional meaning and sense and to use words in such fashion that they would have new meanings. For Mallarmé, words as symbols were to evoke this essence. Mallarmé spent long laborious hours refining his verse, searching for exactly the right word and reorganizing the syntax of his poems. Plagued by the desire to achieve perfection in his poetic creation, he wrote only forty-nine poems. Mallarmé believed that the more ambiguous the sentence structure and the more complex the associations made, the better the poem. What had to be avoided was the telling of a story; the poem was to suggest, to free the imagination. His fascination with language and its infinite possibilities led him to write his experimental poem, *Un Coup de dés jamais n'abolira le hasard* (1897; *A Dice-Throw*, 1958; also as *Dice Thrown Never Will Annul Chance*, 1965), in which the lines of the poem are placed on the page such that it may be read following different patterns and giving different meanings. For Mallarmé as for Verlaine, poetry was music in words. This made it essential for his poetry to be read aloud to reveal the subtle and complex meanings suggested by the words. The essence of his poetry was infused in the sounds of his poetry. Mallarmé's work truly achieved the ultimate expression of Symbolism. Mallarmé regularly shared his theory with his guests in his Tuesday evening gatherings, thus playing a significant role in the creation of Symbolism both as a form of poetry and as a movement.

BIBLIOGRAPHY

Acquisto, Joseph. *French Symbolist Poetry and the Idea of Music*. Burlington, Vt.: Ashgate, 2006. Excellent investigation of the role of music in the development of Symbolism. Studies the approaches of Charles Baudelaire and Stéphane Mallarmé to the function of lyric and the use of memory in Symbolist poetry.

Lloyd, Rosemary. *Baudelaire's World*. Ithaca, N.Y.: Cornell University Press, 2002. Excellent study of Charles Baudelaire's life, theory, and poetry, and of how his work reflects mid-nineteenth century Paris. Also examines the problems of translating poetry.

_____. *Mallarmé: The Poet and His Circle*. Ithaca, N.Y.: Cornell University Press, 2005. Discusses Stéphane Mallarmé's life and his role as the leading Symbolist poet of the period. Translations and explications of his work. Includes "Crise de vers," which explains much of his theory of poetry.

McGuinness, Patrick, ed. *Symbolism, Decadence, and the Fin de Siècle: French and European Perspectives*. Exeter, England: University of Exeter Press, 2000. Good overview of aesthetic activity from 1870 to 1914 in France and its spread throughout Europe. Helps to understand the relationship of Symbolism and Decadence and how both are present in much of the poetry of the period.

Mallarmé, Stéphane. *To Purify the Words of the Tribe: The Major Verse Poems of Stéphane Mallarmé*. Translated by Daisy Aldan. Huntington Woods, Mich.: Sky Blue Press, 1999. Good broad selection of Mallarmé's poems including his tributes to Charles Baudelaire and Paul Verlaine. Also translation of his experimental *Un Coup de dés jamais n'abolira le hasard* (1897; *A Dice-Throw*, 1958; also as *Dice Thrown Never Will Annul Chance*, 1965). Good analysis of Mallarmé's work.

Reynolds, Dee. *Symbolist Aesthetics and Early Abstract Sites of Imaginary Space*. New York: Cambridge University Press, 2008. Excellent chapters on Arthur Rimbaud and Stéphane Mallarmé. Discusses their use of rhythm and the role of imagination. Also defines Symbolism as a term in literary criticism.

Rhodes, S. A. *The Cult of Beauty in Charles Baudelaire*. Vol. 1. Whitefish, Mont.: Kessinger, 2006. Chapter 4 provides an excellent in-depth discussion of Symbolism in Baudelaire's poetry and chapter 2 contains a good examination of the aesthetics of sensation in Baudelaire.

Verlaine, Paul. *The Cursed Poets*. Bilingual ed. Los Angeles: Green Integer, 2001. Important text for its influence on the Symbolist poets. Also good source for poetry of the eight accursed poets.

Shawncey Webb

IMAGISTS

By the end of the nineteenth century, poets in Great Britain and the United States were seeking a new, modern way to write verse. In Britain, the reigning movements in poetry and the arts—Romanticism and Victorianism—seemed to have run their course. Romantic lyric poetry as exemplified by Percy Bysshe Shelley and John Keats, for example, had degenerated (many poets believed) into self-indulgence, so that poets seemed so preoccupied with their own subjectivity that the greater world was largely ignored. The result was a poetry that was precious and clichéd. In other words, poets relied on stock words and phrases such as "thee" and "thou" and "the orb of heaven" that tended to remove poetry from reality, from the day-to-day experience of most people. Poets were, in effect, just repeating what other poets had to say. Victorian poets had made matters worse by writing with sentimentality and decorum, thus eschewing the raw, robust radicalism that poets of Lord Byron's generation had cultivated.

In the United States, poetry as an art was in a kind of limbo. The two greatest American poets of the nineteenth century—Walt Whitman and Emily Dickinson—had largely been ignored by their contemporaries, and the full extent of their contributions to American poetry were discounted in the 1880's and 1890's by what came to be termed the "genteel tradition," one that like the Victorians used poetry to express acceptable sentiments and avoided outspoken experiments. Dickinson and Whitman would not receive their due until the 1920's, after a new generation of writers and critics rediscovered them, seeing in their work the seeds of a bold, new, modern poetry.

Of course, these broad generalizations should not obscure the significant works of poets such as Alfred, Lord Tennyson, and Robert Browning or of the nascent poetry of writers such as Stephen Crane, who died while still quite young and just as he was experimenting with the verse that anticipated Imagism. However, the state of Anglo-American poetry at the end of the nineteenth century seemed moribund to a new generation that would begin to be published in the first two decades of the twentieth century.

The key figure involved in the developed of new experimental forms of poetry, including Imagism, was the American poet and critic Ezra Pound (1885-1972). Finding few sources of encouragement in his native land, Pound settled in London, quickly befriending older, established poets like William Butler Yeats (1865-1939), who seemed eager to write a sharper, grittier, kind of verse that would distinguished them from their nineteenth century predecessors and contemporaries.

THE INFLUENCE OF POUND

Pound used London as his poetry laboratory. He quickly made friends with promising young writers such as Richard Aldington (1892-1962), H. D. (Hilda Doolittle, 1886-1961), John Gould Fletcher (1886-1950), and F. S. Flint (1885-1960)—all of whom would become part of the Imagist movement. Pound also met

Ezra Pound (Getty Images)

a British philosopher, T. E. Hulme (1883-1917), who believed in the revival of classicism, which emphasized not the personality of the writer but the form of the work. The structure of works of art ought to be the poet's concern in an age of science, Hulme argued, and not the poet's feelings per se.

From his talks with Hulme, Pound formulated the cardinal principles of Imagism: direct treatment of subject matter (in practice, this would mean an almost photographic portrayal of objects and scenes) and elimination of any word or phrase that did not absolutely contribute to the presentation of the poem. Another tenet of Imagism was mainly technical advice to poets: Write in musical phrases rather than in rigid meter. Pound was certainly not opposed to traditional forms of poetry such as the sonnet, but the emphasis of his program led to experiments with free verse—lines that did not have end rhymes and that could be of varying lengths and numbers of syllables.

Pound was also one of the first Anglo-American poets to experiment with translations of Japanese poetry and to introduce into Western verse the terse, image-dominated lines of *hokku*: "As cool as the pale wet leaves/ of lily-of-the-valley/ She lay beside me in the dawn." The epigrammatic style served as an antidote to the elaborate and turgid excesses of Romantic and Victorian poetry. Built around a single simile, this short poem, entitled "Alba," functioned as an astringent, ridding the poet's style of any unnecessary word or expression.

Pound inaugurated the Imagist movement with *Des Imagistes: An Anthology*, published in March, 1914. As fiercely as Pound believed in the new poetry, he did little to advance his cause by introducing or campaigning for the work of the writers he had included in *Des Imagistes*. His fellow poets in Great Britain and America were galvanized by his efforts, but they made little headway in attracting readers or in persuading reviewers and publishers that Imagism was a significant departure from past practice that deserved broader attention and approval.

Pound's influence was exerted mainly through journals in England and in the United States, especially in *Poetry*, a magazine established by Chicago poet and editor Harriet Monroe in 1912. It was in this magazine

Philosopher-writer T. E. Hulme, who inspired poet Ezra Pound's development of Imagism. (Hulton Archive/Getty Images)

that Amy Lowell (1874-1925), just beginning her career as a poet, read Pound's strictures about poetry and the requirements of Imagism. She regarded his work as a call to scrap her own rather traditional verse and to begin anew. Her enthusiasm over Pound's pieces in *Poetry* was to fundamentally affect the history of poetry in the United States and abroad in ways Pound had not envisioned, especially in her ability to make poetry a public event that would produce a growing and avid audience not only for Imagism but also for the work of many other modern poets.

THE BEGINNINGS

Lowell, the descendant of a prominent New England family, famous for its achievements in both business and the arts, published her first book of poetry, *A Dome of Many-Coloured Glass*, in 1912. She had been thinking about writing poetry for nearly a decade, although even as a child she wrote poetry and beginning in her twenties lectured in Boston on literary subjects.

The title of her first book, taken from Shelley's famous poem, "Adonais" mourning the death of John Keats, reflected Lowell's love of Romantic literature and her adherence to traditional forms of poetry. However, her first volume excited little interest among reviewers and won her a very small audience. The disappointed Lowell, perusing the pages of *Poetry* magazine, became excited by Pound's extolling of Imagism. Virtually immediately, Lowell decided to jettison the writing of conventional poetry, and in the spring of 1913, she set out for London, the site, she later explained in *Tendencies in Modern American Poetry* (1917), of the most exciting developments in modern verse.

In London, Lowell met with Pound, who introduced her to his Imagist colleagues: Aldington, H. D., Flint, and Fletcher. Lowell would also meet other remarkable writers in Pound's circle as well as D. H. Lawrence (1885-1930), with whom she would correspond to the end of her life. Lowell quickly ascertained that many of these poets resented Pound's high-handed methods. They were also dismayed that their new poetry had so little impact on Anglo-American readers. To Pound's outrage, Lowell set about corralling this disaffected group, promising to put them into print in the United States and in general furthering the Imagist cause. She had both the promotional know-how and the financial resources to make her a creditable alternative to Pound.

Lowell lacked only bona fides as an Imagist poet herself. Industrious and an avid learner, she was producing Imagist poems before she returned to the United States in the fall of 1913. By 1915, Lowell had produced the first of three Imagist anthologies, featuring her work and that of Aldington, H. D., Flint, Lawrence, and Fletcher. Pound excluded himself, deeply resenting Lowell's takeover of a movement he believed belonged to him.

The work of these six poets in the Imagist anthologies is broadly representative of the modern poetry that Pound was promulgating. However, Lowell, a keen publicist, made sure that her three volumes contained prefaces that set out the Imagist program, thus linking the efforts of individual poets to a grand vision of the way modern poetry, especially free verse, was making literary history. Unlike Pound, Lowell made no effort

to dictate to her colleagues. Thus, each Imagist anthology was composed of poems that each poet deemed worthy of inclusion. Pound scorned this democratic, Imagist confederation, calling it "Amygism," by which he meant not only to criticize Lowell's outsize ego but also to express his disapproval of what he deemed her crass popularizing of poetry, which, in his view, diluted the power and ultimately the quality of the poems presented as examples of Imagism.

As the Imagist anthologies demonstrate, however, the poetry was of exceptional quality. Not every poem met Pound's highest standards, but to Lowell that seemed less important than her efforts to make poetry a vital part of life. She wanted not only to energize contemporary poetry, but also to increase the numbers of readers and institutions that could support the careers of poets and make poetry itself count for more in the lives of her fellow Americans.

A consideration of the individual poets who published in the Imagist anthologies provides the best way to comprehend the experiments, achievements, and ambitions of the Imagist movement.

RICHARD ALDINGTON

The youngest of the Imagist poets, Richard Aldington sought a way back to the Greeks. He admired the austerity of Greek art, and as an Imagist, he sought to write unadorned verse, the opposite of the opulent, flowing lines associated with Victorian poets such as Tennyson. Similarly, Aldington wanted to avoid the self-referential qualities of Romantic poetry, in which the poet becomes the hero of his own work.

Some of Aldington's best poetry was the result of his service in World War I. He brought to his description of that war a stark, brutal, and precise power of observation. Although Imagists eschewed the open expression of their feelings, their poetry could still be intense and the product of personal emotion and experience. Tor example, in "Soliloquy-I," Aldington describes the horrors of war: "Dead men should be so still, austere,/ And beautiful,/ Not wobbling carrion roped upon a cart . . . ." Aldington's avidity for Greek art is suggested in his desire to see the dead in repose like figures in classical sculpture. The full shock of war is reflected in choosing the word "carrion," the word for the rotting flesh of animals, including human beings. Although the poet is disgusted with this scene of horror, he does not, in fact, make his aversion explicit, allowing, in true Imagist fashion, the wording of the understated line to carry the weight of his emotions. The poet wishes to aestheticize the world, to make it beautiful, Aldington implies. However, the reality of war thwarts the aesthete's purposes. A true Imagist, the poet presents the indelible image of a body tied to a moving vehicle. This is no refined tableau of war, but war in all its immediacy and grim fatality.

Like other Imagists, Aldington wrote in free verse; that is, he did not use end rhymes or lines of equal length. Thus, "And beautiful" is given its own line in "Soliloquy-I," with no attempt to provide an even, balanced rhythm. On the contrary, the poem stops and starts in lines of uneven length—in this case it does so to emphasize the abruptness of war and the staccato nature of his thoughts in this horrid, shifting panorama of gore. The poet's tone is clipped, and he is, so to speak, short with himself and upset that war so overturns his aestheticism, his desire for what dead men "should" look like. War, in other words, is presented as an affront to the poet, a breakup in the pattern of life and art as he would wish to experience it. A reluctant witness to war, the Imagist poet must nevertheless record what he sees, and in recording what he sees, he must allow his emotions and perceptions to inhere in his choice of words without forcing the scene to conform to the sentiments he wishes to express.

H. D.

Born in Bethlehem, Pennsylvania, H. D. befriended Pound when he was attending the University of Pennsylvania. Later they renewed their acquaintance in 1911 when she arrived in London. It was Pound who persuaded her to sign herself "H. D. Imagiste," and when she married Aldington, the circle of Imagists became all that tighter. H. D., like Aldington, however, was willing to break with Pound over the promotion of Imagism, lending her genius to all three of Lowell's Imagist anthologies.

Glenn Hughes has called H. D. the perfect Imagist—a judgment many critics have ratified. She exemplified the movement in short, terse poems such as "Oread," a densely metaphorical six-line poem that begins "Whirl up, sea—/ whirl your pointed pines." Rep-

etition, or what Lowell liked to call "return," is evident in the poet's use of whirl to evoke the jagged swirls of the sea, seen in the poem as a kind of pine forest swaying—an exact, quite literal picture. Pines do often come to a point and they create a sort of wave effect in heavy winds. In other words, the metaphorical and literal tend to merge in H. D.'s spare, austere verse, which derives, in part, from her sharing Aldington's admiration for the unadorned style of classical poetry.

Critics have sometimes expressed reservations about H. D.'s poetry of isolated images, finding it cold, if vivid, and they are hard put to find a meaning in her literal/metaphorical poems. Like Lowell, who was also accused of writing without passion, H. D. believed that her Imagism was full of emotion brought to bear on a world that readers ought to be able to observe objectively in her poems. In "Oread," the poet does exhibit her own feelings in lines such as "hurl your green over us." This address to the sea, in other words, is about not only the poet's but also humanity's intense attraction to the immensity and power of nature, to the basic elements (water and land) of life. This is hardly, in other words, a poem that is simply devoted to description.

JOHN GOULD FLETCHER

Of all the Imagists at work in London, John Gould Fletcher had the most profound and immediate impact on Lowell. Her conversations with him led not only to a major change in her style but also to her conviction that Fletcher and his colleagues deserved a larger audience than Pound was capable of attracting.

Coming to distrust an increasingly erratic Pound, Fletcher shared his poems with Lowell, who saw in them a rhythm, diction, and pattern that represented a decisive break with her nineteenth century models. An excited Lowell would write about London and New York attempting to capture the urban rhythms of Fletcher's book *Irradiations, Sand and Spray* (1915), for which she secured a publisher. Thus, his poem about a rainstorm in the city captures the movement and scenes of modern life in lines such as "Sudden scurry of umbrellas:/ Bending, recurved blossoms of the storm." Here, Fletcher exemplifies an Imagism that is more fanciful than H. D.'s but still anchored in an actual moment. The literal becomes metaphorical swiftly and economically with the umbrellas taking the shape of a kind of flower show, fashioned out of the poet's observation of people opening their umbrellas. The mass movements of people make it look as though the umbrellas have a life of their own, like flowers bowed and reshaped by rain.

F. S. FLINT

The least well known of the Imagists, poet and critic F. S. Flint, served the movement best in several highly regarded critical essays. Only a few of his poems survive as excellent examples of Imagism, for he tended too often toward padding his lines to suit certain rhythms to the detriment of the overall force and coherence of his work. His poetry seems too much like one of his favorites, Keats—for example, Flint favors the Romantic lyric far more than the hard-edged images of H. D. Thus, in his poem "London," he rejects the daylight images of a pale green sky and birds hopping on a lawn and prefers to think of his beautiful city by moonlight: "among the stars,/ I think of her/ and the glow her passing/ sheds on men." While the images seem pedestrian, the lines do reflect the Imagist concentration on the value of short lines that segregate images to enhance their maximum impact. His rhythms too are refreshing, far more relaxed than the intensity of Romantic lyrics, and without a rigid rhyme scheme, he achieves a natural cadence that suited the Imagists' notion of what modern poetry should look like.

D. H. LAWRENCE

A fine poet and novelist, D. H. Lawrence never really considered himself an Imagist, but Lowell, realizing Lawrence was a great artist, persuaded him to join the movement, and he was grateful for her efforts in promoting his work. To Lowell, Lawrence deserved inclusion in her anthologies because certain of his poems did conform to the Imagist credo. Indeed, in a letter to him, she quoted an example of his Imagism: "The morning breaks like a pomegranate/ In a shining crack of red." Lawrence brought incredible energy to Imagism, a dynamism Lowell saw reflected in these lines, which crackle with the kind of exuberance and explosiveness that was Imagism at its boldest and best.

AMY LOWELL

Although Amy Lowell, like H. D., has been called an unemotional poet—Robert Frost's verdict was that she was a writer content to simply report what she observed—in fact she brought an erotic intensity to Imagism: "You are an almond flower unsheathed/ Leaping and flickering between budded branches," she writes in "White and Green." Fletcher's influence is felt in her effort to capture the movement and shapes of nature as an index of her own passionate mood. The budded branches suggest the bursting and blossoming of love without Lowell's ever making her feelings the focus of her lines.

A good deal of Lowell's finest Imagist poems are set in gardens (she had a beautiful garden and estate in Brookline, Massachusetts) that become metaphors for her exploration of a remarkable range of subjects. Her masterpiece, "Patterns," written in 1917, evokes in the setting of Flanders not only the wars of the seventeenth century and World War I but also the life of a woman caught in the pattern that a woman of her time is supposed to follow and the pattern of war that takes her beloved away from her.

Amy Lowell was a leading voice of the Imagists. (Library of Congress)

THE END

Lowell felt that by 1920, after the publication of three Imagist anthologies, the work of Imagism per se had been accomplished. In other words, the principles and practices of the Imagist poet had become a part of modern poetry and the need for a separate movement no longer seemed urgent or even necessary. H. D. and the other Imagists would continue to write poems that exemplified the movement, but these poets ranged far from a strict adherence to the program Pound initially established—as did Pound himself. No account of modern poetry can ignore the pervasive influence of Imagism while at the same time acknowledging that the movement had limited aims and in the end had to supersede itself by having it poets engage in producing other examples of modern poetry.

BIBLIOGRAPHY

Aldington, Richard. *Life for Life's Sake*. New York: Viking, 1941. Chapter 9 discusses Aldington's involvement with the Imagists.

Fletcher, John Gould. *Life Is My Song*. New York: Rinehart & Winston, 1937. Describes Fletcher's relationship with Lowell, the development of his Imagist poetry, and its influence on her work.

Hughes, Glenn. *Imagism and the Imagists: A Study in Modern Poetry*. Stanford, Calif.: Stanford University Press, 1924. Still one of the standard studies. Hughes interviewed the Imagists and wrote separate chapters on the movement and on individual poets. His work is a deft combination of literary history, literary criticism, and biography. His bibliography includes many contemporary reactions to Imagism.

Jones, Peter, ed. *Imagist Poetry*. New York: Penguin, 2002. Contains an informative introduction as well as selections from T. E. Hulme's influential Imagist poems, the work of the major Imagist poets but also of others writing in the Imagist tradition such as William Carlos Williams and Marianne Moore.

Lowell, Amy. *Tendencies in Modern American Poetry*. Boston: Houghton-Mifflin, 1917. Includes a long, perceptive chapter on H. D. and John Gould Fletcher by the leader of the Imagist movement.

Pratt, William, ed. *The Imagist Poem*. Ashland, Oreg.: Story Line Press, 2001. A revision and expansion of a work first published in 1963. Includes an informative introduction and bibliography, selections from the work of major Imagist poets as well as work by major poets such as T. S. Eliot and Carl Sandburg, who were influenced by the Imagist movement.

Carl Rollyson

MODERNISTS

The English-language poets of the first forty years of the twentieth century who called themselves modernists developed their movement in response to a number of discoveries, disappointments, and disillusions in the nineteenth and early twentieth century.

In the nineteenth century, scientific discoveries led to the development of photography, which made the mimetic value of painting and sculpture less important. Artists, thus liberated, developed Impressionism, stressing the effects of light and color at a moment in time, and post-Impressionism, asserting that significant rendering eludes mere representation. In the realm of poetry, this trend can be seen in the dramatic monologue, which came to prominence in the mid-nineteenth century. This poetic form rendered the world through the distorted vision of driven people, as in "My Last Duchess" by Robert Browning (1812-1889), in which the duke matter-of-factly reveals that he ordered his wife murdered because she was gracious to people. The Romantic William Wordsworth (1770-1850) recounted the moral wisdom of nature, and John Keats (1795-1821) declared with magnificent grace that truth and beauty are mysteriously one; but in the dramatic monologue, the poet no longer mines objective truth or prophetically conveys higher values. The duke's story reveals a perverse aspect of human character. Punctuated in such a manner as to render the rhymed couplets almost invisible, it is true, ugly and extraordinary, grimly captivating disillusioning great poetry.

The eighteenth century economist Adam Smith had theorized that under capitalism, enlightened self-interest would lead entrepreneurs to secure increasing wealth by satisfying people's needs, adequately rewarding workers, and supporting the state that protects their property. In the nineteenth century, technology based on new scientific discoveries led to industrialization, which produced goods faster and in higher quantities. However, the human condition failed to improve. Workers were exploited, and in time, they revolted, leading to the development of communism. The theory and ideals behind capitalism, industrialism, and communism contrasted with the reality, producing disillusionment.

Other sources of disillusion and disappointment were challenges to firmly held beliefs and ideas. In the nineteenth century, Charles Darwin and Alfred Russel Wallace independently created theories of evolution that contradicted both the biblical Adam and Eve story in which God created all living things in less than a week and the seemingly irrefutable idea that causes precedes effects. The idea that accidental congruence (fortunate combination of genes) rather than intentional design led to a species' survival brought into question the belief in a beneficent God who created life, who would punish evil and reward the good after death. In addition, in the early part of the twentieth century, scientist Albert Einstein, with his theory of relativity, challenged the most fundamental phenomenal elements of perception—time, which seems to pass in a fixed manner, and space, which seems unchanging in extension.

INFLUENCES AND PRECURSORS

The veneration of individuals and individualism, represented by Romanticism in the arts, capitalism economically, and democracy politically; of the Christian God; and of conventional scientific wisdom were all challenged in the nineteenth century. Disappointment and disillusionment were the order of the day. Among those trying to deal with the fallout were poets in England, the United States, and on the continent.

In the United States, Walt Whitman (1819-1892), the poet of democracy, anticipated the modernists by developing expansive free verse that he thought suited to the great American experiment in freedom. Not far north of New York, Whitman's base, the cloistered New England poet Emily Dickinson (1830-1886) developed an equally distinct voice. Using dashes instead of punctuation, she closeted away terse, insightful poems in ballad form, filled with telling ironies, often underscored by off (or slant) rhymes and words that almost rhymed, producing dissonances that reinforced the troubling thoughts they conveyed.

In France, inspired by the scandalously sexual poetry of Charles Baudelaire (1821-1867) and his translations of Edgar Allan Poe (1809-1849), the avant-garde Symbolists, Stéphane Mallarmé (1842-1898), Arthur Rimbaud (1854-1891), and Paul Verlaine (1844-1896) wrote shockingly challenging poetry. Trusting imagination more than the mundane world, seeking correspondences to the transcendent, and abandoning direct description in favor of indirect language, they embraced musical language in their poetry. Beginning about 1916, the more revolutionary Dadaists attacked art and memory, freeing words from their meanings and thus moving them into the realm of abstraction. Dada poets constructed poems by piecing random words together. In 1918, Tristan Tzara (1896-1963) wrote the "Manifeste Dada 1918" ("Dada Manifesto 1918"), with the purported aim of abolishing the future through Dada. Following on Dadaism, in the 1920's, Surrealism slid back toward meaning through the Freudian unconscious, receiving its manifesto from André Breton (1896-1966), who advocated morality-beauty-and-reason-free thought that accessed the unconscious.

In Germany, the Prague-born poet Rainer Maria Rilke (1875-1926) brought a blend of Impressionism and mysticism into German poetry, and the manifesto "On Literary Expressionism" (1911), by Kasimir Edschmid (1890-1966), regarded humanity as both elevated and deplorable and declared that the function of poetry was to convey that condition.

In Italy, poet Filippo Tommaso Marinetti (1876-1944) embraced the outrageous. In his Futurist manifesto "Manifeste de Futurisme" (1909), published in *Le Figaro*, he valued emerging power, war, machinery, and speeding objects. Denouncing women and praising the beauty of speed, Marinetti supported the allies in World War I and the Fascist Benito Mussolini thereafter. His manifesto established the general terms for the theory and practice of the entire Futurist movement.

Surrealists, from left, André Breton, Paul Éluard, Tristan Tzara (founder of Dada), and Benjamin Péret in a signed photograph from 1932.
(©Stefano Bianchetti/CORBIS)

THE BEGINNINGS

Modernist poets, who wrote in English, were influenced by and responded to the events and movement of the nineteenth and early twentieth centuries. They committed themselves to the present, often reacting to or agreeing with continental writers, and also sought inspiration from earlier literature, such as the poetry of ancient Greece, medieval Italy and France, and seventeenth century England. They also examined the work of Gerard Manley Hopkins (1844-1889), a heretofore little published Jesuit who was conservative in content and challengingly innovative in images and sprung rhythm, and the tightly ordered poetry of Thomas Hardy (1840-1928), despite his religious leanings, which accepted the Darwinian idea that chance was the organizing principle of the universe.

IMAGISTS

In 1912, Ezra Pound (1885-1972) marked up a poem by H. D., signed it "H. D. Imagiste," and submitted it to *Poetry* magazine, thereby founding the Imagist movement. Imagist poetry is characterized by subjective or objective presentation rather than description of the poem's material, a parsimonious use of language, and rhythms determined by musical phrase rather than metrical considerations. Pound edited an anthology of Imagist poetry, *Des Imagistes: An Anthology* (1914) and wrote the essay "Imagisme" (1914), which was published in *Poetry* magazine and served as an Imagist manifesto. Because of his interest in presentation, Pound was intrigued to learn that each Chinese word is an ideogram, a stylized visual presentation of its meaning. Pound turned the literal translations of Chinese poetry made by Ernest Fenollosa (1853-1908) into splendid translations in *Cathay: Translations by Ezra Pound for the Most Part from the Chinese of Rihaku, from the Notes of the Late Ernest Fenollosa and the Decipherings of the Professors Mori and Ariga* (1915). Pound would later abandon Imagism, and Amy Lowell (1874-1925), a member of a distinguished American family of poets, became the new leader and voice of the movement. She wrote some of the most distinguished free verse of the period.

WILLIAM BUTLER YEATS

William Butler Yeats (1865-1939) was once approached by Pound, who told him that although he was the greatest living poet writing in English, he did not write concretely. Yeats, always intrigued by new ideas and helpful to youths who admired him as well as those who attacked him, asked Pound what he meant. Pound pointed out abstract words in Yeats's published verse, and Yeats amended his writing and made a commitment to reworking his poetry that characterized the rest of his life.

Yeats, born Protestant and Anglo-Irish, was intent on leading a poetic and artistic life in predominantly Roman Catholic Ireland. Regarding Christianity and its permutations as but one useful mythology, he explored Irish myth, legend, and history, and Greek and Indian mythology; involved himself in occult movements; sought comparative analyses; and experimented with psychic transport and automatic writing to discover truths about the human condition that Christian faiths could not access. Yeats saw modern life as reflective of events in the distant past. In love with the beautiful Maud Gonne, who admired his poetry and acted in his plays but did not return his love, Yeats made her into a contemporary Helen in "No Second Troy."

T. S. ELIOT

T. S. Eliot (1888-1965), like Pound an American expatriate who considered contemporary life a thing of disarray, had read chapters of the epic novel *Ulysses* (1922), by James Joyce (1882-1941), in *Little Review*. In the work, Joyce had created a heroic antihero, Leopold Bloom, as a version of Odysseus, the main character in Homer's *Odyssey* (c. 725 B.C.E.; English translation, 1614). Eliot dubbed Joyce's innovation the mythical method and argued that Joyce had structured his novel about disorganized modern life by drawing on a work that came from a magnificently ordered past. Eliot had already written "The Love Song of J. Alfred Prufrock" (1915), a dramatic monologue in which the tormented protagonist, balding and insecure, compares himself unfavorably to Hamlet and anticipates going to a party, speaking deeply, and then proposing to a sophisticated woman there, only to be rebuffed.

After lionizing Joyce, Eliot drafted what, with Pound's editorial help, would become *The Waste Land* (1922). This short epic about the social disasters that followed World War I is based on the legend of the Fisher King, whose wound left his land sterile. *The*

Waste Land, filled with what Eliot called objective correlatives of despair and written while he was recovering from a nervous breakdown, presents the godless world that followed World War I, full of failures embodied in characters such as Lil, who lost her teeth and is advised by a friend who would like Lil's husband for herself to pretty up for Albert, who is coming home, or be ready to lose him. In keeping with Eliot's conviction that literature is always written in relation to the tradition that preceded it, the poem begins in April, the springtime month that poet Geoffrey Chaucer celebrated for the awakening it engendered in plants, animals, and people, but that Eliot regarded as the cruelest month because it breeds awareness of loss that displaces the peaceful death of winter. Ultimately, Eliot sought refuge in tradition, renounced American citizenship, and embraced England and the Anglican Church.

THE AMERICAN MODERNISTS

American modernists Robert Frost (1874-1963), Wallace Stevens (1879-1955), William Carlos Williams (1883-1963) and Marianne Moore (1887-1972) were more balanced than Eliot. Though Frost wrote metrically and compared free verse to playing tennis without a net, his first book, *A Boy's Will* (1913) was positively reviewed by Pound. Frost's graceful style and the attractive rural settings of his poems played off against the profound insights into human loss, pain, and error that he shared with the less accessible modernists. Stevens, an insurance executive, replaced traditional values and the God of the past with an engagement in life and an appreciation of objects such as the sun, which provided an image of what gods ought to be. Williams, a dedicated physician, celebrated simple things in short free-verse lines of powerful rhythmic value. He claimed to deplore iambic pentameter, but if one strings together the initial lines of his famous tribute to the wheelbarrow, one finds a wonderfully musical iambic pentameter line that ends acceptably in an unstressed syllable. Moore, who conceived of poetry as imaginary gardens containing real toads, was the acting editor of *The Dial* from 1925 to 1929. She wrote crisp, witty poems, often in syllabic verse, counting the number of syllables per line but not stress or syllable length.

T. S. Eliot. His The Waste Land *(1922) remains one of the most significant works of modernist poetry.* (Archive Photos/ Getty Images)

HIGH MODERNISM

The 1920's was the period of high modernism, followed by a socially responsible group of younger modernists led by W. H. Auden (1907-1973), who, under Eliot's influence, early on wrote in blank verse and then, following Yeats, turned to brilliantly controlled regular forms devoted to political and moral issues and love. Auden then famously expressed the wish that if unequal love was his destiny, then he wanted to be the one who loved more. Moving in the opposite direction from Eliot, Auden renounced British citizenship and adopted the United States, where the moral and socially conscious Archibald MacLeish (1892-1982) and E. E. Cummings (1894-1962) had taken up the modernist tradition. MacLeish, in "Ars Poetica," declared that the poem does not mean but is, and Cummings further extended the relation of form to content, sometimes adding appearance to sound, placing elevated words higher and words that fall lower down on the page than the rest of their lines.

THE END OF MODERNISM

Despite the grim events occurring in the world, the modernists did not abandon hope. They shared a thirst for meaning, order, and commitment in a world that had lost them. Pound, Eliot, and Yeats moved to the right in search of it. Pound embraced fascism, supported the Axis during World War II, and was tried for treason. Declared insane, he was incarcerated at St. Elizabeths Hospital, where he continued to work on his *Cantos* (1925-1972). He was awarded the first Bollingen Prize in 1949 for *The Pisan Cantos* (1948). With the intercession of fellow modernists, Pound was released in 1958. The once bellicose advocate of radical artistic and political movements fell silent, expressing fragments of regret in verse about his anti-Semitism.

Modernists lived on and continued to write after World War II, but their movement had reached an end: They had declared themselves modern. The new generation saw itself as postmodern. The quest to respond to discoveries and confront disappointments, disillusionments, and disasters by embracing them or transcending them through unique visions or engagement with the past, to make things new with concrete images and shocking subject matter or forms, was over. What had been shocking had become everyday matters in the world that emerged after World War II. A great period of twentieth century poetry had ended.

BIBLIOGRAPHY

Bradbury, Malcolm, and James McFarlane, eds. *Modernism: A Guide to European Literature, 1890-1930*. 1976. Reprint. London: Penguin Books, 1991. A comprehensive survey of which only the preface is new in the second printing.

Chefdor, Monique, Ricardo Quinnones, and Albert Wachtel, eds. *Modernism: Challenges and Perspectives*. Champaign: University of Illinois Press, 1986. Contains essays by major critics, moving from pre- to postmodernism.

Kenner, Hugh. *The Pound Era*. Berkeley: University of California Press, 1971. A magisterial study, centered on Pound, of pattern-seeking explorations of the period.

Lewis, Pericles. *The Cambridge Introduction to Modernism*. New York: Cambridge University Press, 2007. A general introduction to modernism.

Perkins, David. *A History of Modern Poetry: From the 1890's to the High Modernist Mode*. Cambridge, Mass.: Harvard University Press, 1976. Surveys the variety of forms in the period through the study of more than one hundred poets.

Albert Wachtel

HARLEM RENAISSANCE

The Harlem Renaissance, also known as the New Negro movement and dating from approximately 1919 to 1935, is recognized as one of the most important and productive periods in the history of American literature, art, and culture. From the movement came some of the finest music, literature, and art of the twentieth century.

At the end of World War I, black veterans returning to their southern homelands found little change. Despite having served their country, they were afforded no special recognition for their sacrifices and were faced with the same poor living conditions and threats of lynchings and public humiliation that existed before the war. Meanwhile, urban areas in the North and West had profited somewhat from the war with an upswing in new industries. In addition, the decline in immigration from Europe had created a severe labor shortage, which opened up employment opportunities.

In search of economic stability, better lives, and better education for their children, African Americans left the South for industrial centers such as Pittsburgh and Detroit and for cities such as Chicago and New York City. The greatest number of African Americans went to New York City, which had always been a cultural mecca and already had a large black population in Harlem. Harlem's boundaries had been greatly expanded in 1910 when African American real estate agents and church groups had bought large tracts of land, so housing was available to the black migrants, though they faced greatly inflated rental charges. This influx brought problems. Established residents did not embrace the change, seeing the newcomers as interlopers who would try to take their jobs. Eventually, the wide variety of people from different backgrounds provided opportunities for cultural growth and diversity.

Harlem had already been a center for political activism, where silent marches—and some louder ones—protesting injustice had taken place. Marcus Garvey, charismatic leader of the Back to Africa movement, had his headquarters there, and both the National Urban League and the National Association for the Advancement of Colored People (NAACP) had offices there. The National Urban League's *Opportunity: A Journal of Negro Life*, a periodical designed to stimulate pride in past racial achievements and hope for the future, and the NAACP's *Crisis*, edited by historian, journalist, and social critic W. E. B. Du Bois, both provided avenues for sharing ideas. Many writers had come to Harlem intending to turn the lives of migrants into novels and short stories. Alone, these writers might not have created the Renaissance community. However, two very influential leaders—Alain Locke, philosopher, writer, and educator, and Charles Johnson, the director of research for the Urban League—orchestrated a plan for turning the area into a literary haven, calling out to promising writers from other states and offering prize incentives for the best work. Both felt that unfortunate stereotypes could be changed by showing what African Americans were capable of in literature, art, and music. With white publishers begin-

Philosopher-writer Alain Locke helped inspire the start of the Harlem Renaissance in 1925. (Time & Life Pictures/Getty Images)

ning to open their doors to black authors, the stage was set: Harlem became a vibrant site of artistic experimentation.

The migrants from the South had brought with them the music of New Orleans and St. Louis, and jazz and blues clubs opened in Harlem. These clubs attracted both blacks and whites and were excellent places to meet and plan strategies, talk over works in progress, display art, drink, and listen to musicians such as Bessie Smith, Louis Armstrong, Billie Holiday, Cab Calloway, and Duke Ellington. One of the most noted venues, the Cotton Club, practiced its own kind of discrimination. Its entertainers had to be light-skinned. Thus, Josephine Baker, whose act featured a banana skirt, had to go to Europe to achieve fame.

The art world exploded with new experimental expression, brighter colors, and freer forms. The colors became bolder, more alive, and more apt to attract attention and elicit discussion; paintings were everywhere. Artists and art lovers met at coffeehouses, where they shared and generated new ideas.

Writers, in particular, benefited from the camaraderie. They tried out ideas and established salons, often under the auspices of white benefactors, where they read and critiqued one another's works. It became known that the African American was in "vogue," a term that distressed some intellectuals because it implied a temporary condition. It was true that some white patrons simply liked the exotic feel of being associated with another race. One unkind rumor suggested that Zora Neale Hurston was paid to attend white parties and act like an African American. Writers gave talks, took part in symposiums, and generally enjoyed the star status. In addition, theaters began employing black actors and producing works by black playwrights. By the mid-1920's, Harlem had indeed become the epicenter for change and freedom. For more than a decade thereafter, it was abuzz with excitement and seriousness of purpose. Locke felt that the urban setting helped African Americans appreciate the great variety of perspectives and ambitions among them, as Harlem was home to business

professionals, preachers, outcasts, students, and criminals, as well as those involved in the arts.

In March, 1924, the National Urban League hosted a dinner to honor the emerging array of talented black writers. Du Bois urged Harlem writers to attend and meet with white writers and publishers. This gathering had a huge impact. White-run publishing companies were now more eager to solicit manuscripts from black authors.

In 1925, Locke and Johnson were asked to edit a black artisans edition of *Survey Graphic*, a national magazine devoted to social issues and cultural affairs. The issue, "Harlem: Mecca of the New Negro," became a landmark in the Black Arts movement. It featured works by Countée Cullen (1903-1946), Langston Hughes (1902-1967), Du Bois (1868-1963), James Weldon Johnson (1871-1938), and Jean Toomer (1894-1967). Encouraged, Locke expanded the intro-

Harlem Renaissance writers, from left, Jessie R. Fauset, Langston Hughes, and Zora Neale Hurston in front of a statue of Booker T. Washington in Tuskegee, Alabama, in 1927. (The Granger Collection, New York)

duction and used the magazine as the basis for an anthology that included works by Claude McKay (1889-1948), Hurston (1891-1960), and Jessie R. Fauset (1882-1961). The anthology, *The New Negro: An Interpretation* (1925), gave Locke the reputation of being the architect, or, as he preferred to be called, the "midwife" of the Harlem Renaissance.

Locke hoped that greater exposure would demonstrate that African Americans had cultural awareness and self-confidence and in no way were of lesser intelligence or creativity than whites. He hoped to dispel the stereotypes in literature of Uncle Tom or Uncle Remus—no more grinning mammies or faithful family retainers willing to sacrifice themselves to preserve the status of their white employers and no more stock figures, African Americans shuffling to do service, or acting dumb to entertain. The New Negro movement aimed to set those stereotypes to rest. The New Negro spoke his mind, had confidence, and fought back. Mainly, Locke hoped that the image of the humble, self-effacing, always accommodating African American would fade, to be replaced by a self-assertive, independent individual who resisted domination. Arts and letters, Locke believed, could serve to raise racial consciousness.

THE WRITERS AND THEIR WORKS

The poetry of the Harlem Renaissance was the most celebrated, coming from the minds of sensitive, culturally aware, honest, and skilled poets who, by virtue of the genre, had to make each word count. Sometimes those words cut deeply, though not without reason. They opened eyes to outrages and called for action. There were no dominant themes in the poetry, though much of it explored Harlem and race in the United States. Some works protested racial injustice, but most avoided overt protests or propaganda, focusing instead on the psychological and social impact of race. At the time, writers were more interested in acquainting the white public with the lives of African Americans. They wanted to demonstrate these individuals' great capacity for deep thoughts, for grappling with problems, and for seeking truth, justice, and beauty.

This period of artistic and cultural blossoming was sometimes fraught with problems, mainly among those African Americans who were concerned with their public image now that works by black writers were receiving wider white readership. The purpose of writing and the obligations of writers came into question. Poets in particular seemed to divide into three groups: those who wanted to pattern their works after the great masters, thinking it made little sense to try to improve upon perfection; those who wanted to write in the language of the people, to stick with the vernacular of the common man and woman; and those who favored telling the truth about African American life, the delights as well as the horrors.

Many African American poets modeled their works on literary classics, especially favoring allusions that required readers to work toward understanding. Some writers were accused of catering to the white taste for seedy tales of degradation. They presented African American life as it was lived by a portion of the community: scam artists, gamblers, heavy drinkers, and carousers. Hughes was criticized for writing of the "low downs," the ordinary people. Hurston used black dialect to convey the essence of her characters and was told that she was bringing the race down.

Du Bois had high expectations and rules for writers, saying that they had a social responsibility to present African Americans in their best light and that their works should be "uplifting." He thought that all writing should be propaganda. He found the new realism too gritty. However, the new writers felt the constraints too limiting. They wanted their literary talent to discredit the stereotypes. Mainly they wanted to counteract the postcard images of happy darkies in the cotton fields grinning instead of tending to the wounds, invisible to the public, created by the sharp briars of the plant. They wanted the balance of a bookie or a pimp, acting as some real people act. The concept of creating works that were spiritually uplifting went against the artistic ideal of showing life as it is, and some writers would not yield to pressure from the intellectuals.

COUNTÉE CULLEN

Poet Countée Cullen liked traditional verse forms such as the sonnet because his mainstream education exposed him to the literature he loved. He became known as the black John Keats. His works appeared structured, even gentle, but his words conveyed the system of discrimination so prevalent in those days. In "For a Lady I Know," he slaps at white womanhood, while undoubtedly delighting service workers. He says, "She even thinks that up in heaven/ Her class lies late and snores// While poor black cherubs rise at seven/ to do celestial chores." In "Incident," the subject is far more painful. He tells of riding in a public conveyance in Baltimore when he was a boy, just eight, and smiling at another boy who had been staring at him. In response, the child stuck out his tongue and called him "nigger." The last stanza captures the impact of the incident: "I saw the whole of Baltimore/ From May until December;/ Of all the things that happened there/ That's all that I remember."

CLAUDE MCKAY

In 1922, Claude McKay broke the color barrier when a white-owned firm published his poetry collection *Harlem Shadows* to high acclaim. The title poem speaks of the old Harlem, with its "girls who pass to bend and barter at desire's call." However, he speaks of these prostitutes affectionately, calling them lasses, "little dark girls . . . in slippered feet" who work from dusk to dawn, brought down by poverty to use their "timid little feet of clay, the sacred brown feet." His work has been credited with being the forerunner in the shift in African American poetry to modernism and to the New Negro movement.

McKay wrote a strong protest poem that called for African Americans, if cornered by the oppressor, to die with dignity. In "If We Must Die," he urges African Americans, without identifying race, not to allow themselves to be "hunted and penned" like hogs, but to stand nobly like men. Though "pressed to the wall," dying, they should fight back so that even in death they will be honored by the cowards who outnumber them. In "America," McKay wrote with great affection for his native country, saying that "Although she feeds me bread of bitterness/ And sinks into my throat her tiger's tooth," he must "confess" that he loves "this cultured hell that tests" his youth. Her "vigor" and "bigness" give him the strength to stand up against any hatred.

LANGSTON HUGHES

The most widely known and respected poet of the period was Langston Hughes. His early works reflected the music of African Americans, the soul, and the jazz. In 1925, while busing tables in the District of Columbia, Hughes slipped a famous poet a few of his works. Headlines the next day announced the discovery of a new poet. One of the poems was "The Weary Blues," which became the title of his first collection, published in 1926 when he was twenty-four years old. The individual poems—"The Weary Blues," "Dream Variations," "The Negro Speaks of Rivers," "A Black Pierrot," "Water Front Streets," "Shadows in the Sun," and "Our Land"—come together like an opus. Hughes used the free-style rhythms of blues and jazz, music that reached into the souls of black people. His "The Weary Blues" conveyed weariness with such lines as "Droning a drowsy syncopated tune/ Rocking back and forth to a mellow croon/ I heard a Negro play" and "He did a lazy sway . . ./ . . ./ With his ebony hands on each ivory key/ He made that poor piano moan with melody/ O Blues!" and "Swaying to and fro on his rickety stool/ He played that sad raggy tune. . . ." The use of alliteration in "droning/drowsy" and the long slow sadness of such words as "mellow," "croon," "lazy," "sway," and "crooned that tune" spoke of exhaustion, physical but also almost certainly emotional.

Hughes was most adept at including what was not exactly a threat, but definitely an expression of a limit to the tolerance of those who are asked to wait for the right time to realize their hopes. In "Harlem," he asks:

> What happens to a dream deferred?
>   Does it dry up
> like a raisin in the sun?
> Or fester like a sore—
> And then run?
> Does it stink like rotten meat?
> Or crust and sugar over—
> like a syrupy sweet?
>
>   Maybe it just sags
> like a heavy load.
>
> *Or does it explode?*

The setting aside of that one line in italics tells the whole story, serving as a warning that perhaps a kind of violence is inevitable.

In another work, "I, Too, Am America," Hughes relates a veiled threat: A young man is always expected to eat in the kitchen when his employers have company. He says that he attempts to ignore the slight, knowing that the good food will nourish his body and help him to grow strong, and that one day he will already be at the dining room table when the company arrives and no one will dare send him off to the kitchen, not only because he has become strong and could resist them but also because they will realize that he is beautiful and will be ashamed. His title and last line, "I, too, am America," say it all.

JAMES WELDON JOHNSON

James Weldon Johnson hoped his poems would afford greater appreciation of preachers and lead to a reassessment of African Americans. His *God's Trombones: Seven Negro Sermons in Verse* (1927) was made up of an opening prayer and sermons often given by preachers. He used a scholarly style to show whites that religion is important to blacks and that black preachers are social and intellectual leaders in the community. In a powerful retelling of the Creation as it appears in the Bible, he has God walking out into a great black emptiness, his smile bringing on the light. God rolls the light in his hands to make first the sun and then the moon and stars. He throws the world between the sun and the moon and then walks on it to make hills and valleys. There follow all the lakes and flowers, until he realizes he is lonely. So he scoops up some clay from the bed of a river and makes a man.

A BLACK AWAKENING

While courted by wealthy whites and invited to parties, most of the black poets stayed true to their form and did not let their messages be toned down. Not fearful of losing their popularity, they portrayed life as it was and kept their patronage. In poetry, African Americans found a way to further the oral tradition and the stories told through hymns and folk music. No longer necessary were the seemingly innocuous lyrics of such works as "follow the drinking gourd" (look to the Big Dipper for the escape route to the North) or musical maps to the Underground Railroad. Now poets could speak truth and reflect the reality of black life. They produced some remarkable works that went beyond the horrors that African Americans experienced and to the

heart of all who have suffered, felt lost and afraid, and been hurt by life circumstances or unfairness.

The Harlem Renaissance was called a period of great cultural, artistic, and literary achievement, but it was also a time of awakening, when blacks, seeing chances for better lives, took them; when pride in being black became a factor; and when celebrations and recognition of black artists gave the general populace good feelings. Many of the stars of the Harlem Renaissance were either homosexual or bisexual, but for the most part, their sexual proclivities remained hidden, lest publishers or readers wane. The silent awareness among them fostered a strong bond that helped to unite them in their writings on particular themes. They could allude to their sexual feelings without letting the public in on their secrets. Works required much reading between the lines.

The Harlem Renaissance changed the way African Americans were perceived by others and how they viewed themselves. It produced poetry and fiction that will endure because these works went beyond skin tone to the hearts of humanity and to the human condition that weathers external changes.

BIBLIOGRAPHY

Chapman, Abraham. "The Harlem Renaissance in Literary History." *CLA Journal* 11, no. 1 (September, 1967): 38-58. A personal accounting of Chapman's dismay at the scant attention paid to the Renaissance and its writers.

_____, ed. *Black Voices: An Anthology of African American Literature*. New York: New American Library, 1968. The introduction to Chapman's classic collection still stands as one of the most comprehensive statements regarding the long history of blacks in literature.

Gates, Henry Louis, Jr., and Evelyn Brooks Higginbotham, eds. *Harlem Renaissance Lives, from the African American National Biography*. New York: Oxford University Press, 2009. This is a compendium of the main features of the Harlem Renaissance, its germination, and the major artists, writers, and musicians involved. The introduction by Cary D. Wintz is especially valuable.

Lewis, David Levering. *When Harlem Was in Vogue.*

New York: Alfred Knopf, 1981. This remains the standard work on the Harlem Renaissance. It reads as a narrative, involving the reader in the day-to-day details while covering all the salient points.

Major, Clarence, ed. *The Garden Thrives: Twentieth Century African-American Poetry*. New York: HarperPerennial, 1996. A good collection of the major poems, with commentary and an introduction by a leading authority in black literature.

Gay Pitman Zieger

BEAT POETS

The label "beat" designates a group of writers and their friends and affiliates who met at Columbia University in New York and gained fame and notoriety in the period between 1944 and 1961 as the Beat generation. The meaning and origin of the word "beat" are subject to some debate, and explanations range from "downtrodden" and "weary of the world" to "beatific" and "angelic." However, there is general agreement that Jack Kerouac (1922-1969) first used the term in 1948 to characterize himself and a small group of friends: Allen Ginsberg (1926-1997), William Burroughs (1914-1997), Neal Cassady (1926-1968), and Herbert Huncke (1915-1996), with Cassady and Huncke serving mainly as early literary models and muses for their writer friends. A little later, Gregory Corso (1930-2001) joined them. Closely associated with this pioneering group were Lucien Carr (1925-2005), who introduced Kerouac, Ginsberg, and Burroughs to one another, and John Clellon Holmes (1926-1998), whose novel *Go* (1952) is the first semifactual chronicle of the early life of the Beats.

The name "Beat generation" was designed not only to signify the downtrodden, renegade position the young men were proud to hold in an increasingly conformist, status-conscious, and materialistic society but also to hint at their affinity to the lost generation, a similarly disaffected group of American writers in the period after World War I. Like many artists and intellectuals of their time, the early Beat poets were disillusioned because the end of Word War II had not led to a spiritual and cultural reawakening. On the contrary, the Cold War and its threat of nuclear annihilation loomed over the nation, part of the expansion of American capitalist influence in the world with the help of an ever-more-powerful military-industrial complex. The main goal of McCarthyism—a campaign to drive out communist sympathizers led by Senator Joseph McCarthy in the mid-1950's—was to enlist Americans in the struggle against communism, and its hostility was not limited to communism and its sympathizers but extended to all individualists and those who deviated from the white Protestant norm. Therefore, it should come as no surprise that U.S. senator Joseph McCarthy once branded the Beat generation as one of the greatest dangers in the United States.

The early Beat poets were confronted by the problem faced by all individualists in repressive societies, namely, how to maintain their autonomy and integrity as individuals against the overwhelming pressure to conform and to fit in. The answer was an open flouting of accepted social, sexual, and literary norms; the confrontation of a cold, mechanistic world with unabashed romanticism; and a return to traditional American forms of literary expression in reaction to the prevailing modernist poetry and the New Criticism that supported it. Most Beat poets agreed with the assessment of William Carlos Williams (1883-1963) that T. S. Eliot's *The Waste Land* (1922) had set back American

Allen Ginsberg (©Allen Ginsberg/CORBIS)

poetry by twenty years; they fully intended to correct this misstep by writing spontaneous, open-form Dionysian poetry in defiance of the prevailing structured Apollonian poetry of the formalists.

The Beat poets therefore saw themselves not only as a literary movement but also as a counterculture movement in which the abandonment of the literary forms and structures of formalist poetry was the obvious external parallel to their rejection of the values of American mainstream culture. Rather than using political activism as an agent for change, which would have meant the sacrifice of their individualism to a collective, they chose to remain an open, interactive collection of individuals, united only by their opposition to prevailing social conditions within very widely varying parameters: the subjugation of form to content; the rejection of traditional Christianity for more mystical, meditative religions, such as Buddhism and Hinduism; an attraction to and identification with oppressed minorities; the belief in spontaneous, unrevised expression (first thought/best thought); and the liberation of preconscious truth from centuries of rational and social brainwashing, with the aid of meditation or hallucinogens. Only when this spiritual liberation of the individual had been achieved would meaningful social change be possible.

LITERARY ANTECEDENTS

Despite their carefully cultivated image as "holy barbarians," the Beat poets were well read, and their work is full of intertextual references to past and contemporary writers whom they saw as their literary ancestors. Most of those mentioned are writers who saw themselves as being in conflict with their mainstream cultures. Of particular importance to the Beat poets were the British Romantic poets Percy Bysshe Shelley (1792-1822) and especially William Blake (1757-1827), whom Ginsberg claims to have seen and heard in hallucinatory visions in 1948 and whom he considered a powerful influence on his early poetry. Blake's "dark Satanic mills" surely served as an inspiration for Ginsberg's figure of Moloch in his masterpiece "Howl" (1955). The works of American Romantic poet Henry David Thoreau (1817-1862), with their anticonformist, antitechnological message, were among the fa-

vorite books of many Beat poets, and the free-verse prophetic poetry of Walt Whitman (1819-1892) clearly inspired Ginsberg's best poems, including "Howl."

Beat poetry also contains frequent references to the French Symbolist poets. Arthur Rimbaud (1854-1891), in particular, fascinated many of them with his wild Bacchantic poetry and his dissolute lifestyle, including his homosexuality, which frightened the bourgeoisie of his time.

Closer to their own era, Dadaism and Surrealism directly influenced the works of the Beat poets, since a number of them had direct contact with Dadaist and Surrealist poets. Kenneth Rexroth (1905-1982) and Lawrence Ferlinghetti (born 1919) translated their poetry; Ginsberg and Corso are said to have met Marcel Duchamp (1887-1968), and Ginsberg allegedly kissed Duchamp's shoe at the occasion. What attracted the Beats to all of these earlier poets was their flouting of social and literary convention, as well their shocking the timid and conventional bourgeoisie with their abrasive and often vulgar attacks on middle-class morality.

THE BEAT MOVES WEST

During the formative years of the Beat poets, roughly between 1945 and 1955, the literary establishment took no notice of them at all. Only Kerouac and Holmes managed to publish substantial works (*The Town and the City*, 1950, and *Go*, respectively), while Corso languished in jail and Burroughs moved first to Texas and from there to Algiers and Mexico, writing novels that would be published much later. During these years, the original New York Beat poets were discussing and exchanging books while traveling across the United States and abroad, gathering material for their future publications, and exchanging their works-in-progress in manuscript form and debating their merit heatedly in coffeehouses and jazz clubs. While the Beat poets toiled in almost complete obscurity during these years, nearly all the works that brought them fame and notoriety were completed before 1956, including Kerouac's novels *On the Road* (1957), *The Dharma Bums* (1958), *Visions of Cody* (1960, 1972), and *The Subterraneans* (1958), as well as his long, epic poem, *Mexico City Blues* (1959). During the same period, Ginsberg attracted the attention of the poet Williams.

He sent some of his poems to Williams, who became Ginsberg's mentor. Despite all this creative activity, none of the New York Beat poets managed to break into the very exclusive and snobbish New York literary establishment, firmly controlled by the academic formalist poets, and it became apparent to Ginsberg that a change of scenery was necessary.

Following Kerouac, who did some of his best writing while living with Cassady and his wife in San Francisco, Ginsberg moved in with the Cassadys for a while but then took a job with a marketing firm in downtown San Francisco in 1954. Armed with a letter of introduction by Williams, he discovered an already vibrant bohemian literary community presided over by Rexroth and consisting of a group of poets who were trying to revive earlier open forms of poetry and who emphasized spoken poetry, often accompanied by jazz, over the printed form. As a bonus, James Laughlin, the publisher of *New Directions* magazine, gave them an outlet for their avant-garde poetry that had not been available to the Beat poets in New York, where their West Coast counterparts were known as eccentric provincials. It is this fortuitous meeting of the youthful, iconoclastic East Coast Beat poets with the more established so-called First San Francisco Renaissance that led to the genesis of Beat literature as it is presently defined; indeed, this melding of East Coast and West Coast avant-garde poetry is sometimes and confusingly called the Second San Francisco Poetry Renaissance, although the label Beat generation is the more frequently used term. The New York Beat poets were now supplemented by the likes of Ginsberg's lover and life partner Peter Orlovsky (born 1933), Gary Snyder (born 1930), Michael McClure (born 1932), Ferlinghetti, Philip Whalen (1923-2002), and Lew Welch (1926-1971), as well as former members of the now defunct Black Mountain College, such as Charles Olson (1910-1970) and Robert Creeley (1926-2005). Apart from confirming the New York Beat poets in their formal innovations—in the direction of open-verse forms, as well as toward spontaneity and spoken poetry—the West Coast Beats instilled in them a greater awareness of Native American and Latino cultures and reinforced their incipient interest in Asian mysticism and ecological themes.

FROM ANONYMITY TO FAME

The breakthrough for the Beat poets that eventually catapulted them to national fame occurred on October 7, 1955, at the Six Gallery in San Francisco at a poetry reading that has become an integral part of the Beat legend. The reading was suggested by McClure to Ginsberg, who at first refused, claiming that he had nothing to contribute; he changed his mind after composing the first part of "Howl." The participants in the reading represent an interesting cross-section of all the elements of Beat literature. Rexroth, the elder statesman of the first poetry renaissance, was the moderator and introduced the poets. His friend and cohort, Philip Lamantia (1927-2005), read not his own surrealistic poems but the work of a recently deceased friend, and three members of the younger West Coast generation read poems that illustrated their ecological and mystical contribution to Beat literature. McClure recited "Point Lobos Animism" and "For the Death of One Hundred Whales," both of which have been frequently anthologized; Snyder read "A Berry Feast"; and Whalen recited "Plus Ça Change." Also present was an increasingly intoxicated Kerouac, who refused to read his own work but cheered the other poets on; he recounts the event in his novel *The Dharma Bums*.

The crowning point of the evening, however, was Ginsberg's first reading of "Howl," which produced a sensation and almost single-handedly catapulted the Beat poets to fame. Ferlinghetti, who had opened City Lights Bookstore in 1953, had recently expanded it into a publishing venture and asked Ginsberg for permission to publish the poem in a famous telegram modeled after the one Ralph Waldo Emerson (1803-1882) sent to Whitman at the occasion of the first appearance of *Leaves of Grass* (1855), exactly one century before. Having read what are now parts 1 and 3 of the final version, Ginsberg quickly completed parts 2 and 4 ("Footnote to Howl"), and the complete work was published by Ferlinghetti as number four of the Pocket Poets series in 1956, after considerable revision. This slim volume, *Howl, and Other Poems*, remains in print more than fifty years later and is without question the most famous and enduring work of Beat poetry.

"Howl" is a very cleverly structured work, amaz-

(Left to right) Bob Donlin, Neal Cassady, Allen Ginsberg, Robert LaVinge, and Lawrence Ferlinghetti at Ferlinghetti's City Lights Book-store, a central gathering place for the Beat poets, in San Francisco. (©Allen Ginsberg/CORBIS)

ingly so, since it was written in a drug-assisted frenzy and under the influence of Kerouac's theory of spontaneous, unrevised composition. The first part presents a nightmarish vision of modern America, in which the speaker prophetically envisions "the best minds of my generation" marginalized and driven to desperate acts or landing in mental institutions for their "deviant" lifestyles. The second part identifies those elements in contemporary society that are responsible for this dire state of affairs: materialism, conformity, and mechanization leading to a cataclysm. The metaphor for these forces is Moloch, the biblical idol to whom the Canaanites sacrificed children. The speaker claims that the characters portrayed in part 1 have been sacrificed to this idol. Moloch is also the name of an industrial, demoniac figure in Fritz Lang's film *Metropolis* (1927), which Ginsberg acknowledges as a direct influence. Part 3 uses a specific person, Ginsberg's friend Carl Solomon, with whom he spent some time in a New York mental hospital, as an illustration for the pernicious in-

fluence of Moloch. The hellish vision of the first three parts is finally mitigated by part 4, the "Footnote to Howl," that ends the poem on a note of redemption by declaring that even this nightmarish work is part of a divine plan and therefore "holy."

THE GOLDEN AGE

News of the events at the Six Gallery reading quickly reached the East Coast, despite the fact that "Howl" did not appear in print until a year later. For the first time, the Eastern establishment showed some interest in the West Coast poets, and *The New York Times* sent Richard Eberhart, an establishment poet and academic, to write a report on the San Francisco Renaissance. In "West Coast Rhythms," published in *The New York Times Book Review* (September 2, 1956), Eberhart noted that with regard to the Beat poets, "Ambiguity is despised, irony is considered weakness, the poem as a system of connotations is thrown out in favor of long-line denotative statements. . . . Rhyme is outlawed. Whitman is the only god worthy of emulation." About Ginsberg, he wrote:

> The most remarkable poem of the young group is "Howl" . . . a howl against everything in our mechanistic civilization which kills the spirit. . . . It is Biblical in its repetitive grammatical build-up. . . . It lays bare the nerves of suffering and spiritual struggle. Its positive force and energy come from a redemptive quality of love, although it destructively catalogues evils of our time from physical deprivation to madness.

While this was a considerable step forward, most Eastern reviewers and critics remained scathing in their condemnation of the West Coast "barbarians." What really attracted the attention of the public to the Beat poets was a series of highly publicized obscenity trials, most notably the one involving Ginsberg's "Howl" in 1957. The judge's decision that "Howl," despite many objectionable passages, was not obscene because it had "some redeeming social importance" created a sensation and forever changed pornography laws and prosecutions in the United States. Ferlinghetti, whose City Lights Publishers was a codefendant in the trial, facetiously recommended a medal for the prosecutor, because more than ten thousand copies of the book were sold during and immediately after the trial.

The "Howl" trial made instant celebrities of Ginsberg and his friends, particularly as the attacks on them by the literary establishment intensified. The years from the reading of "Howl" in 1955 until 1961 can be considered the golden age of Beat poetry, with Beat poets suddenly finding publishing outlets for their hitherto unpublished work, being hounded by the media, and even finding themselves in demand with advertising agencies. Ginsberg traveled the country, giving readings of "Howl" to enthusiastic audiences, and Corso published the collections still considered his best: *The Vestal Lady on Brattle, and Other Poems* (1955), *Gasoline* (1958), and *The Happy Birthday of Death* (1960). In 1958, Diane di Prima (born 1934) published her first collection of poems, *This Kind of Bird Flies Backward*, starting a long and prolific career, and Ferlinghetti's *A Coney Island of the Mind*, which many consider his best collection, appeared in print. Finally, Kerouac, known to many readers only

for his autobiographical novels, published his poetic masterpiece, *Mexico City Blues*. Most of his other poems were published posthumously, collated and edited by his friends, particularly Ginsberg.

Mexico City Blues is a long epic poem, composed of 242 cantos, whose content parallels that of Kerouac's fourteen autobiographical novels dealing with what has become known as the Duluoz legend. Although Kerouac's novels are written in prose and thus use some conventions of narrative prose, *Mexico City Blues* abandons any pretense of a plot line. Indeed, Kerouac repeatedly insisted that he was a poet who happened to write long lines that looked like prose. *Mexico City Blues* is difficult to read, particularly without having read his novels first; it deals to a large extent with Kerouac's internal struggles while turning from Catholicism to Buddhism and his search for the truth through meditation. Therefore, the poem is laced with references to religious dogma, in addition to the intertextual references to philosophical and literary works. The casual reader can still enjoy the poem by approaching it as a piece of improvisational jazz music, as the title would suggest, and concentrate more on the rhythm and the sounds than on traditional literary interpretation.

THE BEGINNING OF THE END

Paradoxically, the rise to fame and notoriety of the Beat poets was at the same time the beginning of their decline as a literary movement, though individual members of the group continued to publish work of high quality well into the next century. The literary establishment, which saw the Beat poets as threatening intruders in "their" carefully guarded territory, continued to savage and disparage them in academic journals and other publications. However, since comparatively few people ever read these pieces, they had little or no impact on the public. More devastating was a switch in tactics to ridicule and parody, since it was conducted in the mass media, particularly film and television.

On April 2, 1958, the word "beatnik" appeared for the first time, in an article in the *San Francisco Chronicle*, six months after the launch of the Russian satellite Sputnik. By adding the Russian suffix *-nik* to the word "Beat," the effect, if not the intent, was to depict the

Beats as communistic and unpatriotic. This article, together with two feature articles in *Life* magazine, helped create the cartoon character of the Beatnik—in opposition to the middle-class squares—that became a staple of films and television programs in the years to follow. These cartoon characters reduced the serious social and poetic concerns of the Beat poets to a set of superficial, silly externals that have survived to this day: berets, goatees, sunglasses, poetry readings, coffeehouses, slouches, and "cool, man, cool" slang, as popularized by Maynard G. Krebs, the television character played by Bob Denver in *The Many Loves of Dobie Gillis* (1959-1963).

Adding to the detrimental effect of the Beatnik parody was the increasing absorption of the Beat legend into American mainstream commercial culture, which resulted in the slow disintegration of the Beat poets as a group, precipitated by some highly publicized squabbles and jockeying for position. Rexroth felt slighted by the media attention received by Kerouac, Ginsberg, and Burroughs, and he wrote a series of scathing articles and reviews of Kerouac's work. Corso felt equally neglected and expressed his discontent in several interviews. Kerouac himself became more and more distraught by his inability to reconcile his self-created public image as peripatetic rebel and loner with his yearning for stability and status and began drinking heavily. His appearances on talk shows added to the parodistic image of the stoned, dissolute Beatnik.

THE BEAT GOES ON

After the golden age (1955-1961), there was a noticeable diaspora in the Beat community, during which the individual members began to pursue their own interests and careers, many of them in academic positions. This diaspora was preceded by a flourish of important publications of Beat poetry in 1961 and 1962. Snyder, who had joined a Buddhist monastery in 1956, published *Myths and Texts* (1960), which contains some of his best poems. Burroughs, after experimenting with his "cut-up" technique, published *Naked Lunch* and *The Ticket That Exploded* in 1962, the former leading to another famous obscenity trial a few years later. Ginsberg's other masterpiece, his long confessional poem "Kaddish," was published in *Kaddish,*

and Other Poems, 1958-1960 (1961). Most notably, however, a substantial number of Beat poems were included in Donald Allen's anthology *The New American Poetry: 1945-1960* (1961), the first time a mainstream collection had considered the Beat poets part of the canon. Further evidence for the increasing absorption of the Beat poets into the mainstream can be seen in the awarding of a Guggenheim Fellowship to Ginsberg in 1963-1964, Snyder's accepting a faculty position at the University of California, Berkeley, in 1964, and Scribner's publishing the first critical study of the movement, *The Beat Generation: The Tumultuous '50s Movement and Its Impact on Today* (1969), by Bruce Cook.

The death of the triumvirate of Beat poetry—Kerouac in 1969, Ginsberg and Burroughs in 1997—gave rise to new scholarly interest in the Beat poets and produced a flood of biographies, memoirs, and critical studies. A number of English departments at colleges and universities have courses on the Beat generation, and most of the major work and collections of the Beat poets are still in print. Critics and scholars agree that while the creative period of the Beat poets as an identifiable movement with common goals and aspirations was relatively short, its influence is still felt in the twenty-first century. The trend toward performance-oriented, spontaneous, open-form poetry continues unabated, notably in the popular poetry slam, and there is consensus that the Beat poets directly affected political and social progress in the areas of ecology, gay and lesbian rights, and drug legislation.

BIBLIOGRAPHY

Charters, Ann, ed. *The Beats: Literary Bohemians in Postwar America.* 2 vols. Detroit: Gale Group, 1983. Very comprehensive documentary volume on the most important Beat poets. Good introductions, samples of critical articles, and correspondence.

Hemmer, Kurt, ed. *Encyclopedia of Beat Literature.* New York: Facts On File, 2007. Contains hundreds of entries on all the major figures and great works of the Beat movement, by distinguished Beat scholars and friends of the Beat generation.

Theado, Matt, ed. *The Beats: A Documentary Volume.* Detroit: Gale Group, 2001. An invaluable reference work for scholars and students. Contains copies and facsimiles of letters, articles, and essays by major and minor Beat poets.

Tytell, John. *Naked Angels: The Lives and Literature of the Beat Generation*. New York: McGraw-Hill, 1976. One of the earliest histories of the Beat movement, thorough but maybe a little too uncritically adoring.

Waldman, Anne, ed. *The Beat Book: Poems and Fiction of the Beat Generation*. Boston: Shambhala, 1996. A good introductory anthology of Beat literature by a former member of the group. Valuable introduction and bibliographical material.

Watson, Steven, ed. *The Birth of the Beat Generation: Visionaries, Rebels, and Hipsters, 1944-1960*. New York: Pantheon, 1995. A very good study of the beginnings and the heyday of the movement, with excellent layout and great pictorial material, and supporting marginal text.

Franz G. Blaha

CONFESSIONAL POETS

With the publication of Robert Lowell's *Life Studies* in 1959, the term "confessional" began to be used to refer to poetry that drew from and described the poet's own experiences, often including some type of psychological breakdown or mental health treatment as well as familial conflict rendered in a dramatic manner. This was a major departure from the high modernism of the first half of the twentieth century, wherein poets such as William Butler Yeats, T. S. Eliot, Ezra Pound, and Wallace Stevens sought to impress their learnedness on readers, frequently using Greek and Latin and referring to artists and works of art that would be familiar only to readers with similar educational backgrounds. The modernist poets used poetry as "an escape from personality," as Eliot said, not as a way to express personality, a primary motive of confessional poets. Although the term "confessional" refers to the content of the poems rather than the techniques used by confessional poets, they themselves argued that they were just as artistically and technically conscious as their modernist predecessors but more direct and accessible in their subject matter.

This departure from the detachment of modernism created controversy, and confessional poetry was not widely accepted as a legitimate art form at the time of its origin. More traditional poets and critics considered it to be solipsistic, even narcissistic, and its subject matter, such as bodily functions and taboos, inappropriate. Over the years, however, confessional poetry has become recognized as a type of art that illustrates the idea of the personal becoming political, offering insight into psychological upheaval and family drama as well as what writer William Faulkner described as "the human heart in conflict with itself." The technical proficiency recognized in the work of modernist poets has also been noted in that of confessional poets, particularly in the tension that is created through the use of traditional form and nontraditional subject matter. Four poets in particular are known for this skill and for being pioneers in the confessional mode: Robert Lowell, W. D. Snodgrass, Sylvia Plath, and Anne Sexton.

ROBERT LOWELL

Often known as the founder of confessional poetry, Robert Lowell (1917-1977) was the product of an upper-class Boston family that included Amy Lowell, a Pulitzer Prize-winning poet, and his great-granduncle James Russell Lowell, a poet and ardent abolitionist. Robert attended but did not graduate from Harvard University, at one point deciding to leave for Tennessee to camp on the lawn of a poet whom he idolized, James Tate.

Under the influence of modernist poets such as Yeats, Eliot, and Pound, Lowell had developed an appreciation for their dedication to classical form and became proficient in it but felt the need to break away from what he described as the "distant, symbol-ridden, and willfully difficult" poems that he was crafting. In *Life Studies*, his collection of poetry and prose that became known as a landmark of confessional poetry, he experimented with a new style and received great acclaim for it. Beginning with the poem "Beyond the Alps," written in classical style, complete with exact rhyme ("sponge/lunge," "snow/go," and "gongs/belongs"), this volume traces Lowell's familial influences from childhood to adulthood. Showing the complacency that is a luxury of the wealthy, Lowell describes the tradition of the grand tour of Europe that would be typical for a family such as his, confiding, ". . . I envy the conspicuous/ waste of your grandparents on their grand tours—/ long-haired Victorian sages accepted the universe, / while breezing on their trust funds through the world." With references to Paris, Rome, Catholicism, and Greek mythology, Lowell upheld the classical tradition yet gave hints of the confessional in his references to his family. In the prose piece "91 Revere Street," Lowell chronicles the trials and travails of his early upbringing with an overbearing, class-conscious mother and a father who could not decide whether he wanted to retire from the navy, compounded by the pressure Lowell's mother put on his father to retire so that the family could start collecting from his trust fund. Rather than being traumatized by their late-night arguments, Lowell describes eagerly anticipating them. Perhaps even then he was considering them as material for future writing.

In later years, when he attended Harvard University, Lowell dedicated a poem to one of his peers, Delmore Schwartz, also attending Harvard at the time. In "To Delmore Schwartz," he describes the poets' difficulties with daily domestic duties, including ". . . keep[ing] the furnace lit!/ Even when we had disconnected it." Lowell refers to a visit from T. S. Eliot's brother, Henry Ware, and describes his and Schwartz's views of themselves as the next great poets, although the specter of madness is lurking underneath for both of them, with "cigarette smoke circling the paranoid." Lowell quotes Schwartz as saying "*'We poets in our youth begin in sadness;/ thereof in the end comes despondency and madness.'*" This anticipates the mental illness for which Lowell was treated and to which Schwartz succumbed.

"My Last Afternoon with Uncle Devereux Winslow" chronicles Lowell's relationship with his grandfather. At the very beginning of the poem, he demonstrates their closeness with his childhood complaint: "I won't go with you. I want to stay with Grandpa!" His parents with their "watery martini pipe dreams at Sunday dinner" simply cannot compete, since "Nowhere was anywhere after a summer/ at my Grandfather's farm." He admires the "works of [his] Grandfather's hands" and the décor of his house, which "was manly, comfortable," unlike himself at five and a half in his "formal pearl gray shorts," feeling like a ". . . stuffed toucan/ with a bibulous, multicolored beak." This feeling of ridiculousness and inadequacy is also a subject of confessional poetry. In "Dunbarton," another poem about his grandfather, Lowell describes their comfort together, with his grandfather finding "his grandchild's fogbound solitudes/ sweeter than human society" and stopping ". . . at the *Priscilla* in Nashua/ for brownies and root beer." Even raking leaves with his grandfather was an adventure for Lowell, as they "defied the dank weather/ with 'dragon' bonfires." The poem ends with an image of physical closeness and nurturing: "In the mornings I cuddled like a paramour/ in my Grandfather's bed." In "Grandparents," he yearns for his deceased grandfather to once again "Have me, hold me, cherish me!," showing a desperation for love that he did not feel from his parents and that he seems to have known he might never have again.

W. D. SNODGRASS

Although he studied under Lowell, W. D. Snodgrass (1926-2009) did not consider himself a confessional poet. In fact, he disliked the term because of its religious connotation and because critics associated it with writing as therapy. However, Snodgrass is widely considered one of the founding members of the confessional movement, primarily because of *Heart's Needle* (1959), a collection of poems chronicling his divorce and his loss of custody of his daughter as a result.

In "Papageno," dedicated to Janice, his wife at the time, Snodgrass describes how he "went to whistle up a wife" but that his mouth was "padlocked for a liar" and that he ". . . could not speak/ To hush this chattering, blue heart." He beckons to his future wife, "Come take this rare bird into hand;/ In that deft cage, he might sing true." Signs of tension appear when the speaker in "Riddle" says, "You have the damnedest friends and seem to think/ You have some right to think. . . ." Still, the couple has ". . . grown/ Closely together where most people shrink." It seems that they are too close for comfort, although the speaker suggests, ". . . if there's a world between/ Us, it's our own." Ironically, physical distance is emphasized in "Song," with the speaker describing how he and his "woman" are inextricably linked through the ". . . rich/ soil, friable and humble,/ where all our murders rot,/ where our old deaths crumble." This image of mortality is reinforced by the speaker's description of his reach as "far from you, wide and free,/ though I have set my root/ in you and am your tree." This seems to be a desperate attempt to hold onto that which is slipping away.

The long title poem, "Heart's Needle," chronicles a father's estrangement from his daughter in the aftermath of a divorce, Snodgrass's own experience. To mark the passage of time, he uses an image of himself and his daughter digging a garden when she is three years old. He advises her to pay attention to the growing sprouts: "You should try to look at them, every day/ Because when they come to full flower/ I will be away." He compares himself and his former wife to ". . . cold war soldiers that/ Never gained ground, gave none, but sat/ Tight in their chill trenches."

They ". . . sever and divide/ Their won and lost land. . . ." The speaker compares the child to a wishbone and shows a desire for the child to choose sides when he boldly suggests, "It may help that a Chinese play/ Or Solomon himself might say/ I am your real mother."

The father is frustrated at his inability to control the situation, lamenting that he cannot tell his daughter ". . . why/ the season will not wait;/ the night I told you I/ must leave, you wept a fearful rate/ to stay up late." His frustration is exemplified in ". . . broken lines// of verses . . ." that he "can't make." During the same year, although the child is still three years old, he notices, "You are already growing/ Strange to me." He watches her ". . . chatter about new playmates, sing/ Strange songs . . ." and even admits, "You bring things I'd as soon forget." He recalls a night when his daughter had a fever and "wheezed for breath," as if she were drowning. The speaker then gives his daughter the cruel truth: "Child, I have another wife,/ another child. We try to choose our life." Pushing his daughter on a swing— where he must "shove" her away, then see her "return again," "drive" her off again, then "stand quiet" until she comes—is a metaphor for the push-pull relationship between himself and his child, as he must relinquish her at certain times and may regain her only when permission is granted. The father is chagrined at his lack of parenting skills, describing himself as an "absentee bread-winner" who takes his daughter to eat in local restaurants and buys ". . . what lunches we could pack/ in a brown sack." He eventually learns to ". . . fry/ omelettes and griddlecakes so I// could set you supper at my table." He relates, "As I built back from helplessness,/ when I grew able,/ the only possible answer was/ you had to come here less." The father and daughter indulge themselves with sweets at Halloween, and he craves them after she leaves.

As the father and daughter grow more distant from each other and friends ask how she is doing, the speaker admits, ". . . I don't know// or see much right to ask./ Or what use it could be to know." Her pictures above his desk seem "much the same." Despite their geographical closeness, he feels them growing apart, observing how "The world moves like a diseased heart/ packed with ice and snow./ Three months now we have been apart/ less than a mile. I cannot fight/ or let you go."

"They" have said that if he loved her, he would leave and find his own "affairs." However, he and his daughter again visit the zoo, looking at the bears and raccoons, "punished and cared for, behind bars," stretching "thin black fingers" out to them. He ends the poem with a commitment to permanence: "And you are still my daughter." He is determined not to let his daughter slip away the way he let his wife slip out of his grasp.

SYLVIA PLATH

Like Lowell, under whom she studied, Sylvia Plath (1932-1963) was an apprentice to the classical form and heavily influenced by Yeats, Pound, and Eliot. She had her first poem published at age eight. Plath was raised by a single mother after her father died when she was ten. Her symbolic killing of the image she created of him in her mind is chronicled in her poem "Daddy," in which the speaker describes her attempts to "get back" to her father by killing herself and how she made a "model" of him, "A man in black with a Meinkampf look," to cope with his death.

Plath was an overachiever throughout her school years and won many prizes for her poetry before she enrolled in Smith College. While in college, she won a coveted guest editorship at *Mademoiselle* magazine. She graduated from Smith College in 1954 with the highest honors and also won a Fulbright scholarship to study at Oxford University. In 1953, Plath attempted suicide, and throughout her life, she struggled with mental illness, including manic and depressive episodes; she eventually succeeded in committing suicide. Despite the emotional and mental inconsistency she experienced, Plath was a prolific and respected poet during her lifetime. However, the posthumous publication of *Ariel* (1965), a collection containing her most highly skilled and dramatic poems, gained her the fame that would make her practically a legend. It also generated a great deal of controversy regarding the circumstances of her death following the breakup of her marriage to Ted Hughes, one of Great Britain's most important poets. This controversy and speculation has eclipsed her poetry at times, but astute critics have recognized the brilliance of her technical skill and practically mystical ability to evoke profound responses from readers, as exemplified in *Ariel*.

"Morning Song" (from *Ariel*) begins with the promise of hope, with the speaker addressing her child: "Love set you going like a fat gold watch." However, like the speaker of Snodgrass's "Heart's Needle," the mother feels estranged from her child, claiming "I'm no more your mother/ Than the cloud that distills a mirror to reflect its own slow/ Effacement at the wind's hand." Rather than providing the image of nurturing that readers might expect in a poem spoken by a mother to her child, the poet shows a mother noting her lack of connection to her child and perhaps even consciously distancing herself from her child to cope with the challenges of motherhood. In "The Rabbit Catcher" (from *Winter Trees*, 1971), the trap itself is used as a metaphor for a constricted marriage: "Tight wires between us,/ Pegs too deep to uproot, and a mind like a ring/ Sliding shut on some quick thing." Even more grotesquely, "The Applicant" (from *The Collected Poems*, 1981) parodies the "selling" of marriage, particularly in the 1950's and 1960's, with a promise that is unfulfilled, comparing the prospective wife to a suit, "Black and stiff, but not a bad fit./ Will you marry it?/ It is waterproof, shatterproof, proof/ Against fire and bombs through the roof./ Believe me, they'll bury you in it." This product comes with a further guarantee: "in twenty-five years she'll be silver,/ In fifty, gold./ A living doll, everywhere you look./ It can sew, it can cook,/ It can talk, talk, talk." The cultural critique of a poem such as this has earned Plath a reputation for stridency and bitterness. The fact that she would examine marriage in such an uncompromising manner and present it as another "bill of goods" that is "sold" to the American public shows her inventiveness and courage to refute what was considered the sanctity of marriage.

The risk taking continues with "Lady Lazarus" (from *Ariel*), one of Plath's most striking poems, in which the speaker boasts of her suicide attempts: "I have done it again./ One year in every ten/ I manage it—" In her references to Nazism ("... skin/ Bright as a Nazi lampshade") and the circus, with "The peanut-crunching crowd/ Shoves in to see// ... / The big strip tease," Plath combined metaphors to create a surreal and grotesque scene in which the suicide attempt itself is a performance, and the speaker has "nine times to die," like a cat. The speaker boasts:

Dying
Is an art, like everything else.
I do it exceptionally well.

I do it so it feels like hell.
I do it so it feels real.

She even compares it to a calling and admits that it is the "... theatrical// Comeback in broad day," the "miracle" that "knocks [her] out." However, there is a sacrifice to be made, "... a charge// For the eyeing of her scars ..." and the "hearing" of her heart, as well as a charge for a piece of her hair or clothes. Despite being picked apart by prurient onlookers, she rises like a phoenix, "Out of the ash" with her "red hair," and she "eats men like air." Not only is suicide not treated as socially unacceptable or a taboo subject, but instead it is glorified in this poem. Plath portrays suicide as a vocation that holds a fascination for those who witness it as well as those who experience it, anticipating the public's response to Plath's own suicide.

ANNE SEXTON

Like Snodgrass and Plath, Anne Sexton (1928-1974) was a student of Lowell. In fact, she and Plath were in a workshop with him at the same time. However, unlike Plath, Sexton started writing poetry relatively late in life, after several suicide attempts and institutionalization, when her therapist suggested that she write as a form of therapy. She also saw a Public Broadcasting Service program on sonnets, wrote one herself, and was so pleased with the results that she decided to enroll in a poetry workshop, where she met her lifelong friend, the poet Maxine Kumin. She started to publish her work and win prizes for it. Although some critics considered the subject matter of Sexton's poems, which included menstruation and abortion, inappropriate and even offensive, others appreciated her directness and risk taking as well as her technical proficiency.

All My Pretty Ones (1962) is one of the best examples of confessional poetry in its willingness to address subjects often considered inappropriate for poetry at the time. The title poem shows ambivalence toward the death of a parent. After her mother's death, the speaker finds photographs among her deceased father's things.

Anne Sexton (AP/Wide World Photos)

Rather than cherishing the pictures, the speaker says, "I'll never know what these faces are all about./ I lock them into their book and throw them out." She addresses her father as ". . . my drunkard, my navigator,/ my first lost keeper, to love or look at later," and then finds a five-year diary that her mother kept, chronicling her husband's "alcoholic tendency." Ultimately, the speaker reconciles with her father, deciding, "Whether you are pretty or not, I outlive you,/ bend down my strange face to yours and forgive you."

In "Starry Night" (from *All My Pretty Ones*), inspired by Vincent van Gogh's painting of the same title, the speaker describes how ". . . one black-haired tree slips/ up like a drowned woman into the hot sky" while "The town is silent" and "The night boils with eleven stars." "Oh starry starry night!" the speaker proclaims, "This is how/ I want to die." The line is repeated in the second stanza, after a description of the moon bulging "to push children, like a god, from its eye," with "the old unseen serpent swallow[ing] up the stars." This surreal image reveals the personification of the scene in

which the speaker projects herself, expressing how she wants to die: "into that rushing beast of the night,/ sucked up by that great dragon, to split/ from my life with no flag,/ no belly,/ no cry." Unlike the speaker in Plath's "Lady Lazarus," this speaker does not want to go out with a theatrical bang but rather by being sucked into a vortex and vaporized. The glamorization of death makes this poem controversial. A similar attitude can be found in "Her Kind" (from *To Bedlam and Part Way Back*, 1960), in which Sexton describes how a "possessed witch" who has done her "hitch" is "misunderstood" and "is not ashamed to die." Readers would more likely expect her to not be afraid to die; the use of the word "ashamed" implies that there could be a reason for shame, such as suicide, often considered a cowardly way to die. Sexton's treatment of it flies in the face of that.

"The Abortion" and "Woman with Girdle" (both from *All My Pretty Ones*) bring up subjects that some consider best avoided in poetry. With the refrain "*Somebody who should have been born/ is gone*" in "The Abortion," Sexton creates an ambiguous meaning similar to the feelings a woman might have following the procedure. There is a sense of loss, that an event that should have occurred has not, yet the woman relates in a matter-of-fact manner, "I changed my shoes, and then drove south." Although she wonders "when the ground would break" and "how anything fragile survives," she does not seem to regret her decision, although she considers herself a coward for not saying what she means, or what she describes as "this baby that I bleed." In "Woman with Girdle," Sexton lingers on the parts of a woman's body that she is trying to conceal with the girdle that was such a popular undergarment at the time that Sexton wrote the poem. The speaker directly addresses the woman (who could be a woman reading the poem) by noting, "Your midriff sags toward your knees;/ your breasts lie down in air." As the woman stands in her "elastic case," the speaker notices how she "roll[s] down the garment" and exposes her "belly, soft as pudding," similar to the way that Sexton and other confessional poets exposed the "underbelly" of society in the 1950's and 1960's through their art.

BIBLIOGRAPHY

Davison, Peter. *The Fading Smile: Poets in Boston, from Robert Frost to Robert Lowell to Sylvia Plath, 1955-1960.* New York: Alfred A. Knopf, 1994. Describes the environment in which confessional poets worked with and learned from each other in poetry workshops as well as their social interactions with each other in the vibrant literary climate of Boston from 1955 to 1960.

Kirsch, Adam. *The Wounded Surgeon: Confession and Transformation in Six American Poets.* New York: W. W. Norton, 2005. Argues that the technical prowess of poets Robert Lowell, Elizabeth Bishop, John Berryman, Randall Jarrell, Delmore Schwartz, and Sylvia Plath, similar to a surgeon's discipline and skill, has been overshadowed by their confessional subject matter and tumultuous lives.

Middlebrook, Diane Wood. "What Was Confessional Poetry?" In *The Columbia History of American Poetry*, edited by Jay Parini. New York: Columbia University Press, 1993. Describes the origins, subjects, and themes of confessional poetry as well as representative poets and their work.

Holly L. Norton

New York School

The New York School of poets was born in the United States in the late 1950's. Its central members—Frank O'Hara (1926-1966), Kenneth Koch (1925-2002), James Schuyler (1923-1991), and John Ashbery (born 1927)—shared common experiences and interests, which provided their mutual affinity with the momentum necessary to make their writings seem like a movement. O'Hara, Koch, and Schuyler had served in World War II. Schuyler had lived with and worked as a typist for W. H. Auden, on whose poetry Ashbery wrote his senior thesis while an undergraduate at Harvard, where he met O'Hara and Koch. All of them were enamored of the French Surrealists. O'Hara and Ashbery were knowledgeable devotees of the New York art scene and moved in its circles, guaranteeing the influence on their poetry (and drama and criticism) of the ideas and methods at work in the paintings of New York expressionists such as Jackson Pollock and Willem de Kooning.

Indeed, it was from the New York School of painters that gallery director John Bernard Myers took the New York School name and applied it to the poets in 1961 in an overt act of public-relations strategy. However, it was probably inevitable that such a moniker would adhere to the poets. One reason that the poets who make up the New York School, as well as critics, have regarded the New York label as spurious is that, for its founding members, only some of them had grown up in or near the city and some of them lived there only intermittently. About its role as a state of mind common to the poets, however, there has been little dispute. The city, with its intricate network of universities, publishing houses, public-reading forums, and bohemian cachet served as the physical and metaphorical fulcrum of their activity. Its energetic cosmopolitan rhythms and heightened artistic atmosphere, redolent as they were of endless activity and stimulating innovation, enlivened their work and linked even the movement's most stylistically disparate participants.

Despite its beginnings in the underground avant-garde, the New York School saw its more persistent and prolific members embraced by the mainstream literary community. None was embraced more than Ashbery. Nineteen years after winning the Yale Younger Poets Prize in 1956, his book *Self-Portrait in a Convex Mirror* (1975) won the National Book Award, the National Book Critics Circle Award, and a Pulitzer Prize. From 2001 to 2003, he served as the poet laureate of New York State. Schuyler became the second New York School alumnus to win the Pulitzer Prize, in 1981, for his book *The Morning of the Poem* (1980). Koch, who after Ashbery was probably the best-known member of the New York School, did not receive a major award until he won the Shelley Memorial Award in 1994, followed by the Bollingen Prize in 1995 for *One Train* (1994). He was a member of the American Academy of Arts and Letters and enjoyed a long career as a popular university instructor. From 1953 to 1958, he was a lecturer at Rutgers University. In 1959, he was hired as an assistant professor by Columbia University, and he became one of its most popular teachers during his nearly forty-year tenure.

Some observers trace the gradual unraveling of the New York School of poets to 1966, the year that O'Hara was killed by a dune buggy on Fire Island. Certainly O'Hara's death struck the movement a blow, but by then, the movement he had helped launch had taken on a life of its own. With the publication in 1970 of *An Anthology of New York Poets*, edited by Ron Padgett and David Shapiro, the New York School had grown to include too many poets for one volume to encompass. In the decade that followed, the members of the school "graduated" into various careers that in many cases led them well beyond the city.

The central figures among the New York School of poets wrote in a variety of other genres. O'Hara, Ashbery, Koch, and Schuyler wrote plays. O'Hara published four volumes of art criticism. Ashbery translated the work of French poets. Koch wrote a well-received series of books intended to interest students in writing poetry. Schuyler was a novelist. The school's less famous members were equally diverse. Barbara Guest (1920-2006) wrote plays. Kenward Elmslie (born 1929) wrote for the musical theater. Edwin Denby

(1903-1983) was best known as a ballet critic. Aram Saroyan (born 1943), the master of the one-word poem, developed into a writer of prose. Ed Sanders (born 1939) became famous as the leader of the Fugs, a psychedelic folk band. Taken as a whole, the poets of the New York School considered no literary genre to be unsuitable for the exercising of their talents.

AN ANTHOLOGY OF NEW YORK POETS

An Anthology of New York Poets, a six-hundred-page volume that has come to be regarded as the Bible of the New York School of poets, contains 374 poems written by twenty-seven poets over a period of two decades. Judging from the preface by editors Padgett and Shapiro, the process of deciding which poets and which of their poems to include must have resembled, admittedly on a lower metaphysical scale, the selecting of canonical texts. There was a sense that the book would come to represent not only the best work of the individual poets but also the movement as a whole. Some of the poets (Ashbery and Koch in particular) would publish works that superseded the poems included in this anthology. However, for the majority of the poets involved, even those who continued to write prolifically, inclusion in this anthology would represent their only moment on the national stage.

Padgett and Shapiro seem to have been guided in their selection in part by a desire to represent the movement's diversity. There are one-word (even one-letter) poems by Saroyan and traditional sonnets by Denby, playfully transparent poems by O'Hara, explication-defying fragments by Clark Coolidge, plainspoken journal-like poems by Ted Berrigan, and buoyantly lyrical fantasias by Elmslie, "found" poetry by John Giorno, prose poetry by Schuyler, haiku-like elegance by Bernadette Mayer, and frank profanity by Sanders.

The diversity was no ruse. The poets did, however, share common elements, the most obvious of which might be the sense that they were not bound by any of the rules that had accumulated during the previous five hundred years of Western poetry. A poet of the New York School could observe convention, play with it, pillage it for parts, or ignore it altogether. The same freedom applied to subject matter. From baseball and sunglasses (Tom Clark) to highbrow allusions (Shapiro), nothing was off limits.

In a sense, the poetry represented the fulfillment of Walt Whitman's all-encompassing vision. Unlike Whitman's poems, however, the bulk of this anthology's verse has not aged well. Much that no doubt seemed liberating, spontaneous, and fresh in the 1950's and 1960's now seems puerile, insular, and slapdash, the writing of poets so afraid that all work and no play would make them dull boys that they opted instead for all play and no work.

THE WORLD ANTHOLOGY

The World was one of the periodicals most responsible for publishing the works of the younger, lesser-known poets of the New York School. Deliberately amateurish in appearance—its pages were typewritten, mimeographed, and stapled together—its very look invited an experimental informality unwelcome in the more prestigious journals in which older New York School poets had begun to appear.

The World Anthology (1969) was edited by Anne Waldman, a poet who, with Allen Ginsberg, John Cage, and Diane di Prima, would found the Jack Kerouac School of Disembodied Poetics at Naropa University in Boulder, Colorado, five years later. Many of the poets whose work the anthology contains—including Michael Brownstein, Joseph Ceravolo, Dick Gallup, and Peter Schjeldahl—would also have work published a year later in *An Anthology of New York Poets*. As a result, *The World Anthology* seems in retrospect like a first draft, an insufficiently edited template from whose mistakes Padgett and Shapiro would learn in preparing their collection.

One of the more obvious differences between the two books is Waldman's enjoyment of "list poems." Although there is nothing remarkable about the fifteen verbs that make up Larry Fagin's "Fifteen Things I Do Every Day," Ted Berrigan's marginally more elaborate "Ten Things I Do Every Day" (its verbs contain direct objects) hints at the mysteries beneath the mundane. To Waldman's credit, she included Berrigan's "The Avant-Garde Literary Award," a deadpan parody of the type of insufficiently developed experiments that take up many of the pages that follow.

Nevertheless, *The World Anthology* is noteworthy for introducing the work of Jim Carroll, a New York poet who, despite being passed over by Padgett and

Shapiro, would go on to considerable acclaim as a poet, a memoir writer, and a rock-and-roll singer. Of the five Carroll selections, "From the Basketball Diaries" was a conflation of journal entry and prose poem unique among the works of his peers.

THE COLLECTED POEMS OF FRANK O'HARA

In the poems of O'Hara, one observes the deceptively casual discussion of unconventional subject matter that, more than any other single characteristic, set the tone for the New York School of poetry. As might be expected, the solidification of O'Hara's body of work after his death in 1966 has allowed critical analysis to accumulate to the point that, in quantity if not in quality, it now competes with the poetry itself for the attention of the novice reader of O'Hara. The dividing line between those who see his poetry as profound and those who see it as trivial has become increasingly sharp. Reasons for this division can be found in any number of O'Hara's poems. However, those reasons are brought into particularly clear focus by two poems: "The Day Lady Died" and "Why I Am Not a Painter." The subject of the first exemplifies O'Hara's willingness to write about pop culture, the latter his willingness to write about the act of writing.

O'Hara wrote "The Day Lady Died" in 1959, when the cultural allusions suitable to poetry were those that had stood the test of time. T.S. Eliot's *The Waste Land* (1922) and Ezra Pound's *Cantos* (1925-1972), which together dominated the poetry world, freely cited ancient rituals, foreign languages, mythology, and religion. O'Hara's devoting a poem to the death of the jazz singer Billie Holiday (whose nickname was Lady Day) risked sounding of insolence, an insolence intensified by O'Hara's not referring to Holiday's death until just before the poem's end, after having dragged the listener through twenty-four lines of daily minutiae.

This shaggy-dog approach is, admittedly, clever. The speaker experiences Holiday's death as a shock, and O'Hara's circuitousness re-creates the effect. On the other hand, the poem is both manipulative and misleading. The title leads readers to expect the poem to be about the singer's death and therefore a kind of eulogy. It turns out to be about the speaker and his feelings, making the reader, and maybe Holiday, the butt of a joke.

"Why I Am Not a Painter" plays a similar game, but it does so at the poet's own expense. In the poem, O'Hara visits a painter at work on a painting called *Sardines*. By the time the painting is finished, the artist has eliminated the sardines, making the painting a representation of its subject's absence. Later, the poet becomes so obsessed with writing a poem about the color orange that he overshoots, and the poet ends up with pages worth of prose from which all references to orange have vanished. He divides it into twelve poems and calls it *Oranges* (1953). Eventually, the reader realizes that "Why I Am Not a Painter," like *Sardines* and *Oranges*, contains nothing about its titular subject. Besides being a good joke, it puts forth the very interesting idea that no work of art is finished until all traces of whatever inspired it have disappeared.

A WAVE

In "The Ecclesiast," a poem from *Rivers and Mountains* (1966), Ashbery wrote, "The monkish and the frivolous alike were to be trapped in death's capacious claw/ But listen while I tell you about the wallpaper—" These lines adequately summarize his verse.

Ashbery published *A Wave* in 1984, nearly one decade after his reputation as an important contemporary poet had been established by his winning a Pulitzer Prize for *Self-Portrait in a Convex Mirror*. *A Wave* did not win a Pulitzer, but it did win a Lenore Marshall Poetry Prize and the Bollingen Prize, indicating the return of Ashbery's work to a favor after what some critics considered a period of creative stasis. Creative stasis is, in a sense, both the subject—in *A Wave* and elsewhere—of his poetry and its form.

"Stasis" may seem like a peculiar term to describe poetry that with its long, flowing lines, surrealistic swirls, and polysyllabic vocabulary, appears to undulate. However, like the "wallpaper" in "The Ecclesiast," all that actually undulates in Ashbery's verse is a recurring pattern of designs that only appears to move when examined up close. Viewed from a distance, it becomes a static facade. The wall that it covers, the room of which the wall is a part, and the people in the room (the "monkish" and the "frivolous") do not interest Ashbery, and therefore go unconsidered.

Ashbery was also an art critic, so it is not surprising that the illusion of motion conveyed by static surfaces should appeal to his aesthetic sense. What is surprising, and disappointing, is that a poet as obviously gifted as Ashbery should be content to pass off art criticism as art. There are, in most of his poems, lines that live and portend an imminent insight. More often than not, however, they are negated by the lines that follow, leaving the residue of depths unexplored at the poem's end.

Some critics have remarked that the sentences and sometimes the very lines in a typical Ashbery poem could be rearranged at random and still have the same effect, and in longer poems such as "A Wave," the 684-line title poem, the accusation is especially hard to deny. Like the world in T. S. Eliot's "The Hollow Men" (1925), it begins with a bang ("To pass through pain and not know it,/ A car door slamming in the night") and ends with a whimper ("But all was strange"). In a poem so long, reversing the whimper and the bang would have made little difference.

The same cannot be said of "At North Farm," the first piece in *A Wave*. The Godot-like "someone [who] is traveling furiously toward you" at the beginning of the poem never arrives, but the suspense of his arriving in the first stanza intensifies the "mixed feelings" of his failure to arrive in the second. Restricting himself to the length (although not the meter or the rhyme scheme) of a sonnet, Ashbery has little room to meander. It is an all too rare example of an Ashbery poem in which everything matters.

THE COLLECTED POEMS OF KENNETH KOCH

"There are certainly big differences in our poetry," Ashbery once said, comparing his work to that of Koch, "but we had somehow the same attitude: that you could fool around in poetry, which was not the case with most of our contemporaries." By "our contemporaries," Ashbery meant the poets of the 1950's, those who had grown up in the shadow of half a century's worth of manifestly serious—even ominous—poetry. Amid such company, the possibility of "fooling around in poetry" must have looked very appealing.

Few poets made fooling around look more appealing than Koch did, as is evident from *The Collected Poems of Kenneth Koch*. "Sleet machines!" he exclaimed in "The Chase," one of his earliest poems. "I approach you like a moth dizzy with materials,/ Disk! disk! public peaces of entertainment!" The wordplay in the lines of

John Ashbery (Getty Images)

his poems seldom subsided for long, and when it did, it did so only to cast Koch's next mirthful eruption, which was never far away, into sharper relief. The "elephant man" in another early poem, "The Circus," "speaks giddily, to every one of the circus people he passes,/ He does not know what he is saying, he does not care...."

Like the dizzy moth and the insouciant elephant man, Koch had so much fun in his poems that often the idea that readers not in on his jokes might not be having fun seems not to have occurred to him. His signposts in "You Were Wearing," a brief surrealist romp through Western civilization, are easy enough to recognize (Edgar Allan Poe, Herman Melville, Abraham Lincoln, and Dick Tracy), but as with many poets of the New York School, his verse often seems tailored to entertain the poets of the New York School. To read it is to feel like an eavesdropper at a very lively party.

It is therefore perhaps not surprising that, of his many pieces, the one most widely anthologized is "Variations on a Theme by William Carlos Williams," a parody of another, even more widely anthologized poem, Williams's "This Is Just to Say." Unlike the bulk of Koch's work, "Variations on a Theme by William Carlos Williams" has as its subject something well known to the public and therefore presents readers with no epistemological obstacles. It is also a parody in form as well as in content. Capitalizing on the most common objection to Williams's poem—that surely a twenty-eight-word apology about having eaten someone else's plums does not rise to the level of poetry—Koch multiplies its length and writes not one parody but four. Each is funny on its own ("I chopped down the house that you had been saving to live in next summer," "I gave away the money that you had been saving to live on for the next ten years"), but together, and arranged so that the humor builds and the funniest of the four parodies ends the poem with a bang, Koch's "variations" become not only funny but also immune to the charge that they are too brief to be taken seriously.

BIBLIOGRAPHY

Herd, David. *John Ashbery and American Poetry*. New York: Palgrave Macmillan, 2001. Less a biography of Ashbery than an analysis of what he as a poet has in common with a quality of intellect and thought traceable to the eighteenth century. Herd attempts to understand the irony that Ashbery is simultaneously one of the West's most celebrated poets and one of its least understood.

Kane, Daniel. *All Poets Welcome: The Lower East Side Poetry Scene in the 1960's*. Berkeley: University of California Press, 2003. An evocatively detailed description of the anything-goes atmosphere that prevailed in New York City's lower East Side when the "second generation" of the New York School of poets were beginning to make their mark both in print and on stage. Includes a compact disc of audio clips of the poetry readings.

_____. *What Is Poetry: Conversations with the American Avant-Garde*. New York: Teachers & Writers Collaborative, 2003. Includes biographical information about and revealing interviews with John Ashbery, Kenneth Koch, and Bernadette Mayer (as well as experimentally inclined poets not associated with the New York School), each of whom Kane sees as belonging to a uniquely American "avant-garde tradition."

Koch, Kenneth, and Ron Padgett. *Wishes, Lies, and Dreams: Teaching Children to Write Poetry*. New York: HarperCollins, 1999. Arguably the most influential of the several books that Koch wrote or cowrote on making the writing of verse look possible and appealing to students. Contains many examples of the student writing that Koch's imaginative approach inspired.

Lehman, David. *The Last Avant-Garde: The Making of the New York School of Poets*. New York: Knopf, 1999. An account of the friendship of John Ashbery, Kenneth Koch, Frank O'Hara, and James Schuyler and the development of that friendship into a font of energetic energy. Lehman captures the careening spirit of the two-decade period in which a seminal moment engendered a movement. He also illustrates the poets' vital ties to the broader New York art culture (specifically the visual arts) and the great extent to which those connections served as conduits for mutual inspiration.

Padgett, Ron, and David Shapiro, eds. *An Anthology of New York Poets*. New York: Random House, 1970. This anthology begins with a nine-page preface by Padgett that captures what the twenty-seven poets contained in the book thought of the New York School label (not much) and their place in the history, and the future, of American letters. The preface also reprints Frank O'Hara's semiserious "Personism: A Manifesto."

Perloff, Marjorie. *Frank O'Hara: Poet Among Painters*. Chicago: University of Chicago Press, 1998. O'Hara's style, personality, and ancillary artistic passions exercised a greater influence on the poets of the New York School than those of any other individual. Making use of numerous previously unavailable writings, Perloff paints the most vivid and intimate portrait to date of O'Hara as a polymath of the avant-garde. Includes detailed analysis of several of O'Hara's best-known poems.

Ward, Geoffrey. *Statutes of Liberty: The New York School of Poets*. New York: Palgrave Macmillan, 2001. A pioneering work in the understanding of the New York School, focusing primarily on John Ashbery, Frank O'Hara, and James Schuyler.

Arsenio Orteza

MOVEMENT POETS

The Movement consisted of a group of like-minded English poets, loosely associated together in the mid-1950's. Their intention was to redirect the course of English poetry away from the neo-Romantic Symbolist and Imagistic poetry of William Butler Yeats and Dylan Thomas. At the same time, they also disavowed the modernist poetry of the 1920's and 1930's, represented by T. S. Eliot, Ezra Pound, and W. H. Auden. Instead, they sought to place English poetry back into the tradition last represented by Thomas Hardy, of formal verse and accessible meaning, modestly covering everyday experience.

Of this group of poets, Philip Larkin (1922-1985) emerged as the most popular. His poetry did a good deal to re-engage poetry with a more popular audience. Other poets, such as Kingsley Amis (1922-1995) and John Wain (1925-1994), made wider names for themselves as novelists, especially as part of the group known as the Angry Young Men. Many of the group were academics, and their critical writings helped shape the course of British literature for the next two decades.

HISTORY

Poetry in England in the first part of the twentieth century had been subject to various conflicting movements. Before World War I, it was dominated by Georgian poetry, a formal, romantic poetry that was the legacy of Victorian poets such as Alfred, Lord Tennyson, and Matthew Arnold. It tended to be nostalgic and rural. The continuing exponent of this formal and traditional verse in England was Hardy (1840-1928). He wrote on everyday events and meetings, often with a gentle irony or sadness. His poetry made philosophical references at a general level but did not engage directly with issues of the day. It was retiring and understated, lyrical, and mellifluous, using traditional imagery and verse forms. The poetry of Yeats (1865-1939), an Anglo-Irish poet, also was as influential. Yeats had developed a private mythology but could write politically as well. His imagery was much more symbolic and his tonalities were much more varied and original than those of Hardy.

The trauma of World War I and the new awareness created by psychoanalysis and modern science produced a quite different movement in literature, usually termed modernism. The poetic exponents of modernism were at odds with the Hardy-Yeats axis of Romanticism, and they sought to produce a much more loosely formed and structured verse that could at the same time capture everyday speech and the symbolic disassociation felt by members of the fractured postwar society. The leading exponent of modernism in England was Eliot. His *The Waste Land* (1922) became one of the iconic poems of the twentieth century.

The difficulties of 1920's modernism, as exemplified in such poets as Pound, gave way in the 1930's to a more direct political verse, reflecting the rise of extreme right- and left-wing ideologies, as well as growing social problems emerging during and after the Great Depression of the 1930's. English poets, such as Auden and Louis MacNeice, still used modernist tropes and tonalities, but more directly.

In the late 1930's and early 1940's, particularly through the war years of 1939 to 1945, there was something of a romantic reaction to modernism, in the gushing, energetic verse of the Welsh poet Thomas, which sparked of a neo-Romantic wave. Poets were returning to an earthier, even rural subject matter and imagery, and expressing greater concern to create music and a rich, dense, more emotional imagery. At times, mythological themes were incorporated, as in a school of writing sometimes called the Apocalyptics, which included David Gascoyne, Vernon Watkins, and Kathleen Raine.

THE MOVEMENT

The Movement arose as a reaction to both modernism and this neo-Romanticism, grounded in the aftermath of World War II. There was a general desire to avoid any heroic sentiments at all and to live in the ordinary here-and-now, which in postwar Britain was rather bleak and austere, with everything rationed and with an uncertain future. As a country, Britain had been bankrupted by the war and was about to lose its empire and its superpower status, but it was determined to lay the foundations of a solid welfare state and a less class-ridden society. The Cold War was about to begin, and harsh reality took the place of political idealism.

As a poetic movement, the Movement had no strong cohesion to it, no obvious "school" existing around one or two central figures. It was rather a group of young poets whose education had been completed or inter-rupted during the war. Many of them were academics, many from working-class or lower-middle-class back-grounds, who had all managed a university education at Oxford or Cambridge, mainly through gaining aca-demic scholarships. Most of them met at various times and were aware of each others' work, although some denied they belonged to any "movement" at all.

Various events brought about cohesion and caused the literary culture of the day to label the group as the Movement. One such event was the publication in 1952 of *Purity of Diction in English Verse* by the young aca-demic Donald Davie (1922-1995). Davie argued that English poetry should return to the Augustan era of the late eighteenth century, abandon modernism as an ab-erration, and redefine itself in terms of an older classi-cal tradition, lost after Hardy died.

However, it is possible to go back to the war years, to the meeting of Larkin and Amis, then two young Oxford undergraduates. Both were studying English, loved jazz, and were "scholarship boys" from modest backgrounds. Though Larkin was under the influence of Yeats at the time, both Larkin and Amis disliked elit-ism and pretentiousness. Publication of their poems in *Oxford Poetry 1949* (1949), an anthology edited by Amis, brought them acquaintance with other young po-ets, such as Wain and Elizabeth Jennings (1926-2001). Other young poets, such as D. J. Enright (1920-2002) and Thom Gunn (1929-2004), also began writing verse that tried to be formal, precise, and unpretentious. They were influenced by the formal criticism of William Empson and F. R. Leavis, leading English professors at Cambridge University who stressed truthfulness of emotion and sincerity of tone.

In 1951, the Oxford academic F. W. Bateson began publication of the journal *Essays in Criticism*, which was to embrace poetry and criticism along the lines Davie was suggesting. The next year, John Lehman and Wain were hosting *New Soundings*, a monthly program of poetry readings by these new poets on the British Broadcasting Corporation. Their verse began to be published in various magazines, and then in three small presses: the Fortune Press in Oxfordshire, the Univer-sity of Reading Press, and the Marvell Press in northern England. By this time, most of the poets had found jobs in provincial universities or at Oxford and Cambridge. Enright found a post in Japan, from where he edited *Po-ets of the 1950's: An Anthology of New English Verse* (1955). He included his own poetry, together with that of Amis, Davie, Wain, Robert Conquest, Jennings, Larkin, and John Holloway.

On October 1, 1954, the London cultural journal *The Spectator* ran a main article by its literary editor, J. D. Scott, titled "In the Movement." Scott surveyed the contemporary literary scene in an attempt to find a significant cultural shift in British society in the 1950's. He noted the anti-idealism of this "Movement," and the name stuck. Shortly after, Conquest, another of the Movement poets as well as a rising Sovietologist, was asked to produce an anthology of new poetry. His *New Lines: An Anthology* (1956-1963) contained work by nine young poets who became known as the Movement poets. They were the eight included by Enright in his anthology, with the addition of Thom Gunn, the youngest of the group.

Some, like Gunn and Larkin, denied their member-ship in any such group. How long the group existed is debatable. Some members, including Gunn and Davie, went to the United States in the early 1960's, where they became caught up in other influences and found different styles. Others became better known for their novels or academic work, such as Wain, Amis, and Holloway. However, Enright, Jennings, and particu-larly Larkin were writing in what was recognizably the same style during the next decade and even after. Of all the poets, Larkin, although a desperately shy man who spent much of his life as a librarian at Hull University in the north of England, well away from the centers of cul-tural influence, gained the greatest fame and prestige.

THE POETRY

It is difficult to generalize about the style, content, or imagery of Movement poetry. With nine poets as members, any general statement is likely to find an exception. The poets were all born in the 1920's, nearly all to uncultured ("philistine") families, often with blue-collar fathers or grandfathers. For the most part, their childhoods were spent in obtaining academic educations that allowed them to gain places at the prestigious universities of Oxford or Cambridge. There they encountered the elite, class-ridden society that predominated in the arts in England at the time, and they reacted against it. They also reacted, at some point in their early writing careers, against the wordy, inflated style represented for them by the alcoholic Welsh poet Thomas, who died in 1952.

Their poetic reaction took the form of formal verse, tightly patterned, as against the free-verse style represented by Thomas. Often they returned to eighteenth century patterns, with the ironic tone that accompanied that verse. The irony was subversive, mocking, often self-deprecating. It was very aware of elitism, inflated language and attitudes. Poetic utterance came as understatement, often tentatively expressed. "Perhaps" was a favorite word. Big claims were avoided; it was the smaller details of everyday life that became significant topics, expressed in ordinary, everyday language. Often the language would have some colloquial expression in it to produce an anticlimax.

Above all, a rigorous self-examination was conducted to produce as honest a piece of writing as was possible. Thus, a poem would often move away from the poet's perception of his emotional reaction to a situation or person, to peel away layers of false sensibility and to arrive at the poet's genuine response. Sometimes this honesty took the form of an aggressive philistinism, a refusal to be "poetic" or "artsy." Larkin made a point of emphasizing his own provinciality and rejected the London cultural snobbery for the ordinary truth of everyday provincial life. However, there are plenty of poems about paintings and foreign scenes that suggest the poets were, in fact, perfectly well cultured. The philistinism sometimes became a pose in itself.

The other feature of Movement poets was a refusal to make political, philosophical, or theological statements, in contrast to preceding verse. In the end, this produced a rather limited range of topics, and many po-

ets later broke away from this, though Larkin did not. The poets seemed content with life as it was in postwar Britain, however unexciting and drab.

NEW LINES

These features are best exemplified in *New Lines*, the anthology edited by Conquest. Each poet was represented by eight to ten poems, creating a total of seventy-five poems. Some of the poems included became iconic of the Movement: Larkin's "Church Going" and "Toads," Jenning's "Afternoon in Venice," Gunn's "On the Move," Amis's "Against Romanticism," Davie's "Limited Achievement," and Wain's "Eighth Type of Ambiguity." Davie's "Remembering the Thirties" speaks exactly for the Movement, while its reference to "a neutral tone" being preferred pays homage to Hardy, who wrote a poem with that title.

Conquest wrote a significant introduction to explain the Movement, pointing to what he considered the corruption of the previous decade's poetry: its self-indulgence, inflated emotions, and so on. By contrast, the new poetry is "free from both mystical and logical compulsions" but concentrates on "the real person." Interestingly, he claims George Orwell's no-nonsense realism as a significant influence.

Enright's "On the Death of a Child" is a good example of this. Written with Thomas's poem on the death of a child as a subtext, Enright's poem avoids the big gestures of grief that typified Thomas. "The big words fail to fit," he writes. They take up "improper room." Enright is not being callous—indeed, of all the Movement poets, he is the most sympathetic to human suffering. It is just that he wants to avoid the inflated gesture.

Jennings well exemplifies the tight construction of the poems. Her poems typically consist of three stanzas with regular metric and rhyming schemes. Often the construction of thought is logical: A, B, and therefore C, as in "Identity." Her topic is human relationships, and the sense that a person's identity is perhaps less important than the identity others construct of that person in love and friendship. Typical relationship topics, such as breakups, are often handled in an impersonal or ironic way, as in Holloway's "Elegy for an Estrangement." The seven stanzas consist of ten lines each, with a regular though unobtrusive rhyme scheme and a complex though regular metrical pattern. Such disciplined verse had been absent from English poetry for many years.

THE NEW POETRY

Another influential anthology was *The New Poetry*, edited by A. Alvarez and published by Penguin in 1962. It is sometimes claimed that this is anthology was created in reaction to *New Lines* and was an attempt to introduce the poetry of the American poets John Berryman and Robert Lowell and the new English poet Ted Hughes, to counteract the influence of the Movement poets. However, this would be a mistake, as the anthology includes work from Enright, Davie, Larkin, Amis, Wain, and Gunn. In fact, the contributions of Enright (ten poems) and Larkin (eight) are substantial, as is that of Gunn (seventeen). Only two of Enright's poems were repeats from the previous anthology, and only one of Larkin's. Larkin's very fine "Whitsun Weddings" is included, as is Davie's "The Mushroom Gatherers." Davie's "Under St. Paul's" demonstrates his breaking out of the tight Movement mold. It is a big, incantatory statement, at times more like the work of Gerard Manley Hopkins than that of Hardy. Davie, in fact, was the first Movement poet to write against the Movement, seeing its limitations and internal contradictions. Gunn's large contributions— "Lofty at the Palais de Danse" and "Lines for a Book"—show the "philistine" stance, which threatens to become a pose. However, his "Helen's Rape" shows the persistent influence of Yeats, an influence seen more subtly in Larkin.

PHILIP LARKIN

Larkin's first volume of verse, *The North Ship* (1945, revised 1946) was indeed very Yeatsian. His second volume, *The Less Deceived*, published in 1955, seemed very different, the embodiment of the Movement's stance, ironic, self-deprecating, writing on real people in real moments of time. The often anthologized "Church Going" is typical of the "less deceived" stance of the poet. He goes into a church; he is not sure why, but presumably to look at its historical architecture. He ponders if there is a deeper reason. His stance is determinedly secular, philistine, yet there is a sense of a tradition lost and the need for the numinous, which he is both embarrassed by and fascinated with.

The title poem of *The Whitsun Weddings* (1964) is about another rite of passage. Ironically, "whitsun" is the feast of Pentecost, when the Holy Spirit was given to the church and when confirmees were received into the church. Larkin's determined secularity stands out against this. However, weddings represent love, and as a bachelor, Larkin remains an embarrassed observer. The railroad journey he is on becomes a symbol of life itself, of which he is an observer, outside its real experiences. Other major themes of Larkin were aging and dying.

Larkin's poetry has been praised for its discipline and honesty and its tentative exploring of ordinary life. Fellow poet Andrew Motion has noted the latent idealism behind the mask of deprecating irony in Larkin's poetry and remarks on the conflicted emotions in its sadness and nostalgia. Larkin's refusal to publish anything but the achieved poem, revised to perfection, has meant his output has been small but of a consistently high standard. The other Movement poets had no difficulty recognizing him as their best and, in fact, their most continuing standard bearer.

LATER DEVELOPMENTS

Larkin's poetry was modeled on that of Hardy, though still influenced by Yeats. However, Hardy's range is limited, and many Movement poets soon felt that limitation. Gunn's poetry, now based on his California experiences and the first signs of the 1960's counterculture experience, was soon being bracketed with that of Hughes, as much more elemental, violent, and unconstrained. As the influence of Hughes and Lowell grew in England, that of the Movement poets lessened. Their underlying egalitarianism became expressed more through their novels, such as Wain's *Hurry on Down* (1953; pb. in U.S. as *Born in Captivity*) and Amis's *Lucky Jim* (1954), or through the new Angry Young Men drama of John Osborne.

Davie found himself returning to his religious roots, which as a young man had been merely "nonconformist" in a secular way. In this, he joined Jennings, always a devoted Catholic, who began increasingly exploring her faith and the effects of various mental breakdowns. Enright continued to write restrained, controlled poetry, but as he was working in the Far East, his subject matter appeared somewhat exotic. Conquest and Holloway pursued other careers as diplomats or academics. *New Lines II: An Anthology* (1963), edited by Conquest, included many new poets outside the Movement, some of whom had been antagonistic to it.

It was thus left to Larkin to continue the Movement into the 1960's and beyond. However, his very retiring nature and the paucity of his output meant his influence on poetry was less than it might have been. However, his residual influence, and that of the Movement as a whole, brought a healthy discipline back to English verse, probably best seen in the work of Motion, who later became poet laureate, a post that Larkin had previously refused. Davie, Jennings, and Larkin were all in turn entrusted with significant volumes in the Oxford Books of Verse series.

BIBLIOGRAPHY

Bradley, Jerry. *The Movement: British Poets of the 1950's*. New York: Twayne, 1993. Part of the English Authors series, this book devotes a general chapter to the Movement, and separate chapters to each of the nine main members, followed by a very useful bibliography.

Davie, Donald. *Purity of Diction in English Verse*. London: Chatto & Windus, 1952. This is the groundbreaking text that acted as a manifesto for the Movement. Davie went on to publish many other critical studies and became an acclaimed university teacher in Great Britain and the United States.

Leader, Zachary. *Amis*. New York: Pantheon, 2006. A very full biography of Kingsley Amis, setting him in the context of the 1950's and examining his wider influence, as well as his friendships with other Movement poets.

_____, ed. *The Movement Reconsidered: Essays on Larkin, Amis, Gunn, and Their Contemporaries*. New York: Oxford University Press, 2009. A collection of original essays by distinguished poets, critics, and scholars from Great Britain and the United States, seeking to reassess the Movement and to place it in a wider sociohistorical context.

Morrison, Blake. *The Movement*. New York: Oxford University Press, 1980. This is the first full-length study of the group as a whole, written while its members were all still alive and publishing.

Motion, Andrew. *Philip Larkin: A Writer's Life*. London: Faber & Faber, 1993. A fairly biographical account building on an earlier 1983 biography. Motion brings out Larkin's latent Romanticism and the tension this caused him with his antiromantic writings.

Swarbrick, Andrew. *Out of Reach: The Poetry of Philip Larkin*. New York: St. Martin's Press, 1995. A sensible analysis of Larkin's poetry, with one chapter devoted to his particular relationship with the Movement. He builds on the groundbreaking work on Larkin by Andrew Motion.

David Barratt

BLACK MOUNTAIN SCHOOL

Black Mountain School describes a group of poets who emerged in the 1950's. Poets who are included in this group typically have displayed an avant-garde, postmodern poetic style at some time and have had a direct connection with Black Mountain College, have published works in *Black Mountain Review* (first a Black Mountain College publication and later a journal issued from 1954 to 1957), or were associated with a publishing company of a former Black Mountain College student.

Donald Allen, editor of *The New American Poetry: 1945-1960* (1961), was one of the first writers to employ the term "Black Mountain School." In the anthology, Allen categorized the included poets based on their geographic location, such as the Black Mountain School, New York School, and San Francisco Renaissance Poets. Allen identified eleven poets as being original members of the Black Mountain School. Black Mountain, North Carolina, was a part of the background of each of these eleven poets. Most of them had studied or taught at Black Mountain College. A number had works in the *Black Mountain Review*—either the Black Mountain College publication or the journal issued from 1954 to 1957. Many of them had employed open-form verse. Several had published with a publishing company associated with a former Black Mountain College student.

BLACK MOUNTAIN COLLEGE

Situated in Buncombe County, North Carolina, the community of Black Mountain took its name from the mountain range wherein it nestles. The Black Mountains are a part of the Blue Ridge Mountains of the Southern Appalachians, which extend into West Virginia, North and South Carolina, Tennessee, and Georgia. Black Mountain is about fifteen miles east of Asheville.

The population of the village of Black Mountain was about 750 in 1933 when John Andrew Rice, Jr. (1888-1968), and several other dedicated individuals founded the experimental Black Mountain College. Rice served as its first rector. Rice's father, a

Methodist minister, had been the president of Columbia College in Columbia, South Carolina, and a founding faculty member of Southern Methodist University in Dallas, Texas. Rice's mother was Annabelle Smith, the sister of U.S. senator Ellison Durant ("Cotton Ed") Smith. Rice took many ideas for teaching from Webb School, the college preparatory boarding school that he attended (1905-1908) in Bell Buckle, Tennessee. Rice advocated classroom discussion techniques, student-centered teaching, and a minimum of formal lecture.

A graduate of Tulane University, Rice received a Rhodes Scholarship to Oxford University. At Oxford, he met Frank Aydelotte, who would later be a president of Swarthmore College, and Frank's sister Nell Aydelotte. Rice married Nell in 1914 after his Oxford graduation; they had two children before their divorce and his remarriage.

Rice taught one year at Webb School before entering the doctoral program at the University of Chicago. The progressive educator became a controversial faculty member at the University of Nebraska (1920-1927); conflicts led to his departure. Rice's employment at New Jersey College for Women also involved controversy and lasted only two years. After a year in England on a Guggenheim Fellowship, Rice taught at Rollins College in Winter Park, Florida. His controversial teaching methods, his opposition to fraternities and sororities, and his objections to college policies resulted in his resignation after three years. This time, however, some colleagues and students resigned with him and began planning an experimental institution: Black Mountain College.

Rice and the other founders of Black Mountain College intended for its faculty to operate and own the school. The model for governing Black Mountain College would be democratic. There would be no outside trustees overseeing the college; instead, a council—selected by the faculty and students—would offer suggestions. Both faculty and students would participate in all aspects of the college: governance, farmwork, construction, and even kitchen detail. The founders envisioned an innovative college that would emphasize John Dewey's principles of progressive education. Social, cultural, and experiential activities would enhance learning and teaching. Important curricular emphases were the liberal arts, the fine arts, and literature. To complete their course of study, the students would have to pass oral examinations administered by outside examiners. There would be no normal degrees or graduation ceremonies at Black Mountain College. The seclusion of the mountain environment encouraged creativity, community, democracy, individuality, and learning.

FACILITIES OF BLACK MOUNTAIN COLLEGE

The facilities of Black Mountain College were unlike those of most colleges and universities. From 1933 to 1941, the founders of Black Mountain College rented the Young Men's Christian Association's Blue Ridge Assembly buildings, just south of the village of Black Mountain; these facilities had been in use primarily as a summer conference center. A three-story building, an assembly hall, plentiful rooms, and a view of the mountains seemed an ideal environment for the new college.

At its 1933 opening, Black Mountain College had twenty-one students. Over the years, as the college received increasing national recognition, enrollment grew, reaching nearly one hundred students yearly. The campus soon needed to expand. During the late 1930's, the faculty began consulting with Walter Gropius—the German architect who founded the Staatliches Bauhaus School in Germany—and other architects to plan a larger, modern campus for Black Mountain College. Because of the impending war, however, the time for an extensive building project was not right. Still, the college was ready for some changes.

In 1940, the faculty requested that Rice tender his resignation. That year, Black Mountain College began the process of relocating to Lake Eden, just across the valley from the Blue Ridge Assembly location. The newly purchased Lake Eden property had originally been a summer camp and resort; it included a lakeside dining hall, two lodges, and several small cottages. The college enlisted the American architect A. Lawrence Kocher to devise a simple plan for the expansion of Black Mountain College. During 1940-1941, students and faculty of Black Mountain College constructed the Studies Building, a faculty cottage for music teacher Heinrich Jalowetz and his wife, and some other buildings for the campus. The college remained in this Eden Lake location until it closed in 1957.

THE IMPACT OF THE TIMES

In the 1920's, the educator Dewey developed his principles of progressive education, which contrasted with the traditional lecture method of teaching. His progressive teaching model—which featured student-centered learning—was used by many Black Mountain instructors. Black Mountain College's curriculum and teaching methods incorporated many of Dewey's ideas.

When Black Mountain College opened in the 1930's, the United States was in the Great Depression. In its establishment and operation, the college had to consider the financial situation of potential students. Having the students and faculty work together was not just advantageous to the students and the school; it was a necessity for the survival of the institution.

World affairs also affected Black Mountain College. In Germany, Adolf Hitler was rising in power. He and his Nazi regime opposed the Staatliches Bauhaus School, which combined crafts and the arts in its teachings and operated from 1919 to 1933. The Nazis supported traditional architectural designs and opposed the cosmopolitan, modernistic designs advocated by the Bauhaus group. In the early 1930's in Berlin, the married couple of Josef Albers, a Bauhaus artist, and Anni Albers, a weaver and textile designer, endured a search and interrogation by Nazi agents. Knowing of the pressures on the Bauhaus and its staff, Black Mountain College invited the Albers family to come to North Carolina. Neither artist could speak any English, but they readily made the trip to the Blue Ridge Mountains to begin a new life and escape political pressures. Their innovative ideas positively affected the curriculum of Black Mountain College and the work of the students. When the Staatliches Bauhaus in Berlin closed under Nazi pressure, many of its teachers and students tried to flee to the United States. As the persecution of intellectuals and artists throughout the European continent continued, even more teachers and students left their homelands for the United States; some settled in the Blue Ridge Mountains.

Although students at Black Mountain College could choose many of their courses, each enrollee had to take the drawing course taught by Josef Albers. Because of its outstanding faculty—including the Bauhaus stage designer and graphic artist Xanti Schawinsky—and its innovative approaches to instruction, curriculum, and governance, the college began to gain national and world recognition. Black Mountain College became a center for transmitting the Bauhaus philosophy, for teaching innovations, for emphasizing the importance of art to one's education, and for stressing the liberal arts, particularly literature.

Many famous people began to visit the campus and to participate in its programs for days or weeks at a time. One such visitor was Buckminster Fuller, the creator of the geodesic dome; he built the first dome on the campus of Black Mountain College. Other noted guests of the college included educator Dewey, Albert Einstein, the artist Jackson Pollock, and the writers Thornton Wilder, Aldous Huxley, William Carlos Williams, and Henry Miller. The faculty and students encouraged this outside interest and the direct involvement of their guests in the instruction.

EARLY PUBLICATIONS

Black Mountain College began publishing the *Black Mountain Review* in 1951. This journal featured the work of faculty and students of Black Mountain College. The publication, however, did not operate for long. Another journal with the same title, *Black Mountain Review*, was issued from 1954 to 1957. This journal's title reflected its place of publication rather than any affiliation with the college. However, Robert Creeley—a Black Mountain poet and a former teacher at Black Mountain College—did serve as its editor for a while.

Another journal, *Origin*, published in 1951 by Cid Corman (1924-2004), featured the works of many of the original poets of the Black Mountain School. The contributing editor of *Origin* was Charles Olson, a faculty member and a rector at Black Mountain College as well as one of the original Black Mountain poets.

THE ORIGINAL MEMBERS

Allen's anthology, *The New American Poetry: 1945-1960*, included eleven poets in the Black Mountain poets section: Olson, Creeley, Robert Duncan, Edward Dorn, Denise Levertov, Larry Eigner, Paul Blackburn, John Wieners, Jonathan Williams, Joel Oppenheimer, and Hilda Morley.

CHARLES OLSON

Charles Olson (1910-1970) was a professor and rector (1951-1957) at Black Mountain College. Born in Worcester, Massachusetts, Olson had studied at both Harvard and Wesleyan. With a Guggenheim Fellowship, he continued studying the works of Herman Melville. Olson's ideas about poetry were an important part of the style of the avant-garde poets of the Black Mountain School. Olson devised the theory of projective verse and wrote of it in a 1950 essay. He proclaimed that a poem is energy; the poet transfers or projects the energy from its source through the poem to the reader. The source of the energy varies from poem to poem, but

Charles Olson (©Allen Ginsberg/CORBIS)

the purpose of the poem is discharging the energy. Olson stressed that the length of the line is the breath of the poet. He noted that the poet could narrow the unit of structure to fit an utterance or breath; as a result of this contraction, the poetic diction might employ a distinctive style, for instance "yr" for "your."

There is not one poetic style that is followed by all the Black Mountain poets; they do, however, seem committed to open form. Open form replaced the traditional closed poetic forms used by earlier writers. The poetry of the Black Mountain poets could no longer be evaluated using the criteria of effective use of traditional poetic rules and conventional forms. Many essayists and critics still classify contemporary poets who work in projective verse, who use open form, and who attend to utterance or breath as members of the Black Mountain School.

In addition to producing his theory of projective verse, Olson was a prolific writer. More than one hundred of his shorter poems appeared in *Archaeologist of Morning: The Collected Poems Outside the Maximus Series* (1970), published by Cape Goliard in London. Olson's most sustained poetic effort, however, was *The Maximus Poems* (1953-1983), a sequence published in numerous volumes. In 1987, the University of California Press published *The Collected Poems of Charles Olson: Excluding "The Maximus Poems." Selected Poems* (1997) was edited by Creeley, another original Black Mountain poet.

ROBERT CREELEY

Robert Creeley (1926-2005) was born in Arlington, Massachusetts. He lived in Asia, Europe, and Latin America before coming to teach at Black Mountain College in 1955 and serving as editor of *Black Mountain Review* from 1955. When Creeley left two years later when the college closed, he became the Black Mountain poets' link to Allen Ginsberg and the Beat poets and the poets of the San Francisco Renaissance. Two collections capture most of Creeley's poetic works: *The Collected Poems of Robert Creeley, 1945-1975* (1982) and *The Collected Poems of Robert Creeley, 1975-2005* (2006).

ROBERT DUNCAN

Robert Duncan (1919-1988) taught at Black Mountain College from 1955 through 1957. Born in Oakland,

California, this Black Mountain poet later became a leader of the San Francisco Renaissance. Two collections of Duncan's poems that include individualistic spellings (utterances) are *Derivations: Selected Poems, 1950-1956* and *The First Decade: Selected Poems, 1940-1950*, both published by Fulcrum Press in London in 1969.

EDWARD DORN

Reared in the rural poverty of Villa Grove, Illinois, during the Great Depression, Edward Dorn (1929-1999) studied at the University of Illinois and at Black Mountain College (1950-1955). Dorn, with Duncan, Creeley, and Olson, became a Black Mountain poet. Olson influenced Dorn's concept of poetry, and Creeley was one of Dorn's final examiners at Black Mountain College.

After traveling and settling in the Pacific Northwest, Dorn produced his first book of poetry: *The Newly Fallen*, published in 1961 by Totem Press. He wrote the autobiographical *The Rites of Passage: A Brief History*, published in 1965 by Frontier Press and revised as *By the Sound* in 1971. He became known for his mock Western epic, *Gunslinger I* (1968), *Gunslinger II* (1969), and *Gunslinger Book III* (1972). *Way More West: New and Selected Poems* (2007) presents a selection of Dorn's work over his entire career.

DENISE LEVERTOV

Born in Ilford, Essex, England, Denise Levertov (1923-1997) served as a nurse during World War II. After the war, she married an American writer and moved to the United States, where she became associated with the Black Mountain poets, especially Olson and Duncan. Her poetry collections include *Here and Now* (1957), *The Sorrow Dance* (1966), and *The Great Unknowing: Last Poems* (1999), as well as the career-spanning *Collected Earlier Poems, 1940-1960* (1979), *Poems, 1960-1967* (1983), and *Poems, 1968-1972* (1987).

LARRY EIGNER

Larry Eigner (1927-1996) had cerebral palsy from birth. He lived in Massachussets until 1978, when he moved to Berkeley. *Black Mountain Review* published some of his poetry, and Creeley's Divers Press published Eigner's first book, *From the Sustaining Air* (1953). Eigner wrote more than forty volumes of poetry. In 2010, Stanford University Press published *The Collected Poems of Larry Eigner.*

PAUL BLACKBURN

Paul Blackburn (1926-1971) lived in St. Albans, Vermont, from his birth until 1940, when he moved to Greenwich Village with his mother. He began writing poetry and studied at New York University. In 1945, he joined the U.S. Army, then spent his service time in Colorado. In 1947, he returned to New York University, transferred to the University of Wisconsin, Madison, and graduated in 1950. During his college studies, he began corresponding with the poet Ezra Pound and visited him several times in Washington, D.C. Through Pound, Blackburn met the Black Mountain poets Creeley, Corman, Levertov, Olson, Oppenheimer, and Williams.

Blackburn published *Proensa* (1953), a translation of Provençal poetry, and *The Dissolving Fabric* (1955), a book of original poems, with Creeley's Divers Press. Some of Blackburn's poems appeared in Creeley's *Black Mountain Review.* Blackburn, however, did not write only open-form poetry. He experimented with other types of writing, for example, that were typical of the New York School of poets.

He published thirteen books of original poetry, including *The Nets* (1961) and *The Cities* (1967), and five major works of translation. In addition, twelve other books appeared posthumously, including *The Collected Poems of Paul Blackburn* (1985) from Persea Books.

JOHN WIENERS

John Wieners (1934-2002) was born in Massachusetts and earned his bachelor's degree from Boston College. After hearing Olson read in 1954, Wieners enrolled at Black Mountain College and studied with Olson and Duncan from 1955 to 1956. Although Allen classified Wieners as a Black Mountain poet, Wieners also participated (1958-1960) in the San Francisco Renaissance, another of the geographic categories that Allen used in his 1960 anthology.

After living in New York and Boston, Wieners traveled with Olson to the Spoleto Festival in Italy and to the Berkeley Poetry Conference. Wieners enrolled in the graduate program at State University of New York at Buffalo, worked as a teaching fellow with Olson, and earned an endowed chair of poetics (1965-1967). He

published *The Hotel Wentley Poems* in 1958 and was briefly institutionalized in 1960. The Gallery Upstairs Press in Buffalo published his *Pressed Wafer* in 1967. In the spring of 1969, Wieners was again institutionalized. His *Asylum Poems (For My Father)*, published in 1969, reflects that experience. His poems are collected in *Selected Poems, 1955-1984* (1985).

Wieners continued to write and to publish. He was versatile and produced lyrical poetry, prose, and journals. *Kidnap Notes Next, Selected Notebook Entries, 1988-1999* (2002), a collection of poems and journal entries, appeared posthumously. Bookstrap Press in Massachusetts published *A Book of Prophecies* (2007) after a researcher found Wieners's unpublished manuscript in the archives at Kent State.

JONATHAN WILLIAMS

Jonathan Williams (1929-2008) is another original Black Mountain poet who studied at Black Mountain College. In 1951, Williams founded the Jargon Society, which has published poetry, prose, and art for more than fifty years.

Born in Asheville, North Carolina, Williams was never far from Black Mountain. His press published works by three of the original Black Mountain poets: Olson, Duncan, and Creeley. The last of the original Black Mountain Poets, he died on March 16, 2008.

JOEL OPPENHEIMER

Joel Oppenheimer (1930-1988) was a member of both the New York School and the Black Mountain School and a columnist for the *Village Voice* (1969-1984). Born in Yonkers, New York, Oppenheimer attended Cornell University (1948), the University of Chicago (one semester), and Black Mountain College (1950-1953). Oppenheimer studied with Dorn and with Olson; he also worked in the print shop of Black Mountain College. Oppenheimer returned to New York after 1953, worked in a print shop there, and continued to write poetry—in his own style.

In 1988, Oppenheimer published *Names and Local Habitations: Selected Earlier Poems, 1951-1972* through the Jargon Society, founded by Black Mountain poet Williams. His later works are gathered in *The Collected Later Poems of Joel Oppenheimer* (1997). Oppenheimer published numerous volumes of poems, starting in 1956 with *The Dutiful Son,* as well as a volume of short stories and two works of nonfiction in his lifetime. *Drawing from Life*, a collection of his columns for the *Village Voice*, was published posthumously in 1997.

HILDA MORLEY

Hilda Auerbach Morley (1916-1998) was born to Russian parents in New York City. She composed poetry from an early age, and as a young woman, she corresponded with William Butler Yeats. She studied at the University of London. In 1945, she married the abstract painter Eugene Morley, who taught at Black Mountain College. Her connection with this abstract expressionist affected her poetry, as did her association with other poets at the college. The Morleys divorced in 1949. Three years later, Morley married Stefan Wolpe, a German composer and professor at Black Mountain College. Hilda's contact with Black Mountain College through both her husbands and through her studies there enhanced her writings.

With the help of Black Mountain poet Levertov, Morely published her first volume, *A Blessing Outside Us* (1976), with Pourboire Press. Other volumes followed before her 1998 death from a fall in London.

IN RETROSPECT

Although Black Mountain College existed only from 1933 until 1957 and fewer than twelve hundred students were enrolled there, the college became a noted experimental institution for the arts and literature. A remarkable number of literary achievements by its students and teachers ensured its reputation.

Those considered to be Black Mountain poets typically had direct contact with this college, its faculty, its related publishers, and its curriculum. Black Mountain poets left their mark on both American and British poetry. Modern American projectivist poets include Charles Potts (born 1943), who studied with Dorn. British poets influenced by the Black Mountain school include J. H. Prynne (born 1936) and Tom Raworth (born 1938).

BIBLIOGRAPHY

Allen, Donald. *The New American Poetry: 1945-1960*. New York: Grove Press, 1960. Classifies the included poets according to geographic locations and lists eleven poets as being Black Mountain poets.

Duberman, Martin B. *Black Mountain: An Exploration in Community*. 1972. Reprint. Evanston, Ill.: Northwestern University Press, 2009. Includes commentary and interaction with the people, the community, and the history of Black Mountain College.

Harris, Mary Emma. *The Arts at Black Mountain College*. 1987. Reprint. Cambridge, Mass.: MIT Press, 2002. Traces the history of Black Mountain College, includes a roster of faculty and students, and examines the Black Mountain poets and their styles.

Katz, Vincent, et al. *Black Mountain College: Experiment in Art*. Cambridge, Mass.: MIT Press, 2002. Includes a history of Black Mountain College with comments by and interaction with the people of the college.

Anita Price Davis

GREEN MOVEMENT POETS

Although primarily a warning against pesticides, Rachel Carson's *Silent Spring* (1962) made both the public and the government aware of technology's deleterious effects on the environment. It thereby provides a convenient date for the beginning of the Green movement, the greatest influence on subsequent nature poetry. The Green movement rests on three assumptions: that civilization has alienated itself from the environment erroneously, that the resulting damage has threatened humanity with possible extinction, and that collective action is required to repair this and establish a sustainable culture. Previous nature poetry generally expressed the first of these assumptions, but generally concluded that only the quality of life, not its very existence, was at stake.

For example, although Pulitzer Prize winner Gary Snyder (born 1930) eventually earned a very prominent place in the Green movement, his *Riprap* (1959) came a few years too early to be a part of it. Consequently, in this work, Snyder merely urges a return to nature in much the manner of previous poets, especially the Chinese mountain poets. In "The Late Snow & Lumber Strike of the Summer of Fifty-four," Snyder laments his no longer being a lumberjack, because his unemployment distances him from the wilderness as he goes back to look for work in Seattle. What it does not do is consider the environmental impact of logging as it was then practiced—the kind of concern the Green movement came to expect.

PRECURSORS

Despite this clear difference between Green movement poets and earlier nature poets, the movement has devoted much attention to these precursors. It interprets early nature poets, because of their extreme sensitivity to the environment, as having already been more responsive to grave dangers than the general public. At the conclusion of the dramatic poem *Faust: Eine Tragödie, zweiter Teil* (pb. 1833; *The Tragedy of Faust, Part Two*, 1838) by Johann Wolfgang von Goethe (1749-1832), for example, the protagonist uses demons to drain wetlands for agriculture. The project

results in the death of an aged couple who will not relocate, and its digging becomes that of Faust's own grave. Does such skepticism about technological progress (coupled with Goethe's standing as a naturalist) make him a Green movement poet? Conversely, as an exponent of Faustian striving, was he a major voice for human domination of nature? Axel Goodbody's *Nature, Technology, and Cultural Change in Twentieth-Century German Literature: The Challenge of Ecocriticism* (2007) faces the dilemma in forty-one pages on Goethe as an "ecophilosophical inspiration." Similarly, as pioneers of Romantic nature poetry, William Wordsworth and other Lake poets are cited for anticipating the Green movement in Bryan L. Moore's *Ecology and Literature: Ecocentric Personification from Antiquity to the Twenty-first Century* (2008) and Nicholas Roe's *The Politics of Nature: William Wordsworth and Some Contemporaries* (2002). Other studies of precursors include Gyorgi Voros's *Notations of the Wild: Ecology in the Poetry of Wallace Stevens* (1996) and M. Jimmie Killingsworth's *Walt Whitman and the Earth: A Study in Ecopoetics* (2004). Indeed, whether in ecocriticism or in such anthologies of ecopoetry as editor Astley Neil's *Earth Shattering: Ecopoems* (2007), a considerable share of space is usually given to works before 1962.

A major reason for this is that the Green movement's threefold argument is considerably strengthened if it can suggest (even with reservations) that the poets affiliated with the movement are part of a long line, all of whom correctly intuited an increasing need for environmentalism. The problem, of course, is that a real difference in tone usually divides Romantic from Green movement poetry: The former tends to depict nature as nurturing and forgiving (in that it could then still heal itself), whereas the latter generally sees it as ravaged. Even Snyder's medieval, Far Eastern models (which have been extremely influential on many Green movement poets) come from an age before massive pollution and suburbanization; therefore, they inevitably have almost nothing to say about these.

The Green movement's search for precursors is poignantly exemplified in the poem "Chord" (1988) by W. S. Merwin (born 1927). The poem juxtaposes the life of John Keats with the deforestation of Hawaii. Probably, Keats was consciously quite oblivious to the latter, in that he never wrote of it. Merwin's title "Chord," however, may imply that in some way the two resonate with each other, as if Keats, attuned to nature, had an unconscious awareness of its beginning plight, while dying young of tuberculosis.

Because of this fascination with precursors, Green movement writers tend to be very much aware of Romantic poetry, which influences them, albeit in a disguised way. Their poetic descriptions of the present are often anti-Romantic, parodying the older style or reversing it (for example, terseness substituted for verbosity, ugliness for prettiness). Their poems recollecting their own childhoods tend to suggest a Romantic kinship with nature but stripped of the sentimental and idyllic, as in "Oxcart Man" (1977) by Donald Hall (born 1928). Furthermore, these recollections of a better past contrast implicitly with the present contaminated environment. They also occasionally foreshadow threats to nature, as in "The Thought-Fox" (1957) by Ted Hughes (1930-1998)—which also foreshadows the style of his subsequent ecopoems. The poem concerns cubs that he as a child unsuccessfully tried to keep alive. In their longing for a return of the beautiful past, Green movement poets engage in several major struggles: science versus technology, spirituality versus materialism, conservationism versus postmodernism, ecofeminism versus patriarchy, and action versus apathy.

SCIENCE VERSUS TECHNOLOGY

The Green movement has used science to support its arguments while attacking the devastation caused by science's by-product, technology. For example, Snyder's "What Happened Here Before" (1975) narrates his homestead's history for 300 million years (described in scientific terms) but culminates with an assault on the environment by machines. This reliance on science coupled with an irritation with technology distinguishes Green poetry from its precursors. Whereas, for example, the ecopoet Wendell Berry (born 1934) has devoted numerous essays and poems to the scientif-

ically documented problems of monoculture (single-crop agriculture), Oliver Goldsmith's *The Deserted Village* (1770) is occasioned by that technology, yet almost completely ignores it, instead lamenting that nature is no longer being subdued by virtuous Christian farmers.

Even monumental discoveries very relevant to the Green movement, however, do not always slip easily into poetry. Hughes learned this by way of his poem "The Lobby Under the Carpet" (1992), inspired by a 40 percent worldwide drop in male fertility because of pollution. Hughes was so appalled by this that he sent a letter to the British prime minister urging action, yet he had to admit that the resulting poem he wrote about the statistic was not one of his best. Thereafter, he tended to shy away from such literal propagandizing in verse. Similarly, the Green poet A. R. Ammons (1926-2001) generally decreased the scientific vocabulary he used in his poems and always employed it in an ironic and playful manner, as in "Hairy Belly" (1987), in which the word "gravity" means both field force and moral seriousness.

Scientific scrutiny of nature, nonetheless, has sometimes increased poetic empathy with it. "The Wellfleet Whale" (1983), by Stanley Kunitz (1905-2006), for example, begins with the notion that whale song itself constitutes a poetic language—an idea dependent on Roger Payne's having discovered that song during the 1960's. That discovery also probably contributed to "For a Coming Extinction" (1967) by Merwin, in which it underlies the image of the dying whale's bewilderment echoing like that song throughout the ocean.

Perhaps the greatest master of turning scientific ideas into ecopoetry is Santa Fe's poet laureate Arthur Sze (born 1950), a second-generation Chinese American, who left the Massachusetts Institute of Technology to study humanities at the University of California, Berkeley. He learned the discipline of concise, concrete images from translating Chinese classical poetry. In "The Leaves of a Dream Are the Leaves of an Onion" (1987), he pairs neutrinos, quarks, and Galapagos ecology, among other things, with subjectively perceived events or objects in such a way that, by the end, the reader intuits a complex, multilevel system of affinities and tensions that organize the cosmos. The title for

The Quark and the Jaguar: Adventures in the Simple and Complex (1994) by the 1969 Nobel Prize winner in physics, Murray Gell-Mann, comes from Sze's poem. Sze's ecological worries often manifest conspicuously, as in "The String Diamond" (1998), in which he lists thirty endangered species in a long column, occupying a whole page; however, it also functions as a love poem, for he is unusually skilled in connecting the scientific and humanistic.

Another bridge between the two areas is Mario Petrucci (born 1958). With an undergraduate degree in physics from Cambridge, a doctorate in opto-electronics from University College London, and postgraduate work in environment and literature from Middlesex University, Petrucci has worked hard toward a reconciliation between science and literature, through both his poetry books and his fostering of ecologically oriented creativity events for college students and children. He has also issued poetry books and films about the 1986 Chernobyl nuclear accident.

SPIRITUALITY VERSUS MATERIALISM

In connecting science to the humanities, the Green movement has often adapted ideas from the world's religions and continued their struggle against materialism. One of religion's functions has been to interpret reality while defining the human experience, a function that in later years has also been performed by science. In this sense, religion and science have a joint function, although the major ecopoets are eclectic in their approaches to combining the two. Snyder, who loved the wilderness since his childhood, is among those (including his friend Allen Ginsberg) closely associated with Buddhism. The draw of Buddhism is that it pioneered in the protection of animals—a concern first called deep ecology by the philosopher Arne Naess in 1973. Snyder, who practiced Zen Buddhism in Japan, draws metaphors from diverse religious traditions, especially Native American beliefs. Hughes's wide-ranging eclecticism conjoins his ecological position with many shamanic and animistic ideas. Sze frequently alludes to Daoist divination in his multifarious poems, but as a teacher at the Institute of Indian Arts (and someone once married to a Hopi), he more often refers to Native American beliefs. Native American poets such as the

Chickasaw poet Linda Hogan (born 1947) and the Choctaw poet Jim Barnes (born 1933) build ecopoetic metaphors from tribal beliefs. Hogan's "All Winter" (1988) describes her participation with all life as well as with her massacred ancestors crying from the earth. Barnes's "A Season of Loss" (1985) presumes that his tribe once had a special relationship with nature but considers that as lost, concomitant with partial assimilation. Hogan's "The Truth Is" (1986) describes her mixed heritage as giving her one Chickasaw hand and one white one. Berry is a Christian, but he is opposed to organized Christianity. In his 1993 essay "Christianity and the Survival of Creation," he criticizes Christianity for having done too little for the creation. In his nonfiction work *The Gift of Good Land* (1981), he argues that God's gift of this world to humanity is contingent on our preserving the rest of creation. The poems of his *A Timbered Choir: The Sabbath Poems, 1979-1997* (1998) take Romantic adaptations of God's closeness to nature and further adapt them into support of the Green movement.

Of at least equal importance to the Green movement

Wendell Berry (©Dan Carraco/Courtesy, North Point Press)

poets' adapting and interweaving worldviews is their taking from these traditions methods of contemplation. Their meditative practices may be as unassuming as Sze's "Acanthus" (2005), where to appreciate the Turkish coast, the speaker of the poem simply shuts his eyes, thereby tapping his unconscious reservoirs of memory and desire, finding resolution not in material possession but in the poem itself. More obtrusive, nature poems of Ginsberg even as far back as his "Sunflower Sutra" (1955) borrow from Whitman a hypnotically repetitive style, with a potential for inducing trance, particularly in his chant-like delivery. Merwin's "Fox Sleep" (1992) adapts a Zen koan—a paradoxical device for deepening meditation by confusing the conscious mind. Indeed, the ecopoetic tendency is to overcome ego-centered consciousness, as in Berry's 1995 poem "Amish Economy," in which an Amish character says that his goal is not to find himself but to lose himself in nature.

CONSERVATIONISM VERSUS POSTMODERNISM

Green movement poets tend to ally themselves not merely with external nature but also with the unconscious depths in each person and with certain archaic spiritual approaches to both. In this large sense, the movement is conservationist: It seeks to preserve the oldest portions of the world and the mind against civilization's attempts to bring these under conscious control. Not these goals but rather the methods employed to advance them bring the Green movement in conflict with postmodernism (a skeptical trend in the humanities since the 1960's).

Postmodernism's method is to argue playfully that the selfish, imperialistic world control sought by humanity, particularly since the early nineteenth century, is inherently impossible because language does not describe reality, no self exists, and everything (including gender) that seems real to people is merely a social construct. The postmodern approach is thus relatively passive, an effort to debate people into inaction (since action has proven disastrous). In contrast, Green movement poets insist that people really can know that the environment is being destroyed, and poetic words might move the masses to combat this destruction. Snyder's *The Practice of the Wild* (1990) and Berry's *Standing*

by Words: Essays (2005) combat the postmodern position. Ammons's poem "Construing Deconstruction" (1996) derides postmodernism. This conflict, however, does not mean that the ecopoets have a naïve faith in all language. Ammons's book-length poem *Garbage* (1993), for example, admits that words often fulfill the same unintellectual function that grooming does among baboons. His poem "Essay on Poetics" (1970), however, contends that the chief problem with language comes from humanity's separation from nature, which detaches words from the intuition of wholeness that poets derive unconsciously from their affinity with the ecosystem. The disagreement between the Green movement and postmodernism resembles that between Buddhist meditation masters and Buddhist theoreticians: The former (like the Green movement poets) have felt that they encountered reality, whereas the latter (like the postmoderns) have emphasized the importance of exposing the unreality of all appearances. In other words, the disagreement may not just reflect the ecopoets' dedication to action but also derive from the meditative contemplation of nature common in ecopoetry.

ECOFEMINISM VERSUS PATRIARCHY

This tension between conservationism and postmodernism also colors that intertwining of ecology and feminism: ecofeminism. Ecofeminists see a similarity between male domination of nature and of women. "Litter. Wreckage. Salvage" (1988), by Daphne Marlatt (born 1942), for instance, depicts woman as a depreciated commodity who can gain self-knowledge by identifying with a polluted world. Comparably, in Hogan's "Bees in Transit: Osage County" (1985), she parallels Osage women murdered for oil and a beehive destroyed in commercial transportation. Such a matching tends to make postmodern feminists nervous, because it might be construed as positing an essential similarity between all women and "mother nature." Postmodern feminists abhor this idea because it imposes an old-fashioned limitation on each woman's right to construct her own sexual identity. They tend to object to such images as the skirted Earth in *Sleeping in the Forest* (1978) by Mary Oliver. Whereas postmodernism shies away from being locked in battle (or anything

Linda Hogan (©Christopher Felver/CORBIS)

mals and vegetation but also the equality of men and women. He accomplished enough along this line that some ecofeminists have applauded his work, as with Ursula K. Le Guin's tribute poem "Naming Gary" and Anne Waldman's "Voyant," dedicated to him in *Gary Snyder: Dimensions of a Life* (1991), edited by Jon Halper.

ACTION VERSUS APATHY

Green movement poets have done much to change the reputation of the poet from reclusive aesthete to public activist. As a model of this new role, Snyder has frequently given poetry readings at universities and other venues, partly as a way of raising ecological consciousness. In 1976, he delivered "Mother Earth, Her Whales" to an audience of three thousand on California's Whale Day at a symposium organized by Governor Jerry Brown. At the 1977 Lindisfarne Conference, Snyder performed his ecopoetry as a concert, with musical improvisations between the stanzas, all recorded for release as an album. In 1984, he was one of the leaders of Anarchism, Buddhism, and Political Economy, a forum for four hundred that originated the Recovery of the Commons Project, designed both for the preservation of physical wilderness and humanity's psychological commonality. Snyder also made a four-part lecture on "Ecology and Poetry" presented on YouTube.com.

A large area of eco-activism is popular music, some of it with lyrics of award-winning quality. For example, the Creek poet and musician Joy Harjo (born 1951) performs with the Arrow Dynamics Band. Her album *Winding Through the Milky Way* was released in 2009. On the academic front, the cause has been supported by such journals as *Ecopoetics* and *ISLE* (*Interdisciplinary Studies in Literature and Environment*) as well as by the proliferation of courses on ecology and literature. Poetry slams have often chosen ecology as the topic for their competitions. Snyder and other poets, including Merwin, have recorded their performances. Ecopoets have been particularly active in making protests against nuclear proliferation and pollution. Denise Levertov (1923-1997), who wrote "An English Field

else), ecofeminism feels the need to struggle against patriarchal domination of the earth, as in Hogan's "Naming of Animals." It condemns the arrogance of the biblical Adam in imposing his names on animals and on Eve. Indeed, in a 1990 interview with Patricia Smith, Hogan noted how non-Indian culture often compares women and Native Americans to animals.

Only gradually did male ecopoets embrace ecofeminism. In *Riprap*, Snyder is writing not only before the ecological movement but also before the modern feminist movement. For example, *Riprap*'s chauvinist "Praise for Sick Women" begins with lines that might be interpreted as meaning that women cannot think. Diane di Prima (born 1934) responded with her poem "The Practice of Magical Evocation," playfully chiding Snyder's sexism. Subsequently, however, Snyder embraced the new political awareness. In his preface to Peter Blue Cloud's *Turtle, Bear, and Wolf* (1976), he not only declares the equality of humanity with aniin the Nuclear Age" (1981), devoted much of her later life to teach-ins and related activism against war and pollution. Of course, the literary significance of Green movement poetry does not rest on peripheral happenings and media events inspired by it but rather in its having renewed nature poetry with a sense of how fragile and imperiled nature itself has become.

BIBLIOGRAPHY

Bryson, J. Scott. *Ecopoetry: A Critical Introduction.* Salt Lake City: University of Utah Press, 2002. A collection of essays: four on precursors, twelve on individual Green movement poets, and a final one on ecology in "identity poetry" (works directed toward a particular ethnicity or gender orientation).

Felstiner, John. *Can Poetry Save the Earth? A Field Guide to Nature Poems.* New Haven, Conn.: Yale University Press, 2009. A study of diverse precursors and Green movement poets.

Frazier, Jane. *From Origin to Ecology: Nature and the Poetry of W. S. Merwin.* Madison, N.J.: Fairleigh Dickinson University Press, 1999. Examines Merwin's use of a "disembodied narrator" and other devices to present the world in a nonegotistic manner.

Gifford, Terry. *Green Voices: Understanding Contemporary Nature Poetry.* New York: Manchester University Press, 1995. A study of British ecopoetry, contrasting it to its precursors.

Murphy, Patrick D. *A Place for Wayfaring: The Poetry and Prose of Gary Snyder.* Corvallis: Oregon State University Press, 2000. A biographically oriented introduction to Snyder's ecopoetics.

Rasula, Jed. *This Compost: Ecological Imperatives in American Poetry.* Athens: University of Georgia Press, 2002. Looking at both precursors and Green movement poets, Rasula uses "compost" as a metaphor for the way poetry reprocesses and renews both the external physical and the internal psychological worlds.

Scigaj, Leonard M. *Sustainable Poetry: Four American Ecopoets.* Lexington: University Press of Kentucky, 1999. Relying heavily on the philosophy of Maurice Merleau-Ponty, Scigaj examines the poetry of A. R. Ammon, Wendell Berry, W. S. Merwin, and Gary Snyder, taking their side against postmodernism.

Shuman, Joel James, and L. Roger Owens, eds. *Wendell Berry and Religion: Heaven's Earthly Life (Culture of the Land).* Lexington: University Press of Kentucky, 2009. A collection of essays on Berry's interrelated theology and ecology.

Suiter, John. *Poets on the Peaks: Gary Snyder, Philip Whalen, and Jack Kerouac.* Washington, D.C.: Counterpoint, 2003. Well-illustrated with photos by its author, this book details the 1950's wilderness experiences that later brought these Beat writers into ecopoetry.

Tan, Joan Qionglin. *Han Shan, Chan Buddhism, and Gary Snyder's Ecopoetic Way.* Eastbourne, England: Sussex Academic Press, 2009. Comparison of Snyder with his most important Chinese source, Han Shan.

James Whitlark

CRITICISM AND THEORY

CRITICISM FROM PLATO TO ELIOT

The criticism of poetry has always played an influential role in the development of poetry in Western civilization, from the time of the ancient Greeks and Romans up through the Renaissance, neoclassic, and Romantic periods and into the twenty-first century. By articulating the general aims and ideals of poetry and by interpreting and evaluating the works of particular poets, critics throughout the ages have helped shape the development of poetry. Poets, for their part, have often attempted to meet—or to react against—the stated aims and ideals of the prevailing critical theories. Some poets have also formulated and practiced the criticism of poetry, producing a closer and more vital relationship between criticism and poetry. For the student, the study of poetic theory and criticism can be not only an interesting and fruitful study in itself, but also a valuable aid in the attempt to understand the historical development of poetry.

The following review is organized chronologically, divided into six main sections: classical critics, Renaissance critics, neoclassic critics, Romantic critics, Victorian critics, and modern critics. The focus is primarily on English critics, though the ancient Greeks and Romans are included because they represent the classical tradition inherited and built on by the English. Significant American contributors to the mainstream of poetic theory and criticism are, with the exception of Edgar Allan Poe, restricted to the twentieth century and beyond. In this essay, T. S. Eliot is the only American critic treated in depth, though even his contributions are seen as a continuation of the English tradition.

Criticism of poetry can appear in many different forms but can be categorized one of two basic ways: Theoretical criticism, or poetic theory, is the articulation of general principles and tenets of poetry, usually regarding the nature, aims, and ideals of poetry, but also covering techniques and methods. Practical criticism, on the other hand, is the application of these principles and tenets to the tasks of interpreting and evaluating particular works of poetry. Both theoretical and practical criticism can be focused on any of four different aspects of poetry: the poem itself, the relationship of the poem to that which it imitates, the poet's relationship to the poem, and the relationship of the poem to the audience. M. H. Abrams designated these four types of criticism as objective, mimetic (after the Greek word *mimesis*, for imitation), expressive, and pragmatic. A recognition of the critic's orientation as either theoretical or practical and as objective, mimetic, expressive, or pragmatic can help the student of criticism comprehend the contribution of the critic to the history of criticism.

CLASSICAL CRITICS

Four works of poetic theory by ancient Greek and Roman theorists have had a profound influence on the course of Western literature in general and poetry in particular: Plato's *Politeia* (fourth century B.C.E.; *Republic*, 1701), Aristotle's *De poetica* (c. 334-323 B.C.E.; *Poetics*, 1705), Horace's *Ars poetica* (c. 17 B.C.E.; *The Art of Poetry*), and Longinus's *Peri hypsous* (first century C.E.; *On the Sublime*, 1652). In these four works are many critical theories that make up the classical tradition inherited by English letters. The two most important of these theories address the relationship of poetry to that which it imitates and the relationship of poetry to its audience. The central Greek concept of poetry is that of *mimesis*: Poetry, like all forms of art, imitates nature. By nature, the Greeks meant all of reality, including human life, and they conceived of nature as essentially well ordered and harmonious and as moving toward the ideal. Hence, poetry seeks to imitate the order and harmony of nature. Of equal importance to the mimetic concept of poetry is the Greek belief that poetry has a moral or formative effect on its audience. Poetry achieves this effect by making the reader more aware of reality and thereby more aware of his or her own nature and purpose. The Roman theorists, in turn, accepted these basic concepts of poetry. Neither the Greeks nor the Romans were very interested, however, in the expressive relationship between the poet and the poem (involving such questions as what takes place in the poet during the creative act of writing poetry), though they do make occasional comments on this aspect of poetry.

PLATO

In book 9 of the *Republic*, Plato (c. 427-347 B.C.E.), the great Greek philosopher, discusses the role of poets and poetry in the ideal society. His ideas regarding poetry are valuable, not because they clarify poetic issues, but because they raise serious objections to poetry that later critics are forced to answer. Indeed, Plato states that poets and poetry should be banished from the ideal society for two reasons: Poetry represents an inferior degree of truth, and poetry encourages the audience to indulge its emotions rather than to control them. The *Republic* is written in the form of a dialogue, and in book 10, Socrates (speaking for Plato) convinces Glaucon of these two objections to poetry. He arrives at the first objection by arguing that poetry, like painting, is an imitation of an imperfect copy of reality and, therefore, is twice removed from ultimate truth. Reality, or ultimate truth, Plato believed, exists in universal ideas or eternal forms and not in the particular concrete objects of this world of matter. A table or a bed, for example, is a concrete but imperfect copy of the eternal form of the table or the bed. A painter who paints a picture of the particular table or bed is thus imitating not the reality (the eternal form), but an imperfect copy of the eternal form. The poet, in writing a poem about the table or the bed—or about any other imperfect concrete manifestation of reality—is also removed from reality, and therefore the poem represents an inferior degree of truth.

The second objection to poetry raised by Plato stems from his belief that human lives should be governed by reason rather than by emotions. Poetry, Plato believed, encourages the audience to let emotions rule over reason. As an example, Socrates cites the fact that those who listen to tragic passages of poetry indulge in the feelings created by the poem and are pleased by the poet who moves them the most. However, if similar tragic events took place in their own lives, they would strive to be stoical and would be ashamed to be so emotional.

Plato's objections to poetry raise serious questions: Does poetry represent an inferior degree of truth? Does it have a harmful social or moral effect? More generally, and in a sense more important, his objections raise the question of whether poetry can be interpreted and evaluated on grounds other than the philosophical, moral, and social grounds he uses. In other words, can poetry be interpreted and evaluated on poetic grounds? Later critics, beginning with Aristotle, argue that it is possible to construct a general theory by which to interpret and evaluate poetry on poetic grounds.

ARISTOTLE

The *Poetics* of Aristotle (384-322 B.C.E.), as Walter Jackson Bate has remarked, stands out not only as the most important critical commentary of the classical period but also as the most influential work of literary criticism in the entire period of Western civilization. Thus it is essential for the student of poetic theory and criticism to have a grasp of Aristotle's basic ideas concerning poetry, especially those that refute Plato's objections and those that help establish a general theory by which poetry can be interpreted and evaluated on poetic grounds.

"Poetics" means a theory or science of poetry, and accordingly, Aristotle begins his discussion in a scientific manner:

> I propose to treat of Poetry in itself and of its various kinds, noting the essential quality of each; to inquire into the structure of the plot as requisite to a good poem; into the number and nature of the parts of which a poem is composed; and similarly into whatever else falls within the same inquiry. (This and following quotations of the *Poetics* are translations by S. H. Butcher.)

It is important to note that the word "poetry" (the Greek word is *poiesis*, which means "making") is used by Aristotle in a generic sense, to refer to all forms of imaginative literature, including drama, and not in the specific sense in which it is used by modern critics to refer to a form of literature distinct from drama and fiction. Unfortunately, the *Poetics* is not complete (either Aristotle never finished it or part of it was lost). As it now stands, the work contains an extensive analysis of tragedy, an account of the sources and history of poetry, and scattered remarks on comedy, epic poetry, style, and language. It also contains an evaluative comparison of tragedy and epic poetry and a discussion of critical difficulties in poetry. Despite its incompleteness and its lack of any discussion of lyric poetry, the *Poetics* is an extremely important document of poetic theory.

First of all, the *Poetics* is important because it refutes Plato's objections to poetry, though it is uncertain whether Aristotle considered the *Poetics* to be a direct reply to Plato. (As a student of Plato at Athens, he must have been aware of Plato's objections, but the *Poetics* is thought to have been written after Plato's death and therefore not intended as a direct reply.) The key to Aristotle's refutation of Plato's first objection—that poetry represents an inferior degree of truth—is in his interpretation of the Greek concept that poetry is an imitation of nature. It is known from Aristotle's philosophical works that he believed that reality exists, not solely in universal ideas or eternal forms (as Plato believed), but rather in the process by which universal ideas work through and give form and meaning to concrete matter. For example, the reality of a table for Aristotle is not in the universal idea of a table but in the process by which the idea of a table gives form to the wood that goes into the particular table. Hence, in observing the process of nature, the poet observes reality, not an inferior copy of it. Furthermore, the poet's act of imitation, for Aristotle, is not mere slavish copying, as it seems to be for Plato. (Plato implies that the poet is concerned with making realistic copies of the objects of the world of matter rather than with representing universal ideas.) Rather, Aristotle apparently saw the act of poetic imitation as a duplication of the process of nature or reality. That is, poetry is an imitation of the process of universal ideas or forms working through concrete matter. For example, a universal idea of human suffering gives shape to language, characters, and action in a tragic poem.

Poetry for Aristotle is both *poiesis* and *mimesis*, making and imitating. Hazard Adams, in *The Interests of Criticism* (1969), explains it in this way:

> To Aristotle, then, there is no contradiction between poet, or maker, and imitator. The two words, in fact, define each other. The poet is a maker of plots, and these plots are imitations of actions. To imitate actions is not to mirror or copy things in nature but to make something in a way that nature makes something—that is, to have imitated nature.

As for Plato's second objection to poetry—that it encourages emotional and irrational responses—Aristotle's theory of catharsis provides a means of refutation. Catharsis (*katharsis*), a term used by the Greeks in both medicine and religion to mean a purgation or cleansing, is apparently used by Aristotle (there is some disagreement) to mean a process that the audience of a tragedy undergoes. Tragedy excites the emotions of pity and fear in the audience and then, through the structure of the play, purges, refines, and quiets these emotions, leaving the audience morally better for the experience. While Aristotle's comments on catharsis are restricted to tragedy, they seem to be applicable to various kinds of literature. Poetry, Aristotle's ideas suggest, does not simply encourage its audience to indulge their emotions, as Plato contended, but rather it engages their emotions so that they may be directed and refined, thus making the audience better human beings.

The *Poetics*, then, is a significant document in the history of poetic theory because it refutes the specific objections to poetry raised by Plato. It has another significance, however, just as important and closely related to the first: It demonstrates the possibility of establishing a general theory by which poetry can be analyzed and evaluated on poetic grounds rather than on the philosophical, moral, or social grounds used by Plato. Aristotle's analysis of tragedy, his evaluative comparison of tragedy and epic poetry, and his discussion of critical difficulties in poetry all contribute to establishing such a general theory of poetry.

In his analysis of tragedy, which takes up the better part of the *Poetics*, Aristotle enumerates the parts of tragedy (plot, character, thought, diction, song, and spectacle), ranks them in importance, and analyzes each (though he devotes most of his discussion to plot, which he calls "the soul of a tragedy"). In addition to breaking down the parts of a tragedy, he explains how the parts must interrelate with one another and form a unified whole, "the structural union of the parts being such that, if any one of them is displaced or removed, the whole will be disjointed and disturbed." Although his structural analysis is largely restricted to tragedy (he touches on epic poetry), it has the far-reaching effect of demonstrating that every form of literature, including all types of poetry, is made up of parts that ideally should interrelate with one another and form a harmonious and unified whole that is aesthetically pleasing to the audience.

In comparing tragedy with epic poetry, Aristotle concludes that tragedy is the higher art because it is more vivid, more concentrated, and better unified than epic poetry, and that it "fulfills its specific function better as an art—for each art ought to produce, not any chance pleasure, but the pleasure proper to it." Aristotle thus demonstrates, in making this judgment, that poetry can be judged by its poetic elements (such as vividness, concentration, and unity) and its aesthetic effects (the pleasure proper to it).

In one of the last sections of the *Poetics*, Aristotle discusses five sources of critical objections to artistic works, including poetry. Works of art are censured for containing things that are (1) impossible, (2) irrational, (3) morally hurtful, (4) contradictory, and (5) contrary to artistic correctness. Aristotle shows that each of the critical objections can be answered, either by refuting the objection or by justifying the presence of the source of the objection. In several cases, the refutation or justification is made on aesthetic grounds. For example, he says that the artist or poet may describe the impossible if the desired artistic effect is achieved. Here also, then, Aristotle shows that poetry can be analyzed and judged as poetry according to a general theory of poetry.

In summary, the *Poetics* of Aristotle is of primary importance in the history of criticism because it answers Plato's charges against poetry and because it demonstrates to later critics how a general theory of poetry can be established.

HORACE

The greatest Roman contribution to the history of poetic theory is a work by the poet Horace (65-8 B.C.E.), usually titled *The Art of Poetry* but known originally as *Epistle to the Pisos* because it was written as a verse letter to members of the Piso family. Perhaps because it was written in the form of a letter, Horace's work lacks the systematic approach and profundity of Aristotle's treatise and the vigorous thought of Plato's dialogue. Despite these differences, as well as a lack of originality (Horace was restating—perhaps actually copying from an earlier treatise—already accepted poetic prin-

ciples and tenets), *The Art of Poetry* is valuable for its influence on later ages, in particular the Renaissance and the neoclassic age. Poets and critics of those times found in Horace's graceful verse letter many of the classical poetic aims and ideals, such as simplicity, order, urbanity, decorum, good sense, correctness, good taste, and respect for tradition. In addition, Horace's urbane style and witty tone provided his admirers with a writing model.

Horace comments on a wide variety of literary concerns, ranging from the civilizing effect of poetry to the poet's need for study and training as well as genius and natural ability, though he does not explore any of these in appreciable depth. Some of the concerns are specific to drama (for example, a play should have five acts), but others relate to poetry in general. The most famous statement in *The Art of Poetry* is that the "aim of the poet is to inform or delight, or to combine together, in what he says, both pleasure and applicability to life. . . . He who combines the useful and the pleasing wins out by both instructing and delighting the reader" (translated by Bate). This idea that poetry is both pleasing and formative extends back to the Greeks and has retained a central position in poetic theory through the ages. Another important concept that pervades Horace's letter is that of decorum, which is defined as the quality of fitness or propriety in a literary work. All elements in the work should be fitted to one another: character to genre, speech and action to character, style of language to genre, and so on. Horace's statements on decorum, the separation of poetic genres, the use of past models for imitation, and the formative effect of poetry became cornerstones of neoclassic theory in the seventeenth and eighteenth centuries.

LONGINUS

The fourth classical work to have an important influence on English poetry and criticism is *On the Sublime*, a fragmentary treatise generally attributed to Greek philosopher and rhetorician Longinus (flourished first century C.E.). Although the work is mostly a treatise on the principles of rhetoric, it does contain passages of poetic theory.

The author lists five sources of the "sublime," which Bate defines as an "elevation of style, or that which lifts literary style above the ordinary and commonplace to the highest excellence" (*Criticism: The Major Texts*, 1970). The effect of the sublime on the audience is the result of characteristics possessed by the poet: "the power of forming great conceptions" and "vehement and inspired passion" (translated by W. Rhys Roberts). The other three sources are poetic techniques, which the poet must practice and execute: figurative language, noble diction, and the dignified and elevated arrangement of words.

On the Sublime was published in the sixteenth century by an Italian critic, and its popularity among poets and critics of Europe and England reached a peak in the later half of the eighteenth century. Commentators attribute the popularity of *On the Sublime* to its combined appeal to the traditional classical interests and to the emerging romantic interests of the eighteenth century. That is, on the one hand, the author of the work stresses the classical values of studying and practicing the techniques of writing poetry, of imitating past models, and of creating balanced and unified works of poetry, while on the other hand, he stresses the Romantic values of inspiration, imagination, and emotion, both in the poet who creates the poetry and in the reader who is emotionally transported by sublime passages.

RENAISSANCE CRITICS

During the Middle Ages, scholars had little interest in the literary elements of poetry and valued it, if at all, for its religious and philosophical meanings. Even the great Italian poets of the late Middle Ages—Dante, Petrarch, and Giovanni Boccaccio—state in their critical works that the value of poetry is in its religious and moral teachings.

With the Renaissance, however, there came a renewed interest in the literary qualities of poetry. At first, the interest was restricted to studies of technical matters, such as meter, rhyme, and the classification of figures. These studies did not, however, solve what some scholars called the fundamental problem of Renaissance criticism: the justification of poetry on aesthetic or literary grounds. The solution to the problem was contained in classical literary theory, so that, with the rediscovery of Aristotle's *Poetics* (it had been lost to Western Europe during the Middle Ages) and with the study of Horace's *The Art of Poetry*, Renaissance

critics were able to formulate a theory that justified poetry on literary grounds and demonstrated its value for society. In Italy, this theory was developed by such critics as Antonio Minturno, Bernardino Daniello, and Francesco Robortelli. In England, it was most eloquently and persuasively articulated in the late sixteenth century by Sir Philip Sidney in the *Defence of Poesie* (1595), which Bate calls "the most rounded and comprehensive synthesis we have of the Renaissance conception of the aim and function of literature."

Sir Philip Sidney (1554-1586) was neither a full-time poet nor a full-time critic; nevertheless, he is recognized as the first great English poet-critic. The *Defence of Poesie*, written in the early 1580's and published posthumously, is Sidney's sole piece of sustained literary criticism, but it so well provided the needed aesthetic defense of poetry that Sidney's reputation as the foremost English critic of the Renaissance rests securely on it. The essay is an impressive reflection of Sidney's classical education both in its structure and style and in its ideas. The structure, as Kenneth Myrick (*Sir Philip Sidney as a Literary Craftsman*, 1935) pointed out, is that of a classical oration, and the graceful and persuasive style is adapted perfectly to the structure. The ideas, while shaped by Sidney's mind, are derived from the great classical theorists: Aristotle, Plato, and Horace. In addition, the essay shows the influence of Italian literary criticism and contemporary Christian religious thought.

The *Defence of Poesie* (also published as *An Apologie for Poetry*) is a justification of poetry in the generic sense, that is, of all imaginative literature, and was occasioned by various puritanical attacks on poetry, such as Stephen Gosson's *The School of Abuse* (1579), which was dedicated to Sidney. Not only does Sidney refute the puritanical charges against poetry, but he also argues that poetry is the most effective tool of all human learning in leading people to virtuous action. His essay is devoted to establishing proof for this thesis.

Sidney begins to line up his proof by presenting a historical view of poetry, in which he asserts that poetry is the most ancient and esteemed form of all learning. Poetry, he says, was "the first light-giver to ignorance, and first nurse, whose milk by little and little enabled [peoples] to feed afterwards of tougher knowledges." The first books were books of poetry, and these led to other kinds of books, such as history, philosophy, and science. Hence, poetry is the great educator. Accordingly, poets have enjoyed a place of esteem in most civilizations throughout history. The names given to poets (such as the Roman name *vates*, meaning prophet or diviner) is further proof of the honor accorded poets and poetry.

Following his historical view, Sidney offers a definition of poetry and an analysis of the nature and function of poetry—all of which is designed to buttress his argument that poetry, more than any other kind of learning, leads humankind to virtuous actions. It is important to notice in this part of Sidney's argument that he is making a direct connection between the aesthetic quality of poetry and its moral effect—a connection that has its origin in classical theory.

With obvious debts to Aristotle and Horace, Sidney defines poetry as "an art of imitation . . . that is to say, a representing, counterfeiting, or figuring forth—to speak metaphorically, a speaking picture; with this end, to teach and delight." In imitating, Sidney says, the poet is not restricted to nature. He may "mak[e] things either better than Nature bringeth forth, or, quite anew, forms such as never were in Nature," such as demigods and other fantastic creatures. The result is that the poet creates a "golden" world, whereas nature's world is of brass. Poetry, in other words, creates an ideal world and, thereby, "maketh us know what perfection is." In giving us a "speaking picture" of perfection, poetry moves us to virtuous action. The various genres of poetry—epic, satire, elegy, pastoral, comedy, and so on—present various versions of the ideal.

Neither history nor philosophy, according to Sidney, is equal to poetry in its ability to move humankind to virtuous action. History is tied to the actual, "the particular truth of things" or "what is," and philosophy, conversely, is concerned with the universal or the ideal, "the general reason of things" or "what should be." Hence, history fails to show humankind a universal truth or ideal for which to aspire, and philosophy, while possessing the universal truth or ideal, presents it in abstract and general terms, rather than in concrete and particular terms, and thus fails to reach most of human-

kind. Poetry, on the other hand, "coupleth the general notion with the particular example," that is to say, embodies the universal truth in a concrete image or situation and, in so doing, affects its readers emotionally as well as intellectually and moves them to virtuous action.

After establishing proof for his thesis that poetry is the most effective tool of human knowledge in leading humankind to virtuous action, Sidney turns to a refutation of the charges against poetry. He lists four specific charges: first, that there are "more fruitful knowledges" than poetry; second, that poetry is "the mother of lies"; third, that poetry is "the nurse of abuse, infecting us with many pestilent desires"; and fourth, that "Plato banished [poets] out of his Commonwealth." Sidney overturns the first charge by stating that, since no knowledge "can both teach and move [mankind to virtue] so much as Poetry," then none can be as fruitful as poetry. As for the second charge, that poetry lies, Sidney states that the poet does not lie because he does not affirm anything that is false to be true. By this, Sidney means that the poet does not attempt to deceive his audience into believing that what his poetry presents is actual or real. Rather, he offers his poem as an imaginary picture of the ideal, or "what should be." Sidney refutes the third charge, the puritanical charge that poetry is harmful because it increases sinful desires, by asserting that the fault lies, not in poetry itself, but in the abuse of poetry. When poetry is abused, it is harmful; but, used rightly, it is beneficial. In refuting the fourth charge, that Plato banished the poets, Sidney argues that Plato was "banishing the abuse, not the thing"; that is, Plato was upset by the mistreatment of gods in poetry. In *Iōn* (fourth century B.C.E.; *Ion*, 1804), Sidney claims, Plato gave "high and rightly divine commendation to Poetry."

The *Defence of Poesie* also expresses many of the neoclassic ideas and concerns that were to be treated more fully by critics in the seventeenth and eighteenth centuries: the separation and ranking of genres, the need for decorum in poetry, and the use of ancient classical models and critical authorities. It is, however, in the defense and justification of literature on aesthetic as well as moral grounds that Sidney's essay deserves its high place in the history of criticism.

NEOCLASSIC CRITICS

In the two centuries following Sidney's *Defence of Poesie*, neoclassic poetic theory flourished in England. During this period, and especially from the mid-seventeenth to the late eighteenth century, England produced a number of able exponents of neoclassicism. Some of these critics, following the lead of French critics, insisted on a rather strict form of neoclassic theory and critical practice, turning the ancient classical principles into hard-and-fast rules. The two greatest critics of this period, however, rose above this rule mongering and inflexibility, so that their criticism has been of permanent value. They are John Dryden and Samuel Johnson.

JOHN DRYDEN

John Dryden (1631-1700) is known as the founder of English criticism, an honorary title given to him by Samuel Johnson because Dryden was the first English critic to produce a large body of significant literary criticism. Almost all of it, however, is practical criticism, that is, criticism that examines particular literary works and particular problems in literary technique and construction. (Dryden often wrote about his own poems and plays.) Dryden rarely, if ever, treated in depth the larger theoretical issues of literature, such as the aims and ideals of literature, the nature of imitation, the creative process, and the moral and aesthetic effects of literature on the audience. He did write on these issues, but in passing rather than in depth. Furthermore, in no single piece of criticism did Dryden develop a general theory of literature (as Aristotle and Sidney did) as a standard by which to investigate particular works of literature.

Some literary historians are repelled by Dryden's lack of an explicitly stated general theory of literature, especially because his scattered remarks on theoretical issues are sometimes inconsistent or even contradictory. For example, on the matter of the ends of poetry, he says several times that delight is the most important end. This statement from "A Defence of *An Essay of Dramatic Poesy*" (1668) is typical: "for delight is the chief, if not the only, end of poesy: instruction can be admitted but in second place, for poesy instructs as it delights." In other pieces, however, he expresses a different opinion: "Let profit [instruction] have the preeminence of honour, in the end of poetry" (*A Discourse Concerning the Original and Progress of Satire*, 1693); and "The chief design of Poetry is to instruct" ("A Parallel of Poetry and Painting," 1695). In still other pieces, Dryden merges the two ends: "To instruct delightfully is the general end of all poetry," he states in "The Grounds of Criticism in Tragedy" (1679).

Although some commentators see Dryden's lack of an explicitly stated general theory of literature to be a weakness that results in inconsistent statements and judgments, others see it as a strength that affords him flexibility and allows him to evaluate individual pieces of literature on their own merits rather than against a theoretical standard. These latter commentators point out that much questionable neoclassic criticism resulted from an inflexible adherence to general principles and rules.

Most of Dryden's criticism, as well as being practical rather than theoretical, pertains to drama rather than to poetry and is, therefore, outside the purview of this essay. His best and most famous piece, for example, is *Of Dramatic Poesie: An Essay* (1668), a comparative analysis of ancient, modern, French, and English drama, examined in the light of neoclassical dramatic principles and rules by four different speakers. It might be argued that it is his criticism of drama that gives Dryden his high ranking among literary critics; nevertheless, he is also at times an astute reader and judge of poetry.

"Preface to *Fables Ancient and Modern*" (1700) is Dryden's best-known commentary on poetry. Written in an informal, discursive style that Dryden perfected, the essay serves as an introduction to Dryden's translations of fables by Homer, Ovid, Boccaccio, and Geoffrey Chaucer. Dryden's method is largely comparative: He compares Homer to Vergil, Ovid to Chaucer, and Chaucer to Boccaccio, revealing the characteristics of the poets and the beauties of their poems. In addition, Dryden comments on the history and the development of poetry, pointing out relationships among various poets, such as Dante, Petrarch, Edmund Spenser, and John Milton, as well as those mentioned above. In doing all of this, Dryden gives a sense of the achievement of poetry in general and of Chaucer in particular. Chaucer, Dryden says, is "the father of English poetry." He was "a perpetual fountain of good sense," and he "follow'd Nature everywhere." In examining *The Canterbury Tales* (1387-1400), Dryden finds a rich variety of characters representing "the whole English nation." It is to Chaucer's magnificent cast of characters that Dryden applies the proverb: "Here is God's plenty."

Although it is impossible to summarize Dryden's critical position because it frequently shifted and because it was not explicitly stated, it is possible to summarize his critical concerns and to list the characteristics he values as a critic of poetry. First, he was concerned more with the practice of poetry than with theory. He liked to examine particular poems and specific literary problems. Second, in examining particular poems, he felt that the critic's business is not "to find fault," but "to observe those excellencies which should delight a resonable reader" ("The Author's Apology for Heroic Poetry and Poetic License," 1677). Third, he was interested in genres—satire, epic poetry, and so on. He considered, as did most neoclassic critics, heroic (epic) poetry to be the highest type of poetry (partially because of the mistaken neoclassic notion that Aristotle ranked epic over tragedy). In "The Author's Apology for Heroic Poetry and Poetic License," an essay influenced by Longinus's *On the Sublime*, Dryden calls heroic poetry "the greatest work of human nature."

The characteristics that Dryden values as a critic of poetry are unity, simplicity, decorum, wit, grace, urbanity, good sense, and the like. As a poet, he often embodied these characteristics in his own poetry. Thus, in both his poetry and his criticism, Dryden stands out as the preeminent model of neoclassic poetic theory of the seventeenth century.

JOSEPH ADDISON AND ALEXANDER POPE

Between Dryden and Johnson, there were two English critics who deserve mention, Joseph Addison (1672-1719) and Alexander Pope (1688-1744). Addison contributed to English neoclassic criticism through the essays he wrote for popular periodicals of his day, such as *The Tatler* (1709-1710) and *The Spectator* (1711-1712, 1714), which he published with Richard Steele. Addison wrote both theoretical pieces on such poetic matters as wit, taste, and imagination, and pieces of practical criticism on such poems as Milton's epic, *Paradise Lost* (1667, 1674), and the medieval ballad "Chevy Chase." As a body, the essays express the prevailing notions of English neoclassic criticism.

Alexander Pope, a poet of the first rank, is the author of *An Essay on Criticism* (1711), a verse essay written in heroic couplets and modeled on Horace's *The Art of Poetry* and such contemporary pieces as *L'Art poétique* (1674; *The Art of Poetry*, 1683), by the French critic Nicolas Boileau-Despréaux. Pope's essay contains no new critical ideas, nor does it explore traditional ideas in any appreciable depth. It is, however, commendable for its expression of the prevailing neoclassic principles and tenets and for its liberal interpretation. Pope's couplet on wit is a good example of his ability to express ideas succinctly: "True wit is Nature to advantage dress'd;/ What oft' was thought, but ne'er so well express'd." His discussion ranges from the characteristics and skills needed by the critic to various critical methods and principles. A reading of Pope's essay is an excellent introduction to English neoclassic criticism.

SAMUEL JOHNSON

Samuel Johnson (1709-1784) has been called the "Great Cham" of eighteenth century English literary criticism. If to Sidney belongs the honor of writing the first great piece of English literary criticism and to Dryden that of being the first great practicing English critic, then to Johnson belongs the honor of being the first "complete" English literary critic. Johnson was expert in all forms of literary criticism: He formulated and explained literary theory, edited texts and practiced the principles of sound textual criticism (criticism that seeks to date texts, to settle questions of authorship, and to establish the author's intended text, free from errors and unauthorized changes), explained the historical development of poetry, examined and evaluated particular literary works in relation to genre and in terms of literary aims and ideals, and wrote literary biography. Johnson's criticism appears in a variety of sources, ranging from the monumental *The Lives of the Poets* (1779-1781) to the preface and notes to *The Plays of William Shakespeare* (1765), from the narrative *Rasselas, Prince of Abyssinia: A Tale by S. Johnson* (1759) to the essays in *The Rambler* (1750-1752) and *The Idler* (1758-1760), two periodicals he published. In addition to his critical work, he wrote poetry, a play (*Irene: A Tragedy*, pr. 1749), and a great many moral and social essays and meditative works; he also compiled a dictionary of the English language and edited a collection of Shakespeare's works.

Johnson firmly believed in the classical idea that poetry is an imitation of nature, having as its ends instruction and delight. The nature that the poet imitates, however, should be "general nature." In the preface and notes to *The Plays of William Shakespeare*, he states: "Nothing can please many, and please long, but just representations of general nature." By general nature, Johnson means what is universal and permanent, that is, what is true for all people in all ages. In *Rasselas, Prince of Abyssinia*, the philosopher Imlac explains:

> The business of a poet . . . is to examine, not the individual, but the species; to remark general properties and large appearances; he does not number the streaks of the tulip, or describe the different shades in the verdure of the forest. He is to exhibit in his portraits of nature such prominent and striking features, as recall the original to every mind. . . . [He] must disregard present laws and opinions, and rise to general and transcendental truths, which will always be the same.

By imitating general nature, the poet instructs and delights the audience. Johnson believed that instruction, or what Bate calls "the mental and moral enlargement of man," was the more important end of poetry, but he realized that poetry could best instruct by delighting. Hence, he repeatedly makes such statements as that "the end of poetry is to instruct by pleasing" (preface and notes to *The Plays of William Shakespeare*).

As a practicing critic, Johnson examined and evaluated poetry primarily in the light of this principle that poetry is an imitation of general nature with the purpose of instructing and delighting. He also investigated poetry in terms of the prevailing neoclassic notions regarding the conventions and techniques of the various genres. He believed, however, that "there is always an appeal open from criticism to nature" (preface and notes to *The Plays of William Shakespeare*), so that he never approved of conventions and techniques for their own sakes. In fact, he frequently rejected the rigid neoclassic rules as being in violation of the laws of nature. The poet's duty, he felt, was to imitate nature and life, not to follow critical rules. It was on this principle that

Johnson rejected Milton's "Lycidas," a pastoral elegy. The pastoral elements, he felt, divorced the poem from nature, truth, and life. Finally, as a practicing critic, Johnson strove for impartiality, seeking to discover "the faults and defects" of a poem, as well as its "excellencies." By giving a balanced and impartial account of a poet's work, Johnson established credibility as a critic.

The Lives of the Poets is a set of fifty-two critical biographies of English poets, varying greatly in length and written as prefaces to the works of these poets collected and published by a group of London booksellers. The poets are all from the seventeenth and eighteenth centuries and range from Abraham Cowley to Thomas Gray, Johnson's contemporary. Johnson's general method is to sketch the poet's life and character, analyze his works, and estimate his achievement, but he also discusses a variety of poetic issues, such as diction, wit, and the conventions of genre, and by covering the poets of more than a century, he effectively establishes the history of English poetry from the mid-seventeenth to the mid-eighteenth century. A review of several of the more famous biographies will give an idea of Johnson's methods and critical prowess.

In his biographical account of Pope, Johnson includes a description of Pope's method of composition. It serves as a description of the quintessential neoclassic poet (and may be compared to that of the Romantic poet found in various pieces of Romantic criticism). Johnson says that Pope's method of poetic composition "was to write his first thoughts in his first words, and gradually to amplify, decorate, rectify, and refine them." Pope's nearly exclusive use of the heroic couplet resulted in "readiness and dexterity," and his "perpetual practice" led to a "systematical arrangement" of language in his mind. Johnson recounts the rumor that, before sending a poem to be published, Pope would keep it "under his inspection" for two years, and that he always "suffered the tumult of imagination to subside, and the novelties of invention to grow familiar." Johnson's description of Pope emphasizes the neoclassic poet's belief in the importance of practice, labor, revision, and the use of reason over imagination.

Johnson devotes a great part of his biography of Milton to a long analysis of *Paradise Lost*, Milton's epic. In neoclassic fashion, he examines the poem in light of the requirements of the epic genre: moral instruction, fable or plot, significance of subject matter, characters, use of the probable and marvelous, machinery, episodes, integrity of design, sentiments, and diction. His judgment is that, in terms of fulfilling the requirements of an epic, *Paradise Lost* ranks extremely high. There are faults in the poem, however, the chief one being "that it comprises neither human actions nor human manners. The man and woman [Adam and Eve] who act and suffer are in a state which no other man or woman can ever know." The result is that the reader cannot identify with the characters or the actions, so that the poem lacks "human interest." Nevertheless, *Paradise Lost*, in Johnson's final judgment, "is not the greatest of heroick poems, only because it is not the first."

In his biography of Cowley, Johnson gives an account of the seventeenth century Metaphysical poets, a term he is credited with coining. His account of them is to a great extent denigrating: They "will, without great wrong, lose their right to the name of poets, for they cannot be said to have imitated anything; they neither copied nature nor life." They were, however, men of learning and wit, and this admission leads Johnson to a penetrating examination of the essence of wit. After rejecting Pope's definition of wit ("What oft' was thought, but ne'er so well express'd") because it "reduces [wit] from strength of thought to happiness of language," Johnson offers his own definition as that "which is at once natural and new" and "though not obvious . . . acknowledged to be just." He finds, though, that the Metaphysical poets do not possess wit defined as such. Rather, their wit is "a kind of *discordia concors*; a combination of dissimilar images, or discovery of occult resemblances in things apparently unlike. . . . The most heterogeneous ideas are yoked by violence together." It is a tribute to Johnson's critical powers that this definition of Metaphysical wit continues to be applied, despite the fact that his general estimate of Metaphysical poetry is no longer accepted.

Johnson is the last—and arguably the greatest—of the neoclassic critics of poetry. In another sense, though, he is apart from them. By appealing to nature and reason and common sense—in other words, by re-

turning to classical literary principles—he almost singlehandedly overturned the tendencies of extreme neoclassic critics to codify and regularize all aspects of literature. Johnson is, in effect, a great proponent of the classical view of poetry.

ROMANTIC CRITICS

Romantic criticism represents a sharp movement away from the concerns and values of neoclassic criticism. Whereas the neoclassic critic is concerned with the mimetic relationship of poetry to the nature or reality that it imitates and with the pragmatic relationship of poetry to its audience, the Romantic critic focuses primarily on the expressive relationship of the poet to poetry. The neoclassic critic sees poetry as an imitation of nature designed to instruct and delight; the Romantic critic sees poetry as an expression of the creative imagination. In examining poetry, the neoclassic critic turns to matters of genre, techniques, conventions, and effects of poetry; the Romantic turns back to the poet, the imagination, and the creative process. When the Romantic critic does turn to the mimetic relationship, he focuses on the organic and beneficent qualities of nature, and when he looks at the pragmatic relationship, he is especially interested in the connection between feelings and moral response.

WILLIAM WORDSWORTH

In 1798, William Wordsworth (1770-1850) published, with Samuel Taylor Coleridge, a volume of poetry titled *Lyrical Ballads*. For many literary historians, this publication is the watershed between neoclassicism and Romanticism, and the preface that Wordsworth wrote for the second edition (1800) of *Lyrical Ballads* is the manifesto of the English Romantic movement. In this preface, Wordsworth presents definitions and descriptions of the poet, the creative process, and poetry. He also discusses, among other things, the differences between poetry and prose and the effect of poetry on its readers.

Wordsworth defines the poet as "a man speaking to men," suggesting by this phrase that the poet does not differ in kind from others. He does, however, differ in degree: He has "a more lively sensibility, . . . a greater knowledge of human nature, . . . a greater promptness to think and feel without immediate external excitement, and a greater power in expressing such thoughts and feelings as are produced in him in that manner." In short, the poet is, for Wordsworth, one who responds to life and nature with intense feelings and thoughts and is capable of expressing his or her feelings and thoughts poetically.

"[A]ll good poetry," Wordsworth says, "is the spontaneous overflow of powerful feelings," a definition that, at first glance, seems to be the very antithesis of the neoclassical view that poetry is the expression of restrained emotion and clear thought and the result of labor and revision. This definition of poetry is, however, sharply qualified by Wordsworth's description of the creative process. The poet, he says, does not compose poetry spontaneously on the occasion of having an emotional experience. Rather, the emotional experience of the poet must first resolve itself into tranquillity, during which the poet reflects on his or her emotional experience:

> the emotion is contemplated till, by a species of reaction, the tranquility gradually disappears, and an emotion, kindred to that which was before the subject of contemplation, is gradually produced, and does itself actually exist in the mind. In this mood successful composition generally begins.

In other words, raw emotion is not enough for poetic composition. The emotion must be refined in a period of tranquillity by thoughts, which themselves are the representatives of past feelings. When the tranquillity modulates back into emotion, composition can begin.

Though Wordsworth does not make it explicit in this passage on the creative process, it can be inferred from the passage and from statements he makes in his poems that the faculty by which the poet creates poetry is the imagination. Like the other Romantics, Wordsworth exalts imagination over reason (itself exalted by the neoclassicists) and assigns to it a variety of functions, which Bate sums up in his introduction to Wordsworth in *Criticism*:

> We have, then, in the imagination, an ability to draw upon all the resources of the mind: to centralize and unify sense impressions, to combine them with intuitions of form and value, and with realizations won from past experience.

In *The Prelude: Or, The Growth of a Poet's Mind* (1850), his long, autobiographical poem, Wordsworth says that the imagination "Is but another name for absolute power/ And clearest insight, amplitude of mind/ And Reason in her most exalted mood."

One of Wordsworth's principal aims in the preface to *Lyrical Ballads* is to explain the poetic and philosophical bases for the kind of poems he had written. The purpose, he says, "was to choose incidents and situations from common life, and to relate or describe them . . . in a selection of language really used by men." The incidents would be made interesting by "a certain coloring of imagination, whereby ordinary things should be presented to the mind in an unusual aspect" and "by tracing in them . . . the primary laws of our nature." He goes on to say that he chose to depict "[h]umble and rustic life" in his poems because those who live in such circumstances are closer to nature and its formative and beneficial influences. Their feelings and passions reach a maturity from being "incorporated with the beautiful and permanent forms of nature," and their language is purified because they "hourly communicate with the best objects [that is, those of nature] from which the best part of language is originally derived." The effect of reading such poetry as Wordsworth has prescribed is that "the understanding of the Reader must necessarily be in some degrees enlightened, and his affections strengthened and purified." This poetic and philosophical notion—that poetry should imitate the purified language and the beautiful passions and feelings of those who live simple lives in a close relationship to nature—is known as Romantic naturalism. Wordsworth's idea that a poetry of Romantic naturalism will have a profound moral effect on its readers is a central tenet of Romantic poetics.

Wordsworth's poetry of "[h]umble and rustic life" is in opposition to the eighteenth century poetry that depicted a polite, urban society. His espousal of a "language really used by men" is in opposition to the language of eighteenth century poets, known as "poetic diction." Poetic diction is marked by personification, periphrasis, Latinisms, archaisms, invocations, and the like, and is based on the notion that, as Thomas Gray put it, "the language of the age is never the language of poetry." Wordsworth sought, in his poetry and in his preface, to break down the prevailing distinction between the language of poetry and the language of everyday life because he believed that an artificial poetic language prevents the poet from capturing "the essential passions of the heart." For Wordsworth, "the language of a large portion of every good poem, even of the most elevated character, must necessarily, except with reference to the metre, in no respect differ from that of good prose." This idea, in turn, leads him to the controversial notion that meter and rhyme are superadditions to the poem. They are added by the poet to increase the reader's pleasure and to balance the emotional excitement produced by imagery and language with the calmness produced by the regularity of meter and rhyme. This notion that meter and rhyme are superadditions to a poem conflicts, however, with the more accepted concept that all elements of a poem are essential to forming a unified whole.

Wordsworth's importance as a literary critic does not go much beyond the contribution of the preface to *Lyrical Ballads*. Nevertheless, the role that this document played in the Romantic movement and the importance that it has in the total body of Romantic criticism are great indeed.

SAMUEL TAYLOR COLERIDGE

Samuel Taylor Coleridge (1772-1834) is, by far, the greatest of the Romantic critics of poetry: He wrote more theory and practical criticism, ranged farther across critical terrain, and pondered critical problems more deeply than did the other Romantic critics. It is also true, however, that he is not always clear about his ideas, left some of them incomplete, and borrowed some concepts from critics and philosophers, especially the Germans, without proper attribution. The fact that his literary ideas frequently move into philosophical areas also makes it difficult for the student of literature to grasp fully his literary positions. His key literary concepts appear in a variety of publications, the major ones being *Biographia Literaria* (1817) and his lectures on William Shakespeare.

Like the other Romantic critics, Coleridge is interested less in the rules and conventions of poetry than in the nature of the poet, the imagination, and the creative process. He is also deeply interested in the question of what makes a poem a poem.

Poetry for Coleridge is the product of the creative imagination of the poet. He makes this clear when he states in chapter 14 of *Biographia Literaria* that the question "What is poetry? is so nearly the same question with, what is a poet? that the answer to the one is involved in the solution to the other." He then describes the poet, not by what he is, but by what he does:

> The poet, described in *ideal* perfection, brings the whole soul of man into activity, with the subordination of its faculties to each other, according to their relative worth and dignity. He diffuses a tone and spirit of unity, that blends, and (as it were) *fuses*, each into each, by that synthetic and magical power, to which we have exclusively appropriated the name of imagination.

Coleridge has thus moved from poetry back to the poet and then to the imagination.

Coleridge spent a great deal of critical effort in attempts to define the imagination because he felt that a concept of the imagination was central to his poetic theory. Some of his key statements, besides the one quoted above, are that the imagination is the "reconciling and mediatory power" that joins reason to sense impressions and thereby "gives birth to a system of symbols" ("The Statesman's Manual," 1816); that it is "that sublime faculty by which a great mind becomes that on which it meditates" ("Shakespeare as a Poet Generally"); and that it "reveals itself in the balance or reconciliation of opposite or discordant qualities" (*Biographia Literaria*, chapter 14). He also distinguishes between the primary and secondary imagination in chapter 13 of *Biographia Literaria*. The primary imagination is "the living Power and prime Agent of all human Perception, and as a repetition in the finite mind of the eternal act of creation in the infinite I AM." By this latter phrase, he apparently means that the imagination is godlike in its ability to create. The secondary imagination, he explains, differs in degree but not in kind from the primary imagination. Essentially, Coleridge seems to say that the imagination is creative, empathetic, perceptive, harmonizing, synthesizing, symbolizing, and reconciling.

One of Coleridge's key literary concepts that has been fully embraced by modern critics is that of organic form. Although the theory is not original with Coleridge

(Aristotle advocated it), he was the first important English critic to elaborate on it. In one of his Shakespeare lectures, Coleridge distinguishes between "organic" form and "mechanic" form:

> The form is mechanic, when on any given material we impress a pre-determined form, not necessarily arising out of the properties of the material; as when to a mass of wet clay we give whatever shape we wish it to retain when hardened. The organic form, on the other hand, is innate; it shapes, as it develops, itself from within, and the fulness of its development is one and the same with perfection of its outward form. Such as the life is, such is the form. ("Shakespeare's Judgment Equal to His Genius")

Nature, for Coleridge (as for Aristotle), is the model of organic form. Poetry imitates nature's organic process of giving unifying form to all of its diverse elements. A poem, for Coleridge, is like a plant, a living organism, synthesizing all of its diverse elements—imagery, rhythm, language, and so on—into a harmonious and organic whole.

Coleridge also wrote a great amount of criticism on particular poets—Dante, Shakespeare, John Donne, Milton, Wordsworth, and many others. The greater part of it, however, is on Shakespeare and Wordsworth. Much of his criticism on Wordsworth is negative. He objects (in *Biographia Literaria*) to Wordsworth's preface, in particular to what he sees as Wordsworth's attempt to present his poetic theory as applicable to all poetry rather than to a particular kind. Despite his objections, Coleridge considers that his fellow Romantic poet ranks just behind Shakespeare and Milton in greatness.

Coleridge's investigations of particular poets are almost always interesting, but his greatness as a critic lies in his contributions to the theories of the creative imagination and the organic nature of poetry.

PERCY BYSSHE SHELLEY

The poetic theories of Percy Bysshe Shelley (1792-1822) are contained, for the most part, in his essay *A Defence of Poetry* (1840), which he wrote in response to Thomas Love Peacock's satirical attack on poetry in an essay titled *The Four Ages of Poetry* (1820). Shelley's essay shows the influence of Neoplatonism combined with Romantic notions of the organic character of nature, and it bears a resemblance to Sidney's *Defence of Poesie*, especially in its defense of poetry on moral and aesthetic grounds. Although the greater part of the essay is given over to a descriptive history of poetry, it is typically Romantic in its discussion of the nature of the poet, the poetic process, the creative imagination, and the importance of sympathy and feeling in the development of the moral faculty.

Shelley's claims for the poet are very grand: "A poet participates in the eternal, the infinite, and the one." The poet unites the two vocations of legislator and prophet, not in the sense of making social laws and foretelling the future, but in the sense that the poet "beholds intensely the present as it is, . . . [and] beholds the future in the present." Hence, "[A] poem is the very image of life expressed in its eternal truth."

The faculty by which the poet discovers these Platonic laws that govern nature is not reason (which Plato championed) but imagination. Reason, for Shelley, is the "principle of analysis" that dissects, divides, enumerates, and distinguishes objects of nature, whereas imagination is the "principle of synthesis" that grasps the totality of nature in all of its organic character and perceives its value and quality. Poetry, for Shelley, is "the expression of the imagination"; it is not "produced by labour and study," as it was for the neoclassicists. The poet cannot create poetry at will, "for the mind in creation is as a fading coal," which is blown into "transitory brightness" by a power within the poet that comes and goes without warning. Even as the poet is composing, his inspiration is waning, and because inspiration is so fleeting, "the most glorious poetry . . . is probably a feeble shadow of the original conceptions of the poet." This Romantic notion—that the conception is perfect and the execution or composition is imperfect according to its distance from the conception—is the very opposite of the neoclassic notion that the poet approaches perfection through labor and revision.

The effect of poetry on the reader is, according to Shelley, morally formative, not because poetry is or should be didactic, but because it engages the reader's emotions. Shelley echoes the other Romantic critics, especially William Hazlitt, when he states that "[t]he great instrument of moral good is the imagination." The imagination—strengthened and enlarged by reading poetry—enables the reader to move away from his own selfish concerns and sympathetically identify with others, thus developing his moral faculty.

JOHN KEATS

John Keats (1795-1821) was not a professional critic nor did he set down his critical ideas about poetry in a systematic fashion, as did Wordsworth, Coleridge, and Shelley. He expressed his poetical ideas—which are profound and suggestive—sporadically in his personal letters to family and friends. In a letter concerning a personal matter, he would suddenly express his ideas about poetry, the poet, the creative imagination, and other related issues in which he was passionately interested.

Keats describes the nature of the poet to his friend Richard Woodhouse, in a letter of October 27, 1818. The poet, he says, "has no Identity"; rather, he is always "filling some other Body," that is, identifying with someone or something else with which he is poetically engaged—a character, a tree, the sun, a bird, or autumn. The poet, for Keats, is like the chameleon: He changes his color to adjust to his environment. Keats distinguishes this sort of poet from "the Wordsworthian or egotistical sublime," by which he seems to mean the poet who is intent on projecting his own feelings onto other things, instead of entering into the nature of other things.

The power by which the poet is capable of sympathetically identifying with other people and things is labeled by Keats "negative capability." At its simplest, negative capability allows the poet to negate his own personality in order to identify with and understand another person or thing. The understanding, however, is not one of reason but of feeling. Keats says that negative capability is at work "when a man is capable of being in uncertainties, Mysteries, doubts, without any irritable reaching after fact & reason" (December 21 or 27, 1817). Stated another way (in the same letter): "With a great poet the sense of Beauty overcomes every other consideration."

Beauty and truth are the chief aims of art and poetry, according to Keats. He says that the "excellence of every Art is its intensity, capable of making all disagreeables evaporate, from their being in close relationship with Beauty and Truth" (December 21 or 27, 1817).

Another function of the imagination for Keats (besides that of negative capability) is that of apprehending beauty and translating it into truth. In a letter of November 22, 1817, he states that "What the imagination seizes as Beauty must be truth." Abstract truth—truth gained through "consequitive reasoning"—is not as valuable for Keats as truth embodied in the concrete forms of beauty and experienced with the senses and emotions. This belief that truth must be concretely experienced leads Keats to state that if poetry "is not so fine a thing as philosophy—[it is] For the same reason that an eagle is not so fine a thing as a truth" (March 19, 1819).

Several other Romantic critics deserve mention, though there is not space to describe their contributions in detail. In England, Hazlitt wrote widely on literary matters and promulgated many of the ideas that make up the Romantic theory of poetry. In Germany, A. W. von Schlegel and his brother Friedrich articulated the aims and accomplishments of German Romanticism. Poe is recognized as the leading American Romantic critic, though there is substantial disagreement about the real value of his critical ideas. His most famous critical work is "The Poetic Principle" (1848), which urges that beauty, and not truth, is the proper aim of poetry.

VICTORIAN AND MODERN CRITICS

Criticism of poetry became increasingly diverse in the nineteenth century. In the last half of that century, it ranged from the classical, moral, and humanist interests of Matthew Arnold to the impressionistic, art for art's sake theories of Walter Pater and Oscar Wilde and the historical, sociological, and biographical methods of the French critics Hippolyte Taine and Charles-Augustin Sainte-Beuve. In the twentieth and twenty-first centuries, critics widened the scope of literary criticism by applying methods and terminology from a variety of other disciplines to the history and interpretation of literature. This diversity makes it difficult to identify the "great" critics of poetry in the Victorian and modern periods, but certainly two in particular stand out: Arnold and Eliot.

MATTHEW ARNOLD

Matthew Arnold (1822-1888) is the major literary critic of the last half of the nineteenth century. He was a poet, a professor of poetry at Oxford, and an inspector of schools. Furthermore, he perceived his role as critic as extending far beyond literary matters into social, educational, moral, and religious areas, so that he is, in effect, a critic of culture in a broad sense. For this reason, it is imperative to understand his ideas about culture to understand his ideas about poetry and criticism.

In "Sweetness and Light" (a chapter from *Culture and Anarchy*, 1869), Arnold defines culture as "a study of perfection, and of harmonious perfection, general perfection, and perfection which consists in becoming something rather than in having something, in an inward condition of the mind and spirit, not in an outward set of circumstances." In other words, culture is not the possession of certain knowledge or information; rather, it is a condition or habit of being that can be applied to everyday life. Arnold equates the "pursuit of perfection," which is the goal of culture, with the "pursuit of sweetness and light," metaphors for beauty and truth.

The way to culture's goal of perfection, to beauty and truth, is "to know the best which has been thought and said in the world." (Arnold repeats this phrase with some variations in different essays.) When Thomas Huxley, a scientist, accused Arnold of limiting the sources of culture to literature (Huxley believed that scientific knowledge is as effective as literary knowledge in attaining culture), Arnold responded in "Literature and Science" (1882) by stating that all literature—including scientific, social, political, as well as imaginative—contributes to the pursuit of culture. Nevertheless, Arnold goes on to say, a literary education is superior to a scientific education. There is a need in life, Arnold says, for knowledge, and science satisfies this need by providing one with facts about humans and nature. There is also, however, a great need to relate knowledge to "our sense for conduct" and "our sense for beauty," and this, Arnold contends, science cannot do. Literature, on the other hand, does have the power of relating new knowledge to people's senses of conduct and beauty. Arnold means that literature, because it unites the universal with the particular and because it affects the emotions as well as the intellect, can show people how to apply new ideas morally in their conduct and aesthetically in the way they perceive the world.

Arnold's most famous definition of literature is that it is "a criticism of life," a definition that he repeatedly uses in his critical works and consistently applies to poetry under his inspection. Arnold means by this phrase that poetry should address the moral question of "how to live." It should provide an ideal by which people can measure their own lives. In another famous phrase that Arnold uses in various essays, he says that great poetry is "the noble and profound application of ideas to life." The purpose of poetry, he says in "The Study of Poetry" (1880), is "to interpret life for us, to console us, to sustain us," a function that he likens to that of religion. Indeed, to an age in which religious faith had been badly shaken by the findings of science, Arnold solemnly offered poetry as a source of consolation and sustenance.

Criticism, as well as poetry, plays a central role in Arnold's concept of culture. In "The Function of Criticism at the Present Time" (1864), Arnold defines criticism as "a disinterested endeavor to learn and propagate the best that is known and thought in the world, and thus to establish a current of fresh and true ideas." Arnold is speaking here of all types of criticism, not only literary criticism, and the ideas generated by disinterested criticism will be ideas relating to all fields of knowledge and will contribute to the attainment of culture. The task in every critical endeavor, according to Arnold, is "to see the object as in itself it really is," and in evaluating new ideas the duty of the critic is "to be perpetually dissatisfied . . . while they fall short of a high and perfect ideal."

Arnold's method as a practicing critic of poetry is seen in a number of essays. The most famous—and most controversial—of these is "The Study of Poetry," an introduction to a collection of English poetry. In the essay, Arnold rejects two traditional methods of evaluating poetry: the "historic estimate," which judges a poem by its historical context, and the "personal estimate," which relies on a critic's personal taste and preferences to judge a poem. In place of these, Arnold proposes the "touchstone" method: The critic compares lines of the poem under consideration with "lines and expressions of the great masters"—Homer, Dante, Shakespeare, Milton. Such lines, which the critic should keep stored in his mind, will serve as "an infallible touchstone for detecting the presence or absence of high poetic quality, and also the degree of this quality, in all other poetry which we may place beside them."

The chief objection raised to Arnold's "touchstone" method is that it appears to place more value on the individual parts (lines) than on the interrelationship of the parts and the total design and unity of the poem. This may not, in fact, have been Arnold's intention. In other critical works, he emphasizes the importance of total design and unity. For example, in his preface to *Poems* (1853), he praises the quality of total design in poems, and he disparages "poems which seem to exist merely for the sake of single lines and passages; not for the sake of producing any total-impression." He cites Keats's *Isabella* (1820) as a poem without total design. In *Matthew Arnold: A Survey of His Poetry and Prose* (1971), Douglas Bush suggests that Arnold may have meant that "a line or two [the touchstone] may recall the texture and total character of a long poem—which he assumes that his readers know," so that in effect the critic using the touchstone method is not comparing individual lines but complete poems.

"The Study of Poetry" is also controversial in some of its judgments of English poets. In the latter half of the essay, Arnold uses the touchstone method to evaluate most of the major English poets from Chaucer to Robert Burns. In examining each poet, Arnold looks for "high seriousness," a quality he does not define but which is obviously related to his notion that poetry should be "a criticism of life." Shakespeare and Milton, in Arnold's view, are classics of English poetry because they possess "high seriousness." Chaucer, on the other hand, is not a classic of English poetry because he lacks "high seriousness." This judgment conflicts with past judgments of Chaucer (such as Dryden's), and it is all the more controversial in the light of the fact that Arnold judges Gray to be a classic poet with "high seriousness." Also controversial is Arnold's judgment that Dryden and Pope are not classics of English poetry. Instead, "they are classics of our prose" because they possess the qualities of great prose: "regularity, uniformity, precision, balance."

The survey of English poetry in "The Study of Poetry" stops with Burns (who falls short of being judged

a classic), but Arnold makes judgments of later English poets in other essays, most of which can be found in the two volumes of *Essays in Criticism* (1865 and 1888). He ranks Wordsworth directly behind Shakespeare and Milton in poetical greatness because Wordsworth "deals with more of *life* than [other poets] do; he deals with *life*, as a whole, more powerfully" ("Wordsworth"). Lord Byron, in Arnold's opinion, ranks right behind Wordsworth. The strengths of Byron are his "splendid and puissant personality, . . . his astounding power and passion . . . and deep sense for what is beautiful in nature, and for what is beautiful in human action and suffering." Byron lacks, however, the "great artist's profound and patient skill in combining an action or in developing a character." This and his other faults—such as "his vulgarity, his affectation"—keep him from achieving in his poetry "a profound criticism of life" ("Byron").

Of Keats's poetry, Arnold's opinion is that it "is abundantly and enchantingly sensuous" and possesses "natural magic" equal to that of Shakespeare. He lacks, on the other hand, the "faculty of moral interpretation" and "high architectonics" (by which Arnold means the ability to create a total design) necessary for the great poet. Had Keats not died early, he might, in Arnold's view, have developed into a great poet because he undoubtedly had the "elements of high character" ("Keats"). Arnold's essay on Shelley is a review of a recent biography of the Romantic poet. Arnold rejects the biographer's unqualified veneration of Shelley and "propose[s] to mark firmly what is ridiculous and odious in . . . Shelley . . . and then to show that our former beautiful and lovable Shelley nevertheless survives." He concludes the essay by repeating his now-famous description of Shelley (first used in his essay on Byron): Shelley is "a beautiful *and ineffectual* angel, beating in the void his luminous wings in vain" ("Shelley").

Arnold's literary interests extended beyond English poetry. He also wrote about Celtic literature, the poetry of Homer, of Heinrich Heine and Johann Wolfgang von Goethe, and the works of Count Leo Tolstoy, as well as about many other authors and literary topics. Through all of his critical writings, Arnold maintained the position of the classicist, asserting the broad moral value of humane arts and letters in a world in which proponents of science, on one hand, and proponents of the art for art's sake movement, on the other, were threatening to eclipse classical literary ideals.

T. S. ELIOT

T. S. Eliot (1888-1965) deserves the title of great critic because of the range and depth of his criticism. A gifted poet and playwright who gave up his American citizenship to become a naturalized British subject, Eliot wrote on a diversity of literary topics. Because of this diversity, his critical work is very difficult to summarize. Rather than attempting to encompass all of his views regarding poetry and criticism, the following discussion presents a rough classification of his critical works and a detailed explanation of several of his key poetic concepts. If Eliot's critical works on drama and dramatists and those dealing with topics other than literature, such as culture and religion, are excluded, most of the remaining works can be classified into three groups: works dealing with the nature of criticism, works dealing with the nature of poetry, and works dealing with individual poets.

The first group includes such works as "The Perfect Critic" and "Imperfect Critics" (both from *The Sacred Wood*, 1920), "The Function of Criticism" (1923), and *The Use of Poetry and the Use of Criticism: Studies in the Relation of Criticism to Poetry in England* (1933). One of the purposes of the latter work is to explore "the relation of criticism to poetry" from the Elizabethan age to the modern period, and it includes essays on many of the great critics of poetry. Eliot's ideas about the criticism of poetry are many and diverse, but on the whole they contributed greatly to modern formalistic or New Criticism by insisting on the primacy of the poem itself. In the introduction to *The Use of Poetry and the Use of Criticism*, Eliot states that criticism addresses two questions: "What is poetry?" and "Is this a good poem?" At a time when literary critics were often concerned with historical and biographical aspects, Eliot's statement served to remind critics that poetry itself should be the primary concern of the critic.

The second group of critical works includes such essays as "The Social Function of Poetry," "The Music of Poetry," and "The Three Voices of Poetry" (all contained in the first section of *On Poetry and Poets*,

1957). As with the first group, Eliot's range in this group is wide. Almost any aspect of poetry interests him—relatively small matters such as the use of blank verse to larger issues such as the difference between "classic" and "romantic." Probably the two most influential essays in the group are "Tradition and the Individual Talent" and "The Metaphysical Poets" (both in *Selected Essays*, 1932, 1950).

The English poets about whom Eliot writes in the third group of critical works include Andrew Marvell, Milton, Dryden, William Blake, Byron, Algernon Charles Swinburne, and William Butler Yeats. Especially noticeable in these works is Eliot's extensive use of quotations from the poetry to illustrate his observations. This practice is in keeping with his idea that the critic should focus on the poetry. Also noticeable are Eliot's attempts to reshape the reigning view of English poets (especially to downgrade Milton and to elevate the Metaphysical poets and Dryden). Eliot believed that one of the ends of criticism is "the correction of taste."

Several of Eliot's poetic concepts have become very important in modern poetics and therefore deserve special attention. These concepts concern the nature of the poet and the poetic process, the nature of poetry, and the idea of tradition. Eliot developed these ideas throughout several works, the most important of which are "Tradition and the Individual Talent" and "The Metaphysical Poets."

In "Tradition and the Individual Talent" Eliot says that "[t]he poet's mind is in fact a receptacle for seizing and storing up numberless feelings, phrases, images, which remain there until all the particles which can unite to form a new compound are present together." The difference between a poet and an ordinary person, Eliot explains, is that the poet has the ability to form these chaotic elements into a unified whole:

> When a poet's mind is perfectly equipped for its work, it is constantly amalgamating disparate experience; the ordinary man's experience is chaotic, irregular, fragmentary. The latter falls in love, or reads Spinoza, and these experiences have nothing to do with each other, or with the noise of the typewriter or the smell of cooking; in the mind of the poet these experiences are always forming new wholes. ("The Metaphysical Poets")

To explain the actual creative process of composing poetry, Eliot uses a scientific analogy, which has the effect of emphasizing the objectivity and intensity of the process. He compares the creative act of composing poetry to the scientific act of forming sulphurous acid:

> When the two gases previously mentioned [oxygen and sulphur dioxide] are mixed in the presence of a filament of platinum, they form sulphurous acid. This combination takes place only if the platinum is present; nevertheless the newly formed acid contains no trace of platinum, and the platinum itself is apparently unaffected; has remained inert, neutral, and unchanged. ("Tradition and the Individual Talent")

The two gases represent the emotions and feelings and other experiences that the poet has stored up. The filament of platinum represents his mind or creative faculty, and the sulphurous acid is the poem. The objectivity of the process is stressed in the fact that the poem (the sulphurous acid) shows "no trace" of the poet's mind (the platinum) and that his mind is "unchanged" by the experience of writing the poem. Eliot further emphasizes this objectivity (called "aesthetic distance" by formalistic critics) in his statement, following the analogy that "the more perfect the artist, the more completely separate in him will be the man who suffers and the mind which creates."

Eliot calls this process of composing poetry the "process of depersonalization" because it deemphasizes the poet's personality and personal emotions. "Poetry," he states in "Tradition and the Individual Talent," "is not a turning loose of emotion, but an escape from emotion; it is not the expression of personality, but an escape from personality." This does not mean, however, that poetry for Eliot is not intense. There is intensity involved, but "it is not the 'greatness,' the intensity, of the emotions, the components, but the intensity of the artistic process, the pressure, so to speak, under which the fusion takes place, that counts." The result of such an intense artistic process is an impersonal aesthetic emotion, that is, an "emotion which has its life in the poem and not in the history of the poet." Eliot expounds on this idea of an impersonal aesthetic emotion in his essay "Hamlet and His Problems":

The only way of expressing emotion in the form of art is by finding an "objective correlative"; in other words, a set of objects, a situation, a chain of events which shall be the formula of that *particular* emotion; such that when the external facts, which must terminate in sensory experience, are given, the emotion is immediately evoked.

The ideal poet for Eliot, then, is one who keeps his creative self separate from his personal self and who creates an impersonal artistic emotion in his poetry through the "objective correlative" formula. In order to be such a poet, it is necessary for him to "surrender . . . himself . . . to something which is more valuable," that is, to tradition. Tradition, for Eliot, involves the "historical sense," that is, "a perception, not only of the pastness of the past, but of its presence." The historical sense gives the poet a feeling for the "simultaneous existence" and "simultaneous order" of all literature from Homer on, and it will make clear to him how his own work must fit into this literary tradition while at the same time expressing his "individual talent."

With regard to the English literary tradition, Eliot worked to overturn the prevailing opinion that the line of great English poets extended from Shakespeare to Milton to Wordsworth and excluded the Metaphysical poets (Donne, Marvell, and others) and the neoclassic poets, especially Dryden. (Arnold was the critic most responsible for the prevailing opinion, especially by his designation of Dryden and Pope as "classics of prose" and not of poetry, and his praise of Wordsworth, but Johnson's view that the Metaphysical poets were more "wits" than poets had stuck through the nineteenth century and contributed to the prevailing opinion.) Eliot argues that the Metaphysical poets "were the direct and normal development of the precedent age," that is the Elizabethan age, and not "a digression from the main current" of English poetry. These poets, like their Elizabethan predecessors, "possessed a mechanism of sensibility which could devour any kind of experience." They had the ability to unite thought and feeling, so that in their poetry "there is a direct sensuous apprehension of thought, or a recreation of thought into feeling." After the Metaphysical poets, "a dissociation of sensibility set in, from which we have never recovered" ("The Metaphysical Poets").

This "dissociation of sensibility"—the separation of thought and feeling in poetry—was "aggravated," Eliot says, by Milton and Dryden. Milton perfected an impassioned language but dispensed with wit, whereas Dryden developed an intellectual wit lacking an emotional element. Both were fine poets, but their followers lacked their poetic qualities and only "thought and felt by fits, unbalanced." Eliot touches on this thesis again in his essays on Milton, Dryden, and Marvell, but he does not develop it further in his essays on the Romantic poets. Nevertheless, his theory of poetic sensibility has become one of the leading theories regarding the historical development of English poetry.

Other modern critics of poetry perhaps deserve to be ranked as great critics, but it is fitting to end this essay with Eliot because he is the latest in a long line of great English critics who are also poets. It is not essential, of course, that a critic also be able to write poetry, but the fact that so many of the great English critics—from Sidney to Eliot—have also been poets has undoubtedly increased the perception, sensitivity, range, and flexibility of English criticism.

BIBLIOGRAPHY

Ashton, Rosemary. *The Life of Samuel Taylor Coleridge: A Critical Biography.* Cambridge, Mass.: Blackwell Publishers, 1996. Examines Coleridge's complex personality, from poet, critic, and thinker to feckless husband and guilt-ridden opium addict, placing his life within the context of both British and German Romanticism.

Baines, Paul. *The Complete Critical Guide to Alexander Pope.* New York: Routledge, 2000. This introduction offers basic information on the author's life, contexts, and works, and outlines the major critical issues surrounding Pope's works, from the time they were written to the end of the twentieth century.

Bate, Walter Jackson. *Samuel Johnson.* New York: Harcourt Brace Jovanovich, 1979. This Pulitzer Prize-winning biography has shrewd psychological assessments of Johnson's early and major poems.

Christensen, Allan C. *The Challenge of Keats: Bicentenary Essays, 1795-1995.* Atlanta: Rodopi, 2000. These essays reexamine some of the criticisms and exaltations of Keats in order to deliver an appraisal of the historical and cultural contexts of Keats's work and an in-depth discussion of the influences on Keats and his relationships with other poets.

Collini, Stefan. *Matthew Arnold: A Critical Portrait.* Rev. ed. New York: Oxford University Press, 2008. A new edition of a classic study. An afterword, created for this edition, considers Arnold's influence on later critics. Includes an updated bibliography.

Day, Gary. *Literary Criticism: A New History.* Edinburgh, Scotland: Edinburgh University Press, 2008. A reliable overview, enlivened with details about the lives and times of the critics and with the author's often unconventional opinions. Bibliography and index.

Fulford, Tim. *Landscape, Liberty, and Authority: Poetry, Criticism, and Politics from Thomson to Wordsworth.* New York: Cambridge University Press, 2006. This innovative study demonstrates how landscape descriptions reflected the critical views and political opinions of various writers during a historical period marked by rapid change.

Gelber, Michael Werth. *The Just and the Lively: The Literary Criticism of John Dryden.* Manchester, England: Manchester University Press, 1999. Gelber provides a complete study of Dryden's criticism. Through a detailed reading of each of Dryden's essays, he explains and illustrates the unity and the development of Dryden's thought.

Habib, M. A. R. *A History of Literary Criticism: From Plato to the Present.* Malden, Mass.: Wiley-Blackwell, 2005. This award-winning book, praised for its comprehensiveness, lucidity, and accessibility, is divided into eight chronological sections. It offers explanations of literary theories, discussions of writers and their works, and close readings of important texts, and serves as an excellent introduction to the subject. Bibliography and index.

Harrison, Stephen, ed. *The Cambridge Companion to Horace.* New York: Cambridge University Press, 2007. Essays by various scholars discuss such subjects as the themes of Horace's works, his poetics, his wide range of genres, contemporary reactions to his poetry, and his later influence. Introduction by the editor. Dateline, list of works cited, and index.

Leitch, Vincent B., ed. *The Norton Anthology of Theory and Criticism.* New York: Norton, 2001. An extensive collection of critical works from classical times to the end of the twentieth century. Includes general introduction, headnotes, annotations, and bibliographies.

Martin, Peter. *Samuel Johnson: A Biography.* London: Weidenfeld and Nicolson, 2008. A well-researched, insightful study of the man many consider England's greatest literary critic. Illustrated. Maps.

Murray, A. David, ed. *The Cambridge Companion to T. S. Eliot.* New York: Cambridge University Press, 1994. Seventeen essays by noted scholars on such subjects as Eliot's life and thought, his works, and his literary, social, and political criticism. The final chapter is a review of Eliot studies, with a selected bibliography. Chronology.

Murray, Chris, ed. *Encyclopedia of Literary Criticism.* 2 vols. Chicago: Fitzroy Dearborn, 1999. Based on Salem Press's four-volume *Critical Survey of Literary Theory* (1987), this indispensable reference expands on the original publication, adding 117 new entries. It covers more than 250 world critics through the ages in lengthy essays that survey their lives, introduce their literary theory, and list both primary and secondary works. Articles on concepts, chronological periods, and movements range from ancient times to the present and are worldwide in scope. Contains copious finding aids (alphabetized, chronological, and categorized lists) and a thorough subject index.

Stillinger, Jack. *Romantic Complexity: Keats, Coleridge, and Wordsworth.* Urbana: University of Illinois Press, 2008. A collection of major essays by a distinguished scholar and specialist in the Romantic period. Among the subjects discussed are multiple texts, varied readings, editing and revising, collaboration, and the influence of one writer on another.

Wellek, René. *A History of Modern Criticism: 1750-1950.* 8 vols. New Haven, Conn.: Yale University Press, 1992. This massive work is still considered a standard history of literary criticism. Wellek conceives of literary study as comprising three areas: criticism, theory, and history. He covers the later eighteenth century; the Romantic age; the "age of transition"; the later nineteenth century; the first half of the twentieth century in England; the first half of the twentieth century in America; German, Russian, and Eastern European criticism in the first half of the twentieth century; and French, Spanish, and Italian criticism in the same period.

Michael L. Storey

ARCHETYPAL AND PSYCHOLOGICAL CRITICISM

Historically, an archetypal approach to poetry is derived from Sir James George Frazer's work in comparative anthropology, *The Golden Bough* (1890; 2 vols.), 1911-1915 (12 vols.), and from the depth psychology of Carl Jung. Frazer discovered certain repetitive cultural patterns that transcended time and place appearing in widely different myths and literatures. Jung posited the existence of a collective unconscious within each individual, a racial memory that held a variety of archetypes. The archetypes or recurrent patterns and images had to do with birth, death, rebirth, marriage, childhood, old men, magnanimous mothers, heroes and villains, male and female, love and revenge, and countless others. A type of person, a type of action, a type of relationship were so embedded within an individual's history that any new appearance was imbued with the force and richness of every past occurrence. When literature possesses such archetypes, its potency is magnified.

An archetypal critic of poetry can employ Jungian psychology as an extraliterary body of knowledge, in contrast to the archetypal criticism represented by Northrop Frye, in which archetypes do not refer to anything outside literature but to a larger unifying category within literature itself. Even though the term "archetypal" is relevant to both Jung and Frye, their critical intentions differ. A Jungian approach to poetry seeks to wrest meaning from the poem by referring specific images, persons, and patterns to broader, richer archetypes. A Frye approach assumes that there is a totality of structure to literature represented by a variety of common literary archetypes. It is the critic's job to connect individual works to the total structure of literature by way of the recognition of archetypes. Thus, one archetypal approach, Jungian, involves content and meaning, and the other, derived from Frye, involves systematic literary form.

It is only the Jungian variety of archetypal criticism that has relevance for a distinctively psychological approach to literature. A Jungian archetype is an inherited racial pattern or disposition residing in a layer of the unconscious that all persons share. It is brought to light by

the poet's imaginative transformation of the archetype into a symbol, a symbol that appears in the poem. All depth psychologies, which postulate the existence of an unconscious, are predicated on the notion that a symbol emerging from an unconscious level may manifest itself in a poem. Freudians, however, do not interpret humanity's psychological base as the collective unconscious; their symbols emerge from the personal unconscious and therefore have no connection with archetypes. Within the psychoanalytic group, there are a number of schools and therefore a number of psychological approaches to poetry. After discussing the Jungian approach (which is both archetypal and psychological), Frye's approach, and the varieties of psychoanalytic approaches, discussion will focus on the phenomenological approach, which owes nothing to archetype or symbol.

A JUNGIAN APPROACH TO POETRY

Jung deals specifically with literature in the following essays: "The Type Problem in Poetry" "The Phenomenology of the Spirit in Fairytales," "On the Relation of Analytical Psychology to Poetry," and "Psychology and Literature." What ties Jung's discussion of literature to psychology is the symbol. The inexplicable part of the symbol is, according to Jung, a manifestation of certain "inherited" structural elements of the human psyche. These elements or archetypes are revealed in dreams, visions, or fantasies and are analogous to the figures one finds in mythology, sagas, and fairytales.

In "Psychology and Literature," Jung mentions those "visionary artists" who seem to allow us "a glimpse into the unfathomed abyss of what has not yet become." Beyond Jung's specific focus on symbol as revealed in literature as a basis for certain hypotheses and finally for an entire depth psychology that may be applied in turn to literature itself, Jung's study of the nature of symbol gives him an especially perceptive understanding of the nature of literature. Jung has no concern for the specific form, the presentation of symbols in literature; it is not possible to distinguish the symbolic processes of the poet from those of anyone else. The symbolic richness of a work as illuminated by the Jungian approach, therefore, does not itself make the work successful. A Jungian methodology, however, can be said to reinforce the notion of a symbolic unity of a work in the sense that it can make explicit certain image-patterns that may be obscure.

The Freudian attacks on Jung's view of art are strident and somewhat muddled. Frederick Crews believes that invoking the Jungian system is contradictory—a view presented at length in Edward Glover's *Freud or Jung?* (1950). For Jung, art represents necessary contact with the personal unconscious, as in the case of psychological art, and with the collective unconscious, as in the case of visionary art. While Sigmund Freud's artist is a person who turns from the real world to a fantasy life that permits him (or her) to express his erotic wishes, Jung's artist is not driven to art because of such unfulfilled desires but achieves his art through a natural encountering of energies existing on two levels of the unconscious and through a manifestation of archetypal energy by means of unique symbols.

With Freud, no universal, inherited archetypes exist; therefore, no continuum of comparable symbols can be traced in literature except those that refer to the personal unconscious and specifically to repressed energy therein. Symbols in Freud's view represent instinctual needs and are always defined within a limited model of the human personality—one in which no real growth beyond childhood takes place. On the other hand, Jung's consideration of archetype and symbol as emerging from a nonpathological relationship between consciousness and two levels of the unconscious goes beyond Freud's notion that all art is the sublimation of repressed drives.

The Jungian approach has been criticized for reducing the artist to a mere instrument of the archetype. This criticism, however, is based on a confusion between the archetype and the symbol, the observable image representing the archetype; it is an image that cannot be fully grasped and that does not fully realize the archetype. The archetype may be considered autonomous, since it does not depend on the conscious mind. The symbol that the imagination grasps, however, is manifested in accord with the volitions of the conscious mind. Actual

pictorial and verbal images owe their aesthetic aspects not to the uncontrollable forces of the archetype but to the forming disposition of the conscious mind. A Jungian approach to literature casts light on the symbolic aura of a literary work as well as on the creative process itself. Such revelation in turn, from a psychological view, acquaints humans with unconscious levels that humans themselves cannot reach and encourages a continuation of human growth. As in Norman Holland's reader-response approach, the Jungian critic-reader possesses a personality that develops through literature, although the literary text in the Jungian view is certainly a repository for symbols that transcend the personal.

A JUNGIAN APPROACH TO "THE SICK ROSE"

> O Rose, thou art sick!
> The invisible worm
> That flies in the night,
> In the howling storm,
>
> Has found out thy bed
> Of crimson joy,
> And his dark secret love
> Does thy life destroy.

The design accompanying this poem, "The Sick Rose" (1794) by William Blake, pictures the worm in human form. Two other human figures are pictured in lamenting postures. A Jungian interpretation of this poem brings in archetypes of Anima and Animus and Shadow. In Jung's view, the human male must assimilate his contrasexual self, his female Anima, and the human female must assimilate her contrasexual self, her male Animus. The totally individuated person is androgynous on the psychic level and is able to utilize energies from male and female contrasexual portions of the psyche. In this poem, the worm is the rose's Animus and she is his Anima. Both are clearly divided, obdurate in their own sexual identities. Divided so, there is no mutual sexual interaction, no sexual dynamic. Instead, the rose has a "bed of crimson joy" that obviously must have been hidden, since the worm has to journey to find it. The Shadow archetype is formed in the personal unconscious by repressed desires. In this poem, the rose has clearly repressed sexual desire since she hides from her male counterpart and thus allows him but one entrance—as a ravager. His love is dark and secret from the perspective of the rose. He is indeed a shadow figure emerging from the night, a shadow of the rose's own unconscious.

FRYE'S ARCHETYPAL CRITICISM

Frye's archetypes connect "one poem with another and thereby [help] to unify and integrate our literary experience" (*Anatomy of Criticism: Four Essays*, 1957). Literature, in Frye's view, is an expression of a person's imaginative transformation of his (or her) experiences. Ritual and myth were the first creative expressions, beginning as stories about a god and developing into what Frye calls "a structural principle of storytelling" (*The Educated Imagination*, 1963). Essential mythic patterns or archetypes manifested themselves in literature. Writers in various periods drew upon these archetypes, modifying them in accordance with the conventions of their own day and the force of their own personalities.

The archetypal literary critic views the entire body of literature as a self-contained universe of these archetypes, an autonomous and self-perpetuating universe that is not effectively interpreted by extraliterary analogues. Frye believes that by confining criticism to an exploration of essential archetypes recurring throughout literature, he is developing a "science" of literary criticism, a science that recognizes that literature, like all art, is self-referential and that the function of criticism is to bring past imaginative transformations of human experiences into the present and to explore the parameters of present transformations. According to Frye, the critic is scientific in his study of literature, although his mission is not to proclaim literature as science but to make man's imaginative transformations of his experience, his literature, "a part of the emancipated and humane community of culture."

Frye discerned four basic types of imaginative transformations of experience in literature. These types first developed as mythic patterns expressing humanity's attempt to humanize the world. The imagination fuses the rhythms of human life with the cycle of nature and then invests the whole with variable emotional import. The fused natural-human cycle is one in which a youthful spring declines into winter and death. Frye then relates literature to the following mythic structure: Romance is synonymous with dawn, spring, and birth; comedy is synonymous with the zenith, summer, and marriage; tragedy is synonymous with sunset, autumn, and death; satire is synonymous with darkness, winter, and dissolution.

Frye defines commentary as "the translating of as much as possible of a poem's meaning into discursive meaning" ("Literary Criticism"). Such allegorical commentary, however, is not the aim of criticism, which, in Frye's view, is to identify the poem. Like a cultural anthropologist, the literary critic places the poem within its proper literary context. The first context is the total canon produced by the poet under consideration. The second context is historical. For example, John Keats's poetry must be understood within the broader context of Romanticism. Beyond considering the poet's historical context, the critic must consider the genre. Tragedy, Frye says, is a "kind of literary structure," a genre exemplified throughout literary history. The critic must also pay attention to the allusions within the poem itself. John Milton's *Lycidas* (1638) for example, reveals historical ties both in its form—pastoral elegy—and in its imagery. These ties are within literature itself. Allusions in a poem by Milton are to a poem by Vergil.

Poems in Frye's Romantic mode possess a vision of the heroic, either religious or secular, with which the poet himself is identified. Gerard Manley Hopkins's "The Windhover" (wr. 1877, pb. 1918) presents a view of Jesus as hero, while Walt Whitman's *Passage to India* (1871) presents the poet as hero. The poet of the romantic mode seeks the imaginative transformation of the natural world, as do Andrew Marvell in "The Garden" (wr. c. 1660) and William Butler Yeats in "Sailing to Byzantium" (1927). The poets in the comic mode, however, are satisfied with the world as it is, as in Keats's major odes. The tragic mode involves loss and reconciliation through some effort to make sense out of loss, as in Milton's *Lycidas*, Percy Bysshe Shelley's *Adonais* (1821), and Hopkins's "The Wreck of the Deutschland" (1918). The ironic poet does not achieve imaginative transformation of the world through supernatural help but rather achieves a vision of a shattered world. Emily Dickinson's poetry, T. S. Eliot's *The Waste Land* (1922), and Robert Frost's "Stopping by Woods on a Snowy Evening" (1923) are examples.

In Frye's criticism, mythic images were the first and clearest expressions of a relationship between humans and their world. Literature is thus a "direct descendant of mythology," and biblical and classical mythologies are central myths in Western literature. What the poetry critic of archetypal persuasion ultimately does is to explore archetypal connections, recurrent patterns, in literature. As criticism continues to explore the structure of literature rather than its content, it eventually encompasses literature as a whole as its content. Once this is achieved—when criticism has a hold on literature as a whole—questions regarding the purpose of literature, its relationship to society, and its connections with discursive literature can be tackled.

Frye has been criticized for ignoring the critic's task of evaluation, for separating literature from life, for ignoring the individuality of a work by emphasizing its archetypal relations with other literature, and for creating, in *Anatomy of Criticism*, a literary work rather than a critical theory that has practical applications. Frye is criticized for assuming that literary discourse and poetic vision are unique and separable from all modes of extraliterary thought and discourse. Frye's views here are traced to the German idealist tradition, in which the words of the poet are somehow autonomous, free of referential meaning. Frye's view of literature is criticized because literature is seen as the ultimate goal of culture, as superior to the objective world because it transcends it by way of the imagination. The liberally educated person has replaced an unsatisfying world with its imaginative transformation—literature. What is celebrated in Frye, according to critic Frank Lentricchia,

> is a fantastical, utopian alternative to the perception of a degraded social existence: a human discoursing free of all contingency, independent of all external forces, a discoursing empowered by unconditioned human desire.

A FRYE APPROACH TO "THE SICK ROSE"

In "Blake's Treatment of the Archetype" (1950), Frye comments on Blake's powerfully integrated the-

ory of art and of the unity of symbol and archetype in Blake's work. Frye places Blake in the anagogic phase of symbolic meaning, in which the total ritual of humanity, the total dream of humanity, is represented. Blake's "The Sick Rose" is interlocked with his entire canon; in itself it re-creates the "total form of verbal expression" of his work ("Levels of Meaning in Literature"). Blake's symbols are anagogic symbols, symbols that turn outward toward the macrocosm of his entire myth and inward toward any individual work (in this case "The Sick Rose") that expresses the unity of desire and reality, of dream and ritual.

Only religious myths have achieved this combination of personal dream or desire and reality or ritual. Romance, a phase just below the anagogic phase, reflects a conflict rather than a unity of desire and reality. It also employs archetypes that do not have a limitless range of reference, as do the "monads" of the anagogic phase. If "The Sick Rose" is placed within a mythical rather than anagogic phase of symbolic meaning, the rose and the worm would have correspondences to other roses and worms in literature but would not be true representations of the visionary apocalyptic kind of poetry that Blake's is. The location of the poem within Frye's anatomy depends upon a proper location of Blake's entire work within that anatomy. All the richness of the proper fit can be brought to bear on "The Sick Rose." Thus, finding the proper niche for the poem rather than interpreting it as a unique, unconnected entity is the task of Frye's critical anthropologist.

PSYCHOANALYTIC APPROACHES: FREUD

Freud's views of the relationship between art and psychoanalysis were presented in his "Delusion and Dreams in Jensen's *Gradiva*" (1907) and in "The Relationship of the Poet to Daydreaming" (1908). The forbidden wishes of dream, associated with the psychosexual stages (oral, anal, phallic, and genital), appear in the literary work but are disguised by distracting aspects of aesthetic form. The superegos of both reader and author are circumvented, and art serves to release unconscious forces that might otherwise overwhelm the ego. The critic's job is to delve below the surface of a distracting literary facade and point out the lurking fantasies. Freud himself began, in his book on Leonardo da Vinci, a stage of psychoanalytic criticism that has been termed "genetic reductionism," or the discussion of a work in terms of the author's neurosis.

Genetic reductionism has been and remains a primary focus of psychoanalytic criticism in spite of a general recognition that the danger for psychoanalysis is the lure of a simplistic and mechanistic interpretation. The dispute here is between those who hold that literature is autonomous, existing independently of a creator's emotional disposition, and those who hold that a psychoanalytic critic can "show how a writer's public intention was evidently deflected by a private obsession" (Frederick Crews). A psychoanalytic examination of the author's wishes and anxieties, in the view of antipsychoanalytic criticism, ignores the variety and ontology of literature. Crews argues, nevertheless, that there does exist a certain range of problems that psychoanalytic assumptions illuminate.

Freud also initiated a psychoanalytic interpretation of particular characters in his work on Wilhelm Jensen's *Gradiva* (1918) and in his discussion of oedipal complexes displayed by certain characters in Sophocles' *Oedipus Tyrannus* (c. 429 B.C.E.; English translation, 1715) and William Shakespeare's *Hamlet: Prince of Denmark* (pr. c. 1600-1601, pb. 1603). While most contemporary psychoanalytic critics deplore genetic reductionism, there is debate regarding the treatment of characters as real people. Critics on one side of the spectrum tend to put a character on the analyst's couch, talk about the character's childhood, and totally neglect other aspects of the literary work. Opposing critics contend that while readers do indeed experience characters as human beings, the critic must use psychoanalysis so as to understand fully the character in relation to other aspects of the work.

In Freud's view, literature was like dream—a symbolic expression of the unconscious whose original meaning could be interpreted. This interest in the relationship between the writer and his or her work, in the creative process itself and its importance in interpreting a work, remains an interest of contemporary psychoanalysts and psychoanalytic critics. Freud's original view of creativity has been refashioned in various ways, and psychoanalytic critics now fall into various camps.

Freud's view of the work of literature as a product of the author's sublimated desires has been challenged by an emphasis upon the literary work as "the potential space between the individual and the environment," by an emphasis upon the reader whose own "identity theme" fashions meaning from a work of art, and by an emphasis on preconscious and conscious involvement with literary creation (D. W. Winnicott). These views have been termed, respectively, "object-relations," "reader-response" (based on the work of Norman Holland), and "ego psychology." The psychoanalyst Jacques Lacan has also created a unique approach to literature.

A FREUDIAN APPROACH TO "THE SICK ROSE"

The focus in this approach is immediately upon the poet. The question is, What "dark secret" repressed by the poet has found release in this poem? The poem is a mere symptom of the poet's neurotic desires. The rose can be viewed as a female whose "bed of crimson joy" is "found out." This is no healthy, natural sexual act, however, because the "worm" or phallus "flies in the night," in a "howling storm," and destroys his beloved with "his dark secret love." At the root of the poem, therefore, is the incestuous desire of the poet. The secret love of the poet here is his mother.

EGO PSYCHOLOGY

Freud's view of literature-as-symptom emerging from the id is modified by ego psychologists who recognize creativity as a function of the ego. For the ego psychologists, literature in the service of the ego reflects the ego's mission of mediating between self and others, between id and superego. Symbols from the id are therefore shaped in literature so as to be communicable beyond the intrapsychic level. The movement in ego psychology is away from literature as raw wish fulfillment of the author and toward the literary text as a manifestation of id instinct and ego-monitoring. Literary critics utilizing ego psychology seek in the text not the disguised wish or wishes of the author but their transformation by the ego in the direction of something beyond the personality of the author, something of thematic import, communicable and succeeding or not succeeding depending upon the author's gifts or skills.

The ego psychoanalyst analyzing poetry emphasizes ego functions rather than id impulses. In what ways, this critic asks, does the poem display the ego's assertion of control by allowing repressed instincts an outlet? A discovery of what instincts are latent does not lead the critic into the entire poem, but a study of the poem as a manifestation of an ego directing the release of repressed instincts does.

AN EGO PSYCHOLOGIST'S APPROACH TO "THE SICK ROSE"

For the critic applying the theories of ego psychology, incest may remain the repressed desire of the poem, but the way in which the conscious ego expresses that hidden desire in the form of the poem itself is the proper subject matter of the critic. The poet distances himself (or herself) from the poem by adopting a censorious tone. The directness and clarity of poetic style also reveal the wise perceptiveness of the poet with regard to the sexual plight of rose and worm. Thus, both tone and style point to the ego's mastery over a repressed desire of the id, and a search for such ego mastery results in an analysis of the poem. The poet's perceptiveness does not lie in the core fantasy of incest but in his view of love that must be invisible, which must emerge only at night. The poet's perceptiveness lies in his understanding that a covert sexuality injures and ultimately destroys both sexual partners. His censoriousness lies in his view that such clandestine sexuality is "unethical," that it works against humanity and the individual human life. The instinctual base remains incest but it has been controlled by the ego's fashioning of the poem, making the poem something other than the wish that inspired it.

READER-RESPONSE CRITICISM

Norman Holland, in *The Dynamics of Literary Response* (1968), emphasizes the instinctual drives of the id rather than the monitoring, controlling powers of the ego, although, unlike early Freudian interpreters of literature, he posits an ego that mediates between the id and the superego and whose mediation is the form of the work itself. The form of a literary work is indeed comparable to the ego defenses against the assault of the id, but it is this assault that is the hidden, determining root of the work. A core fantasy is the base of every literary work, and the writer, through form, defends against it, tries to shape it in the direction of redeemable social, moral, and intellectual value. The eye of the critic, in Holland's view, is on the core fantasy, on the id, while the eye of the ego psychologist-critic is on the ego's manipulation of the id through literary form. The core fantasy critic seeks out the core fantasy and demonstrates the author's artistry in shaping and disguising it. The reader accepts both the core fantasy, which he or she may share, and the devices employed to contain the fantasy. Thus, the reader achieves pleasure by possession of the fantasy as well as by having it controlled. The reader, in the view of the ego psychologist-critic, attains pleasure primarily through the pattern of ego control expressed in the literary work.

In Holland's later work (*Poems in Persons: An Introduction to the Psychoanalysis of Literature*, 1973, and *Five Readers Reading*, 1975), he places the pertinent core fantasy in the mind of the reader rather than in the text. Readers extract meaning from the text in accordance with their "identity themes." Readers may be directed by their own desires to seek such themes in the texts they read. Finding them, readers may deal with them as they do in their own lives. They may also attend the author in transforming a core fantasy into something socially acceptable or intellectually significant. Holland believes that through the literary text the readers confront themselves, engaging in acts of self-discovery by analyzing what they as readers have said about a text. Throughout the three faces of psychoanalysis that Holland identifies—psychology of the unconscious (id), of the ego, and of the self—readers have always been structuring the text by means of their own intentions. A realization of this fact enables readers to make use of literature as an opportunity to gain self-knowledge.

A critical approach to poetry based on Holland's later work would begin with a description of the critic-reader's own responses to the poem. These responses, determined by the critic-reader's identity theme, direct an analysis of the poem. A dialectic then takes place between the objective reality of the poem, a common store of shareable realities, and the critic.

A READER-RESPONSE CRITIC'S APPROACH TO "THE SICK ROSE"

The reader-response critic approaches the poem by focusing on those personal connections made in the poem. Such an interpretation is not necessarily the same thing as a literal interpretation, for example, that the poem is about the perils of gardening. From the reader-response view, this poem would be seen as a poem only about gardening by a gardener. It is quite possible in the first line of the poem, "O Rose, thou art sick," for a reader to think of someone named Rose, perhaps a mother or a sister or a lover, who was or is or may be sick. The "invisible worm" becomes a disease, such as cancer, that has struck the reader-critic's beloved suddenly, perhaps in the full bloom of life, in bed of "crimson joy." Now, this cancer slowly destroys the beloved.

Given this personal reading, what can the poem do to assert its own existence? The reader-critic must first be willing to entertain the notion that perhaps the poem is not about Rose's bout with cancer. The poet has used the word "love." The poem asserts itself, if given a chance, by its words, and the word here is "love." This love "flies in the night" "in the howling storm"—it emerges from Nature. Thus, in spite of the apparent ludicrousness of such a subjective beginning, the reader-critic is led toward an acceptance of this love as natural. It is in the nature of things to die, or to love sexually. Neither death nor sexuality can be repressed wisely. In this instance, the path of subjectivity is modified by the poem itself. As this dialectic continues, the original subjectivity of the reader-critic is modified, and the interpretation becomes more "objective" though determined by the identity theme of the reader-critic. What the poem is connects with what the reader is, and the result is a thoroughly human form of comprehension.

OBJECT-RELATIONS THEORY

Object-relations theory does not hold, as do traditional psychological and ego psychological theories, that a literary work is the product of psychic conflict. It argues, rather, that a literary work is the place where the writer's wishes and the culture around him or her meet. Rather than emphasizing the literary work as narcissistic wish fulfillment, object-relations critics emphasize those aspects of a literary work that are not the author's self, which lead toward a world outside the writer. This outside world of convention and tradition is transformed by the writer, he or she having accepted what is outside his or her own self. The literary work as an object is an extension of the writer, somewhat as a teddy bear, for example, is an extension of a child. Both teddy bear and literary work are invested with illusions; yet they are objects in the world. In the case of the child, the teddy bear is something like the mother's breast, although significantly it is another object. Similarly, the literary work is wish fulfillment and yet an object that is not pure wish fulfillment but a place where wishes and world meet, an object representing a "collective love affair with the world."

A critical approach to poetry based on an object-relations theory would not focus on the poem as an expression of intrapsychic conflict but as the ground in which the poet's wishes and the outside world meet. In what ways does the poem signify the internal desires of the poet? In what ways does it stand as a transformation of those desires into what is outside the poet? The meeting of internal and external is the poem.

AN OBJECT-RELATIONS CRITIC'S APPROACH TO "THE SICK ROSE"

The object-relations critic views the poem as a meeting ground of the poet's fantasies and the surrounding environment—in this case, late eighteenth century England. If incest is on the unconscious mind of the poet—Blake—he has presented it as nothing more specific than "dark secret love," a phrase that has meaning in the context of an England in which hypocrisy with regard to sexuality was increasing. If the poet were really expressing a desire to unite sexually with his mother, then the poem would serve as an illusionary connection between himself and his mother. The poem as object, however, is clearly a transitional object rather than a complete illusion of the poet. The poem is a transition between the poet's desire for uncensored sexuality and the moral prohibitions against sexuality that were prevalent in the poet's day.

JACQUES LACAN

Lacanian psychoanalysis once again resurrects the sole supremacy of the id in the creative process. Indeed, the unconscious itself is structured as a language, and therefore both the conscious and the unconscious are identically rooted. Literary discourse, like ordinary discourse, is symbolical and subjective. Rather than the id being a source of instinctual drives that appear disguised in literature, specifically in the language of literature, the Lacanian id is a reservoir of words that determine perceptions.

Lacanian literary interpretation depends upon tracing literary language to a constitutive language of the unconscious. It depends upon relating significant words in the literary text to words signified in the unconscious. The unconscious is structured not according to innate laws but originally according to the image of another, someone whom the child is dependent upon (usually the mother). This desire to remain secure is fulfilled when the child constructs his (or her) unconscious in accordance with the significant other. The "discourse" of the other becomes the discourse of the child's unconscious, which is fictional insofar as it is not the child's but another's.

In Lacan's view, the ego is composed of a *moi*, which is unconscious, overriding the other but determined by it; and the *je*, which is identified with spoken language and culture. The discourse of the *moi* permeates the discourse of the *je*. The symbolic, subjective *moi* permeates the apparent logical discourse of the *je*. The Lacanian literary critic seeks to go from the discourse of the *je* to the discourse of the *moi*, from a symbolical consciousness to a symbolical unconsciousness. The discourse of the *moi*, of the unconscious, is weakly and elusively manifest in the surface of the literary text. Both signifiers and signifieds are available in the surface of the text, and the act of literary interpretation attempts to reconstruct, wherever possible, the connection between signifiers and signifieds. It is an act that seeks to uncover what unconscious desires determine the details of the literary text.

A LACANIAN APPROACH TO "THE SICK ROSE"

A Lacanian interpretation attempts to break through the language of the *je* and reach the symbolical unconscious of the *moi*. The literal language of the *je* in this poem has to do with gardening, with the destruction of a rose by a worm that is invisible to the naked eye.

When readers probe more deeply, they discover that the poem is really "talking" about human sexuality. The poet, Blake, clearly reveals his symbolic intent in his depiction of human figures in the design accompanying the poem. A Lacanian analysis probes below the level of the language of the *je* in poems apparently not symbolical and not intended to be symbolical by the poet, whose surface language seems to mean no more than it says. The "invisible worm" as a phallus signifies a flaccid phallus. The erect, firm phallus *lies* not *flies* in the night. The "dark secret love" cannot be consummated with the flaccid phallus, and thus the *moi*, formed by a desire to please the mother, describes in this poem the fulfillment in words of a desire the reality of which the words themselves belie.

PSYCHOANALYTIC APPROACHES:
CRITICAL OVERVIEW

Alan Roland and Frederick Crews, among others, have provided criticism of various psychoanalytic approaches to literature. Roland objects to the correlation of literary work and daydream. The literary work, in his view, goes far beyond the author's fantasies and the imagery of dream. Poetic metaphor and the structure of paradox are essential components of the literary work but not of dream. According to Roland, literary form must be freed from the notion that it is synonymous with the ego's defenses. Defense is viewed as only part of form. Object-relations critics do not limit the author's fantasies to those of a psychosexual stage, but they fail, in Roland's view, to integrate their exploration of fantasies with what the work may mean on its highest level. In opposition to Holland's view of the reader, Roland feels that, besides a core fantasy, a literary work possesses an abstract meaning, a total vision formally created. The relationship between these two levels should be described by the critic. In Roland's view, the core fantasy within the reader's mind is apparently affected by the critic's efforts.

Crews sees as reductionist the views that Holland expresses in *The Dynamics of Literary Response*, although he admits that Holland is sensitive to literary form and very cautious about making an "armchair diagnosis of authors." Holland's reductionism lies in his view of literature as subterfuge for forbidden thoughts. Crews also maintains that no one goes to criticism to discover the "identity theme" of the critic but rather to learn more about literature as a meaning-creating enterprise.

In the final analysis, according to Crews, Holland's focus on the reader is yet another example of academic objectivity being attacked by subjectivists, by those who argue that the interpretation of literature is a private affair. Crews finds no real remedy for contemporary psychoanalytic criticism, not even ego psychology. Eventually, all psychoanalytic critics realize that their interpretations say more about themselves than about the text, that "they have reduced literature to the rigid and narrow outlines of their own personalities." A psychoanalytic critic, according to Crews, must bear in mind that his or her method is reductive and that there are many aspects of a work excluded from his or her approach.

In his essay "Anaesthetic Criticism" (1970), Crews goes beyond a discussion of the dangers of reductionism in psychoanalytic criticism and defends it against antideterministic critics. He considers the "informal taboo" placed on extraliterary theories by many academic critics. Frye, the most influential antideterministic critic, in Crews's view, advocates an inductive survey of literary works, in which no external conceptual framework is considered. Literature, in Frye's archetypal view, is its own progenitor; although Crews terms such a belief "a common fantasy among writers, a wish that art could be self-fathered, self-nurturing, self-referential, purified of its actual origins in discontent." Such a "fantasy," of course, is no less common among critics than among writers. In essence, critics who deplore the search for causes and effects are anti-intellectual, preferring a literary approach in which references to extraliterary analogues are at once disclaimed. Finally, in Crews's view, criticism that ignores the affective element of literature and accentuates the role of form over chaos, of genre conventions and the like, is anaesthetic criticism. Crews concludes that regardless of the dangers of reductionism in the application of psychoanalysis to literature, the approach is more efficacious than that of such antideterministic critics as Frye.

PHENOMENOLOGICAL PSYCHOLOGY

In the case of a phenomenological psychology, a delineation of a *Lebenswelt*, or human life-world of a character, a speaker in a poem, or an author, is in each case a delineation of consciousness. The phenomenologist's desire is to return to lived experiences and bracket, or set aside, presuppositions. Such experiences are not understood by an examination of external behavior but by an examination of psychic reality, or consciousness. Because consciousness is always consciousness of something, intentionality with regard to external reality being always implicit, a focus on a person in literature or on the author him- or herself, on various self-revelations, reveals the *Lebenswelt*.

To the phenomenological psychologist, literary accounts—poetry, drama, or fiction—are personal records, descriptions of psychic reality that aid in achieving a psychological understanding of both behavior and phenomenal experience. Through a phenomenological approach to poetry, which emphasizes various portrayals of self by both poetic speakers and the poet (portrayals of others, of objects and time), it is possible both to define and to reveal meaning in the poem as a whole.

The poetic consciousness involves the poet's own intentions, which are tied to his or her own human life-world and his or her own particular arrangement of phenomena. Although such an arrangement is unique to each poet, a patterning presided over by his or her own poetic consciousness, such consciousness, by virtue of its intentionality, is directed to and tied to objects comprising the reader's natural universe. The very process of poetic construction and patterning reveals the experiential foundation of the reader's world and illuminates rather than mirrors disparate objects and impressions. The critic of poetry has little interest in poetry as a source of phenomenal experience, as an exploration of psychic-subjective reality. Rather, he or she utilizes the phenomenological perspective to define the relationship between intentionality and aesthetic patterning or form.

The relationship between intentionality and form cannot be defined until the *Lebenswelt* of each speaker or persona in the poem is defined, leaving the poet's own *Lebenswelt* discernible. Thus, the phenomenological perspective enables the critic to analyze speakers and personae by means of their perceptions of the world and eventually to distinguish aspects of the poem that are derived from intentions not of any speaker or persona but of the poet. Nothing less than the entire poem is revealed.

A PHENOMENOLOGICAL PSYCHOLOGICAL APPROACH TO "THE SICK ROSE"

In "The Sick Rose" it is possible to discern two "characters" almost immediately—worm and rose. It is also possible to discern a speaker, who may or may not be the poet, and, somewhere behind it all, the poet. Neither worm nor rose is a true character since they do not reveal their own perceptions. Focus must be placed on the speaker of the poem, who reveals himself in his revelation regarding the worm and the rose. In spite of the conventional perception that a rose is beautiful, the speaker finds, in the very first line, that this rose is sick. "She" is sick because "her" life is being destroyed by the dark secret love of an invisible worm. In the mind of the speaker of the poem, the worm is "the" and not "a" worm; in the mind of the speaker of the poem, the worm is obviously someone or some specific thing. If "someone" is first considered, it is someone up to no good, someone evil. That evil has been created not through hate but through love, although a dark secret love. A bright, open love is a love that can be displayed in society without fear of censure. A dark, secret love is that sexual love that must go on behind closed doors, which cannot be lawfully witnessed. The worm in this speaker's mind is a diabolical figure bringing death through sexuality to the rose. When one begins to separate poet from speaker, it is clear that the speaker himself is "sick."

The poet's *Lebenswelt* is not restricted to this one poem. In the case of Blake, it is revealed in the totality of the work he has titled *Songs of Innocence and of Experience* (1794). "The Sick Rose" is a song of experience. Most often the speakers within poems of experience are themselves victims of what Blake considered to be the "evils" of experience. In the phenomenological approach, critics employ what is known of the poet as revealed in his or her other work as a gloss on the poem under consideration. Biographical information becomes important so that the *Lebenswelt* of the

poet can be defined. The reader-critic's intention is to know enough about the poet's mode of perception to be able to distinguish the poet from speakers or personae in his or her poems. The richness of the poem is then revealed as a rhetorical juxtaposition of victimized speaker and critical poet.

In another experience poem, "The Garden of Love," a speaker returns to the garden of love, which previously bore so many sweet flowers, and discovers that it is filled with graves, that priests have bound with briars the speaker's joys and desires. This bound speaker is the speaker of "The Sick Rose." In the poet's view, "the" worm may be a priest, or he may be conventional religion's notion of god. The rose of perfect beauty, in its bed of crimson joy, is destroyed by a priest's or a conventionally perceived god's repressive dark secret love—a love that binds the speaker's joys and desires, a love that is fatal. A dark secret love makes love dark and secret. Only a human victimized as this speaker is victimized can construct a god for him- or herself who binds and shackles and is then considered loving because of those acts. The love of an institutionalized religion's god, a god outside humanity itself, is, in this poet's view, not love but death.

NEW APPLICATIONS

At the beginning of the twenty-first century, many critics were still finding psychological and archetypal theories useful. Archetypal criticism has been found especially helpful in studies of the ritual poetry of groups such as Native Americans, the First Nations peoples, and the Maori. It has also been applied to other religious traditions, especially those that emphasize the mystical and the transformational.

Archetypal criticism is also basic to gender studies. Feminists explicitly identify women as sacred figures, earth-mothers, or divine goddesses, and point out how poets implicitly use archetypes to define or to elevate the status of women. Other writers identify traditional male archetypes, such as gods and heroes. Both archetypal and psychological theories can be applied to poems about the search for the self and to the related theme of metamorphosis. Thus, twenty-first century critics continue to utilize and to develop new variations on these theoretical approaches to literature.

BIBLIOGRAPHY

Ackerman, Robert. *The Myth and Ritual School: J. G. Frazer and the Cambridge Ritualists*. New York: Garland, 1991. The author points out that though Sir James George Frazer is often the only person mentioned in connection with the Cambridge ritualists, the achievements of Jane Ellen Harrison, Gilbert Murray, F. M. Cornford, and A. B. Cook should not be minimized. This volume is an analysis of their works. Notes, bibliography, and index.

Agha-Jaffar, Tamara. *Women and Goddesses in Myth and Sacred Text*. New York: Longman, 2004. A reader that focuses on eighteen incarnations of the Great Goddess in cultures throughout the world. Glossaries provided for each chapter. Includes a time line.

Bynum, Caroline Walker. *Metamorphosis and Identity*. New York: Zone Books, 2005. Examines the use of the themes of metamorphosis, hybridity, and personal identity, primarily in medieval literature, with special attention to poets such as Dante.

Campbell, Joseph. *The Hero with a Thousand Faces*. 3d ed. Novato, Calif.: New World Library, 2008. By pointing out the relevance of ancient myths not only to scholars and writers but to general readers, Campbell became a major influence on twentieth century culture. This edition of his best-known book includes additional illustrations and a comprehensive bibliography.

Cobb, Noel. *Archetypal Imagination: Glimpses of the Gods in Life and Art*. Hudson, N.Y.: Lindisfarne Press, 1992. Maintains that the soul should not be thought of as an individual possession but as a universal phenomenon, best understood in the works of artists and mystics, such as Dante, Rumi, Rainer Maria Rilke, and Gabriel García Lorca.

DiPasquale, Theresa M. *Refiguring the Sacred Feminine: The Poems of John Donne, Aemilia Lanyer, and John Milton*. Pittsburgh, Pa.: Duquesne University Press, 2008. Four Christian archetypes— Ecclesia, the Blessed Virgin Mary, Divine Wisdom, and the soul as bride of Christ—were utilized by Renaissance poets in their interpretations of the sacred feminine. This study examines their use of these archetypes as reflections of their attitudes toward women, especially women in the church.

Frazer, Sir James George. *The Golden Bough: A Study in Magic and Religion*. Rev. ed. Edited by Robert Fraser. New York: Oxford University Press, 2009. An important revision of a classic study. In it, for the first time, passages have been restored that the author and his wife omitted from their 1922 abridged version, fearing that they would arouse controversy. Excellent introduction and notes.

Frye, Northrop. *The Secular Scripture, and Other Writings on Critical Theory, 1976-1991*. Edited by Joseph Adamson and Jean Wilson. Toronto, Ont.: University of Toronto Press, 2006. Some of Frye's most important works about literary and critical issues, produced during the last fifteen years of his life.

Gill, Glen Robert. *Northrop Frye and the Phenomenology of Myth*. Toronto, Ont.: University of Toronto Press, 2006. The author explains why he considers Frye's theories vastly superior to those of Carl Jung, Joseph Campbell, and Mircea Eliade. A thoughtful, well-researched book and an excellent overview of twentieth century mythological theory.

Impastato, David, ed. *Upholding Mystery: An Anthology of Contemporary Christian Poetry*. New York: Oxford University Press, 1996. A collection of poems, all by critically acclaimed writers, that deal with such themes as transformation, suffering, death, presence, grace, and holiness. The editor, a psychiatrist accustomed to dealing with problems affecting the mind, turns his analytical skills to the even more complex concerns of the soul.

Jung, Carl. *The Essential Jung*. Rev. ed. Edited by Anthony Storr. Princeton, N.J.: Princeton University Press, 1999. The original publication, which appeared in 1983, was made up of annotated extracts from Jung's works, arranged to reveal the development of his thought, and included an excellent introduction by the editor. It continues to be ranked as the best book with which to begin the study of Jung. Bibliography updated for this edition.

Lodge, David, and Nigel Wood. *Modern Criticism and Theory*. 3d ed. New York: Longman, 2008. An introduction to literary study, consisting of extracts from the works of specialists in literary criticism, each preceded by an introduction and followed by suggestions for further reading. Includes references to Web sources. Two tables of contents, one chronological and one thematic. Glossary of terms.

Natanson, Maurice Alexander. *The Erotic Bird: Phenomenology in Literature*. Princeton, N.J.: Princeton University Press, 1998. By applying phenomenology to the interpretation of several major literary works, the author defines the theory and demonstrates its usefulness in literary criticism. Recommended for those approaching the subject for the first time.

Pratt, Annis V. *Archetypal Patterns in Women's Fiction*. Bloomington: Indiana University Press, 1981. A feminist study, demonstrating how myths and archetypes influence the development of social attitudes and how both ancient ideas and newer views are reflected in poetry. Bibliography and index.

Robinson, Peter. *Twentieth Century Poetry: Selves and Situations*. New York: Oxford University Press, 2005. Analyzes the complex relationship between the poet or the poet's assumed self and the immediate environment. The authors' theories are applied to a number of poets, including Ezra Pound and Elizabeth Bishop. Bibliographical references and index.

Tsur, Reuven. *On the Shore of Nothingness: Space, Rhythm, and Semantic Structure in Religious Poetry and Its Mystic-Secular Counterpart—A Study in Cognitive Poetics*. Exeter, England: Imprint Academic, 2003. The author applies his theory of cognitive poetics to various kinds of poetry, ranging from meditations and poems describing mystical experiences to descriptions of creation. Focus is not on theology but on how poets utilize words and structure to re-create nonverbal experiences. Index.

Warner, Marina. *Fantastic Metamorphoses, Other Worlds: Ways of Telling the Self*. New York: Oxford University Press, 2004. Argues for the importance of metamorphosis in life and in art. Theories are illustrated with such works as the paintings of Bosch and the poetry of Ovid, Dante, and Samuel Taylor Coleridge. Also deals with the issue of identity, given the ongoing processes of creation, evolution, growth, and decay. Lavishly illustrated.

Weber, Samuel. *Return to Freud: Jacques Lacan's Dislocation of Psychoanalysis*. Translated by Michael Levine. New York: Cambridge University Press, 2008. The first English version of a major work, revised and updated by the author. A thorough exploration of Lacan's thought, indicating how he was influenced by his interpretation of Freud and also by the structuralism of Ferdinand de Saussure.

Welch, John. *Spiritual Pilgrims: Carl Jung and Teresa of Avila*. New York: Paulist Press, 1982. Compares the meaning of the spiritual life as seen by two important figures, one a noted psychologist, the other a canonized mystic.

Wright, Elizabeth. *Psychoanalytic Criticism: A Reappraisal*. 2d ed. New York: Routledge, 1998. In this updated version of a standard text, the author surveys both the opposition to psychoanalytic criticism and its increasing influence on critical theory and practice, including its relationship to feminism. References, suggestions for further reading, and index.

Joseph Natoli
Updated by Rosemary M. Canfield Reisman

CULTURAL CRITICISM

In his handbook *Cultural Criticism* (1995), Arthur Asa Berger points out that cultural criticism is best understood as an activity rather than a system. In its broadest terms, cultural criticism is the study of culture in all of its forms—literary, political, sociological, economic, moral, and religious. The history of cultural criticism from the nineteenth century to the twenty-first century reveals that the role of the cultural critic has changed radically, in part because the term "culture" has had and continues to have many meanings; it is not possible, therefore, to state with certainty that any two cultural critics who write about poetry will agree on the terms for their analysis or arrive at similar conclusions about a given poem.

For example, cultural critics of the nineteenth and early twentieth centuries often employed the term "culture" to mean a sense of refinement and an elevated awareness of the moral or aesthetic dimensions of life. Later exponents of cultural criticism often viewed culture in a more anthropological sense—that is, as the collective behavior of a group—and, hence, displayed interest in revealing the relationship of art, including poetry, to the society that produced it. Many late twentieth century critics saw their primary role as critics of the high culture celebrated by their predecessors. Generally speaking, however, cultural critics employ one or more psychological, political, economic, philosophical, or historical approaches to analyze a poem either as a literary work whose form and content might make it universally accessible and meaningful, or as an artifact of a particular time and place that carries the values of the society in which it was produced.

THE ROOTS OF CULTURAL CRITICISM

It is possible to trace the roots of cultural criticism to the works of such Enlightenment figures as German philosophers Friedrich Schiller and Johann Gottfried von Herder, as well as such English Romantics as William Hazlitt and Samuel Taylor Coleridge. These writers sought to define "culture" and to explain how it operated as a kind of elevating force for poetry. Built on the works of these thinkers, the practice of modern cultural criticism rose to prominence during the Victorian era. The three writers most often cited as cultural criticism's first theorists among English-speaking writers are Thomas Carlyle, John Ruskin, and Matthew Arnold. Carlyle, however, tended to focus on historical, political, and moral issues and had little to say directly about literature. Ruskin initially concentrated on art and architecture before expanding his studies to include critiques of social practices. By contrast, Arnold's writings on culture almost always center on the importance of literature as a means by which culture is observed, valued, and transmitted. As a consequence, his work is frequently cited as the starting point for examining the intersection of literary criticism and cultural criticism.

Concerned by what he perceives as the increasing vulgarization of society, Arnold seeks to promote a program of self-improvement and social reform that would save civilization from the dehumanizing forces of industrialization. The key to avoiding a downward social and moral spiral, Arnold suggests in his *Culture and Anarchy* (1869), lies in the acquisition and preservation of culture, which he defines as the "love" and "study" of perfection. For Arnold, to study culture means "getting to know, on all the matters which most concern us, the best which has been thought and said in the world." Hence, the effort to achieve and preserve culture is at once an aesthetic and a moral activity. Arnold argues that poems worthy of attention and study are those that contribute to promoting the ends of culture as he defines it.

As a literary critic, Arnold is concerned with establishing standards by which poems may be judged as contributing to the perpetuation of culture—that is, as containing ennobling or insightful ideas expressed in memorable language. He places great value on poetry that displays qualities of what he calls "high seriousness." The best poetry is characterized by emotional restraint and deals with subjects of notable import. Arnold's ideal poets are Homer, Dante, and William Shakespeare. Although he was personally attracted to William Wordsworth's poetry, he is critical of the emotional excesses displayed by the Romantics, which included Wordsworth, and even repudiated some of his own early poetry as being too self-indulgent. The rigorous criteria he sets forth in his essays on poetry and criticism offer guidance for identifying from the multitude of imaginative works published throughout history a small number that should be considered of enduring value. The work of Arnold and his successors in the humanist tradition of cultural criticism eventually produced the notion of a "canon" of literary works that have influenced the development of culture (specifically Western culture). Arnold and his disciples argued that these works should be widely read by those wishing to improve themselves morally and aesthetically.

THE HUMANIST AND MORALIST TRADITION

Arnold's ideas had great influence in shaping both literary study and broader discussions of culture both in Great Britain and in the United States. The first notable American disciples were a group of writers known as the New Humanists. Chief among the group are Irving Babbitt, Paul Elmer More, and Stuart Sherman.

Dedicated to the promotion of so-called high culture, these writers evaluated poetry using Arnoldian standards. In a number of writings Babbitt attacks the Romantics for their emotional excess and for promoting what he describes as the celebration of the "native" over the more refined civilization that in his view marks humankind's greatest achievements. More, in his *Shelburne Essays* (1904-1921; 11 vols.), insists that great poetry can be appreciated only when readers have a highly developed historic sense. More also devoted considerable energy to rehabilitating the neoclassic poet Alexander Pope, whose satires depend on readers' knowledge of the social and political milieu to be fully effective. For More, Pope's *Epistle to Dr. Arbuthnot* (1735) is substantially more valuable than any work by the Romantics because it treats great human themes with exceptional insight and skill. Although not a New Humanist, the critic Edmund Wilson also contributed to cultural criticism in essays and collections that stress the social dimensions of literature, especially modern literature.

The successors of the New Humanists were the New York Intellectuals, a group of more than two dozen philosophers, sociologists, historians, and literary critics, including the influential writer-critic Lionel Trilling. Throughout his career Trilling expressed interest in the way literature reflects social values and simultaneously shapes them. Trilling tends to value literature that reflects qualities such as sincerity and authenticity, although he frequently found merit in the more experimental work produced by his contemporaries.

One of the most influential and controversial cultural critics of the first decades of the twentieth century was Cambridge scholar F. R. Leavis. As a critic of culture, Leavis railed against modernist trends toward mass production and democratization that emphasized a "watering down" of intellectual accomplishments. Committed to developing an antidote to this trend, Leavis offers in several works a program for the establishment of a university curriculum that would prepare a small group of intellectuals to resist and reverse trends toward what he saw as insidious proletarian standards of intellectual attainment and moral conduct. Leavis sees the study of literature as central to that education, because literature provides a vehicle for understanding and appreciating the moral dimension of humankind. Literature can also serve as a check against any ideology—especially Marxism—that promotes notions of equality based on economic measures at the expense of intellectual advancement. Hence, for Leavis the study of poetry becomes part of a moral imperative to preserve civilization. The best poems are those with discernible social context; these poems can help people understand what is valuable to them personally and to society as a whole.

In *New Bearings in English Poetry: A Study of the Contemporary Situation* (1932), Leavis takes great pains to show the reciprocal effects of poets and the intellectual milieu in which they work. His review of William Butler Yeats's career and his commentary on T. S. Eliot's *The Waste Land* (1922) reveal his bias for poetry that reflects the age in which it is written, even when the poet was highly critical of his times, as was Eliot.

Beginning in the 1920's, a major challenge to the hegemony of cultural criticism was mounted both in Europe and in the United States. Led by the Russian formalists, European critics developed the practice of structural criticism, arguing that the primary role of the critic is to understand the ways in which literature is crafted and the ways its construction (both form and rhetoric) works to influence readers.

In the United States, the principal challenge to cultural criticism came from the New Critics, a group that advocated an apolitical, atemporal reading of literature, especially poetry, and which stressed its formal and aesthetic qualities. New Critics insisted that truly great poetry was timeless and self-referential, and that it did not necessarily depend on the milieu in which it was composed for its meaning. New Criticism became the dominant mode of critical inquiry during the 1940's in the United States and England and maintained its place of prominence for several decades. It was celebrated as an effective counter to the cultural critics' approach to literature, which the New Critics believed was not sufficiently detached from social, political, or ideological matters.

In the 1990's, however, a number of studies, such as Mark Jancovich's *The Cultural Politics of the New Criticism* (1993), revealed the biases of the New Critics, whose promotion of political and moral detachment in the study of literature reflects attitudes consistent with American political ideology at the time.

POSTSTRUCTURALIST AND POSTMODERN CULTURAL CRITICISM

An important step toward expanding the scope of studies by cultural critics occurred during the 1960's. Academics influenced by Marxist and other leftist ideologies began highlighting the unspoken ideology behind mainstream ideas about high culture, exposing its inherently elitist, racist, and gender-biased view of society that privileged certain elite groups while marginalizing most others. The study of culture as a critique of mainstream society was the principal aim of the Centre for Contemporary Cultural Studies, established in 1964 by Richard Hoggart at the University of Birmingham in England. Hoggart and his colleagues applied a variety of new and traditional theories to examinations of literary works to expose the ideology behind them. In the view of these new cultural critics, any literary work had value as a cultural text. As a consequence, the academic study of poetry changed not only

in its methodology but also in its selection of subject matter. Practitioners of the then-new cultural studies, for example, were as apt to study song lyrics as they were sonnets.

This new form of cultural criticism had been influenced by numerous philosophical studies of culture, largely European in origin. The Frankfurt School, a group of writers and thinkers guided by Marxist ideology, produced a series of leftist tracts on the inherent weaknesses of Western society and its principal institutions; their work came to be known as critical theory. Writings by members Max Horkheimer, Theodor W. Adorno, Erich Fromm, Herbert Marcuse, and Walter Benjamin began to have an influence on literary studies shortly after the end of World War II. Another impetus for a revaluation of the idea of culture was provided by the Italian critic Antonio Gramsci, who promoted the notion that critics should be engaged directly with social issues and should use their work as weapons for social change.

Cultural commentary by such French theorists as Jacques Derrida, Roland Barthes, Jacques Lacan, and Michel Foucault, as well as by the Belgian theorist Paul de Man, have had perhaps the greatest impact on American cultural critics, who have been strong in replacing old-style literary criticism with a more broadly based, interdisciplinary form of inquiry. The application of Marxist-style critiques of the Western canon in literature has had a profound effect on the study of poetry during the final four decades of the twentieth century, and has continued to shape literary criticism within academic institutions into the twenty-first century.

As Terry Eagleton explains in *The Idea of Culture* (2000), postmodern cultural critics have substituted Arnold's definition of cultural criticism as a search for the best that has been thought and said with a mandate to provide a critique of a given society's dominant ideology. Hence, rather than celebrate works that seem to uphold traditional humanist and Western values, they often point out the inadequacies, prejudices, or other shortcomings represented, often unconsciously, in such works.

Poststructuralist cultural critics, for example, see themselves at odds with two important critical traditions: humanism, with its totalizing morality disguised as aesthetics, and New Criticism, which insists on re-moving a literary text from its context (historical, polit-ical, or sociological) to consider the text exclusively as an aesthetic object. Poststructuralist critics examine poetry to determine the influence of cultural biases on the production and understanding of texts, often con-structing radically new interpretations or revealing hid-den subtexts that reshape conventional thinking about a poem's meaning. Often applying theories of decons-truction and other poststructuralist theories, they cham-pion readings of poems that highlight the indeter-minacy of meaning. Poststructuralist cultural critics investigate the connections of individual poems with other realms of knowledge—literature, history, sociol-ogy, economics, science, and technology—to expose the ideology or belief systems at work within the cul-ture that influenced the poet either overtly or uncon-sciously. Hence, any critical enterprise that attempts to apply methodologies of historical, political, ethical, economic, scientific, or sociological inquiry on poetry can be viewed as cultural criticism. One of the im-portant by-products of cultural criticism has been to explain how poems written in the past can take on cultural significance to contemporary readers.

Although not strictly a postmodern critic, the figure who most influenced cultural criticism in England dur-ing the second half of the twentieth century was Ray-mond Williams. Approaching literary study from a sociological perspective, and heavily influenced by Marxist theory, Williams treats art (including poetry) as part of the process by which a society creates con-ventions and institutions and communicates shared val-ues. Williams also explored the differences between high culture (the kind Arnold, Leavis, and the New Hu-manists touted) and mass culture. In numerous books published between the 1950's and his death in 1988, Williams examined the power structures at work be-hind individual texts that helped shape a work's aes-thetic appeal and its social or political message. For ex-ample, in *The Country and the City* (1973), Williams provides readings of a number of celebrated "country house" poems of the seventeenth century. Earlier read-ings of these poems tend to stress the poet's desire to celebrate the house and its owner, usually a wealthy no-bleman, and to contrast the serenity of country life with the hustle and bustle of public affairs. Williams's leftist readings demonstrate how authors of these poems use a number of rhetorical strategies and literary tropes to gloss over the inequities of the social system that sustained the maintenance of these estates for the pleasure of the wealthy and elite.

CULTURAL CRITICISM AND THE CANON

The first generations of cultural critics helped shape the literary canon—those works of literature generally described as most important and most worthy of being read and taught. Later cultural critics challenged the very notion of a canon, consciously expanding their focus to include neglected or marginalized works to demonstrate how poetry and fiction previously ex-cluded from serious study actually helps reveal the bi-ased nature of both canonical works and the ideologies that influenced critics in promoting them as great litera-ture. Where Arnold, Leavis, and their fellow humanists and moralists valued poems that seemed to be universal in appeal, modern cultural critics celebrate difference and diversity in poetry.

Most poststructuralist cultural critics are leftist but not necessarily Marxist. They reject any attempt to read poetry as part of a comprehensive worldview or to have poetry's meanings limited by any one critical approach. Poststructuralists are often concerned with who or what has been marginalized in a text and with discrepancies in a work that seem to challenge the dominant political or moral ideology at work during the time a poem was written. The new generation of cultural critics shares affinities with scholars engaged in ethnic, race, gender, gay and lesbian, and class studies, in that it is particu-larly interested in what texts reveal about issues of oppression, discrimination, marginalization, or exclu-sion. In fact, some of the best cultural criticism comes from feminists, who have painstakingly exposed the male-centered ideology that has dominated Western culture. The efforts of feminist cultural critics have led to the rediscovery of a number of early women poets, for example, whose work provides insights into politi-cal, social, and moral issues important at the time these works were composed.

The foregoing discussion is not meant to suggest that traditional or conservative cultural criticism has disappeared or fallen out of favor. A notable contingent of intellectuals, including Allan Bloom and E. D. Hirsch, Jr., continues to trumpet the superiority of Western civilization and culture. The former two have written about literature, including poetry, and have lauded the Western canon as developed and codified during the nineteenth and early twentieth centuries. Bloom's *Shakespeare's Politics* (1964) is an example of mainstream conservative cultural criticism of dramatic poetry, examining the political philosophy of four plays. Hirsch's major contribution to cultural criticism is *Cultural Literacy: What Every American Needs to Know* (1987), which contains an extended argument in favor of the study of canonical texts.

BIBLIOGRAPHY

Berger, Arthur Asa. *Cultural Criticism: A Primer of Key Concepts.* Thousand Oaks, Calif.: Sage, 1995. Provides useful discussions of the way various literary, psychological, sociological, and political theories may be employed by those who practice cultural criticism. Offers succinct definitions of many terms used by cultural critics.

Brantlinger, Patrick. *Crusoe's Footprints: Cultural Studies in Britain and America.* New York: Routledge, 1990. Studies the growth of cultural studies as an academic practice, describing its links with leftist ideologies, feminism, and other poststructuralist methodologies. Explains the significance of cultural studies to the practice of literary criticism.

Eagleton, Terry. *The Idea of Culture.* 2000. Reprint. Malden, Mass.: Blackwell, 2005. Examines the phenomenon of postmodern cultural criticism, providing a brief history of the development of cultural studies and exploring the competing ideologies that have appropriated the term "culture" to privilege their value systems.

Haslett, Moyra. *Marxist Literary and Cultural Theories.* New York: St. Martin's Press, 2000. Discusses the ways a variety of Marxist analyses of literature and culture work to offer a critique of individual works, including poems, and of the ideology they represent or refute. Includes an extended cultural critique of an eighteenth century poem as an example of these theories in practice.

Johnson, Lesley. *The Cultural Critics: From Matthew Arnold to Raymond Williams.* London: Routledge & Kegan Paul, 1979. Explains the rise of modern cultural criticism and its links with literary studies. Provides summaries of the ideas of the most important British cultural theorists of the nineteenth and twentieth centuries.

Kaplan, Harold. *Poetry, Politics, and Culture: Argument in the Work of Eliot, Pound, Stevens, and Williams.* New Brunswick, N.J.: Transaction, 2006. Excellent example of contemporary cultural criticism. Examines methods used by four important American poets to shape the way poetry should be written so it could serve as a catalyst for defining, preserving, or reshaping social and moral value systems.

Leitch, Vincent B. *Cultural Criticism, Literary Theory, Poststructuralism.* New York: Columbia University Press, 1992. Constructs a system for cultural criticism by employing techniques from poststructuralism and other new theories. Explains why cultural criticism is necessary because poetry is always engaged with cultural, political, moral, and sociological issues.

Lenhart, Gary. *The Stamp of Class: Reflections on Poetry and Social Class.* Ann Arbor: University of Michigan Press, 2006. A series of interconnected essays provide a cultural critique of the practice of poetry and the influence of class structure on the production of verse.

Rubin, Joan Shelby. *Songs of Ourselves: The Uses of Poetry in America.* Cambridge, Mass.: Belknap Press, 2007. Work by a cultural historian exploring the influence of poetry on the lives of Americans. Pays special attention to the social uses for which poetry has been employed, particularly poems included in school textbooks and anthologies for classroom use.

Said, Edward W. *The World, the Text, and the Critic.* 1983. Reprint. London: Vintage, 1991. Collection of essays by one of the first practitioners of postmodern cultural criticism and an acknowledged leading scholar of postcolonial studies. Individual essays demonstrate how cultural criticism is practiced in examining literary works.

Laurence W. Mazzeno

Feminist Criticism

Any survey of feminist criticism will most likely be fraught with difficulties, the most serious of which is the attempt to avoid reductionism. This introduction to feminist criticism attempts to identify key figures, central concerns, and general movements. Such an attempt is a strategic move to organize a vital and growing body of work into some sort of scheme that can be collated and presented. Despite the existence of American, French, and British feminisms, for example, no such clear-cut schools or movements exist in a fixed way. The various writers included in this essay, and the various trends and movements discussed, share many positions and disagree on many important points. Such agreements and disagreements have less to do with nationality than with the rapid changes occurring in feminist criticism.

Three general perspectives on feminism are summarized here, as reflected in the work of American, French, and British writers. The work of two pivotal feminist writers, Simone de Beauvoir and Virginia Woolf, is discussed at some length, and there is also an attempt to isolate a few general trends and issues within the feminist movement.

Feminism has diverse goals, many of which overlap in the work of individual writers. This work is filled with pitfalls and temptations: Because women are participants in their cultures, the thinking (and writing) of women cannot be separated from the methods of the cultures in which they live, nor can women be separated from their races or sexual orientations. Furthermore, feminist criticism may be combined with other methods of criticism, such as deconstruction, psychoanalytic criticism, and Marxist criticism. Generally, however, feminist writers are concerned with the political, social, and cultural equality of women and with researching the effects of gender upon writing—determining how the writing of women differs from the writing of men.

Gender systems

Feminist critics have produced a variety of models to account for the production, reproduction, and maintenance of gender systems. They discuss the female writer's problems in defining herself in the conventional structures of male-dominated society, structures that restrict the possibilities of women and impose standards of behavior upon women personally, professionally, and creatively. Again, to generalize, once women experience themselves as subjects, they can attempt to undermine the social, cultural, and masculine subject positions offered them.

Feminist critics may, for example, reexamine the writing of male authors (an approach associated with American feminists) and, in particular, reexamine the great works of male authors from a woman's perspective in an attempt to discover how these great works reflect and shape the ideologies that subjugate women. Through this reexamination, feminist critics carefully analyze the depictions of female characters to expose the ideology implicit in such characterizations. They may also seek to expose the patriarchal ideology that permeates great works and to show how it also permeates the literary tradition. This particularly American approach is seen in the works of Kate Millett, Judith Fetterley, and Carolyn Gold Heilbrun.

Gynocriticism

A second approach used by American feminists is termed "gynocriticism." This method of inquiry takes as its subject the writings of women who have produced what Elaine C. Showalter, who coined the term "gynocriticism," calls "a literature of their own." A female literary tradition is examined to discover how women writers have historically perceived themselves and their cultures. Other goals of gynocriticism are to preserve and chronicle the history of women's writing and to rediscover lost or neglected women writers. Showalter describes feminine writing as a form of the general experience of minority cultures, cultures that are also "Others" and whose members are struggling to find a place usually reserved for white males. This leads to the problem of multiple marginalization, since some men and women may be Others in terms of ethnicity and sexual orientation as well. In particular, the place within feminism of women of color is a controversial issue, as black writers such as Phillis Wheatley, Toni Morrison, Gwendolyn Brooks, and Nikki Giovanni challenge and enter the canon. Other practitioners of gynocriticism include Patricia Meyer Spacks and Susan Gubar.

LANGUAGE

Feminist writers may also focus on language, defining it as a male realm and exploring the many ways in which meaning is created. This language-based feminism is typically associated with French feminism. Such feminists may conceive of language as phallocentric, arguing that language privileges the masculine by promoting the values appreciated and perpetuated by male culture. Such a language-based approach typically attempts to reveal a relationship between language and culture, or, more specifically, the way the politics of language affects and even determines women's roles in a culture. Radical French feminists may associate feminine writing with the female body, so that the repression of female sexual pleasure is related to the repression of feminine creativity in general. French feminists insist that once women learn to understand and express their sexuality, they will be able to progress toward a future defined by the feminine economy of generosity as opposed to the masculine economy of hoarding. Such a position has drawn criticism from other feminists, because it seems to reduce women to biological entities and fosters (though it reverses) a set of binary oppositions—female/male. French feminists include Julia Kristeva, Annie Leclerc, Xaviere Gauthier, and Marguerite Duras.

Interestingly, differences between the French and English languages involve complicated feminist issues. The English language distinguishes between sex and gender, so that human beings are either female or male by sex and feminine or masculine by gender. The feminine/masculine opposition permits some fluidity, so that androgyny can become a central, mediating position between the two extremes. The distinction between male and female, however, is absolute. The way the English language categorizes people has itself created a debate within feminism, about naming. In the French language, by comparison, the concepts of femininity and femaleness are included in the same word.

POLITICAL AND SOCIAL AGENDAS

Finally, British feminists have tended to be more historically oriented than have French and American feminists. British critics tend to be materialistic and ideological; they look carefully at the material conditions of historical periods and consider such conditions as central to understanding literature. Literature, in this model, is culturally produced. Some British feminists consider that an American opposition to male stereotypes has produced a feminine reaction that has led to an ignorance of real differences among women's races, social classes, and cultures. British feminists also emphasize that women's development of individual strategies to obtain real power within their political, social, or creative arenas is actually a negative move. They argue that such examples mystify male oppression and perpetrate the myth that, somehow, male oppression creates for women a world of special opportunities.

Generally, the British position encourages historical and political engagement to promote social change. This model of activism contrasts with the American and French models, which focus primarily on sexual difference. A typical strategy of the British approach is to examine a text by first placing the text in its historical context and then exposing the patriarchal ideologies that structure the text and govern the depiction of women characters. Because of historical oppression, the women characters tend either to be silent or to be mouthpieces for men's myths. British feminists include Judith Newton and Deborah Rosenfelt.

HISTORY

Feminist criticism owes much to the work of French philosopher and critic Beauvoir and to English writer and critic Woolf, two founders of contemporary feminist thought. Beauvoir, whose best-known and perhaps most important work is *Le Deuxième Sexe* (1949; *The Second Sex*, 1953), explored the many ways in which women are defined and limited in relation to men. Such limiting, Beauvoir contends, cannot be avoided in a male-dominated culture; even women perceived as independent are still negatively affected by the ideas and the relations of male society. Western society in general, for Beauvoir, is patriarchal and denies freedom of expression to women. In this patriarchal society, women become Others, viewed not as they are but as projections of male needs and subordinate to male expectations. Her approach tends toward a Marxist model in identifying an economic and political limiting of women with sexism in literature. Beauvoir finds in literature reflections of a more general socioeconomic oppression of women. Her approach emphasizes art's mimetic quality: Through its powers of reflection, art yields valuable insights into the sexism that is culturally prevalent.

The otherness examined by Beauvoir and other feminist writers is a condition of women, so that the characteristic of identity for women is separation. Constituted through a male gaze, the feminine exists as something that is inexpressible. Women function as objects of the male gaze. Therefore, women's bodies are vehicles for ambivalent feelings toward the mother. These problems extend into the Western philosophical tradition, so that Western (usually male) thinkers express their philosophical positions as essential and universal while embracing a center that is unexamined and male.

In her essay *A Room of One's Own* (1929), Woolf introduced many topics that have become vital to feminist critics. She contends that art is a collective product, incorrectly romanticized in theory as individual and personal. Woolf's conceptualization of a metaphorical "room," a female place, merges the introspection often associated with female discourse and the social sanctuary within which a woman may achieve her potential. Woolf helped to establish the broad range of feminist criticism, from cultural critique to discourse. The most important portion of *A Room of One's Own* ironically and satirically traces the lost career of William Shakespeare's "sister," whose creativity had no outlet in the sixteenth century. Woolf problematizes the structures of the male ego, its rituals, titles, and institutions, which are created at the expense of Others. This ironic introduction sets the stage in the text for a historical discussion of women writers and the problems they had in pursuing their careers. Furthermore, in her discussion of women novelists of the nineteenth century, especially George Eliot, Charlotte Brontë, and Jane Austen, Woolf foreshadows contemporary research on language.

Woolf further argues that a woman writer should write as a woman and as a woman who is not self-conscious of her gender. Ever-aware of the alienating and repressive effects of the myths created around women, Woolf also attempted to avoid creating alternative myths. She sets forth in her work the attempt to discover a collective concept of subjectivity that would foreground identity constructs, and she argues that such a concept of subjectivity is a characteristic of women's writing. Other women writers, however, seem more interested in the alienation created by structures that permit women restricted and repressive roles only, roles as Others, in society.

In her writing, Woolf is striving, like later feminists, to uncover the effects of a phallocentric culture that idolizes the autonomous and rational ego. She also attempts to offer an alternative to this idolatry, an alternative that emphasizes subjectivity and connectedness, if in a historically fluid context. Through her struggle to redefine women, she tries to avoid simply reversing the binary oppositions that polarize men and women into specific categories. She does not argue for a reversal of these categories.

GENDER RULES AND RELATIONS

Since the time of Beauvoir and Woolf, the naming and interrogating of phallocentrism has become more assured. Feminist critics are challenging stereotypical masculine virtues, no longer accepting them as measures of virtue and excellence. One strategy many feminist critics adopt is to locate both men and women within a larger context; men and women are both captives of gender, in interrelated, but in vastly different, ways. Though men may appear to be the masters under the rules of gender, they are not therefore free, for like women, their gender expression is tightly controlled by sociocultural "rules."

If both men and women are influenced by gender, then the conceptualizations of women and the conceptualizations of men must be examined in terms of gender relations. Feminist critical models are complex and often contradictory. Claims about the centrality of gender relations in the formation of self, knowledge, and power relations, and the relationships of these areas to one another, continue to be debated. Feminist critics have developed many theories of how gender systems are created and perpetuated, how they dominate, and how they maintain themselves. Each of the theories, however, identifies a single process or set of processes as vital to gender relations. Influential feminist theorists have suggested the centrality of the sexual division of labor, childbearing and child-rearing practices, and various processes of representation (including aesthetic and language processes, for example). Such positions address the meanings and nature of sexuality and the relationship of sexuality to writing, the importance and implications of differences among women writers, and the effects of kinship and family organizations. Each of these many theories and debates has crucial implications for an understanding of knowledge, gender, power, and writing.

Juliet Mitchell has argued for the importance of Freudian theories to feminist theories of gender relations. Her work entails a defense of Lacanian psychoanalysis. She argues that Freud's work on the psychology of women should be read as a description of the inevitable effects on feminine psychic development of patriarchal social power. Dorothy Dinnerstein and Nancy Chodorow contribute to this psychoanalytical approach a larger account of the unconscious and its role in gender relations. They also examine the traditional sexual division of labor in the West, how this tradition has been passed on, and how it influences male-female relations.

MALE VERSUS FEMALE DISCOURSE

Hélène Cixous and Luce Irigaray find fundamental psychological differences between men and women. They have concluded that women are more influenced by pre-Oedipal experience and believe that the girl retains an initial identification with her mother, so that the relationship between mother and daughter is less repressed than that of the mother and son. This retention affects women's selves, so that they remain fluid and interrelational. As a result of this difference between men and women, masculine writing has an ambivalent response to women. Women tend to remain outside or on the fringes of male discourse, and feminine pleasure poses the greatest challenge to masculine discourse. Masculine discourse is also logocentric and binary; its meaning is produced through hierarchal, male-dominated, binary oppositions. Masculine discourse creates a situation in which feminine discourse is characterized by omissions and gaps. Latent in these gaps and omissions are conflicting feelings regarding sexuality, motherhood, and autonomy.

An important question raised by feminist criticism is whether there is a gender-based women's language that is significantly and inevitably different from the language of men. In *Language and Woman's Place* (1975), Robin Lakoff argues that there is more to "speaking like a woman" than simply vocabulary. Examining syntactical patterns of a typical female and evaluating the frequency with which women use tag questions, she concludes that the traditional powerlessness of women in Western society is reflected in many aspects of women's language. Other theorists who are interested in differences between male and female languages explore sociolinguistic issues, such as the practice of women assuming their fathers' names at birth and their husbands' names when married, the frequency with which women are addressed by familiar names, the frequency of interruption in speech between men and women, and the large number of pejorative terms applicable to women. Writers interested in these latter linguistic areas are Cheris Kramarae and Julia Penelope Stanley.

In this conflict between male and female discourse, writing may be an anticipatory, therapeutic experience of liberation. Writing may return to a woman her repressed pleasure. It may also create a collective space in which women writers may speak of and to women. Gayatri Chakravorty Spivak explores discourse and literature in general as discursive practices. In her *In Other Worlds: Essays in Cultural Politics* (1987) she shows the tendency in Western cultures to universalize particular examples into human examples. Spivak examines feminism in relation to British imperialism in India and then situates feminist criticism within middle-class academia. This approach argues that what has been assumed to be universal truth is in fact the Western colonial or male conception of truth, a perspective that distorts or ignores the experiences of Others. The goal of such a critical perspective is to authenticate the expression of Others based on individual experience and shared understanding and to call into question the accepted definitions of truth and meaningful discourse.

DIFFERENCES AMONG WOMEN

Another concern that has become important in feminist criticism is the differences among women themselves. A model that presumes a universal feminine experience requires that women, unlike men, be free from cultural and racial determination. Under such a model, the barriers to shared experience created by race, class, gender, and sexuality are somehow cleared away when one is a woman. Women of color, such as critic Barbara Smith, argue that one cannot assume that there is one universal feminine experience or writing. For example, the sexuality of black women tends to be represented as natural, primitive, and free from traditional cultural inhibitions; this assumption has been invoked both to justify and to deny the sexual abuse of black women and the lack of respect given to them. In general, Smith criticizes other feminists for excluding or ignoring women of color. She also observes that both black and white male scholars working with black authors neglect women.

Furthermore, it is not possible to discuss a universal experience of motherhood. Racism affects women of color differently from the way it affects white women, especially in the effort to rear children who can be self-sufficient and self-respecting. These troubles are inherent in a culture that holds as natural the binary opposition white/black, wherein white is the privileged term. This opposition is deeply rooted in the colonial history of Western civilization. Women of color cannot be exempt from the insidious consequences of this binary opposition, and white women cannot participate in productive dialogue with women of color whenever this traditional opposition is ignored.

LESBIAN FEMINIST CRITICISM

Another friction within the feminist movement involves lesbian feminist criticism. Just as women of color have considered themselves excluded, lesbian feminists consider themselves excluded, not only by the dominant white male culture but also by heterosexual females. Authors concerned with this problem include Bonnie Zimmerman and Adrienne Rich. In fact,

Rich provides a definition of "lesbianism" so broad that it encompasses most of feminine creativity.

FEMINIST PSYCHOANALYTIC CRITICISM

In the 1970's a general movement toward psychoanalysis and toward women reading men and one another occurred within feminism. This movement is exemplified in the writings of such feminists as Mary Jacobs, Jane Gallop, and Juliet Richardson. For feminist theorists, the limitations of traditional theories accounting for the origins of oppression had been uncovered. Writers in the 1970's became very interested in, for example, the positioning of women within repressive sexual and political discourses. Many feminist writers have become interested in the establishment of an identity that involves both separation and connection, so that a binary relationship is not created and one is not perceived as a threat. In such a new relationship, women would no longer need, for example, to attempt to create an Oedipal triangle through their children. Each gender might develop less threatening relations to the other.

READING DIFFERENCES

In regard to women reading men and one another, Annette Kolodny investigated methodological problems from an empiricist stance. She concludes that women do read differently from men. Her essay "A Map for Rereading: Or, Gender and the Interpretation of Literary Texts" (1980) examines how the two contrasting methods of interpretation appear in two stories and how the differences between masculine and feminine perspectives are mirrored in the reaction of readers to the two stories (Charlotte Perkins Gilman's "The Yellow Wallpaper," 1892, and Susan Glaspell's "A Jury of Her Peers," 1927). Judith Fetterley's work also presents a model for gender differences in reading. In *The Resisting Reader: A Feminist Approach to American Fiction* (1978), she argues against the position that the primary works of American fiction are intended, and written, for a universal audience and that women have permitted themselves to be masculinized in order to read these texts. One of the first steps, Fetterley contends, is for women to become resisting, rather than assenting, readers.

VARIETIES OF FEMINISM

Feminism has engaged in and with other branches of criticism, including Marxist criticism and deconstruction. Nancy K. Miller and Peggy Kamuf, for example, have incorporated deconstructive approaches in their work. Judith Lowder Newton and Lillian Robinson have incorporated Marxism.

The movement toward alternative ways of writing, however, involves drastic changes in the relationship between public and private and the traditional opposition between emotional and rational. Such an attempt in literature was heralded by Woolf's writing (for example, *The Waves* in 1931 and *To the Lighthouse* in 1927) and may be read in the work of Muriel Spark (*The Hothouse by the East River*, 1973), Angela Carter (*The Passion of New Eve*, 1977), Toni Morrison (*The Bluest Eye*, 1970), Alice Walker (*Meridian*, 1976), Marge Piercy (*Woman on the Edge of Time*, 1976), Margaret Atwood (*The Edible Woman*, 1969), Joanna Russ (*The Female Man*, 1975), and Fay Weldon (*The Life and Loves of a She-Devil*, 1983), among others.

Perhaps the most agreed-upon accomplishment of feminist criticism (though even in this agreement there is caution) has been finding and identifying a variety of feminine traditions in literature. Numerous women writers have been "rediscovered," introduced into the literary canon, and examined as important to the literary tradition. This interest in expanding the study of literature by women has had a significant impact in colleges and universities. Indeed, feminist criticism, by the beginning of the twenty-first century, had joined with other traditions—Native American, African American, Asian American, lesbian and gay—in an ongoing effort to celebrate and express diversity in investigations of identity.

BIBLIOGRAPHY

Beauvoir, Simone de. *The Second Sex*. 1949. Reprint. Introduction by Deirdre Blair. New York: Random House, 1990. In this famous work, the author considers thoughtfully just what it means to be a woman, thus setting the stage for the modern feminist movement. Includes an index.

Christian, Barbara. *New Black Feminist Criticism, 1985-2000*. Edited by Gloria Bowles, M. Guilia Fabi, and Arlene R. Keizer. Urbana: University of Illinois Press, 2007. A collection of essays and reviews by one of the founders of black feminist literary criticism, ranging in subject matter from pedagogical issues and questions of definition to analyses of specific writers. Includes bibliographical references and an index.

Eagleton, Mary, ed. *Feminist Literary Theory: A Reader*. Reprint. Cambridge, Mass.: Blackwell, 2000. A revised and expanded edition of a classic text, featuring additions to every section and an added chapter on postmodernist theories of subjectivity. Fully indexed.

Federico, Annette, ed. *Gilbert and Gubar's "The Madwoman in the Attic" After Thirty Years*. Columbia: University of Missouri Press, 2009. A thirty-year retrospective on a classic work of feminist literature and literary criticism (see below). Includes a foreword by Sandra M. Gilbert.

Frost, Elisabeth A. *The Feminist Avant-Garde in American Poetry*. Iowa City: University of Iowa Press, 2003. Discusses the works of Gertrude Stein, Mina Loy, Sonia Sanchez, Susan Howe, and Harryette Mullen. Includes a bibliography and an index.

Frost, Elisabeth A., and Cynthia Hogue, eds. *Innovative Women Poets: An Anthology of Contemporary Poetry and Interviews*. Iowa City: University of Iowa Press, 2006. Interviews in which fourteen diverse poets comment on their poetry and their poetic theories. Includes selections from their poetry. Each interview is preceded by a brief introduction.

Gilbert, Sandra M., and Susan Gubar. *The Madwoman in the Attic: The Woman Writer and the Nineteenth-Century Literary Imagination*. 2d ed. New Haven, Conn.: Yale University Press, 2000. A landmark work, reissued with a revealing new introduction by the original authors.

_____, eds. *Feminist Literary Theory and Criticism: A Norton Reader*. New York: W. W. Norton, 2007. Represents more than one hundred writers and scholars, dating from the Middle Ages to the twenty-first century. An indispensable collection.

Greer, Germaine. *Slip-Shod Sibyls: Recognition, Rejection, and the Woman Poet*. London: Penguin, 1996. A poignant account of the plight of women poets before the twentieth century, who were often treated as freaks of nature but because of their lack of education produced works that were neither original nor of high enough quality to be admitted to the canon.

Kinnahan, Linda A. *Lyric Interventions: Feminism, Experimental Poetry, and Contemporary Discourse.* Iowa City: University of Iowa Press, 2004. Examines how such social and cultural factors as nation, gender, and race influence the lyric subject. The author discusses linguistically experimental poetry by American and British writers, including Barbara Guest, Kathleen Fraser, Erica Hunt, Alison Saar, M. Nourbese Philip, and Carol Ann Duffy. Includes a bibliography and an index.

Langdell, Cheri Colby. *Adrienne Rich: The Moment of Change.* Westport, Conn.: Praeger, 2004. A biographical and critical study of one of America's most important poets, showing how her poetry reflects each radical transformation in her ideology, including her adoption of radical feminism and her later conversion to postmodern Marxism. Includes biographical references and an index.

Lepson, Ruth, ed. *Poetry from "Sojourner": A Feminist Anthology.* Urbana: University of Illinois Press, 2004. A collection of nearly 150 poems published in the prominent feminist journal *Sojourner*, some by such well-known poets as Nikki Giovannni and Adrienne Rich, others by women whose only recognition has come from their work's appearance in *Sojourner*. Includes an index.

Mills, Sara. *Feminist Stylistics.* New York: Routledge, 2005. A study of feminist stylistics, utilizing both literary and nonliterary texts. In the first part of the volume, the author considers several theoretical issues; in the second section, she discusses analysis at the level of the word, the phrase or sentence, and the complete discourse. Includes a glossary, notes, a bibliography, and an index.

Rooney, Ellen, ed. *The Cambridge Companion to Feminist Literary Theory.* New York: Cambridge University Press, 2006. Provides extracts representing a wide range of historical periods and drawn from various disciplines to demonstrate how language reflects assumptions about gender. The book is divided into six thematic sections, each with an introduction. Includes a bibliography of extracts and an index. A well-organized, accessible guide to the subject.

Showalter, Elaine. *Inventing Herself: Claiming a Feminist Intellectual Heritage.* New York: Scribner, 2001. Examines the lives of famous women, from Mary Wollstonecraft to Princess Diana, many of them feminist writers and critics, but all, feminist or not, determined to be independent.

Smith, Barbara, ed. *Home Girls: A Black Feminist Anthology.* 1983. Reprint. New Brunswick, N.J.: Rutgers University Press, 2000. A collection of works by thirty-two black and lesbian activists from the United States and the Caribbean. Includes a new preface, updated biographies, and a bibliography.

David L. Erben

FORMALISTIC CRITICISM

The formalist approach to poetry was the most influential in American criticism during the 1940's, 1950's, and 1960's, and it is still often practiced in literature courses in colleges and universities in the United States. Its popularity was not limited to American literary criticism.

In France, formalism has long been employed as a pedagogical exercise in reading literature in the universities and in the *lycées*. In England in the 1940's and 1950's, formalism was associated with an influential group of critics writing for a significant critical periodical, *Scrutiny*, the most prominent of whom was F. R. Leavis. There also was a notable formalist movement in the Soviet Union in the 1920's, and, although championed by René Wellek in the United States, its influence at that time was primarily limited to Slavic countries.

The formalist approach in the United States was popularized by John Crowe Ransom, Allen Tate, Robert Penn Warren, and Cleanth Brooks, all four southerners, all graduates of Vanderbilt University, and all, in varying degrees, receptive to the indirections and complexities of the modernism of T. S. Eliot, James Joyce, and William Butler Yeats. The critical method of Ransom, Tate, Warren, and Brooks that came to be known as New Criticism, was, in part, developed to explicate the modernism of Eliot, Joyce, and Yeats. A fifth critic, R. P. Blackmur, not directly associated with the Vanderbilt group, made important contributions to the formalist reading of poetry in *The Double Agent* (1935) and in essays in other books. He did not, however, develop a distinctive formalist method.

FORMALISM IN THE HISTORY OF LITERARY CRITICISM

Formalism is clearly a twentieth century critical phenomenon in its emphasis on close readings of literary texts, dissociated from extrinsic references to authors or to their society. There had been a formalist tendency before in the history of literary criticism, but it did not, as in twentieth century formalism, approach exclusivity in its emphasis on the structure of the work itself. Aristotle's analysis in *De poetica* (c. 334-323

B.C.E.; *Poetics*, 1705) of the complex tragic plot as having a tripartite division of reversal, recognition, and catastrophe is one of the most valuable formalist analyses of the structure of tragedy ever made.

That Aristotle's approach to poetics was not intrinsic but extrinsic, however, was made clear by his twentieth century followers, the Chicago Neo-Aristotelians Ronald S. Crane and Elder Olson. They were the harshest critics of what they regarded as the limited critical perspective of modern formalists, pointing out that an Aristotelian analysis was characteristically in terms of four causes. These were the formal cause (the form that the work imitates), the material cause (the materials out of which the work is made), the efficient cause (the maker), and the final cause (the effect on the reader or audience). Crane charged in *Critics and Criticism: Ancient and Modern* (1952) that the New Criticism is concerned with only one of these causes, language, in order to distinguish poetic from scientific and everyday uses of language, but was unable to distinguish among the various kinds of poetry. It is true that formalism is largely concerned with literature as a verbal art. This single-mindedness has been its strength in explication as well as its weakness as a critical theory.

Two key concepts in the literary theory of the English Romantic period may have been influential on twentieth century formalism. Although the New Critics were professedly anti-Romantic, following Eliot's call for impersonality in modern poetry, their stress on the meaning of the total poem, rather than the meaning centered in a specific part, probably owes something to the concept of organic form, assumed by most Romantics and stated explicitly by Samuel Taylor Coleridge in his defense of William Shakespeare. This is the concept that a poem grows like a living organism, its parts interrelated, its form and content inseparable; the total work is thus greater than the sum of its parts. This concept was assumed by all the New Critics except Ransom, who viewed "texture" as separate from structure.

The formalist view of creativity is of a rage brought to order through submission to the discipline of form. A good poem is characterized by tensions that are usually reconciled. The most detailed statement of this view by a New Critic is in Warren's essay "Pure and Impure Poetry" (1943), in which Warren gives a long list of resistances or "tensions" in a good poem. The origin of this idea lies in Romantic critical theory. Warren's statements, as well as Tate's discussion of tension in his essay "Tension in Poetry" (1938), undoubtedly owe much to chapter 14 of Coleridge's *Biographia Literaria* (1817), in which he describes the distinctive quality of the creative imagination of the poet as revealing itself "in the balance or reconciliation of opposite or discordant qualities."

The strongest twentieth century influences on formalism in the United States and in England were the early essays of Eliot, especially those in *The Sacred Wood* (1920), and two books by I. A. Richards, *Principles of Literary Criticism* (1924) and *Practical Criticism: A Study of Literary Judgement* (1929). Eliot, influenced by the anti-Romanticism of T. E. Hulme in *Speculations: Essays and Humanism and the Philosophy of Art* (1924), called for a theory of the impersonal in the modernist view of poetry to rectify the personality cults of Romantic and Victorian poetry, and he even detailed how to impersonalize personal emotions through the use of "objective correlatives." Eliot's intention was to redirect critical attention from the poet to the work of art, which he declared to be autotelic, or self-contained, a fictive world in itself. It was this pronouncement of Eliot, more than any statement in his essays in the 1920's, which had the strongest influence on the development of formalist criticism.

Eliot also devised his own version of a Cartesian "split" between logic and untrustworthy feelings, his theory that a dissociation of sensibility took place in English poetry in the late seventeenth century. John Donne had a unified sensibility capable of devouring any kind of experience. In the Metaphysical poet "there is a direct sensuous apprehension of thought": They could think feelings and feel thoughts. The New Critics were to develop a formalist approach to poetry that could show this kind of sensibility at work. To a formalist such as Brooks in *Modern Poetry and the Tradition* (1939), Metaphysical poetry was the proper tradition in which to fit modern poetry, and critical

techniques were needed to explicate the complexities of poetry in the tradition. He provided a model for formalist explication in a brilliant analysis of parallelisms and ironic contrasts used functionally by Eliot in *The Waste Land* (1922).

THE FORMALIST DEFENSE OF POETRY

Formalism in the United States and England may have evolved in reaction to nineteenth century literary thought and practice as a method of understanding a modernist literature that was indirect, impersonal, complex, and autotelic. As far as the New Critics were concerned, however, their formalism was a defense of poetry in an age of science. Their criticism can quite properly be regarded as an "apology" for poetry in the tradition of Sir Philip Sidney and Percy Bysshe Shelley. An "apology" is a formal defense of poetry in an age thought to be hostile to the poetry of its own time. Sidney apologized for poetry at a time when Puritans were attacking drama and voicing suspicions as to whether poetry could and did advance morality. Shelley defended the value of poetry in an age that was beginning to turn to prose, assuming that the golden age of poetry was over. In this tradition the New Critics apologized for poetry in an age of logical positivism, when scientific method was regarded as the sole means to truth, and poetry was being limited to mere emotive effects.

In his *Principles of Literary Criticism*, Richards sought to find a place for poetry in an age of science by emphasizing the psychological effects of poetry on the personality of the reader. In *Practical Criticism*, he documented the helplessness of his graduate students when confronted with an unidentified poem to explicate, making a case for a literary criticism that specialized in explicating the text. Richards seemed, however, at least in the earlier book, to be in agreement with the positivistic view that poetry was a purely emotive use of language, in contrast to science, which was the language of factual assertion. Although influenced by Richards, the New Critics attempted to counter his apparent denial of a cognitive dimension of poetry. They did this through their formalism, staying inside the poem in their explications and declaring it characteristic of the poet's use of language to direct the reader to meanings back inside the poem rather than to referents outside the poem.

Brooks contended that poets are too direct at pointing to everyday referents outside the poem, and that the meanings of a poem cannot be wrenched outside the context of the poem without serious distortions. He was making a case for meaning in the poem and at the same time was keeping poetry out of direct competition with science. In a poem, he asserted, apparently referential statements are qualified by ambiguities, paradoxes, and ironies so that the knowledge offered cannot stand as a direct proposition apart from the poem itself. This is why it does not matter that John Keats in a famous sonnet credits Hernán Cortés, not Vasco Núñez de Balboa, with the first sighting by a European of the Pacific Ocean. What Keats writes is true to the poem, not to historical fact, and he does not intend a truth claim to be taken outside the poem and examined for factual accuracy. Murray Krieger argued quite plausibly in *The New Apologists for Poetry* (1956) that the New Critics might be called "contextualists" because of their insistence on getting meaning in context and from the context.

Each major New Critic was in his own way trying to establish that poetry offers a special kind of knowledge and does not compete with the more referential knowledge that Richards found characteristic of scientific assertions. Their apology for poetry committed them to formalism, to directing critical attention intrinsically to the structure of the poem rather than extrinsically to referents outside. Ransom, in *The World's Body* (1938) and *The New Criticism* (1941), even departed from the concept of organic form to argue that the main difference between scientific and poetic language was that while both had "structure," only the latter had "texture," details that are interesting in themselves. Through "texture" the poet expresses his or her revulsion against the inclination of science to abstract and to categorize by giving his or her reader the particulars of the world, the "sensuous apprehension of thought" that Eliot had admired in the Metaphysical poets. To Ransom, this was knowledge of "the world's body." Ransom's single most important contribution to formalism was his often anthologized essay, "Poetry: A Note on Ontology" (1934).

The most philosophically inclined of the New Critics, Tate, also made a specific claim that literature offers a special kind of knowledge, more complete than the knowledge of science; it is experiential knowledge rather than the abstracted, shorthand version of experience given by science. Tate argued that a special characteristic of poetic language is the creation of "tension," a kind of balance between the extremes of too much denotation and literalness and too much connotation and suggestiveness. A good poem possesses both a wealth of suggestiveness and a firm denotative base. In his essay "Tension in Poetry," he provided examples of tension as a kind of touchstone for critical judgments.

In "Pure and Impure Poetry," Warren presented his own version of the concept of tension, one closer to Coleridge's than Tate's was. Warren was also influenced by Richards's concept of a "poetry of inclusion" (in turn derived from Coleridge), a poetry that contains its own oppositions. Warren believed that such an "impure" poet writing in modern times must "come to terms with Mercutio," that is, use irony to qualify direct propositions, much as Shakespeare used the realistic, bawdy jests of Mercutio to counter the sentimental love poetry in *Romeo and Juliet* (pr. c. 1595-1596, pb. 1597). Such irony is accessible only through formalist analysis of the poem itself, a close reading of the text. As a formalist, Warren believed, as the other New Critics did, in a less accessible meaning beyond the usual public meaning.

THE PRACTICE OF FORMALISM

Brooks was the most consistent practicing formalist and the most influential as well, whether in collaboration with Warren, in their popular textbooks, *Understanding Poetry: An Anthology for College Students* (1938) and *Understanding Fiction* (1943), or in his own studies in formalism, *Modern Poetry and the Tradition* and *The Well Wrought Urn: Studies in the Structure of Poetry* (1947). In *Modern Poetry and the Tradition*, Brooks extended Eliot's concept of tradition to a selective history of poetry from seventeenth century Metaphysical poetry to twentieth century modernism. The proper tradition for the modern poet was the Metaphysical tradition because "hard" Metaphysical conceits conveyed both thought and feeling and maintained a proper balance, in contrast to the excessive emotion in much Romantic poetry and the excessive rationalism in much neoclassical poetry. Brooks wrote the book to show the relationship between Metaphysical and modern poetry and to explain modern poetry to readers whose understanding of poetry was primarily based on Romantic poetry.

Brooks's next book, *The Well Wrought Urn*, was slightly revisionist, expanding the tradition to include some of the best works of Romantic and Victorian poetry, and even a major poem of the neoclassical period, Alexander Pope's *The Rape of the Lock* (1712, 1714). The test for admission to the tradition is again a careful formalist analysis, revealing, in unexpected places, tensions and paradoxes—although the formalist technique has been refined and even expanded. Brooks contended that poetry is "the language of paradox," evident even in a poem such as William Wordsworth's "Composed upon Westminster Bridge, September 3, 1802" (1807). The paradox central to the structure of the poem is that a city, London, is enabled to "wear the beauty of the morning," a privilege that Wordsworth usually reserves for nature. The city is also paradoxically most alive with this surprising beauty when it is asleep, as it is on this occasion. Brooks conceded that Wordsworth's employment of paradox might have been unconscious, something he was driven to by "the nature of his instrument," but paradox can also be conscious technique, as it was in John Donne's "The Canonization" (1633).

Brooks's analysis of "The Canonization" is a model of formalist method, as his analysis of Eliot's *The Waste Land* had been in his previous volume. The poem is complex but unified, an argument dramatically presented but a treatise on the important subject of divine and profane love as well. The tone, an important element of meaning, is complex, scornful, ironic, and yet quite serious. Also central in the poem is the "love metaphor," and basic to its development is the paradox of treating profane love as if it were divine love. Such a treatment permits the culminating paradox in the speaker's argument for his love: "The lovers in rejecting life actually win to the most intense life." In this poem, technique has shaped content: The only way in which the poet could say what the poem says is by means of paradox.

Brooks made another major contribution to formalist practice in *The Well Wrought Urn*. He demonstrated the importance of the dramatic context as the intrinsic referent for meaning in a poem. Even the simplest lyric has some of the drama of a play. There are within a poem a speaker, an occasion, sometimes an audience, and a conflict—in a lyric usually a conflict of attitudes. Brooks declared in the chapter "The Problem of Belief and the Problem of Cognition" that a poem should not be judged by the truth or falsity "of the idea which it incorporates, but rather by its character as drama. . . ." The formalist as New Critic, most fully represented by an explication according to Brooks's formula, is concerned with this drama in the poem, with how the conflict of attitudes is resolved, with paradox and how it is central to argument in poetry, with metaphor and how it may be the only permissible way of developing the thought of the poem. He is concerned with technique in a verbal art, and these techniques make possible the poetic communication of what becomes the content.

Ranking with *The Well Wrought Urn* as a major formalist document is René Wellek and Austin Warren's *Theory of Literature* (1949). When it was published, the intention of the book was to argue for the use of intrinsic approaches to literature, drawing on New Criticism, Russian Formalism, and even phenomenology, in conjunction with literary history and the history of ideas, then the dominant approaches. Its value today is as a source book of formalist theory, just as Brooks's *The Well Wrought Urn* is a source book of formalist practice. Wellek and Warren make the distinction between the scientific use of language, ideally purely denotative, and the literary use of language, not merely referential but expressive and highly connotative, conveying the tone and attitude of speaker and writer. Form and content are regarded as inseparable: Technique determines content. Reference to the Russian Formalists reinforces the New Critics on this point. Meter, alliteration, sounds, imagery, and metaphor are all functional in a poem. Poetry is referential but the references are intrinsic, directed back inside the fictive world that is being created.

THE DECLINE OF FORMALISM

The influence of formalism reached its peak in the 1950's and began to decline in the 1960's. In England, *Scrutiny* suspended publication; although Leavis continued to publish, his criticism became less formalistic and more Arnoldian. In the United States, the New Critics also became less formalistic, and their formalism was taken over by followers who lacked the explicative genius of Ransom, Tate, Brooks, and Warren.

Warren had always published less formal criticism than his colleagues, and in the 1960's he turned his attention even more to fiction and, especially, to writing poetry. Tate, never as fond as the others of critical explications, continued to write essays of social and moral significance, moving in and out of Catholicism and the influence of Jacques Maritain. His best critical explication remained that of his own poem, "Ode to the Confederate Dead" (1937), an exploration of the creative process as well as a formalistic analysis. He died in 1979. Ransom continued to edit the most important new critical journal, *Kenyon Review*, until his retirement from Kenyon College; he then returned to something he had put aside for many years—his poetry. In the few essays that he wrote in the years just before his death in 1974, his Kantian interests preoccupied him more and more. Brooks wrote one more book that might be called formalistic, *A Shaping Joy: Studies in the Writer's Craft* (1971), but he turned most of his attention to his two major books on William Faulkner, *William Faulkner: The Yoknapatawpha Country* (1963) and *William Faulkner: Toward Yoknapatawpha and Beyond* (1978). In these works, Brooks brilliantly discusses Faulkner's novels, but it is clear that his interest is more in the relationship of Faulkner's fiction to his Southern society than in formalist analysis.

Newer critical approaches appeared, none of which was content to remain within the structure of the poem itself—the archetypal criticism of Northrop Frye, the phenomenological criticism of Georges Poulet and J. Hillis Miller, the structuralism of Roland Barthes, and the deconstruction of Jacques Derrida. The latter were influential but were more concerned with the modes of literary discourse than with the explication of texts, and they were better with fiction than with poetry.

During the protest movement of the later 1960's,

formalism fell into disrepute because of its lack of concern for the social and political backgrounds of literary works. Ironically, the New Critics were accused of empiricism and scientism in the analysis of literature. Nevertheless, twentieth century formalism has had a seemingly permanent influence on the teaching of literature in the United States, just as it has in France. Most literature introductory courses remain primarily formalistic in their approaches.

The New Critics taught a generation of students the art of close reading of the text. They warned readers against fallacies and heresies in reading and teaching poetry, and the lessons seem to have been widely learned. Although they used paraphrase masterfully themselves, they warned against "the heresy of paraphrase." The prose statement should not be regarded as the equivalent of the meaning of the poem. They attacked and seemingly permanently damaged the positivistic view that would limit poetry to the emotions only—what they called the affective fallacy. As Brooks declared in *The Well Wrought Urn*, "Poetry is not merely emotive . . . but cognitive. It gives us truth. . . ." Formalism did not prevent, but did restrict, practice of the biographical fallacy, studying the poet instead of his or her works.

The most controversial fallacy exposed by the New Critics was the intentional fallacy, against which all the formalists warned. Monroe C. Beardsley and William K. Wimsatt, who stated (in *The Verbal Icon: Studies in the Meaning of Poetry*, 1954) what was implicit in formalism all along, may have gone too far in seeming to exclude the poet from throwing any light at all on the meaning of his or her poem; they did, however, warn against finding the meaning of a work in some prose statement by the author before or after he or she wrote it. Formalism has made the point that the actual intention of a poem can be determined only from an explication of the poem itself. Few literary critics today would regard the poem as a fictive world that is sufficient unto itself. Poems have thematic and psychological contexts as well as verbal and dramatic contexts. Formalist analyses were too innocent of the linguistic structures of the language that poetry used. Nevertheless, no modern critical approach has revealed more of the richness of meaning potentially available within a poem.

BIBLIOGRAPHY

Beck, Charlotte H. *Robert Penn Warren, Critic*. Knoxville: University of Tennessee Press, 2006. A chronological study of Warren's development as a critic, noting that though his main interest was the text itself, he often took into account the biographical and historical background. Although Warren thought of himself primarily as a writer, it is now evident that he was among the most important critics of the twentieth century.

Brooks, Cleanth. *Modern Poetry and the Tradition*. 1939. Reprint. Chapel Hill: University of North Carolina Press, 1979. A study of the relationship between modern poetry and the established tradition, notably in the poetry of Robert Frost, Archibald MacLeish, W. H. Auden, T. S. Eliot, and W. B. Yeats. One of the author's most influential books.

_____. *The Well Wrought Urn: Studies in the Structure of Poetry*. Rev. ed. London: Methuen, 1968. Ten chapters of this volume are devoted to close readings of poems by John Donne, William Shakespeare, John Milton, Alexander Pope, William Wordsworth, John Keats, Yeats, Eliot, and Alfred, Lord Tennyson. Brooks attacks the custom of paraphrasing poems, which he argues eliminates the ambiguities and paradoxes that are inherent in any worthwhile literary work. Includes two appendixes and index.

Brooks, Cleanth, and Robert Penn Warren. *Understanding Poetry*. 4th ed. Reprint. Fort Worth, Tex.: Heinle & Heinle, 2003. Demonstrates the New Critical approach to poetry, which shows students how to utilize their own analytical skills, as well as their imaginations, in mastering the meaning of a poem and its implications. A landmark work. Includes an index.

Cowan, Louise. *The Southern Critics: An Introduction to the Criticism of John Crowe Ransom, Allen Tate, Donald Davidson, Robert Penn Warren, Cleanth Brooks, and Andrew Lytle*. Dallas, Tex.: Dallas Institute of Humanities and Culture, 1997. A concise introduction to the Southern Critics, with emphasis on Ransom, Tate, and Davidson, who founded the movement.

Davis, Garrick, ed. *Praising It New: The Best of the New Criticism*. Athens: Ohio University Press, 2008. This long-overdue collection contains key essays by the most influential poet-critics of the early and mid-twentieth century, from Eliot and Pound to Brooks, Tate, Warren, and Hugh Kenner. Each of the four sections is preceded by an overview. Brief biographies and selected bibliographies in the appendix.

Empson, William. *Seven Types of Ambiguity*. 3d ed. London: Pimlico, 2004. After explaining at length the various functions of ambiguous wordings, using examples from major poets from Shakespeare and Chaucer to Hopkins and Eliot, the author considers the usefulness of ambiguity in criticism. One of the key documents of the New Criticism. Originally published in 1930.

Ransom, John Crowe. *The New Criticism*. 1941. Reprint. Westport, Conn.: Greenwood Press, 1980. Looks at the criticism of I. A. Richards, Empson, Eliot, and Ivor Winters, all of whom he calls new critics because they attempt to ascertain the true meaning of a poem, rather than merely relating background information. The school derived its name from the title of this volume.

Richards, I. A. *Practical Criticism: A Study of Literary Judgement*. 1929. Reprint. Edited by John Constable. New York: Routledge, 2001. Explains how to use the new technique of close reading to come to a full understanding of a literary work. Suggests how best to teach this technique to students.

_____. *Principles of Literary Criticism*. 1924. 2d ed. New York: Routledge, 2002. A reissue of a classic work. After pointing out the deficiencies in then-current critical practices, Richards advances his own psychologically based theory of aesthetics.

Tate, Allen. *Essays of Four Decades*. 1968. 3d ed. Wilmington, Del.: ISI Books, 1999. A collection of nearly fifty essays by the celebrated poet and critic and one of the major exponents of the New Criticism. Includes a new introduction by Louise Cowan.

Wellek, René, and Austin Warren. *Theory of Literature*. 3d ed. New York: Harcourt Brace Jovanovich, 1984. Long popular as a textbook for graduate studies, this volume is notable for its precision and clarity. Divided into four parts, covering definitions, the evaluation of evidence, extrinsic information, and intrinsic forms, such as styles and genres. Includes a section on literary history. Notes, bibliography, and index.

Wimsatt, William K., and Monroe C. Beardsley. *The Verbal Icon: Studies in the Meaning of Poetry.* 1954. Reprint. Lexington: University Press of Kentucky, 1989. Noted for its explanation of the "Principle of Autonomy," which holds that a creative work should not be judged on the basis of whether or not it fulfilled the artist's purpose. Ends with the chapter "Poetry and Christian Thinking."

Winchell, Mark Royden. *Cleanth Brooks and the Rise of Modern Criticism.* Charlottesville: University Press of Virginia, 1996. A biography of the life and career of Brooks, as well as a sympathetic history of New Criticism, detailing its rise and its decline, which is more evident in the publications of its opponents than in actual educational practice. An essential volume for any student of the history of literary criticism.

Richard J. Calhoun

LINGUISTIC CRITICISM

In many ways, linguistic criticism is a legacy of the work done in the early twentieth century by Ferdinand de Saussure, the great French theorist whose posthumously published work has been the point of departure for all modern structuralism, not only in linguistics but also in anthropology and other disciplines. American structural linguistics, the principles and research program for which were laid down by Leonard Bloomfield in his *Language* (1933), was concerned with establishing the structure—phonological, morphological, syntactical, and semantic—of languages conceived as systematic wholes. It dealt with what Saussure's *Cours de linguistique generale* (1916; *Course in General Linguistics*) called the *langue*, the system of a limited repertoire of sounds, on whose differentiation differences of meaning depend, and of a limited number of kinds of sentence elements that can be combined in certain orders and hierarchical relationships, as distinguished from *parole*, particular utterances. To elicit these elements and rules of combination for a given language, linguists depended primarily on speech rather than on written texts. Furthermore, Bloomfieldian linguists tended to concentrate their efforts on the description of "exotic" languages rather than of English. Meanwhile, literary critics focused their attention on particular written texts, deemed literary, and were concerned with the interpretation and evaluation of these works of individual writers.

Poems and other literary works are, of course, works of verbal art whose medium is language, and this fact suggested to some linguists a potential for the application of linguistics to the study of literature. The techniques developed by linguists for the analysis of language could be applied to the language of literary texts. The linguist could bring to bear on these texts an expertise that the literary critic did not have. Much of the work that has been done involving the application of linguistics to the study of literary texts falls under the heading of stylistics, the study of literary style. Early contributions in linguistic stylistics tended to carry the animus of bringing a new objectivity to a field that had hitherto been merely impressionistic in its methods;

however, later work has generally recognized both the inevitability and the value of a subjective component in stylistic analysis. While the interest of literary criticism and, for the most part, stylistics, is in particular literary texts, modern poetics, which traces its roots to Russian Formalism (a movement in literary scholarship originating in Russia around 1915 and suppressed there about 1930), is instead interested in the question of the nature of literariness or poeticity. The study of poetics is closely related to the study of linguistics.

Besides application of the specific techniques and categories of one or another kind of linguistics for studying the language of literary texts, another kind of application of linguistics to the study of literature has been of great importance: Linguistics has been taken as a model for the study of literary structures, such as narrative, that are not intrinsically linguistic but are translatable into other media. Students of literature have identified constituents of such structures and formalized descriptive rules for their combination by analogy with linguists' descriptions of the structure of a language (*langue*). In thus adopting the structuralist approach derived from Saussure, literary critics have participated in a transdisciplinary movement affecting all the human sciences. A discussion of structuralism in literary studies, however, is outside the scope of this survey of linguistic approaches to poetry, which will be limited to applications of the techniques and categories of linguistic analysis to the language of poetic texts. Even within these limits, this survey does not purport to cover all the significant work. The contributions discussed below—which include both general, programmatic pieces and specific, descriptive studies—do not by any means represent all the important figures in the field or even the full range of relevant work by those cited; they are simply examples of various linguistic approaches to poetry from the early 1950's to the early 1980's.

BEGINNINGS

When, in 1951, the linguists George L. Trager and Henry Lee Smith, Jr., published *An Outline of English*

Structure, a description of English phonetics, morphology, and syntax such as had been made of many exotic languages, the linguist Harold Whitehall immediately saw the possibility of application to the study of English literature, and went so far as to say that "no criticism can go beyond its linguistics." Specifically, he saw that Trager and Smith's account of stress, pitch, and juncture—as each having four functionally distinguishable levels in English—would be valuable to students of meter and rhythm of English verse. The rhythm of lines could presumably be much more precisely described in terms of four levels of stress rather than in the two normally recognized in traditional metrics. Such an application of Trager and Smith's findings for modern American speech to the study of verse in English was actually made by Edmund L. Epstein and Terence Hawkes, who found in a body of iambic pentameter verse a vast number of different stress-patterns according to the four-level system. The question of the relevance of such descriptive analysis to the meaning and aesthetic value of the poetry in question was not raised in these early applications of linguistics to literature.

Archibald A. Hill, who did practical work in the application of linguistics to literature in the 1950's, saw linguistic analysis of a text in terms of such factors as word order and stress as operating on a preliterary level, but considered them to be a useful preliminary to analysis in terms of literary categories such as images. Not unlike the New Critics, he approached a poem as a structured whole and sought to interpret it with minimal reference to outside knowledge such as biographical information, but he differed from the New Critics in thinking it best to begin with specifically linguistic formal details. In a 1955 discussion of Gerard Manley Hopkins's "The Windhover" (wr. 1877, pb. 1918), Hill took an analysis of Hopkins's stress and word order, considered in relation to general English usage, as the basis for resolving ambiguities and determining emphases at particular points—and applied it, as an aid to interpretation of at least local meaning.

ROMAN JAKOBSON

In 1958, the Conference on Style was held at Indiana University, in which a group of linguists, literary critics, and psychologists presented and discussed papers on issues relevant to the matter of style in language. This conference, the papers of which were published in 1960 in a collection titled *Style in Language*, edited by Thomas A. Sebeok, proved to be something of a watershed for the application of linguistics to the study of poetry. Roman Jakobson's presentation on the relation of linguistics to poetics still remains a point of reference for work on the language of poetry. While the focus of the New Critics and some linguists working on literature was on the individual poem considered as an autonomous structured whole, the concern of poetics, as Jakobson sets it forth, is with the differentiating characteristics of poetic language. He argues that inasmuch as poetics deals with problems of verbal structure, it lies wholly within the field of linguistics, "the global science of verbal structure." He offers a functional definition of poetic language in terms of the constitutive factors of any act of verbal communication, enumerating six such factors—the addresser, the message, the addressee, the context, the contact between addresser and addressee, and the code (the rules of the language, also of a certain register, dialect, and so on) in accord with which the message is constructed. In any given utterance or text, focus will be on one of these factors primarily, though to a lesser extent on others, and the predominant function of the utterance or text can be defined accordingly. Jakobson defines the poetic function of language as "focus on the message for its own sake," stressing that the poetic function is not confined to poetry (appearing also, for example, in political slogans and advertising jingles) and that poetry involves functions of language other than the poetic; different genres, for example, are partially characterized by the relative importance of the referential, emotive, or conative (focus on the addressee) functions.

Contending that "the verbal structure of a message depends predominantly on [its] predominant function," Jakobson then studies the effect of the poetic function on the linguistic structure of a text. His famous account of the differentiating feature of language in which the poetic function predominates over the other functions depends on the fact that making an utterance or constructing a text always involves two operations: selection from among a series of items that are syntactically and semantically equivalent and the combination of the selected items into a meaningful sequence of words. "The poetic function," runs Jakobson's formulation, "projects the principle of equivalence from the axis of selection into the axis of combination." In verse, for example, every syllable becomes equivalent to every other syllable, every stress to every other stress, as units of measure. A passage of verse is characterized by the repetition of equivalent units.

Jakobson goes on to cite some of the kinds and operations of equivalence in a broad range of poetry of many different languages, in the process providing what amounts to a program for research on poetic language. All metrical systems, he says, use "at least one (or more than one) binary contrast of a relatively high and relatively low prominence"; he gives examples of meters "based only on the opposition of syllabic peaks and slopes (syllabic verse)," meters based "on the relative levels of the peaks (accentual verse)," and meters based "on the relative length of the syllabic peaks or entire syllables (quantitative verse)." Besides features invariably present in lines in a given meter, optional features will be likely to occur, and these, Jakobson maintains, form part of the metrical system to be described by the linguist. A full description should not, as traditional descriptions of meters typically do, exclude any linguistic feature of the verse design. Jakobson cites, as an example of a feature that ought not to be ignored, the "constitutive value of intonation in English meters," "the normal coincidence of syntactic pause and pausal intonation" with line-ending, such that, even when frequent, enjambment is felt as a variation.

Word boundaries and grammatical boundaries may also be among the defining characteristics of a line in a given verse tradition, even if such boundaries are not marked by any distinguishable phonetic features. (Jakobson does not specify a method for ascertaining that the enumeration of relevant features has been exhaustive.) What have generally been treated as deviations from a metrical pattern should, according to Jakobson, form part of the description of the pattern, for they are variations allowed by the rules of the given meter.

For rhyme as well as meter Jakobson emphasizes that linguistic analysis should not be limited to sound alone. The similarity of sound between rhyme words throws into relief their grammatical and semantic relations. Whether rhyme words are of the same or different grammatical classes, whether their syntactical functions are the same or different, whether they have a semantic relationship of similarity or antithesis, are all questions relevant to the operation of rhyme in the poetry in question. Poets and schools of poetry that use rhyme differ in favoring or opposing rhyming words of the same grammatical class and function, and grammatical rhymes operate differently from antigrammatical ones.

While repetition is an important aspect of the sound of poetry, a sound can be important, Jakobson points out, without being repeated: A sound with a single occurrence in a prominent position against a contrasting background and in a thematically important word should not be neglected. Analysis of the sound in poetry must take into account both the phonological structure of the language in question and which of the distinctive features of phonemes (voiced/voiceless, nasal/oral, and so on) are taken into account in the particular verse convention. Besides meter, rhyme, alliteration, and other forms of reiteration that are primarily of sound, though also involving syntactic and semantic aspects, poetic language is characterized by other forms of parallelism . For example, lines may be grammatically parallel, inviting semantic comparison between words in corresponding positions, which may be perceived as having a metaphorical or quasimetaphorical relationship. Concentration on lexical tropes to the exclusion of the syntactical aspect of poetic language is, according to Jakobson, not warranted:

> The poetic resources concealed in the morphological and syntactic structure of language, briefly the poetry of grammar, and its literary product, the grammar of poetry, have been seldom known to critics and mostly disregarded by linguists but skillfully mastered by creative writers.

MICHAEL RIFFATERRE

Jakobson asserted "the right and duty of linguistics to direct the investigation of verbal art in all its compass and extent," and provided a program for such research. At about the same time, Michael Riffaterre was concerning himself with the problem that a linguistic analysis of a poetic text could provide only a linguistic description of it and could not distinguish which of the features isolated were operative as part of the poem's style. In a 1959 paper, "Criteria for Style Analysis," he endeavored to supply a technique for distinguishing stylistic features of a text from merely linguistic features without stylistic function.

Riffaterre's argument is based on the dual assumption—diametrically opposed to Jakobson's notion of the nature of poetic language—that the literary artist works to ensure the communication of his or her meaning, and that this end can be achieved through reduction of the predictability of elements, so that the reader's natural tendency to interpolate elements that seem predictable from the context will be frustrated, and he or she will be held up and forced to attend to unpredictable elements. The linguistic elements that are to be taken into account in the stylistic analysis of a literary work are precisely these unpredictable elements, which Riffaterre calls stylistic devices or SD's.

While Riffaterre is apparently confident of the efficacy of this means for getting reader-attention, at least one investigator of style in poetry (Anne Cluysenaar) cites an instance in which readers failed to notice an unpredictable phrase, simply substituting what they would have expected for what was actually there in the text. Not content that the analyst of style should rely simply on his own subjective impressions as to the location of stylistic devices in a literary text, Riffaterre recommends the use of informants, readers of the text in question, including critics and editors of the text as well as lay readers. In using informants' responses, the analyst of style should, according to Riffaterre, empty them of such content as value judgments and take them as mere indicators of possible sites of stylistic devices. The resultant enumeration should then be verified, by checking whether the points identified coincide with points where a pattern established by a preceding stretch of text has been broken; if so, they are stylistic devices and should be submitted to linguistic analysis by the stylistician.

In choosing to compare parts of a given text with each other, Riffaterre departed from the practice, become common at the time, of taking ordinary language—a very vague entity—as a norm with which to compare the text. His examples show, however, that he has not been able to dispense altogether with reference to language usage outside the text in question, for items can be interpreted as unpredictable in a given context only with respect to knowledge or experience of usage in a similar context elsewhere. Besides the fact of departure from a pattern established by a preceding stretch of text, another phenomenon can, according to Riffaterre, help confirm the identification of a stylistic device: This is the presence of a cluster of independent stylistic devices, which together highlight a particular passage.

In a well-known paper published in *Yale French Studies* in 1966, Riffaterre assesses an analysis by Jakobson and Claude Lévi-Strauss of the poem "Les Chats" (1847; *The Cats*, 1955) of Charles Baudelaire. Jakobson and Lévi-Strauss had scanned the text on several levels—meter, phonology, grammar, and meaning—discovering equivalences of various kinds, which they took as constitutive of several simultaneous structural divisions of the poem. Riffaterre contends that many of the linguistic equivalences they identify cannot be taken as stylistic features, as elements of the poetic structure, because they would not be perceived in the process of reading. Only such equivalences as would be perceptible should be taken as pertaining to the poetic structure of the text. Equivalences on one level alone generally will not be perceived as correspondences; grammatical parallelism, for example, will need to be reinforced by correspondence in metrical position.

TRANSFORMATIONAL-GENERATIVE GRAMMAR

With the development of transformational-generative grammar by Noam Chomsky and others, beginning with Chomsky's 1957 book *Syntactic Structures*, came new kinds of linguistic approaches to literature. The theory of transformational-generative grammar is based on the assumption that native speakers of a language internalize grammatical rules for their language such that they are able to produce unlimited numbers of grammatical sentences they have never heard before and to judge a given sentence as grammatical or ungrammatical (or as more or less grammatical, more or less complex).

There is the further assumption that the grammar should reflect native speaker intuitions of relation between superficially different sentences, as between a given declarative sentence in the active voice and its passivization, and of ambiguity as to the construction of certain sentences: In the former case, the superficially different sentences are taken as having the same "deep structure"; in the latter, the surface structure of the given sentence is taken as able to have been reached by two or more different routes, from two or more different deep structures. A transformational-generative grammar of a given language ideally consists of an ordered set of rules for the generation of all possible grammatical sentences in the language; besides phrase-structure rules, it includes ordered series of obligatory and optional transformational rules that transform an underlying "kernel sentence" or set of kernel sentences into a surface structure.

The surface structure/deep structure distinction was taken, in early efforts at the application of transformational-generative grammar to the study of literary texts such as Richard Ohmann's, as a confirmation and clarification of the traditional distinction between form and content. A writer's style could be accounted for by the nature of the optional transformations he chose. Ohmann adheres to the position of early transformational-generative theory that different surface structures produced by the choice of different optional transformations have the same content, but he contradicts himself when he says that each writer will make characteristic choices and that these choices correlate with the writer's way of looking at experience. Likewise, regarding deviance in poetic language from usage restrictions on categories of words, he holds that the kinds of deviance employed by a poet will reflect his or her vision; the kinds of deviance found in Dylan Thomas's poetry, Ohmann suggests, reflect his sense of nature as personal, the world as process.

One of the first linguists to apply transformational-generative grammar to the study of style in poetry was Samuel Levin. Levin was interested in the fact that poetry contains sentences and phrases that a native speaker might consider ungrammatical or semigrammatical. In a 1965 paper called "Internal and External Deviation in Poetry," he takes external deviation in syntax, that is, deviation from a norm of syntactical usage lying outside the text in question, as ungrammaticality; in other words, he assumes that it involves sentences that the grammar of the language in question would not generate. Among such sentences he recognizes degrees of deviance or ungrammaticality. He does not find the notion of the probability of a given element at a given point in the text (transitional probability) helpful in rationalizing this sense of degrees of deviance because of the unfeasibility of calculating transitional probabilities for the occurrence of a given word after a given sequence of preceding words. His approach is to determine what kinds of changes would have to be made in the rules of the grammar to make it generate the deviant sentences or phrases, assuming that it does not do so. These would be deemed more or less grammatical depending on the number of ungrammatical sentences that the changes entailed would generate.

In the case of a phrase such as E. E. Cummings's "anyone lived in a pretty how town" (1940), the number of ungrammatical sentences would be large, since either "how" would have to be added to the class of adjectives, or adverbs would have to be allowed to occur in the place of the second adjective in the sequence determiner plus adjective plus adjective plus noun, changes involving large classes. In the case of Thomas's phrase, "Rage me back," however, "rage" would simply have to be added to the subclass of transitive verbs taking "back" (mostly verbs of motion). Hence, the Cummings example is less grammatical than the example of Thomas. In like manner, the Thomas example produces a sense of richness through the conflation of the verb "rage" with notions of transitivity and motion, while Cummings's phrase leaves a sense of diffuseness because what is added to "how" is so unspecific. Levin notes that the former kind of ungrammaticality occurs more frequently than the latter in poetry and considers it akin to metaphor in its operation.

J. P. Thorne shares Levin's interest in the occurrence in poetry of sentences that would not be generated by the grammar; indeed, he says at one point that such sentences form the subject matter of stylistics. Where Levin takes single sentences and phrases from poetry and considers how the grammar would have to be modified to generate each sentence, however, Thorne proposes taking whole poems and constructing a grammar for the language of each poem. The grammar for a poem should be constructed on the same principles as the grammar for the language as a whole, the point being to compare the two and discover how the one differs from the other. A good poet, in Thorne's view, will invent a new language, differing from the standard language not (or not primarily) in surface structure, but in deep structure, that is, on the level of meaning. The poet will invent a new language to be able to say things that cannot be said in the standard language. In reading a good poem, the reader learns a new language. The grammar that one constructs for this new language will make explicit one's intuitions about its structure. One must decide which features of the poem's language are features of that language and which are features merely of the sample, when the sample (the poem) is all of the language there is. One's assignments of words to categories in this grammar and formulation of selection rules for their co-occurrence will reflect one's interpretation of the poem.

In a 1965 paper, "Stylistics and Generative Grammars," Thorne sketches a grammar for Cummings's poem "anyone lived in a pretty how town." Thorne also suggests that it may be illuminating to construct grammars for poems in which the language does not seem so manifestly ungrammatical, such as John Donne's "A Nocturnal upon St. Lucy's Day" (1633), where animate subjects have verbs normally selected by inanimate subjects, and inanimate subjects have verbs normally selected only by animate subjects. In a 1970 paper, "Generative Grammar and Stylistic Analysis," Thorne finds a similar deviation from the selection rules for Standard English in Theodore Roethke's poem "Dolor" (1943), where there are constructions such as "the sadness of pencils," which attach to concrete, inanimate nouns adjectives that normally select animate nouns or a subcategory of abstract nouns including "experience" and "occasion"; he points out that the decision whether to assimilate "pencils" and the other nouns so used in the poem to the category of animate nouns or to the particular subcategory of abstract nouns will depend on how one reads the poem.

Early efforts at applying transformational-generative grammar to literature have been recognized as limited by (1) the theory's separation of syntax from semantics (that is, of consideration of sentence structure from questions of meaning); (2) the assumption in early versions of the theory that the transformations that produced different surface structures from a single underlying structure did not affect the meaning; (3) the failure to extend analysis beyond the level of the sentence; and (4) the treatment of literary (especially poetic) language as characterized by ungrammatical constructions, deviations from the supposed norm of everyday speech. With these limitations, transformational-generative grammar could not illuminate the relation between form and content in poetry or relate formal description to interpretation. It did not offer a means of discussing the connections within and cohesiveness of a text as a whole. It had nothing to say about poetry in which the language was not in any sense ungrammatical. Much of the irritation of literary critics with early applications of transformational-generative grammar to literature is attributable to limitations in the applications resulting from limitations in the early versions of the theory.

CATEGORY-SCALE GRAMMAR

Besides transformational-generative grammar, other modes of syntactical analysis developed by modern linguistics have been used in approaches to poetry. One of these is category-scale grammar, developed by M. A. K. Halliday and set forth in his 1961 paper "Categories of the Theory of Grammar." Category-scale grammar analyzes English syntax in terms of a hierarchically ordered enumeration or "rank-scale" of units: sentence, clause, group, word, morpheme. Halliday introduces the notion of rank-shift to refer to cases where a unit operates as a structural member of a unit of the same or lower rank; for example, a clause can be part of another clause or of a group (phrase). Category-scale grammar has been commended to students of literary style as making possible a clear and accurate description of the infrastructuring of the language and helping to discover and specify where the structural complexity of a text resides. Halliday himself has advocated the linguistic study of literary texts, arguing that this should be a comparative study and that it is not enough to discover, say, the kinds of clause structures in a given text, but that their relative frequencies in that text should then be compared with those in other texts, other samples of the language.

In a 1964 paper, Halliday illustrates the sort of treatment he recommends with a discussion of two features of the language of William Butler Yeats's "Leda and the Swan" (1928)—the use of "the" and the forms and nature of the verbs. "The" is a deictic (a word that points to or identifies); its particular function is to identify a specific subset, by reference to the context (either of the text itself or of the situation of its utterance), to elements of the rest of the modifier or of the qualifier of the noun it modifies, or to the noun modified itself. In nominal groups where there are other modifying elements preceding the noun or a qualifier following it, "the" usually (in samples of modern English prose referred to by Halliday) specifies by reference to the rest of the modifier or the qualifier. While "Leda and the Swan" has a high proportion of such nominal groups in comparison with another Yeats poem, in only one of them does "the" function in the usual way; in all the rest it specifies by reference not to anything else in the nominal group, but to the title. "Leda and the Swan" is also found to differ markedly in the handling of verbs from both another Yeats poem and a poem by Alfred, Lord Tennyson. A high proportion of verbs, including especially the lexically more powerful, are "deverbalized" by occurring as participles in bound or rank-shifted clauses or as modifiers of a noun (rather than as finite verbs in free clauses).

John Sinclair's 1966 paper "Taking a Poem to Pieces" is the sort of analysis recommended by Halliday. Further, it represents an effort to remedy linguists' neglect of poetry in which the language is not describable as ungrammatical or deviant. Sinclair hypothesizes that even in poetry, where the language is apparently unremarkable, grammatical and other linguistic patterns are operating in a more complex way than could be described—or even perceived—with traditional terms. He uses the terms of category-scale grammar to describe the language of a short poem by Philip Larkin called "First Sight" (1956).

Beginning with the highest unit of syntax, the sentence, Sinclair sets forth the syntactical structure of Larkin's text: first the sentence structure (the nature and arrangement of the constituent clauses), then the clause structure (the nature and arrangement of the constituent groups and rank-shifted clauses), then the structure of the groups (the arrangement and relations of the constituent words and rank-shifted higher structures). He shows that the language of Larkin's poems represents a restricted selection from among the wide range of possibilities afforded by the language. Its stylistic character can be in part accounted for by the persistent selection of certain constructions normally occurring with lower frequency.

It is on the level of the clausal constitution of its sentences that Larkin finds the particular quality of the language of "First Sight" to lie. In what he calls everyday English, in sentences that contain a free clause and a bound clause, the most common arrangement is an uninterrupted free clause followed by a bound clause; discontinuous structure (that is, a free clause interrupted by a bound clause) and the sequence of bound clause followed by free clause are both less common. Of the four sentences in Larkin's poem, only the last has the generally most common arrangement of free clause followed by bound clause. Thus, while this poem's language is not deviant in such a way as to require a special grammar to describe it, it is distinguished by the relative frequency of certain otherwise unremarkable structures.

In a 1972 paper, "Lines About 'Lines,'" Sinclair attempts to integrate stylistic description with interpretation and develop theoretical principles and a methodology for stylistic analysis. He assumes that the analyst must begin with a critical understanding of the text; then look for patterns at successive levels; in each case where a pattern is found, relate it to the meaning; and finally synthesize the findings of form-meaning relationships. Sinclair hypothesizes that there will be "intersection points" of form and meaning and adopts the term "focusing categories" or "focats" for such points. The focats found in the analysis of a given text will be initially taken as pertaining to that text alone, but assumed to be general if subsequently encountered in numerous texts.

In this case, Sinclair takes as his example for analysis William Wordsworth's famous "Tintern Abbey" (1798). He finds two focats operative in the poem. One, the introduction of an optional element in a syntactical structure not yet complete, he calls arrest. The other, which he calls extension, is essentially the continuation of a potentially completed structure by an element not syntactically predictable from any of the preceding elements. Sinclair argues convincingly that arrest and extension do indeed represent instances of significant interrelation of formal structure and meaning in "Tintern Abbey." These two focats also seem to be likely candidates for generality (occurrence in numerous texts).

GENERATIVE METRICS

Many of the examples of linguistic approaches to poetry so far considered here have been studies of the language, especially the syntax, of individual poems. Besides focusing on individual texts, however, linguists have also addressed themselves to more general phenomena of poetic language, such as meter and metaphor.

Beginning with a 1966 paper by Morris Halle and Samuel Jay Keyser, a generative metrics was developed, devoted almost exclusively to accentual-syllabic verse, principally iambic pentameter. Halle and Keyser draw an analogy between the native speaker of a language, who has internalized a set of logically ordered rules in accord with which he or she produces grammatical sentences, and the poet, whom they assume to have similarly internalized a set of rules in accord with which he or she produces metrical lines. Generative metrics does away with the notion of the metrical foot and replaces the hodgepodge of rules and exceptions of traditional metrics with a brief and ordered sequence of systematically related rules. This sequence of rules governs the realization of an abstract pattern in an actual text. The pattern is represented as consisting of positions rather than feet, each position corresponding to a single syllable. The rules for actualization of the pattern are presented as alternatives arranged in an order from least to greatest metrical "complexity" (greatest to least strictness).

DAVID CRYSTAL: TONE-UNITS

A very different approach to metrics has been taken by the British linguist David Crystal, who, in a 1971 paper, proposed a model for the description of English verse that is supposed to encompass both accentual-syllabic and free verse and to distinguish both from prose. He takes the line, rather than the syllable or the foot, as the basic unit of verse, and hypothesizes that the line normally consists, in performance, of a single complete "tone-unit." A tone-unit is the basic unit of organization of intonation in an utterance; since intonation functions in part to signal syntactical relations, tone-unit boundaries coincide with syntactical—generally clause—boundaries.

SPEECH ACT THEORY

Transformationalists have approached metaphor as deviance through violation of selection restriction rules (rules formalizing acceptable collocations—for example, that for verbs with certain semantic features the subject must be animate). One interprets metaphors, according to this view (espoused, for example, by Robert J. Matthews in a 1971 paper), by deemphasizing those semantic features entailed in the selection restriction violation.

In the 1970's and 1980's, there was a growing recognition that properties such as metaphoricity, previously assumed to be peculiar to literary language, pertain as well to conversational usage; also, not only the formal features of a text but also the situational context and the speaker-hearer (or writer-reader) relationship were now seen as relevant to its operation.

Growing interest in speech act theory (developed by J. L. Austin and John R. Searle) is a reflection of the concern for context-sensitive analysis of utterances or texts. According to speech act theory, besides performing a locutionary act (that is, producing a grammatical utterance), a speaker will perform one or another kind of illocutionary act (such as asserting, ordering, promising) and possibly a perlocutionary act (that is, bringing about a certain state in the hearer). Besides being grammatical or ungrammatical, an utterance will be appropriate or inappropriate in the given situation; appropriateness conditions—internalized rules of language use that speakers assume to be in force—can be formulated.

While the Austinian treatment of appropriateness conditions is to define them in relation to particular speech acts in particular contexts, H. Paul Grice has generalized the notion of appropriateness, developing rules intended to apply to all discourse. His cooperative principle, which a participant in a speech exchange supposedly will normally assume his or her interlocutor to know and to be trying to observe and expecting him or her to observe also, is "Make your conversational contribution such as is required, at the stage at which it occurs, by the accepted purpose or direction of the talk-exchange in which you are engaged." At the same time, linguists have been extending the purview of their discipline in ways that bring it into close accord with speech act philosophy. Since 1968, post-Chomskyan generative semantics (as developed by George Lakoff, Robin Lakoff, Charles Fillmore, and others) has extended the notion of speaker competence to embrace the ability to perform appropriate speech acts in particular situations, as well as phonology and syntax. In addition, sociolinguists are concerned with language use.

How do these developments in linguistics and allied fields relate to the study of literature, particularly poetry? Mary Louise Pratt claims (in *Toward a Speech Act Theory of Literary Discourse*, 1977) that, with these developments, linguistics is for the first time able to describe literary discourse in terms of the literary speech situation, to define it in terms of use rather than of intrinsic features, and to relate it to other kinds of language use. She cites studies showing that features assumed by poeticians to be exclusively attributes of literary discourse occur in conversation as well; specifically, structural and stylistic features such as are found in fiction also occur in "natural narratives." These formal similarities, she thinks, can be in part explained by the fact that with both natural narratives and literary works, the speech exchange situation is one in which the hearer or reader is a voluntary, nonparticipant audience. She also considers it important to take into account that the reader normally knows that a literary work was, and was intended to be, published, and assumes it was composed in writing with an opportunity for deliberation, hence that it is more likely to be worthwhile than casual utterances; because of these assumptions on the part of the reader, a literary work can get away with being "difficult," and with making considerable demands on its audience.

Pratt attempts to adapt the categories of speech act theorists to accommodate literary discourse and relate it to other kinds of speech acts. She considers that many, if not all, literary works, together with exclamations and natural narratives, fall into the class of speech acts that have been characterized as thought-producing (as opposed to action-producing), representative (representing a state of affairs), or world-describing (as opposed to world-changing). She sees exclamations, natural narratives, and literary works together as constituting a subclass of representative speech acts that are characterized by "tellability," that is, by the unlikelihood or problematical nature of the state of affairs represented (whether fictional or not). This characteristic she holds to pertain as much to lyric poetry as to novels and short stories. The subclass is further characterized by (1) detachability from any immediate speech context (this is obvious for literary works, which generally have no immediate relation to the situation in which the reader happens to find him- or herself) and (2) a tendency to elaborate on the state of affairs represented. Indeed, Pratt suggests that this elaboration is what literary works chiefly do.

SOCIOLINGUISTICS

Roger Fowler, a British linguist, advocated and practiced the application of linguistics to the study of literary texts since the 1960's; his early work in this field includes a paper (published in the 1966 collection *Essays on Style and Language*, which he edited) showing, with a rich variety of examples, that verse of a given meter can have very different rhythmical movements, depending on the relationships of the grammatical units with the lineation. In his 1981 volume *Literature as Social Discourse: The Practice of Linguistic Criticism*, Fowler argues that linguistic description of literary texts should concern itself with the sociocultural context. He exemplifies the sort of description, essentially sociolinguistic, that he advocates in a treatment (in the same volume) of Wordsworth's poem "Yew-Tree" (1798).

Fowler's treatment is in answer to a reading of this poem by critic Riffaterre. Riffaterre concentrates on the lexical aspect of the poem's language, showing that it consists basically of variations on "yew-tree" through translation of certain of its semantic components from "tree-code" into other codes—for example, "snake-code" in the lines, "Huge trunks! and each particular trunk a growth/ Of intertwisted fibres serpentine/ Upcoiling, and inveterately convolved." Fowler contends that by neglecting the matters of register (and what it implies of the activity of the speaker of the poem vis-à-vis an addressee) and of the reader's sequential experience of the text, Riffaterre has failed to give sufficient weight to the shift from a geographical guide register to Miltonic loftiness in these lines. This and other shifts of register in the poem are, he contends, significant, central to its meaning.

NEW DIRECTIONS

Besides speech act theory and sociolinguistics, later work on the development of a linguistic theory of discourse saw applications to literature. Teun A. van Dijk, for example, has done work on a grammar taking the text, rather than the sentence, as the structure to be described, and including a "pragmatic" component that would specify appropriateness conditions for discourses.

BIBLIOGRAPHY

Carter, Ronald, ed. *Language and Literature: An Introductory Reader in Stylistics*. 1982. New ed. New York: Routledge, 1991. Chapters in this important study include "Systemic Grammar and Its Use in Literary Analysis" by Chris Kennedy and "Stylistics and the Teaching of Literature" by M. H. Short.

Dijk, Teun A. van. *Discourse Studies*. 5 vols. Thousand Oaks, Calif.: Sage, 2008. This classic study examines the major fields of discourse studies, including grammar, stylistics, conversation analysis, narrative analysis, argumentation, psychology of comprehension, ethnography of speaking, and media.

Searle, John R. *Expression and Meaning: Studies in the Theory of Speech Acts*. 1979. Reprint. New York: Cambridge University Press, 2008. An updated follow up to Searle's classic work, *Speech Acts* (1969). In this later study, Searle extends his speech-acts analysis and also examines "the relation between the meanings of sentences and the contexts of their utterance."

_____. *Speech Acts: An Essay in the Philosophy of Language*. 1969. Reprint. New York: Cambridge University Press, 1977. Searle's classic work in the philosophy of language. This study further develops the foundational work of J. L. Austin, *How to Do Things with Words* (1962).

Toolan, Michael. *Narrative: A Critical Linguistic Introduction*. 2d ed. New York: Routledge, 2001. Asks and analyzes such questions as "What is narrative?" and "What do we mean by 'narrative structure.'" Includes bibliography and index.

Weber, Jean Jacques, ed. *The Stylistics Reader: From Roman Jakobson to the Present*. 1996. Reprint. New York: St. Martin's Press, 1998. This study "documents the significant impact of linguistic theory on literary studies," featuring essays on formalist, functionalist, affective, pedagogical, pragmatic, critical, feminist, and cognitive approaches in stylistics.

Eleanor von Auw Berry

MARXIST CRITICISM

Marxist criticism uses the terms and tools of Marxist philosophy to explain the production and meaning of literature. Based on the writings of Karl Marx and Friedrich Engels from the middle of the nineteenth century, Marxist criticism flourished in the 1920's and 1930's (Vladimir I. Lenin, Leon Trotsky, and Mao Zedong all wrote on literature) and was refined after World War II using more sophisticated poststructuralist theory and the rediscovered writings of Georg Lukács, Walter Benjamin, Mikhail Bakhtin, Antonio Gramsci, and other European critics.

Marx and Engels left no systematic study of literature, although they both discussed literature extensively in reviews and letters. Later critics have built their theory on Marx and Engels's understanding of the crucial roles of social class and class struggle in every phase of human history, and the interdependence of the socioeconomic foundations or "base" of any society and its "superstructure" of law, religion, art, and other manifestations of culture and civilization. In Marxist criticism, social class is a key determining factor. An understanding of medieval poetry, for example, might start with the aristocratic and feudal class structure of that society. History is the story of the struggles between social classes—in modern times, and in Western culture, between a dominant bourgeoisie and an emerging proletariat. Literature, like all cultural products, plays a role in that struggle, whether the makers of literature are aware of that role or not.

Given such sweeping historical and political views, it is not surprising that Marxist criticism is often best at explaining larger literary movements: for example, how the development of the novel followed the emergence of the middle class (and thus increased leisure time for reading) in the eighteenth century; the rise of modernism in Anglo-American literature at the beginning of the twentieth century; or the function of a literary canon in any culture. Marxist criticism may be closest in practice to sociological criticism, in its study, for example, of the actual social conditions and relations that produce works of art; to New Historicism, in the understanding of the layers of meaning in any society; and to feminist criticism, because both feminist and Marxist criticism challenges power structures—feminist critics usually in the name of gender issues and Marxists more generally in terms of social class. All four of these critical schools have come to be subsumed by the end of the twentieth century under what is usually called cultural studies, and many contemporary literary critics use analytical tools from all four, especially in speaking about issues of race, gender, and social class in literary works and movements.

The Marxist critic is best at showing the important role that ideology plays in any literary work. "Ideology" is the term used to identify the shared beliefs and values held by any particular culture, and one of its functions, as the British critic Terry Eagleton has defined it, "is to legitimate the power of the ruling class in society; in the last analysis, the dominant ideas of a society are the ideas of its ruling class." Marxist critics attempt to identify the key ideological concepts at play in any work (the anti-Semitism and bizarre economic views of the American poet Ezra Pound in the 1930's, for example) at the same time that they try to avoid reductive critical interpretations (for example, that those horrific political views must necessarily cripple the poetry he produced in that period). Since all literature is finally ideological—even when the author denies it—the task of the Marxist critic is to evaluate a literary work in part as the transcription of a complex reaction among a writer and the prevailing material conditions, class relations, and dominant values of that writer's world. This Marxist literary practice—particularly the use of ideological analysis—has become influential on nearly all other critical disciplines.

EMERGENCE OF POETRY

Given its interest in larger socioliterary movements and its belief in the interdependent relationship between literature and society, it is not surprising that much earlier Marxist criticism focused not on individual poems, but on the emergence of poetry as a literary genre. One of the first full-length studies of the origins of poetry was Christopher Caudwell's *Illusion and Reality: A Study of the Sources of Poetry* (1937), in which the young British Marxist, who died fighting in the Spanish Civil War near the time his book was published, mixed insights into the sources of poetry with some rather crude analyses. George Thomson was a major disciple of Caudwell, and his *Marxism and Poetry* (1945) was a much more developed study that argued the organic relationships between work and consciousness, between inspiration and collective expression. Even the rhythm of poetry, Thomson argued, could finally be traced to the use of tools in work.

Probably the best study of the origins of poetry appeared in the Austrian critic Ernst Fischer's *Von der Notwendigkeit der Kunst* (1959; *The Necessity of Art: A Marxist Approach*, 1963), which describes the history of the arts from a Marxist perspective and includes, in its analysis of everything from the collective origins of art to the modern conditions of alienation and mystification, a number of poetry topics, including William Shakespeare and the Romantic poets. (See "The world and language of poetry," in Fischer's chapter "Content and Form.") A similarly valuable work a few years later was Raymond Williams's study of English literature that touches on various poets and poetic forms over thousands of years. Fischer and Williams proved how valuable Marxism could be in exploring the complex and symbiotic relationship between art and literature (including poetry), on one hand, and the societies out of which they came, on the other.

THEORIES OF POETIC FORM

The development of theories of poetic form, beyond the study of the emergence of poetry as a genre, began around the mid-twentieth century. The prolific American critic Margaret Schlauch wrote *Modern English and American Poetry: Techniques and Ideologies* (1956), which illustrated, as much as anything, the multiple pressures Marxist criticism suffered during the Cold War years between 1947 and 1991. A few years later, however, Peter Demetz published *Marx, Engels, und die Dichter: Zur Grundlagenforschung des Marxismus* (1959; *Marx, Engels, and the Poets: Origins of Marxist Literary Criticism*, 1967), which established the interest in poetry the founders of Marxism had, looking in particular at Marx and Engels's comments on Shakespeare, Johann Wolfgang von Goethe,

and Honoré de Balzac. Henri Arvon's *L'Esthéthique marxiste* (1970; *Marxist Esthetics*, 1973) firmly established the importance of formal questions in Marxist criticism, and the following year, Fredric Jameson published his groundbreaking *Marxism and Form: Twentieth-Century Dialectical Theories of Literature* (1971), a work that would have a profound influence, not only on Marxist critics but also on much poststructuralist criticism as well. Drawing on the twentieth century Marxist theory of Theodor Adorno, Benjamin, Herbert Marcuse, Ernst Bloch, Jean-Paul Sartre, and other critics, Jameson developed what he called a dialectical criticism. Jameson established the primacy of theoretical and formal issues in Marxist criticism. Dismissing earlier crude and reductive Marxist practice, Jameson built an aesthetic theory that was sophisticated (if at times difficult to understand) and that built on the best of his European models.

Another important Marxist theorist has been Eagleton, who, in a dozen books in the last quarter of the twentieth century, incorporated the theory of Pierre Macherey, Adorno, and other critics to create a poststructuralist Marxist criticism that is both theoretically supple and capable of dealing with a wide range of literature, including poetry. Eagleton's best works include *Criticism and Ideology: A Study in Marxist Literary Theory* (1976), *Marxism and Literary Criticism* (1976), and *Literary Theory: An Introduction* (1983).

The Marxist study of individual poems operates of course under the same requirements as any critical approach and often begins by resembling formalist criticism—that is, by trying to understand the particular pattern of words, lines, and stanzas that make up the poem, and the structure of its meaning. Only after this kind of formal analysis has been completed (or at least acknowledged) does the Marxist critic turn to the larger ideological questions that tend to define the discipline to produce the distinctive analyses Marxist criticism can make.

POETRY AND IDEOLOGY

Rarely does literature reveal its own ideological biases, but older poetry tends to give them up more easily than contemporary verse. In 1839, for example, the American Henry Wadsworth Longfellow published "A Psalm of Life," and this hymn of faith and courage

("Life is real! Life is earnest!/ And the grave is not its goal") was to become one of the most popular poems in the English language over the next century, with its famous concluding stanza, "Let us, then, be up and doing,/ With a heart for any fate;/ Still achieving, still pursuing,/ Learn to labor and to wait." Viewing the poem in terms of its ideological content, the Marxist critic would be able to link the poem's values to an emergent industrial capitalism in the first half of the nineteenth century, for the poem was clearly encouraging the development of a work ethic needed in the textile mills of New England, as elsewhere.

Forty years later, Eliza Cook, in a poem titled "Work" that appeared in *McGuffey's Fifth Eclectic Reader* in 1879, urged, "Work, work, my boy, be not afraid;/ Look labor boldly in the face;/ Take up the hammer or the spade,/ And blush not for your humble place." This might strike the modern reader as a rather crude job-recruitment poster for child labor, but by the twentieth century, such blatant hymns to work would be harder to find. More common might be a poem like "The Golf Links" (1917), where Sarah N. Cleghorn could write, with much irony, "The golf links lie so near the mill/ That almost every day/ The laboring children can look out/ And see the men at play." Here social classes and the tensions between them are revealed, and the inequities that gap signifies are made the subject of the poem, heightened by the incongruous inversion of roles (boys working, adults playing). The ideological assumptions of Longfellow and Cook and other earlier American writers have been turned on their heads in Cleghorn's poem, to reveal what an unchecked industrial capitalism had become by the end of the nineteenth century—and how few good writers can any longer subscribe to its values.

Even narrative poetry is ideological, according to the precepts of Marxist criticism. In one of the most popular poems produced at the end of the nineteenth century, the American Edward Rowland Sill (in imitation of his master, the British Victorian poet Alfred, Lord Tennyson) could create the heroic battle scene depicted in "Opportunity" (1880), in which, in a dream, the narrator sees the troops of the "Prince" forced back in a "furious battle." A cowardly foot soldier compares his plight to that of the prince—"Had I a sword of keener steel—/ That blue blade that the king's son bears"—throws away his sword, "And lowering crept away and left the field":

> Then came the king's son, wounded, sore bestead,
> And weaponless, and saw the broken sword,
> Hilt-buried in the dry and trodden sand,
> And ran and snatched it, and with battle-shout
> Lifted afresh he hewed his enemy down,
> And saved a great cause that heroic day.

Translated into the socioeconomic conditions of the late nineteenth century, this heroic narrative clearly becomes a cry of encouragement to the working masses: Take your "opportunity" while you can, and ignore the horribly inequitable conditions around you. The poem urges workers to apply themselves in spite of class differences and working conditions: Do not aspire, the poem argues: instead, perspire. Clearly, these are the values of a dominant capitalist class, which needs a willing proletarian workforce to operate its machines; the fewer complaints, the better the machines will run. Late nineteenth century American poetry is filled with such encouragements to those toiling in mill and mine. Like the Horatio Alger myth circulating through dime novels, or Russell Conwell's lecture "Acres of Diamonds," delivered thousands of times during the same period, the values of the author of "Opportunity" and other poets—like their belief in the work ethic—came from the dominant ideology of a capitalist ruling class. Poetry is never free of ideology, the Marxist critic argues; here, at the end of the nineteenth century and before the advent of labor unions and other protections for workers, it was in full display.

It is more difficult of course to do this kind of Marxist analysis with poetry at the beginning of the twenty-first century (because reader, poet, and critic are all part of the same ideological moment), but the Marxist critic strives to do something similar with any poem: to recognize its formal structures—the patterns of sound and meaning that make up the totality of the poem—but also to go beyond and beneath these structures to uncover the underlying ideological values and assumptions out of which this poem has emerged. Such an analysis demands sensitivity to formal questions, but additionally it demands an awareness of the role that class values and ideals, along with the assumptions and stereotypes of race and gender, play in any society.

BIBLIOGRAPHY

Eagleton, Terry. *Marxism and Literary Criticism*. 2d ed. New York: Routledge, 2002. A cogent summary of the major areas of present-day Marxist criticism. Includes a new preface by the author. First published 1976.

Eagleton, Terry, and Drew Milne, eds. *Marxist Literary Theory: A Reader*. Cambridge, Mass.: Blackwell, 1996. An extensive collection of principal texts in the Marxist literary tradition. An introduction by Eagleton traces the evolution of Marxist criticism and speculates as to its future. In a second introduction, Milne examines the relationship between Marx's writings and the Marxist movement.

Goldstein, Philip. *The Politics of Literary Theory: An Introduction to Marxist Criticism*. Tallahassee: Florida State University Press, 1990. A comprehensive overview of both Marxist theory and opposed critical theories, from the New Criticism of Cleanth Brooks and René Wellek; through those of feminism, reader-response, Raymond Williams, and Fredric Jameson; to recent "Marxist versions of deconstruction" (Eagleton, Michael Ryan, Gayatri Chakravorty Spivak).

Haslett, Moyra. *Marxist Literary and Cultural Theories*. New York: St. Martin's Press, 2000. Divided into two parts, "Key Theories" and "Applications and Readings." The second section includes the long chapter "A Labouring Woman Poet in the Age of Pope: Mary Leapor's 'Crumble-Hall'" (1751), which propounds a Marxist reading of this eighteenth century poem. An annotated bibliography describes sixteen seminal Marxist theoretical works, including volumes by Eagleton, Jameson, and Williams.

Jameson, Fredric. *Marxism and Form: Twentieth-Century Dialectical Theories of Literature*. Princeton, N.J.: Princeton University Press, 1971. This work established Marxist aesthetics as a legitimate form of poststructuralist literary theory. Includes chapters on Theodor Adorno, "Versions of a Marxist Hermeneutic"; Georg Lukács; and Jean-Paul Sartre, and ends with the essay "Towards Dialectical Criticism," which attempts to build a modern Hegelian model for literary criticism.

Klages, Mary. *Literary Theory: A Guide for the Perplexed*. New York: Continuum, 2007. A general introduction to literary theory, including Marxist literary criticism and theory, for students new to the field.

Leitch, Vincent B. "Marxist Criticism in the 1930's." In *American Literary Criticism Since the 1930's*. 2d ed. New York: Routledge, 2010. Leitch explores, among other topics in American literary criticism, the world of Marxist literary criticism in the 1930's in the United States.

Paananen, Victor, ed. *British Marxist Criticism*. New York: Garland, 2000. Part of the Wellesley Studies in Critical Theory, Literary History, and Culture series. Contains major works by eight British Marxist critics, each preceded by an introductory essay. Includes separate annotated bibliographies.

Puchner, Martin. *Poetry of the Revolution: Marx, Manifestos, and the Avant-Gardes*. Princeton, N.J.: Princeton University Press, 2006. Shows how Marxism and Marxist views of art and literature evolved from one manifesto to the next, culminating in the avant-garde movement, which the author argues may retain its vigor, if in a somewhat different form. Illustrated. Bibliographical references and index.

Venuti, Lawrence. *Our Halcyon Dayes: English Prerevolutionary Texts and Postmodern Culture*. Madison: University of Wisconsin Press, 1989. Venuti's study is "a Marxist intervention into Renaissance studies" that includes the chapter "Cavalier Love Poetry and Caroline Court Culture," in which Thomas Carew, Richard Lovelace, John Suckling, Ben Jonson, and other period poets are examined in detail.

Williams, Raymond. *The Country and the City*. 1973. Reprint. London: Hogarth Press, 1993. A classic study of country and city as subject and theme in literature from Andrew Marvell to D. H. Lawrence. Also a nostalgia and a polemic against a "loss of the organic society" of the past. Argues that capitalism as a mode of production "is the basic process of most of what we know as the history of country and city." Considers pastoral poetry, dark views of the city, and stereotypes of "innocent" country and "wicked" town.

David Peck

New Historicism

With a simple declarative statement, noted Renaissance scholar Stephen Greenblatt laid the foundation for what would become New Historicism, a mode of cultural inquiry that would change the direction of literary theory in the final two decades of the twentieth century. In his seminal volume *Shakespearean Negotiations: The Circulation of Social Energy in Renaissance England* (1988), Greenblatt acknowledges, "I began with the desire to speak to the dead."

Desire is the keystone of New Historical inquiry, which aims to explore the past through its documents and to do so not as objective observers governed solely by reason, but as subjective participants fully cognizant that scholarly impartiality is impossible. Human interests are never far from human emotions, thus, human passion governs human inquiry. New Historicism, in its efforts to examine the material and ideological elements that governed people's lives in specific time periods, is "conversing with the dead" through examining literary and historical texts; but this conversation is controlled by the living. In their approach to the past, New Historians can be considered time-traveling reporters. Primarily, these critics are interested in how literature functions as a political tool, as a by-product of power, and as part of cultural reproduction.

New Historicism is characterized by a desire to understand not only the work of literature—indeed, any creative work—but also the context in which the work was composed. In particular, New Historicism wants to understand the cultural ideologies (belief systems) present at the time a work was formed. For New Historicists, the question is not solely, What is this poem about? but What cultural contexts informed the writing of this poem? Answers to the latter question are discerned through consideration of related texts from the same time period. Unlike New Criticism, a theoretical predecessor that insisted a literary work stand independent of its author, culture, and era, New Historicists insist the opposite. A work can be understood only by considering it in the surrounding framework of ideas circulating at the time of its composition. In contrast, the art for art's sake movement, frequently associated with New Criticism, sought to distance art and literature from the cultural contexts of their derivation.

New Historians refuse to place literature in a vacuum, apart from power structures. They seek to establish a relationship between sources of power within a society and the works of art and literature produced by a society. New Historicists are not seeking "truths" about civilization. Indeed, truths for New Historians are not givens; rather, truths are cultural constructs. What is "true" in a society depends on who or what is in power. For New Historicists, history is not a neat compilation of events over time, but a complex and tangled record of the evolution of ideas. They ask questions such as, What were humans thinking, when were they thinking it, and why were they thinking it? During the Renaissance, for example, why did people believe in the Great Chain of Being, in which pampered kings and queens were only one link from God and hardworking peasants only one link above beasts? For the New Historicists, textual analysis can never reveal the truths of a society or an age, but it may provide clues to an understanding of the social construction of truth.

Despite its emergence and popularity in Renaissance studies, New Historical approaches can be applied to various genres and eras of literature. All types of cultural "texts," from novels to comic books, from films to postcards, from architecture to furnishings, can be accessed and analyzed through the methodologies of New Historicism. For the purposes of this overview, examples of New Historical methods will be drawn primarily from poetry.

Historical criticisms

The word "new" seemingly separates New Historicism as a mode of inquiry from "old" historical approaches, but the claim that there are "old" and "new" approaches is perhaps a misnomer. Many traditional historical approaches to literary and cultural analysis are still in practice; this fact suggests that they are not outdated, nor have they been replaced by New Historicism. To better understand how New Historicism is distinct from its predecessors and contemporaries in the field of historical inquiry, it is important to understand the ways in which their various theories and methodologies diverge.

Traditional historical inquiry suggests that to understand a work of literature, the scholar must first investigate the author's life and background, the society in which the author lived, and the prevailing ideas of the time. Traditional historical critics give preeminence to the literary text, with historical texts providing supporting background material. For instance, an understanding of the sewer system, or the lack of one, in eighteenth century London elucidates the black humor of Jonathan Swift's poem "A Description of a City Shower" (1710), which lists in graphic detail the various items of refuse that wash through the streets of the city during a rainstorm. As Steven Lynn points out in *Texts and Contexts: Writing About Literature with Critical Theory* (1994), "The modern reader who is unaware of the sanitary problems in Swift's day may find the poem's imagery incredible." Thus, one aspect of traditional historical criticism is to prove the veracity of a literary text. The content of the poem is valid because historical data supports its description of a London street at the time in which the poem was composed.

Biographical criticism is closely connected to historical criticism as it relates the author's life events or beliefs to the work produced. However, despite connections between lived experiences and creative expression, it is simplistic to equate the life of the poet with his or her poetry, and then go no further. American poet Sylvia Plath's "Daddy" (1966) conjures up images of a brutish father, but her biography provides no such evidence of abuse; the fact that her father died when she was a child seems the most injurious of his crimes. Still, this fact allows an entry into the poem, and information about her subsequent relationships with men provides even greater insight. Biographical research allows scholars to connect the "Daddy" of the title with various men in Plath's life; it becomes a metaphor for the men who rejected the poet over her lifetime, and not her particular birth father.

There are significant differences between New Historicism and traditional historical research. Historians generally believe in documented facts and a linear progression of civilization. They believe certain eras can be characterized by a specific belief system; for instance, the Great Chain of Being is considered by traditional historians to be an organizing principle for Elizabethan society. New Historicists resist such codifying and are more likely to eschew facts and reveal the flaws in grand schematics.

Another important difference is the New Historicist's predilection for minutiae rather than for extant texts, and their tendency to reach "local" conclusions rather than proclaim overarching judgments. Rather than explicate an entire work like John Milton's twelve-book *Paradise Lost* (1667), a New Historicist will focus on a few lines of various texts, perhaps a passage from book 1 of *Paradise Lost*, a paragraph from a religious treatise of the era, and a paragraph from a surviving letter from Milton to his daughter, and then treat the three partial texts as equals. Unlike traditional historical approaches that rely on historical information as a subtext for greater understanding of a literary work, New Historicism refuses to privilege either the literary or the historical text. Instead, practitioners of New Historicism explore a history of ideas that employs the technique of cross-reading. Literary texts are read to glean history and historical texts are read to understand literature.

ORIGINS AND FOUNDERS

The decade of the 1980's marked the emergence of New Historicism as a recognized mode of inquiry in literary and cultural studies. It followed on the heels of and in reaction to New Criticism (1940's-1970's), which maintained that the text of a literary work was sacrosanct. New Critics focused exclusively on properties integral to a poem, particularly its formal and linguistic qualities, and rejected biographical or historical contexts as unnecessary to an understanding and appreciation of a poem. The poet, the era, and the circumstances of a poem's composition were of no concern to the New Critics. The poem, in and of itself, provided the key to understanding.

Prior to the influx of new critical approaches, literary scholars had engaged in historical research, but the New Historicism that emerged in the 1980's was unlike its forerunners. Practitioners of New Historicism were informed by other more radical criticisms that developed in the 1970's, including reader-response, feminist, and Marxist approaches. Questioning the status quo was a common practice on university and college campuses, where many emerging theorists, such as French philosopher-historian Michel Foucault and American literary historian Greenblatt, were professors. Particularly in light of the Civil Rights and women's movements and of organized opposition to the Vietnam War, rethinking the status quo was popular in higher education. Foucault, Greenblatt, and others extended this line of questioning back through time and reexamined accepted historical truths. This reexamination led to their publications as New Historicists: Foucault's *Surveiller et punir: Naissance de la prison* (1975; *Discipline and Punish: The Birth of the Prison*, 1977) and Greenblatt's *Shakespearean Negotiations*. Foucault had been questioning social institutions since the early 1960's, publishing, among other works, *Folie et déraison: Histoire de la folie à l'âge classique* (1961; *Madness and Civilization: A History of Insanity in the Age of Reason*, 1965), which examines the social construction of madness and its accompanying discourse over a number of centuries, and *Naissance de la clinique: Une Archéologie du regard médical* (1963; *The Birth of the Clinic: An Archaeology of Medical Perception*, 1973), which looks at the establishment of medical hospitals and the training of doctors, again across an extended period of time. New Historicism was the new name for his approach, but Foucault preferred to think of himself as just another French intellectual. New Historicists embraced his ideas and borrowed liberally from his terminology as they engaged in countercultural inquiries of their own.

BELIEFS AND METHODOLOGIES

While its main founder, Greenblatt, is a noted Renaissance scholar associated with the field of English literature, the range of New Historicists is vast. In addition to literary scholars, New Historicism includes cultural critics, anthropologists, and historians, all of whom work across the curriculum, utilizing methods from various disciplines and sharing epistemological tools. Given this diversity of backgrounds, interests, and methods, it is not surprising that disagreements emerge among New Historicists. Even Greenblatt regrets the term "New Historicism"; he prefers to call his approach a poetics of culture.

In his introduction to *The New Historicism* (1989), editor H. Aram Veeser identifies five epistemological threads that connect practitioners of New Historicism. First, Veeser notes that "every expressive act is embedded in a network of material practices," suggesting that even a simple couplet at the end of a sonnet, a type of expressive act, is the product of the cultural milieu from which it originated. Second, he notes that "every act of unmasking, critique and opposition uses the tools it condemns and risks falling prey to the practice it exposes," an admission that any claim to objective inquiry is a fallacy. New Historicists are vulnerable to and operate within the same cultural power grids that produced the texts they study. There is no still-point in the universe from which to conduct textual analyses. Critics, like the writers whose works they study, are the products of a particular culture and age. New Historicists are cognizant of their inherent biases and frequently acknowledge them in the course of their writings.

Veeser's third observation is "that literary and nonliterary 'texts' circulate inseparably," a recognition of the interdependence of texts, ranging from poetry to legal writings, composed in the same time period. Veeser's fourth point, "that no discourse, imaginative or archival, gives access to unchanging truths, nor expresses inalterable human nature," points out perhaps the one constant in the history of human ideas and social structures: These ideas and structures are subject to change. The trajectory of social structures is not an evolutionary line of progress necessarily, but a chaotic diaspora of beliefs and practices. Human history is messy, as is writing about the texts that are both byproducts and chronicles of that history. Point five, "that a critical method and a language adequate to describe culture under capitalism participate in the economy they describe," is related to the second point. Most New Historicists, even those who espouse socialism, are the products of capitalism, the dominant economic ideology of the twentieth and early twenty-first centuries. In the process of describing and analyzing the texts that capitalism has produced, or even the texts that predate capitalism, they cannot escape the system they critique.

In brief, New Historicists approach a text from a contextual standpoint, identifying ideologies that informed its composition. They look at interconnections between historical and literary texts. For instance, they consider how changes in the rights of women as revealed in a legal document produced in the Elizabethan age connect to the portrayal of women in light verses composed in the same period. New Historicists consider the systems of meaning—whether economic, medical, educational, legal, religious, or political—available to the writer at the time the work was composed and consider how the work is a product of these systems. Furthermore, New Historicists are not averse to skipping eras and showing relationships between cultures and practices across time and space. New Historicists do this not to suggest linear progression; rather, they do this to emphasize the randomness of coincidental events over the development of linked patterns.

TERMINOLOGY

A number of terms appear frequently in scholarship by New Historicists and in works about New Historicism. Crucial to an understanding of New Historicism are the following terms: "discourse," "power," "representations," and "self-positioning." "Discourse" refers to a vocabulary associated with a particular group of people with a shared knowledge. The discourse allows members to communicate with each other, define standards for outsiders, and keep those who do not share their specialized knowledge out of the discussion. Discourses exist in areas such as law, medicine, higher education, and sports. Foucault's three-volume *Histoire de la sexualité* (1976-1984; *History of Sexuality*, 1978-1987, 3 vols.), for example, notes the frequency with which psychiatrists and sexologists invented new terms for human sexual behavior, determining what was acceptable and what was reprehensible through this vocabulary. Foucault further notes how views toward sexuality shifted as a result of this specialized and expanding discourse.

"Power," along with ethics and truth, is a means by which humans are subjugated by the societies in which they exist. Foucault believes that power is a construct, not a reality. Power is associated with knowledge; to possess knowledge, particularly specialized knowledge, as is the case with government leaders, surgeons, and college professors, for example, is to be able to wield power over others. Power gives one the authority to determine whether something is true or false, acceptable or repugnant, valid or invalid. For New Historicists, truth is a construct backed by power.

The idea and term "representations" is central to New Historicism, so much so that the title of the journal founded by Greenblatt is *Representations*. "Representation" means that which is opposed to reality. Because New Historicists question the nature of reality—because reality is often defined by those in power—the preferred term to describe phenomena is "representations." History becomes not just one story, but many stories through representations. How people from diverse backgrounds and times view events differs dramatically. No single representation can claim the truth. Similarly, self-positioning refers to the fallibility of the scholar who cannot step outside history to evaluate the phenomena of humanity. The term is a reference to the inevitable subjectivity of all human inquiry.

OPPOSITION

The popularity of New Historicism continues to grow, as evidenced by the increasing number of scholarly articles and books that employ this method of inquiry, including Greenblatt's *Will in the World: How Shakespeare Became Shakespeare* (2004), which reached a popular audience and became a best seller. However, New Historicism's detractors are also increasingly evident. Opponents object to the ideological scrutiny under which works of literature are placed by New Historicists, including their emphasis on socially constructed and socially enforced belief systems. Detractors argue that such a politically charged focus detracts from an enjoyment and appreciation of poems, plays, short fiction, and novels. They argue, for example, that they want to read Sir Philip Sidney's sonnet sequence *Astrophel and Stella* (1591), not as evidence of repressive sexual politics in the sixteenth century, but as a classic love story. Other critics, who hark back to New Criticism, desire a return to textual meaning. More traditional methods of historical criticism aim toward the recovery of a text's original meaning; New

Historicists question the very notion of an obtainable meaning. The author's intentions, often the product of social forces beyond the writer's control or ken, are irrecoverable.

Late twentieth century conservative pundits George Will and William Bennett perceive something much more sinister at work in New Historicism: the complete eradication of shared cultural values. New Historicism is argued to be a vehicle by which liberal intellectuals disrupt any semblance of aesthetic norms. Greenblatt countered this perception in an interview, noting that

> One thing that's very puzzling about the ferocity of some of these attacks is that—though they're often mounted in the name of American culture, what George Will calls our "social cement"—they seem to me oddly hostile to democratic currents in America, to our ability to absorb lots and lots of different things and make them our own.

BIBLIOGRAPHY

Gallagher, Catherine, and Stephen Greenblatt. *Practicing New Historicism*. Chicago: University of Chicago Press, 2000. A clearly written work that focuses its examination on five central New Historicist themes: the "recurrent use of anecdotes, preoccupation with the nature of representations, fascination with the history of the body, sharp focus on neglected details, and skeptical analysis of ideology."

Greenblatt, Stephen. *The Greenblatt Reader*. Edited by Michael Payne. Malden, Mass.: Blackwell, 2005. This reader gathers Greenblatt's most important New Historicist writings, including his works about "culture, Renaissance studies, and Shakespeare." Also includes essays on storytelling and miracles. Counters assertions that New Historicism fails to embrace ideas of literary and aesthetic value.

Laden, Sonja. "Recuperating the Archive: Anecdotal Evidence and Questions of 'Historical Realism.'" *Poetics Today* 25, no. 1 (Spring, 2004): 1-28. Examines the role of anecdotal evidence in New Historicist writing. Explores connections between literary artifacts, literary scholarship, and historical discourse within New Historicist practices.

Lynn, Steven. "Connecting the Text: Biographical, Historical, and New Historical Criticism." In *Texts and Contexts: Writing About Literature with Critical Theory*. 5th ed. New York: Pearson Longman, 2008. Delineates assumptions and strategies associated with New Historical practices in literary criticism. Provides examples as well.

Robson, Mark. *Stephen Greenblatt*. New York: Routledge, 2008. A biographical study of New Historicism's early practitioner, Stephen Greenblatt. Examines his foundational works as well as key concepts in the practice, including context, cultural poetics, power and subversion, thick description, and the anecdote.

Ryan, Michael. "History." In *Literary Theory: A Practical Introduction*. 2d ed. Malden, Mass.: Blackwell, 2007. Introduces New Historicism in the context of traditional historical methods and other emerging historical practices. Applies New Historical methods to literary works, including poems by Elizabeth Bishop.

Veeser, H. Aram, ed. *The New Historicism*. New York: Routledge, 1989. Anthology of classic New Historicist essays, including entries by Stephen Greenblatt, Jane Marcus, and Gayatri Chakravorty Spivak, and a helpful introduction that defines New Historicism and places the movement in a theoretical context.

_____. *The New Historicism Reader*. New York: Routledge, 1994. In the introduction to this collection of now-classic essays, Veeser examines New Historicism's "allies and opponents, surveys related fields, and identifies now-emerging New Historicist themes."

Wilson, Scott. "The Economimesis of New Historicism (Or, How New Historicism Displaced Theory in English Literature Departments)." *Journal for Cultural Research* 11, no. 2 (April, 2007): 161-174. Posits why New Historicism has gained ground in academia while other theoretical models of literary analysis have fallen from favor.

Dorothy Dodge Robbins

POSTCOLONIAL CRITICISM

Postcolonial criticism analyzes and critiques the literature, poetry, drama, and prose fiction of writers who are subjects of countries that were governed by or that were colonies of other nations, primarily England and France, and, to a lesser extent, the United States. Postcolonial criticism deals mainly with the literatures of Africa, Asia, and the Caribbean by analyzing the interactions between the culture, customs, and history of indigenous peoples and of the colonial power that governs. Postcolonial criticism is part of a larger field called cultural studies, or race and ethnicity studies.

To understand the importance of postcolonial literature, a reader should understand the scope of European involvement in the lives of people around the world. Between the fifteenth and nineteenth centuries, European countries conquered, governed, and otherwise had interests in the majority of nations around the world. Colonialism had begun principally through mercantilism and the protection of mercantile companies, such as the British East India Company, by the British navy and the navies of other trading countries. By the mid-twentieth century, however, domination by Europe began to end, as colonized countries staged successful independence movements. By 1980, Britain had lost all but a few of its colonial holdings; Hong Kong remained British until 1997 and Australia remained British until 1999.

Postcolonial literary criticism is a recent development. Formerly known as commonwealth studies, postcolonial literary studies includes examinations of works by authors from colonized nations. After nationalism, indigenous novelists and poets finally were able to express freely their own thoughts and feelings about the effects of the long-term conquest of their peoples, their traditions, and their customs. Although some literature from the East originated in these early days of colonial rule, the great mass of postcolonial literature began as colonies gained their independence.

EDWARD SAID

A list of the most influential postcolonial critics would have to begin with Edward W. Said (1935-2003), whose *Orientalism* (1978) is considered a foundational work in postcolonial studies. Said has a special place in postcolonial studies in part because of the uniqueness of his birth and education. He was born in Jerusalem while it was still a British protectorate, and he was educated in Egypt, England, and in the United States, where he received his doctorate from Harvard University. He taught at Columbia University for many years, won a number of honors, and was well-regarded in his profession.

In *Orientalism,* Said argues that Europeans have always been prejudiced against people of the Orient (the East), a prejudice that led to the formation of images of the East and of Easterners that were both mistaken and romanticized. Because of their view of the Orient, Europeans, and later Americans, began to feel justified in their conquest of the East, particularly the nations of the Middle East. Said, however, also denounces the Middle East for accepting the prejudiced values of the West regarding the Orient. In *Orientalism*, Said focuses on the ideas that become commonplace when the people raised in a governing culture, such as England, are mistakenly educated about the people of the country they dominate, such as India.

Said argues that even though Europeans were interested in the nations they governed and even made efforts to learn about the people, language, and cultural history of their colonies, nevertheless, European understandings and attitudes were often mistaken. One of the most common mistakes of the Orientalists, as Said calls the colonizers of the East, is their misguided view of the Orient itself. Said argues that, for example, Orientalists most often see a series of opposites between the two cultures. That is, they believe that the culture of the European country is normal and that the culture of its colony is simply a mirror-image of, and inferior to, the governing nation. To the Orientalist, therefore, the culture of the governed people is less than normal, or subnormal.

To take another example, Oriental males are often portrayed as weak and effeminate; nevertheless, they are considered a threat to European women, and European women are considered by the Orientalist to be drawn to the mysterious males of the East. To understand this dichotomy, one might consider an image from popular culture: the 1920's Italian film star Rudolph Valentino, whose most famous role was as an Arabian sheik who abducted European and American women. This image of the Arabian sheik, one of the most popular images of the 1920's, found resonance with many people, who then formed their own ideas of what a "sheik of Araby" was like from these film portrayals.

Still another example of Orientalist views of the East is the stereotype of the Asian or Arab woman as exotic, highly sexed, and eager for domination by a European conqueror. To an Orientalist, the East is always compared to the West, but this comparison always considers the East inferior. That is, where the West is progressive, the East is backward, where the West values unity and friendship, the East is untouchable and alien, where the West is strong and unconquerable, the East is weak, merely awaiting the domination of the West. Thus, Said seems to suggest that to the Orientalist, the East and its people are alien.

Orientalism as well as Said's 1993 book, *Culture and Imperialism*, provoked much debate, both pro and con, among historians, but there is no denying the special place of these works in the canon of postcolonial literary criticism. In these works, Said attempts to show how these ideas of the past are clearly presented in the writings of authors of the colonial period, and how the literature of the former colonies has perhaps progressed somewhat beyond the errors of the past. Even if a mistaken worldview is somehow a part of human nature, in that people yearn for the fantastic and exotic instead of sameness among the world's peoples, Said contends that such a view prevents an honest relationship among peoples of varied cultures.

WRITERS AND CRITICS FROM THE DEVELOPING WORLD

Any study of postcolonial criticism should include a number of well-known and well-respected writers from Africa, India, and other former colonies. Some of the major names to be considered are Frantz Fanon, Chinua Achebe, Ngugi Wa Thiong'o, Jamaica Kincaid, and Salman Rushdie, among a host of others.

Fanon was a leading intellectual of the twentieth century. Born in Martinique, his work describes the role that intellectuals ought to play in the struggle against colonialism. He was active during World War II, fighting against supporters of the French Vichy government, which cooperated with the Nazis in subjugating the French. He was decorated for his efforts, but after the war found himself regarded not as a French war hero but primarily as a black man. He had expected respect but found disdain; he was seen as "the other," a person feared and dismissed. He began to despair, as his education—he had begun studying medicine before the war—his language skills, and his elegant demeanor did not keep him from being treated as an exotic and alien specimen.

Fanon's first book, *Peau noire, masques blancs* (1952; *Black Skin, White Masks*, 1967), examines the effects of racism on the psyches of people of color. He describes the anger and pain he feels after his attempts to remake himself into a "white man" with black skin are rebuffed. He then travels to Africa to find the antidote to his psychological pain. In 1953, he finished medical training and moved to Algeria to work as a psychiatrist. In Algeria he experienced revolution firsthand, as Algerians fought for independence from France. Fanon wrote about his experiences as a part of the Algerian struggle. His works include *L'An V de la révolution algérienne* (1959; *Studies in a Dying Colonialism*, 1965), *Les Damnés de la terre* (1961; *The Wretched of the Earth*, 1963), and *Pour la révolution africaine* (1964; *Toward the African Revolution*, 1976). Fanon died from leukemia at the age of thirty-six.

AFRICA

Many of the countries of Africa were fighting for independence in the twentieth century, beginning with South Africa in 1910 and leading up to Eritrea in the 1990's. However, African nations began to accelerate their demands for independence following World War II. Writers soon took up the challenge of moving the nations into a new age.

Chinua Achebe was born in Nigeria and graduated from that country's University College in 1953. Although a speaker of Igbo, he writes in English, making him one of the most widely read African writers. Because he began to write before Nigerian independence, he had experienced both colonial and postcolonial life. He is considered by some to be the founder of modern African literature. *Things Fall Apart* (1958), his first novel, shows life from an African point of view. *No Longer at Ease* (1960) and *Arrow of God* (1964) show the effect of colonial government on Igbo society and on Nigeria, as well as on other newly independent African nations. Nigeria became a republic in 1963, but only three years passed before a military junta seized power. Achebe's 1966 novel, *A Man of the People*, correctly foreshadows the unrest that followed independence. A later novel, *Anthills of the Savannah* (1987), contrasts the actual government corruption with the idealism and dreams of the disenchanted public.

In addition to his novels, Achebe has written short stories, children's books, and poetry, including *Beware, Soul Brother, and Other Poems* (1971; published in the United States as *Christmas in Biafra, and Other Poems*, 1973). His *Morning Yet on Creation Day* (1975) is a collection of essays reflecting his thoughts and disillusionment with the state of his nation. Achebe considers such critical questions as, Is there such a thing as African literature? What is the role of the writer in African society? He even wonders if an African literature is possible. The essays were originally published between 1962 and 1972, when, in his enthusiasm for African literature, he led the initiative for the Heinemann's African Writer's series. Early on, Achebe saw great promise for African literature, but the ensuing years have brought not a flowering of literature in Africa but modern, struggling societies that are too chaotic to support writers and poet's efforts.

Another name often mentioned in the litany of African postcolonial critics is Ngugi Wa Thiong'o, who was born in Kenya. He writes in Gikuyu, although much of his earlier work is in English. He has written fiction, plays, short stories, and essays in criticism and children's literature. He is the founding editor of the Gikuyu-language journal *Mutiiri*. Ngugi went to the United States in 1977 after serving time in prison in Kenya. He taught at Yale and New York universities, holding professorships in comparative literature and performance studies. He also taught at the University of California, Irvine. His works in English include the play *The Black Hermit* (pr. 1962, pb. 1968); novels

Weep Not, Child (1964), *The River Between* (1965), and *A Grain of Wheat* (1967); and the nonfiction works *Homecoming: Essays on African and Caribbean Literature, Culture, and Politics* (1972) and *Penpoints, Gunpoints, and Dreams: Toward a Critical Theory of the Arts and the State in Africa* (1998), an essay on the critical state of African literature.

Taban lo Liyong is a Ugandan poet. He attended Howard University and the University of Iowa Writers' Workshop, where he graduated in 1968, the first African to do so. When Taban finished his education, dictator Idi Amin was ruling Uganda, so the young Taban moved to Kenya and began teaching at the University of Nairobi. Later, he taught in New Guinea, Australia, Japan, and South Africa. He maintains that his experiences in many cultures have made him more diverse in his worldview than many fellow African writers. He has published more than twenty books, including books of poetry: *Frantz Fanon's Uneven Ribs, with Poems More and More* (1971), *Another Nigger Dead: Poems* (1972), and *Ballads of Underdevelopment: Poems and Thoughts* (1976). His nonfiction works include *The Last Word: Cultural Synthesis* (1969) and *Another Last Word* (1990); he also wrote the novel *Meditations in Limbo* (1970).

Henry Owuor-Anyumba was a music historian born in Kenya. He taught at the University of Nairobi along with Ngugi and Taban. In 1968, the three professors wrote a paper, "On the Abolition of the English Department" (1968), which has since become famous as a position paper on the place of English in postcolonial literature. They argued, in part, that if the university needed to teach a single culture, that culture should be African, not a distillation of British literature, language, and linguistics. They asserted that African literature should be at the center of the curriculum.

The professors further suggested that the Department of English be abolished, and that a department of African languages and literatures take its place. They called for a mandatory study of French as the example from European language and of Swahili as a universal African language. They called for study of African oral traditions in literature and for the addition of the literatures of other nations, including those of the Caribbean and the Americas. The University of Nairobi began to offer a languages and literatures program with elements of these suggestions as part of their course offerings.

INDIA, PAKISTAN, AND THE CARIBBEAN

An important contributor to postcolonial writing is V. S. Naipaul, a native of Trinidad and Tobago. His Hindu family emigrated to Trinidad and Tobago as indentured servants. Naipaul's father was a journalist and loved literature. Naipaul attended Queen's Royal College in Trinidad and Tobago and later studied literature at Oxford, graduating in 1953. He later worked for the British Broadcasting Corporation and wrote for *The New Statesman*.

A House for Mr. Biswas (1961), Naipaul's first major novel, was based in part on his father's life and on his own childhood in Trinidad and Tobago. When Naipaul went to India later, he was struck by how foreign it seemed to him, although it had always been the family dream to go back to India some day. What he discovered was that living in the West Indies had made it impossible for him to ever experience the "real India" he had heard so much about from his immigrant grandfather. His disappointment was the basis for the nonfiction work *An Area of Darkness: An Experience of India* (1964). His next work, the novel *Mr. Stone and the Knights Companion* (1963), is set in England.

At this point, Naipaul began to feel the pressure of his dual heritage and began to see his duty as a postcolonial writer. The collection *In a Free State* (1971) won the Booker Prize and was quite a change for Naipaul. Transcending the boundaries of genre, the work consists of short stories, a novella, and two excerpts from a travel diary. The thread that ties all the parts together is the fear that an individual in a newly decolonized world can never be free. All of his works portray his alienation, uncertainty, and self-mockery. In 1990, he received a British knighthood.

Another postcolonial Caribbean writer is Jamaica Kincaid (born Elaine Cynthia Potter Richardson in Antigua). As a teenager, she worked as an au pair in New York. She attended Franconia College, worked as a photographer, and wrote articles for *Ingenue* magazine. She has written several novels, and one of her books, *A Small Place* (1988), is a nonfiction work that focuses on the problems that Antigua encountered during its transition to full independence from British rule in 1981. In this book, Kincaid argues that in many ways, conditions in Antigua worsened after independence. Her criticism of the government and the "elected dynasty" of the Vere Cornwall Bird family, which ruled until 2004, led to her book being banned in Antigua.

Another name often associated with the new postcolonial writers is Salman Rushdie, an Indian novelist and essayist, born in Mumbai (Bombay). Rushdie went to school in England, getting his degree from Cambridge. After graduation, he moved to Pakistan. His novel *Midnight's Children* (1981) follows the lives of the children born at midnight on Independence Day in India in 1947. It won the Booker Prize. The novel *Shame* (1983) won the Prix du Meilleur Livre Étranger in 1984 and was among the finalists for the Booker Prize in fiction. In 1988, he published *The Satanic Verses*, leading to accusations of blasphemy and the issuance of a fatwa against Rushdie by the Islamic Iranian government in 1989. He was forced to go into hiding under the protection of the British government. Even while in hiding, Rushdie continued to write. His works include *Haroun and the Sea of Stories* (1990), a children's fable that won a Writers' Guild Award; *Imaginary Homelands: Essays and Criticism, 1981-1991* (1991); *East, West: Stories* (1994), a book of short stories; and *The Moor's Last Sigh* (1995), a novel about a young man descended from the last Moorish ruler in Andalucía, Spain.

Rushdie is a major part of the postcolonial criticism movement, as he shows in *Midnight's Children*, a story of the years following independence. Here the hero moves from a childhood of hope and enthusiasm to adulthood filled with disillusion and despair. The hero's journey mirrors the political realities of the period of emergency rule established by Prime Minister Indira Gandhi in 1975.

Rushdie does not spare Pakistan in his dark portrayal of postcolonial times: *Shame* mirrors political reality as Rushdie uses Muhammad Zia-ul-Haq's actual rise to power in Pakistan as the inspiration for the novel's fantastic country (which, he claims, is not Pakistan). The novel depicts a nation of fools who have no sense of values, who are brutal and cruel while still being ridiculous. The Pakistani government eventually banned the novel.

A recurring image through much postcolonial literature is of a great cataclysm that follows independence in the former colonies. What happens to the colonies when they finally reach their much longed freedom and independence, so that they cannot escape an inevitable fall into anarchy and despair? One might question whether ineptitude, inexperience in governing, or greed has caused the strife that is the reality of independence for so many newly created nations. One might ask whether there are other reasons.

BIBLIOGRAPHY

Al-Dabbagh, Abdulla. *Literary Orientalism, Postcolonialism, and Universalism*. New York: Peter Lang, 2010. Argues that many classics of English literature "contain a sympathetic portrayal of the East." Examines Oriental literature to show its significant impact on English literature and to show "the striking manner in which" these works "have been absorbed and appropriated into British culture."

Bery, Ashok. *Cultural Translation and Postcolonial Poetry*. New York: Palgrave Macmillan, 2007. Included in this book on postcolonial poetry are critical essays on Judith Wright, Les Murray, Louis MacNeice, Seamus Heaney, A. K. Ramanujan, and Derek Walcott.

Gikandi, Simon, ed. *Encyclopedia of African Literature*. New ed. New York: Routledge, 2009. Contains almost seven hundred alphabetically arranged entries on specific writers and movements, regional and linguistic literary traditions, institutions of literary production, historical and cultural issues, and theoretical concepts.

Gordon, Lewis R., T. Denean Sharpley-Whiting, and Renée T. White, eds. *Fanon: A Critical Reader*. 1996. Reprint. Malden, Mass.: Blackwell, 1999. This critical reader contains a number of works by Fanon.

Harrison, Nicholas. *Postcolonial Criticism: History, Theory, and the Work of Fiction*. Malden, Mass.: Blackwell, 2003. Chapters in this study include "Colonialism and Colonial Discourse," "Racism, Realism, and the Question of Historical Context," and "Writing and Voice: Women, Nationalism, and the Literary Self."

Killam, K. D., and Ruth Rowe, eds. *The Companion to African Literatures*. 2000. Reprint. Oxford, England: James Currey, 2010. Alphabetically arranged entries on African authors, works, languages and literatures, genres and subgenres, and relations between literature and politics and religion. Includes maps, a country-author guide, a select list of topics and themes, and suggestions for further reading.

McLeod, John. *Beginning Postcolonialism*. 2d ed. New York: Manchester University Press, 2010. An excellent, readable resource for undergraduate students new to postcolonial studies and literature.

Newell, Stephanie. *West African Literatures: Ways of Reading*. New York: Oxford University Press, 2006. The selections in this study of West African literatures reflect various approaches to literature and differing views on colonialism.

Patke, Rajeev S. *Postcolonial Poetry in English*. New York: Oxford University Press, 2006. Includes chapters on the postcolonial poetry of South Asia and Southeast Asia, the Caribbean, and black Africa, as well as the "settler countries."

Tong, Rosemarie. *Feminist Thought: A More Comprehensive Introduction*. 3d ed. Boulder, Colo.: Westview Press, 2009. This introductory study of feminist thought includes the chapter "Multicultural, Global, and Postcolonial Feminism." A good starting place for readers new to postcolonial thought from a feminist perspective.

Julia M. Meyers

QUEER THEORY

The mode of literary and cultural analysis known as queer theory was established in the early 1990's as an outgrowth of numerous theoretical developments from the twentieth century covered by the broad umbrella of poststructuralism. Queer theory began as a reaction to a series of binary distinctions it has questioned, challenged, or outright denied, including male versus female, sex versus gender, nature versus nurture, and heterosexual versus homosexual. The term "queer," as a word of indeterminate meaning and with negative connotations, reinforces the challenges it brings to the texts under investigation. In practice, queer theory demands repeated, nearly infinite, reevaluation of the standard that is established or assumed by texts both literary and cultural. Queer theory is complex, playful, and elusive, making it difficult both to comprehend and to apply, causing some concern about its viability. Because forcing confrontation to expose power relationships is part of its mission, and because it proceeds by testing arguments rather than positing them, queer theory has proven largely indifferent to such accusations.

SEX AND GENDER AND THE BEGINNINGS OF QUEER THEORY

Contributing to queer theory's emergence is the differentiation between sex and gender made by feminist thinkers, including Simone de Beauvoir and Luce Irigaray. Complications to those precepts have been raised by feminist literary and cultural critics such as Eve Kosofsky Sedgwick and Judith Butler. Their arguments are predicated upon premises generally current among postmodernists and specifically articulated by French psychoanalysts Jacques Lacan and Michel Foucault. The fact that queer theory appeared at a historical point in response to specific philosophers suggests to some that it may be culturally bound and might become irrelevant, but its immediate, broad application to a variety of disciplines argues for its continuation as a viable and relevant method of textual analysis.

Beauvoir's claim that "one is not born, but rather becomes, a woman" summarizes for many early feminists the distinction between the biological factors commonly used to identify a person's sex and the social pressures that form a person's gender. While biological sex was then commonly held to be easily categorized and understood, an assumption that would soon be challenged, social constructions were immediately recognized as shifting, variable, and indeterminate. Feminists have since engaged in systematic explorations of the social pressures to which women are subjected, perhaps in complicity with the patriarchy, and which men and women alike, either consciously or otherwise, perpetuate. Lesbian and gay theorists adopt similar models to explore tendencies and behaviors sometimes rooted in biological distinction, other times being culturally conditioned. The distinction has likewise been fostered by those who would like to reduce behaviors and identities to the influence of either nature or nurture so they can "normalize" sexual identities and orientations.

While recent work suggests a more complex model of interaction, early feminist, lesbian, gay, bisexual, and transgender activists tended to hold either a constructionist view, arguing that a person's sexual and gender identities can be formed by his or her environment, or an essentialist view, which claims that sexuality and gender are genetically encoded or biologically self-evident. Both approaches have also been found useful by those who define gender roles in ways they term "traditional" and who advocate male-female, monogamous relationships as the only viable mode of sexual identity or orientation, who consider a genitalia-focused sexual act as the only possible expression of desire, and who treat any person without a clear, binary gender role or sexual orientation as a victim or as willfully disobedient.

At various times, both the constructionist view and the essentialist view have been supported implicitly by the scientific community. Psychoanalysts, psychiatrists, and psychologists embracing the constructionist view engage in inquiries to determine the causes of sexual identification and behavior. In the past, constructionists labeled androgynes, hermaphrodites, and homosexuals as mentally ill; but still today, some clinicians regularly prescribe treatments ranging from counseling to drug therapy aimed at "curing the disease" or "normalizing the subject." Other medical practitioners faced with a wide range of possible combinations among external genitalia, internal sexual organs, and XY chromosomal patterns through which to determine a person's gender prefer to conduct surgery to assign the patient a clear gender, even if doing so means long-term hormone therapy or infertility, coupled with confusion and even anxiety about a gender chosen sometimes by the patient, sometimes by the parents, and sometimes by the surgeon alone. Scientists embracing essentialism continue their search for a master gene that determines sexual identity as well as for a so-called gay gene that determines sexual orientation.

PUSHING THE BOUNDARIES OF NORMAL VERSUS QUEER

Queer theory has generally refused both the constructivist and the essentialist approach as well as the binary logic that governs sexual identification and orientation, preferring to expose the internal logic of each system by locating—often by pushing against it—a boundary between the normal and the deviant, exploring the nature and consequence of deviance and the ways the normal uses the deviant to reinforce its own normality. In these arguments, queer theorists follow poststructuralists, who reject the basis and terms of the Western systems of logic and rational argumentation institutionalized by the dialectic discourses of Plato, who inscribed the Socratic dialogues.

At its foundation, this challenge is brought to language itself, most radically by linguist Ferdinand de Saussure and philosopher Jacques Derrida. Saussure argues that there is no natural connection between a word, which he calls a signifier, and its definition, which he calls the signified. Derrida notes that because the relationship between a word and its definition can only be arbitrary, that relationship is not fixed or stable but subject to what he terms slippage, the process of defining a word by using other words, which in turn have to be defined. So the meaning of an idea is never fixed; it is always in a state of flux that depends on the chain of terms used to elaborate it. Queer theorists apply similar logic to sexual identity, gender roles, and desire, argu-

ing that each depends on a network of relationships established along a specific historical trajectory and resisting fixed definitions that are at the very least arbitrary, are potentially meaningless, and serve an imbalanced and repressive power structure aimed at regulating desire, sex, and thus identity. The term "queer," adopted by analysts working in this mode, is the cause of much debate.

Historically, the term "queer" has been both ambiguous and derogatory. In the field of queer studies, the term "queer" is generally embraced precisely because of its ambiguity and derogatoriness; the term unsettles the audience, provokes argument, and challenges definitions of what is normal. In practice, queer theory seeks to define, first and foremost, itself. The questions it addresses include what is the meaning of the term "queer"; how does the term intersect with and deviate from similar concepts such as gay, lesbian, and transgender; and what is the potential impact of "queer" upon "normal" (for example, of "queering" something). While such definitional strategies generally characterize a burgeoning field of study, queer theory demands that these strategies remain central foci of its analyses so that the mode of inquiry can remain at the margins of disciplinary discourse, constantly questioning what constitutes the standard.

NORMALIZING QUEER THEORY

Ironically, queer theory's basis has been threatened by its very popularity. Within a few years of its emergence on the critical field, it has entered the annals of academia as a regular mode of investigation, spawning conferences, books, journals, and courses of study across many disciplines. This proliferation has led some to wonder how such a "trendy" theoretical approach, so readily institutionalized by a historically understood center of power, can continue to define itself as marginal.

This question is further complicated by the potential application of queer theory to any number of intellectual disciplines. For example—greatly simplifying arguments that have taken shape throughout the twentieth century—the Austrian psychoanalyst Sigmund Freud argued that sexuality and desire are key to identity. A student of his school, Lacan, later argued that desire is encoded in language. In turn, Lacan's ideas were modified by French literary theorist Roland Barthes and cultural philosophers Felix Guattari and Gilles Deleuze. Finally, Foucault argued how language functions as the instrument of power. When these arguments are combined, as they are in queer discourse, any linguistic act becomes an instance of power that establishes identity and is subject to a queer analysis. Such a broad application threatens the unity and basis of queer theory by separating it from its original discourses of sex, gender, and desire. Queer theoreticians have recently found themselves in the position of establishing what queer theory is not, trying to prevent a total dissolution of the method that operates by unraveling possible identifications and power relationships.

Still, it remains within queer theory's "nature" to be always teetering on the precipice of oblivion. From the biblical narrative of Sodom and Gomorrah, completely destroyed because of an unidentified history of sexual perversion, to the twentieth century rhetoric surrounding HIV-AIDS, queer discourse has ever hovered at the edges of annihilation. Some argue that obliteration and obsolescence are part of its nature too because homosexual acts are not procreative, thereby separating desire from creation and continuity. While critics charge that the queer model of intellectual inquiry or artistic endeavor is therefore consumptive or even self-destructive, queer theory freely and playfully explores the pleasures found, for example, in both the making and the enjoying of an art object even when devoid of practical application.

The creation of the theory itself is predicated upon two works published in 1990: Sedgwick's *Epistemology of the Closet* and Butler's *Gender Trouble: Feminism and the Subversion of Identity*. Sedgwick's analysis challenges the methodology that separates homosexuality from heterosexuality as the exclusive basis for sexual orientation, locating in the origin of each term an epistemological shift that affects every domain of Western thought. While Sedgwick warns that by historicizing sexuality one runs the risk of eradicating alternate forms of reality, she explores the implications of the ability to precisely date the first use of the term "homosexual" and the fact that its opposite, "heterosexual," while supposedly the normal tendency, was

coined many years after and in opposition to the earlier, "deviant" word. Sedgwick argues that by distilling sexual identification to one element of the pleasure paradigm, and that by establishing an oppositional scheme by which to label it, the Western world has reinforced the power structure based squarely upon patriarchy and its ability to control reproduction. This power remains, even though its tenuous hold on society is continually exposed through discourses ranging from the faulty logic governing the U.S. Supreme Court decision to allow states the authority to define and outlaw sexual acts between consenting adults (*Bowers vs. Hardwick*, 1986) to the prejudices feminists routinely discover in the literary canon.

Like Sedgwick, Butler began her career as a feminist theorist and believes that her explorations of sexual orientation and gender identity are warranted both because feminists have historically examined the ways language itself constructs and maintains sexual difference and male power and because feminists must identify the category of person they wish to represent before they can be reasonably expected to achieve their political goals. She speculates on the possibility that by arguing that women are subjected to male power, even by claiming to represent women at all, feminists are actually upholding the very binary logic that divides human beings into two sexual categories—one dominant, one subservient—thereby perpetuating the patriarchal power they seek to eradicate.

Butler acknowledges the extent to which her arguments depend upon observations made by French theoretician Foucault, who first identified the logic by which binary oppositions operate and subjugate. In *Histoire de la sexualité* (1976-1984; 3 vols.; *The History of Sexuality*, 1978-1987, 3 vols.) Foucault denies the readily accepted explanation for the prevalence of sexual discourse in modern society, that sexuality has been repressed and therefore strives to make itself known. Instead, he argues that even those with the power to repress sexuality generate discourse about it to silence it, not by denying its existence but by enfolding it within its own linguistic structures of confession and inquiry. In his later work *L'Archéologie du savoir* (1969; *The Archaeology of Knowledge*, 1972), Foucault argues that power structures interface with one another and uphold themselves by generating language surrounding the definition of "the normal" but focusing on the abnormal, the disruptive, or the liminal (that which exists at the margins). Foucault notes that these terms are defined only in opposition to a supposed standard, and that they thereby encompass within themselves the norms they supposedly defy. He thus introduces areas of discourse in which the oppositions tend to break down and in which the standards can be exposed and challenged without being simply reversed.

Butler raises several questions about the social construction of gender, but rather than counter these questions with biological arguments, she asserts that social constructions are radically uncertain, almost to the point of unintelligibility. Butler in particular criticizes the distinctions between the mind, the body, and the world; the first two established by Plato, the last added by French philosopher René Descartes, author of the infamous formulation *Cogito, ergo sum*, or "I think, therefore I am." Butler claims that modern discoveries about the roles played by language and perspective in determining truth prove that there can be no distinction between the mental activity, its material substance, and the culture in which it lives, and that, therefore, any notion of sexual identity, whether derived from bodily characteristics or social indoctrination, is necessarily fabricated. Butler speculates that if sex and gender can be distinguished from one another, as they were by earlier feminists, then gender certainly has no causal relationship to sex and may not have any connection to it whatsoever. She opens the possibility that sex itself is not a natural, biological distinction but may be the product of discourse about sex and therefore may be constructed by and for the service of the power that holds some sexes in thrall.

Butler further argues that both sex and gender are subject to the demands and strictures of what she calls performance. Performance is not simply a matter of deciding which sex or gender role one wants to adopt, nor is it the enacting of specific behaviors along a scale of femininity or masculinity. Instead, performance is the product of a complicated interaction between an individual and his or her environment. It is always changing and never definitive, but it is still necessary to the production of identity and the development of relation-ships. Still, Butler recognizes that people need an identity on which to base their sense of self and to interact with the world in which they live. Therefore, she argues, people construct a gender identity for themselves by performing it. That construction is not stable because people change their performance in response to internal and external pressures. Others interpret the performance and convey their interpretations to the performer, in turn affecting the performance. Butler's argument thus displaces the agent of sexual identification, so that neither the individual nor his or her society is wholly responsible for the construction of sexual identity. Rather, both the person and society work together or in conflict along a scale of gendered possibilities.

Butler's insights dovetail with arguments made by speech-act and reader-reception theorists, who claim that texts perform their meaning in concert with their readers, thus laying the foundation for a broad application of queer theory. By parsing the moves made by a text to constitute the reader's interpretation of sex, gender, and desire, queer theoreticians expose and thereby challenge the power structures that establish and maintain sexual difference. So a "queer reading" might explore the implications of poet and playwright William Shakespeare's sonnets in praise of a young man's physical beauty, in light of the fact that Shakespeare was married and his wife had given birth to three children. A queer analysis, too, could explore the social pressure that keeps pseudonymous female author George Eliot's character Dorothea Brooke (*Middlemarch*, 1872) obligated to her dead husband's scholarship, considering that Eliot was ostracized from learned society for living with a married man. Finally, queer theoreticians may take up seemingly abstract topics such as race, democracy, or the aesthetic and explore how the experiences or perspectives of gays, lesbians, bisexuals, or transgendered persons alter the conceptions of spurious or tacit definitions and standards.

QUEER THEORY'S DETRACTORS AND CRITICS

The methodology of queer theory questions what people believe they know about sex, identity, and desire to expose and challenge unspoken assumptions. Because queer theory refuses the standards adopted by the text and then posits alternatives, often only to undermine them, it has been accused of being petty and querulous, and even illogical. Queer theory both ignores and embraces these accusations in its quest to escape the rules governing philosophical inquiry in the West. Likewise, queer theory has been criticized for its focus on the freakish, abnormal, and fetishist, and for proceeding in a tone alternatively described as campy, hysterical, or "screaming." When they choose to respond, queer theoreticians argue that only by exploring life at the margins can they hope to define the boundaries that uphold power, and that by calling attention to the performative features of argument, they hope to undermine the perhaps more subtle but no more legitimate rhetorical strategies employed by those who claim to be reasonable, rational, and objective.

Finally, in response to charges that queer theory coins terms illogically or unnecessarily, or that it employs complex or even faulty grammatical structures, queer theorists argue that nouns or adjectives used to specify genders or sexual orientations cannot be defined because they refer to such a complex network of objects and experiences. Even the very syntax of language upholds the binary logic of power structures that govern gender and desire, and thus must be defied by those not privileged to speak within or against the system.

Despite the many criticisms that queer theory employs an unnecessary and even exclusionary elitism predicated upon its erudite treatment of texts, that it is overly playful in its handling of serious arguments, and that its intentionally loose treatment of grammar make it unreadable, inapplicable, or irrelevant, queer theory remains a vibrant and productive area of interdisciplinary inquiry. It remains possible that scientific discoveries about sexuality and gender may alter understandings of identity so that its logic becomes utterly nonsensical. Likewise, historical developments may shift the mechanisms of power away from sex and gender. It seems more likely though that the kinds of radical uncertainty, relentless questioning, and rejection of standards performed by queer theory will become the only conceivable model of intellectual inquiry, normalizing queer theory to the point that it too will have to be challenged from an entirely new model.

BIBLIOGRAPHY

Berlant, Lauren, and Michael Warner. "What Does Queer Theory Teach Us About X?" *PMLA* 110, no. 3 (May, 1995): 343-349. An attempt to define queer theory by establishing what it does not do, including the ways it is not useful or practical, while defending that inutility as key to its function.

Butler, Judith. *Gender Trouble: Feminism and the Subversion of Identity.* 1990. Reprint. New York: Routledge, 2008. A foundational text in queer theory that challenges the definitions of "sexuality," "sex," and "gender," locating all three concepts in what Butler describes as performance.

Differences: A Journal of Feminist Cultural Studies 3, no. 2 (Summer, 1991). Special issue on queer theory edited by Teresa de Lauretis. A collection of essays that explores the basis of queer theory and demonstrates its applicability across academic disciplines.

Edelman, Lee. *No Future: Queer Theory and the Death Drive.* Durham, N.C.: Duke University Press, 2004. Edelman questions the viability of a theory—namely queer theory—that opposes convention simply for the sake of opposing convention, exploring the nihilistic impulse and the anti-energy that govern the discipline.

Fuss, Diana, ed. *Inside / Out: Lesbian Theories, Gay Theories.* New York: Routledge, 1991. A collection of essays examining queer identity formation, performance, and interpretation.

Hall, Donald E. *Queer Theories.* New York: Palgrave Macmillan, 2003. A thorough, readable summary of the origins, applications, and range of queer theory.

Halperin, David M. *One Hundred Years of Homosexuality, and Other Essays on Greek Love.* New York: Routledge, 1989. Halperin questions the utility of a historicized perspective for queer theoreticians, particularly the extent to which homosexual identities are culturally constructed and therefore limited and limiting.

Huffer, Lynne. *Mad for Foucault: Rethinking the Foundations of Queer Theory.* New York: Columbia University Press, 2009. Huffer reevaluates Michel Foucault's *Folie et déraison* (1961; *Madness and Civilization*, 1965; fully translated as *History of*

Madness, 2006) to argue that it was this early work that should be considered a foundational text in queer theory.

Jagose, Annamarie. *Queer Theory: An Introduction.* 1996. Reprint. New York: New York University Press, 2007. A clear, concise overview of the historical and factual circumstances surrounding the intellectual model.

O'Rourke, Michael. *Derrida and Queer Theory*. New York: Palgrave Macmillan 2010. The first book-length study of critic Jacques Derrida in relation to queer theory. Examines queer theory's "debts to Derrida" and seeks "queer moments" in Derrida's writings.

Rubin, Gayle S. "Thinking Sex." In *The Lesbian and Gay Studies Reader*, edited by Henry Abelove, Michèle Aina Barale, and David M. Halperin. New York: Routledge, 1993. Gayle S. Rubin, in this classic essay, explores whether sex/gender and politics are perhaps the same, and she examines the ways sexual identities are used to enforce power.

L. Michelle Baker

STRUCTURALIST AND POSTSTRUCTURALIST CRITICISM

Space and spatial form traditionally bear directly upon the visual arts, and only metaphorically, by virtue of the tradition of the sister arts (*Ut pictura poesis*), upon literature. The language of literary criticism is rich in spatially metaphorical terms such as "background," "foreground," "local color," "form," "structure," "imagery," and "representation." The opposition of literal and metaphorical spatiality in literature could be accounted for as a residual effect of Gotthold Ephraim Lessing's classic and influential attack in the eighteenth century on the *Ut pictura poesis* tradition.

Lessing maintained an absolute distinction between the verbal and visual arts based on a belief that an essential difference between poetry and painting is the divergent perceptions of their signs: The proper domain of language is temporal, since its signs are sequential, unfolding one by one in linear fashion along a time line, whereas the proper domain of painting, whose signs are simultaneous images juxtaposed in space, is spatial.

The modern mind, nurtured in Einsteinian physics, would have no trouble collapsing the mutual exclusivity of Lessing's categorization by way of the notion of space-time, in which the description of an object consists not merely of length, width, and height but also of duration. The fourth dimension is the inclusion of change and motion; space is defined in relation to a moving point of reference.

If time and space are not viewed as mutually exclusive, then Lessing's categories cannot maintain the absolute distinction he desired to establish between the verbal/temporal and the visual/spatial arts. A painting, in fact, is not perceived as a whole instantaneously; rather the eye moves across the picture plane, assimilating and decoding in a process not unlike that of reading, which likewise entails movement over spatial form: the words written on the page. Given this interpretation of space and time, literary criticism of the second half of the twentieth century radically redefined the nature of the relationship between the sister arts.

The seminal theoretical work in Anglo-American studies on literature as a spatial art is Joseph Frank's essay "Spatial Form in Modern Literature" (1945). Frank asserts that in the literature of modernism (Gustave Flaubert, James Joyce, T. S. Eliot, Ezra Pound), spatial juxtaposition is favored over normal linear chronology, marking the evolution toward a radical dislocation of the theory that language is intrinsically sequential. The formal method of modern literature is architectonic-spatial rather than linear-temporal, in that meaning is seen to arise ex post facto from the contiguous relation among portions of a work, rather than simply being represented in a temporal and progressive unfolding. The theory that the modern text has its own space by virtue of the simultaneous configuration of its elements—words, signs, sentences—in temporal disposition, is then extended to language in general in the model of meaning predominant in the critical movement known as structuralism.

STRUCTURAL LINGUISTICS: SAUSSURE

Structuralism is a method of investigation that gained popularity in the 1960's in Paris and in the 1970's in the United States through the writings of anthropologist Claude Lévi-Strauss, social historian and philosopher Michel Foucault, critic Roland Barthes, and psychoanalyst Jacques Lacan, among others. The diversity of the list is accounted for by the fact that structuralism grew out of structural linguistics, whose methods were considered applicable to several disciplines. Analysis is structuralist when the meaning of the object under consideration is seen to be based on the configuration of its parts, that is, on the way the elements are structured, contextually linked.

The linguistic theory grounding structuralism, and, by extension, literary criticism in the structuralist vein, is that of Ferdinand de Saussure (1857-1913). Saussurian linguistics considers the basic unit in the production of meaning to be the sign, an entity conceived of as a relationship between two parts; the signified or mental, conceptual component, lies behind the signifier, or phonetic, acoustical component. The signifier is a material manifestation of what is signified, of a meaning. Any given sign will be conceived of spatially, inasmuch as it always occupies a particular semantic and phonetic territory whose boundaries mark the limits of that space, thus allowing meaning to "take place"; that is, allowing the sign to function. For example, the phonetic space within which "tap" remains operable is always relative to a limit beyond which it would no longer differ from "top" or "tape." Likewise, its semantic space would be defined in terms of differentiation from other signs verging on "tap" semantically, such as "strike," "knock," "hit," and "collide." Thus, the value of the sign is neither essential nor self-contained but rather is contingent upon its situation in a field of differential relations, in the absence of which meaning would not arise.

Comparable to Frank's attribution of spatial form to modern literature by virtue of its atemporality, Saussurian linguistics renders language spatial in promoting synchrony over diachrony as its procedural method. The synchronic study of language, whose basic working hypothesis is that there exists an underlying system structuring every linguistic event, would reconstruct language as a functional, systematic whole at a particular moment in time, in contrast to the diachronic method of nineteenth century linguists interested in etymologies, the evolution of language over the course of time. Space becomes a linguistic activity in structural linguistics through investigation under ahistorical conditions of the synchronic structures governing the language system and through the notion of the sign as constitutive of a space of differential relations. Applied to the analysis of poetic texts, this theoretical groundwork accords the written work a space of its own in which meaning is produced. The pervasive influence of structural linguistics, specifically in the analysis of poetic texts, might be traced to the investigation in the early 1960's by Roman Jakobson of what he termed the "poetic function" of language.

ROMAN JAKOBSON

Jakobson designates the poetic function (one of six possible functions fulfilled by any utterance) as "the focus on the message for its own sake"; it is distinct from the referential or mimetic function dominating in normal linguistic usage, where the meaning to which signs refer is directly conveyed (represented) by virtue of a univocal rapport between signifier (sound) and signified (meaning). The exchange of signs (communica-

tion) is not problematic. Whereas referential or mimetic language would focus on an exterior referent, the nature of the poetic function is introversion. The poetic function reaches its apex in poetry, according to Jakobson: "a complex and indivisible totality where everything becomes significant, reciprocal, converse, correspondent . . . in a perpetual interplay of sound and meaning."

The poetic text is characterized by a high degree of patterning; its principal technique of organization is parallel structure: Patterns of similarity are repeated at each level of the text (phonetic, phonological, syntactic, semantic, and so on), such that the grammatical structure is seen as coextensive with the level of meaning or signification. In his analysis of William Blake's "Infant Sorrow" (1794), for example, Jakobson uncovers a network of ten nouns contained in the poem—evenly divided into five animates and five inanimates, and distributed among the couplets of the poem's two quatrains according to a principle of asymmetry:

> Anterior couplets: 3 animates, 2 inanimates
> Outer couplets: 3 animates, 2 inanimates
> Posterior couplets: 2 animates, 3 inanimates
> Inner couplets: 2 animates, 3 inanimates

Recalling "a remarkable analogy between the role of grammar in poetry and the painter's composition," Jakobson compares what he terms the manifestly spatial treatment opposing animates and inanimates in the poem to the converging lines of a background in pictorial perspective. The tension in the grammatical structure between animate and inanimate nouns underscores the tension between birth and the subsequent experience of the world on the poem's semantic level.

This type of structural analysis is characterized by the codification and systematization of the structural patterns grounding textual space, resulting in an immanent rather than transcendent reading of that space, one that reconstructs the rules governing the production of meaning rather than uncovering an essential meaning of that text. The tendency is toward all-encompassing systematic accountability in which every detail supplies information. The poem is interpreted as a highly structured network of interacting parts; it is a space closed off from "normal" language, a polysemic discourse whose semiotic play eventuates meaning within its borders, and not by virtue of an exterior referent or a priori idea that the poem is to convey. Structuralism thus implies the rejection of a purely phenomenological approach to language as expression, as denotation. As Vincent Descombes remarks in *Modern French Philosophy* (1980),

> if a poetic utterance presents the construction that it does, this is not at all that some lived state (regret, desire) has elicited this particular form of expression in which to speak its meaning. . . . The poet listens not so much to the stirrings of his heart as to the prescriptions of the French language, whose resources and limitations engender a poetics which governs the poem.

The poem as productive textual space signals the dissolution of the notion of the author as a univocal source of meaning and intentionality situated outside the text and, thus, marks a radical shift away from critical analysis that would determine meaning as controlled by authorial intent or ultimately by the sociological, historical, or psychological influences structuring that intent.

DECONSTRUCTION AND POSTSTRUCTURALISM

The tendency in literary criticism of the 1970's to examine the unquestioned assumptions of structuralism came to be called deconstruction, or poststructuralism. It is largely influenced by the writings of Jacques Derrida, whose examination of the Western concept of representation (of language as referential, mimetic) is responsible in large part for the highly philosophical bent of poststructuralist criticism.

Poststructuralism does not offer an alternate comprehensive system of textual analysis as a replacement for structuralist methodology; rather, it supplements tenets of structuralism. It is not a system, but rather a particular use of language that recognizes the involvement of any discourse, itself included, in paradoxes that might be repressed but cannot be resolved. Whereas structuralism tends to view textual space in the final analysis as the configuration of a unified and stable semantic space—a system actualized by its structure in which every detail is functional—for the poststructuralist a fully coherent and adequate system is impos-

sible. The system in which all coheres depends on exclusion: the repression of elements that will not fit. For example, in the analysis of "Infant Sorrow" on the basis of grammatical categories, Jakobson is able to ignore the pronoun "I" in his discussion of animate and inanimate nouns. Taken into account, "I" alters Jakobson's numeric scheme, undermining the specific nature of the parallel structures claimed to function in the poem.

When textual space is made to function systematically, it is only by the synthesis or exclusion of elements otherwise disruptive of the system. Such unified totality and closure are illusory from a poststructuralist point of view, which sees textual space effecting a meaning that is always at least double, marked by unresolvable tension between what a discourse would appear to assert and the implications of the terms in which the assertions are couched. Inscription, the writing per se, is thereby not seen as a neutral form at the service of meaning, but a signifying force threatening the determination of signification. In its attention to the graphic force of a word, its "letteral" meaning, poststructuralism would not pass off writing as mere transcription of the spoken word. In some sense dealing with any discourse as if it were concrete poetry, it recognizes the participation of the medium—the letter, the word as plastic form—in its own definition. Signification would be seen to be constantly displaced along a multiplicity of signifying trajectories whose transformations "anagrammatically" engender new possibilities: A signifier might verge on another, perhaps contradictory, signifier that it resembles phonetically or graphically; it may disengage other signifiers by way of semantic similarity; the visual impact of the word or letter on the page might cut a significant figure; signifying combinations might arise from mere juxtaposition of elements without any other apparent connection.

No longer conceived as the transparent carrier of a message, the signifier/word/inscription menaces the establishment of ultimate signification. Poststructuralism thus supplements the structuralist attack on the authority of the writing subject to include the dissolution of the illusion of mastery on the part of the critic. To the poststructuralist, the text is a space of semantic dispersal, a space of dissemination forever in flux, never to be completely controlled and mastered. From this standpoint, structuralist methodology is thought to be overly reductionist in its resolution of the text into a set of structuring components, too akin to the effort of archetypal criticism, or to Romantic notions of the work as an organic whole, albeit in structuralism an architectural one. Although it might be said in defense of structuralism that the analysis of structure is purely formal, that an essence (nature of being) is not ascribed to particular structures, structuralist readings imply essentiality by the air of puzzle-solving involved in their uncovering of the semiotic unity of a work, its essential governing principles. Structures are implicitly privileged with the status of eschatological presence; language's suggestive power, the disruptive force of its inscription, is attenuated for the sake of form: that is, of defining the system.

Poststructuralism would regard, for example, the emphasis in structuralist linguistics on synchrony as an attempt to exclude linguistic force and change that might undermine the fixity of systematic analysis. Following the implications of structuralism's principle of difference, of meaning produced by virtue of relational differences, one cannot escape the conclusion that the practice of language is implicitly diachronic, temporal, and historical because the principle is undeniably one of combination, selection, and exclusion. If meaning for the structuralist is the product of relational differences rather than derivative of an intrinsic permanent value attached to a word in itself, then it can never be fully present all at once at a given moment; no single word/gesture/expression/signifier is in and of itself capable of initiating the difference necessary for significance to operate. Like motion, meaning cannot be completely grasped in a present moment that would exclude a past and a future moment, and thus the structuralist principle of difference implies a paradoxically double movement at the "origin" of meaning that is repressed in favor of the oneness and synchrony establishing textual space as an unproblematic domain of simultaneous, systematic relationships.

The structuralist concept of textual space does attribute spatiality to language and not merely to a particular use of it ("modern literature"). It establishes a synchronic stable space containing the movement of

signification guaranteeing that the text will be something other than nonsense. Language is dealt with as a spatial phenomenon, but to the exclusion of temporal movement and flux, which might trigger disorder or nonsense. In other words, a protest against Lessing's separation of the verbal and visual arts by way of structuralism seems only to reverse the categories of space and time and thus remain within the mode of oppositional thinking: Language is synchronic when diachronicity is ignored, spatial when temporal movement is repressed. In an effort to exceed the limitations of oppositional thinking, poststructuralism supplements the principle of difference with what Derrida terms the *différance* operative in the textual dissemination of signification.

DIFFERENCE = *DIFFÉRANCE*

Différance is a neologism whose graphic play (in French) combines the meaning of "*différance*" (*difference*), with which it is exactly equivalent phonetically, and "deferring." It articulates meaning as a complex configuration incorporating both a passive state of differences and the activity of differing and deferring that produces those differences. *Différance* is consequently inconceivable in terms of binary opposition: Like motion, it is neither simply absent nor present, neither spatial (differing in space) nor temporal (deferring in time). "Espacement" (spacing), a comparable Derridean term, indicates both the passive condition of a particular configuration or disposition of elements, and the gesture effecting the configuration, of distributing the elements in a pattern.

Like the Einsteinian concept of space-time, *différance* and spacing (articulated along the bar of binary opposition that would separate space and time, active and passive) disrupt the comfort of thinking within a purely oppositional mode. Derrida demonstrates such lack of guarantees in his reading of "hymen" in the poetry of Stéphane Mallarmé. An undecidable signifier whose meaning cannot be mastered, "hymen" is both marriage as well as the vaginal membrane. Whereas hymen as virginity is hymen without hymen/marriage, hymen as marriage is hymen without hymen/virginity. Hymen, then, articulates both difference (between the interior and exterior of a virgin, between desire and its consummation), and, at the same time, the abolition of difference in the consummation of marriage; it is the trace of a paradoxical abolition of difference between difference and nondifference.

Within a structuralist framework, meaning produced by textual space, albeit ambiguous or polysemic, is in the final analysis recuperable. Ambiguity is controlled as the various strands of meaning are enumerated and accounted for. Poststructuralism views the implications of such practice as problematic. On the one hand, meaning is claimed to be the product of semiotic play governed by a principle of difference (signaling the dissolution of the control of the writing subject) that implicates a definition of the sign in which meaning floats among signifiers rather than existing a priori as an essence—the signified. On the other hand, by enclosing this textual play within the boundaries of the "poetic" and seeking out and privileging structures informing that play, a very classical definition of the sign is implied in which the signifier serves ultimately as a vehicle representing an eschatological presence: an ultimate signified that arrests play and closes off the movement of signification. Dissemination, *différance*, and spacing would splay the fixed borders that characterize criticism's structuring of the movement of signifiers within poetic space so as to explicate texts.

Sign, like symbol, ultimately refers back to a single source, a signified assuring of the determination of meaning; with the poststructuralist gloss on signifier as signifying trace, there can be no return to a simple origin. Signifying trace would articulate an effect of meaning without the illusion of understanding provided by binary opposition. Trace (again, like motion), cannot be determined as simply either present or absent. Giving evidence of an absent thing that passed by, trace "in itself" contains its other which it is not (the absent thing). It paradoxically "is" what it is not, inasmuch as its presence (its identity) depends on alluding to an absence (its nonidentity to the absent thing leaving the trace) from which it distinguishes itself. Its meaning or identity is thus split from the beginning, already always involved in a paradoxical movement of *différance*. The origin of meaning or identity is then not single; the first trace of anything is first only in deferring to a second in relation to which it becomes

first—and in that sense it is more of a third. The poststructuralist endeavor is a recognition of the intractable paradox of the nonsingle point of origin of the difference that inaugurates any signifying system. *Différance* is, then, not so much a concept as an opening onto the possibility of conceptualization.

IMAGE AND *DIFFÉRANCE*

A recapitualization of Pound's theory of the image as a generative and dislocating force in Joseph Riddel's "Decentering the Image" is a useful gloss on *différance*. Like spacing, which is both configuration and the gesture effecting that configuration, Pound's image is both a visual representation (form) and a displacement or trope (force); it is a cluster of figures in a space of relational differences and a transformative machine articulating movement across the differential field. The image is not an idea, not the mere signifier of a signified, but rather a constellation of radical differences, a vortex whose form as radiating force resists the synthesis and collapse of differences into oneness and unity. Whereas formalist, archetypal, and structuralist criticism tends to privilege implicitly master structures, assuring a totalization of the poem's fragments, Pound's vortex would disrupt the assurance of an originating signified in its refusal to be resolved into the unity of presence, to be fully present at a given moment. As the signifying trace is always already split at its origin, constituted in a present moment/space by absence, so too is Pound's vortex always already an image; that is, a field of relations, originally a text, the reinscription of a past into a present text, a vector, a force always already multiple and temporalizing.

There is, then, no continuity between origin and image as there is with symbol and the conventional sign. A poem is not recuperable in synthesizing totality and must be read somewhat in the manner of a rebus, whose play of signifiers annuls/refuses a simple reading, provoking, instead, reinterpretations and reopenings.

POSTSTRUCTURALISM VS. STRUCTURALISM

The poststructuralist critique of the frame that structuralism would draw around poetic discourse provokes reinterpretation of structuralist discourse. Because the principle of difference provides for theoretically unlimited play of the sign within the textual space, what prevents that movement from exceeding its borders, that force from spilling out of its form? How can one unproblematically draw borders around different language functions, keeping the play of the poetic—that introverted self-referential "focus on the message for its own sake"—framed off from the mimetic referential space of common linguistic usage?

The controversy between structuralism and poststructuralism indicated by such questioning is not a simple dispute over methodological technique in the analysis of poetry. Deconstruction of structuralist discourse betrays the ideological move involved in fixed framing: the strategy of setting up distinctions to shelter "rational" discourse from the vagaries of the poetic.

Relegation of textual play to the poetic seemingly protects the language of critical discourse from irrational forces, guarantees it the possibility of lucidity, of the impression that language is under control—mastered by the critic. Meaning as *différance*/spacing dissolves the illusion of the possibility of purely logical discourse unfettered by the anomalies of the poetic, of a purely literal language unhampered by figural machinations. Furthermore, *différance* annuls the very distinction classically affirmed between literal and figurative. Signification would be neither purely literal nor metaphoric; there would be no literal truth represented by a sign because the very possibility of representation depends on metaphor: In representing an absent in a present, in transferring the literal reference signified, the sign "tropes" and metaphorizes (*metapherein*—to carry over, transfer). Likewise, if purely metaphoric meaning were possible, then there would be a literal meaning of metaphor to which metaphor would refer metaphorically.

Whereas for structuralism, space structures meaning, delineating its borders and giving it form, poststructuralism demonstrates that closure of meaning is illusory. Meaning as spacing/*différance* is neither fixed nor absolute but kept in motion by the figural, the figural both as metaphor usurping the position of the sign's would-be literal referent, and as inscription, whose graphic impact on the page engenders disruptive anagrammatic combinations. Poststructuralism traces the catachresis at play in the space of discourse, be it

poetic, philosophic, or critical. The signifying traces at play in the text are catachrestic in their deconstruction of the illusion of literal terms whose eschatological presence would stop the movement of signification. Catachresis—the metaphor created when there is no literal term available (such as the foot of the table)—is traditionally considered a form of abuse and misapplication. Poststructuralism demonstrates such misapplication as the condition of language: The sign necessarily fails to hit the mark; the signifier is always something other than its signified in order that language might operate.

BIBLIOGRAPHY

Bloom, Harold, et al. *Deconstruction and Criticism.* 1979. Reprint. New York: Continuum, 2005. Five essays by leading postmodern theorists, including Paul de Man, Jacques Derrida, Geoffrey Hartman, and J. Hillis Miller.

Culler, Jonathan. *Structuralist Poetics: Structuralism, Linguistics, and the Study of Literature.* 2d ed. New York: Routledge, 2002. When it first appeared in 1975, this book introduced the concept of approaching a literary work by analyzing its structure. In a preface written for this edition, Culler defends his ideas against subsequent criticism.

Habib, M. A. R. *A History of Literary Criticism: From Plato to the Present.* Malden, Mass.: Wiley-Blackwell, 2005. An award-winning book, praised for its comprehensiveness, lucidity, and accessibility. Explains literary theories, discusses writers and their works, and offers close readings of major texts. Almost forty pages are devoted to structuralism and deconstruction. Bibliography and index.

Harland, Richard. *Superstructuralism: The Philosophy of Structuralism and Post-Structuralism.* New York: Routledge, 2003. Discusses all the major superstructuralists, including Ferdinand de Saussure, Roland Barthes, Michel Foucault, and Jacques Derrida. Notes, bibliography, and index.

Leitch, Vincent B., ed. *The Norton Anthology of Theory and Criticism.* 2d ed. New York: Norton, 2010. An extensive collection of critical works, including several by leading structuralists and poststructuralists. Includes general introduction, head notes, and annotations, as well as a bibliography of modern and contemporary critical movements.

McQuillan, Martin, ed. *Deconstruction: A Reader*. New York: Routledge, 2001. Sixty essential texts by writers from Karl Marx and Martin Heidegger to Jacques Derrida. Introduction by the editor. Extensive bibliographical references and index.

Rivkin, Julie, and Michael Ryan, eds. *Literary Theory: An Anthology*. 2d ed. Malden, Mass.: Blackwell, 2004. One entire section of this massive volume is devoted to essays about structuralism, linguistics, and narratology by such eminent scholars as Jonathan Culler, Ferdinand de Saussure, Roman Jakobson, and Michel Foucault. Bibliography and index.

Selden, Raman, Peter Widdowson, and Peter Brooker. *A Reader's Guide to Contemporary Literary Theory*. 5th ed. Harlow, England: Pearson Longman, 2005. A clear and balanced guide to a complex subject. Bibliography and index.

Sturrock, John. *Structuralism*. 2d ed. Malden, Mass.: Wiley-Blackwell, 2008. Sturrock's work has long been admired for its lucidity and its impartiality. In his introduction to this new edition, the French theorist Jean-Michel Rabaté points out recent developments in the critical reception of structuralism.

Williams, James. *Understanding Poststructuralism*. Montreal: McGill-Queen's University Press, 2006. Each chapter of this work concentrates on a key text, summarizing the main points and providing an analysis of the arguments advanced. The major criticisms of the movement are also noted and evaluated. Serves as an ideal introduction to the theory and the methodology of poststructuralism. Includes discussion questions, bibliography, and index.

Nancy Weigel Rodman

RESOURCES

EXPLICATING POETRY

Explicating poetry begins with a process of distinguishing the poem's factual and technical elements from the readers' emotional ones. Readers respond to poems in a variety of ways that may initially have little to do with the poetry itself but that result from the events in their own lives, their expectations of art, and their philosophical/theological/psychological complexion.

All serious readers hope to find poems that can blend with the elements of their personal backgrounds in such a way that for a moment or a lifetime their relationship to life and the cosmos becomes more meaningful. This is the ultimate goal of poetry, and when it happens—when meaning, rhythm, and sound fuse with the readers' emotions to create a unified experience—it can only be called the magic of poetry, for something has happened between reader and poet that is inexplicable in rational terms.

When a poem creates such an emotional response in readers, then it is at least a partial success. To be considered excellent, however, a poem must also be able to pass a critical analysis to determine whether it is mechanically superior. Although twenty-first century criticism has tended to judge poetic works solely on their individual content and has treated them as independent of historical influences, such a technique often makes a full explication difficult. The best modern readers realize that good poetry analysis observes all aspects of a poem: its technical success, its historical importance and intellectual force, and its effect on readers' emotions.

Students of poetry will find it useful to begin an explication by analyzing the elements that poets have at their disposal as they create their art: dramatic situation, point of view, imagery, metaphor, symbol, meter, form, and allusion. The outline headed "Checklist for Explicating a Poem" (see page 790) will help guide the reader through the necessary steps to a detailed explication.

Although explication is not a science, and a variety of observations may be equally valid, these step-by-step procedures can be applied systematically to make the reading of most poems a richer experience for the reader. To illustrate, these steps are applied below to a difficult poem by Edwin Arlington Robinson.

Luke Havergal

Go to the western gate, Luke Havergal,
There where the vines cling crimson on the wall,
And in the twilight wait for what will come.
The leaves will whisper there of her, and some, 4
Like flying words, will strike you as they fall;
But go, and if you listen, she will call.
Go to the western gate, Luke Havergal—
Luke Havergal. 8

No, there is not a dawn in eastern skies
To rift the fiery night that's in your eyes;
But there, where western glooms are gathering,
The dark will end the dark, if anything: 12
God slays Himself with every leaf that flies,
And hell is more than half of paradise.
No, there is not a dawn in eastern skies—
In eastern skies. 16

Out of a grave I come to tell you this,
Out of a grave I come to quench the kiss
That flames upon your forehead with a glow
That blinds you to the way that you must go. 20
Yes, there is yet one way to where she is,
Bitter, but one that faith may never miss.
Out of a grave I come to tell you this—
To tell you this. 24

There is the western gate, Luke Havergal
There are the crimson leaves upon the wall.
Go, for the winds are tearing them away,—
Nor think to riddle the dead words they say, 28
Nor any more to feel them as they fall;
But go, and if you trust her she will call.
There is the western gate, Luke Havergal—
Luke Havergal.

E. A. Robinson, 1897

STEP I-A: *Before reading*

1. "Luke Havergal" is a strophic poem composed of four equally lengthened stanzas. Each stanza is long enough to contain a narrative, an involved description or situation, or a problem and resolution.

2. The title raises several possibilities: Luke Havergal

CHECKLIST FOR EXPLICATING A POEM

I. THE INITIAL READINGS
   A. Before reading the poem, the reader should:
      1. Notice its form and length.
      2. Consider the title, determining, if possible, whether it might function as an allusion, symbol, or poetic image.
      3. Notice the date of composition or publication, and identify the general era of the poet.
   B. The poem should be read intuitively and emotionally and be allowed to "happen" as much as possible.
   C. In order to establish the rhythmic flow, the poem should be re-read. A note should be made as to where the irregular spots (if any) are located.

II. EXPLICATING THE POEM
   A. *Dramatic situation.* Studying the poem line by line helps the reader discover the dramatic situation. All elements of the dramatic situation are interrelated and should be viewed as reflecting and affecting one another. The dramatic situation serves a particular function in the poem, adding realism, sur-realism, or absurdity; drawing attention to certain parts of the poem; and changing to reinforce other aspects of the poem. All points should be considered. The following questions are particularly helpful to ask in determining dramatic situation:
      1. What, if any, is the narrative action in the poem?
      2. How many personae appear in the poem? What part do they take in the action?
      3. What is the relationship between characters?
      4. What is the setting (time and location) of the poem?
   B. *Point of view.* An understanding of the poem's point of view is a major step toward comprehending the poet's intended meaning. The reader should ask:
      1. Who is the speaker? Is he or she addressing someone else or the reader?
      2. Is the narrator able to understand or see everything happen-ing to him or her, or does the reader know things that the narrator does not?
      3. Is the narrator reliable?
      4. Do point of view and dramatic situation seem consistent? If not, the inconsistencies may provide clues to the poem's meaning.
   C. *Images and metaphors.* Images and metaphors are often the most intricately crafted vehicles of the poem for relaying the poet's message. Realizing that the images and metaphors work in harmony with the dramatic situation and point of view will help the reader to see the poem as a whole, rather than as disas-sociated elements.
      1. The reader should identify the concrete images (that is, those that are formed from objects that can be touched, smelled, seen, felt, or tasted). Is the image projected by the poet consistent with the physical object?
      2. If the image is abstract, or so different from natural imag-ery that it cannot be associated with a real object, then what are the properties of the image?
      3. To what extent is the reader asked to form his or her own images?

   4. Is any image repeated in the poem? If so, how has it been changed? Is there a controlling image?
   5. Are any images compared to each other? Do they reinforce one another?
   6. Is there any difference between the way the reader perceives the image and the way the narrator sees it?
   7. What seems to be the narrator's or persona's attitude to-ward the image?
   D. *Words.* Every substantial word in a poem may have more than one intended meaning, as used by the author. Because of this, the reader should look up many of these words in the dictio-nary and:
      1. Note all definitions that have the slightest connection with the poem.
      2. Note any changes in syntactical patterns in the poem.
      3. In particular, note those words that could possibly function as symbols or allusions, and refer to any appropriate sources for further information.
   E. *Meter, rhyme, structure, and tone.* In scanning the poem, all elements of prosody should be noted by the reader. These ele-ments are often used by a poet to manipulate the reader's emotions, and therefore they should be examined closely to arrive at the poet's specific intention.
      1. Does the basic meter follow a traditional pattern such as those found in nursery rhymes or folk songs?
      2. Are there any variations in the base meter? Such changes or substitutions are important thematically and should be identified.
      3. Are the rhyme schemes traditional or innovative, and what might their form mean to the poem?
      4. What devices has the poet used to create sound patterns (such as assonance and alliteration)?
      5. Is the stanza form a traditional or innovative one?
      6. If the poem is composed of verse paragraphs rather than stanzas, how do they affect the progression of the poem?
      7. After examining the above elements, is the resultant tone of the poem casual or formal, pleasant, harsh, emotional, authoritative?
   F. *Historical context.* The reader should attempt to place the poem into historical context, checking on events at the time of composition. Archaic language, expressions, images, or symbols should also be looked up.
   G. *Themes and motifs.* By seeing the poem as a composite of emotion, intellect, craftsmanship, and tradition, the reader should be able to determine the themes and motifs (smaller recurring ideas) presented in the work. He or she should ask the following questions to help pinpoint these main ideas:
      1. Is the poet trying to advocate social, moral, or religious change?
      2. Does the poet seem sure of his or her position?
      3. Does the poem appeal primarily to the emotions, to the in-tellect, or to both?
      4. Is the poem relying on any particular devices for effect (such as imagery, allusion, paradox, hyperbole, or irony)?

could be a specific person; Luke Havergal could represent a type of person; the name might have symbolic or allusive qualities. Thus, "Luke" may refer to Luke of the Bible or "Luke-warm," meaning indifferent or showing little or no zeal. "Havergal" could be a play on words. "Haver" is a Scotch and Northern English word meaning to talk foolishly. It is clear from the rhyme words that the "gal" of Havergal is pronounced as if it had two "l's," but it is spelled with one "l" for no apparent reason unless it is to play on the word "gal," meaning girl. Because it is pronounced "gall," meaning something bitter or severe, a sore or state of irritation, or an impudent self-assurance, this must also be considered as a possibility. Finally, the "haver" of "Havergal" might be a perversion of "have a."

3. Published in 1897, the poem probably does not contain archaic language unless it is deliberately used. The period of writing is known as the Victorian Age. Historical events that may have influenced the poem may be checked for later.

STEP I-B: *The poem should be read*

STEP I-C: *Rereading the poem*

The frequent use of internal caesuras in stanzas 1 and 2 contrast with the lack of caesuras in stanzas 3 and 4. There are end-stopped lines and much repetition. The poem reads smoothly except for line 28 and the feminine ending on lines 11 and 12.

STEP II-A: *Dramatic situation*

In line 1 of "Luke Havergal," an unidentified speaker is addressing Luke. Because the speaker calls him by his full name, there is a sense that the speaker has assumed a superior (or at least a formal) attitude toward Luke and that the talk that they are having is not a casual conversation.

In addition to knowing something about the relationship in line 1, the reader is led to think, because of the words "go to the western gate," that the personae must be near some sort of enclosed house or city. Perhaps Luke and the speaker are at some "other" gate, since the western gate is specifically pointed out.

Line 2 suggests that the situation at the western gate is different from that elsewhere—there "vines cling crimson on the wall," hinting at some possibilities

about the dramatic situation. (Because flowers and colors are always promising symbols, they must be carefully considered later.)

The vines in line 2 could provide valuable information about the dramatic situation, except that in line 2 the clues are ambiguous. Are the vines perennial? If so, their crimson color suggests that the season is late summer or autumn. Crimson might also be their natural color when in full bloom. Further, are they grape vines (grapes carry numerous connotations and symbolic values), and are the vines desirable? All of this in line 2 is ambiguous. The only certainty is that there is a wall—a barrier that closes something in and something out.

In lines 1-3, the speaker again commands Luke to go and wait. Since Luke is to wait in the twilight, it is probably now daylight. All Luke must do is be passive because whatever is to come will happen without any action on his part.

In line 4, the speaker begins to tell Luke what will happen at the western gate, and the reader now knows that Luke is waiting for something with feminine characteristics, possibly a woman. This line also mentions that the vines have leaves, implying that crimson denotes their waning stage.

In line 5, the speaker continues to describe what will happen at the western gate: The leaves will whisper about "her," and as they fall, some of them will strike Luke "like flying words." The reader, however, must question whether Luke will actually be "struck" by the leaves, or whether the leaves are being personified or being used as an image or symbol. In line 6, the speaker stops his prophecy and tells Luke to leave. If Luke listens, "she" will call, but if he does not, it is unclear what will happen. The reader might ask the questions, to whom is "she" calling, and from where?

In summarizing the dramatic situation in stanza 1, one can say that the speaker is addressing Luke, but it is not yet possible to determine whether he or she is present or whether Luke is thinking to himself (interior monologue). The time is before twilight; the place is near a wall with a gate. Luke is directed to go to the gate and listen for a female voice to call.

From reading the first line in the second stanza, it is apparent that Luke has posed some kind of question, probably concerned with what will be found at the western gate. The answer given is clearly not a direct answer to whatever question was asked, especially as the directions "east" and "west" are probably symbolic. The reader can expect, however, that the silent persona's response will affect the poem's progress.

Stanza 3 discloses who the speaker is and what his relationship is to Luke. After the mysterious discourse in stanza 2, Luke has probably asked "Who are you?" The equally mysterious reply in stanza 3 raises the issue of whether the voice speaking is a person or a spirit or whether it is Luke's imagination or conscience.

Because the voice says that it comes out of the grave, the reader cannot know who or what it is. It may be a person, a ghost, or only Luke's imagination or conscience. Obviously the answer will affect the dramatic situation.

In line 18, the reader learns that the speaker is on a particular mission: "to quench the kiss," and the reader can assume that when the mission is complete he or she will return to the grave. This information is sudden and shocking, and because of this sharp jolt, the reader tends to believe the speaker and credit him or her with supernatural knowledge.

In stanza 4, it becomes apparent that Luke and the speaker have not been stationary during the course of the poem because the western gate is now visible; the speaker can see the leaves upon the wall (line 26).

The wind is blowing (line 27), creating a sense of urgency, because if all the leaves are blown away they cannot whisper about "her." The speaker gives Luke final instructions, and the poem ends with the speaker again pointing toward the place where Luke will find the female persona.

In summary, one can say that the dramatic situation establishes a set of mysterious circumstances that are not explained or resolved on the dramatic level. Luke has been told to go to the western gate by someone who identifies himself or herself as having come from the grave in order to quench Luke's desire, which seems to be connected with the estranged woman, who is, perhaps, dead. The dramatic situation does not tell whether the commanding voice is an emissary from the woman or from the devil, or is merely Luke's conscience; nor does it suggest that something evil will happen to Luke at the western gate, although other elements in the poem make the reader afraid for him.

The poet, then, is using the dramatic situation to draw the reader into questions which will be answered by other means; at this point, the poem is mysterious, obscure, ambiguous, and deliberately misleading.

STEP II-B: *Point of view*

There are a number of questions that immediately come to mind about the point of view. Is the speaker an evil seducer, or is he or she a friend telling Luke about death? Why is the poem told from his or her point of view?

From a generalized study, readers know that the first-person singular point of view takes the reader deep into the mind of the narrator in order to show what he or she knows or to show a personal reaction to an event.

In "Luke Havergal," the narrator gives the following details about himself and the situation: a sense of direction (lines 1 and 9); the general type and color of the vegetation, but not enough to make a detailed analysis of it (line 2); a pantheistic view of nature (line 4); a feeling of communication with the leaves and "her" (lines 5 and 6); a philosophic view of the universe (stanza 2); the power to "quench the kiss," a sense of mission, and a home—the grave (line 18); special vision (line 20); a sense of destiny (lines 21 and 22); and a sense of time and eternity (lines 27 through 29).

Apparently, the narrator can speak with confidence about the western gate, and can look objectively at Luke to see the kiss on his forehead. Such a vantage point suggests that the speaker might represent some aspect of death. He also knows the "one way to where she is," leaving it reasonable to infer that "she" is dead.

There is another possibility in regard to the role of the speaker. He might be part of Luke himself—the voice of his thoughts, of his unconscious mind—or of part of his past. This role might possibly be combined with that of some sort of spirit of death.

The poem, then, is an internal dialogue in which Luke is attempting to cope with "she," who is probably dead and who might well have been his lover, though neither is certain. He speaks to another persona, which is probably Luke's own spirit which has been deadened by the loss of his lover.

Once it is suggested that Luke is a man who is at the depth of despair, the dramatic situation becomes very important because of the possibility that Luke may be driving himself toward self-destruction.

The dramatic situation, therefore, may not be as it originally seemed; perhaps there is only one person, not two. Luke's psychological condition permits him to look at himself as another person, and this other self is pushing Luke toward the western gate, a place that the reader senses is evil.

If the voice is Luke's, then much of the mystery is clarified. Luke would have known what the western gate looked like, whereas a stranger would have needed supernatural powers to know it; furthermore, Luke had probably heard the leaves whispering before, and in his derangement he could believe that someone would call to him if he would only listen.

Establishing point of view has cleared up most of the inconsistencies in this poem's dramatic situation, but there is still confusion about the grave and the kiss. It is easy to make the grave symbolically consistent with point of view, but the reader should look for other possibilities before settling on this explanation.

In stanzas 1 and 2, there is no problem; the dramatic situation is simple and point of view can be reconciled since there is no evidence to prove that another person is present. If, however, the voice is that of Luke's other self, then why has it come from the grave, and where did the kiss come from? At this point, it is not possible to account for these inconsistencies, but by noting them now, the reader can be on the alert for the answers later. Quite possibly accounting for the inconsistencies will provide the key for the explication.

STEP II-C: *Images and metaphors*

Finding images in poems is usually not a difficult task, although seeing their relation to the theme often is. "Luke Havergal" is imagistically difficult because the images are introduced, then reused as the theme develops.

In stanza 1, the reader is allowed to form his or her own image of the setting and mood at the western gate; most readers will probably imagine some sort of mysterious or supernatural situation related to death or the dead. The colors, the sound of the words, and the particular images (vines, wall, whispering leaves) establish the relationship between the living and the dead as the controlling image of the entire poem.

Within the controlling death-in-life image, the metaphors and conceits are more difficult to handle. Vines clinging crimson on the wall (line 2) and waiting in the twilight for something to come (line 3) are images requiring no particular treatment at this point, but in lines 4 and 5 the reader is forced to contend directly with whispering leaves that are like flying words, and there are several metaphorical possibilities for this image.

First, there is the common image of leaves rustling in a breeze, and in a mysterious or enchanted atmosphere it would be very easy to imagine that they are whispering. Such a whisper, however, would ordinarily require a moderate breeze, as a fierce wind would overpower the rustling sound of leaves; but there is more ambiguity in the image: "The leaves will whisper there for her, and some,/ Like flying words, will strike you as they fall."

Because of the syntactical ambiguity of "some,/ Like flying words, will strike," the reader cannot be sure how close or literal is the similarity or identity of "leaves" and "words." The reader cannot be completely sure whether it is leaves or words or both that will strike Luke, or whether the sight of falling leaves might be forcing him to recall words he has heard in the past. There is a distinct metaphoric connection between leaves and words, however, and these in some way strike Luke, perhaps suggesting that the words are those of an argument (an argument in the past between Luke and "her" before her death) or perhaps meant to suggest random words which somehow recall "her" but do not actually say anything specific.

In stanza 2, the poet forces the reader to acknowledge the light and dark images, but they are as obscure as the falling leaves in stanza 1. The dawn that the reader is asked to visualize (line 9) is clear, but it is immediately contrasted with "the fiery night that's in your eyes"; Luke's smoldering, almost diabolic eyes are imagistically opposed to the dawn.

Line 11 returns to the western gate, or at least to the "west," where twilight is falling. The "western glooms" become imagistic as the twilight falls and depicts Luke's despair. Twilight is not "falling," but dark is "gathering" around him, and glooms not only denotes darkness but also connotes Luke's emotional state.

The paradox in line 12, "The dark will end the dark," beckons the reader to explore it imagistically, but it is not easy to understand how darkness relieves darkness, unless one of the two "darknesses" is symbolic of death or of Luke's gloom. With this beckoning image, the poet has created emphasis on the line and teases with images which may really be symbols or paradoxes. The same thing is true for lines 13 and 14, which tempt the reader to imagine how "God slays Himself" with leaves, and how "hell is more than half of paradise."

The beginning of stanza 3 does not demand an image so much as it serves to tell where the narrator comes from, and to present the narrator's method for quenching the kiss. Line 19, however, presents an image that is as forceful as it is ambiguous. The kiss, which may be the kiss of the estranged woman, or "the kiss of death," or both, flames with a glow, which is also paradoxical. The paradox, however, forms an image which conveys the intensity of Luke's passion.

Stanza 4 returns to the imagery of stanza 1, but now the whispering leaves take on a metaphorical extension. If the leaves are whispering words from the dead, and if the leaves are "her" words, then once the wind tears all the leaves away, there will no longer be any medium for communication between the living and the dead. This adds a sense of urgency for Luke to go to the western gate and do there what must be done.

In summary, the images in "Luke Havergal" do more than set the mood; they also serve an important thematic function because of their ambiguities and paradoxical qualities.

STEP II-D: *Words*

Because the poem is not too old, the reader will find that most of the words have not changed much. It is still important, however, for the reader to look up words as they may have several diverse meanings. Even more important to consider in individual words or phrases, however, is the possibility that they might be symbolic or allusive.

"Luke Havergal" is probably not as symbolic as it at first appears, although poems that use paradox and allusion are often very symbolic. Clearly the western gate is symbolic, but to what degree is questionable. No doubt it represents the last light in Luke's life, and once he passes beyond it he moves into another type of existence. The west and the twilight are points of embarka-

tion; the sun is setting in the west, but even though the sun sets, there will not be a dawn in the east to dispel Luke's dark gloom. Traditionally the dark, which is gathering in the west, is symbolic of death (the west is also traditionally associated with death), and only the dark will end Luke's gloom in life, if anything at all can do it.

There is one important allusion in the poem, which comes in stanza 3; the kiss which the speaker is going to quench may be the "kiss of death," the force that can destroy Luke.

In both concept and language, stanza 3 is reminiscent of the dagger scene and killing of Duncan (act 2, scene 1) in William Shakespeare's *Macbeth* (pr. 1606). Just before the murder, Macbeth has visions of the dagger:

> Art thou not, fatal vision, sensible
> To feeling as to sight? or art thou but
> A dagger of the mind, a false creation,
> Proceeding from the heat-oppressed brain?
> I see thee yet, in form as palpable
> As this which now I draw.
> Thou marshall'st me the way that I was going

And a few lines later (act 2, scene 2) Lady Macbeth says:

> That which hath made them drunk hath made me bold;
> What hath quench'd them hath given me fire.

The reversal in point of view in "Luke Havergal" gives the poem added depth, which is especially enhanced by the comparison with Macbeth. The line, "That blinds you to the way that you must go" is almost a word-for-word equivalent of "Thou marshall'st me the way that I was going," except that in "Luke Havergal" whoever is with Luke is talking, while Macbeth himself is talking to the dagger.

The result of the allusion is that it is almost possible to imagine that it is the dagger that is talking to Luke, and the whole story of Macbeth becomes relevant to the poem because the reader suspects that Luke's end will be similar to Macbeth's.

The words of Lady Macbeth strengthen the allusion's power and suggest a male-female relationship that is leading Luke to his death, especially since, in the resolution of *Macbeth*, Lady Macbeth goes crazy and whispers to the spirits.

If the reader accepts the allusion as a part of the poem, the imagery is enhanced by the vivid descriptions in *Macbeth*. Most critics and writers agree that if a careful reader finds something that fits consistently into a poem, then it is "there" for all readers who see the same thing, whether the poet consciously put it there or not. Robinson undoubtedly read and knew Shakespeare, but it does not matter whether he deliberately alluded to *Macbeth* if the reader can show that it is important to the poem.

There is a basic problem with allusion and symbol that every explicator must resolve for himself: Did the poet intend a symbol or an allusion to be taken in the way that a particular reader has interpreted it? The New Critics answered this question by coining the term "intentional fallacy," meaning that the poet's *intention* is ultimately unimportant when considering the finished poem. It is possible that stanza 3 was not intended to allude to *Macbeth*, and it was simply by accident that Robinson used language similar to Shakespeare's. Perhaps Robinson never read *Macbeth*, or perhaps he read it once and those lines remained in his subconscious. In either case, the reader must decide whether the allusion is important to the meaning of the poem.

STEP II-E: *Meter, rhyme, structure, and tone*

Because "Luke Havergal" is a poem that depends so heavily on all the elements of prosody, it should be scanned carefully. Here is an example of scansion using the second stanza of the poem:

> Nŏ, thére/ ĭs nót/ ă dáwn/ ĭn eás/tĕrn skiés
> Tŏ ríft/ thĕ fíe/rў níght/ thăt's ín/ yŏur éyes;
> Bŭt thére,/ whĕre wés/tĕrn glóoms/ ăre gáth/ĕrĭng,
> Thĕ dárk/ wĭll énd/ thĕ dárk,/ ĭf ăn/ўthĭng:
> Gŏd sláys/ Hĭmsélf/ wĭth éve/rў léaf/ thăt flíes,
> Ănd héll/ ĭs móre/ thăn hálf/ ŏf pár/ădĭse.
> Nŏ, thére/ ĭs nót/ ă dáwn/ ĭn eást/ĕrn skiés—
> Ĭn eás/tĕrn skíes.

The basic meter of the poem is iambic pentameter, with frequent substitutions, but every line except the last in each stanza contains ten syllables.

The stanza form in "Luke Havergal" is very intri-

cate and delicate. It is only because of the structure that the heavy *a* rhyme (*aabbaaaa*) does not become monotonous; yet it is because of the *a* rhyme that the structure works so well.

The pattern for the first stanza works as follows:

Line	Rhyme	Function
1	a	Sets up ideas and images for the stanza.
2	a	Describes or complements line 1.
3	b	Lines 3, 4, and 5 constitute the central part of the mood and the fears. The return to the a rhyme unifies lines 1-5.
4	b	
5	a	
6	a	Reflects on what has been said in lines 1-5; it serves to make the reader stop, and it adds a mysterious suggestion.
7	a	Continues the deceleration and reflection.
8	a	The repetition and dimeter line stop the stanza completely, and the effect is to prepare for a shift in thought, just as Luke's mind jumps from thought to thought.

Stanza 2 works in a similar manner, except for lines 13 and 14, which tie the stanza together as a couplet. Thus, lines 13 and 14 both unify and reflect, while lines 15 and 16 in the final couplet continue to reflect while slowing down.

Lines	Rhyme	Function
9 and 10	a	Opening couplet.
11 and 12	b	Couplet in lines 11-12 contains the central idea and image.
13 and 14	a	Couplet in 13-14 reflects on that in 11-12, but the autonomy of this third couplet is especially strong. Whereas in stanza 1, only line 5 reflects on the beginning of the stanza to create unity, this entire couplet is now strongly associated with the first, with the effect of nearly equating Luke with God.
15 and 16	a	Final couplet reflects on the first and completes the stanza.

Stanza 3 works in the same manner as stanza 2, while stanza 4 follows the pattern of stanza 1.

Each stanza is autonomous and does not need the others for continuation or progression in plot; each stanza appears to represent a different thought as Luke's mind jumps about.

The overall structure focuses on stanza 3, which is crucial to the theme. Stanzas 1 and 2 clearly present the problem: Luke knows that if he goes he will find "her," and the worst that can happen is that the darkness will remain. With stanza 3, however, there is a break in point of view as the narrator calls attention to himself.

With stanza 4 there is a return to the beginning, reinforced by the repetition of rhyme words; the difference between stanzas 4 and 1 is that the reader has felt the impact of stanza 3; structurally, whatever resolution there is will evolve out of the third stanza, or because of it.

The stanza form of "Luke Havergal" achieves tremendous unity and emphasis; the central image or idea presented in the *b* lines is reinforced in the remainder of the stanza by a tight-knit rhyme structure. There are several types of rhymes being used in the poem, all of which follow the traditional functions of their type. Stanza 1 contains full masculine end rhyme, with a full masculine internal rhyme in line 2 (*There where*). Lines 2 and 3 contain alliteration (*c* in line 2, *t* in line 3) also binding the lines more tightly.

With "go" occurring near the end of stanza 1 and "No" appearing as the first word in stanza 2, this rhyme becomes important in forming associations between lines. Lines 9, 10, 15, 16, and 18 form full masculine end rhyme, with line 14 "paradise" assonating with a full rhyme. Lines 11 and 12 are half falling rhymes; these lines also contain a full internal rhyme ("there," "where") and alliteration (*g* and *w* in line 11). "Dark" in line 12 is an exact internal rhyme. The *l* and *s* in "slays" and "flies" (line 14) create an effect similar to assonance; there is also an *h* alliteration in line 15.

In stanza 3, the plosive consonants *c* and *q* make an alliterative sound in line 18, binding "come" and "quench" together; there is also an *f* alliteration in line 19. All the end rhymes are full masculine in stanza 3 except line 21, which assonates. Stanza 4 contains full masculine end rhyme, with one internal rhyme ("they

say") in line 28, one alliteration in line 29, and consonance ("will call") in line 30.

In addition to its function in developing the stanza, rhyme in "Luke Havergal" has important influence on sound, and in associating particular words and lines.

In lines 1 and 2 of "Luke Havergal," there are a number of plosive consonants and long vowels, in addition to the internal rhyme and *c* alliteration. The cadence of these lines is slow, and they reverberate with "cling" and "crimson." The tone of these lines is haunting (which is consistent with the situation), and the rhythm and sound of the poem as a whole suggest an incantation; the speaker's voice is seductive and evil, which is important to the theme, because if Luke goes to the gate he may be persuaded to die, which is what the voice demands.

Through its seductive sound, the poem seems to be having the same effect on the reader that it does on Luke; that is, the reader feels, as Luke does, that there is an urgency in going to the gate before all the leaves are blown away, and that by hearing "her" call, his discomfort will be relieved. The reader, unable to see the evil forces at work in the last stanza, sympathizes with Luke, and thinks that the voice is benevolent.

Whereas sound can be heard and analyzed, tone is a composite of a number of things that the reader can feel only after coming to know the poem. The poet's attitude or tone may be noncommittal or it may be dogmatic (as in allegory); sometimes the tone will affect the theme, while at other times it comes as an aside to the theme.

Poems that attempt to initiate reform frequently have a more readily discernible tone than poems that make observations without judging too harshly, although this is not always true. "Luke Havergal" is, among other things, about how the presence of evil leads toward death, but the poet has not directly included his feelings about that theme. If there is an attitude, it is the poet's acceptance of the inevitability of death and the pain that accompanies it for the living.

Perhaps the poet is angry at how effectively death can seduce life; it is obvious that Robinson wants the poem to haunt and torment the reader, and in doing so make him or her conscious of the hold death has on humanity.

Luke must meet death part way; he must first go to

the gate before he can hear the dead words, which makes him partly responsible for death's hold over him. The tone of "Luke Havergal" is haunting and provocative.

STEP II-F: *Historical context*

Finished in December, 1895, "Luke Havergal" was in Robinson's estimation a Symbolist poem. It is essential, then, that the explicator learn something about the Symbolist movement. If his or her explication is not in accord with the philosophy of the period, the reader must account for the discrepancy.

In a study of other Robinson poems, there are themes parallel to that of "Luke Havergal." One, for example, is that of the alienated self. If Robinson believes in the alienated self, then it is possible that the voice speaking in "Luke Havergal" is Luke's own, but in an alienated state. This view may add credence to an argument that the speaker is Luke's past or subconscious, though it by no means proves it. Although parallelisms may be good support for the explication, the reader must be careful not to misconstrue them.

STEP II-G: *Themes and motifs, or correlating the parts*

Once the poem has been placed in context, the prosodic devices analyzed, and the function of the poetical techniques understood, they should be correlated, and any discrepancies should be studied for possible errors in explication. By this time, every line should be understood, so that stating what the poem is about is merely a matter of explaining the common points of all the area, supporting it with specific items from the poem, secondary sources, other poems, other critics, and history. The reader may use the specific questions given in the outline to help detail the major themes.

BIBLIOGRAPHY

Coleman, Kathleen. *Guide to French Poetry Explication*. New York: G. K. Hall, 1993.

Gioia, Dana, David Mason, and Meg Schoerke, eds. *Twentieth-Century American Poetics: Poets on the Art of Poetry*. Boston: McGraw-Hill, 2003.

Hirsch, Edward. *How to Read a Poem and Fall in Love with Poetry*. New York: Harcourt Brace, 1999.

Kohl, Herbert R. *A Grain of Poetry: How to Read Contemporary Poems and Make Them a Part of Your Life*. New York: HarperFlamingo, 1999.

Lennard, John. *The Poetry Handbook: A Guide to Reading Poetry for Pleasure and Practical Criticism*. 2d ed. New York: Oxford University Press, 2006.

Martínez, Nancy C., and Joseph G. R. Martínez. *Guide to British Poetry Explication*. 4 vols. Boston: G. K. Hall, 1991-1995.

Oliver, Mary. *A Poetry Handbook*. San Diego, Calif.: Harcourt Brace, 1994.

Preminger, Alex, et al., eds. *The New Princeton Encyclopedia of Poetry and Poetics*. 3d rev. ed. Princeton, N.J.: Princeton University Press, 1993.

Ryan, Michael. *A Difficult Grace: On Poets, Poetry, and Writing*. Athens: University of Georgia Press, 2000.

Statman, Mark. *Listener in the Snow: The Practice and Teaching of Poetry*. New York: Teachers & Writers Collaborative, 2000.

Steinman, Lisa M. *Invitation to Poetry: The Pleasures of Studying Poetry and Poetics*. Walden, Mass.: Wiley-Blackwell, 2008.

Strand, Mark, and Eavan Boland, eds. *The Making of a Poem: A Norton Anthology of Poetic Forms*. New York: W. W. Norton, 2000.

Wolosky, Shira. *The Art of Poetry: How to Read a Poem*. New York: Oxford University Press, 2001.

Walton Beacham

Language and Linguistics

Most humans past the infant stage have a spoken language and use it regularly for understanding and speaking, although much of the world's population is still illiterate and cannot read or write. Language is such a natural part of life that people tend to overlook it until they are presented with some special problem: They lose their sight or hearing, have a stroke, or are required to learn a foreign language. Of course, people may also study their own language, but seldom do they stand aside and view language for what it is—a complex human phenomenon with a history reaching back to humankind's beginnings. A study of the development of one language will often reveal intertwinings with other languages. Sometimes such knowledge enables linguists to construct family groups; just as often, the divergences among languages or language families are so great that separate typological variations are established.

True language is characterized by its systematic nature, its arbitrariness of vocabulary and structure, its vocality, and its basis in symbolism. Most linguists believe that language and thought are separate entities. Although language may be necessary to give foundation to thought, it is not, in itself, thinking. Many psychologists, however, contend that language is thought. An examination of language on the basis of these assertions reveals that each language is a purely arbitrary code or set of rules. There is no intrinsic necessity for any word to sound like or mean what it does. Language is essentially speech, and symbolism is somehow the philosophical undergirding of the whole linguistic process. The French author Madame de Staël (1766-1817) once wrote, in describing her native language, that language is even more: "It is not only a means of communicating thoughts, feeling and acts, but an instrument that one loves to play upon, and that stimulates the mental faculties much as music does for some people and strong drink for others."

Origin of Language

How did language originate? First, the evidence for the origin of language is so deeply buried in the past that it is unlikely that people shall ever be able to do more than speculate about the matter. If people had direct knowledge of humankind's immediate ancestors, they should be able to develop some evolutionary theory and be able to say, among other things, how speech production and changes in the brain are related. Some linguists maintain that language ability is innate, but this assertion, true though it may be, rests on the assumption of a monogenetic theory of humanity's origin. Few scholars today are content with the notion that the human race began with Adam and Eve.

According to the Bible, Adam is responsible for human speech. Genesis reports:

> And out of the ground the Lord God formed every beast of the field, and every fowl of the air, and brought them unto Adam to see what he would call them; and whatsoever Adam called every creature, that was the name thereof. And Adam gave names to all cattle, and to the fowl of the air, and to every beast of the field.

If the story of Adam and Eve is taken literally, one might conclude that their language was the original one. Unfortunately, not even the Bible identifies what this language was. Some people have claimed that Hebrew was the first language and that all the other languages of the world are derived from it; Hebrew, however, bears no discernible relationship to any language outside the Hamito-Semitic group. Besides, any so-called original language would have changed so drastically in the intervening millennia before the onset of writing that it would not bear any resemblance to ancient Hebrew. Whatever the "original" language was—and there is every reason to believe that many languages sprang up independently over a very long span of time—it could not sound at all like any language that has been documented.

Many theories of the origin of language have been advanced, but three have been mentioned in textbooks more frequently than others. One, the "bow-wow" or echoic theory, insists that the earliest forms of language were exclusively onomatopoeic—that is, imitative of the sounds of animals and nature, despite the fact that the so-called primitive languages are not largely composed of onomatopoeic words. Furthermore, some measure of conventionalization must take place before echoisms become real "words"; individual young children do not call a dog a "bow-wow" until they hear an older child or adult use the term. Another theory, called the "pooh-pooh" or interjectional theory, maintains that language must have begun with primitive grunts and groans—that is, very loose and disjointed utterances. Many have held that such a theory fits animals better than humans; indeed, this kind of exclamatory speech probably separates humans quite clearly from the animals. Still another theory, dubbed the "ding-dong" theory, claims that language arose as a response to natural stimuli. None of these theories has any strong substantiation. Some linguists have suggested that speech and song may have once been the same. The presence of tones and pitch accent in many older languages lends some plausibility to the idea; it is likely that language, gestures, and song, as forms of communication, were all intertwined at the earliest stages.

Is it a hopeless task to try to discover the origin of language? Linguists have continued to look into the question again, but there is little chance that more than a priori notions can be established. It has been suggested, for example, that prehumans may have gradually developed a kind of grammar by occasionally fitting together unstructured vocal signals in patterns that were repeated and then eventually understood, accepted, and passed on. This process is called compounding, and some forms of it are found in present-day gibbon calls.

THE HISTORY OF LANGUAGE STUDY

In the history of language study, a number of signposts can be erected to mark the path. The simplest outline consists of two major parts: a prescientific and a scientific period. The first can be dispensed with in short order.

The earliest formal grammar of any language is a detailed analysis of classical Sanskrit, written by the Indian scholar Pānini in the fourth century B.C.E. He called it the Sutras (instructions), and in it, he codified the rules for the use of proper Sanskrit. It is still an authoritative work. Independently of Pānini, the ancient Greeks established many grammatical concepts that strongly influenced linguistic thinking for hundreds of years. Platonic realism, although by today's standards severely misguided in many respects, offered a number of useful insights into language, among them the basic division of the sentence into subject and predicate, the recognition of word stress, and the twofold classification of sounds into consonants and vowels. In the third century B.C.E., Aristotle defined the various parts of speech. In the next century, Dionysius Thrax produced a grammar that not only improved understanding of the sound system of Greek but also classified even more clearly the basic parts of speech and commented at length on such properties of language as gender, number, case, mood, voice, tense, and person. At no time, though, did the Hindu and Greek scholars break away from a focus on their own language to make a comparison with other languages. This fault was also largely one of the Romans, who merely adapted Greek scholarship to their own needs. If they did any comparing of languages, it was not of the languages in the Roman world, but only of Latin as a "corrupt" descendant of Greek. In sum, the Romans introduced no new concepts; they were, instead, content to synthesize or reorganize their legacy from ancient Greece. Only two grammarians come to mind from the fourth and fifth centuries of the Roman Empire—Priscian and Donatus, whose works served for centuries as basic texts for the teaching of Latin.

The scientific period of language study began with a British Sanskrit scholar, Sir William Jones, who headed a society organized in Calcutta for the exploration of Asia. In 1786, he delivered a paper in which he stated that

the Sanskrit language . . . [was] more perfect than the Greek, more copious than the Latin, and more exquisitely refined than either; yet [bore] to both of them a stronger affinity . . . than could possibly have been produced by accident; so strong, indeed, that no philologer could examine them all three without believing them to have sprung from some common source, which, perhaps, no longer exists.

He went on to say that Germanic and Celtic probably had the same origin. His revolutionary assertion that Sanskrit and most of the languages of Europe had descended from a single language no longer spoken and never recorded first produced considerable scholarly opposition, but shortly thereafter set the stage for comparative analysis. He insisted that a close examination of the "inner structures" of this family of languages would reveal heretofore unsuspected relationships.

Franz Bopp, a German born in 1791 and a student of Oriental languages, including Sanskrit, was the founder of comparative grammar. In his epochmaking book *Über das Conjugationssystem der Sanskritsprache in Vergleichung mit jenem der griechischen, lateinischen, persischen und germanischen Sprache* (1816), he demonstrated for all time what Jones and Friedrich von Schlegel and other researchers had only surmised. A young Danish contemporary named Rasmus Rask corroborated his results and established that Armenian and Lithuanian belong to the same language group, the Indo-European. The tool to establish these relationships was the "comparative method," one of the greatest achievements of nineteenth century linguistics. In applying this method, linguists searched in the various languages under investigation for cognates—words with similar spelling, similar sound, and similar meaning. They then set up sound correspondences among the cognates, much like looking for the lowest common denominator in a mathematical construction, from which the original linguistic forms could be constructed.

The German linguist Jakob Grimm (one of the Brothers Grimm known for books of fairy tales) took Rask's work one step further and, in a four-volume work published between 1819 and 1822, showed conclusively the systematic correspondences and differences between Sanskrit, Greek, and Latin, on one hand, and the Germanic languages, on the other hand. The formulation of this system of sound changes came to be known as Grimm's law, or the First Sound Shift, and the changes involved can be diagramed as follows:

Proto-Indo-European: *bh dh gh b d g p t k*
Proto-Germanic: *b d g p t k f Θ h*

Where the Indo-European, as transmitted through Latin or Greek, had a *p* sound (as in *piscis* and *pēd*), the German-based English word has an *f* ("fish" and "foot");

the Latinate *trēs* becomes the English "three." In addition to the changes described above, another important change took place in the Germanic languages. If the *f Θ h* resulting from the change of *p t k* stood after an unaccented vowel but before another vowel, they became voiced fricatives, later voiced stops, as in the pair *seethe : sodden*. This change also affected *s*, yielding *z*, which later became *r* (Rhotacism) and explains, for example, the alternations in *was : were*. It was described by Karl Verner, a Danish linguist, and is known appropriately as Verner's law. There are one or two other "laws" that explain apparent exceptions to Grimm's law, illustrating the basic regularity of Grimm's formulations. At the very end of the nineteenth century, the neo-Grammarians, led by Karl Brugmann, insisted that all exceptions could be explained—that, in fact, "phonetic laws are natural laws and have no exceptions." Even those studying the natural sciences do not make such a strong assertion, but the war cry of the neo-Grammarians did inspire scholars to search for regularity in language.

The German language itself underwent a profound change beginning probably in the far south of the German-speaking lands sometime during the fifth century, causing a restructuring of the sounds of all of the southern and many of the midland dialects. These became known, for geographical reasons, as High German, while those dialects in the north came to be known as Low German. Six consonants in various positions were affected, but the most consistently shifted sounds were the Indo-European *b*, which in English became *p* and in German *pf*, and the *d* to *t* and *ts*. For example, the Latin *decim* became the English "ten" and the German *zehn*.

In the course of the nineteenth century, all such changes were recognized, and scholars were enabled to identify and diagram the reflex languages of Indo-European into five subgroups known as *satem* languages and four known as *centum* languages. This division is significant both geographically—the *satem* languages are located clearly to the east of where the original home of the Indo-Europeans probably was—and linguistically—the *satem* languages have, among other characteristics, *s* sounds where the *centum* languages have *k* sounds (the word *centum* is pronounced

---

THE *SATEM* LANGUAGES

Indo-Iranian	Earliest attested form, Sanskrit; modern languages include Hindi, Bengali, and Persian.
Albanian	Spoken by a small number of Balkan people.
Armenian	Spoken by a small number of people in that country.
Slavic	Divided into East Slavic (Great Russian, the standard language; Little Russian or Ukrainian; White Russian, spoken in the region adjacent to and partly in modern-day Poland); West Slavic (Czech, Slovak, Polish); South Slavic (Slovenian and Serbo-Croatian; Bulgarian).
Baltic	Lithuanian and Lettic, spoken in the Baltic states.

---

with an initial hard *c*). The very words *satem* and *centum*, meaning "hundred" in Avestan (an Indo-Iranian language) and Latin, respectively, illustrate the sound divergence.

INDO-EUROPEAN LANGUAGES

The original home of the Indo-Europeans is not known for certain, but it is safe to say that it was in Europe, and probably close to present-day Lithuania. For one thing, the Lithuanians have resided in a single area since the Neolithic Age (2500-2000 B.C.E.) and speak a language of great complexity. Furthermore, Lithuania is situated on the dividing line between *centum* and *satem* languages. One would also assume that the original home was somewhere close to the area where the reflex languages are to be found today and not, for example, in Africa, Australia, or North or South America. For historical and archaeological reasons, scholars have ruled out the British Isles and the peninsulas of southern Europe. Last, there are indications that the Indo-Europeans entered India from the northwest, for there is no evidence of their early acquaintanceship with the Ganges River, but only with the Indus (hence "Indo-"). Certain common words for weather conditions, geography, and flora and fauna militate in favor of a European homeland.

Scholars have classified the Indo-European languages as a family apart from certain other languages on the basis of two principal features: their common word stock and their inflectional structure. This type of classification, called genetic, is one of three. Another, called geographical, is usually employed initially. For example, if nothing whatsoever was known about American Indian languages, one might divide them into North American and South American, Eastern North American and Western North American, and perhaps some other geographical categories. A third variety of classification, called typological, is possible only when a good deal is

---

THE *CENTUM* LANGUAGES

Greek (Hellenic)	Attic, Ionic, and Doric, formerly spoken throughout the eastern areas around the Mediterranean; modern Greek.
Italic	Latin; modern Italian, French, Spanish, Portuguese, Catalan, Sardinian, Romanian, and Rhaeto-Romanic.
Celtic	Modern Welsh, Cornish, Breton, Irish, and Scots Gaelic.
Germanic (Teutonic)	East Germanic (Gothic, now extinct); North Germanic (Danish, Norwegian, Swedish, Icelandic); West Germanic (Low German: English, Dutch, Frisian, Plattdeutsch; High German: standard German).
In addition	Several extinct Indo-European languages, such as Tocharian and the Anatolian languages, especially Hittite.

---

known about the structure of a language. The four main types of languages arrived at through such classification are inflectional, meaning that such syntactic distinctions as gender, number, case, tense, and so forth are usually communicated by altering the form of a word, as in English when *-s* added to a noun indicates plurality but, when added to a verb, singularity; agglutinative, meaning that suffixes are piled onto word bases in a definite order and without change in phonetic shape (for example, Turkish *evlerimden*, "house-s-my-from"); isolating, meaning that invariable word forms, mostly monosyllabic, are employed in variable word order (for example, Chinese *wŏ*, meaning, according to its position in the utterance, "I," "me," "to me," or "my"); and incorporating or polysynthetic, meaning that a sentence, with its various syntactic features, may be "incorporated" as a single word (for example, Eskimo /a: wlisa-utiss?ar-siniarpu-na/, "I am looking for something suitable for a fish-line").

OTHER LANGUAGES

Although the Indo-European languages have been studied in more detail than other language families, it is possible to classify and describe many of the remaining language families of the world, the total comprising more than twenty-seven hundred separate languages. In Europe and Asia, relatively few languages are spoken by very large numbers of people; elsewhere many distinct languages are spoken by small communities. In Europe, all languages are Indo-European except for Finnish, Estonian, Hungarian, and Basque. The last-named is something of a mystery; it appears to predate Indo-European by such a long period that it could conceivably be descended from a prehistoric language. The first three belong to the same family, the Finno-Urgic. Sometimes Turkish is added to the group, and the four are called the Ural-Altaic family. All are agglutinative.

The most extensive language family in eastern Asia is the Sino-Tibetan. It consists of two branches, the Tibeto-Burman and Chinese. Mandarin is the language of the northern half of China, although there are three different varieties—northern, southwestern, and southern. In the south, there is a range of mutually unintelligible dialects. All are isolating in structure.

In other parts of Asia are found the Kadai family, consisting of Thai, Laotian, and the Shan languages of Burma, and in southern Asia, the Munda languages and Vietnamese. The latter has a considerable number of speakers.

Japanese and Korean are separate families, even though cultural relationships between the two countries have produced some borrowing over the years. Japanese is essentially agglutinative.

On the continent of Africa, the linguistic family of prime importance is the Hamito-Semitic family. Hebrew, Arabic, and some of the languages of Ethiopia make up the Semitic side. There are four Hamitic languages: Egyptian, Berber, Cushitic, and Chad. All exhibit some inflectional characteristics. In addition to these languages, Hausa, an important trade language, is used throughout the northern part of the continent.

In central and southern Africa, the Niger-Congo language family is dominant. The largest subgroup of this family is Bantu, which includes Swahili in central and eastern Africa, Kikuyu in Kenya, and Zulu in the south. Most appear to be either agglutinative or polysynthetic.

The Malayo-Polynesian languages are spoken as original tongues all the way from Madagascar to the Malay Peninsula, the East Indies, and, across the Pacific, to Hawaii. Many seem to be isolating with traces of earlier inflections.

The Indian languages of the Americas are all polysynthetic. Until recently, these Indian languages were classified geographically. Many of the North American languages have been investigated, and linguists group them into distinct families, such as Algonquian, Athabaskan, Natchez-Muskogean, Uto-Aztecan, Penutian, and Hokan.

MODERN LANGUAGES

In addition to the distinction between prescientific and scientific periods of language study, there are other divisions that can help clarify the various approaches to this vast topic. For example, the entire period from earliest times until the late nineteenth century was largely historical, comparative at best, but scarcely truly scientific in terms of rigor. Beginning with the neo-Grammarians Brugmann and Delbrück, the stage was set for what may be called a period of general or descriptive linguistics. Languages were examined not only diachronically—that is, historically—but also synchronically, where a segment or feature of language was scrutinized without regard to an earlier stage. The most important names associated with this descriptive school are those of N. S. Trubetzkoy and Roman Jakobson. Strongly influenced by the theories of the Swiss linguist Ferdinand de Saussure, they examined each detail of language as a part of a system. In other words, they were ultimately more interested in the system and the way it hung together than in each individual detail. These scholars were members of the European school of linguistic thought that had its origin in Jakobson's Prague circle. Across the Atlantic, their most important counterpart was Leonard Bloomfield, who, in 1933, published his classic linguistics text, *Language*. Like his contemporary, Edward Sapir, Bloomfield began as a comparativist in Germanic linguistics, then studied American Indian languages, and finally became an expert in the general principles of language. Bloomfield's theory of structuralism has been criticized for its resemblance to the psychological theory of behaviorism, which restricts itself to the observable and rejects the concept of mind.

Since the 1930's, there has been a steady procession of American linguists studying and reporting on the sounds and grammatical features of many different languages, in some sense all derivative from the foundation laid by the phonemicists beginning with Saussure and Bloomfield. Kenneth Pike's tagmemics, in part an attempt to present language behavior empirically through a description at each level of grammatical form, evolved directly out of descriptive linguistics. In 1957, Noam Chomsky launched transformational-generative grammar, concerned at first only with syntax, but later also with phonology. Considerable tension has developed between structuralists and transformational-generative grammarians, concerning not only syntactic analysis but also the representation of sounds. For some, stratificational grammar provides a connection, through strata or levels of description, among descriptive, tagmemic, and computational analyses.

THE TECHNICAL SIDE OF LANGUAGE

A language is made up of its sound system, grammar, and vocabulary. The former two may differ considerably from language family to language family, but there is a workable range in the extent and type of sounds and grammatical functions. The inventory of significant sounds in a given language, called phonemes, extends from about twenty to about sixty. English has forty-six, including phonemes of pitch, stress, and juncture. If the grammatical facts of a complicated language can be written out on one or two sheets of paper, the grammar of English can be laid out on the back of an envelope. In short, some languages are simpler phonologically or grammatically than others, but none is so complicated in either respect that every child cannot learn his or her language in about the same time.

The study of the sounds of which speech is made up became scientific in method by the end of the nineteenth century, when Paul Passy founded the International Phonetic Association. Down to the present day, articulatory phonetics has borne a close relationship to physiology in the description of the sounds of speech according to the organs producing them and the position of these organs in relation to surrounding structures.

By the mid-1920's, phoneticians realized that the unit of description of the phonology of a language had to be a concept rather than some physical entity. The term phoneme was chosen; it designates a minimally significant sound unit, an abstraction around which cluster all the phonetic realizations of that generalized sound. Thus, the English phoneme /p/ represents all recognizably similar pronunciations of [p], with more or less or no aspiration depending on position within a word or the speech habits of a given speaker. In other words, it designates a class of sounds distinct from others in the language. It carries no meaning as such, but it serves to distinguish one sound from another and, together with other phonemes, produces morphemic, or meaning, differences. Thus /p/, /i/, and /n/ are separate phonemes, but, taken together, make up a morpheme—the word *pin*—which is distinct, by virtue of a single phoneme, from, say, /bin/, "bin," or /tin/ "tin." Sometimes, morphemes show relations between words, as when -*s* is added to a noun to indicate plurality or possession or to a verb to indicate singularity.

The sound system and grammar of a language are thus closely related. Grammar, at least for Indo-European languages and many others, can be defined as consisting of a morphology and syntax, where, expressed simply, the former refers to the words and their endings and the latter to the order of words. Accompanying the words are, however, other features of language that can alter meaning. It matters, for example, whether the stress occurs on the first or second syllable of the word *pervert* or *permit*. If the stress falls on the first syllable, the word is a noun; if on the second, it is a verb. It matters whether the last few sounds of an utterance convey an upturn or a downturn and trail-off, for a question or a statement may result. It matters also what the pitch level is and whether juncture is present. These features, too, are phonemic.

To function in a language, one must have control of close to 100 percent of the phonology and 75 percent or more of the grammar, but a mere 1 percent of the vocabulary will enable the speaker to function in many situations. For a speaker of a language the size of English, a vocabulary of six thousand words will suffice. Possessing a vocabulary implies an unconscious knowledge of the semantic relationship to the phonology and grammar of the language. One theory of the word regards the word as a compound formed of two components: a physical element, the sequence of sounds of speech; and a semantic element, the amount of meaning expressed by the segment of speech. The first is called the formant, the second the morpheme. The word "cook" /kuk/ is one morpheme expressed by one formant—the formant consisting of one syllable, a sequence of three phonemes. In the plural of "cook," -*s* is a formant that is not even a syllable. In fact, a formant is not even necessarily a phoneme, but can be the use of one form instead of another, as in "her" instead of "she." There is no reason that the same formant, such as -*s*, cannot express more than one morpheme: "cooks" (noun) versus "cook's" versus "cooks" (verb). The same morpheme can also be expressed by more than one formant; there are, for example, many different formants for the plural, such as basis/bases, curriculum/curricula, datum/data, ox/oxen, child/children, man/men, woman/women, cherub/cherubim, monsignore/monsignori.

The distinction in morphology made above between words and their endings needs further amplification. An examination of a stanza from Lewis Carroll's "Jabberwocky" (from *Alice's Adventures in Wonderland*, 1865) illustrates the manner in which the poet uses formants with no evident meaning to the average speaker:

> 'Twas brilling, and the slithy toves
> Did gyre and gimble in the wabe;
> All mimsy were the borogoves,
> And the mome raths outgrabe.

Alice herself remarks that the words fill her head with ideas, but she does not know what they are. There is a rightness about the way the poem sounds because the endings, the structural morphemes, are correctly placed. When the message is of primary importance and the speaker knows the language only imperfectly, the structural morphemes may be incorrect or missing and a string of pure message morphemes may be the result: Her give man bag money.

Message morphemes have their own peculiar properties, limiting their use to certain contexts, regardless of the accuracy of the combined structural morphemes. To illustrate this principle, Chomsky composed the sentence "Colorless green ideas sleep furiously." The subject is "colorless green ideas"; the predicate, "sleep furiously." This sentence has the same structure as any sentence of the shape: adjective/adjective/noun/intransitive verb/adverb. However, there is something semantically troubling. How can one describe something green as colorless? Can ideas be green? How can an intransitive verb that describes such a passive activity be furiously involved in an action?

Chomsky's example was designed to combine structural familiarity with semantic impossibility. It is possible to devise similar sentences that, though semantically improbable, could conceivably be used by an actual speaker. The sentence "Virtue swims home every night" attributes to an abstract noun an action performed by animate beings, and poses other difficulties as well (in what setting can one swim home?), yet such strange semantic violations, given a meaningful context, are the stuff of poetry.

Indeed, semantic change actually occurs with a

measure of frequency in the history of a language. It is usually of two types. Words that are rather specific in meaning sometimes become generalized; for example, Latin *molīna* (gristmill) originally meant "mill" but expanded to cover "sawmill," "steel mill," even "diploma mill." Many words in English of very broad meanings, such as "do," "make," "go," and "things," derive from words of more specific notions. At the same time, the opposite often happens. Words that once were very general in meaning have become specific. Examples include *deer*, which formerly meant merely "animal" (compare German *Tier*), and *hound*, "dog," now a particular kind of dog. Sometimes, words undergo melioration, as in the change in *knight*, meaning originally a "servant," to "king's servant," or pejoration, as in the change in *knave*, meaning "boy" (compare German *Knabe*), to "rascal."

Perhaps the most significant force for change in language is analogy. It is occasioned by mental associations arising because of similarity or contrast of meaning and may affect the meaning or the form of words or even create new words. Most verbs in English are regular and form their preterit and past participles by the addition of *-ed* (or *-t*), as "dream, dreamed, dreamt," and not by vowel change, as in "drink, drank, drunk." New words taken into the language, as well as some of the irregular ones already in use, will usually become regular. It is by no means unusual to hear a child use analogy in forming the past of, say, "teach" or "see" as "teached" and "see'd" instead of "taught" and "saw." Since most English nouns form their plural by the addition of *-s*, it is to be expected that unfamiliar words or words with little-used, learned plural forms will be pluralized in the same way: for example, "memorandums" (or "memos") for *memoranda*, "stadiums" for *stadia*, "gymnasiums" for *gymnasia*, "prima donnas" for *prime donne*, and "formulas" for *formulae*. Sometimes a resemblance in the form of a word may suggest a relationship that causes a further assimilation in form. This process is known as folk etymology and often occurs when an unfamiliar or foreign word or phrase is altered to give it a more meaningful form. There are many examples: "crayfish" comes from Old French *crevisse* (crab), but *-visse* meant nothing and thus was changed to the phonetically similar *-fish*; a hangnail is not a (fin-

ger)nail that hangs, but one that hurts (from Old English *ang*); the second element of "titmouse" has nothing to do with a mouse, but comes from Middle English *mose*, the name for several species of birds.

There are many other processes in language by which changes are brought about. Among them are several of great importance: assimilation, dissimilation, conversion, back formation, blending, and the creation of euphemisms and slang.

Assimilation causes a sound to change in conformance with a neighboring sound, as in the plural of "kit" with [-s] (/kits/), as opposed to the plural of "limb" with [-z] (/limz/), or in the preterit and participial forms of regular verbs: "grazed" [greyzd], but "choked" [čowkt].

Dissimilation is the opposite process, whereby neighboring sounds are made unlike, as in "pilgrim" from Latin *peregrīnus*, where the first *r* dissimilates.

Conversion is the change of one part of speech or form class into another, as the change from noun to verb: The nouns "bridge," "color," and "shoulder" are converted to verbs in "to bridge a gap," "to color a book," and "to shoulder a load."

A back formation occurs when a word is mistakenly assumed to be the base form from which a new word is formed, as in "edit" from "editor," "beg" from "beggar," "peddle" from "pedlar."

Some words are blends: "flash" + "blush" = "flush"; "slight" (slim) + "tender" = "slender"; "twist" + "whirl" = "twirl"; "breakfast" + "lunch" = "brunch."

Euphemisms are words and expressions with new, better-sounding connotations—for example, to "pass away" or "breathe one's last" or "cross the river" for "to die"; "lingerie" or "intimate wear" for "underwear"; "acute indigestion" for "bellyache."

Slang consists of informal, often ephemeral expressions and coinages, such as "turkey" for "stupid person," "blow away" for "to kill," and "kook," meaning "odd or eccentric person," from "cuckoo."

All three constituents of language change over a long period of time—sounds, structure, and vocabulary—but each language or dialect retains its distinctiveness. The most durable and unchanging aspect of language is writing, of which there are two major varieties: picture writing, also called ideographic writing, and alphabetic writing. The former kind of writing began as actual pictures and developed gradually into ideograms linked directly to the objects or concepts and having no connection with the sounds of the language. The latter variety began as symbols for syllables, until each symbol was taken to represent a single spoken sound. Although alphabetic writing is much more widespread and easier to learn and use, ideographic writing has the advantage of maintaining cultural unity among speakers of dialects and languages not mutually intelligible. An alphabetic writing system can, over time, act as a conservative influence on the spoken language as well as provide valuable etymological clues. Ideographic writing can be, and often is, seen as art capable of conveying messages separate from speech. Both systems are vehicles for the transmission of history and literature without which civilization would falter and perish.

THE SOCIAL SIDE OF LANGUAGE

The social side of language is inextricably linked to behavior. It is concerned with the use of language to create attitudes and responses toward language, objects, and people. For example, certain overt behaviors toward language and its users can create unusual political pressures. The insistence by the Québecois on French as the primary, if not sole, language of their province of Canada has led to near secession and to bitter interprovincial feelings. The creation of modern Hebrew has helped to create and sustain the state of Israel. The Irish are striving to make Irish the first language of that part of the British Isles. The Flemish urge full status for their variety of Dutch in the Brussels area. African Americans sometimes advocate clearer recognition of black English. Frisians, Bretons, Basques, Catalans, and Provençals are all insisting on greater acceptance of their mother tongues.

Within a language or dialect, there can be specialized vocabulary and pronunciation not generally understood. The term "dialect" is commonly taken to mean a regional variety of language or one spoken by the undereducated, but, strictly speaking, it is differentiated from language as such, being largely what people actually speak. Some dialects differ so substantially from standard, national tongues that, to all intents and

purposes, they are languages in their own right. The term "vernacular" is similar in that it designates everyday speech as opposed to learned discourse. "Lingo" designates, somewhat contemptuously, any dialect or language not readily comprehended. "Jargon" is specialized or professional language, often of a technical nature; in this context, the term "cant," as in "thieves' cant," is virtually synonymous with "jargon." Closely related to these two terms is the term "argot," referring to the idiom of a closely knit group, as in "criminal argot." Finally, "slang," discussed above, refers to the colorful, innovative, often short-lived popular vocabulary drawn from many levels of language use, both specialized and nonspecialized.

Words, like music, can produce moods. They can raise one's spirits or lower them. They can stir up discontent or soothe human anger. They can inspire and console, ingratiate and manipulate, mislead and ridicule. They can create enough hatred to destroy but also enough trust to overcome obstacles. While a mood may originate in physical well-being or physical discomfort and pain, language can express that mood, intensify it, or deny it. Language can be informative (emotionally neutral), biased (emotionally charged), or propagandistic (informatively neutral).

Language is informative when it states indisputable facts or asks questions dealing with such facts, even though those facts are very broad and general. One can also inform with misstatements, half-truths, or outright lies. It does not matter whether the statement is actually true or false, only that the question can be posed.

Language often reflects bias by distorting facts. Frequently, the substitution of a single derogatory term is sufficient to load the atmosphere. Admittedly, some words are favorably charged for some people, unfavorably for others. Much depends on the context, word and sentence stress, gestures, and former relationship.

Language can be propagandistic when the speaker desires to promote some activity or cause. The load that propaganda carries is directly proportional to the receiver's enthusiasm, bias, or readiness to be deceived. Almost invariably, propaganda terms arise out of the specialized language of religion, art, commerce, education, finance, government, and so forth. Propaganda is a kind of name calling, using words from a stock of esoteric and exclusive terms. Not many people are thoroughly familiar with the exact meanings of words such as "totalitarian," "fascist," "proletarian," and "bourgeois," but they think they know whether these words are good or bad, words of approval or disapproval. The effect is to call forth emotions as strong as those prompted by invectives.

The language of advertising achieves its effectiveness by conveniently combining information, bias, and propaganda. A good advertisement must gain immediate attention, make the reader or listener receptive to the message, ensure its retention, create a desire, and cause the person to buy the product without setting up resistance. Advertising must, moreover, link the product to "pleasant" or "healthy" things. In advertising circles, there is no widespread agreement as to which is more important: the avoidance of all associations that can create resistance or the creation of desire for a particular object. Even if the latter is regarded as the prime objective, it is still important to avoid resistance. The most powerful tools of the advertiser are exaggeration and cliché. The words generally used in ads deal with the basic component and qualities of a product, while the qualifiers are hackneyed and overblown: lather (rich, creamy, full-bodied); toothpaste (fights cavities three ways, ten ways, tastes zesty); cleanser (all-purpose, powerful, one-step); coffee (full of flavor buds, brewed to perfection, marvelous bouquet). The danger of advertising is evident when its pathology carries over into other areas of life. Every culture must be on guard against the effect of advertising on the health of its citizenry and the shaping of its national image. Even foreign policy can be the victim of advertising that stresses youth over maturity, beauty of body over soundness of mind, physical health over mental serenity, or the power of sex appeal over everything else.

In the latter part of the twentieth century, language began to be closely examined by certain groups aiming to rid it of inherent prejudice. Of all of these groups, perhaps feminists have had the greatest effect on the vocabulary, and even the structure, of languages that differentiate along sex lines. A vociferous contingent of women contend that the symbols of perception—words—give both meaning and value to the objects they define and that many of these words are loaded with a male-chauvinist aspect. For example, words with the affix *-man* are being avoided or paired with *-woman* or *-person:* "congressman"/"congresswoman," "chairman"/"chairwoman"/"chairperson." In some instances, gender is eliminated altogether: "humankind" for "mankind," "chair" for "chairman" or "chairwoman." There are many more techniques employed to desexualize English; some even involve tampering with personal pronouns, a much less likely area for success. Nevertheless, any language can cope with any pressing linguistic problem. The impetus for a solution begins with the individual or a small group, but the community as a whole often applies brakes to change that is too rapid or drastic, dramatizing the fact that language exists not for the individual alone but for the community as a whole.

APPLICATIONS

Almost everybody is intimately acquainted with at least one language. Everybody can produce the sounds and sound combinations of his or her language and understand the meanings of the sounds produced by other speakers. Everybody knows which sounds and sound combinations are allowable and which do not fit the language. Sentences that are grammatically or semantically unacceptable or strange are easily recognized. Despite this intuitive or unconscious knowledge of one's language, the average native speaker cannot comment authoritatively on the sound system or the structure of his or her language. Furthermore, there are no books containing the complete language of English or Arabic or Mandarin Chinese in which all possible sentences and sound combinations are listed. Instead, people must rely largely on dictionaries for a list of words and on grammars and linguistic texts for a statement of rules dealing with sounds, morphology, and syntax. To study one's language as an object or phenomenon is to raise one's consciousness of how language functions.

Some people have a professional need to know a lot about a language as opposed to simply being able to use it. Some of the more obvious examples include language teachers, speech therapists, advertising writers, communications engineers, and computer programmers. Others, such as the anthropologist or the historian, who often work with documents, employ their knowledge as an ancillary tool. The missionary may have to learn about some very esoteric language for which there is no grammar book and perhaps even no writing. The psychologist studies language as a part of human behavior. The philosopher is often primarily interested in the "logical" side of language. Students of foreign languages can benefit greatly from linguistic knowledge; they can often learn more efficiently and make helpful comparisons of sounds and structures between their own and the target language.

Translation and interpretation are two activities requiring considerable knowledge about language. Strictly speaking, the terms are not interchangeable; translation refers to the activity of rendering, in writing, one language text into another, whereas interpretation is oral translation. Translation is of two kinds, scientific and literary, and can be accomplished by people or machines. In general, machine translation has been a disappointment because of the grave difficulties involved in programming the many complexities of natural language. Interpretation is also of two kinds: legal and diplomatic. Whereas the legal interpreter requires a precise knowledge of the terminology of the court and must tread a thin line between literal and free interpretation, the diplomatic interpreter has the even more difficult task of adding, or subtracting, as circumstances dictate, allusions, innuendos, insinuations, and implications. Interpretation is accomplished in two ways: simultaneously with the speaker, or consecutively after a given segment of speech.

One of the important questions before linguistics is: Does linguistics aid in the study and appreciation of literature? Many would automatically assume that the answer is an unqualified yes, since the material of which literature is made is language. There are others, however, who find linguistic techniques of analysis too mechanical and lacking in the very feeling that literature tries to communicate. Probably most thoughtful people would agree that linguistics can make a contribution in tandem with more traditional analytical approaches, but that alone it cannot yet, if ever, disclose the intrinsic qualities of great literary works.

By one definition at least, literature consists of texts constructed according to certain phonological, morpho-logical, and syntactic restrictions, where the result is the creation of excellence of form and expression. For poetry in the Western tradition, for example, the restriction most frequently imposed is that of rhythm based on stress or vowel quantity. In other cultures, syntactic and semantic prescriptions can produce the same effect.

For both poetic and prose texts, the discovery and description of the author's style are essential to analysis. In contrast to the methods of traditional literary criticism, linguistics offers the possibility of quantitative stylistic analysis. Computer-aided analysis yields textual statistics based on an examination of various features of phonology and grammar. The results will often place an author within a literary period, confirm his region or dialect, explain the foreign-vocabulary influences, describe syllabication in terms of vowel and consonant count, list euphemisms and metaphors, and delineate sentence structure with regard to subordinating elements, to mention some of the possibilities. All of these applications are based on the taxemes of selection employed by an individual author.

Of all literary endeavors, literary translation seems to stand in the closest possible relationship to linguistics. The translator must perform his task within the framework of an awareness, be it conscious or intuitive, of the phonology, syntax, and morphology of both the source language and the target language. Like the linguist, he should also be acquainted in at least a rudimentary fashion with the society that has produced the text he is attempting to translate. His work involves much more than the mechanical or one-to-one exchange of word for word, phrase for phrase, or even concept for concept. The practice of translation makes possible the scope and breadth of knowledge encompassed in the ideal of liberal arts, and without translation relatively few scholars could claim knowledge and understanding of many of the world's great thinkers and literary artists.

BIBLIOGRAPHY

Akmajian, Adrian, et al. *Linguistics: An Introduction to Language and Communication.* Cambridge, Mass.: MIT Press, 2001. The first part of this work deals with the structural and interpretive parts of language, and the second part is cognitively oriented and includes chapters on pragmatics, psychology of language, language acquisition, and language and the brain.

Beekes, Robert S. P. *Comparative Indo-European Linguistics: An Introduction*. Philadelphia: John Benjamins, 1996. Examines the history of Indo-European languages and explores comparative grammar and linguistics.

Cavalli-Sforza, L. L. *Genes, Peoples, and Languages*. Berkeley: University of California Press, 2001. Cavalli-Sforza was among the first to ask whether the genes of modern populations contain a historical record of the human species. This collection comprises five lectures that serve as a summation of the author's work over several decades, the goal of which has been nothing less than tracking the past hundred thousand years of human evolution.

Chomsky, Noam. *Language and Thought*. Wakefield, R.I.: Moyer Bell, 1998. Presents an analysis of human language and its influence on other disciplines.

Lycan, William G. *Philosophy of Language: A Contemporary Introduction*. 2d ed. New York: Routledge, 2008. Introduces nonspecialists to the main issues and theories in the philosophy of language, focusing specifically on linguistic phenomena.

Pinker, Stephen. *The Language Instinct: How the Mind Creates Language*. New York: HarperPerennial Modern Classics, 2009. Explores how humans learn to talk, how the study of language can provide insight into the way genes interact with experience to create behavior and thought, and how the arbitrary sounds people call language evoke emotion and meaning.

Ruhlen, Merritt. *The Origin of Language: Tracing the Evolution of the Mother Tongue*. New York: John Wiley & Sons, 1996. Provides an accessible examination of nearly 100,000 years of human history and prehistory to uncover the roots of the language from which all modern tongues derive.

Trudgill, Peter. *Sociolinguistics: An Introduction to Language and Society*. 4th ed. New York: Penguin Books, 2007. Examines how speech is deeply influenced by class, gender, and ethnic background and explores the implications of language for social and educational policy.

Vygotsky, Lev S. *Thought and Language*. Edited by Alex Kozulin. Rev. ed. Cambridge, Mass.: MIT Press, 1986. A classic foundational work of cognitive science. Vygotsky analyzes the relationship between words and consciousness, arguing that speech is social in its origins and that only as a child develops does it become internalized verbal thought. Revised edition offers an introductory essay by editor Kozulin that offers new insight into the author's life, intellectual milieu, and research methods.

Yule, George. *The Study of Language*. 4th ed. New York: Cambridge University Press, 2010. Revised edition includes a new chapter on pragmatics and an expanded chapter on semantics; incorporates many changes that reflect developments in language study in the twenty-first century.

Donald D. Hook

GLOSSARY OF POETICAL TERMS

Accentual meter: A base meter in which the occurrence of a syllable marked by a stress determines the basic unit, regardless of the number of unstressed syllables. It is one of four base meters used in English (accentual, accentual-syllabic, syllabic, and quantitative). An example from modern poetry is "Blue Moles" by Sylvia Plath, the first line of which scans: "They're out of the dark's ragbag, these two." Because there are five stressed syllables in this accentually based poem, the reader can expect that many of the other lines will also contain five stresses. See also *Scansion.*

Accentual-syllabic meter: A base meter that measures the pattern of stressed syllables relative to the unstressed ones. It is the most common base meter for English poetry. In the first line of William Shakespeare's sonnet 130, "My mistress' eyes are nothing like the sun," there is a pattern of alternating unstressed with stressed syllables, although there is a substitution of an unstressed syllable for a stressed syllable at the word "like." In the accentual-syllabic system, stressed and unstressed syllables are grouped together into feet.

Allegory: A literary mode in which a second level of meaning—wherein characters, events, and settings represent abstractions—is encoded within the surface narrative. The allegorical mode may dominate the entire work, in which case the encoded message is the work's primary excuse for being, or it may be an element in a work otherwise interesting and meaningful for its surface story alone.

Alliteration: The repetition of consonants at the beginning of syllables; for example, "Large mannered motions of his mythy mind." Alliteration is used when the poet wishes to focus on the details of a sequence of words and to show relationships between words within a line. Because a reader cannot easily skim over an alliterative line, it is conspicuous and demands emphasis.

Allusion: A reference to a historical or literary event whose story or outcome adds dimension to the poem. "Fire and Ice" by Robert Frost, for example, alludes to the biblical account of the flood and the prophecy that the next destruction will come by fire, not water. Without recognizing the allusion and understanding the biblical reference to Noah and the surrounding associations of hate and desire, the reader cannot fully appreciate the poem.

Anacrusis: The addition of an extra unstressed syllable to the beginning or end of a line; the opposite of truncation. For example, anacrusis occurs in the line: "their shoul/ders held the sky/suspended." This line is described as iambic tetrameter with terminal anacrusis. Anacrusis is used to change a rising meter to falling and vice versa to alter the reader's emotional response to the subject.

Anapest: A foot in which two unstressed syllables are associated with one stressed syllable, as in the line, "With the sift/ed, harmon/ious pause." The anapestic foot is one of the three most common in English poetry and is used to create a highly rhythmical, usually emotional, line.

Anaphora: The use of the same word or words to begin successive phrases or lines. Timothy Steele's "Sapphics Against Anger" uses anaphora in the repetition of the phrase "May I."

Approximate rhyme: Assonance and half rhyme (or slant rhyme). Assonance occurs when words with identical vowel sounds but different consonants are associated. "Stars," "arms," and "park" all contain identical *a* (and *ar*) sounds, but because the consonants are different the words are not full rhymes. Half rhyme or slant rhymes contain identical consonants but different vowels, as in "fall" and "well." "Table" and "bauble" constitute half rhymes; "law," "cough," and "fawn" assonate.

Archetype: 1) Primordial image from the collective unconscious of humankind, according to psychologist Carl Jung, who believed that works of art, including poetry, derive much of their power from the unconscious appeal of these images to ancestral memories. 2) A symbol, usually an image, that recurs so frequently in literature that it becomes an element of the literary experience, according to Northrop Frye in his extremely influential *Anatomy of Criticism* (1957).

Assonance: See *Approximate rhyme*

Aubade: A type of poem welcoming or decrying the arrival of the dawn. Often the dawn symbolizes the separation of two lovers. An example is William Empson's "Aubade" (1937).

Ballad: A poem composed of four-line stanzas that alternate rhyme schemes of *abab* or *abcb*. If all four lines contain four feet each (tetrameter), the stanza is called a long ballad; if one or more of the lines contain only three feet (trimeter), it is called a short ballad. Ballad stanzas, which are highly mnemonic, originated with verse adapted to singing. For this reason, the poetic ballad is well suited for presenting stories. Popular ballads are songs or verse that tell tales, usually impersonal, and they usually impart folk wisdom. Supernatural events, courage, and love are frequent themes, but any experience that appeals to people is acceptable material. A famous use of the ballad form is *The Rime of the Ancient Mariner* (1798), by Samuel Taylor Coleridge.

Ballade: A popular and sophisticated French form, commonly (but not necessarily) composed of an eight-line stanza rhyming *ababbcbc*. Early ballades usually contained three stanzas and an envoy, commonly addressed to a nobleman, priest, or the poet's patron, but no consistent syllable count. Another common characteristic of the ballade is a refrain that occurs at the end of each stanza.

Base meter: Also called metrical base. The primary meter employed in poems in English and in most European languages that are not free verse. Based on the number, pattern, or duration of the syllables within a line or stanza, base meters fall into four types: accentual, accentual-syllabic, syllabic, or quantitative. Rhythm in verse occurs because of meter, and the use of meter depends on the type of base into which it is placed.

Blank verse: A type of poem having a base meter of iambic pentameter and with unrhymed lines usually arranged in stichic form (that is, not in stanzas). Most of William Shakespeare's plays are written in blank verse; in poetry it is often used for subject matter that requires much narration or reflection. In both poetry and drama, blank verse elevates emotion and gives a dramatic sense of importance. Although the base meter of blank verse is iambic pentameter, the form is very flexible, and substitution, enjambment, feminine rhyme, and extra syllables can relax the rigidity of the base. The flexi-

bility of blank verse gives the poet an opportunity to use a formal structure without seeming unnecessarily decorous. T. S. Eliot's "Burnt Norton," written in the 1930's, is a modern blank-verse poem.

Cadence: The rhythmic speed or tempo with which a line is read. All language has cadence, but when the cadence of words is forced into some pattern, it becomes meter, thus distinguishing poetry from prose. A prose poem may possess strong cadence, combined with poetic uses of imagery, symbolism, and other poetic devices.

Caesura: A pause or break in a poem, created with or without punctuation marks. The comma, question mark, colon, and dash are the most common signals for pausing, and these are properly termed caesuras; pauses may also be achieved through syntax, lines, meter, rhyme, and the sound of words. The type of punctuation determines the length of the pause. Periods and question marks demand full stops, colons take almost a full stop, semicolons take a long pause, and commas take a short pause. The end of a line usually demands some pause even if there is no punctuation.

Cinquain: Any five-line stanza, including the madsong and the limerick. Cinquains are most often composed of a ballad stanza with an extra line added to the middle.

Classicism: A literary stance or value system consciously based on the example of classical Greek and Roman literature. Although the term is applied to an enormous diversity of artists in many different periods and in many different national literatures, classicism generally denotes a cluster of values including formal discipline, restrained expression, reverence for tradition, and an objective rather than a subjective orientation. As a literary tendency, classicism is often opposed to Romanticism, although many writers combine classical and romantic elements.

Conceit: A type of metaphor that uses a highly intellectualized comparison; an extended, elaborate, or complex metaphor. The term is frequently applied to the work of the Metaphysical poets, notably John Donne.

Connotation: An additional meaning for a word other than its denotative, formal definition. The word "mercenary," for example, simply means a soldier who is paid to fight in an army not of his own region, but connotatively a mercenary is an unprincipled scoundrel who kills for money and pleasure, not for honor and patriotism. Connotation is one of the most important devices for achieving irony, and readers may be fooled into believing a poem has one meaning because they have missed connotations that reverse the poem's apparent theme.

Consonance: Repetition or recurrence of the final consonants of stressed syllables without the correspondence of the preceding vowels. "Chair/star" is an example of consonance, since both words end with *r* preceded by different vowels. Terminal consonance creates half or slant rhyme (see *Approximate rhyme*). Consonance differs from alliteration in that the final consonants are repeated rather than the initial consonants. In the twentieth century, consonance became one of the principal rhyming devices, used to achieve formality without seeming stilted or old-fashioned.

Consonants: All letters except the vowels, *a, e, i, o, u*, and sometimes *y*; one of the most important sound-producing devices in poetry. There are five basic effects that certain consonants will produce: resonance, harshness, plosiveness, exhaustiveness, and liquidity. Resonance, exhaustiveness, and liquidity tend to give words—and consequently the whole line if several of these consonants are used—a soft effect. Plosiveness and harshness, on the other hand, tend to create tension. Resonance is the property of long duration produced by nasals, such as *n* and *m*, and by voiced fricating consonants such as *z, v*, and the voiced *th*, as in "them." Exhaustiveness is created by the voiceless fricating consonants and consonant combinations, such as *h, f*, and the voiceless *th* and *s*. Liquidity results from using the liquids and semivowels *l, r, w*, and *y*, as in the word "silken." Plosiveness occurs when certain consonants create a stoppage of breath before releasing it, especially *b, p, t, d, g, k, ch*, and *j*.

Controlling image/controlling metaphor: Just as a poem may include as structural devices form, theme, action, or dramatic situation, it may also use imagery for structure. When an image runs throughout a poem, giving unity to lesser images or ideas, it is called a controlling image. Usually the poet establishes a single idea and then expands and complicates it; in Edward

Taylor's "Huswifery," for example, the image of the spinning wheel is expanded into images of weaving until the reader begins to see life as a tapestry. Robert Frost's "The Silken Tent" is a fine example of a controlling image and extended metaphor.

Couplet: Any two succeeding lines that rhyme. Because the couplet has been used in so many different ways and because of its long tradition in English poetry, various names and functions have been given to types of couplets. One of the most common is the decasyllabic (ten-syllable) couplet. When there is an end-stop on the second line of a couplet, it is said to be closed; an enjambed couplet is open. An end-stopped decasyllabic couplet is called a heroic couplet, because the form has often been used to sing the praise of heroes. The heroic couplet was widely used by the neoclassical poets of the eighteenth century. Because it is so stately and sometimes pompous, the heroic couplet invites satire, and many poems have been written in "mock-heroic verse," such as Alexander Pope's *The Rape of the Lock* (1712, 1714). Another commonly used couplet is the octasyllabic (eight-syllable) couplet, formed from two lines of iambic tetrameter, as in "L'Allegro" by John Milton: "Come, and trip as we go/ On the light fantastic toe." The light, singsong tone of the octasyllabic couplet also invited satire, and Samuel Butler wrote one of the most famous of all satires, *Hudibras* (1663, 1664, 1678), in this couplet. When a couplet is used to break another rhyme scheme, it generally produces a summing-up effect and has an air of profundity. William Shakespeare found this characteristic particularly useful when he needed to give his newly invented Shakespearean sonnet a final note of authority and purpose.

Dactyl: A foot formed of a stress followed by two unstressed syllables (´ ˘ ˘). It is fairly common in isolated words, but when this pattern is included in a line of poetry, it tends to break down and rearrange itself into components of other types of feet. Isolated, the word "meaningless" is a dactyl, but in the line "Polite/ meaning/less words," the last syllable becomes attached to the stressed "words" and creates a split foot, forming a trochee and an iamb. Nevertheless, a few dactylic poems do exist. "After the/pangs of a / desperate/lover" is a dactyllic line.

Deconstruction: An extremely influential contemporary school of criticism based on the works of the French philosopher Jacques Derrida. Deconstruction treats literary works as unconscious reflections of the reigning myths of Western culture. The primary myth is that there is a meaningful world that language signifies or represents. The deconstructionist critic is most often concerned with showing how a literary text tacitly subverts the very assumptions or myths on which it ostensibly rests.

Denotation: The explicit formal definition of a word, exclusive of its implications and emotional associations (see *Connotation*).

Depressed foot: A foot in which two syllables occur in a pattern in such a way as to be taken as one syllable without actually being an elision. In the line: "To each/ he boul/ders (that have)/fallen/to each," the base meter consists of five iambic feet, but in the third foot, there is an extra syllable that disrupts the meter but does not break it, so that "that have" functions as the second half of the iambic foot.

Diction: The poet's "choice of words," according to John Dryden. In Dryden's time, and for most of the history of English verse, the diction of poetry was elevated, sharply distinct from everyday speech. Since the early twentieth century, however, the diction of poetry has ranged from the banal and the conversational to the highly formal, and from obscenity and slang to technical vocabulary, sometimes in the same poem. The diction of a poem often reveals its persona's values and attitudes.

Dieresis: Caesuras that come after the foot (see *Split foot* for a discussion of caesuras that break feet). They can be used to create long pauses in the line and are often used to prepare the line for enjambment.

Dramatic dialogue: An exchange between two or more personas in a poem or a play. Unlike a dramatic monologue, both characters speak, and in the best dramatic dialogues, their conversation leads to a final resolution in which both characters and the reader come to the same realization at the same time.

Dramatic irony: See *Irony*

Dramatic monologue: An address to a silent person by a narrator; the words of the narrator are greatly influenced by the persona's presence. The principal reason for writing in dramatic monologue form is to control the speech of the major persona through the implied reaction of the silent one. The effect is one of continuing change and often surprise. In Robert Browning's "My Last Duchess," for example, the duke believes that he is in control of the situation, when in fact he has provided the emissary with terrible insights about the way he treated his former duchess. The emissary, who is the silent persona, has asked questions that the duke has answered; in doing so he has given away secrets. Dramatic monologue is somewhat like hearing one side of a telephone conversation in which the reader learns much about both participants.

Duration: The length of the syllables, which is the measure of quantitative meter. Duration can alter the tone and the relative stress of a line and influence meaning as much as the foot can.

Elegy: Usually a long, rhymed, strophic poem whose subject is meditation on death or a lamentable theme. The pastoral elegy uses the natural setting of a pastoral scene to sing of death or love. Within the pastoral setting the simplicity of the characters and the scene lends a peaceful air despite the grief the narrator feels.

Elision: The joining of two vowels into a single vowel (synaeresis) or omitting of a vowel altogether (syncope), usually to maintain a regular base meter. Synaeresis can be seen in the line "Of man's first disobedience, and the fruit," in which the "ie" in "disobedience" is pronounced as a "y" ("ye") so that the word reads dis/o/bed/yence, thereby making a five-syllable word into a four-syllable word. An example of syncope is when "natural" becomes "nat'ral" and "hastening" becomes "hast'ning." Less frequent uses of elision are to change the sound of a word, to spell words as they are pronounced, and to indicate dialect.

Emphasis: The highlighting of or calling attention to a phrase or line or a poem by altering its meter. A number of techniques, such as caesura, relative stress, counterpointing, and substitution can be used.

End rhyme: See *Rhyme*

End-stop: A punctuated pause at the end of a line in a poem. The function of end-stops is to show the relationship between lines and to emphasize particular words or lines. End-stopping in rhymed poems creates more emphasis on the rhyme words, which already carry a great deal of emphasis by virtue of their rhymes. Enjambment is the opposite of end-stopping.

Enjambment: When a line is not end-stopped—that is, when it carries over to the following line—the line is said to be "enjambed," as in John Milton's: "Avenge, O Lord, thy slaughtered saints, whose bones/ Lie scattered on the Alpine mountains cold." Enjambment is used to change the natural emphasis of the line, to strengthen or weaken the effect of rhyme, or to alter meter.

Envoy: Any short poem or stanza addressed to the reader as a beginning or end to a longer work. Specifically, the envoy is the final stanza of a sestina or a ballade in which all the rhyme words are repeated or echoed.

Epic: A long narrative poem that presents the exploits of a central figure of high position.

Extended metaphor: Metaphors added to one another so that they run in a series. Robert Frost's poem "The Silken Tent" uses an extended metaphor; it compares the "she" of the poem to the freedom and bondage of a silken tent. See also *Controlling image/controlling metaphor.*

Eye rhyme: Words that appear to be identical because of their spelling but that sound different. "Bough/ enough/cough" and "ballet/pallet" are examples. Because of changes in pronunciation, many older poems appear to use eye rhymes but do not. For example, "wind" (meaning moving air) once rhymed with "find." Eye rhymes that are intentional and do not result from a change in pronunciation may be used to create a disconcerting effect.

Fabliau: A bawdy medieval verse, such as many found in Geoffrey Chaucer's *The Canterbury Tales* (1387-1400).

Falling rhyme: Rhyme in which the correspondence of sound comes only in the final unstressed syllable, which is preceded by another unstressed syllable. T. S. Eliot rhymes "me-tic-u-lous" with "ri-dic-u-lous" and creates a falling rhyme. See also *Feminine rhyme*; *Masculine rhyme.*

Falling rhythm: A line in which feet move from stressed to unstressed syllables (trochaic or dactyllic). An example can be seen in this line from "The Naming

of Parts," by Henry Reed: "Glistens/like cor/al in/all of the/neighboring/gardens." Because English and other Germanic-based languages naturally rise, imposing a falling rhythm on a rising base meter creates counterpointing.

Feminine rhyme: A rhyme pattern in which a line's final accented syllable is followed by a single unaccented syllable and the accented syllables rhyme, while the unaccented syllables are phonetically identical, as with "flick-er/snick-er" and "fin-gers/ma-lin-gers." Feminine rhymes are often used for lightness in tone and delicacy in movement.

Feminist criticism: A criticism advocating equal rights for women in a political, economic, social, psychological, personal, and aesthetic sense. On the thematic level, the feminist reader should identify with female characters and their concerns. The object is to provide a critique of phallocentric assumptions and an analysis of patriarchal ideologies inscribed in male-centered and male-dominated literature. On the ideological level, feminist critics see gender, as well as the stereotypes that go along with it, as a cultural construct. They strive to define a particularly feminine content and to extend the canon so that it might include works by lesbians, feminists, women of color, and women writers in general.

First person: The use of linguistic forms that present a poem from the point of view of the speaker. It is particularly useful in short lyrical poems, which tend to be highly subjective, taking the reader deep into the narrator's thoughts. First-person poems normally, though not necessarily, signal the use of the first person through the pronoun "I," allowing the reader direct access to the narrator's thoughts or providing a character who can convey a personal reaction to an event. See also *Third person.*

Foot/feet: Rhythmic unit in which syllables are grouped together; this is the natural speech pattern in English and other Germanic-based languages. In English, the most common of these rhythmic units is composed of one unstressed syllable attached to one stressed syllable (an iamb). When these family groups are forced into a line of poetry, they are called feet in the accentual-syllabic metrical system. In the line "My mis/tress' eyes/are noth/ing like/the sun" there are four iambic feet (‿ʹ) and one pyrrhic foot (‿‿), but in the line "Thére whére/the vínes/cling crím/son ón/the wall," there are three substitutions for the iamb—in the first, third, and fourth feet. The six basic feet in English poetry are the iamb (‿ʹ), trochee (ʹ‿), anapest (‿‿ʹ), dactyl (ʹ‿‿), spondee (ʹʹ), and pyrrhus (‿‿).

Form: The arrangement of the lines of a poem on the page, its base meter, its rhyme scheme, and occasionally its subject matter. Poems that are arranged into stanzas are called strophic, and because the strophic tradition is so old, a large number of commonly used stanzas have evolved particular uses and characteristics. Poems that run from beginning to end without a break are called stichic. The form of pattern poetry is determined by its visual appearance rather than by lines and stanzas, while the definition of free verse is that it has no discernible form. Some poem types, such as the sestina, sonnet, and ode, are written in particular forms and frequently are restricted to particular subject matter.

Formalism, Russian: A twentieth century Russian school of criticism that employed the conventional devices used in literature to defamiliarize that which habit has made familiar. The most extreme formalists treated literary works as artifacts or constructs divorced from their biographical and social contexts.

Found poetry: Poems created from language that is "found" in print in nonliterary settings. They can use any language that is already constructed, but usually use language that appears on cultural artifacts, such as cereal boxes. The rules for writing a found poem vary, but generally the found language is used intact or altered only slightly.

Free verse: A poem that does not conform to any traditional convention, such as meter, rhyme, or form, and that does not establish any pattern within itself. There is, however, great dispute over whether "free" verse actually exists. T. S. Eliot said that by definition poetry must establish some kind of pattern, and Robert Frost said that "writing free verse is like playing tennis with the net down." However, some would agree with Carl Sandburg, who insisted that "you can play a better game with the net down." Free verse depends more on cadence than on meter.

Ghazal: A poetic form based on a type of Persian poetry. It is composed of couplets, often unrhymed,

that function as individual images or observations but that also interrelate in sometimes subtle ways.

Gnomic verse: Poetry that typically includes many proverbs or maxims.

Haiku: A Japanese form that appeared in the sixteenth century and is still practiced in Japan. A haiku consists of three lines of five, seven, and five syllables each; in Japanese there are other conventions regarding content that are not observed in Western haiku. The traditional haiku took virtually all of its images from nature, using the natural world as a metaphor for the spiritual.

Half rhyme: See *Approximate rhyme*

Heroic couplet: See *Couplet*

Historical criticism: A school of criticism that emphasizes the historical context of literature. Ernst Robert Curtius's *European Literature and the Latin Middle Ages* (1940) is a prominent example of historical criticism.

Hymn stanza: See *Ballad*

Hyperbole: A deliberate overstatement made in order to heighten the reader's awareness. As with irony, hyperbole works because the reader can perceive the difference between the importance of the dramatic situation and the manner in which it is described.

Iamb: A foot consisting of one unstressed and one stressed syllable (‿ʹ). The line "So lóng/as mén/can bréathe/or éyes/can sée" is composed of five iambs. In the line "Acóld/cóming/we hád/of ít," a trochaic foot (a trochee) has been substituted for the expected iamb in the second foot, thus emphasizing that this is a "coming" rather than a "going," an important distinction in T. S. Eliot's "The Journey of the Magi."

Iambic pentameter: A very common poetic line consisting of five iambic feet. The following two lines by Thomas Wyatt are in iambic pentameter: "I find no peace and all my war is done,/ I fear and hope, I burn and freeze like ice." See also *Foot/feet; iamb*.

Identical rhyme: A rhyme in which the entire final stressed syllables contain exactly the same sounds, such as "break/brake," or "bear" (noun), "bear" (verb), "bare" (adjective), "bare" (verb).

Imagery: The verbal simulation of sensory perception. Like so many critical terms, imagery betrays a visual bias: It suggests that a poetic image is necessarily visual, a picture in words. In fact, however, imagery calls on all five senses, although the visual is predominant in many poets. In its simplest form, an image re-creates a physical sensation in a clear, literal manner, as in Robert Lowell's lines, "A sweetish smell of shavings, wax and oil/ blows through the redone bedroom newly aged" ("Marriage"). Imagery becomes more complex when the poet employs metaphor and other figures of speech to re-create experience, as in Seamus Heaney's lines, "Right along the lough shore/ A smoke of flies/ Drifts thick in the sunset" ("At Ardboe Point"), substituting a fresh metaphor ("A smoke of flies") for a trite one (a cloud of flies) to help the reader visualize the scene more clearly.

Interior monologue: A first-person representation of a persona's or character's thoughts or feelings. It differs from a dramatic monologue in that it deals with thoughts rather than spoken words or conversation.

Internal rhyme: See *Rhyme*

Irony: A figure of speech in which the speaker's real meaning is different from (and often exactly opposite to) the apparent meaning. Irony is among the three or four most important concepts in modern literary criticism. Although the term originated in classical Greece and has been in the vocabulary of criticism since that time, only in the nineteenth and twentieth centuries did it assume central importance. In Andrew Marvell's lines, "The Grave's a fine and private place,/ But none I think do there embrace" ("To His Coy Mistress"), the speaker's literal meaning—in praise of the grave—is quite different from his real meaning. This kind of irony is often called verbal irony. Another kind of irony is found in narrative and dramatic poetry. In the *Iliad* (c. 750 B.C.E.; English translation, 1611), for example, the reader is made privy to the counsels of the gods, which greatly affect the course of action in the epic, while the human characters are kept in ignorance. This discrepancy between the knowledge of the reader and that of the character (or characters) is called dramatic irony. Beyond these narrow, well-defined varieties of irony are many wider applications.

Limerick: A comic five-line poem rhyming *aabba* in which the third and fourth lines are shorter (usually five syllables each) than the first, second, and last lines, which are usually eight syllables each. The limerick's

anapestic base makes the verse sound silly; modern limericks are almost invariably associated with bizarre indecency or with ethnic or anticlerical jokes.

Line: A poetical unit characterized by the presence of meter; lines are categorized according to the number of feet (see *Foot/feet*) they contain. A pentameter line, for example, contains five feet. This definition does not apply to a great deal of modern poetry, however, which is written in free verse. Ultimately, then, a line must be defined as a typographical unit on the page that performs various functions in different kinds of poetry.

Lyric poetry: Short poems, adaptable to metrical variation, and usually personal rather than having a cultural function. Lyric poetry developed when music was accompanied by words, and although the lyrics were later separated from the music, the characteristics of lyric poetry have been shaped by the constraints of music. Lyric poetry sings of the self, exploring deeply personal feelings about life.

Mad-song: Verse uttered by someone presumed to have a severe mental illness that manifests in a happy, harmless, inventive way. The typical rhyme scheme of the mad-song is *abccb*, and the unrhymed first line helps to set a tone of oddity and unpredictability, since it controverts the expectation that there will be a rhyme for it. The standard mad-song has short lines.

Marxist criticism: A school of criticism based on the nineteenth century writings of Karl Marx and Friedrich Engels that views literature as a product of ideological forces determined by the dominant class However, many Marxists believe that literature operates according to its own autonomous standards of production and reception: It is both a product of ideology and able to determine ideology. As such, literature may overcome the dominant paradigms of its age and play a revolutionary role in society.

Masculine rhyme: A rhyme pattern in which rhyme exists in the stressed syllables. "Men/then" constitute masculine rhyme, but so do "af-ter-noons/spoons." Masculine rhyme is generally considered more forceful than feminine rhyme, and while it has a variety of uses, it generally gives authority and assurance to the line, especially when the final syllables are of short duration.

Metaphor: A figure of speech in which two strikingly different things are identified with each other, as in "the waves were soldiers moving" (Wallace Stevens). Metaphor is one of a handful of key concepts in modern literary criticism. A metaphor contains a "tenor" and a "vehicle." The tenor is the subject of the metaphor, and the vehicle is the imagery by which the subject is presented. In D. H. Lawrence's lines, "Reach me a gentian, give me a torch/ let me guide myself with the blue, forked torch of this flower" ("Bavarian Gentians"), the tenor is the gentian and the vehicle is the torch. This relatively restricted definition of metaphor by no means covers the usage of the word in modern criticism. Some critics argue that metaphorical perception underlies all figures of speech. Others dispute the distinction between literal and metaphorical description, saying that language is essentially metaphorical. Metaphor has become widely used to identify analogies of all kinds in literature, painting, film, and even music. See also *Simile*.

Meter: The pattern that language takes when it is forced into a line of poetry. All language has rhythm; when that rhythm is organized and regulated in the line so as to affect the meaning and emotional response to the words, then the rhythm has been refined into meter. Because the lines of most poems maintain a similar meter throughout, poems are said to have a base meter. The meter is determined by the number of syllables in a line and by the relationship between them.

Metrical base. See *Base meter*

Metonymy: Using an object that is closely related to an idea stand for the idea itself, such as saying "the crown" to mean the king. Used to emphasize a particular part of the whole or one particular aspect of it. See also *Synecdoche*.

Mnemonic verse: Poetry in which rhythmic patterns aid memorization but are not crucial to meaning. Ancient bards were able to remember long poems partly through the use of stock phrases and other mnemonic devices.

Mock-heroic: See *Couplet*

Modernism: An international movement in the arts that began in the early years of the twentieth century. Although the term is used to describe artists of widely varying persuasions, modernism in general was characterized by its international idiom, by its interest in cultures distant in space or time, by its emphasis on for-

mal experimentation, and by its sense of dislocation and radical change.

Multiculturalism: The tendency to recognize the perspectives of works by authors (particularly women and non-European writers) who, until the latter part of the twentieth century, were excluded from the canon of Western art and literature. To promote multiculturalism, publishers and educators have revised textbooks and school curricula to incorporate material by and about women, ethnic and racial minorities, non-Western cultures, gays, and lesbians.

Myth: Anonymous traditional stories dealing with basic human concepts and antinomies. Claude Lévi-Strauss says that myth is that part of language where the "formula *tradutore, tradittore* reaches its lowest truth value.... Its substance does not lie in its style, its original music, or its syntax, but in the story which it tells."

Myth criticism: A school of criticism concerned with the basic structural principles of literature. Myth criticism is not to be confused with mythological criticism, which is primarily concerned with finding mythological parallels in the surface action of a narrative.

Narrator: The person who is doing the talking—or observing or thinking—in a poem. Roughly synonymous with persona and speaker. Lyric poetry most often consists of the poet expressing his or her own personal feelings directly. Other poems, however, may involve the poet adopting the point of view of another person entirely. In some poems—notably in a dramatic monologue—it is relatively easy to determine that the narrative is being related by a fictional (or perhaps historical) character, but in others it may be more difficult to identify the "I."

New Criticism: A formalist movement whose members held that literary criticism is a description and evaluation of its object and that the primary concern of the critic is with the work's unity. At their most extreme, these critics treated literary works as artifacts or constructs divorced from their biographical and social contexts.

Occasional verse: Any poem written for a specific occasion, such as a wedding, a birthday, a death, or a public event. Edmund Spenser's *Epithalamion* (1595), which was written for his marriage, and John Milton's "Lycidas," which commemorated the death of his schoolmate Edward King, are examples of occasional verse, as are W. H. Auden's "September 1, 1939" and Frank O'Hara's "The Day Lady Died."

Octave: A poem in eight lines. Octaves may have many different variations of meter, such as ottava rima.

Ode: A lyric poem that treats a unified subject with elevated emotion, usually ending with a satisfactory resolution. There is no set form for the ode, but it must be long enough to build intense emotional response. Often the ode will address itself to some omnipotent source and will take on a spiritual hue. When explicating an ode, readers should look for the relationship between the narrator and some transcendental power to which the narrator must submit to find contentment. Modern poets have used the ode to treat subjects that are not religious in the theological sense but that have become innate beliefs of society.

Ottava rima: An eight-line stanza of iambic pentameter, rhyming *ababababcc*. Probably the most famous English poem written in ottava rima is Lord Byron's *Don Juan* (1819-1824), and because the poem was so successful as a spoof, the form has come to be associated with poetic high jinks. However, the stanza has also been used brilliantly for just the opposite effect, to reflect seriousness and meditation.

Oxymoron: The juxtaposition of two paradoxical words, such as "wise fool" or "devilish angel."

Pantoum: A French form of poetry consisting of four quatrains in which entire lines are repeated in a strict pattern of 1234, 2546, 5768, 7183. Peter Meinke's "Atomic Pantoum" is an example.

Paradox: A statement that contains an inherent contradiction. It may be a statement that at first seems true but is in reality contradictory. It may also be a statement that appears contradictory but is actually true or that contains an element of truth that reconciles the contradiction.

Pentameter: A type of rhythmic pattern in which each line consists of five poetic feet. See also *Accentual-syllabic meter*; *Foot/feet*; *Iamb*; *Iambic pentameter*; *Line*.

Periphrasis: The use of a wordy phrase to describe something that could be described simply in one word.

Persona: See *Narrator*

Phenomenological criticism: A school of criticism that examines literature as an act and focuses less on individual works and genres. The work is not seen as an object, but rather as part of a strand of latent impulses in the work of a single author or an epoch. Proponents include Georges Poulet in Europe and J. Hillis Miller in the United States.

Point of view: The mental position through which readers experience the situation of a poem. As with fiction, poems may be related in the first person, second person (unusual), or third person. (The presence of the words "I" or "we" indicates singular or plural first-person narration.) Point of view may be limited or omniscient. A limited point of view means that the narrator can see only what the poet wants him or her to see, while from an omniscient point of view the narrator can know everything, including the thoughts and motives of others.

Postcolonialism: The literature that emerged in the mid-twentieth century when colonies in Asia, Africa, and the Caribbean began gaining their independence from the European nations that had long controlled them. Postcolonial authors, such as Salman Rushdie, V. S. Naipaul, and Derek Walcott, tend to focus on both the freedom and the conflict inherent in living in a postcolonial state.

Postmodernism: A ubiquitous but elusive term in contemporary criticism that is loosely applied to the various artistic movements that followed the era of so-called high modernism, represented by such giants as writer James Joyce and painter and sculptor Pablo Picasso. In critical discussions of contemporary fiction, postmodernism is frequently applied to the works of writers such as Thomas Pynchon, John Barth, and Donald Barthelme, who exhibit a self-conscious awareness of their modernist predecessors as well as a reflexive treatment of fictional form. Such reflexive treatments can extend to poetry as well.

Prose poem: A poem that looks like prose on the page, with no line breaks. There are no formal characteristics by which a prose poem can be distinguished from a piece of prose. Many prose poems employ rhythmic repetition and other poetic devices not normally found in prose, but others use such devices sparingly if at all. Prose poems range in length from a few lines to three or four pages; most prose poems occupy a page or less.

Psychological criticism: A school of criticism that places a strong emphasis on a causal relation between the writer's psychological state, variously interpreted, and his or her works. A notable example of psychological criticism is Norman Fruman's *Coleridge, the Damaged Archangel* (1971).

Pun: The use of words that have similar pronunciations but entirely different meanings to establish a connection between two meanings or contexts that the reader would not ordinarily make. The result may be a surprise recognition of an unusual or striking connection, or, more often, a humorously accidental connection.

Pyrrhus: A poetic foot consisting of two unstressed syllables, as in the line "Appear/and dis/appear/in the/ blue depth/of the sky," in which foot four is a pyrrhus.

Quatrain: Any four-line stanza. Aside from the couplet, it is the most common stanza type. The quatrain's popularity among both sophisticated and unsophisticated readers suggests that there is something inherently pleasing about the form. For many readers, poetry and quatrains are almost synonymous. Balance and antithesis, contrast and comparison not possible in other stanza types are indigenous to the quatrain.

Realism: A literary technique in which the primary convention is to render an illusion of fidelity to external reality. Realism is often identified as the primary method of the novel form: It focuses on surface details, maintains a fidelity to the everyday experiences of middle-class society, and strives for a one-to-one relationship between the fiction and the action imitated. The realist movement in the late nineteenth century coincides with the full development of the novel form.

Regular meter: A line of poetry that contains only one type of foot. Only the dullest of poems maintain a regular meter throughout, however; skillful poets create interest and emphasis through substitution.

Relative stress: The degree to which a syllable in pattern receives more or less emphasis than other syllables in the pattern. Once the dominant stress in the line has been determined, every other syllable can be assigned a stress factor relative to the dominant syllable. The stress factor is created by several aspects of prosody: the position of the syllable in the line, the position of the syllable in its word, the surrounding syllables, the type of vowels and consonants that constitute the syllable, and the syllable's relation to the foot, base meter, and caesura. Because every syllable will have a different stress factor, there could be as many values as there are syllables, although most prosodists scan poems using primary, secondary, and unstressed notations. In the line "I am there like the dead, or the beast," the anapestic base meter will not permit "I" to take a full stress, but it is a more forceful syllable than the unstressed ones, so it is assigned a secondary stress. Relative to "dead" and "beast," it takes less pressure; relative to the articles in the line, it takes much more.

Resolution: Any natural conclusion to a poem, especially to a short lyric poem that establishes some sort of dilemma or conflict that the narrator must solve. Specifically, the resolution is the octave stanza of a Petrarchan sonnet or the couplet of a Shakespearean sonnet in which the first part of the poem prents a situation that must find balance in the resolution.

Rhyme: A correspondence of sound between syllables within a line or between lines whose proximity to each other allows the sounds to be sustained. Rhyme may be classified in a number of ways: according to the sound relationship between rhyming words, the position of the rhyming words in the line, and the number and position of the syllables in the rhyming words. Sound classifications include full rhyme and approximate rhyme. Full rhyme is defined as words that have the same vowel sound, followed by the same consonants in their last stressed syllables, and in which all succeeding syllables are phonetically identical. "Hat/ cat" and "laughter/after" are full rhymes. Categories of approximate rhyme are assonance, slant rhyme, alliteration, eye rhyme, and identical rhyme.

Rhyme classified by its position in the line includes end, internal, and initial rhyme. End rhyme occurs when the last words of lines rhyme. Internal rhyme occurs when two words within the same line or within various lines recall the same sound, as in "Wet, below the snow line, smelling of vegetation" in which "below" and "snow" rhyme. Initial rhyme occurs when the first syllables of two or more lines rhyme. See also *Masculine rhyme*; *Feminine rhyme*.

Rhyme scheme: A pattern of rhyme in a poem, designated by lowercase (and often italicized) letters. The letters stand for the pattern of rhyming sounds of the last word in each line. For example, the following A. E. Housman quatrain has an *abab* rhyme scheme.

> Into my heart an air that kills
> From yon far country blows:
> What are those blue remembered hills,
> What spires, what farms are those?

As another example, the rhyme scheme of the poetic form known as ottava rima is *ababababcc*. Traditional stanza forms are categorized by their rhyme scheme and base meter.

Rime royal: A seven-line stanza in English prosody consisting of iambic pentameter lines rhyming *ababbcc*. William Shakespeare's *The Rape of Lucrece* (1594) is written in this form. The only variation permitted is to make the last line hexameter.

Romanticism: A widespread cultural movement in the late eighteenth and early nineteenth centuries, the influence of which is still felt. As a general literary tendency, Romanticism is frequently contrasted with classicism or neoclassicism. Although there were many varieties of Romanticism indigenous to various national literatures, the term generally suggests an assertion of the preeminence of the imagination. Other values associated with various schools of Romanticism include primitivism, an interest in folklore, a reverence for nature, and a fascination with the demoniac and the macabre.

Rondeau: One of three standard French forms assimilated by English prosody; generally contains thirteen lines divided into three groups. A common stanzaic grouping rhymes *aabba*, *aabR*, *aabbaR*, where the *a* and *b* lines are tetrameter and the *R* (refrain) lines are dimeter. The rondel, another French form, contains fourteen lines of trimeter with alternating rhyme (*ababab bababab*) and is divided into two stanzas. The rondeau and rondel forms are always light and playful.

Rondel: See *Rondeau*

Rubaiyat stanza: An iambic pentameter quatrain that has a rhyme scheme of *aaba*.

Scansion: The assigning of relative stresses and meter to a line of poetry, usually for the purpose of determining where variations, and thus emphasis, in the base meter occur. Scansion can help explain how a poem

generates tension and offer clues as to the key words. E. E. Cummings's "singing each morning out of each night" could be scanned in two ways: (1) singing/each morn/ing out/of each night or (2) sing/ing each/morning/out of/each night. Scansion will not only affect the way the line is read aloud but also influences the meaning of the line.

Secondary stress: See *Relative stress*

Seguidilla: An imagistic or mood poem in Spanish, which, like a haiku, creates emotional recognition or spiritual insight in the reader. Although there is no agreement as to what form the English seguidilla should take, most of the successful ones are either four or seven lines with an alternating rhyme scheme of *ababcbc*. Lines 1, 3, and 6 are trimeter; lines 2, 4, 5, and 7 dimeter.

Semiotics: The science of signs and sign systems in communication. Literary critic Roman Jakobson says that semiotics deals with the principles that underlie the structure of signs, their use in language of all kinds, and the specific nature of various sign systems.

Sestet: A six-line stanza. A Petrarchan or Italian sonnet is composed of an octave followed by a sestet.

Sestina: Six six-line stanzas followed by a three-line envoy. The words ending the lines in the first stanza are repeated in different order at the ends of lines in the following stanzas as well as in the middle and end of each line of the envoy. Elizabeth Bishop's "Sestina" is a good example.

Shakespearean sonnet: See *Sonnet*

Simile: A type of metaphor that signals a comparison by the use of the words "like" or "as." William Shakespeare's line "My mistress' eyes are nothing like the sun" is a simile that establishes a comparison between the woman's eyes and the sun. See also *Metaphor*.

Slant rhyme: See *Approximate rhyme*

Sonnet: A poem consisting of fourteen lines of iambic pentameter with some form of alternating rhyme and a turning point that divides the poem into two parts. The sonnet is the most important and widely used of traditional poem types. The two major sonnet types are the Petrarchan (or Italian) sonnet and the Shakespearean sonnet. The original sonnet form, the Petrarchan (adopted from the poetry of Petrarch), presents a problem or situation in the first eight lines, the octave, then resolves it in the last six, the sestet. The octave is composed of two quatrains (*abbaabba*), the second of which complicates the first and gradually defines and heightens the problem. The sestet then diminishes the problem slowly until a satisfying resolution is achieved.

During the fifteenth century, the Italian sonnet became an integral part of the courtship ritual, and most sonnets during that time consisted of a young man's description of his perfect lover. Because so many unpoetic young men had generated a nation full of bad sonnets by the end of the century, the form became an object of ridicule, and the English sonnet developed as a reaction against all the bad verse being turned out in the Italian tradition. When Shakespeare wrote "My mistress' eyes are nothing like the sun," he was deliberately negating the Petrarchan conceit, rejoicing in the fact that his loved one was much more interesting and unpredictable than nature. Shakespeare also altered the sonnet's formal balance. Instead of an octave, the Shakespearean sonnet has three quatrains of alternating rhyme and is resolved in a final couplet. During the sixteenth century, long stories were told in sonnet form, one sonnet after the next, to produce sonnet sequences. Although most sonnets contain fourteen lines, some contain as few as ten (the curtal sonnet) or as many as seventeen.

Speaker: See *Narrator*

Split foot: The alteration of the natural division of a word as a result of being forced into a metrical base. For example, the words "point/ed," "lad/der," and "stick/ing" have a natural falling rhythm, but in the line "My long/two-point/ed lad/der's stick/ing through/a tree" the syllables are rearranged so as to turn the falling rhythm into a rising meter. The result of splitting feet is to create an uncertainty and delicate imbalance in the line.

Spondee: When two relatively stressed syllables occur together in a foot, the unit is called a spondee or spondaic foot, as in the line "Appear/and dis/appear/in the/blue depth/of the sky."

Sprung rhythm: An unpredictable pattern of stresses in a line, first described near the end of the nineteenth century by Gerard Manley Hopkins, that results from taking accentual meter is to its extreme. According to Hopkins, in sprung rhythm "any two stresses may either follow one another running, or be divided by one, two, or three slack syllables."

Stanza: A certain number of lines meant to be taken as a unit, or that unit. Although a stanza is traditionally considered a unit that contains rhyme and recurs predictably throughout a poem, the term is also sometimes applied to nonrhyming and even irregular units. Poems that are divided into fairly regular and patterned stanzas are called strophic; poems that appear as a single unit, whether rhymed or unrhymed, or that have no predictable stanzas, are called stichic. Both strophic and stichic units represent logical divisions within the poem, and the difference between them lies in the formality and strength of the interwoven unit. Stanza breaks are commonly indicated by a line of space.

Stichic verse: See *Stanza*

Stress: See *Relative stress*

Strophic verse: See *Stanza*

Structuralism: A movement based on the idea of intrinsic, self-sufficient structures that do not require reference to external elements. A structure is a system of transformations that involves the interplay of laws inherent in the system itself. The study of language is the primary model for contemporary structuralism. The structuralist literary critic attempts to define structural principles that operate intertextually throughout the whole of literature as well as principles that operate in genres and in individual works. The most accessible survey of structuralism and literature is Jonathan Culler's *Structuralist Poetics* (1975).

Substitution: The replacement of one type of foot by another within a base meter. One of the most common and effective methods by which the poet can emphasize a foot. For example, in the line "Thy life/a long/dead calm/of fixed/repose," a spondaic foot (′′) has been substituted for an iambic foot (˘′). Before substitution is possible, the reader's expectations must have been established by a base meter so that a change in those expectations will have an effect. See also *Foot/feet; iamb; spondee.*

Syllabic meter: The system of meter that measures only the number of syllables per line, without regard to stressed and unstressed syllables.

Symbol: Any sign that a number of people agree stands for something else. Poetic symbols cannot be rigidly defined; a symbol often evokes a cluster of meanings rather than a single specific meaning. For example, the rose, which suggests fragile beauty, gentleness, softness, and sweet aroma, has come to symbolize love, eternal beauty, or virginity. The tide traditionally symbolizes, among other things, time and eternity. Modern poets may use personal symbols; these take on significance in the context of the poem or of a poet's body of work, particularly if they are reinforced throughout. For example, through constant reinforcement, swans in William Butler Yeats's poetry come to mean as much to the reader as they do to the narrator.

Synaeresis: See *Elision*

Synecdoche: The use of a part of an object to stand for the entire object, such as using "heart" to mean a person. Used to emphasize a particular part of the whole or one particular aspect of it. See also *Metonymy*.

Tenor: See *Metaphor*

Tercet: Any form of a rhyming triplet. Examples are *aaa bbb*, as used in Thomas Hardy's "Convergence of the Twain"; *aba cdc*, in which *b* and *d* do not rhyme; *aba bcb*, also known as terza rima.

Terza rima: A three-line stanzaic form in which the middle line of one stanza rhymes with the first line of the following stanza, and whose rhyme scheme is *aba bcb cdc*, and so on. Since the rhyme scheme of one stanza can be completed only by adding the next stanza, terza rima tends to propel itself forward, and as a result of this strong forward motion it is well suited to long narration.

Theme: Recurring elements in a poem that give it meaning; sometimes used interchangeably with motif. A motif is any recurring pattern of images, symbols, ideas, or language, and is usually restricted to the internal workings of the poem. Thus, one might say that there is an animal motif in William Butler Yeats's poem "Sailing to Byzantium." Theme, however, is usually more general and philosophical, so that the theme of "Sailing to Byzantium" might be interpreted as the failure of human attempts to isolate oneself within the world of art.

Third person: The use of linguistic forms that present a poem from the point of view of a narrator, or speaker, who has not been part of the events described and is not probing his or her own relationship to them; rather, the speaker is describing what happened without the use of the word "I" (which would indicate first-person narration). A poet may use a third-person point of view, either limited or omniscient, to establish a distance between the reader and the subject, to give credi-

bility to a large expanse of narration, or to allow the poem to include a number of characters who can be commented on by the narrator.

Tone: The expression of a poet's attitude toward the subject and persona of the poem as well as about himself or herself, society, and the poem's readers. If the ultimate aim of art is to express and control emotions and attitudes, then tone is one of the most important elements of poetry. Tone is created through the denotative and connotative meanings of words and through the sound of language (principally rhyme, consonants, and diction). Adjectives such as "satirical," "compassionate," "empathetic," "ironic," and "sarcastic" are used to describe tone.

Trochee: A foot with one stressed syllable and one unstressed syllable ($\acute{\ }\breve{\ }$), as in the line: "Dóuble/dóuble tóil and/tróuble." Trochaic lines are frequently substituted in an iambic base meter in order to create counterpointing. See also *Foot/feet*; *iamb*.

Truncation: The omission of the last, unstressed syllable of a falling line, as in the line: "Týger,/týger/ búrning/bríght," where the "ly" has been dropped from bright.

Vehicle: See *Metaphor*

Verse: A generic term for poetry, as in *The Oxford Book of English Verse* (1939); poetry that is humorous or superficial, as in light verse or greeting-card verse; and a stanza or line.

Verse drama: Drama that is written in poetic rather than ordinary language and characterized and delivered by the line. Verse drama flourished during the eighteenth century, when the couplet became a standard literary form.

Verse paragraph: A division created within a stichic poem (see *Stanza*) by logic or syntax, rather than by form. Such divisions are important for determining the movement of a poem and the logical association between ideas.

Villanelle: A French verse form that has been assimilated by English prosody, usually composed of nineteen lines divided into five tercets and a quatrain, rhyming *aba*, *bba*, *aba*, *aba*, *abaa*. The third line is repeated in the ninth and fifteenth lines. Dylan Thomas's "Do Not Go Gentle into That Good Night" is a modern English example of a villanelle.

BIBLIOGRAPHY

CONTENTS

About This Bibliography 824

General Reference Sources 824
Biographical sources 824
Criticism 824
Poetry dictionaries and
   handbooks 825
Indexes of primary works 825
Poetics, poetic forms,
   and genres 825

English-Language Poetry 826
General reference sources 826
Biographical sources 826
Criticism 826
Dictionaries, histories, and
   handbooks 826
Index of primary works 827
Poetics 827
Postcolonial Anglophone
   poetry 827
Women writers 827
Africa and the Caribbean 827
General 827
Africa 827
Caribbean and West Indian . . . 828
Australia 828
Aboriginal poets 828
Bibliographies 828
Biographical sources 828
Dictionaries, histories, and
   handbooks 828
Women writers 829
Canada 829
Biographical sources 829
Criticism 829
Dictionaries, histories, and
   handbooks 829
Indexes of primary works 830
England 830
Bibliographies 830
Biographical sources 830
Criticism 830
Dictionaries, histories, and
   handbooks 830
History: Old and Middle
   English 831
History: Renaissance
   to 1660 831

History: Restoration (1660)
   through eighteenth
   century 831
History: Nineteenth century 832
History: Twentieth century
   and contemporary 832
Women writers 833
India and South Asia 833
Irish poetry in English 833
Biographical sources 833
Dictionaries, histories, and
   handbooks 833
Women writers 833
New Zealand 833
Scottish poetry in English 834
United States 834
Biographical sources 834
Criticism 834
Dictionaries, histories, and
   handbooks 834
Indexes of primary works 834
History: Colonial to 1800 835
History: Nineteenth century 835
History: Twentieth century
   and contemporary 835
African American:
   Biographical sources 836
African American: Indexes of
   primary works 836
African American: Dictionaries,
   histories, and handbooks 836
African American: Women
   writers 836
Asian American 836
Latino 836
Native American 837
Regional poetry 837
Women writers 837
Welsh poetry in English 837

Foreign-Language Poetry 838
General reference sources 838
Biographical sources 838
Criticism 838
Dictionaries, histories, and
   handbooks 838
Index of primary works 838
Poetics 838
African languages 839
Arabic 839

Caribbean 839
Catalan 839
Celtic languages 839
Irish Gaelic 839
Scottish Gaelic 839
Welsh 839
Chinese 840
Classical Greek and Latin 840
Dutch and Flemish 840
Francophone 841
General 841
Africa and the Caribbean 841
France: Bibliography 841
France: Biographical
   sources 841
France: Criticism 841
France: Dictionaries, histories,
   and handbooks 841
France: Women writers 842
French Canadian 842
German 842
Biographical sources 842
Dictionaries, histories, and
   handbooks 842
Women writers 843
Greek 843
Hebrew and Yiddish 843
Hungarian 844
Indian and South Asian
   languages 844
Italian 844
Biographical sources 844
Dictionaries, histories, and
   handbooks 844
Women writers 844
Japanese 845
Biographical sources 845
Dictionaries, histories, and
   handbooks 845
Korean 845
Persian (Farsi) 845
Scandinavian languages 846
General 846
Danish 846
Icelandic 846
Norwegian 846
Swedish 846
Slavic languages 846
General 846
Albanian 846

Bulgarian 846	*Slovak* 847	*Mexico and Central*
Croatian 846	*Slovene* 848	*America* 848
Czech. 846	*Ukrainian* 848	*South America* 849
Macedonian 847	Spanish and Portuguese 848	*Spain and Portugal* 849
Polish. 847	*General* 848	Tibetan 850
Russian 847	*Africa*. 848	Turkish 850
Serbian 847	*Caribbean*. 848	Vietnamese 850

ABOUT THIS BIBLIOGRAPHY

This bibliography contains three main sections. The first, "General Reference Sources," lists books that treat poetry of all or several languages and countries. The section "English-Language Poetry" includes sources primarily relevant to poetry written in English; it is subdivided into general and country-specific materials, sometimes further grouped by type (biographical, indexes, etc.). The section headed "Foreign-Language Poetry" contains sources primarily relevant to poetry in languages other than English; it is also further subdivided into "General Reference Sources" and then language- or region-specific sources, and again, where appropriate, further subdivided by type of source. Materials that treat bilingual poetry written by U.S. writers are placed in the section on the United States. Sources treating poetry of multilingual geographical areas, such as the Caribbean, Africa, and Latin America, are listed in more than one section, as appropriate. Section headings also indicate, by means of "see also" cross-references, when more than one section is likely to contain relevant sources.

GENERAL REFERENCE SOURCES

BIOGRAPHICAL SOURCES

Colby, Vineta, ed. *World Authors, 1975-1980.* Wilson Authors Series. New York: H. W. Wilson, 1985.

_____. *World Authors, 1980-1985.* Wilson Authors Series. New York: H. W. Wilson, 1991.

_____. *World Authors, 1985-1990.* Wilson Authors Series. New York: H. W. Wilson, 1995.

Cyclopedia of World Authors. 4th rev. ed. 5 vols. Pasadena, Calif.: Salem Press, 2003.

Dictionary of Literary Biography. 254 vols. Detroit: Gale Research, 1978-   .

International Who's Who in Poetry and Poets' Encyclopaedia. Cambridge, England: International Biographical Centre, 1993.

Seymour-Smith, Martin, and Andrew C. Kimmens, eds. *World Authors, 1900-1950.* Wilson Authors Series. 4 vols. New York: H. W. Wilson, 1996.

Thompson, Clifford, ed. *World Authors, 1990-1995.* Wilson Authors Series. New York: H. W. Wilson, 1999.

Wakeman, John, ed. *World Authors, 1950-1970.* New York: H. W. Wilson, 1975.

_____. *World Authors, 1970-1975.* Wilson Authors Series. New York: H. W. Wilson, 1991.

Willhardt, Mark, and Alan Michael Parker, eds. *Who's Who in Twentieth Century World Poetry.* New York: Routledge, 2000.

CRITICISM

Brooks, Cleanth, and Robert Penn Warren. *Understanding Poetry.* 4th ed. Reprint. Fort Worth, Tex.: Heinle & Heinle, 2003.

Classical and Medieval Literature Criticism. Detroit: Gale Research, 1988-   .

Contemporary Literary Criticism. Detroit: Gale Research, 1973-   .

Day, Gary. *Literary Criticism: A New History.* Edinburgh, Scotland: Edinburgh University Press, 2008.

Draper, James P., ed. *World Literature Criticism 1500 to the Present: A Selection of Major Authors from Gale's Literary Criticism Series.* 6 vols. Detroit: Gale Research, 1992.

Habib, M. A. R. *A History of Literary Criticism: From*

Plato to the Present. Malden, Mass.: Wiley-Blackwell, 2005.

Jason, Philip K., ed. *Masterplots II: Poetry Series, Revised Edition*. 8 vols. Pasadena, Calif.: Salem Press, 2002.

Literature Criticism from 1400 to 1800. Detroit: Gale Research, 1984- .

Lodge, David, and Nigel Wood. *Modern Criticism and Theory*. 3d ed. New York: Longman, 2008.

Magill, Frank N., ed. *Magill's Bibliography of Literary Criticism*. 4 vols. Englewood Cliffs, N.J.: Salem Press, 1979.

MLA International Bibliography. New York: Modern Language Association of America, 1922- .

Nineteenth-Century Literature Criticism. Detroit: Gale Research, 1981- .

Twentieth-Century Literary Criticism. Detroit: Gale Research, 1978- .

Vedder, Polly, ed. *World Literature Criticism Supplement: A Selection of Major Authors from Gale's Literary Criticism Series*. 2 vols. Detroit: Gale Research, 1997.

Young, Robyn V., ed. *Poetry Criticism: Excerpts from Criticism of the Works of the Most Significant and Widely Studied Poets of World Literature*. 29 vols. Detroit: Gale Research, 1991.

POETRY DICTIONARIES AND HANDBOOKS

Carey, Gary, and Mary Ellen Snodgrass. *A Multicultural Dictionary of Literary Terms*. Jefferson, N.C.: McFarland, 1999.

Deutsch, Babette. *Poetry Handbook: A Dictionary of Terms*. 4th ed. New York: Funk & Wagnalls, 1974.

Drury, John. *The Poetry Dictionary*. Cincinnati, Ohio: Story Press, 1995.

Kinzie, Mary. *A Poet's Guide to Poetry*. Chicago: University of Chicago Press, 1999.

Lennard, John. *The Poetry Handbook: A Guide to Reading Poetry for Pleasure and Practical Criticism*. New York: Oxford University Press, 1996.

Matterson, Stephen, and Darryl Jones. *Studying Poetry*. New York: Oxford University Press, 2000.

Packard, William. *The Poet's Dictionary: A Handbook of Prosody and Poetic Devices*. New York: Harper & Row, 1989.

Preminger, Alex, et al., eds. *The New Princeton Encyclopedia of Poetry and Poetics*. 3d rev. ed. Princeton, N.J.: Princeton University Press, 1993.

Shipley, Joseph Twadell, ed. *Dictionary of World Literary Terms, Forms, Technique, Criticism*. Rev. ed. Boston: George Allen and Unwin, 1979.

INDEXES OF PRIMARY WORKS

Frankovich, Nicholas, ed. *The Columbia Granger's Index to Poetry in Anthologies*. 11th ed. New York: Columbia University Press, 1997.

_____. *The Columbia Granger's Index to Poetry in Collected and Selected Works*. New York: Columbia University Press, 1997.

Guy, Patricia. *A Women's Poetry Index*. Phoenix, Ariz.: Oryx Press, 1985.

Hazen, Edith P., ed. *Columbia Granger's Index to Poetry*. 10th ed. New York: Columbia University Press, 1994.

Hoffman, Herbert H., and Rita Ludwig Hoffman, comps. *International Index to Recorded Poetry*. New York: H. W. Wilson, 1983.

Kline, Victoria. *Last Lines: An Index to the Last Lines of Poetry*. 2 vols. Vol. 1, *Last Line Index, Title Index*; Vol. 2, *Author Index, Keyword Index*. New York: Facts On File, 1991.

Marcan, Peter. *Poetry Themes: A Bibliographical Index to Subject Anthologies and Related Criticisms in the English Language, 1875-1975*. Hamden, Conn.: Linnet Books, 1977.

Poem Finder. Great Neck, N.Y.: Roth, 2000.

POETICS, POETIC FORMS, AND GENRES

Attridge, Derek. *Poetic Rhythm: An Introduction*. New York: Cambridge University Press, 1995.

Brogan, T. V. F. *Verseform: A Comparative Bibliography*. Baltimore: Johns Hopkins University Press, 1989.

Fussell, Paul. *Poetic Meter and Poetic Form*. Rev. ed. New York: McGraw-Hill, 1979.

Hollander, John. *Rhyme's Reason*. 3d ed. New Haven, Conn.: Yale University Press, 2001.

Jackson, Guida M. *Traditional Epics: A Literary Companion*. New York: Oxford University Press, 1995.

Padgett, Ron, ed. *The Teachers and Writers Handbook*

of Poetic Forms. 2d ed. New York: Teachers & Writers Collaborative, 2000.

Pinsky, Robert. *The Sounds of Poetry: A Brief Guide.* New York: Farrar, Straus and Giroux, 1998.

Preminger, Alex, and T. V. F. Brogan, eds. *New Princeton Encyclopedia of Poetry and Poetics*. 3d ed. Princeton, N.J.: Princeton University Press, 1993.

Spiller, Michael R. G. *The Sonnet Sequence: A Study of*

Its Strategies. Studies in Literary Themes and Genres 13. New York: Twayne, 1997.

Turco, Lewis. *The New Book of Forms: A Handbook of Poetics*. Hanover, N.H.: University Press of New England, 1986.

Williams, Miller. *Patterns of Poetry: An Encyclopedia of Forms*. Baton Rouge: Louisiana State University Press, 1986.

ENGLISH-LANGUAGE POETRY

GENERAL REFERENCE SOURCES
Biographical sources

Bold, Alan. *Longman Dictionary of Poets: The Lives and Works of 1001 Poets in the English Language.* Harlow, Essex: Longman, 1985.

Riggs, Thomas, ed. *Contemporary Poets*. Contemporary Writers Series. 7th ed. Detroit: St. James Press, 2001.

Criticism

Alexander, Harriet Semmes, comp. *American and British Poetry: A Guide to the Criticism, 1925-1978*. Manchester, England: Manchester University Press, 1984.

_____. *American and British Poetry: A Guide to the Criticism, 1979-1990*. 2 vols. Athens, Ohio: Swallow Press, 1995.

Annual Bibliography of English Language and Literature. Cambridge, England: Modern Humanities Research Association, 1920- .

Childs, Peter. *The Twentieth Century in Poetry: A Critical Survey*. New York: Routledge, 1999.

Cline, Gloria Stark, and Jeffrey A. Baker. *An Index to Criticism of British and American Poetry*. Metuchen, N.J.: Scarecrow Press, 1973.

Coleman, Arthur. *Epic and Romance Criticism: A Checklist of Interpretations, 1940-1972*. New York: Watermill Publishers, 1973.

Donow, Herbert S., comp. *The Sonnet in England and America: A Bibliography of Criticism*. Westport, Conn.: Greenwood Press, 1982.

Jason, Philip K., ed. *Masterplots II: Poetry Series, Revised Edition*. 8 vols. Pasadena, Calif.: Salem Press, 2002.

Kuntz, Joseph M., and Nancy C. Martinez. *Poetry Explication: A Checklist of Interpretation Since 1925 of British and American Poems Past and Present.* 3d ed. Boston: Hall, 1980.

Roberts, Neil, ed. *A Companion to Twentieth-Century Poetry*. Malden, Mass.: Blackwell Publishers, 2001.

Walcutt, Charles Child, and J. Edwin Whitesell, eds. *Modern Poetry*. Vol. 1 in *The Explicator Cyclopedia*. Chicago: Quadrangle Books, 1968.

_____. *Traditional Poetry: Medieval to Late Victorian*. Vol. 2 in *The Explicator Cyclopedia*. Chicago: Quadrangle Books, 1968.

The Year's Work in English Studies. London: Blackwell, 1921- .

Dictionaries, histories, and handbooks

Draper, Ronald P. *An Introduction to Twentieth-Century Poetry in English*. New York: St. Martin's Press, 1999.

Gingerich, Martin E. *Contemporary Poetry in America and England, 1950-1975: A Guide to Information Sources*. American Literature, English Literature, and World Literatures in English: An Information Guide Series 41. Detroit: Gale Research, 1983.

Hamilton, Ian, ed. *The Oxford Companion to Twentieth-Century Poetry in English*. New York: Oxford University Press, 1994.

Perkins, David. *From the 1890's to the High Modernist Mode*. Vol. 1 in *A History of Modern Poetry*. Cambridge, Mass.: Belknap-Harvard University Press, 1976.

_____. *Modernism and After.* Vol. 2 in *A History of Modern Poetry.* 2 vols. Cambridge, Mass.: Belknap-Harvard University Press, 1987.

Index of primary works

Poetry Index Annual: A Title, Author, First Line, Keyword, and Subject Index to Poetry in Anthologies. Great Neck, N.Y.: Poetry Index, 1982-   .

Poetics

Brogan, T. V. F. *English Versification, 1570-1980: A Reference Guide with a Global Appendix.* Baltimore: Johns Hopkins University Press, 1981.

Malof, Joseph. *A Manual of English Meters.* Bloomington: Indiana University Press, 1970.

Shapiro, Karl, and Robert Beum. *A Prosody Handbook.* New York: Harper, 1965.

Postcolonial Anglophone poetry (see also Australia; Irish poetry in English; Scottish poetry in English; Welsh poetry in English)

Benson, Eugene, and L. W. Connolly. *Encyclopedia of Post-Colonial Literatures in English.* 2 vols. London: Routledge, 1994.

Bery, Ashok. *Cultural Translation and Postcolonial Poetry.* New York: Palgrave Macmillan, 2007.

Keown, Michelle. *Pacific Islands Writing: The Postcolonial Literatures of Aotearoa/New Zealand and Oceania.* New York: Oxford University Press, 2007.

Lawson, Alan, et al. *Post-Colonial Literatures in English: General, Theoretical, and Comparative, 1970-1993.* A Reference Publication in Literature. New York: G. K. Hall, 1997.

Mohanram, Radhika, and Gita Rajan, eds. *English Postcoloniality: Literatures from Around the World.* Contributions to the Study of World Literature 66. Westport, Conn.: Greenwood Press, 1996.

Patke, Rajeev S. *Postcolonial Poetry in English.* New York: Oxford University Press, 2006.

Ramazani, Jahan. *The Hybrid Muse: Postcolonial Poetry in English.* Chicago: University of Chicago Press, 2001.

Williams, Mark. *Post-Colonial Literatures in English: Southeast Asia, New Zealand, and the Pacific, 1970-1992.* Reference Publications in Literature. New York: G. K. Hall, 1996.

Women writers

Davis, Gwenn, and Beverly A. Joyce, comps. *Poetry by Women to 1900: A Bibliography of American and British Writers.* Toronto: University of Toronto Press, 1991.

Mark, Alison, and Deryn Rees-Jones. *Contemporary Women's Poetry: Reading, Writing, Practice.* New York: St. Martin's Press, 2000.

AFRICA AND THE CARIBBEAN (*see also in the foreign-language section:* AFRICAN LANGUAGES; CARIBBEAN; FRANCOPHONE; SPANISH AND PORTUGUESE)

General

Lindfors, Bernth, and Reinhard Sander, eds. *Twentieth-Century Caribbean and Black African Writers: First Series.* Dictionary of Literary Biography 117. Detroit: Gale Research, 1992.

_____. *Twentieth-Century Caribbean and Black African Writers: Second Series.* Dictionary of Literary Biography 125. Detroit: Gale Research, 1993.

_____. *Twentieth-Century Caribbean and Black African Writers: Third Series.* Dictionary of Literary Biography 157. Detroit: Gale Research, 1996.

Africa

Fraser, Robert. *West African Poetry: A Critical History.* Cambridge, England: Cambridge University Press, 1986.

Killam, Douglas, and Ruth Rowe, eds. *The Companion to African Literatures.* Bloomington: Indiana University Press, 2000.

Lindfors, Bernth. *Black African Literature in English: A Guide to Information Sources.* American Literature, English Literature, and World Literatures in English: An Information Guide Series 23. Detroit: Gale Research, 1979.

_____. *Black African Literature in English, 1977-1981 Supplement.* New York: Africana, 1986.

_____. *Black African Literature in English, 1982-1986.* New York: Zell, 1989.

_____. *Black African Literature in English, 1987-1991.* Bibliographical Research in African Literature 3. London: Zell, 1995.

Ojaide, Tanure. *Poetic Imagination in Black Africa:*

Essays on African Poetry. Durham, N.C.: Carolina Academic Press, 1996.

Ojaide, Tanure, and Tijan M. Sallah, eds. *The New African Poetry: An Anthology*. Boulder, Colo.: Lynne Rienner, 1999.

Parekh, Pushpa Naidu, and Siga Fatima Jagne. *Postcolonial African Writers: A Bio-Bibliographical Critical Sourcebook*. Westport, Conn.: Greenwood Press, 1998.

Scanlon, Paul A., ed. *South African Writers*. Dictionary of Literary Biography 225. Detroit: Gale Group, 2000.

Caribbean and West Indian

Allis, Jeannette B. *West Indian Literature: An Index to Criticism, 1930-1975*. Reference Publication in Latin American Studies. Boston: Hall, 1981.

Arnold, A. James, ed. *A History of Literature in the Caribbean*. 3 vols. Philadelphia: J. Benjamins, 1994.

Bloom, Harold, ed. *Caribbean Women Writers*. Women Writers of English and Their Work. Philadelphia: Chelsea House, 1997.

Breiner, Laurence A. *An Introduction to West Indian Poetry*. Cambridge, England: Cambridge University Press, 1998.

Brown, Stewart, and Mark McWatt, eds. *The Oxford Book of Caribbean Verse*. New York: Oxford University Press, 2005.

Burnett, Paula, ed. *The Penguin Book of Caribbean Verse in English*. London: Penguin Global, 2006.

Dance, Daryl Cumber, ed. *Fifty Caribbean Writers: A Bio-Bibliographical Critical Sourcebook*. New York: Greenwood Press, 1986.

Dawes, Kwame, ed. *Talk Yuh Talk: Interviews with Anglophone Caribbean Poets*. Charlottesville: University Press of Virginia, 2001.

Fenwick, M. J. *Writers of the Caribbean and Central America: A Bibliography*. Garland Reference Library of the Humanities 1244. New York: Garland, 1992.

Herdeck, Donald E., ed. *Caribbean Writers: A Bio-Bibliographical-Critical Encyclopedia*. Washington, D.C.: Three Continents Press, 1979.

Hughes, Roger, comp. *Caribbean Writing: A Checklist*. London: Commonwealth Institute Library Services, 1986.

Jenkins, Lee M. *The Language of Caribbean Poetry: Boundaries of Expression*. Gainesville: University Press of Florida, 2004.

Jordan, Alma, and Barbara Comissiong. *The English-Speaking Caribbean: A Bibliography of Bibliographies*. Reference Publication in Latin American Studies. Boston: Hall, 1984.

Miller, Kei, ed. *New Caribbean Poetry: An Anthology*. Manchester, England: Carcanet, 2007.

Narain, Denise DeCaires. *Contemporary Caribbean Women's Poetry: Making Style*. New York: Routledge, 2002.

AUSTRALIA

Aboriginal poets

Healy, John Joseph. *Literature and the Aborigine in Australia, 1770-1975*. New York: St. Martin's Press, 1978.

Schurmann-Zeggel, Heinz. *Black Australian Literature: A Bibliography of Fiction, Poetry, Drama, Oral Traditions and Non-Fiction, Including Critical Commentary, 1900-1991*. New York: Peter Lang, 1997.

Shoemaker, Adam. *Black Words, White Page*. UQP Studies in Australian Literature. St. Lucia: University of Queensland Press, 1989.

Bibliographies

Hergenhan, Laurie, and Martin Duwell, eds. *The ALS Guide to Australian Writers: A Bibliography*. UQP Studies in Australian Literature. Queensland: University of Queensland Press, 1992.

Webby, Elizabeth. *Early Australian Poetry: An Annotated Bibliography of Original Poems Published in Australian Newspapers, Magazines, and Almanacks Before 1850*. Sydney: Hale, 1982.

Biographical sources

Samuels, Selina, ed. *Australian Literature, 1788-1914*. Dictionary of Literary Biography 230. Detroit: Gale Group, 2001.

Who's Who of Australian Writers. 2d ed. Clayton: National Centre for Australian Studies, 1995.

Dictionaries, histories, and handbooks

Andrews, B. G., and William H. Wilde. *Australian Literature to 1900: A Guide to Information Sources*. American Literature, English Literature, and World Literatures in English: An Information Guide Series 22. Detroit: Gale Research, 1980.

Brins, Nicholas, and Rebecca McNeer, eds. *A Companion to Australian Literature Since 1900*. Rochester, N.Y.: Camden House, 2007.

Elliott, Brian Robinson. *The Landscape of Australian Poetry*. Melbourne: Cheshire, 1967.

Gray, Robert, and Geoffrey Lehmann, eds. *Australian Poetry in the Twentieth Century*. Port Melbourne: William Heinemann Australia, 1991.

Green, H. M. *A History of Australian Literature: Pure and Applied—A Critical Review of All Forms of Literature Produced in Australia from the First Books Published After the Arrival of the First Fleet Until 1950*. Revised by Dorothy Green. 2 vols. London: Angus & Robertson, 1984.

Hergenhan, Laurie. *The Penguin New Literary History of Australia*. New York: Penguin, 1988.

Hooton, Joy, and Harry Heseltine. *Annals of Australian Literature*. 2d ed. Melbourne: Oxford University Press, 1992.

Jaffa, Herbert C. *Modern Australian Poetry, 1920-1970: A Guide to Information Sources*. American Literature, English Literature, and World Literatures in English: An Information Guide Series 24. Detroit: Gale Research, 1979.

Lever, Richard, James Wieland, and Scott Findlay. *Post-colonial Literatures in English: Australia, 1970-1992*. A Reference Publication in Literature. New York: G. K. Hall, 1996.

Lock, Fred, and Alan Lawson. *Australian Literature: A Reference Guide*. 2d ed. Australian Bibliographies. New York: Oxford University Press, 1980.

Pierce, Peter, ed. *The Cambridge History of Australian Literature*. New York: Cambridge University Press, 2009.

Wilde, W. H., Joy Hooton, and Barry Andrews. *The Oxford Companion to Australian Literature*. 2d ed. New York: Oxford University Press, 1994.

Women writers

Adelaide, Debra. *Bibliography of Australian Women's Literature, 1795-1990: A Listing of Fiction, Poetry, Drama, and Non-fiction Published in Monograph Form Arranged Alphabetically by Author*. Port Melbourne: Thorpe with National Centre for Australian Studies, 1991.

Hampton, Susan, and Kate Llewellyn, eds. *The Penguin Book of Australian Women Poets*. New York: Penguin Ringwood, 1986.

CANADA (*see also in the foreign-language section:* FRANCOPHONE)

Biographical sources

Lecker, Robert, Jack David, and Ellen Quigley, eds. *Canadian Writers and Their Works: Poetry Series*. Downsview, Ont.: ECW Press, 1983.

McLeod, Donald, ed. *Canadian Writers and Their Works Cumulated Index Volume: Poetry Series*. Toronto, Ont.: ECW Press, 1993.

New, W. H., ed. *Canadian Writers Before 1890*. Dictionary of Literary Biography 99. Detroit: Gale Research, 1990.

_____. *Canadian Writers, 1890-1920*. Dictionary of Literary Biography 92. Detroit: Gale Research, 1990.

_____. *Canadian Writers, 1920-1959: First Series*. Dictionary of Literary Biography 68. Detroit: Gale Research, 1988.

_____. *Canadian Writers, 1920-1959: Second Series*. Dictionary of Literary Biography 88. Detroit: Gale Research, 1989.

_____. *Canadian Writers Since 1960: First Series*. Dictionary of Literary Biography 53. Detroit: Gale Research, 1986.

_____. *Canadian Writers Since 1960: Second Series*. Dictionary of Literary Biography 60. Detroit: Gale Research, 1987.

Criticism

Platnick, Phyllis. *Canadian Poetry: Index to Criticisms, 1970-1979*. Ontario: Canadian Library Association, 1985.

Dictionaries, histories, and handbooks

Brandt, Di, and Barbara Godard, eds. *Wider Boundaries of Daring: The Modernist Impulse in Canadian Women's Poetry*. Waterloo, Ont.: Wilfrid Laurier University Press, 2009.

Marshall, Tom. *Harsh and Lovely Land: The Major Canadian Poets and the Making of a Canadian Tradition*. Vancouver: University of British Columbia Press, 1979.

Starnino, Carmine, ed. *The New Canon: An Anthology of Canadian Poetry*. Montreal: Véhicule Press, 2006.

Stevens, Peter. *Modern English-Canadian Poetry: A Guide to Information Sources*. American Literature, English Literature, and World Literatures in English: An Information Guide Series 15. Detroit: Gale Research, 1978.

Indexes of primary works

Fee, Margery, ed. *Canadian Poetry in Selected English-Language Anthologies: An Index and Guide*. Halifax, N.S.: Dalhousie University, University Libraries, School of Library Service, 1985.

McQuarrie, Jane, Anne Mercer, and Gordon Ripley, eds. *Index to Canadian Poetry in English*. Toronto: Reference Press, 1984.

ENGLAND (*see also* IRISH POETRY IN ENGLISH; SCOTTISH POETRY IN ENGLISH; WELSH POETRY IN ENGLISH)

Bibliographies

Case, Arthur E. *A Bibliography of English Poetical Miscellanies, 1521-1750*. London: Oxford University Press for the Bibliographical Society, 1935.

Dyson, A. E., ed. *English Poetry: Select Bibliographical Guides*. London: Oxford University Press, 1971.

Biographical sources

Fredeman, William E., and Ira B. Nadel, eds. *Victorian Poets Before 1850*. Dictionary of Literary Biography 32. Detroit: Gale Research, 1984.

_____. *Victorian Poets After 1850*. Dictionary of Literary Biography 35. Detroit: Gale Research, 1985.

Greenfield, John R., ed. *British Romantic Poets, 1789-1832: First Series*. Dictionary of Literary Biography 93. Detroit: Gale Research, 1990.

_____, ed. *British Romantic Poets, 1789-1832: Second Series*. Dictionary of Literary Biography 96. Detroit: Gale Research, 1990.

Hester, M. Thomas, ed. *Seventeenth-Century British Nondramatic Poets: First Series*. Dictionary of Literary Biography 121. Detroit: Gale Research, 1992.

Quinn, Patrick, ed. *British Poets of the Great War: Brooke, Rosenberg, Thomas: A Documentary Volume*. Dictionary of Literary Biography 216. Detroit: Gale Group, 2000.

Sherry, Vincent B., Jr., ed. *Poets of Great Britain and Ireland, 1945-1960*. Dictionary of Literary Biography 27. Detroit: Gale Research, 1984.

_____. *Poets of Great Britain and Ireland, Since 1960*. Dictionary of Literary Biography 40. Detroit: Gale Research, 1985.

Sitter, John, ed. *Seventeenth-Century British Nondramatic Poets: Second Series*. Dictionary of Literary Biography 126. Detroit: Gale Research, 1993.

_____. *Seventeenth-Century British Nondramatic Poets: Third Series*. Dictionary of Literary Biography 131. Detroit: Gale Research, 1993.

_____. *Eighteenth-Century British Poets: First Series*. Dictionary of Literary Biography 95. Detroit: Gale Research, 1990.

_____. *Eighteenth-Century British Poets: Second Series*. Dictionary of Literary Biography 109. Detroit: Gale Research, 1991.

Stanford, Donald E., ed. *British Poets, 1880-1914*. Dictionary of Literary Biography 19. Detroit: Gale Research, 1983.

_____. *British Poets, 1914-1945*. Dictionary of Literary Biography 20. Detroit: Gale Research, 1983.

Thesing, William B., ed. *Late Nineteenth- and Early Twentieth-Century British Women Poets*. Dictionary of Literary Biography 240. Detroit: Gale Group, 2001.

_____. *Victorian Women Poets*. Dictionary of Literary Biography 199. Detroit: Gale Research, 1999.

Criticism

Guide to British Poetry Explication. 4 vols. Boston: G. K. Hall, 1991.

Dictionaries, histories, and handbooks

Courthope, W. J. *A History of English Poetry*. New York: Macmillan, 1895-1910.

Garrett, John. *British Poetry Since the Sixteenth Century: A Student's Guide*. Totowa, N.J.: Barnes & Noble Books, 1987.

Mell, Donald Charles, Jr. *English Poetry, 1660-1800: A Guide to Information Sources*. American Literature, English Literature, and World Literatures in English: An Information Guide Series 40. Detroit: Gale Research, 1982.

Smith, Eric. *A Dictionary of Classical Reference in English Poetry*. Totowa, N.J.: Barnes & Noble, 1984.

Woodring, Carl, and James Shapiro, eds. *The Colum-*

bia History of British Poetry. New York: Columbia University Press, 1993.

History: Old and Middle English

Aertsen, Hank, and Rolf H. Bremmer, eds. *Companion to Old English Poetry*. Amsterdam: VU University Press, 1994.

Beale, Walter H. *Old and Middle English Poetry to 1500: A Guide to Information Sources*. American Literature, English Literature, and World Literatures in English: An Information Guide Series 7. Detroit: Gale Research, 1976.

Brown, Carleton, and Rossell Hope Robbins. *The Index of Middle English Verse*. New York: Columbia University Press for the Index Society, 1943.

Cooney, Helen, ed. *Nation, Court, and Culture: New Essays on Fifteenth Century Poetry*. Dublin: Four Courts Press, 2001.

Hirsh, John C., ed. *Medieval Lyric: Middle English Lyrics, Ballads, and Carols*. Annotated ed. Malden, Mass.: Blackwell, 2005.

Jost, Jean E. *Ten Middle English Arthurian Romances: A Reference Guide*. Boston: G. K. Hall, 1986.

Martinez, Nancy C., and Joseph G. R. Martinez. *Old English-Medieval*. Vol. 1 in *Guide to British Poetry Explication*. Boston: G. K. Hall, 1991.

O'Keeffe, Katherine O'Brien, ed. *Old English Shorter Poems: Basic Readings*. Garland Reference Library of the Humanities 1432. New York: Garland, 1994.

Palmer, R. Barton, ed. and trans. *Medieval Epic and Romance: An Anthology of English and French Narrative*. Glen Allen, Va.: College Publishing, 2007.

Pearsall, Derek. *Old English and Middle English Poetry*. Vol. 1 in *The Routledge History of English Poetry*. London: Routledge, 1977.

Scanlon, Larry, ed. *The Cambridge Companion to Medieval Literature, 1100-1500*. New York: Cambridge University Press, 2009.

History: Renaissance to 1660

Cheney, Patrick, Andrew Hadfield, and Garrett A. Sullivan, Jr., eds. *Early Modern English Poetry: A Critical Companion*. New York: Oxford University Press, 2006.

Frank, Joseph. *Hobbled Pegasus: A Descriptive Bibliography of Minor English Poetry, 1641-1660.*

Albuquerque: University of New Mexico Press, 1968.

Gutierrez, Nancy A. *English Historical Poetry, 1476-1603: A Bibliography*. Garland Reference Library of the Humanities 410. New York: Garland, 1983.

Martinez, Nancy C., and Joseph G. R. Martinez. *Renaissance*. Vol. 2 in *Guide to British Poetry Explication*. Boston: G. K. Hall, 1991.

Post, Jonathan F. S., ed. *Green Thoughts, Green Shades: Essays by Contemporary Poets on the Early Modern Lyric*. Berkeley: University of California Press, 2002.

Ringler, William A., Jr. *Bibliography and Index of English Verse Printed 1476-1558*. New York: Mansell, 1988.

Ringler, William A., Michael Rudick, and Susan J. Ringler. *Bibliography and Index of English Verse in Manuscript, 1501-1558*. New York: Mansell, 1992.

Rivers, Isabel. *Classical and Christian Ideas in English Renaissance Poetry: A Student's Guide*. 2d ed. New York: Routledge, 1994.

History: Restoration (1660) through eighteenth century

Fairer, David. *English Poetry of the Eighteenth Century, 1700-1789*. Annotated ed. Harlow, Essex, England: Longman, 2003.

Foxon, D. F. *English Verse 1701-1750: A Catalogue of Separately Printed Poems with Notes on Contemporary Collected Editions*. 2 vols. Cambridge, England: Cambridge University Press, 1975.

Jackson, J. R. de J. *Annals of English Verse, 1770-1835: A Preliminary Survey of the Volumes Published*. Garland Reference Library of the Humanities 535. New York: Garland, 1985.

Martinez, Nancy C., Joseph G. R. Martinez, and Erland Anderson. *Restoration-Romantic*. Vol. 3 in *Guide to British Poetry Explication*. Boston: G. K. Hall, 1991.

Nokes, David, and Janet Barron. *An Annotated Critical Bibliography of Augustan Poetry*. Annotated Critical Bibliographies. New York: St. Martin's Press, 1989.

Rothstein, Eric. *Restoration and Eighteenth-Century Poetry, 1660-1780*. Vol. 3 in *The Routledge History of English Poetry*. Boston: Routledge & Kegan Paul, 1981.

Sitter, John, ed. *The Cambridge Companion to Eighteenth-Century Poetry.* New York: Cambridge University Press, 2001.

Starr, G. Gabrielle. *Lyric Generations: Poetry and the Novel in the Long Eighteenth Century.* Baltimore: Johns Hopkins University Press, 2004.

History: Nineteenth century

Blyth, Caroline, ed. *Decadent Verse: An Anthology of Late-Victorian Poetry, 1872-1900.* London: Anthem Press, 2009.

Bristow, Joseph, ed. *The Cambridge Companion to Victorian Poetry.* New York: Cambridge University Press, 2000.

Chapman, Alison, ed. *Victorian Women Poets.* Cambridge, England: D. S. Brewer, 2003.

Faverty, Frederic E., ed. *The Victorian Poets: A Guide to Research.* 2d ed. Cambridge, Mass.: Harvard University Press, 1968.

Jackson, J. R. de J. *Poetry of the Romantic Period.* Vol. 4 in *The Routledge History of English Poetry.* Boston: Routledge & Kegan Paul, 1980.

Jordan, Frank, ed. *The English Romantic Poets: A Review of Research and Criticism.* 4th ed. New York: MLA, 1985.

McLane, Maureen N., and James Chandler, eds. *The Cambridge Companion to British Romantic Poetry.* New York: Cambridge University Press, 2008.

Martinez, Nancy C., Joseph G. R. Martinez, and Erland Anderson. *Victorian-Contemporary.* Vol. 4 in *Guide to British Poetry Explication.* Boston: G. K. Hall, 1991.

O'Gorman, Francis, ed. *Victorian Poetry: An Annotated Anthology.* Malden, Mass.: Wiley-Blackwell, 2004.

O'Neill, Michael, and Charles Mahoney, eds. *Romantic Poetry: An Annotated Anthology.* Malden, Mass.: Wiley-Blackwell, 2008.

Reilly, Catherine W. *Late Victorian Poetry, 1880-1899: An Annotated Biobibliography.* New York: Mansell, 1994.

_____. *Mid-Victorian Poetry, 1860-1879: An Annotated Biobibliography.* New York: Mansell, 2000.

Reiman, Donald H. *English Romantic Poetry, 1800-1835: A Guide to Information Sources.* American Literature, English Literature, and World Literature

in English: An Information Guide Series 27. Detroit: Gale Research, 1979.

Richards, Bernard Arthur. *English Poetry of the Victorian Period, 1830-1890.* 2d ed. New York: Longman, 2001.

Roberts, Adam. *Romantic and Victorian Long Poems: A Guide.* Brookfield, Vt.: Ashgate, 1999.

History: Twentieth century and contemporary

Anderson, Emily Ann. *English Poetry, 1900-1950: A Guide to Information Sources.* American Literature, English Literature, and World Literatures in English: An Information Guide Series 33. Detroit: Gale Research, 1982.

Bradley, Jerry. *The Movement: British Poets of the 1950's.* New York: Twayne, 1993.

Broom, Sarah. *Contemporary British and Irish Poetry: An Introduction.* Illustrated ed. New York: Palgrave Macmillan, 2006.

Corcoran, Neil, ed. *The Cambridge Companion to Twentieth-Century English Poetry.* New York: Cambridge University Press, 2007.

Davie, Donald. *Under Briggflatts: A History of Poetry in Great Britain, 1960-1988.* Chicago: University of Chicago Press, 1989.

Dowson, Jane, and Alice Entwistle. *A History of Twentieth-Century British Women's Poetry.* New York: Cambridge University Press, 2005.

Lehmann, John. *The English Poets of the First World War.* New York: Thames and Hudson, 1982.

Martinez, Nancy C., Joseph G. R. Martinez, and Erland Anderson. *Victorian-Contemporary.* Vol. 4 in *Guide to British Poetry Explication.* Boston: G. K. Hall, 1991.

Persoon, James. *Modern British Poetry, 1900-1939.* Twayne's Critical History of Poetry Studies. New York: Twayne, 1999.

Reilly, Catherine W. *English Poetry of the Second World War: A Biobibliography.* Boston: G. K. Hall, 1986.

Schmidt, Michael. *A Reader's Guide to Fifty Modern British Poets.* New York: Barnes & Noble, 1979.

Shields, Ellen F. *Contemporary English Poetry: An Annotated Bibliography of Criticism to 1980.* Garland Reference Library of the Humanities 460. New York: Garland, 1984.

Thwaite, Anthony. *Poetry Today: A Critical Guide to British Poetry, 1960-1992.* New York: Longman with the British Council, 1996.

Tuma, Keith, ed. *Anthology of Twentieth-Century British and Irish Poetry.* Annotated ed. New York: Oxford University Press, 2001.

Women writers

Chapman, Alison, ed. *Victorian Women Poets.* Cambridge, England: D. S. Brewer, 2003.

Dowson, Jane, and Alice Entwistle. *A History of Twentieth-Century British Women's Poetry.* New York: Cambridge University Press, 2005.

Gray, F. Elizabeth. *Christian and Lyric Tradition in Victorian Women's Poetry.* New York: Routledge, 2009.

Jackson, J. R. de J. *Romantic Poetry by Women: A Bibliography, 1770-1835.* Oxford: Clarendon-Oxford University Press, 1993.

INDIA AND SOUTH ASIA

Agrawal, K. A. *Toru Dutt: The Pioneer Spirit of Indian English Poetry—A Critical Study.* New Delhi: Atlantic, 2009.

De Souza, Eunice, ed. *Early Indian Poetry in English: An Anthology, 1829-1947.* New Delhi: Oxford University Press, 2005.

King, Bruce. *Modern Indian Poetry in English.* Rev. ed. New Delhi: Oxford University Press, 2001.

Naik, M. K. *A History of Indian English Literature.* New Delhi: Sahitya Akademi, 1989.

Rama, Atma. *Indian Poetry and Fiction in English.* New Delhi: Bahri Publications, 1991.

Singh, Amritjit, Rajiav Verma, and Irene M. Johsi. *Indian Literature in English, 1827-1979: A Guide to Information Sources.* American Literature, English Literature, and World Literatures in English: An Information Guide Series 36. Detroit: Gale Research, 1981.

Singh, Kanwar Dinesh. *Contemporary Indian English Poetry: Comparing Male and Female Voices.* New Delhi: Atlantic, 2008.

Sinha, R. P. N. *Indo-Anglican Poetry: Its Birth and Growth.* New Delhi: Reliance Publishing House, 1987.

Thayil, Jeet, ed. *The Bloodaxe Book of Contemporary Indian Poets.* Cambridge, Mass.: Bloodaxe, 2008.

IRISH POETRY IN ENGLISH (*see also in the foreign-language section:* CELTIC LANGUAGES)

Biographical sources

Sherry, Vincent B., Jr., ed. *Poets of Great Britain and Ireland, 1945-1960.* Dictionary of Literary Biography 27. Detroit: Gale Research, 1984.

_____. *Poets of Great Britain and Ireland Since 1960.* Dictionary of Literary Biography 40. Detroit: Gale Research, 1985.

Dictionaries, histories, and handbooks

Broom, Sarah. *Contemporary British and Irish Poetry: An Introduction.* Illustrated ed. New York: Palgrave Macmillan, 2006.

Hogan, Robert, ed. *Dictionary of Irish Literature.* Rev. ed. 2 vols. Westport, Conn.: Greenwood Press, 1996.

Schirmer, Gregory A. *Out of What Began: A History of Irish Poetry in English.* Ithaca, N.Y.: Cornell University Press, 1998.

Tuma, Keith, ed. *Anthology of Twentieth-Century British and Irish Poetry.* Annotated ed. New York: Oxford University Press, 2001.

Women writers

Colman, Anne Ulry. *Dictionary of Nineteenth-Century Irish Women Poets.* Galway: Kenny's Bookshop, 1996.

McBreen, Joan, ed. *The White Page = An Bhileog Bhán: Twentieth-Century Irish Women Poets.* Cliffs of Moher, Ireland: Salmon, 1999.

Weekes, Ann Owens. *Unveiling Treasures: The Attic Guide to the Published Works of Irish Women Literary Writers: Drama, Fiction, Poetry.* Dublin: Attic Press, 1993.

NEW ZEALAND

Keown, Michelle. *Pacific Islands Writing: The Postcolonial Literatures of Aotearoa/New Zealand and Oceania.* New York: Oxford University Press, 2007.

Marsack, Robyn, and Andrew Johnstone, eds. *Twenty Contemporary New Zealand Poets: An Anthology.* Manchester, England: Carcaret Press, 2009.

Sturm, Terry, ed. *The Oxford History of New Zealand Literature in English.* Auckland: Oxford University Press, 1991.

Thomson, John. *New Zealand Literature to 1977: A*

Guide to Information Sources. American Literature, English Literature, and World Literatures in English: An Information Guide Series 30. Detroit: Gale Research, 1980.

SCOTTISH POETRY IN ENGLISH (*see also in the foreign-language section:* CELTIC LANGUAGES)

Glen, Duncan. *The Poetry of the Scots: An Introduction and Bibliographical Guide to Poetry in Gaelic, Scots, Latin, and English*. Edinburgh: Edinburgh University Press, 1991.

Mapstone, Sally, ed. *Older Scots Literature*. Edinburgh: John Donald, 2005.

Martin, Joanna. *Kingship and Love in Scottish Poetry, 1424-1540*. Farnham, Surrey, England: Ashgate, 2008.

Scottish Poetry Index: An Index to Poetry and Poetry-Related Material in Scottish Literary Magazines, 1952-   . Edinburgh: Scottish Poetry Library, 1994-2000.

UNITED STATES
Biographical sources

Alfonsi, Ferdinando. *Dictionary of Italian-American Poets*. American University Studies. Series II, Romance Languages and Literature 112. New York: Peter Lang, 1989.

Baughman, Ronald, ed. *American Poets*. Vol. 3 in *Contemporary Authors: Bibliographical Series*. Detroit: Gale Research, 1986.

Conte, Joseph, ed. *American Poets Since World War II: Fourth Series*. Dictionary of Literary Biography 165. Detroit: Gale Research, 1996.

_____. *American Poets Since World War II: Fifth Series*. Dictionary of Literary Biography 169. Detroit: Gale Research, 1996.

_____. *American Poets Since World War II: Sixth Series*. Dictionary of Literary Biography 193. Detroit: Gale Research, 1998.

Greiner, Donald J., ed. *American Poets Since World War II*. Dictionary of Literary Biography 5. Detroit: Gale Research, 1980.

Gwynn, R. S., ed. *American Poets Since World War II: Second Series*. Dictionary of Literary Biography 105. Detroit: Gale Research, 1991.

_____. *American Poets Since World War II: Third Series*. Dictionary of Literary Biography 120. Detroit: Gale Research, 1992.

Quartermain, Peter, ed. *American Poets, 1880-1945: First Series*. Dictionary of Literary Biography 45. Detroit: Gale Research, 1986.

_____. *American Poets, 1880-1945: Second Series*. Dictionary of Literary Biography 48. Detroit: Gale Research, 1986.

_____. *American Poets, 1880-1945: Third Series*. Dictionary of Literary Biography 54. Detroit: Gale Research, 1987.

Criticism

Guide to American Poetry Explication. Reference Publication in Literature. 2 vols. Boston: G. K. Hall, 1989.

Dictionaries, histories, and handbooks

Kamp, Jim, ed. *Reference Guide to American Literature*. 3d ed. Detroit: St. James Press, 1994.

Parini, Jay, ed. *The Columbia History of American Poetry*. New York: Columbia University Press, 1993.

Perkins, George, Barbara Perkins, and Phillip Leininger, eds. *Benét's Reader's Encyclopedia of American Literature*. New York: HarperCollins, 1991.

Shucard, Alan. *American Poetry: The Puritans Through Walt Whitman*. Twayne's Critical History of Poetry Series. Boston: Twayne, 1988.

Waggoner, Hyatt H. *American Poets from the Puritans to the Present*. Rev. ed. Baton Rouge: Louisiana University Press, 1984.

Indexes of primary works

American Poetry Index: An Author, Title, and Subject Guide to Poetry by Americans in Single-Author Collections. Great Neck, N.Y.: Granger, 1983-1988.

Annual Index to Poetry in Periodicals. Great Neck, N.Y.: Poetry Index Press, 1985-1988.

Caskey, Jefferson D., comp. *Index to Poetry in Popular Periodicals, 1955-1959*. Westport, Conn.: Greenwood Press, 1984.

Index of American Periodical Verse. Lanham, Md.: Scarecrow Press, 1971.

Index to Poetry in Periodicals: American Poetic Renaissance, 1915-1919: An Index of Poets and Poems Published in American Magazines and Newspapers. Great Neck, N.Y.: Granger, 1981.

Index to Poetry in Periodicals, 1920-1924: An Index of Poets and Poems Published in American Magazines and Newspapers. Great Neck, N.Y.: Granger, 1983.

Index to Poetry in Periodicals, 1925-1992: An Index of Poets and Poems Published in American Magazines and Newspapers. Great Neck, N.Y.: Granger, 1984.

History: Colonial to 1800

Lemay, J. A. Leo. *A Calendar of American Poetry in the Colonial Newspapers and Magazines and in the Major English Magazines Through 1765.* Worcester, Mass.: American Antiquarian Society, 1972.

Scheick, William J., and JoElla Doggett. *Seventeenth-Century American Poetry: A Reference Guide.* Reference Guides in Literature 14. Boston: G. K. Hall, 1977.

Wegelin, Oscar. *Early American Poetry: A Compilation of the Titles of Volumes of Verse and Broadsides by Writers Born or Residing in North America, North of the Mexican Border, 1650-1820.* 2d ed. 2 vols. New York: Smith, 1930.

History: Nineteenth century

Bennett, Paula, Karen L. Kilcup, and Philipp Schweighauser. *Teaching Nineteenth-Century American Poetry.* New York: Modern Language Association of America, 2007.

Haralson, Eric L., ed. *Encyclopedia of American Poetry: The Nineteenth Century.* Chicago: Fitzroy Dearborn, 1998.

Jason, Philip K. *Nineteenth Century American Poetry: An Annotated Bibliography.* Pasadena, Calif.: Salem Press, 1989.

Lee, A. Robert, ed. *Nineteenth-Century American Poetry.* Critical Studies Series. Totowa, N.J.: Barnes & Noble, 1985.

Olson, Steven. *The Prairie in Nineteenth Century American Poetry.* Norman: University of Oklahoma Press, 1995.

Ruppert, James. *Colonial and Nineteenth Century.* Vol. 1 in *Guide to American Poetry Explication.* Boston: G. K. Hall, 1989.

Sorby, Angela. *Schoolroom Poets: Childhood and the Place of American Poetry, 1865-1917.* Durham: University of New Hampshire Press, 2005.

History: Twentieth century and contemporary

Altieri, Charles. *The Art of Twentieth-Century American Poetry: Modernism and After.* Malden, Mass.: Blackwell, 2006.

Axelrod, Steven Gould, and Camille Roman, eds. *Modernisms, 1900-1950.* Vol. 2 in *The New Anthology of American Poetry.* New Brunswick, N.J.: Rutgers University Press, 2005.

Beach, Christopher. *The Cambridge Introduction to Twentieth-Century American Poetry.* New York: Cambridge University Press, 2003.

Davis, Lloyd, and Robert Irwin. *Contemporary American Poetry: A Checklist.* Metuchen, N.J.: Scarecrow Press, 1975.

Gioia, Dana, David Mason, and Meg Schoerke, eds. *Twentieth-Century American Poetics: Poets on the Art of Poetry.* Boston: McGraw-Hill, 2004.

_____. *Twentieth-Century American Poetry.* Boston: McGraw-Hill, 2003.

Green, Scott E. *Contemporary Science Fiction, Fantasy, and Horror Poetry: A Resource Guide and Biographical Directory.* New York: Greenwood Press, 1989.

Haralson, Eric L., ed. *Encyclopedia of American Poetry: The Twentieth Century.* Chicago: Fitzroy Dearborn, 2001.

Kane, Daniel. *All Poets Welcome: The Lower East Side Poetry Scene in the 1960's.* Berkeley: University of California Press, 2003.

Kirsch, Adam. *The Wounded Surgeon: Confession and Transformation in Six American Poets.* New York: W. W. Norton, 2005.

Leo, John R. *Modern and Contemporary.* Vol. 2 in *Guide to American Poetry Explication.* Boston: G. K. Hall, 1989.

McPheron, William. *The Bibliography of Contemporary American Poetry, 1945-1985: An Annotated Checklist.* Westport, Conn.: Meckler, 1986.

Moramarco, Fred, and William Sullivan. *Containing Multitudes: Poetry in the United States Since 1950.* Critical History of Poetry Series. New York: Twayne, 1998.

Rasula, Jed. *This Compost: Ecological Imperatives in American Poetry.* Athens: University of Georgia Press, 2002.

Shucard, Alan, Fred Moramarco, and William Sullivan. *Modern American Poetry, 1865-1950.* Boston: Twayne, 1989.

Ward, Geoffrey. *Statutes of Liberty: The New York School of Poets.* New York: Palgrave Macmillan, 2001.

African American: Biographical sources

Harris, Trudier, ed. *Afro-American Writers Before the Harlem Renaissance.* Dictionary of Literary Biography 50. Detroit: Gale Research, 1986.

_____. *Afro-American Writers from the Harlem Renaissance to 1940.* Dictionary of Literary Biography 51. Detroit: Gale Research, 1987.

Harris, Trudier, and Thadious M. Davis, eds. *Afro-American Poets Since 1955.* Dictionary of Literary Biography 41. Detroit: Gale Research, 1985.

African American: Indexes of primary works

Chapman, Dorothy Hilton, comp. *Index to Black Poetry.* Boston, G. K. Hall, 1974.

Frankovich, Nicholas, and David Larzelere, eds. *The Columbia Granger's Index to African-American Poetry.* New York: Columbia University Press, 1999.

African American: Dictionaries, histories, and handbooks

French, William P., et al. *Afro-American Poetry and Drama, 1760-1975: A Guide to Information Sources.* American Literature, English Literature, and World Literatures in English: An Information Guide Series 17. Detroit: Gale Research, 1979.

Major, Clarence, ed. *The Garden Thrives: Twentieth Century African-American Poetry.* New York: HarperPerennial, 1996.

Rampersad, Arnold, and Hilary Herbold, eds. *The Oxford Anthology of African-American Poetry.* New York: Oxford University Press, 2005.

Sherman, Joan R. *Invisible Poets: Afro-Americans of the Nineteenth Century.* 2d ed. Urbana: University of Illinois Press, 1989.

Wagner, Jean, and Kenneth Douglas, trans. *Black Poets of the United States: From Paul Laurence Dunbar to Langston Hughes.* Urbana: University of Illinois Press, 1973.

African American: Women writers

Chapman, Dorothy Hilton, comp. *Index to Poetry by Black American Women.* Bibliographies and Indexes in Afro-American and African Studies 15. New York: Greenwood Press, 1986.

Lee, Valerie, ed. *The Prentice Hall Anthology of African American Women's Literature.* Upper Saddle River, N.J.: Pearson Prentice Hall, 2006.

Asian American

Chang, Juliana, ed. *Quiet Fire: A Historical Anthology of Asian American Poetry, 1892-1970.* New York: Asian American Writers' Workshop, 1996.

Chang, Victoria, ed. *Asian American Poetry: The Next Generation.* Urbana: University of Illinois Press, 2004.

Cheung, King-Kok, ed. *An Interethnic Companion to Asian American Literature.* New York: Cambridge University Press, 1997.

Cheung, King-Kok, and Stan Yogi. *Asian American Literature: An Annotated Bibliography.* New York: MLA, 1988.

Huang, Guiyou, ed. *Asian American Poets: A Bio-Bibliographical Critical Sourcebook.* Westport, Conn.: Greenwood Press, 2002.

Yu, Timothy. *Race and the Avant-Garde: Experimental and Asian American Poetry Since 1965.* Stanford, Calif.: Stanford University Press, 2009.

Zhou, Xiaojing. *The Ethics and Poetics of Alterity in Asian American Poetry.* Iowa City: University of Iowa Press, 2006.

Latino

Aragón, Francisco, ed. *The Wind Shifts: New Latino Poetry.* Tucson: University of Arizona Press, 2007.

Bleznick, Donald William. *A Sourcebook for Hispanic Literature and Language: A Selected, Annotated Guide to Spanish, Spanish-American, and United States Hispanic Bibliography, Literature, Linguistics, Journals, and Other Source Materials.* 3d ed. Lanham, Md.: Scarecrow Press, 1995.

Candelaria, Cordelia. *Chicano Poetry: A Critical Introduction.* Westport, Conn.: Greenwood Press, 1986.

Dick, Bruce Allen, ed. *A Poet's Truth: Conversations with Latino/Latina Poets.* Tucson: University of Arizona Press, 2003.

Eger, Ernestina N. *A Bibliography of Criticism of Contemporary Chicano Literature.* Berkeley: Chicano Library Publications, University of California, 1982.

Kanellos, Nicolás, ed. *Biographical Dictionary of Hispanic Literature in the United States: The Literature of Puerto Ricans, Cuban Americans, and Other Hispanic Writers*. New York: Greenwood Press, 1989.

Lomelí, Francisco A., and Carl R. Shirley, eds. *Chicano Writers: First Series*. Dictionary of Literary Biography 82. Detroit: Gale Research, 1989.

_____. *Chicano Writers: Second Series*. Dictionary of Literary Biography 122. Detroit: Gale Research, 1992.

_____. *Chicano Writers: Third Series*. Dictionary of Literary Biography 209. Detroit: Gale Group, 1999.

Martínez, Julio A., and Francisco A. Lomelí, eds. *Chicano Literature: A Reference Guide*. Westport, Conn.: Greenwood Press, 1985.

Native American

Fast, Robin Riley. *The Heart as a Drum: Continuance and Resistance in American Indian Poetry*. Ann Arbor: University of Michigan Press, 1999.

Howard, Helen Addison. *American Indian Poetry*. Twayne's United States Authors Series 334. Boston: Twayne, 1979.

Littlefield, Daniel F., Jr., and James W. Parins. *A Biobibliography of Native American Writers, 1772-1924*. Native American Bibliography Series 2. Metuchen, N.J.: Scarecrow Press, 1981.

_____. *A Biobibliography of Native American Writers, 1772-1924: Supplement*. Native American Bibliography Series 5. Metuchen, N.J.: Scarecrow Press, 1985.

Lundquist, Suzanne Evertsen. *Native American Literatures: An Introduction*. New York: Continuum, 2004.

Porter, Joy, and Kenneth M. Roemer, eds. *The Cambridge Companion to Native American Literature*. New York: Cambridge University Press, 2005.

Rader, Dean, and Janice Gould, eds. *Speak to Me Words: Essays on Contemporary American Indian Poetry*. Tucson: University of Arizona Press, 2003.

Roemer, Kenneth M., ed. *Native American Writers of the United States*. Dictionary of Literary Biography 175. Detroit: Gale Research, 1997.

Ruoff, A. LaVonne Brown. *American Indian Literatures: An Introduction, Bibliographic Review, and Selected Bibliography*. New York: Modern Language Association, 1990.

Wiget, Andrew. *Native American Literature*. Twayne's United States Authors Series 467. Boston: Twayne, 1985.

_____, ed. *Dictionary of Native American Literature*. Garland Reference Library of the Humanities 1815. New York: Garland, 1994.

Wilson, Norma. *The Nature of Native American Poetry*. Albuquerque: University of New Mexico Press, 2000.

Regional poetry

Bain, Robert, and Joseph M. Flora, eds. *Contemporary Poets, Dramatists, Essayists, and Novelists of the South: A Bio-bibliographical Sourcebook*. Westport, Conn.: Greenwood Press, 1994.

Jantz, Harold S. *The First Century of New England Verse*. Worcester, Mass.: American Antiquarian Society, 1944.

Women writers

Davidson, Phebe, ed. *Conversations with the World: American Women Poets and Their Work*. Pasadena, Calif.: Trilogy Books, 1998.

Drake, William. *The First Wave: Women Poets in America, 1915-1945*. New York: Macmillan, 1987.

Gray, Janet, ed. *She Wields a Pen: American Women Poets of the Nineteenth Century*. Iowa City: University of Iowa Press, 1997.

Reardon, Joan, and Kristine A. Thorsen. *Poetry by American Women, 1900-1975: A Bibliography*. Metuchen, N.J.: Scarecrow Press, 1979.

_____. *Poetry by American Women, 1975-1989: A Bibliography*. Metuchen, N.J.: Scarecrow Press, 1990.

WELSH POETRY IN ENGLISH (*see also in the foreign-language section:* CELTIC LANGUAGES)

Conran, Anthony. *Frontiers in Anglo-Welsh Poetry*. Cardiff: University of Wales Press, 1997.

FOREIGN-LANGUAGE POETRY

GENERAL REFERENCE SOURCES

Biographical sources

Jackson, William T. H., ed. *European Writers*. 14 vols. New York: Scribner, 1983-1991.

Kunitz, Stanley, and Vineta Colby, eds. *European Authors, 1000-1900: A Biographical Dictionary of European Literature*. New York: Wilson, 1967.

Magill, Frank N., ed. *Critical Survey of Poetry: Foreign Language Series*. 5 vols. Englewood Cliffs, N.J.: Salem Press, 1984.

_____. *Critical Survey of Poetry: Supplement*. Englewood Cliffs, N.J.: Salem Press, 1987.

Serafin, Steven, ed. *Encyclopedia of World Literature in the Twentieth Century*. 3d ed. 4 vols. Detroit: St. James Press, 1999.

_____. *Twentieth-Century Eastern European Writers: First Series*. Dictionary of Literary Biography 215. Detroit: Gale Group, 1999.

_____. *Twentieth-Century Eastern European Writers: Second Series*. Dictionary of Literary Biography 220. Detroit: Gale Group, 2000.

_____. *Twentieth-Century Eastern European Writers: Third Series*. Dictionary of Literary Biography 232. Detroit: Gale Group, 2001.

Solé, Carlos A., ed. *Latin American Writers*. 3 vols. New York: Scribner, 1989.

Criticism

Coleman, Arthur. *A Checklist of Interpretation, 1940-1973, of Classical and Continental Epics and Metrical Romances*. Vol. 2 in *Epic and Romance Criticism*. 2 vols. New York: Watermill, 1974.

Jason, Philip K., ed. *Masterplots II: Poetry Series, Revised Edition*. 8 vols. Pasadena, Calif.: Salem Press, 2002.

Krstovic, Jelena, ed. *Hispanic Literature Criticism*. Detroit: Gale Research, 1994.

The Year's Work in Modern Language Studies. London: Oxford University Press, 1931.

Dictionaries, histories, and handbooks

Auty, Robert, et al. *Traditions of Heroic and Epic Poetry*. 2 vols. Vol. 1, *The Traditions*; Vol. 2, *Characteristics and Techniques*. Publications of the Modern Humanities Research Association 9, 13. London: Modern Humanities Research Association, 1980, 1989.

Bede, Jean-Albert, and William B. Edgerton, eds. *Columbia Dictionary of Modern European Literature*. 2d ed. New York: Columbia University Press, 1980.

France, Peter, ed. *The Oxford Guide to Literature in English Translation*. New York: Oxford University Press, 2000.

Henderson, Lesley, ed. *Reference Guide to World Literature*. 2d ed. 2 vols. New York: St. James Press, 1995.

Oinas, Felix, ed. *Heroic Epic and Saga: An Introduction to the World's Great Folk Epics*. Bloomington: Indiana University Press, 1978.

Ostle, Robin, ed. *Modern Literature in the Near and Middle East, 1850-1970*. Routledge/SOAS Contemporary Politics and Culture in the Middle East Series. New York: Routledge, 1991.

Prusek, Jaroslav, ed. *Dictionary of Oriental Literatures*. 3 vols. Vol. 1, *East Asia*, edited by Z. Shupski; Vol. 2, *South and South-East Asia*, edited by D. Zbavitel; Vol. 3, *West Asia and North Africa*, edited by J. Becka. New York: Basic Books, 1974.

Pynsent, Robert B., ed. *Reader's Encyclopedia of Eastern European Literature*. New York: Harper-Collins, 1993.

Weber, Harry B., George Gutsche, and P. Rollberg, eds. *The Modern Encyclopedia of East Slavic, Baltic, and Eurasian Literatures*. 10 vols. Gulf Breeze, Fla.: Academic International Press, 1977.

Index of primary works

Hoffman, Herbert H. *Hoffman's Index to Poetry: European and Latin American Poetry in Anthologies*. Metuchen, N.J.: Scarecrow Press, 1985.

Poetics

Gasparov, M. L. *A History of European Versification*. Translated by G. S. Smith and Marina Tarlinskaja. New York: Oxford University Press, 1996.

Wimsatt, William K., ed. *Versification: Major Language Types: Sixteen Essays*. New York: Modern Language Association, 1972.

AFRICAN LANGUAGES (*see also in the English-language section:* GENERAL REFERENCE SOURCES (POSTCOLONIAL); AFRICA AND THE CARIBBEAN; *in the Foreign-language section:* FRANCOPHONE; SPANISH AND PORTUGUESE)

Elimimian, Isaac Irabor. *Theme and Style in African Poetry*. Lewiston, N.Y.: E. Mellen, 1991.

Herdeck, Donald E., ed. *African Authors: A Companion to Black African Writing, 1300-1973*. Dimensions of the Black Intellectual Experience. Washington, D.C.: Black Orpheus Press, 1973.

Killam, Douglas, and Ruth Rowe, eds. *The Companion to African Literatures*. Bloomington: Indiana University Press, 2000.

Limb, Peter, and Jean-Marie Volet. *Bibliography of African Literatures*. Lanham, Md.: Scarecrow Press, 1996.

ARABIC

Allen, Roger. *An Introduction to Arabic Literature*. Cambridge, England: Cambridge University Press, 2001.

Badawi, M. M. *A Critical Introduction to Modern Arabic Poetry*. New York: Cambridge University Press, 1975.

_____. *Modern Arabic Literature*. New York: Cambridge University Press, 1992.

Frolov, D. V. *Classical Arabic Verse: History and Theory of 'Arūd*. Boston: Brill, 2000.

Meisami, Julie Scott, and Paul Starkey, eds. *Encyclopedia of Arabic Literature*. New York: Routledge, 1998.

CARIBBEAN (*see also in the English-language section:* AFRICA AND THE CARIBBEAN; *in the Foreign-language section:* DUTCH AND FLEMISH; FRANCOPHONE; SPANISH AND PORTUGUESE)

Arnold, A. James, ed. *A History of Literature in the Caribbean*. 3 vols. Vol. 1, *Hispanic and Francophone Regions*; Vol. 2, *English and Dutch-Speaking Countries*; Vol. 3, *Cross-Cultural Studies*. Comparative History of Literatures in European Languages 10. Philadelphia: J. Benjamins, 1994.

Berrian, Brenda F., and Aart Broek. *Bibliography of Women Writers from the Caribbean, 1831-1986*. Washington, D.C.: Three Continents Press, 1989.

Fenwick, M. J. *Writers of the Caribbean and Central America: A Bibliography*. Garland Reference Library of the Humanities 1244. New York: Garland, 1992.

Goslinga, Marian. *Caribbean Literature: A Bibliography*. Scarecrow Area Bibliographies 15. Lanham, Md.: Scarecrow Press, 1998.

Herdeck, Donald E., ed. *Caribbean Writers: A Bio-Bibliographical-Critical Encyclopedia*. Washington, D.C.: Three Continents Press, 1979.

CATALAN

Barkan, Stanley H., ed. *Four Postwar Catalan Poets*. Rev. ed. Translated by David H. Rosenthal. Merrick, N.Y.: Cross-Cultural Communications, 1994.

Crowe, Anna, ed. *Light off Water: Twenty-five Catalan Poems, 1978-2002*. Translated by Iolanda Pelegri. Manchester, England: Carcanet Press, 2007.

Rosenthal, David H. *Postwar Catalan Poetry*. Lewisburg, Pa.: Bucknell University Press, 1991.

CELTIC LANGUAGES (*see also in the English-language section:* IRISH POETRY IN ENGLISH; SCOTTISH POETRY IN ENGLISH; WELSH POETRY IN ENGLISH)

Irish Gaelic

McBreen, Joan, ed. *The White Page = An Bhileog Bhán: Twentieth-Century Irish Women Poets*. Cliffs of Moher, Ireland: Salmon, 1999.

Scottish Gaelic

Gifford, Douglas, and Dorothy McMillan. *A History of Scottish Women's Writing*. Edinburgh: Edinburgh University Press, 1997.

Glen, Duncan. *The Poetry of the Scots: An Introduction and Bibliographical Guide to Poetry in Gaelic, Scots, Latin, and English*. Edinburgh: Edinburgh University Press, 1991.

Thomson, Derick S. *An Introduction to Gaelic Poetry*. 2d ed. Edinburgh: Edinburgh University Press, 1989.

Welsh

Jarman, A. O. H., and Gwilym Rees Hughes, eds. *A Guide to Welsh Literature*. 6 vols. Cardiff: University of Wales Press, 1992-2000.

Lofmark, Carl. *Bards and Heroes: An Introduction to Old Welsh Poetry*. Felinfach, Wales: Llanerch, 1989.

Williams, Gwyn. *An Introduction to Welsh Poetry, from the Beginnings to the Sixteenth Century.* London: Faber and Faber, 1953.

CHINESE

Barnstone, Tony, and Chou Ping, eds. *The Anchor Book of Chinese Poetry: From Ancient to Contemporary, the Full 3,000-Year Tradition.* New York: Anchor Books, 2004.

Cai, Zong-qi, ed. *How to Read Chinese Poetry: A Guided Anthology.* Bilingual ed. New York: Columbia University Press, 2007.

Chang, Kang-i Sun, and Haun Saussy, eds. *Women Writers of Traditional China: An Anthology of Poetry and Criticism.* Stanford, Calif.: Stanford University Press, 1999.

Haft, Lloyd, ed. *The Poem.* Vol. 3 in *A Selective Guide to Chinese Literature, 1900-1949.* New York: E. J. Brill, 1989.

Lin, Julia C., trans. and ed. *Twentieth-Century Chinese Women's Poetry: An Anthology.* Armonk, N.Y.: M. E. Sharpe, 2009.

Lupke, Christopher, ed. *New Perspectives on Contemporary Chinese Poetry.* New York: Palgrave Macmillan, 2008.

Lynn, Richard John. *Guide to Chinese Poetry and Drama.* 2d ed. Boston, Mass.: G. K. Hall, 1984.

Nienhauser, William, Jr., ed. *The Indiana Companion to Traditional Chinese Literature.* Bloomington: Indiana University Press, 1986.

Owen, Stephen. *The Making of Early Chinese Classical Poetry.* Cambridge, Mass.: Harvard University Asia Center, 2006.

Wu-chi, Liu. *An Introduction to Chinese Literature.* Bloomington: Indiana University Press, 1966.

Yip, Wai-lim, ed. and trans. *Chinese Poetry: An Anthology of Major Modes and Genres.* 2d ed. Durham, N.C.: Duke University Press, 1997.

CLASSICAL GREEK AND LATIN

Albrecht, Michael von. *Roman Epic: An Interpretive Introduction.* Boston: Brill, 1999.

Braund, Susanna Morton. *Latin Literature.* New York: Routledge, 2002.

Briggs, Ward W. *Ancient Greek Authors.* Dictionary of Literary Biography 176. Detroit: Gale Research, 1997.

_____. *Ancient Roman Writers.* Dictionary of Literary Biography 211. Detroit: Gale Group, 1999.

Budelmann, Felix, ed. *The Cambridge Companion to Greek Lyric.* New York: Cambridge University Press, 2009.

Constantine, Peter, et al., eds. *The Greek Poets: Homer to the Present.* New York: W. W. Norton, 2009.

David, A. P. *The Dance of the Muses: Choral Theory and Ancient Greek Poetics.* New York: Oxford University Press, 2006.

Dihle, Albrecht, and Clare Krojzl, trans. *A History of Greek Literature: From Homer to the Hellenistic Period.* New York: Routledge, 1994.

Green, Ellen, ed. *Women Poets in Ancient Greece and Rome.* Norman: University of Oklahoma Press, 2005.

Harrison, Stephen, ed. *A Companion to Latin Literature.* Malden, Mass.: Blackwell, 2004.

Kessels, A. H. M., and W. J. Verdenius, comps. *A Concise Bibliography of Ancient Greek Literature.* 2d ed. Apeldoorn, Netherlands: Administratief Centrum, 1982.

King, Katherine Callen. *Ancient Epic.* Hoboken, N.J.: Wiley-Blackwell, 2009.

Lefkowitz, Mary R. *The Lives of the Greek Poets.* Baltimore: The Johns Hopkins University Press, 1981.

Lyne, R. O. *Collected Papers on Latin Poetry.* Edited by S. J. Harrison. New York: Oxford University Press, 2007.

Raffel, Burton, trans. *Pure Pagan: Seven Centuries of Greek Poems and Fragments.* New York: Random House, 2004.

West, M. L., trans. *Greek Lyric Poetry.* 1993. Reprint. New York: Oxford University Press, 2008.

DUTCH AND FLEMISH

Meijer, Reinder P. *Literature of the Low Countries: A Short History of Dutch Literature in the Netherlands and Belgium.* New ed. Boston: Nijhoff, 1978.

Nieuwenhuys, Robert. *Mirror of the Indies: A History of Dutch Colonial Literature.* Translated by Frans van Rosevelt, edited by E. M. Beekman. Library of the Indies. Amherst: University of Massachusetts Press, 1982.

Vermij, Lucie, and Martje Breedt Bruyn. *Women Writers from the Netherlands and Flanders*. Amsterdam: International Feminist Book Fair Press/Dekker, 1992.

Weevers, Theodoor. *Poetry of the Netherlands in Its European Context, 1170-1930*. London: University of London-Athlone Press, 1960.

FRANCOPHONE

General

Gilroy, James P., ed. *Francophone Literatures of the New World*. Denver, Colo.: Dept. of Foreign Languages and Literatures, University of Denver, 1982.

Africa and the Caribbean

Blair, Dorothy S. *African Literature in French: A History of Creative Writing in French from West and Equatorial Africa*. New York: Cambridge University Press, 1976.

Brown, Stewart, and Mark McWatt, eds. *The Oxford Book of Caribbean Verse*. New York: Oxford University Press, 2005.

D'Almeida, Irène Assiba, ed. *A Rain of Words: A Bilingual Anthology of Women's Poetry in Francophone Africa*. Translated by Janis A. Mayes. Charlottesville: University of Virginia Press, 2009.

Haigh, Sam, ed. *An Introduction to Caribbean Francophone Writing: Guadeloupe and Martinique*. New York: Berg, 1999.

Hurley, E. Anthony. *Through a Black Veil: Readings in French Caribbean Poetry*. Trenton, N.J.: Africa World Press, 2000.

Larrier, Renée Brenda. *Francophone Women Writers of Africa and the Caribbean*. Gainesville: University Press of Florida, 2000.

Moore, Gerald, and Ulli Beier, eds. *The Penguin Book of Modern African Poetry*. 4th ed. New York: Penguin, 2007.

Ojaide, Tanure. *Poetic Imagination in Black Africa: Essays on African Poetry*. Durham, N.C.: Carolina Academic Press, 1996.

Parekh, Pushpa Naidu, and Siga Fatima Jagne. *Postcolonial African Writers: A Bio-bibliographical Critical Sourcebook*. Westport, Conn.: Greenwood Press, 1998.

France: Bibliography

Kempton, Richard. *French Literature: An Annotated Guide to Selected Bibliographies*. New York: Modern Language Association of America, 1981.

France: Biographical sources

Beum, Robert, ed. *Nineteenth-Century French Poets*. Dictionary of Literary Biography 217. Detroit: Gale Group, 2000.

Sinnreich-Levi, Deborah, and Ian S. Laurie, eds. *Literature of the French and Occitan Middle Ages: Eleventh to Fifteenth Centuries*. Dictionary of Literary Biography 208. Detroit: Gale Group, 1999.

France: Criticism

Coleman, Kathleen. *Guide to French Poetry Explication*. New York: G. K. Hall, 1993.

France: Dictionaries, histories, and handbooks

Acquisto, Joseph. *French Symbolist Poetry and the Idea of Music*. Burlington, Vt.: Ashgate, 2006.

Aulestia, Gorka. *The Basque Poetic Tradition*. Translated by Linda White. Reno: University of Nevada Press, 2000.

Banks, Kathryn. *Cosmos and Image in the Renaissance: French Love Lyric and Natural-Philosophical Poetry*. London: Legenda, 2008.

Bishop, Michael. *Nineteenth-Century French Poetry*. Twayne's Critical History of Poetry Series. New York: Twayne, 1993.

Brereton, Geoffrey. *An Introduction to the French Poets, Villon to the Present Day*. 2d rev. ed. London: Methuen, 1973.

Caws, Mary Ann, ed. *The Yale Anthology of Twentieth-Century French Poetry*. New Haven, Conn.: Yale University Press, 2004.

Dolbow, Sandra W. *Dictionary of Modern French Literature: From the Age of Reason Through Realism*. New York: Greenwood Press, 1986.

France, Peter, ed. *The New Oxford Companion to Literature in French*. New York: Clarendon Press, 1995.

Gaunt, Simon, and Sarah Key, eds. *The Cambridge Companion to Medieval French Literature*. New York: Cambridge University Press, 2008.

_____. *The Troubadours: An Introduction*. New York: Cambridge University Press, 1999.

Levi, Anthony. *Guide to French Literature*. 2 vols. Chicago: St. James Press, 1992-1994.

Moss, Ann. *Poetry and Fable: Studies in Mythological Narrative in Sixteenth-Century France*. New York: Cambridge University Press, 2009.

Palmer, R. Barton, ed. and trans. *Medieval Epic and Romance: An Anthology of English and French Narrative*. Glen Allen, Va.: College Publishing, 2007.

Shaw, Mary Lewis. *The Cambridge Introduction to French Poetry*. New York: Cambridge University Press, 2003.

Switten, Margaret Louise. *Music and Poetry in the Middle Ages: A Guide to Research on French and Occitan Song, 1100-1400*. New York: Garland, 1995.

Thomas, Jean-Jacques, and Steven Winspur. *Poeticized Language: The Foundations of Contemporary French Poetry*. University Park: Pennsylvania State University Press, 1999.

Willett, Laura, trans. *Poetry and Language in Sixteenth-Century France: Du Bellay, Ronsard, Sébillet*. Toronto: Centre for Reformation and Renaissance Studies, Victoria University, 2004.

France: Women writers

Sartori, Eva Martin, and Dorothy Wynne Zimmerman. *French Women Writers: A Bio-bibliographical Source Book*. New York: Greenwood Press, 1991.

Shapiro, Norman R., ed. and trans. *French Women Poets of Nine Centuries: The Distaff and the Pen*. Baltimore: Johns Hopkins University Press, 2008.

French Canadian (see also in the English-language section: Canada)

Blouin, Louise, Bernard Pozier, and D. G. Jones, eds. *Esprit de Corps: Québec Poetry of the Late Twentieth Century in Translation*. Winnipeg, Man.: Muses, 1997.

Platnick, Phyllis. *Canadian Poetry: Index to Criticisms, 1970-1979 = Poésie canadienne: Index de critiques, 1970-1979*. Ontario: Canadian Library Association, 1985.

GERMAN

Biographical sources

Hardin, James, ed. *German Baroque Writers, 1580-1660*. Dictionary of Literary Biography 164. Detroit: Gale Research, 1996.

_____. *German Baroque Writers, 1661-1730*. Dictionary of Literary Biography 168. Detroit: Gale Research, 1996.

Hardin, James, and Will Hasty, eds. *German Writers and Works of the Early Middle Ages, 800-1170*. Dictionary of Literary Biography 148. Detroit: Gale Research, 1995.

Hardin, James, and Siegfried Mews, eds. *Nineteenth-Century German Writers to 1840*. Dictionary of Literary Biography 133. Detroit: Gale Research, 1993.

_____. *Nineteenth-Century German Writers, 1841-1900*. Dictionary of Literary Biography 129. Detroit: Gale Research, 1993.

Hardin, James, and Max Reinhart, eds. *German Writers and Works of the High Middle Ages, 1170-1280*. Dictionary of Literary Biography 138. Detroit: Gale Research, 1994.

_____. *German Writers of the Renaissance and Reformation, 1280-1580*. Dictionary of Literary Biography 179. Detroit: Gale Group, 1997.

Hardin, James, and Christoph E. Schweitzer, eds. *German Writers from the Enlightment to Sturm und Drang, 1720-1764*. Dictionary of Literary Biography 97. Detroit: Gale Research, 1990.

_____. *German Writers in the Age of Goethe, Sturm und Drang to Classicism*. Dictionary of Literary Biography 94. Detroit: Gale Research, 1990.

_____. *German Writers in the Age of Goethe, 1789-1832*. Dictionary of Literary Biography 90. Detroit: Gale Research, 1989.

Dictionaries, histories, and handbooks

Appleby, Carol. *German Romantic Poetry: Goethe, Novalis, Heine, Hölderlin*. Maidstone, Kent, England: Crescent Moon, 2008.

Baird, Jay W. *Hitler's War Poets: Literature and Politics in the Third Reich*. New York: Cambridge University Press, 2008.

Browning, Robert M. *German Poetry from 1750 to 1900*. New York: Continuum, 1984.

_____. *German Poetry in the Age of the Enlightenment: From Brockes to Klopstock*. University Park: Pennsylvania State University Press, 1978.

Dobozy, Maria. *Re-membering the Present: The Medieval German Poet-Minstrel in Cultural Context*. Turnhout, Belgium: Brepois, 2005.

Faulhaber, Uwe K., and Penrith B. Goff. *German Liter-

ature: An Annotated Reference Guide. New York: Garland, 1979.

Hanak, Miroslav John. *A Guide to Romantic Poetry in Germany*. New York: Peter Lang, 1987.

Hofmann, Michael, ed. *Twentieth-Century German Poetry: An Anthology*. New York: Farrar, Straus and Giroux, 2008.

Hutchinson, Peter, ed. *Landmarks in German Poetry*. New York: Peter Lang, 2000.

Leeder, Karen J. *Breaking Boundaries: A New Generation of Poets in the GDR, 1979-1989*. New York: Oxford University Press, 1996.

Mathiew, Gustave, and Guy Stern, eds. *Introduction to German Poetry*. New York: Dover Publications, 1991.

Nader, Andrés José, ed. *Traumatic Verses: On Poetry in German from the Concentration Camps, 1933-1945*. Rochester, N.Y.: Camden House, 2007.

Owen, Ruth J. *The Poet's Role: Lyric Responses to German Unification by Poets from the GDR*. Amsterdam: Rodopi, 2001.

Women writers

Boland, Eavan, ed. and trans. *After Every War: Twentieth-Century Women Poets*. Princeton, N.J.: Princeton University Press, 2004.

Classen, Albrecht, ed. and trans. *Late-Medieval German Women's Poetry: Secular and Religious Songs*. Rochester, N.Y.: D. S. Brewer, 2004.

Harper, Anthony, and Margaret C. Ives. *Sappho in the Shadows: Essays on the Work of German Women Poets of the Age of Goethe, 1749-1832*. New York: Peter Lang, 2000.

GREEK (*see also* CLASSICAL GREEK AND LATIN)

Bien, Peter, et al., eds. *A Century of Greek Poetry, 1900-2000*. Bilingual ed. Westwood, N.J.: Cosmos, 2004.

Constantine, Peter, et al., eds. *The Greek Poets: Homer to the Present*. New York: W. W. Norton, 2009.

Demaras, Konstantinos. *A History of Modern Greek Literature*. Translated by Mary P. Gianos. Albany: State University of New York Press, 1972.

Saïd, Suzanne, and Monique Trédé. *A Short History of Greek Literature*. Translated by Trista Selous et al. New York: Routledge, 1999.

Valaoritis, Nanos, and Thanasis Maskaleris, eds. *An Anthology of Modern Greek Poetry*. Jersey City, N.J.: Talisman House, 2003.

Van Dyck, Karen. *Kassandra and the Censors: Greek Poetry Since 1967*. Ithaca, N.Y.: Cornell University Press, 1998.

HEBREW AND YIDDISH

Alonso Schokel, Luis. *A Manual of Hebrew Poetics*. Subsidia Biblica 11. Rome: Editrice Pontificio Istituto Biblico, 1988.

Alter, Robert. *The Art of Biblical Poetry*. New York: Basic Books, 1985.

Burnshaw, Stanley, T. Carmi, and Ezra Spicehandler, eds. *The Modern Hebrew Poem Itself: From the Beginnings to the Present, Sixty-nine Poems in a New Presentation*. With new afterword, "Hebrew Poetry from 1965 to 1988." Cambridge, Mass.: Harvard University Press, 1989.

Gevirtz, Stanley. *Patterns in the Early Poetry of Israel*. Chicago: University of Chicago Press, 1963.

Kugel, James L. *The Great Poems of the Bible: A Reader's Companion with New Translations*. New York: Free Press, 1999.

Liptzin, Solomon. *A History of Yiddish Literature*. Middle Village, N.Y.: Jonathan David, 1985.

Madison, Charles Allan. *Yiddish Literature: Its Scope and Major Writers*. New York: F. Ungar, 1968.

O'Connor, M. *Hebrew Verse Structure*. Winona Lake, Ind.: Eisenbrauns, 1980.

Pagis, Dan. *Hebrew Poetry of the Middle Ages and the Renaissance*. Berkeley: University of California Press, 1991.

Petersen, David L., and Kent Harold Richards. *Interpreting Hebrew Poetry*. Minneapolis: Fortress Press, 1992.

Watson, Wilfred G. E. *Classical Hebrew Poetry: A Guide to Its Techniques*. 2d ed. Sheffield, England: JSOT Press, 1986.

Wiener, Leo. *The History of Yiddish Literature in the Nineteenth Century*. 2d ed. New York: Hermon Press, 1972.

Zinberg, Israel. *Old Yiddish Literature from Its Origins to the Haskalah Period*. Translated and edited by Bernard Martin. Cincinnati: Hebrew Union College Press, 1975.

HUNGARIAN

Gömöri, George, and George Szirtes, eds. *The Colonnade of Teeth: Modern Hungarian Poetry.* Chester Springs, Pa.: Dufour Editions, 1996.

Kolumban, Nicholas, ed. and trans. *Turmoil in Hungary: An Anthology of Twentieth Century Hungarian Poetry.* St. Paul, Minn.: New Rivers Press, 1996.

Makkai, Adam, ed. *In Quest of the "Miracle Stag": The Poetry of Hungary, an Anthology of Hungarian Poetry in English Translation from the Thirteenth Century to the Present.* Foreword by Árpád Göncz. Urbana: University of Illinois Press, 1996.

Suleiman, Susan Rubin, and Éva Forgács, eds. *Contemporary Jewish Writing in Hungary: An Anthology.* Lincoln: University of Nebraska Press, 2003.

Szirtes, George, ed. *Leopard V: An Island of Sound— Poetry and Fiction Before and Beyond the Iron Curtain.* New York: Random House, 2004.

INDIAN AND SOUTH ASIAN LANGUAGES (*see also* ARABIC; PERSIAN; VIETNAMESE)

Dimock, Edward C., Jr., et al. *The Literatures of India: An Introduction.* Chicago: University of Chicago Press, 1974.

Gerow, Edwin. *Indian Poetics.* Wiesbaden: Harrassowitz, 1977.

Lienhard, Siegfried. *A History of Classical Poetry: Sanskrit, Pali, Prakrit.* Wiesbaden, Germany: Harrassowitz, 1984.

Mahmud, Shabana. *Urdu Language and Literature: A Bibliography of Sources in European Languages.* New York: Mansell, 1992.

Natarajan, Nalini, ed. *Handbook of Twentieth-Century Literatures of India.* Westport, Conn.: Greenwood Press, 1996.

Rajan, P. K., and Swapna Daniel, eds. *Indian Poetics and Modern Texts: Essays in Criticism.* New Delhi: S. Chand, 1998.

Sadiq, Mohammed. *A History of Urdu Literature.* Delhi: Oxford University Press, 1984.

Saran, Saraswiti. *The Development of Urdu Poetry.* New Delhi: Discovery Publishing House, 1990.

ITALIAN

Biographical sources

De Stasio, Giovanna Wedel, Glauco Cambon, and Antonio Illiano, eds. *Twentieth-Century Italian Poets: First Series.* Dictionary of Literary Biography 114. Detroit: Gale Research, 1992.

_____. *Twentieth-Century Italian Poets: Second Series.* Dictionary of Literary Biography 128. Detroit: Gale Research, 1993.

Dictionaries, histories, and handbooks

Bohn, Willard, ed. and trans. *Italian Futurist Poetry.* Toronto: University of Toronto Press, 2005.

Bondanella, Peter, and Julia Conaway Bondanella, eds. *Dictionary of Italian Literature.* Rev. ed. Westport, Conn.: Greenwood Press, 1996.

Cavallo, Jo Ann. *The Romance Epics of Boiardo, Ariosto, and Tasso: From Public Duty to Private Pleasure.* Toronto: University of Toronto Press, 2004.

Condini, Ned, ed. and trans. *An Anthology of Modern Italian Poetry in English Translation, with Italian Text.* New York: Modern Language Association of America, 2009.

Dombroski, Robert S. *Italy: Fiction, Theater, Poetry, Film Since 1950.* Middle Village, N.Y.: Council on National Literatures, 2000.

Holmes, Olivia. *Assembling the Lyric Self: Authorship from Troubador Song to Italian Poetry Book.* Minneapolis: University of Minnesota Press, 2000.

Italian Poets of the Twentieth Century. Florence, Italy: Casalini Libri, 1997.

Kleinhenz, Christopher. *The Early Italian Sonnet: The First Century, 1220-1321.* Collezione di Studi e Testi n.s. 2. Lecce, Italy: Milella, 1986.

Payne, Roberta L., ed. *Selection of Modern Italian Poetry in Translation.* Montreal: McGill-Queen's University Press, 2004.

Zatti, Sergio. *The Quest for Epic: From Ariosto to Tasso.* Translated by Sally Hill with Dennis Looney, edited by Looney. Toronto: University of Toronto Press, 2006.

Women writers

Blum, Cinzia Sartini, and Lara Trubowitz, eds. and trans. *Contemporary Italian Women Poets: A Bilingual Anthology.* New York: Italica Press, 2001.

Frabotta, Biancamaria, ed. *Italian Women Poets*. Translated by Corrado Federici. Toronto: Guernica Editions, 2002.

Stortoni, Laura A., and Mary P. Lillie, eds. *Women Poets of the Italian Renaissance: Courtly Ladies and Courtesans*. New York: Italica, 1997.

JAPANESE

Biographical sources

Carter, Steven D., ed. *Medieval Japanese Writers*. Dictionary of Literary Biography 203. Detroit: Gale Group, 1999.

Hisamatsu, Sen'ichi, ed. *Biographical Dictionary of Japanese Literature*. New York: Harper & Row, 1976.

Dictionaries, histories, and handbooks

Bownas, Geoffrey, and Anthony Thwaite, eds. and trans. *The Penguin Book of Japanese Verse*. Rev. ed. London: Penguin Books, 2009.

Brower, Robert, and Earl Miner. *Japanese Court Poetry*. 1961. Reprint. Stanford, Calif.: Stanford University Press, 1988.

Carter, Steven D., trans. *Traditional Japanese Poetry: An Anthology*. Stanford, Calif.: Stanford University Press, 1991.

_____. *Waiting for the Wind: Thirty-six Poets of Japan's Late Medieval Age*. Reprint. New York: Columbia University Press, 1994.

Miner, Earl Roy, Hiroko Odagiri, and Robert E. Morrell. *The Princeton Companion to Classical Japanese Literature*. Princeton, N.J.: Princeton University Press, 1985.

Morton, Leith. *Modernism in Practice: An Introduction to Postwar Japanese Poetry*. Honolulu: University of Hawaii Press, 2004.

Ooka, Makoto. *The Poetry and Poetics of Ancient Japan*. Translated by Thomas Fitzsimmons. Santa Fe, N.Mex.: Katydid Books, 1997.

Rimer, J. Thomas. *A Reader's Guide to Japanese Literature*. 2d ed. New York: Kodansha International, 1999.

Rimer, J. Thomas, and Van C. Gessel, eds. *The Columbia Anthology of Modern Japanese Literature*. 2 vols. New York: Columbia University Press, 2005-2007.

Rimer, J. Thomas, and Robert E. Morrell. *Guide to Japanese Poetry*. Asian Literature Bibliography Series. 2d ed. Boston, Mass.: G. K. Hall, 1984.

Sato, Hiroaki, ed. and trans. *Japanese Women Poets: An Anthology*. Armonk, N.Y.: M. E. Sharpe, 2007.

Shirane, Haruo. *Traditional Japanese Literature: An Anthology, Beginnings to 1600*. Rev. ed. Translated by Sonja Arntzen et al. New York: Columbia University Press, 2007.

_____, ed. *Early Modern Japanese Literature: An Anthology, 1600-1900*. Translated by James Brandon et al. New York: Columbia University Press, 2002.

KOREAN

Kim, Jaihiun. *Modern Korean Poetry*. Fremont, Calif.: Asian Humanities Press, 1994.

_____. *Traditional Korean Verse Since the 1900's*. Seoul, South Korea: Hanshin, 1991.

Korean Poetry: An Anthology with Critical Essays. Seoul, South Korea: Korean Culture & Arts Foundation, 1984.

Lee, Young-gul. *The Classical Poetry of Korea*. Seoul, South Korea: Korean Culture and Arts Foundation, 1981.

McCann, David R. *Form and Freedom in Korean Poetry*. New York: Brill, 1988.

Who's Who in Korean Literature. Korean Culture & Arts Foundation. Elizabeth, N.J.: Hollym, 1996.

PERSIAN (FARSI)

Husain, Iqbal. *The Early Persian Poets of India (A.H. 421-670)*. Patna, India: Patna University, 1937.

Jackson, A. V. Williams. *Early Persian Poetry, from the Beginnings Down to the Time of Firdausi*. New York: Macmillan, 1920.

Meisami, Julie Scott. *Medieval Persian Court Poetry*. Princeton, N.J.: Princeton University Press, 1987.

Thackston, W. M. *A Millennium of Classical Persian Poetry: A Guide to the Reading and Understanding of Persian Poetry from the Tenth to the Twentieth Century*. Bethesda, Md.: Iranbooks, 1994.

Thiesen, Finn. *A Manual of Classical Persian Prosody: With Chapters on Urdu, Karakhanidic, and Ottoman Prosody*. Wiesbaden, Germany: O. Harrassowitz, 1982.

SCANDINAVIAN LANGUAGES

General

Sjåvik, Jan. *Historical Dictionary of Scandinavian Literature and Theater*. Lanham, Md.: Scarecrow Press, 2006.

Sumari, Anni, and Nicolaj Stochholm, eds. *The Other Side of Landscape: An Anthology of Contemporary Nordic Poetry*. New York: Slope Editions, 2006.

Zuck, Virpi, ed. *Dictionary of Scandinavian Literature*. New York: Greenwood Press, 1990.

Danish

Borum, Poul. *Danish Literature: A Short Critical Survey*. Copenhagen: Det Danske Selskab, 1979.

Rossel, Sven H., ed. *A History of Danish Literature*. Lincoln: University of Nebraska Press, 1992.

Stecher-Hansen, Marianne, ed. *Twentieth-Century Danish Writers*. Dictionary of Literary Biography 214. Detroit: Gale Group, 1999.

Icelandic

Beck, Richard. *History of Icelandic Poets, 1800-1940*. Ithaca, N.Y.: Cornell University Press, 1950.

McTurk, Rory, ed. *A Companion to Old Norse-Icelandic Literature and Culture*. Malden, Mass.: Blackwell, 2005.

Neijman, Daisy, ed. *A History of Icelandic Literature*. Vol. 5 in *A History of Scandinavian Literatures*, edited by Sven H. Rossel. Lincoln: University of Nebraska Press, 2006.

Norwegian

McTurk, Rory, ed. *A Companion to Old Norse-Icelandic Literature and Culture*. Malden, Mass.: Blackwell, 2005.

Naess, Harald S. *A History of Norwegian Literature*. Lincoln: University of Nebraska Press, 1993.

Swedish

Scobbie, Irene. *Aspects of Modern Swedish Literature*. 2d ed. Norwich, England: Norvik Press, 1999.

Forsås-Scott, Helena. *Swedish Women's Writing, 1850-1995*. Atlantic Highlands, N.J.: Athlone, 1997.

Page, Edita, ed. *The Baltic Quintet: Poems from Estonia, Finland, Latvia, Lithuania, and Sweden*. Hamilton, Ont.: Wolsak and Wynn, 2008.

Warme, Lars G., ed. *A History of Swedish Literature*. Vol. 3 in *A History of Scandinavian Literatures*, edited by Sven H. Rossel. Lincoln: University of Nebraska Press, 1996.

SLAVIC LANGUAGES

General

Jakobson, Roman, C. H. van Schooneveld, and Dean S. Worth, eds. *Slavic Poetics: Essays in Honor of Kiril Taranovsky*. Slavistic Printings and Reprintings 267. The Hague: Mouton, 1973.

Mihailovich, Vasa D., comp. and ed. *Modern Slavic Literatures*. 2 vols. Vol. 1, *Russian Literature*; Vol. 2, *Bulgarian, Czechoslovak, Polish, Ukrainian, and Yugoslav Literatures*. New York: F. Ungar, 1972.

Tschizewskij, Dmitrij. *Comparative History of Slavic Literatures*. Translated by Richard Noel Porter and Martin P. Rice, edited by Serge A. Zenkovsky. Nashville, Tenn.: Vanderbilt University Press, 1971.

Albanian

Elsie, Robert. *Dictionary of Albanian Literature*. Westport, Conn.: Greenwood Press, 1986.

_____. *Studies in Modern Albanian Literature and Culture*. East European Monographs 455. New York: Distributed by Columbia University Press, 1996.

Pipa, Arshi. *Contemporary Albanian Literature*. East European Monographs 305. New York: Distributed by Columbia University Press, 1991.

Ressuli, Namik. *Albanian Literature*. Edited by Eduard Lico. Boston: Pan-Albanian Federation of America Vatra, 1987.

Bulgarian

Matejic, Mateja, et al. *A Biobibliographical Handbook of Bulgarian Authors*. Translated by Predrag Matejic, edited by Karen L. Black. Columbus, Ohio: Slavica, 1981.

Croatian

Miletich, John S. *Love Lyric and Other Poems of the Croatian Renaissance: A Bilingual Anthology*. Bloomington, Ind.: Slavica, 2009.

Czech

French, Alfred. *The Poets of Prague: Czech Poetry Between the Wars*. New York: Oxford University Press, 1969.

Kovtun, George J. *Czech and Slovak Literature in English: A Bibliography*. 2d ed. Washington, D.C.: Library of Congress, 1988.

Lodge, Kirsten, ed. and trans. *Solitude, Vanity, Night: An Anthology of Czech Decadent Poetry*. Prague: Charles University, 2007.

Novák, Arne. *Czech Literature*. Translated by Peter Kussi, edited by William E. Harkins. Joint Committee on Eastern Europe Publication Series 4. Ann Arbor: Michigan Slavic Publications, 1976.

Volkova, Bronislava, and Clarice Cloutier, eds. and trans. *Up the Devil's Back: A Bilingual Anthology of Twentieth-Century Czech Poetry*. Bloomington, Ind.: Slavica, 2008.

Macedonian

Osers, Ewald, ed. *Contemporary Macedonian Poetry*. Translated by Eward Osers. London: Kultura/Forest Books, 1991.

Polish

Barańczak, Stanisław, and Clare Cavanagh, eds. and trans. *Polish Poetry of the Last Two Decades of Communist Rule: Spoiling Cannibals' Fun*. Foreword by Helen Vendler. Evanston, Ill.: Northwestern University Press, 1991.

Carpenter, Bogdana, ed. *Monumenta Polonica: The First Four Centuries of Polish Poetry, a Bilingual Anthology*. Ann Arbor: Michigan Slavic Publications, 1989.

Czerniawski, Adam, ed. *The Mature Laurel: Essays on Modern Polish Poetry*. Chester Springs, Pa.: Dufour Editions, 1991.

Czerwinski, E. J., ed. *Dictionary of Polish Literature*. Westport, Conn.: Greenwood Press, 1994.

Grol, Regina, ed. *Ambers Aglow: An Anthology of Contemporary Polish Women's Poetry*. Austin, Tex.: Host, 1996.

Mengham, Rod, et al., trans. *Altered State: The New Polish Poetry*. Ottawa, Ont.: Arc, 2003.

Miłosz, Czesław, ed. *Postwar Polish Poetry: An Anthology*. 3d ed. Berkeley: University of California Press, 1983.

Russian

Blok, Aleksandr. *Us Four Plus Four: Eight Russian Poets Conversing*. New Orleans, La.: UNO Press, 2008.

Bunimovitch, Evgeny, and J. Kates, eds. *Contemporary Russian Poetry: An Anthology*. Translated by Kates. Champaign: Dalkey Archive Press, University of Illinois, 2008.

Cornwell, Neil, ed. *Reference Guide to Russian Literature*. Chicago: Fitzroy Dearborn, 1998.

Kates, J., ed. *In the Grip of Strange Thoughts: Russian Poetry in a New Era*. Brookline, Mass.: Zephyr Press, 2000.

Nabokov, Vladimir Vladimirovich, comp. and trans. *Verses and Versions: Three Centuries of Russian Poetry*. Edited by Brian Boyd and Stanislav Shvabrin. Orlando, Fla.: Harcourt, 2008.

Poggioli, Renato. *The Poets of Russia, 1890-1930*. Cambridge, Mass.: Harvard University Press, 1960.

Polukhina, Valentina, and Daniel Weissbort, eds. *An Anthology of Contemporary Russian Women Poets*. Iowa City: University of Iowa Press, 2005.

Rydel, Christine A., ed. *Russian Literature in the Age of Pushkin and Gogol: Poetry and Drama*. Dictionary of Literary Biography 205. Detroit: Gale Group, 1999.

Tschizewskij, Dmitrij. *History of Nineteenth-Century Russian Literature*. Translated by Richard Noel Porter. Edited by Serge A. Zenkovsky. Nashville, Tenn.: Greenwood Press, 1974.

Wachtel, Michael. *The Cambridge Introduction to Russian Poetry*. New York: Cambridge University Press, 2004.

_____. *The Development of Russian Verse: Meter and Its Meanings*. New York: Cambridge University Press, 1998.

Serbian

Holton, Milne, and Vasa D. Mihailovich, eds. and trans. *Serbian Poetry from the Beginnings to the Present*. New Haven, Conn.: Yale Center for International and Area Studies, 1988.

Simic, Charles, ed. and trans. *The Horse Has Six Legs: An Anthology of Serbian Poetry*. St. Paul, Minn.: Graywolf Press, 1992.

Slovak

Kovtun, George J. *Czech and Slovak Literature in English: A Bibliography*. 2d ed. Washington, D.C.: Library of Congress, 1988.

Kramoris, Ivan Joseph, ed. *An Anthology of Slovak Po-*

etry: A Selection of Lyric and Narrative Poems and Folk Ballads in Slovak and English*. Scranton, Pa.: Obrana Press, 1947.

Petro, Peter. *A History of Slovak Literature*. Montreal: McGill-Queen's University Press, 1995.

Smith, James Sutherland, Pavol Hudik, and Jan Bajanek, eds. *In Search of Beauty: An Anthology of Contemporary Slovak Poetry in English*. Translated by Bajanek. Mundelein, Ill.: Bolchazy-Carducci, 2004.

Slovene

Cooper, Henry R., ed. *A Bilingual Anthology of Slovene Literature*. Bloomington, Ind.: Slavica, 2003.

Jurkovič, Tina, ed. *Contemporary Slovenian Literature in Translation*. Translated by Lili Potpara. Ljubljana, Slovenia: Študentska založba, 2002.

Mokrin-Pauer, Vida. *Six Slovenian Poets*. Translated by Ana Jeinika, edited by Brane Mozetič. Todmorden, Lancashire, England: Arc, 2006.

Zawacki, Andrew, ed. *Afterwards: Slovenian Writing, 1945-1995*. Buffalo, N.Y.: White Pine Press, 1999.

Ukrainian

Cyzevkyj, Dmytro. *A History of Ukrainian Literature: From the Eleventh to the End of the Nineteenth Century*. Translated by Dolly Ferguson, Doreen Gorsline, and Ulana Petyk. Edited by George S. N. Luckyi. 2d ed. New York: Ukrainian Academic Press, 1997.

Piaseckyj, Oksana. *Bibliography of Ukrainian Literature in English and French: Translations and Critical Works, 1950-1986*. University of Ottawa Ukrainian Studies 10. Ottawa: University of Ottawa Press, 1989.

SPANISH AND PORTUGUESE

General

Bleznick, Donald William. *A Sourcebook for Hispanic Literature and Language: A Selected, Annotated Guide to Spanish, Spanish-American, and United States Hispanic Bibliography, Literature, Linguistics, Journals, and Other Source Materials*. 3d ed. Lanham, Md.: Scarecrow Press, 1995.

Newmark, Maxim. *Dictionary of Spanish Literature*. Westport, Conn.: Greenwood Press, 1972.

Sefami, Jacobo, comp. *Contemporary Spanish American Poets: A Bibliography of Primary and Secondary Sources*. Bibliographies and Indexes in World Literature 33. Westport, Conn.: Greenwood Press, 1992.

Woodbridge, Hensley Charles. *Guide to Reference Works for the Study of the Spanish Language and Literature and Spanish American Literature*. 2d ed. New York: Modern Language Association of America, 1997.

Africa

Ojaide, Tanure. *Poetic Imagination in Black Africa: Essays on African Poetry*. Durham, N.C.: Carolina Academic Press, 1996.

Parekh, Pushpa Naidu, and Siga Fatima Jagne. *Postcolonial African Writers: A Bio-bibliographical Critical Sourcebook*. Westport, Conn.: Greenwood Press, 1998.

Caribbean

Brown, Stewart, and Mark McWatt, eds. *The Oxford Book of Caribbean Verse*. New York: Oxford University Press, 2005.

Fenwick, M. J. *Writers of the Caribbean and Central America: A Bibliography*. Garland Reference Library of the Humanities 1244. New York: Garland, 1992.

James, Conrad, and John Perivolaris, eds. *The Cultures of the Hispanic Caribbean*. Gainesville: University Press of Florida, 2000.

Martinez, Julia A., ed. *Dictionary of Twentieth-Century Cuban Literature*. Westport, Conn.: Greenwood Press, 1990.

Mexico and Central America

Agosín, Marjorie, and Roberta Gordenstein, eds. *Miriam's Daughters: Jewish Latin American Women Poets*. Foreword by Agosín. Santa Fe, N.Mex.: Sherman Asher, 2001.

Cortes, Eladio. *Dictionary of Mexican Literature*. Westport, Conn.: Greenwood Press, 1992.

Dauster, Frank N. *The Double Strand: Five Contemporary Mexican Poets*. Louisville: University Press of Kentucky, 1987.

Foster, David William. *Mexican Literature: A Bibliography of Secondary Sources*. 2d ed. Metuchen, N.J.: Scarecrow Press, 1992.

_____, ed. *Mexican Literature: A History*. Austin: University of Texas Press, 1994.

González Peña, Carlos. *History of Mexican Literature*. Translated by Gusta Barfield Nance and Florence Johnson Dunstan. 3d rev. ed. Dallas: Southern Methodist University Press, 1968.

Nicholson, Irene. *A Guide to Mexican Poetry, Ancient and Modern*. Mexico: Editorial Minutiae Mexicana, 1968.

Vicuña, Cecilia, and Ernesto Livon-Grosman, eds. *The Oxford Book of Latin American Poetry: A Bilingual Anthology*. New York: Oxford University Press, 2009.

Washbourne, Kelly, ed. *An Anthology of Spanish American Modernismo: In English Translation, with Spanish Text*. Translated by Washbourne with Sergio Waisman. New York: Modern Language Association of America, 2007.

South America

Agosín, Marjorie, and Roberta Gordenstein, eds. *Miriam's Daughters: Jewish Latin American Women Poets*. Foreword by Agosín. Santa Fe, N.Mex.: Sherman Asher, 2001.

Brotherston, Gordon. *Latin American Poetry: Origins and Presence*. New York: Cambridge University Press, 1975.

Perrone, Charles A. *Seven Faces: Brazilian Poetry Since Modernism*. Durham, N.C.: Duke University Press, 1996.

Rowe, William. *Poets of Contemporary Latin America: History and the Inner Life*. New York: Oxford University Press, 2000.

Smith, Verity, ed. *Encyclopedia of Latin American Literature*. Chicago: Fitzroy Dearborn, 1997.

Stern, Irwin, ed. *Dictionary of Brazilian Literature*. Westport, Conn.: Greenwood Press, 1988.

Vicuña, Cecilia, and Ernesto Livon-Grosman, eds. *The Oxford Book of Latin American Poetry: A Bilingual Anthology*. New York: Oxford University Press, 2009.

Washbourne, Kelly, ed. *An Anthology of Spanish American Modernismo: In English Translation, with Spanish Text*. Translated by Washbourne with Sergio Waisman. New York: Modern Language Association of America, 2007.

Spain and Portugal

Bellver, Catherine G. *Absence and Presence: Spanish Women Poets of the Twenties and Thirties*. Lewisburg, Pa.: Bucknell University Press, 2001.

_____. *Dictionary of the Literature of the Iberian Peninsula*. Cranbury, N.J.: Associated University Presses, 2001.

Florit, Eugenio, ed. *Introduction to Spanish Poetry*. New York: Dover Publications, 1991.

Foster, David Williams, Daniel Altamiranda, and Carmen de Urioste, eds. *Spanish Literature: 1700 to the Present*. Spanish Literature 3. New York: Garland, 2000.

Fox, Gwyn. *Subtle Subversions: Reading Golden Age Sonnets by Iberian Women*. Washington, D.C.: Catholic University of America Press, 2008.

McNerny, Kathleen, and Cristina Enriques de Salamanca, eds. *Double Minorities of Spain: A Bio-bibliographic Guide to Women Writers of the Catalan, Galician, and Basque Countries*. New York: Modern Language Association of America, 1994.

Merwin, W. S., ed. and trans. *Spanish Ballads*. Port Townsend, Wash.: Copper Canyon Press, 2008.

Mudrovic, W. Michael. *Mirror, Mirror on the Page: Identity and Subjectivity in Spanish Women's Poetry, 1975-2000*. Bethlehem, Pa.: Lehigh University Press, 2009.

Penna, Michael L., ed. *Twentieth-Century Spanish Poets: First Series*. Dictionary of Literary Biography 108. Detroit: Gale Research, 1991.

Pérez, Janet. *Modern and Contemporary Spanish Women Poets*. New York: Prentice Hall International, 1996.

St. Martin, Hardie, ed. *Roots and Wings: Poetry from Spain, 1900-1975*. Buffalo, N.Y.: White Pine Press, 2004.

Walters, Gareth. *The Cambridge Introduction to Spanish Poetry*. New York: Cambridge University Press, 2003.

West-Settle, Cecile, and Sylvia Sherno, eds. *Contemporary Spanish Poetry: The Word and the World*. Madison, N.J.: Fairleigh Dickinson University Press, 2005.

Wilcox, John. *Women Poets of Spain, 1860-1990: To-*

ward a Gynocentric Vision. Urbana: University of Illinois Press, 1997.

Winfield, Jerry Phillips. *Twentieth-Century Spanish Poets: Second Series*. Dictionary of Literary Biography 134. Detroit: Gale Research, 1994.

TIBETAN

Cabezon, Jose I., and Roger R. Jackson. *Tibetan Literature: Studies in Genre*. Ithaca, N.Y.: Snow Lion, 1995.

Hartley, Lauran R., and Patricia Schiaffini-Vedani, eds. *Modern Tibetan Literature and Social Change*. Durham, N.C.: Duke University Press, 2008.

Jinpa, Thupten, and Jas Elsner. *Songs of Spiritual Experience: Tibetan Buddhist Poems of Insight and Awakening*. Boston: Shambhala, 2000.

TURKISH

Andrews, Walter G., Jr. *An Introduction to Ottoman Poetry*. Minneapolis: Bibliotheca Islamica, 1976.

Gibb, E. J. W. *A History of Ottoman Poetry*. 6 vols. Cambridge, England: Published and distributed by the Trustees of the "E. J. W. Gibb Memorial," 1963-1984.

VIETNAMESE

Thông, Huynh Sanh, ed. and trans. *An Anthology of Vietnamese Poems: From the Eleventh Through the Twentieth Centuries*. New Haven, Conn.: Yale University Press, 1996.

"Vietnamese Poetry and History." Special issue of *Crossroads: An Interdisciplinary Journal of Southeast Asian Studies* 7, no. 2 (1992).

Maura Ives; updated by Tracy Irons-Georges

GUIDE TO ONLINE RESOURCES

The following sites were visited by the editors of Salem Press in 2010. Because URLs frequently change, the accuracy of these addresses cannot be guaranteed; however, long-standing sites, such as those of colleges and universities, national organizations, and government agencies, generally maintain links when their sites are moved.

Academy of American Poets

http://www.poets.org

The mission of the Academy of American Poets is to "support American poets at all stages of their careers and to foster the appreciation of contemporary poetry." The academy's comprehensive Web site features information on poetic schools and movements; a Poetic Forms Database; an Online Poetry Classroom, with educator and teaching resources; an index of poets and poems; essays and interviews; general Web resources; links for further study; and more.

African Literature and Writers on the Internet

http://www-sul.stanford.edu/depts/ssrg/africa

This page is included in the Africa South of the Sahara site created by Karen Fung of Stanford University. It provides an alphabetical list of links to numerous resources about African poets and writers, online journals and essays, association Web sites, and other materials.

Australian Literature

http://www.middlemiss.org/lit/lit.html

Perry Middlemiss, a Melbourne-based blogger, created this useful resource about Australian writers, including poets, and their works. It features an alphabetical list of authors that links to biographies and lists of their works. The site also provides, for some of the listed works, links to synopses and excerpts.

The Cambridge History of English and American Literature

http://www.bartleby.com/cambridge

This site provides an exhaustive examination of the development of all forms of literature in Great Britain and the United States. The multivolume set on which this site is based was published in 1907-1921 but remains a relevant, classic work. It offers "a wide selection of writing on orators, humorists, poets, newspaper columnists, religious leaders, economists, Native Americans, song writers, and even non-English writing, such as Yiddish and Creole."

The Canadian Literature Archive

http://www.umanitoba.ca/canlit

Created and maintained by the English Department at the University of Manitoba, this site is a comprehensive collection of materials for and about Canadian writers. It includes an alphabetical listing of authors with links to additional Web-based information. Users also can retrieve electronic texts, announcements of literary events, and videocasts of author interviews and readings.

A Celebration of Women Writers

http://digital.library.upenn.edu/women

This site is an extensive compendium on the contributions of women writers throughout history. The "Local Editions by Authors" and "Local Editions by Category" pages include access to electronic texts of the works of numerous writers. Users can also access biographical and bibliographical information by browsing lists arranged by writers' names, countries of origin, ethnicities, and the centuries in which they lived.

Contemporary British Writers

http://www.contemporarywriters.com/authors

Created by the British Council, this site offers profiles of living writers of the United Kingdom, the Republic of Ireland, and the Commonwealth. Information includes biographies, bibliographies, critical reviews, and news about literary prizes. Photographs are also featured. Users can search the site by author, genre, nationality, gender, publisher, book title, date of publication, and prize name and date.

Internet Public Library: Native American Authors

http://www.ipl.org/div/natam

The Internet Public Library, a Web-based collection of resource materials, includes this informational index to writers of Native American heritage. An alphabetical list of authors features links to biographies, lists of works, electronic texts, tribal Web sites, and other online resources. The majority of the writers covered are contemporary Indian authors, but some historical authors also are featured. Users also can retrieve information by browsing lists of titles and tribes. In addition, the site contains a bibliography of print and online materials about Native American literature.

LiteraryHistory.com

http://www.literaryhistory.com

This site is an excellent source of academic, scholarly, and critical literature about eighteenth, nineteenth, and twentieth century American and English writers. It provides numerous pages about specific eras and genres, including individual pages for eighteenth, nineteenth, and twentieth century literature and for African American and postcolonial literatures. These pages contain alphabetical lists of authors that link to articles, reviews, overviews, excerpts of works, teaching guides, podcasts, and other materials.

Literary Resources on the Net

http://andromeda.rutgers.edu/~jlynch/Lit

Jack Lynch of Rutgers University maintains this extensive collection of links to Web sites that are useful to researchers, including numerous sites about American and English literature. This collection is a good place to begin online research about poetry, as it links to other sites with broad ranges of literary topics. The site is organized chronologically, with separate pages about the Middle Ages, the Renaissance, the eighteenth century, the Romantic and Victorian eras, and twentieth century British and Irish literature. It also has separate pages providing links to Web sites about American literature and to women's literature and feminism.

LitWeb

http://litweb.net

LitWeb provides biographies of hundreds of world authors throughout history that can be accessed through an alphabetical listing. The pages about each writer contain a list of his or her works, suggestions for further reading, and illustrations. The site also offers information about past and present winners of major literary prizes.

The Modern Word: Authors of the Libyrinth

http://www.themodernword.com/authors.html

The Modern Word site, although somewhat haphazard in its organization, provides a great deal of critical information about writers. The "Authors of the Libyrinth" page is very useful, linking author names to essays about them and other resources. The section of the page headed "The Scriptorium" presents "an index of pages featuring writers who have pushed the edges of their medium, combining literary talent with a sense of experimentation to produce some remarkable works of modern literature."

Outline of American Literature

http://www.america.gov/publications/books/outline -of-american-literature.html

This page of the America.gov site provides access to an electronic version of the ten-chapter volume *Outline of American Literature*, a historical overview of poetry and prose from colonial times to the present published by the Bureau of International Information Programs of the U.S. Department of State.

Poetry Foundation

http://www.poetryfoundation.org

The Poetry Foundation, publisher of *Poetry* magazine, is an independent literary organization. Its Web site offers links to essays; news; events; online poetry resources, such as blogs, organizations, publications, and references and research; a glossary of literary terms; and a Learning Lab that includes poem guides and essays on poetics.

Poetry in Translation

http://poetryintranslation.com

This independent resource provides modern translations of classic texts by famous poets and also provides original poetry and critical works. Visitors can choose from several languages, including English, Spanish, Chinese, Russian, Italian, and Greek. Original text is available as well. Also includes links to further literary resources.

Poetry International Web

http://international.poetryinternationalweb.org

Poetry International Web features information on poets from countries such as Indonesia, Zimbabwe, Iceland, India, Slovenia, Morocco, Albania, Afghanistan, Russia, and Brazil. The site offers news, essays, interviews and discussion, and hundreds of poems, both in their original languages and in English translation.

Poet's Corner

http://theotherpages.org/poems

The Poet's Corner, one of the oldest text resources on the Web, provides access to about seven thousand works of poetry by several hundred different poets from around the world. Indexes are arranged and searchable by title, name of poet, or subject. The site also offers its own resources, including "Faces of the Poets"—a gallery of portraits—and "Lives of the Poets"—a growing collection of biographies.

Representative Poetry Online

http://rpo.library.utoronto.ca

This award-winning resource site, maintained by Ian Lancashire of the Department of English at the University of Toronto in Canada, has several thousand English-language poems by hundreds of poets. The collection is searchable by poet's name, title of work, first line of a poem, and keyword. The site also includes a time line, a glossary, essays, an extensive bibliography, and countless links organized by country and by subject.

The Victorian Web

http://www.victorianweb.org

One of the finest Web sites about the nineteenth century, the Victorian Web provides a wealth of information about Great Britain during the reign of Queen Victoria, including information about the era's literature. The section "Genre & Technique" includes poetry.

Voice of the Shuttle

http://vos.ucsb.edu

One of the most complete and authoritative places for online information about literature, Voice of the Shuttle is maintained by professors and students in the English Department at the University of California, Santa Barbara. The site provides countless links to electronic books, academic journals, literary association Web sites, sites created by university professors, and many other resources.

Voices from the Gaps

http://voices.cla.umn.edu/

Voices from the Gaps is a site of the English Department at the University of Minnesota, dedicated to providing resources on the study of women artists of color, including writers. The site features a comprehensive index searchable by name, and it provides biographical information on each writer or artist and other resources for further study.

Western European Studies

http://wess.lib.byu.edu

The Western European Studies Section of the Association of College and Research Libraries maintains this collection of resources useful to students of Western European history and culture. It also is a good place to find information about non-English-language literature. The site includes separate pages about the literatures and languages of the Netherlands, France, Germany, Iberia, Italy, and Scandinavia, in which users can find links to electronic texts, association Web sites, journals, and other materials, the majority of which are written in the languages of the respective countries.

ELECTRONIC DATABASES

Electronic databases usually do not have their own URLs. Instead, public, college, and university libraries subscribe to these databases, provide links to them on their Web sites, and make them available to library card holders or other specified patrons. Readers can visit library Web sites or ask reference librarians to check on availability.

Bloom's Literary Reference Online

Facts On File publishes this database of thousands of articles by renowned scholar Harold Bloom and other literary critics, examining the lives and works of great writers worldwide. The database also includes information on more than forty-two thousand literary characters, literary topics, themes, movements, and genres, plus video segments about literature. Users can retrieve information by browsing writers' names, titles of works, time periods, genres, or writers' nationalities.

Canadian Literary Centre

Produced by EBSCO, the Canadian Literary Centre database contains full-text content from ECW Press, a Toronto-based publisher, including the titles in the publisher's Canadian fiction studies, Canadian biography, and Canadian writers and their works series; *ECW's Biographical Guide to Canadian Novelists*; and *George Woodcock's Introduction to Canadian Fiction*. Author biographies, essays and literary criticism, and book reviews are among the database's offerings.

Literary Reference Center

EBSCO's Literary Reference Center (LRC) is a comprehensive full-text database designed primarily to help high school and undergraduate students in English and the humanities with homework and research assignments about literature. The database contains massive amounts of information from reference works,

books, literary journals, and other materials, including more than 31,000 plot summaries, synopses, and overviews of literary works; almost 100,000 essays and articles of literary criticism; about 140,000 author biographies; more than 605,000 book reviews; and more than 5,200 author interviews. It contains the entire contents of Salem Press's MagillOnLiterature Plus. Users can retrieve information by browsing a list of authors' names or titles of literary works; they can also use an advanced search engine to access information by numerous categories, including author name, gender, cultural identity, national identity, and the years in which he or she lived, or by literary title, character, locale, genre, and publication date. The Literary Reference Center also features a literary-historical time line, an encyclopedia of literature, and a glossary of literary terms.

Literary Resource Center

Published by Gale, this comprehensive literary database contains information on the lives and works of more than 130,000 authors in all genres, in all time periods, and throughout the world. In addition, the database offers more than 70,000 full-text critical essays and reviews from some of Gale's reference publications, including *Contemporary Literary Criticism*, *Literature Criticism from 1400-1800*, *Nineteenth-Century Literature Criticism*, and *Twentieth-Century Literary Criticism*; more than 7,000 overviews of frequently studied works; more than 650,000 full-text articles, critical essays, and reviews from about three hundred scholarly journals and literary magazines; more than 4,500 interviews; and about five hundred links to selected Web sites. Users can retrieve information by browsing author name, ethnicity, nationality, and years of birth and death; titles of literary works; genres; selected literary movements or time periods; keywords; and themes of literary works. Literary Resource Center also features a literary-historical time line and an encyclopedia of literature.

MagillOnLiterature Plus

MagillOnLiterature Plus is a comprehensive, integrated literature database produced by Salem Press and available on the EBSCOhost platform. The database contains the full text of essays in Salem's many literature-related reference works, including *Masterplots*, *Cyclopedia of World Authors*, *Cyclopedia of Literary Characters*, *Cyclopedia of Literary Places*, *Critical Survey of Poetry*, *Critical Survey of Long Fiction*, *Critical Survey of Short Fiction*, *World Philosophers and Their Works*, *Magill's Literary Annual*, and *Magill's Book Reviews*. Among its contents are articles on more than 35,000 literary works and more than 8,500 poets, writers, dramatists, essayists, and philosophers; more than 1,000 images; and a glossary of more than 1,300 literary terms. The biographical essays include lists of authors' works and secondary bibliographies, and hundreds of overview essays examine and discuss literary genres, time periods, and national literatures.

Rebecca Kuzins; updated by Desiree Dreeuws

TIME LINE

c. 2000 B.C.E.	The main portion of *Gilgamesh* (*Gilgamesh Epic*, 1917) is written on cuneiform clay tablets. This epic, which is the oldest surviving poem, recounts the exploits of Gilgamesh, the legendary king of Uruk and the first literary hero.
c. 750 B.C.E.	Homer composes the *Iliad* (English translation, 1611), a Greek epic poem that recounts the fall of Troy. This work and Homer's subsequent poem the *Odyssey* (c. 725 B.C.E.; English translation, 1614) will establish the epic poem as a genre in Western literature and will influence European literature and culture for centuries.
c. 700 B.C.E.	The Greek poet Hesiod writes *Erga kai Emerai* (*Works and Days*, 1618), in which the poet instructs his wastrel brother Perses about the virtues of hard work and provides advice about farming techniques.
c. 630 B.C.E.	Sappho, one of the most admired poets of the ancient world, is born on the Greek island of Lesbos.
c. 500 B.C.E.	Vālmīki, whom Indian tradition credits with having invented poetry, composes *Rāmāyaṇa* (*The Ramayana*, 1870-1874). Written in Sanskrit, this poem is the national epic of India and will continue to influence poetry, art, drama, and religion in South and Southeast Asia into the twenty-first century.
c. 498-446 B.C.E.	Pindar produces *Epinikia* (*Odes*, 1656), a collection of odes celebrating the victories of athletes in the Panhellenic festival games.
c. 400 B.C.E.-400 C.E.	The *Mahābhārata* (*The Mahabharata*, 1834), the longest surviving poem in any language, is written in Sanskrit. This epic records political, ethical, mythological, and philosophical thought in ancient India. The *Bhagavadgītā* (*The Bhagavad Gita*, 1785), a Hindu devotional text composed between c. 200 B.C.E. and 200 C.E., is preserved as an interlude in the *Mahābhārata*.
c. 334-323 B.C.E.	Aristotle writes *De poetica* (*Poetics*, 1705), an early work of literary criticism in which he analyzes the essence of poetry and distinguishes its various forms, including the epic, comic, and tragic.
October 15, 70 B.C.E.	Vergil, whom many consider the greatest poet of ancient Rome, is born in Andes, Cisalpine Gaul, near Mantua (now in Italy).
c. 17 B.C.E.	Horace, the premier Roman lyric poet, analyzes the poetic genre in *Ars poetica* (*The Art of Poetry*, 1567), which is included in *Epistles* (c. 20-15 B.C.E.; English translation, 1567). Among his literary theories, Horace praises consistency as the highest virtue of poetry and advises poets to carefully choose each word and incident, as well as the meter of their compositions.
c. 8 C.E.	The Roman poet Ovid composes *Metamorphoses* (English translation, 1567), an epic recounting more than two hundred stories from Greek and Roman mythology, legend, and history.
c. 103 C.E.	Martial, the Roman writer who perfected the genre of epigrammatic poetry, dies in Hispania (now in Spain).
210	Ruan Ji is born in Weishi, China. He will compose eighty-two verses designated as *yonghuai shi* (poems singing of my emotions), which will be studied and imitated by subsequent Chinese poets.
c. 670	Cædmon, the first English poet, composes "Hymn," which combines the meters of Nordic heroic poetry with the subject matter of the Scriptures.

689	Meng Haoran, the first great poet of the Tang Dynasty, is born in Xianyang, China.
701	Li Bo, one of the two greatest poets in Chinese literature, is born in what is now Chinese Turkistan.
712	Du Fu, one of the two greatest poets in Chinese literature, is born in Gongxian, China.
mid-eighth century	*Manyōshū* (*The Collections of Ten Thousand Leaves*, also as *The Ten Thousand Leaves*, pb. 1981, and as *The Manyoshu*, 1940), an anthology of more than 4,500 Japanese poems, is compiled.
c. 1000	*Beowulf*, an Old English epic heroic poem, is composed by an anonymous writer.
c. 1010	The Persian poet Firdusi creates the Iranian national epic, *Shahnamah* (*Sah-name*, 1906), or "the book of kings." Later translations of this epic will influence the work of Western poets.
ninth-twelfth centuries	Anonymous writers compose the Old Norse poems that are collected in the *Poetic Edda*. These poems are primarily preserved in the Icelandic *Codex Regius*, a manuscript written in the thirteenth century. The *Poetic Edda* is the most important source of information on Norse mythology and Germanic heroic legends.
twelfth century	Omar Khayyám, a Persian poet, composes *Rubā'īyāt* (*True Translation of Hakim Omar Khayyam's "Robaiyat,"* 1994; commonly known as *Rubáiyát of Omar Khayyám*). The work is a series of *ruba'i*, or individual quatrains.
twelfth century	*Chanson de Roland* (*The Song of Roland*, 1880), the oldest surviving French medieval epic poem, is written. This epic, recounting the defeat of Count Roland, Charlemagne's nephew, by a Saracen army in 877, is one of about one hundred surviving French *chansons de geste* (songs of heroic action).
c. 1200	*Nibelungenlied* (English translation, 1848) is written in Middle High German by an unknown Austrian monk. This epic poem explores Germanic conceptions of the true values of knighthood.
early thirteenth century	The oldest surviving Spanish epic poem, *Cantar de mío Cid* (*Chronicle of the Cid*, 1846), is composed. This work describes the exploits of the Spanish hero El Cid.
c. 1205	Layamon composes *Brut*, the first major literary work written in Middle English and the first English-language version of the stories of King Arthur and King Lear.
July 20, 1304	Petrarch is born in Arezzo, Tuscany (now in Italy). His work will include vernacular poems in which he celebrates his everlasting love for a woman named Laura.
1320	Hafiz, the master of the *ghazal*, or lyric poem, is born in Shīrāz, Persia (now in Iran).
c. 1320	Dante creates his masterpiece, the three-volume *La divina commedia* (*The Divine Comedy*, 1802). This work describes the poet's journey through the three realms of the Christian otherworld—Hell, Purgatory, and Paradise.
1387-1400	Geoffrey Chaucer writes *The Canterbury Tales*, a collection of comic stories told by a group of pilgrims.
c. 1400	The Pearl-Poet composes *Sir Gawain and the Green Knight*, one of many medieval poems concerning King Arthur and his knights.
1570	Scottish writer Robert Henryson publishes *The Morall Fabillis of Esope, the Phyrgian* (also known as *Fables*, twelve shorter poems of uncertain attribution). These didactic poems retell thirteen of Aesop's animal fables.
1572	*Os Lusíadas* (*The Lusiads*, 1655), Luís de Camões's epic poem about Portugal's expansion, is published.

1572	John Donne is born in London. He will become the best-known of the Metaphysical poets, a group of seventeenth century English writers that includes George Herbert, Andrew Marvell, Thomas Traherne, Henry Vaughan, Richard Crashaw, Abraham Cowley, Sir William Davenant, Sir John Suckling, and Thomas Carew.
1590	Edmund Spencer creates *The Faerie Queene*, his allegorical tribute to Queen Elizabeth I.
1595	*Defence of Poesie* by Sir Philip Sidney is published. In this work of Renaissance literary criticism, Sidney argues for the superiority of poetry over any other aesthetic pursuit.
1609	William Shakespeare's *Sonnets* are published. In addition to being one of the world's greatest dramatists, Shakespeare wrote some of the greatest love poems in the English language.
August 6, 1637	Ben Jonson, the founder of English neoclassical poetry, dies in London. Jonson's verse imitates Roman classical forms and subject matters, foreshadowing a style that would be more commonly employed by eighteenth century British poets.
1644	Matsuo Bashō, considered by many to be the greatest of the haiku poets, is born in Ueno, Igo Province, Japan.
November, 1648	Sor Juana Inés de la Cruz, the major writer of colonial Spanish America, is born in New Spain (now Mexico). She will write more than four hundred poems, as well as plays and prose works.
1650	Anne Bradstreet's *The Tenth Muse Lately Sprung Up in America: Or, Several Poems Compiled with Great Variety of Wit and Learning, Full of Delight* is published. Bradstreet is one of America's foremost colonial poets and the first female poet to be published in America.
1660-1700	During "The Age of Dryden," the prolific John Dryden writes and translates numerous works of literature. His two hundred poems are composed in a variety of genres, including odes, verse epistles, satires, and religious poetry.
1667	The first books of John Milton's *Paradise Lost* are published, with the remaining volumes released in 1674. This work is arguably the greatest epic poem in English.
1712	Alexander Pope publishes his mock-epic poem *The Rape of the Lock*.
June 24, 1729	Edward Taylor, an English-born minister and one of the premier American colonial poets, dies in Westfield, Massachusetts.
1751	Thomas Gray's poem "Elegy Written in a Country Churchyard," one of the most popular works of British literature, is published.
1770	Johann Wolfgang von Goethe publishes *Neue Lieder* (*New Poems*, 1853), his first volume of poetry. In his lyric poetry, Goethe mastered the use of diverse meters, techniques, and styles as had no other German writer before him.
1773	Phillis Wheatley's *Poems on Various Subjects, Religious and Moral* is published. Wheatley is America's first black poet and the second female poet to be published in America, after Anne Bradstreet.
1786	The Kilmarnock edition of Robert Burns's *Poems, Chiefly in the Scottish Dialect*, is published. The poetic works of Burns, who is regarded as the national poet of Scotland, include more than three hundred songs about eighteenth century life in that country.

January 22, 1788	Lord Byron is born in London. His creation of the defiant and brooding "Byronic hero" would exert a profound influence on nineteenth century Romantic sensibility.
1794	William Blake publishes *Songs of Innocence and of Experience*. Blake was one of the earliest English Romantic poets.
1798	William Wordsworth and Samuel Taylor Coleridge anonymously publish *Lyrical Ballads*, a collection of their Romantic poetry that includes the first appearance of Coleridge's poem *The Rime of the Ancient Mariner*. In his preface to the collection, Wordsworth argues that primitivism—the belief that there is an intrinsic "state of nature" from which humankind has fallen into wickedness—is the basis of Romanticism.
1800	German writer Friedrich Schiller composes his best-known poem, "Das Lied von der Glocke" ("The Song of the Bell"), a philosophical ballad in which he projects humankind's mortal existence against the background of the bell's creation.
December 17, 1807	John Greenleaf Whittier is born in Haverhill, Massachusetts. He and several other Americans—Henry Wadsworth Longfellow, James Russell Lowell, Oliver Wendell Holmes, and William Cullen Bryant—would later be known as the Fireside Poets because nineteenth century Americans often gathered around the fireside to hear a family member read these writers' works.
1817	John Keats publishes his first volume of poetry. Keats would die before his twenty-sixth birthday, but in that brief time he would produce some of the greatest Romantic poetry in the English language.
1820	*Ruslan i Lyudmila* (*Ruslan and Liudmila*, 1936), the first long poem by Alexander Pushkin, is published. Pushkin is the first poet to write in a purely Russian style.
1820	*Méditations poétiques* (*Poetical Meditations*, 1839), by Alphonse de Lamartine, hailed as the first masterpiece of French Romantic poetry, is published.
July 8, 1822	Percy Bysshe Shelley drowns in a boating accident in Italy, less than one month before his thirtieth birthday. One of the premier English Romantic poets, Shelley used a wide variety of stanzaic patterns and poetic forms in his work.
1827	*Buch der Lieder* (*Book of Songs*, 1856), by the German poet Heinrich Heine, is published. The most controversial poet of his time, Heine is renowned for his love poetry.
December 10, 1830	Emily Dickinson is born in Amherst, Massachusetts. Although she gained little recognition for her work during her lifetime, Dickinson would later be considered one of America's greatest lyric poets.
1831	French Romantic poet Victor Hugo attains lyrical maturity with the publication of *Les Feuilles d'automne*, in which he treats themes of childhood, nature, and love.
1842	Robert Browning publishes *Dramatic Lyrics*, which includes "My Last Duchess," one of his best dramatic monologues.
October 7, 1849	Edgar Allan Poe dies in Baltimore, Maryland, at the age of forty. Poe's poetry would influence many British poets and writers. He also wrote literary criticism in which he maintained that critics should protect readers from bad poetry and encourage poets to live up to their potential.

1850	The first of the four versions of "The Blessed Damozel" is published in a British magazine. The ballad's author, Dante Gabriel Rossetti, is also a painter and a member of the Pre-Raphaelite Brotherhood of artists. Rossetti's poetry, with its use of medieval settings and painterly detail, exemplifies the Pre-Raphaelite style of art and literature.
1850	Elizabeth Barrett Browning publishes *Poems: New Edition*, which includes *Sonnets from the Portuguese*.
November 5, 1850	Prince Albert selects Alfred, Lord Tennyson, to replace William Wordsworth as England's poet laureate. The appointment is announced after *In Memoriam* (1850), Tennyson's elegy upon the death of his friend Arthur Henry Hallem, was published and became an instant best seller. Tennyson will hold the position of poet laureate for the next forty-two years.
1855	Henry Wadsworth Longfellow, the most popular English-language poet of the nineteenth century, publishes *The Song of Hiawatha*.
1855	The first edition of Walt Whitman's *Leaves of Grass* is published. Whitman radically alters conventional poetry by using free verse and ordinary diction.
1857	The first edition of French poet Charles Baudelaire's *Les Fleurs du mal* (*Flowers of Evil*, 1931) is published. The poems in this collection are characterized by their bold metaphors and bizarre juxtapositions of beauty and ugliness.
1867	Matthew Arnold publishes "Dover Beach," which makes reference to the Victorian debate between religion and science.
1873	*Une Saison en enfer* (*A Season in Hell*, 1932), by Arthur Rimbaud, is published. Rimbaud will become one of the most influential of the French Symbolist poets.
1876	*L'Après-midi d'un faune* (*The Afternoon of a Faun*, 1936), by French Symbolist poet Stéphane Mallarmé, is published. Mallarmé's work influenced younger poets, who hailed him as an exemplar of Symbolism.
1877	Jacint Verdaguer publishes *La Atlántida*, written in the Catalan language. Verdaguer's works exemplify the religious, patriotic, and epic characteristics of the nineteenth century Renaixença, a period of rebirth for Catalan literature and art.
1888	*Azul*, a collection of works by Nicaraguan poet Rubén Darío, is published, receiving praise from both South American and European critics. Darío is one of the founders of the *Modernismo* literary movement, and his poetry features innovative themes, language, meters, and rhymes.
1889	Anna Akhmatov is born near Odessa, Ukraine. She will become one of the leading poets of the Russian Acmeist movement.
1898	Thomas Hardy publishes the first of his eight volumes of poetry, *Wessex Poems, and Other Verses*.
1907	Rudyard Kipling receives the Nobel Prize in Literature.
1908	*A Lume Spento*, the first volume of poetry by Ezra Pound, is published. In the first two decades of the twentieth century, Pound and T. S. Eliot will create the idiom that will characterize modern American and English poetry.

1912	Harriet Monroe founds *Poetry* magazine, which will continue to be issued into the twenty-first century. The magazine will publish works by many of the world's leading poets, including Ezra Pound, T. S. Eliot, Marianne Moore, Carl Sandburg, and Rabindranath Tagore, and will discover such poets as Gwendolyn Brooks, John Ashbery, and James Merrill.
1913	*Alcools: Poèmes, 1898-1913* (*Alcools: Poems, 1898-1913*, 1964), by Guilluame Apollinaire, is published. Apollinaire was one of the first French poets to describe the discontinuity and disorientation of modern society.
1913	Indian poet Rabindranath Tagore receives the Nobel Prize in Literature.
1913-1930	Robert Bridges is poet laureate of the United Kingdom.
April 23, 1915	Rupert Brooke dies while performing his military service during World War I. During this year, Brooke's collection *1914, and Other Poems*, which features five sonnets glamorizing the fate of martyred soldiers, is published.
1918	Sara Teasdale receives the Pulitzer Prize in Poetry for *Love Songs*.
1919-1935	The Harlem Renaissance produces some of the finest African-American literature, music, and art of the twentieth century. Poets associated with this movement include Langston Hughes, Countée Cullen, and Claude McKay.
1922	T. S. Eliot's *The Waste Land* is published. In this influential work, Eliot describes human alienation in the years following World War I.
1923	Irish poet William Butler Yeats is awarded the Nobel Prize in Literature.
1924	*Haru to shura* (*Spring and Asura*, 1973), by Japanese poet Kenji Miyazawa, is released. This collection is the only volume of Miyazawa's poetry published during his lifetime.
1930	*The Bridge*, by Hart Crane, is published. In this lengthy poem, Crane seeks to provide a synthesis of the American identity.
1930	Conrad Aiken receives the Pulitzer Prize in Poetry for *Selected Poems*.
1936	The publication of *Twenty-five Poems* establishes Welsh writer Dylan Thomas as a significant poet.
1936	Patrick Kavanagh publishes his collection *Ploughman, and Other Poems*. Kavanagh will become a major figure in the second generation of the Irish literary revival.
August 19, 1936	Federico García Lorca is executed by members of the Spanish fascist party during the Spanish Civil War. His poetry is characterized by startling images and metaphors drawn from traditional Spanish culture.
October 17, 1938	Les A. Murray is born in Nabiac, New South Wales, Australia. His work will earn him the distinction of being Australia's major poet and also one of the finest poets of his generation writing in English.
1941	Robert Frost receives the Frost Medal from the Poetry Society of America for distinguished lifetime service to American poetry.
1945	Gabriela Mistral is the first Latin American writer to receive the Nobel Prize in Literature.
1945-1946	Louise Bogan serves as America's poet laureate.
1947-1948	Robert Lowell serves as America's poet laureate.
1950	E. E. Cummings receives the Academy of American Poets Fellowship.
1950	Wallace Stevens receives the Bollingen Prize in Poetry.

1951	Gottfried Benn receives the Georg Büchner Prize, the most important literary prize in Germany.
1952	Frank O'Hara's first collection, *A City Winter, and Other Poems*, is published. O'Hara, Kenneth Koch, James Schuyler, and John Ashbery were the central members of the New York School of poets, an influential group of writers during the late 1950's.
1953	Archibald MacLeish and William Carlos Williams receive the Bollingen Prize in Poetry.
1956	"Howl," by Allen Ginsberg, is published. This poem is the best-known work by one of the Beat writers, a group whose other members include poets Kenneth Rexroth, Lawrence Ferlinghetti, Michael McClure, Gregory Corso, and Philip Whalen.
1956	Spanish poet Juan Ramón Jiménez is awarded the Nobel Prize in Literature.
1956	Elizabeth Bishop receives the Pulitzer Prize in Poetry for *Poems: North and South*.
1958	Irish poet Thomas Kinsella receives the Guinness Poetry Award for *Another September*.
1959	Gary Snyder publishes his first collection, *Riprap*. Snyder's environmentally conscious poetry will later make him a member of the Green movement, a group of writers who advocate the need to repair and sustain the damaged environment.
1960	*The Colossus, and Other Poems*, Sylvia Plath's first poetry collection, is published.
1960	Donald Allen's anthology *The New American Poetry: 1945-1960*, is published. This collection contains the work of several poets associated with the Black Mountain School, including Charles Olson, Robert Creeley, Robert Duncan, Edward Dorn, Denise Levertov, Paul Blackburn, Joel Oppenheimer, and Hilda Morley.
1960	Delmore Schwartz receives the Bollingen Prize in Poetry.
1961	"Babii Yar," Yevgeny Yevtushenko's poem castigating Soviet anti-Semitism, is published.
1961	X. J. Kennedy receives the Lamont Poetry Selection (now the James Laughlin Award) for *Nude Descending a Staircase*.
1961	Randall Jarrell receives the National Book Award in Poetry for *The Woman at the Washington Zoo*.
1963	Hans Magnus Enzensberger receives the Georg Büchner Prize, the most important literary prize in Germany.
1964	*Rediscovery, and Other Poems*, the first book by Ghanaian writer Kofi Awoonor, is published.
1965	Philip Larkin receives the Queen's Gold Medal for Poetry.
1965	Marianne Moore is awarded the Academy of American Poets Fellowship.
1965	Henri Coulette receives the Lamont Poetry Selection (now the James Laughlin Award) for *The War of the Secret Agents*.
1965	Theodore Roethke receives the National Book Award in Poetry for *The Far Field*.
1966	*The Circle Game*, a collection of poems and the first critically acclaimed work by Canadian writer Margaret Atwood, is published.
1966	German-born poet Nelly Sachs is awarded the Nobel Prize in Literature.
1967	Anne Sexton is awarded the Pulitzer Prize in Poetry for *Live or Die*.
1968	Nikki Giovanni's first book of poetry, *Black Feeling, Black Talk*, is published to critical acclaim, with some praising her as the "Princess of Black Poetry."

1969	Stevie Smith receives the Queen's Gold Medal for Poetry.
1969	John Berryman receives the National Book Award in Poetry for *His Toy, His Dream, His Rest*.
1971	Chilean poet Pablo Neruda receives the Nobel Prize in Literature.
1972-1984	John Betjeman is poet laureate of the United Kingdom.
1973	Nigerian writer Chinua Achebe publishes *Christmas in Biafra, and Other Poems*.
1974-1976	Stanley Kunitz serves as America's poet laureate. He will hold this position again in 2000-2001.
1975	French-Canadian poet Anne Hèbert receives the Governor-General's Award for *Les Enfants du sabbat* (*Children of the Black Sabbath*, 1977).
1976	Jorge Guillén receives the Miguel de Cervantes Prize, which honors the lifetime achievement of an outstanding writer in the Spanish language.
1976	Australian poet A. D. Hope receives the Christopher Brennan Award in recognition of his lifetime literary achievement.
1978	Josephine Miles receives the Academy of American Poets Fellowship.
1978	Howard Nemerov is awarded the Pulitzer Prize in Poetry for *Collected Poems*.
1979	W. S. Merwin is awarded the Bollingen Prize in Poetry.
1980	Polish writer Czesław Miłosz is awarded the Nobel Prize in Literature.
1981	Carolyn Forché receives the Lamont Poetry Selection (now the James Laughlin Award) for *The Country Between Us*.
1985-1986	Gwendolyn Brooks serves as America's poet laureate.
1986	Wole Soyinka of Nigeria receives the Nobel Prize in Literature.
1986	Yves Bonnefoy is awarded the Goncourt Prize in Poetry by the Goncourt Literary Society of France.
1987	Joseph Brodsky, a Soviet writer exiled in the United States, receives the Nobel Prize in Literature. Brodsky wrote his poetry in Russian, and it was translated into many languages, with the English translations earning him high regard in the West.
1987	Philip Levine receives the Ruth Lilly Poetry Prize, awarded by the Poetry Foundation in recognition of lifetime achievement im English-language poetry.
1990	Mexican writer Octavio Paz is awarded the Nobel Prize in Literature.
1991	Donald Hall receives the Frost Medal from the Poetry Society of America for distinguished lifetime service to American poetry.
1992	West Indian writer Derek Walcott receives the Nobel Prize in Literature.
1992	Mary Oliver receives the National Book Award in Poetry for *New and Selected Poems*.
1993	Thom Gunn receives the Lenore Marshall Poetry Prize from the Academy of American Poets for *The Man with Night Sweats*.
January 20, 1993	Maya Angelou reads her poem "On the Pulse of Morning" during the inauguration of President Bill Clinton.
1994	*Poetry Canada Review* ceases publication. The magazine was founded in 1978 by Clifton Whiten in order to publish and review poetry from across Canada.
1994	Paul Muldoon receives the T. S. Eliot Prize for *The Annals of Chile*. The annual award is given to the best new poetry collection published in the United Kingdom or the Republic of Ireland.

1994	Irish poet Eavan Boland and American poets Linda Hogan and Jack Gilbert are among the five recipients of the Lannan Literary Award for Poetry.
1994	Brigit Pegeen Kelley receives the Lamont Poetry Selection (now the James Laughlin Award) for *Song*.
1995	Irish writer Seamus Heaney receives the Nobel Prize in Literature.
1995	Denise Levertov receives the Academy of American Poets Fellowship.
1997-2000	Robert Pinsky serves as America's poet laureate.
1998	Ted Hughes receives the T. S. Eliot Prize for *Birthday Letters*. The annual award is given to the best new poetry collection published in the United Kingdom or the Republic of Ireland.
1999	Maxine Kumin receives the Ruth Lilly Poetry Prize, awarded by the Poetry Foundation in recognition of lifetime achievement in English-language poetry.
2001	Louise Glück receives the Bollingen Prize in Poetry.
2001	Sonia Sanchez receives the Frost Medal from the Poetry Society of America for distinguished lifetime service to American poetry.
2001	Canadian poet Anne Carson receives the Griffin Poetry Prize for *Men in the Off Hours*.
September 15, 2001	Scott Simon of National Public Radio reads W. H. Auden's poem "September 1, 1939" (with many lines omitted). The poem is relevant to the terrorist attacks on September 11, 2001, and will be widely circulated and discussed.
2002	Sharon Olds receives the Academy of American Poets Fellowship.
2003	Li-Young Lee receives the Academy of American Poets Fellowship.
2003	Eamon Grennan receives the Lenore Marshall Poetry Prize from the Academy of American Poets for *Still Life with Waterfall*.
2006	Nicaraguan writer Claribel Alegría is awarded the Neustadt International Prize for her body of work.
2007	Robert Haas receives the National Book Award in Poetry for *Time and Materials*.
2007-2008	Charles Simic is America's poet laureate.
2009	Harryette Mullen receives the Academy of American Poets Fellowship.
2009	Allen Grossman receives the Bollingen Prize in Poetry.
2009	Linda Gregg receives the Lenore Marshall Poetry Prize from the Academy of American Poets for *All of It Singing: New and Selected Poems*.
January 20, 2009	Elizabeth Alexander reads her poem "Praise Song for the Day" at the inauguration of President Barack Obama.
July 1, 2010	The Library of Congress announces that W. S. Merwin will replace Kay Ryan as the seventeenth poet laureate of the United States. Merwin is the recipient of two Pulitzer Prizes, the National Book Award, and the Bollingen Prize in Poetry.

Rebecca Kuzins

Major Awards

Academy of American Poets Fellowship

The Academy of American Poets awards American poets with fellowships for distinguished poetic achievement. No awards were given between 1938 and 1945, or in 1949 and 1951.

1937: Edwin Markham
1946: Edgar Lee Masters
1947: Ridgely Torrence
1948: Percy MacKaye
1950: E. E. Cummings
1952: Padraic Colum
1953: Robert Frost
1954: Louise Townsend Nicholl and Oliver St. John Gogarty
1955: Rolfe Humphries
1956: William Carlos Williams
1957: Conrad Aiken
1958: Robinson Jeffers
1959: Louise Bogan
1960: Jesse Stuart
1961: Horace Gregory
1962: John Crowe Ransom
1963: Ezra Pound and Allen Tate
1964: Elizabeth Bishop
1965: Marianne Moore
1966: Archibald MacLeish and John Berryman
1967: Mark Van Doren
1968: Stanley Kunitz
1969: Richard Eberhart
1970: Howard Nemerov
1971: James Wright
1972: W. D. Snodgrass
1973: W. S. Merwin
1974: Léonie Adams
1975: Robert Hayden
1976: J. V. Cunningham
1977: Louis Coxe

1978: Josephine Miles
1979: May Swenson and Mark Strand
1980: Mona Van Duyn
1981: Richard Hugo
1982: John Frederick Nims and John Ashbery
1983: James Schuyler and Philip Booth
1984: Richmond Lattimore and Robert Francis
1985: Amy Clampitt and Maxine Kumin
1986: Irving Feldman and Howard Moss
1987: Josephine Jacobsen and Alfred Corn
1988: Donald Justice
1989: Richard Howard
1990: William Meredith
1991: J. D. McClatchy
1992: Adrienne Rich
1993: Gerald Stern
1994: David Ferry
1995: Denise Levertov
1996: Jay Wright
1997: John Haines
1998: Charles Simic
1999: Gwendolyn Brooks
2000: Lyn Hejinian
2001: Ellen Bryant Voigt
2002: Sharon Olds
2003: Li-Young Lee
2004: Jane Hirschfield
2005: Claudia Rankine
2006: Carl Phillips
2007: James McMichael
2008: Brigit Pegeen Kelly
2009: Harryette Mullen

ADONAIS PRIZE FOR POETRY

The Adonais Prize for Poetry, or Premio Adonáis de Poesía, is awarded annually in Spain to an unpublished Spanish-language poem from any country. Created in 1943 by the publishing house Biblioteca Hispánica, the prize was placed in the hands of Ediciones RIALP in 1946.

1943: José Suárez Carreño (Spain)—"Edad del hombre"; Vicente Gaos (Spain)—"Arcángel de mi noche"; Alfonso Moreno (Spain)—"El vuelo de la carne"

1944: no award

1945: no award

1946: no award

1947: José Hierro (Spain)—"Alegría"

1948: no award

1949: Ricardo Molina (Spain)—"Corimbo"

1950: José García Nieto (Spain)—"Dama de soledad"

1951: Lorenzo Gomis (Spain)—"El caballo"

1952: Antonio Fernández Spencer (Dominican Republic)—"Bajo la luz del día"

1953: Claudio Rodríguez (Spain)—"Don de la ebriedad"

1954: José Angel Valente (Spain)—"A modo de esperanza"

1955: Javier de Bengoechea (Spain)—"Hombre en forma de elegía"

1956: María Elvira Lacaci (Spain)—"Humana voz"

1957: Carlos Sahagún (Spain)—"Profecías del agua"

1958: Rafael Soto Verges (Spain)—"La agorera"

1959: Francisco Brines (Spain)—"Las brasas"

1960: Mariano Roldán (Spain)—"Hombre nuevo"

1961: Luis Feria (Spain)—"Conciencia"

1962: Jesús Hilario Tundidor (Spain)—"Junto a mi silencio"

1963: Félix Grande (Spain)—"Las piedras"

1964: Diego Jesús Jiménez (Spain)—"La ciudad"

1965: Joaquín Caro Romero (Spain)—"El tiempo en el espejo"

1966: Miguel Fernández (Spain)—"Sagrada materia"

1967: Joaquín Benito de Lucas (Spain)—"Materia de olvido"

1968: Roberto Sosa (Honduras)—"Los pobres"

1969: Angel García López (Spain)—"A flor de piel"

1970: Pureza Canelo (Spain)—"Lugar común"

1971: José Infante (Spain)—"Elegía y no"

1972: José Luis Alegre Cudos (Spain)—"Abstracción de Mío Cid con Cid Mío"

1973: José Antonio Moreno Jurado (Spain)—"Ditirambos para mi propia burla"

1974: Julia Castillo (Spain)—"Urgencias de un río interior"

1975: Angel Sánchez Pascual (Spain)—"Ceremonia de la inocencia"

1976: Jorge G. Aranguren (Spain)—"De fuegos, tigres, ríos"

1977: Eloy Sánchez Rosillo (Spain)—"Maneras de estar solo"

1978: Arcadio López-Casanova (Spain)—"La oscura potestad"

1979: Laureano Albán (Costa Rica)—"Herencia del otoño"

1980: Blanca Andreu (Spain)—"De una niña de provincias que vino a vivir en un Chagall"

1981: Miguel Velasco (Spain)—"Las berlinas del sueño"

1982: Luis García Montero (Spain)—"El jardín extranjero"

1983: Javier Peñas Navarro (Spain)—"Adjetivos sin agua, adjetivos con agua"

1984: Amalia Iglesias Serna (Spain)—"Un lugar para el fuego"

1985: Juan Carlos Mestre (Spain)—"Antífona de otoño en el valle del Bierzo"

1986: Juan María Calles (Spain)—"Silencio celeste"

1987: Francisco Serradilla (Spain)—"El bosque insobornable"

1988: Miguel Sánchez Gatell (Spain)—"La soledad absoluta de la tierra"

1989: Juan Carlos Marset (Spain)—"Puer profeta"

1990: Diego Doncel (Spain)—"El único umbral"

1991: Jesús Javier Lázaro Puebla (Spain)—"Canción para una amazona dormida"

1992: Juan Antonio Marín Alba (Spain)—"El horizonte de la noche"

1993: María Luisa Mora Alameda (Spain)—"Busca y captura"

1994: Ana Merino (Spain)—"Preparativos para un viaje"

1995: Eduardo Moga (Spain)—"La luz oída"

1996: Rosario Neira (Spain)—"No somos ángeles"

1997: Luis Martínez-Falero (Spain)—"Plenitud de la materia"

1998: Luis Enrique Belmonte (Venezuela)—"Inútil registro"

1999: Irene Sánchez Carrón (Spain)—"Escenas principales de actor secundario"

2000: Joaquín Pérez Azaústre (Spain)—"Una interpretación"

2001: José Antonio Gómez-Coronado (Spain)—"El triunfo de los días"

2002: Adrián González da Costa (Spain)—"Rua dos douradores"

2003: Javier Vela (Spain)—"La hora del crepúsculo"

2004: José Martínez Ros (Spain)—"La enfermedad"

2005: Carlos Vaquerizo (Spain)—"Fiera venganza del tiempo"

2006: Jorge Galán (pseudonym of George Alexander Portillo; El Salvador)—"Breve historia del Alba"

2007: Teresa Soto González (Spain)—"Un poemario (Imitación de Wislawa)"

2008: Rogelio Guedea (Mexico)—"Kora"

2009: Rubén Martín Díaz (Spain)—"El minuto interior"

ANDREI BELY PRIZE

The Andrei Bely Prize in Russian Literature was founded in 1978 and honors literature in various categories, such as poetry, prose, criticism, and humanitarian investigations. The prize is one ruble, a bottle of vodka, and an apple. The poetry winners are listed below.

1978: Victor Krivulin

1979: Elena Shwartz

1980: Vladimir Aleinikov

1981: Alexander Mironov

1982: no award

1983: Olga Sedakova

1984: no award

1985: Alexei Parschikov

1986: no award

1987: Genady Aigi

1988: Ivan Zhdanov

1989: no award

1990: no award

1991: Alexander Gornon

1992: no award

1993: no award

1994: Shamshad Abdulayev

1995: no award

1996: no award

1997: Victor Letsev

1998: Mikhail Eremin

1999: Elena Fanailova

2000: Yaroslav Mogutin

2001: Vasily Filipov

2002: Mikhail Gronas

2003: Mikhail Eisenberg

2004: Elizabeth Mnatsakonova

2005: Maria Stepanova

2006: Alexander Skidan

2007: Aleksei Tvetkov

2008: Vladimir Aristov and Sergei Kruglov

2009: Nikolai Kononov

BOLLINGEN PRIZE IN POETRY

Administered by Yale University Library, this award is given to an American poet. Awarded every two years since 1963.

1949: Ezra Pound

1950: Wallace Stevens

1951: John Crowe Ransom

1952: Marianne Moore

1953: Archibald MacLeish and William Carlos
    Williams
1954: W. H. Auden
1955: Léonie Adams and Louise Bogan
1956: Conrad Aiken
1957: Allen Tate
1958: E. E. Cummings
1959: Theodore Roethke
1960: Delmore Schwartz
1961: Yvor Winters
1962: John Hall Wheelock and Richard Eberhart
1963: Robert Frost
1965: Horace Gregory
1967: Robert Penn Warren
1969: John Berryman and Karl Shapiro
1971: Richard Wilbur and Mona Van Duyn
1973: James Merrill
1975: A. R. Ammons

1977: David Ignatow
1979: W. S. Merwin
1981: Howard Nemerov and May Swenson
1983: Anthony Hecht and John Hollander
1985: John Ashbery and Fred Chappell
1987: Stanley Kunitz
1989: Edgar Bowers
1991: Laura Riding Jackson and Donald Justice
1993: Mark Strand
1995: Kenneth Koch
1997: Gary Snyder
1999: Robert Creeley
2001: Louise Glück
2003: Adrienne Rich
2005: Jay Wright
2007: Frank Bidart
2009: Allen Grossman

CHRISTOPHER BRENNAN AWARD

First awarded in 1974, the Christopher Brennan Award (formerly the Robert Frost Prize) recognizes an Australian poet for lifetime achievement. The Fellowship of Australian Writers sponsors the award, which is named after the poet Christopher Brennan.

1974: R. D. Fitzgerald
1976: A. D. Hope
    Judith Wright
1977: Gwen Harwood
1979: Rosemary Dobson
1980: John Blight
1982: Vincent Buckley
1983: Bruce Dawe
    Les A. Murray
1988: Roland Robinson
1991: Elizabeth Riddell
1992: R. A. Simpson

1993: Geoffrey Dutton
1994: Judith Rodriguez
1995: Robert Adamson
    Thomas Shapcott
1996: Dorothy Hewett
1998: Jennifer Maiden
1999: Kevin Hart
2001: Dorothy Porter
2003: Philip Salom
2004: Kris Hemensley
2006: Geoff Page
2008: John Kinsella

GEORG BÜCHNER PRIZE

Given yearly by the Deutsche Akademie für Sprache und Dichtung to German-language authors, the Georg Büchner Prize is the most important literary prize in Germany. Created in 1923 to be given to visual artists, poets, actors, and singers, in 1951 it became a general literary prize. The list below includes only poets who have received the award.

1929: Carl Zuckmayer
1932: Albert H. Rausch
1945: Hans Schiebelhuth
1946: Fritz Usinger
1948: Hermann Heiss
1950: Elisabeth Langgässer
1951: Gottfried Benn
1954: Martin Kessel
1955: Marie Luise Kaschnitz
1956: Karl Krolow
1957: Erich Kästner
1959: Günter Eich
1960: Paul Celan
1963: Hans Magnus Enzensberger
1964: Ingeborg Bachmann
1965: Günter Grass
1969: Helmut Heissenbüttel

1970: Thomas Bernhard
1976: Heinz Piontek
1977: Reiner Kunze
1979: Ernst Meister (posthumous)
1984: Ernst Jandl
1985: Heiner Müller
1987: Erich Fried
1991: Wolf Biermann
1993: Peter Rühmkorf
1995: Durs Grünbein
1996: Sarah Kirsch
1997: Hans Carl Artmann
2000: Volker Braun
2001: Friederike Mayröcker
2002: Wolfgang Hilbig
2006: Oskar Pastior (posthumous)

MIGUEL DE CERVANTES PRIZE

Spain's ministry of culture awards its prize to honor the lifetime achievement of an outstanding writer in the Spanish language. Recipients, nominated by the language academies of Spanish-speaking countries, can be of any nationality. The list below includes only poets who have received the award.

1976: Jorge Guillén (Spain)
1978: Dámaso Alonso (Spain)
1979: Jorge Luis Borges (Argentina) and Gerardo Diego (Spain)
1981: Octavio Paz (Mexico)
1982: Luis Rosales (Spain)
1983: Rafael Alberti (Spain)
1990: Adolfo Bioy Casares (Argentina)
1992: Dulce María Loynaz (Cuba)

1996: José García Nieto (Spain)
1998: José Hierro (Spain)
2001: Álvaro Mutis (Colombia)
2002: José Jiménez Lozano (Spain)
2003: Gonzalo Rojas (Chile)
2005: Sergio Pitol (Mexico)
2006: Antonio Gamoneda (Spain)
2007: Juan Gelman (Argentina)
2009: José Emilio Pacheco (Mexico)

T. S. ELIOT PRIZE

Administered by the Poetry Book Society, this annual award is given to the best new poetry collection published in the United Kingdom or the Republic of Ireland.

1993: Ciaran Carson—*First Language*
1994: Paul Muldoon—*The Annals of Chile*
1995: Mark Doty—*My Alexandria*
1996: Les A. Murray—*Subhuman Redneck Poems*
1997: Don Paterson—*God's Gift to Women*
1998: Ted Hughes—*Birthday Letters*
1999: Hugo Williams—*Billy's Rain*
2000: Michael Longley—*The Weather in Japan*
2001: Anne Carson—*The Beauty of the Husband*

2002: Alice Oswald—*Dart*
2003: Don Paterson—*Landing Light*
2004: George Szirtes—*Reel*
2005: Carol Ann Duffy—*Rapture*
2006: Seamus Heaney—*District and Circle*
2007: Sean O'Brien—*The Drowned Book*
2008: Jen Hadfield—*Nigh-No-Place*
2009: Philip Gross—*The Water Table*

FLAIANO PRIZE

The Flaiano Prize (Premio Flaiano) is an Italian international award recognizing achievement in the fields of theater, cinema, television, and literature (novels, poetry, and literary criticism). Below are the winners of the Poetry Prize.

1986: Maria Luisa Spaziani
1987: Luciano Luisi
1988: Elio Filippo Accrocca
1989: Pietro Cimatti, Vivian Lamarque, Benito Sablone
1990: Edoardo Albinati, Dario Bellezza, Vico Faggi
1991: Renzo Barsacchi, Isabella Scalfaro, Massimo Scrignòli
1992: Marco Guzzi, Luciano Roncalli, Mario Trufelli
1993: Attilio Bertolucci, Cesare Vivaldi

1994: Piero Bigongiari
1995: Seamus Heaney
1996: Yves Bonnefoy
1997: Miroslav Holub
1998: Lawrence Ferlinghetti
1999: Yang Lian
2000: Derek Walcott
2001: Charles Tomlinson
2002: Adonis

FROST MEDAL

Awarded by the Poetry Society of America to a poet for distinguished lifetime service to American poetry. Awarded annually since 1984.

1930: Jessie Rittenhouse
1941: Robert Frost
1942: Edgar Lee Masters
1943: Edna St. Vincent Millay
1947: Gustav Davidson
1951: Wallace Stevens
1952: Carl Sandburg
1955: Leonora Speyer
1967: Marianne Moore

1971: Melville Cane
1974: John Hall Wheelock
1976: A. M. Sullivan
1984: Jack Stadler
1985: Robert Penn Warren
1986: Allen Ginsberg and Richard Eberhart
1987: Robert Creeley and Sterling Brown
1988: Carolyn Kizer
1989: Gwendolyn Brooks

1990: Denise Levertov and James Laughlin
1991: Donald Hall
1992: Adrienne Rich and David Ignatow
1993: William Stafford
1994: A. R. Ammons
1995: John Ashbery
1996: Richard Wilbur
1997: Josephine Jacobsen
1998: Stanley Kunitz
1999: Barbara Guest
2000: Anthony Hecht

2001: Sonia Sanchez
2002: Galway Kinnell
2003: Lawrence Ferlinghetti
2004: Richard Howard
2005: Marie Ponsot
2006: Maxine Kumin
2007: John Hollander
2008: Michael S. Harper
2009: X. J. Kennedy
2010: Lucille Clifton

GOLDEN WREATH AWARD

Struga Poetry Evenings, a major international poetry festival in Macedonia, presents its award to living poets for lifetime achievement.

1966: Robert Rozhdestvensky (Soviet Union)
1967: Bulat Okudzhava (Soviet Union)
1968: László Nagy (Hungary)
1969: Mak Dizdar (Bosnia and Herzegovina)
1970: Miodrag Pavlović (Serbia)
1971: W. H. Auden (United States)
1972: Pablo Neruda (Chile)
1973: Eugenio Montale (Italy)
1974: Fazıl Hüsnü Dağlarca (Turkey)
1975: Léopold Senghor (Senegal)
1976: Eugène Guillevic (France)
1977: Artur Lundkvist (Sweden)
1978: Rafael Alberti (Spain)
1979: Miroslav Krleža (Croatia)
1980: Hans Magnus Enzensberger (Germany)
1981: Blaže Koneski (Macedonia)
1982: Nichita Stănescu (Romania)
1983: Sachchidananda Hirananda Vatsyayan Agyey (India)
1984: Andrey Voznesensky (Soviet Union)
1985: Yannis Ritsos (Greece)
1986: Allen Ginsberg (United States)
1987: Tadeusz Różewicz (Poland)

1988: Desanka Maksimović (Serbia)
1989: Thomas W. Shapcott (Australia)
1990: Justo Jorge Padrón (Spain)
1991: Joseph Brodsky (United States)
1992: Ferenc Juhász (Hungary)
1993: Gennadiy Aygi (Chuvash Republic)
1994: Ted Hughes (England)
1995: Yehuda Amichai (Israel)
1996: Makoto Ooka (Japan)
1997: Adunis (Syria)
1998: Lu Yuan (China)
1999: Yves Bonnefoy (France)
2000: Edoardo Sanguineti (Italy)
2001: Seamus Heaney (Northern Ireland)
2002: Slavko Mihalić (Croatia)
2003: Tomas Tranströmer (Sweden)
2004: Vasco Graça Moura (Portugal)
2005: W. S. Merwin (United States)
2006: Nancy Morejón (Cuba)
2007: Mahmoud Darwish (Palestine)
2008: Fatos Arapi (Albania)
2009: Tomaž Šalamun (Slovenia)
2010: Ljabomir Levčev (Bulgaria)

GONCOURT PRIZE IN POETRY

The Goncourt Literary Society of France, also known as the Goncourt Academy, has awarded its prize in poetry since 1985.

1985: Claude Roy
1986: Yves Bonnefoy
1987: no award
1988: Eugène Guillevic
1989: Alain Bosquet
1990: Charles Le Quintrec
1991: Jean-Claude Renard
1992: Georges-Emmanuel Clancier
1993: no award
1994: no award
1995: Lionel Ray
1996: André Velter
1997: Maurice Chappaz

1998: Lorand Gaspar
1999: Jacques Réda
2000: Liliane Wouters
2001: Claude Esteban
2002: Andrée Chedid
2003: Philippe Jaccottet
2004: Jacques Chessex
2005: Charles Dobzynski
2006: Alain Jouffroy
2007: Marc Alyn
2008: Claude Vigée
2009: Abdellatif Laabi

GOVERNOR GENERAL'S LITERARY AWARDS

Presented by the Canada Council for the Arts annually to the best English-language and French-language books in seven categories, including poetry. This list comprises works published in English.

1981: F. R. Scott—*The Collected Poems of F. R. Scott*
1982: Phyllis Webb—*The Vision Tree: Selected Poems*
1983: David Donnell—*Settlements*
1984: Paulette Jiles—*Celestial Navigation*
1985: Fred Wah—*Waiting for Saskatchewan*
1986: Al Purdy—*The Collected Poems of Al Purdy*
1987: Gwendolyn MacEwen—*Afterworlds*
1988: Erin Mouré—*Furious*
1989: Heather Spears—*The Word for Sand*
1990: Margaret Avison—*No Time*
1991: Don McKay—*Night Field*
1992: Lorna Crozier—*Inventing the Hawk*
1993: Don Coles—*Forests of the Medieval World*
1994: Robert Hilles—*Cantos from a Small Room*
1995: Anne Szumigalski—*Voice*
1996: E. D. Blodgett—*Apostrophes: Woman at a Piano*

1997: Dionne Brand—*Land to Light On*
1998: Stephanie Bolster—*White Stone: The Alice Poems*
1999: Jan Zwicky—*Songs for Relinquishing the Earth*
2000: Don McKay—*Another Gravity*
2001: George Elliott Clarke—*Execution Poems*
2002: Roy Miki—*Surrender*
2003: Tim Lilburn—*Kill-Site*
2004: Roo Borson—*Short Journey Upriver Toward Oishida*
2005: Anne Compton—*Processional*
2006: John Pass—*Stumbling in the Bloom*
2007: Don Domanski—*All Our Wonder Unavenged*
2008: Jacob Scheier—*More to Keep Us Warm*
2009: David Zieroth—*The Fly in Autumn*

This list comprises works published in French.

1981: Michel Beaulieu—*Visages*
1982: Michel Savard—*Forages*

1983: Suzanne Paradis—*Un Goût de sel*
1984: Nicole Brossard—*Double Impression*

1985: André Roy—*Action writing*

1986: Cécile Cloutier—*L'Écouté*

1987: Fernand Ouellette—*Les Heures*

1988: Marcel Labine—*Papiers d'épidémie*

1989: Pierre DesRuisseaux—*Monème*

1990: Jean-Paul Daoust—*Les Cendres bleues*

1991: Madeleine Gagnon—*Chant pour un Québec lointain*

1992: Gilles Cyr—*Andromède attendra*

1993: Denise Desautels—*Le Saut de l'ange*

1994: Fulvio Caccia—*Aknos*

1995: Émile Martel—*Pour orchestre et poète seul*

1996: Serge Patrice—*Le Quatuor de l'errance*, followed by *La Traversée du désert*

1997: Pierre Nepveu—*Romans-fleuves*

1998: Suzanne Jacob—*La Part de feu*, preceded by *Le Deuil de la rancune*

1999: Herménégilde Chiasson—*Conversations*

2000: Normand de Bellefeuille—*La Marche de l'aveugle sans son chien*

2001: Paul Chanel Malenfant—*Des Ombres portées*

2002: Robert Dickson—*Humains paysages en temps de paix relative*

2003: Pierre Nepveu—*Lignes aériennes*

2004: André Brochu—*Les jours à vif*

2005: Jean-Marc Desgent—*Vingtièmes siècles*

2006: Hélène Dorion—*Ravir: Les lieux*

2007: Serge Patrice Thibodeau—*Seul on est*

2008: Michel Pleau—*La Lenteur du monde*

2009: Hélène Monette—*Thérèse pour joie et orchestre*

THE GRIFFIN POETRY PRIZE

The Griffin Poetry Prize is given by Canada each year, beginning in 2001, to collections by one living Canadian poet and one living international poet writing in the English language. Lifetime Recognition Awards to poets from all countries and languages were added in 2006.

2001: Anne Carson—*Men in the Off Hours* (Canada); Nikolai Popov and Heather McHugh, translation of *Glottal Stop: 101 Poems by Paul Celan* (international)

2002: Christian Bök—*Eunoia* (Canada); Alice Notley—*Disobedience* (international)

2003: Margaret Avison—*Concrete and Wild Carrot* (Canada); Paul Muldoon—*Moy Sand and Gravel* (international)

2004: Anne Simpson—*Loop* (Canada); August Kleinzahler—*The Strange Hours Travelers Keep* (international)

2005: Roo Borson—*Short Journey Upriver Toward Oishida* (Canada); Charles Simic—*Selected Poems, 1963-2003* (international)

2006: Sylvia Legris—*Nerve Squall* (Canada); Kamau Brathwaite—*Born to Slow Horses* (international); Lifetime Recognition Award, Robin Blaser

2007: Don McKay—*Strike/Slip* (Canada); Charles Wright—*Scar Tissue* (international); Lifetime Recognition Award, Tomas Tranströmer

2008: Robin Blaser—*The Holy Forest: Collected Poems of Robin Blaser* (Canada); John Ashbery—*Notes from the Air: Selected Later Poems* (international); Lifetime Recognition Award, Ko Un

2009: A. F. Moritz—*The Sentinel* (Canada); C. D. Wright—*Rising, Falling, Hovering* (international); Lifetime Recognition Award, Hans Magnus Enzensberger

2010: Karen Solie—*Pigeon* (Canada); Eilean Ni Chuilleanain—*The Sun-fish* (international); Lifetime Recognition Award, Adrienne Rich

JNANPITH AWARD

The Indian literary and research organization Bharatiya Jnanpith presents its annual award for lifetime achievement in literature, including poetry, written by an Indian citizen in any of several Indian languages.

1965: G. Sankara Kurup
1966: Tarashankar Bandopadhyaya
1967: Kuppali V. Puttappa and Umashankar Joshi
1968: Sumitranandan Pant
1969: Firaq Gorakhpuri
1970: Viswanatha Satyanarayana
1971: Bishnu Dey
1972: Ramdhari Singh Dinkar
1973: Dattatreya R. Bendre and Gopinath Mohanty
1974: Vishnu S. Khandekar
1975: P. V. Akilandam
1976: Ashapurna Devi
1977: K. Shivaram Karanth
1978: Sachchidananda H. V. Ajneya
1979: Birendra K. Bhattacharya
1980: S. K. Pottekkatt
1981: Amrita Pritam
1982: Mahadevi Varma
1983: Maasti V. Ayengar
1984: Thakazhi S. Pillai
1985: Pannalal Patel
1986: Sachidananda Routroy

1987: V. V. S. Kusumagraj
1988: C. Narayana Reddy
1989: Qurratulain Hyder
1990: V. K. Gokak
1991: Subhash Mukhopadhyaya
1992: Naresh Mehta
1993: Sitakant Mahapatra
1994: U. R. Anantha Murthy
1995: M. T. Vasudevan Nair
1996: Mahasweta Devi
1997: Ali Sardar Jafri
1998: Girish Karnad
1999: Nirmal Verma and Gurdial Singh
2000: Indira Goswami
2001: Rajendra Shah
2002: D. Jayakantan
2003: Vinda Karandikar
2004: Rahman Rahi
2005: Kunwar Narain
2006: Ravindra Kelekar and Satya Vrat Shasti
2007: Akhlaq Mohammed Khan (Shahryar)
2008: O. N. V. Kurap

LANNAN LITERARY AWARD FOR POETRY

The Lannan Literary Awards are a series of awards and literary fellowships given out in various fields by the Lannan Foundation. Established in 1989, the awards "honor both established and emerging writers whose work is of exceptional quality."

1989: Cid Corman, George Evans, Peter Levitt
1990: Derek Mahon, Seamus Heaney
1991: William Bronk, Chrystos, Pattiann Rogers, Herbert Morris
1992: A. R. Ammons, Thomas Centolella, Killarney Clary, Suzanne Gardinier, Susan Mitchell, Luis J. Rodriguez
1993: Cyrus Cassells, Denise Levertov, Benjamin Alire Saenz
1994: Simon Armitage, Eavan Boland, Linda Hogan, Jack Gilbert, Richard Kenney

1995: Hayden Carruth, Carol Ann Duffy, Arthur Sze, Li-Young Lee
1996: Anne Carson, Lucille Clifton, William Trevor, Donald Justice
1997: Ken Smith
1998: Frank Bidart, Jon Davis, Mary Oliver
1999: Dennis O'Driscoll, C. D. Wright, Louise Glück
2000: Herbert Morris, Jay Wright
2001: no award
2002: Alan Dugan, Peter Dale Scott
2003: no award

2004: Peter Reading
2005: Pattiann Rogers
2006: Bruce Weigl

2007: no award
2008: August Kleinzahler
2009: no award

JAMES LAUGHLIN AWARD

The Academy of American Poets gives this annual award to a poet for the publication of an outstanding second poetry collection. Originally known as the Lamont Poetry Selection, the name was changed in 1995 to honor poet and publisher James Laughlin.

1954: Constance Carrier—*The Middle Voice*
1955: Donald Hall—*Exiles and Marriages*
1956: Philip Booth—*Letter from a Distant Land*
1957: Daniel Berrigan, S. J.—*Time Without Number*
1958: Ned O'Gorman—*The Night of the Hammer*
1959: Donald Justice—*The Summer Anniversaries*
1960: Robert Mezey—*The Lovemaker*
1961: X. J. Kennedy—*Nude Descending a Staircase*
1962: Edward Field—*Stand Up, Friend, with Me*
1963: no award
1964: Adrien Stoutenberg—*Heroes, Advise Us*
1965: Henri Coulette—*The War of the Secret Agents*
1966: Kenneth O. Hanson—*The Distance Anywhere*
1967: James Scully—*The Marches*
1968: Jane Cooper—*The Weather of Six Mornings*
1969: Marvin Bell—*A Probable Volume of Dreams*
1970: William Harmon—*Treasury Holiday*
1971: Stephen Dobyns—*Concurring Beasts*
1972: Peter Everwine—*Collecting the Animals*
1973: Marilyn Hacker—*Presentation Piece*
1974: John Balaban—*After Our War*
1975: Lisel Mueller—*The Private Life*
1976: Larry Levis—*The Afterlife*
1977: Gerald Stern—*Lucky Life*
1978: Ai—*Killing Floor*
1979: Frederick Seidel—*Sunrise*
1980: Michael Van Walleghen—*More Trouble with the Obvious*
1981: Carolyn Forché—*The Country Between Us*
1982: Margaret Gibson—*Long Walks in the Afternoon*
1983: Sharon Olds—*The Dead and the Living*

1984: Philip Schultz—*Deep Within the Ravine*
1985: Cornelius Eady—*Victims of the Latest Dance Craze*
1986: Jane Shore—*The Minute Hand*
1987: Garrett Kaoru Hongo—*The River of Heaven*
1988: Mary Jo Salter—*Unfinished Painting*
1989: Minnie Bruce Pratt—*Crime Against Nature*
1990: Li-Young Lee—*The City in Which I Love You*
1991: Susan Wood—*Campo Santo*
1992: Kathryn Stripling Byer—*Wildwood Flower*
1993: Rosanna Warren—*Stained Glass*
1994: Brigit Pegeen Kelly—*Song*
1995: Ralph Angel—*Neither World*
1996: David Rivard—*Wise Poison*
1997: Tony Hoagland—*Donkey Gospel*
1998: Sandra Alcosser—*Except by Nature*
1999: Tory Dent—*HIV, Mon Amour*
2000: Liz Waldner—*A Point Is That Which Has No Point*
2001: Peter Johnson—*Miracles and Mortifications*
2002: Karen Volkman—*Spar*
2003: Vijay Seshadri—*The Long Meadow*
2004: Jeff Clark—*Music and Suicide*
2005: Barbara Jane Reyes—*Poeta en San Francisco*
2006: Tracy K. Smith—*Duende*
2007: Brenda Shaughnessy—*Human Dark with Sugar*
2008: Rusty Morrison—*the true keeps calm biding its story*
2009: Jennifer K. Sweeney—*How to Live on Bread and Music*

GRACE LEVEN PRIZE FOR POETRY

The Grace Leven Prize for Poetry was established in 1947 by William Baylebridge in the name of his benefactor. The award is given to "the best volume of poetry published in the preceding twelve months by a writer either Australian-born, or naturalised in Australia and resident in Australia for not less than ten years."

1947: Nan McDonald—*Pacific Sea*

1948: Francis Webb—*A Drum for Ben Boyd*

1949: Judith Wright—*Woman to Man*

1951: Rex Ingamells—*The Great South Land*

1952: R. D. Fitzgerald—*Between Two Tides*

1953: Roland Robinson—*Tumult of the Swans*

1954: John Thompson—*Thirty Poems*

1955: A. D. Hope—*The Wandering Islands*

1957: Leonard Mann—*Elegaic, and Other Poems*

1958: Geoffrey Dutton—*Antipodes in Shoes*

1959: R. D. Fitzgerald—*The Wind at Your Door: A Poem*

1960: Colin Thiele—*Man in a Landscape*

1961: Thomas Shapcott—*Time on Fire*

1962: R. D. Fitzgerald—*South-most Tree*

1963: Ian Mudie—*The North-Bound Rider*

1964: David Rowbotham—*All the Room*

1965: Les Murray and Geoffrey Lehmann—*The Ilex Tree*

1966: William Hart-Smith—*The Talking Clothes: Poems*

1967: Douglas Stewart—*Collected Poems, 1936-1967*

1968: David Campbell—*Selected Poems, 1942-1968*

1969: Randolph Stow—*A Counterfeit Silence: Selected Poems*

1970: Bruce Beaver—*Letters to Live Poets*

1971: James McAuley—*Collected Poems, 1936-1970*; Judith Wright—*Collected Poems, 1942-1970*

1972: Peter Skrzynecki—*Head-waters*

1973: Rodney Hall—*A Soapbox Omnibus*

1974: David Malouf—*Neighbours in a Thicket: Poems*

1975: Gwen Harwood—*Selected Poems* (1975)

1976: John Blight—*Selected Poems, 1939-1975*

1977: Robert Adamson—*Selected Poems*

1978: Bruce Dawe—*Sometimes Gladness: Collected Poems, 1954-1978*

1979: David Campbell—*The Man in the Honeysuckle*

1980: Les Murray—*The Boys Who Stole the Funeral*

1981: Geoffrey Lehmann—*Nero's Poems: Translations of the Public and Private Poems of the Emperor Nero*

1982: Vivian Smith—*Tide Country*

1983: Peter Porter—*Collected Poems*

1984: Rosemary Dobson—*The Three Fates, and Other Poems*

1985: Robert Gray—*Selected Poems, 1963-1983* Chris Wallace-Crabbe—*The Amorous Cannibal*

1986: Rhyll McMaster—*Washing the Money: Poems with Photographs*

1987: Elizabeth Riddell—*Occasions of Birds, and Other Poems*

1988: John Tranter—*Under Berlin*

1989: Dorothy Hewett—*A Tremendous World in Her Head*

1990: Les Murray—*Dog Fox Field*

1992: Kevin Hart—*Peniel* Gary Catalano—*Empire of Grass*

1993: Philip Hodgins—*The End of the Season*

1995: Kevin Hart—*New and Selected Poems*; Jemal Sharah—*Path of Ghosts: Poems, 1986-93*

1997: John Kinsella—*The Undertow: New and Selected Poems*

2001: Geoff Page—*Darker and Lighter*

2002: Kate Lilley—*Versary*

2003: Stephen Edgar—*Lost in the Foreground*

2004: Luke Davies—*Totem*

2005: Noel Rowe—*Next to Nothing*

2006: Alan Gould—*The Past Completes Me: Selected Poems, 1973-2003*

2007: Robert Adamson—*The Goldfinches of Baghdad*

2008: Alan Wearne—*The Australian Popular Song Book*

2010: Judith Beveridge—*Storm and Honey*

RUTH LILLY POETRY PRIZE

This annual prize, awarded by the Poetry Foundation, recognizes lifetime achievement in English-language poetry.

1986: Adrienne Rich
1987: Philip Levine
1988: Anthony Hecht
1989: Mona Van Duyn
1990: Hayden Carruth
1991: David Wagoner
1992: John Ashbery
1993: Charles Wright
1994: Donald Hall
1995: A. R. Ammons
1996: Gerald Stern
1997: William Matthews
1998: W. S. Merwin

1999: Maxine Kumin
2000: Carl Dennis
2001: Yusef Komunyakaa
2002: Lisel Mueller
2003: Linda Pastan
2004: Kay Ryan
2005: C. K. Williams
2006: Richard Wilbur
2007: Lucille Clifton
2008: Gary Snyder
2009: Fanny Howe
2010: Eleanor Ross Taylor

LENORE MARSHALL POETRY PRIZE

Awarded by the Academy of American Poets annually to a poet for the publication in the United States of an outstanding poetry collection.

1975: Cid Corman—*O/I*
1976: Denise Levertov—*The Freeing of the Dust*
1977: Philip Levine—*The Names of the Lost*
1978: Allen Tate—*Collected Poems, 1919-1976*
1979: Hayden Carruth—*Brothers, I Loved You All*
1980: Stanley Kunitz—*The Poems of Stanley Kunitz, 1928-1978*
1981: Sterling A. Brown—*The Collected Poems of Sterling A. Brown*
1982: John Logan—*The Bridge of Chance: Poems, 1974-1980*
1983: George Starbuck—*The Argot Merchant Disaster*
1984: Josephine Miles—*Collected Poems, 1930-1983*
1985: John Ashbery—*A Wave*
1986: Howard Moss—*New Selected Poems*
1987: Donald Hall—*The Happy Man*
1988: Josephine Jacobsen—*The Sisters: New and Selected Poems*
1989: Thomas McGrath—*Selected Poems, 1938-1988*
1990: Michael Ryan—*God Hunger*
1991: John Haines—*New Poems, 1980-1988*
1992: Adrienne Rich—*An Atlas of the Difficult World*

1993: Thom Gunn—*The Man with Night Sweats*
1994: W. S. Merwin—*Travels*
1995: Marilyn Hacker—*Winter Numbers*
1996: Charles Wright—*Chickamauga*
1997: Robert Pinsky—*The Figured Wheel: New and Collected Poems, 1966-1996*
1998: Mark Jarman—*Questions for Ecclesiastes*
1999: Wanda Coleman—*Bathwater Wine*
2000: David Ferry—*Of No Country I Know: New and Selected Poems and Translations*
2001: Fanny Howe—*Selected Poems*
2002: Madeline DeFrees—*Blue Dusk*
2003: Eamon Grennan—*Still Life with Waterfall*
2004: Donald Revell—*My Mojave*
2005: Anne Winters—*The Displaced of Capital*
2006: Eleanor Lerman—*Our Post-Soviet History Unfolds*
2007: Alice Notley—*Grave of Light: New and Selected Poems, 1970-2005*
2008: Henri Cole—*Blackbird and Wolf*
2009: Linda Gregg—*All of It Singing: New and Selected Poems*

MASAOKA SHIKI INTERNATIONAL HAIKU PRIZE

Beginning in 2000, the Haiku Grand Prize and several Haiku Prizes have been given every two years at the International Haiku Symposium to raise international awareness of the poet Masaoka Shiki and his chosen form, the haiku. Ehime Prefecture, birthplace of the poet, sponsors the award.

2000: Grand Prize — Yves Bonnefoy (France); Haiku Prize — Li Mang (China), Bart Mesotten (Belgium), Robert Speiss (United States), Kazuo Sato (Japan)

2002: Grand Prize — Cor van den Neuvel (United States); Haiku Prize — Satya Bhushan Verma (India), Shigeki Wada (Japan)

2004: Grand Prize — Gary Snyder (United States);

Haiku Prize — Hidekazu Masuda (Brazil), Ko Reishi (Taiwan), Bansei Tsukushi (Japan)

2006: No awards

2008: Grand Prize — Tota Kaneko (Japan); Haiku Prize — Biwao Kawahara (Japan); Sweden Award: Sonoo Uchida (Japan), O-Young Lee (South Korea)

NATIONAL BOOK AWARD IN POETRY

Awarded by the National Book Foundation to an American poet for the publication of the best book of poetry during the year. Not awarded from 1984 to 1990.

1950: William Carlos Williams—*Paterson: Book III and Selected Poems*

1951: Wallace Stevens—*The Auroras of Autumn*

1952: Marianne Moore—*Collected Poems*

1953: Archibald MacLeish—*Collected Poems, 1917-1952*

1954: Conrad Aiken—*Collected Poems*

1955: Wallace Stevens—*The Collected Poems of Wallace Stevens*

1956: W. H. Auden—*The Shield of Achilles*

1957: Richard Wilbur—*Things of the World*

1958: Robert Penn Warren—*Promises: Poems, 1954-1956*

1959: Theodore Roethke—*Words for the Wind*

1960: Robert Lowell—*Life Studies*

1961: Randall Jarrell—*The Woman at the Washington Zoo*

1962: Alan Dugan—*Poems*

1963: William Stafford—*Traveling Through the Dark*

1964: John Crowe Ransom—*Selected Poems*

1965: Theodore Roethke—*The Far Field*

1966: James Dickey—*Buckdancer's Choice: Poems*

1967: James Merrill—*Nights and Days*

1968: Robert Bly—*The Light Around the Body*

1969: John Berryman—*His Toy, His Dream, His Rest*

1970: Elizabeth Bishop—*The Complete Poems*

1971: Mona Van Duyn—*To See, to Take*

1972: Frank O'Hara—*The Collected Poems of Frank O'Hara* and Howard Moss—*Selected Poems*

1973: A. R. Ammons—*Collected Poems, 1951-1971*

1974: Allen Ginsberg—*The Fall of America: Poems of These States* and Adrienne Rich—*Diving into the Wreck: Poems, 1971-1972*

1975: Marilyn Hacker—*Presentation Piece*

1976: John Ashbery—*Self-Portrait in a Convex Mirror*

1977: Richard Eberhart—*Collected Poems, 1930-1976*

1978: Howard Nemerov—*The Collected Poems of Howard Nemerov*

1979: James Merrill—*Mirabell: Book of Numbers*

1980: Philip Levine—*Ashes*

1981: Lisel Mueller—*The Need to Hold Still*

1982: William Bronk—*Life Supports: New and Collected Poems*

1983: Galway Kinnell—*Selected Poems* and Charles Wright—*Country Music: Selected Early Poems*

1991: Philip Levine—*What Work Is*

1992: Mary Oliver—*New and Selected Poems*

1993: A. R. Ammons—*Garbage*

1994: James Tate—*A Worshipful Company of Fletchers*

1995: Stanley Kunitz—*Passing Through: The Later Poems*

1996: Hayden Carruth—*Scrambled Eggs and Whiskey: Poems, 1991-1995*

1997: William Meredith—*Effort at Speech: New and Selected Poems*

1998: Gerald Stern—*This Time: New and Selected Poems*

1999: Ai—*Vice: New and Selected Poems*

2000: Lucille Clifton—*Blessing the Boats: New and Selected Poems, 1988-2000*

2001: Alan Dugan—*Poems Seven: New and Complete Poetry*

2002: Ruth Stone—*In the Next Galaxy*

2003: C. K. Williams—*The Singing*

2004: Jean Valentine—*Door in the Mountain: New and Collected Poems, 1965-2003*

2005: W. S. Merwin—*Migration: New and Selected Poems*

2006: Nathaniel Mackey—*Splay Anthem*

2007: Robert Hass—*Time and Materials*

2008: Mark Doty—*Fire to Fire: New and Collected Poems*

2009: Keith Waldrop—*Transcendental Studies: A Trilogy*

NEUSTADT INTERNATIONAL PRIZE FOR LITERATURE

Awarded biennially since 1970, this award sponsored by the University of Oklahoma honors writers for a body of work. The list below includes only poets who have received the award.

1970: Giuseppe Ungaretti (Italy)

1974: Francis Ponge (France)

1976: Elizabeth Bishop (United States)

1978: Czesław Miłosz (Poland)

1980: Josef Škvorecky (Czechoslovakia/Canada)

1982: Octavio Paz (Mexico)

1984: Paavo Haavikko (Finland)

1990: Tomas Tranströmer (Sweden)

1992: João Cabral de Melo Neto (Brazil)

1994: Edward Kamau Brathwaite (Barbados)

2000: David Malouf (Australia)

2002: Alvaro Mutis (Colombia)

2004: Adam Zagajewski (Poland)

2006: Claribel Alegría (Nicaragua/El Salvador)

2010: Duo Duo (China)

NEW SOUTH WALES PREMIER'S LITERARY AWARDS

Established in 1979, the New South Wales Premier's Literary Awards includes the Kenneth Slessor Prize for poetry.

1980: David Campbell—*Man in the Honeysuckle*

1981: Alan Gould—*Astral Sea*

1982: Fay Zwicky—*Kaddish, and Other Poems*

1983: Vivian Smith—*Tide Country*

1984: Les A. Murray—*The People's Other World*

1985: Kevin Hart—*Your Shadow*

1986: Robert Gray—*Selected Poems, 1963-83*

1987: Philip Hodgins—*Blood and Bone*

1988: Judith Beveridge—*The Domesticity of Giraffes*

1989: John Tranter—*Under Berlin*

1990: Robert Adamson—*The Clean Dark*

1991: Jennifer Maiden—*The Winter Baby*

1992: Elizabeth Riddell—*Selected Poems*

1993: Les A. Murray—*Translations from the Natural World*

1994: Barry Hill—*Ghosting William Buckley*

1995: Peter Boyle—*Coming Home from the World*

1996: Eric Beach—*Weeping for Lost Babylon*; J. S. Harry—*Selected Poems*

1997: Anthony Lawrence—*The Viewfinder*

1999: Lee Cataldi—*Race Against Time*

2000: Jennifer Maiden—*Mines*

2001: Ken Taylor—*Africa*

2002: Alan Wearne—*The Lovemakers*

2003: Jill Jones—*Screens Jets Heaven: New and Selected Poems*

2004: Pam Brown—*Dear Deliria: New and Selected Poems*

2005: Samuel Wagan Watson—*Smoke Encrypted Whispers*

2006: Jaya Savige—*Latecomers*

2007: John Tranter—*Urban Myths: 210 Poems*

2008: Kathryn Lomer—*Two Kinds of Silence*

2009: L. K. Holt—*Man Wolf Man*

NIKE AWARD

Established in 1997 and sponsored by the Polish newspaper Gazeta Wyborcza *and the consulting company NICOM, the NIKE Literary Award (Nagroda Literacka NIKE) is given to the best book by a single living author writing in Polish published the previous year. It is open to works in all literary genres. Only poetry collections that have received the jury award are listed below.*

1998: Czesław Miłosz—*Piesek przydrożny* (*Road-side Dog*)

1999: Stanisław Barańczak—*Chirurgiczna precyzja* (surgical precision)

2000: Tadeusz Różewicz—*Matka odchodzi* (mother is leaving)

2003: Jarosław Marek Rymkiewicz—*Zachód słonca w Milanówku* (sunset in Milanówek)

2009: Eugeniusz Tkaczyszyn—*Dycki for Piosenka o zaleznosciach i uzaleznieniach* (song of dependency and addiction)

NOBEL PRIZE IN LITERATURE

Awarded annually since 1901, this prize is given to an author for his or her entire body of literary work. The list below includes only the poets who have been so honored.

1901: Sully Prudhomme

1906: Giosuè Carducci

1907: Rudyard Kipling

1913: Rabindranath Tagore

1923: William Butler Yeats

1945: Gabriela Mistral

1946: Hermann Hesse

1948: T. S. Eliot

1956: Juan Ramón Jiménez

1958: Boris Pasternak

1959: Salvatore Quasimodo

1960: Saint-John Perse

1963: George Seferis

1966: Nelly Sachs

1969: Samuel Beckett

1971: Pablo Neruda

1974: Harry Martinson

1975: Eugenio Montale

1977: Vicente Aleixandre

1979: Odysseus Elytis

1980: Czesław Miłosz

1984: Jaroslav Seifert

1986: Wole Soyinka

1987: Joseph Brodsky

1990: Octavio Paz

1992: Derek Walcott

1995: Seamus Heaney

1996: Wisława Szymborska

2005: Harold Pinter

2009: Herta Müller

PEN/Voelcker Award for Poetry

The PEN/Voelcker Award for Poetry is given biennially to an American poet whose distinguished body of work represents a notable and accomplished presence in U.S. literature.

1994: Martín Espada
1996: Franz Wright
1998: C. K. Williams
2000: Heather McHugh

2002: Frederick Seidel
2004: Robert Pinsky
2006: Linda Gregg
2008: Kimiko Hahn

Poet Laureate Consultant in Poetry

An appointment is given through the Library of Congress to a poet who then serves as the United States' official poet, or poet laureate.

1937-1941: Joseph Auslander
1943-1944: Allen Tate
1944-1945: Robert Penn Warren
1945-1946: Louise Bogan
1946-1947: Karl Shapiro
1947-1948: Robert Lowell
1948-1949: Léonie Adams
1949-1950: Elizabeth Bishop
1950-1952: Conrad Aiken
1952: William Carlos Williams (did not serve)
1956-1958: Randall Jarrell
1958-1959: Robert Frost
1959-1961: Richard Eberhart
1961-1963: Louis Untermeyer
1963-1964: Howard Nemerov
1964-1965: Reed Whittemore
1965-1966: Stephen Spender
1966-1968: James Dickey
1968-1970: William Jay Smith
1970-1971: William Stafford
1971-1973: Josephine Jacobsen
1973-1974: Daniel Hoffman
1974-1976: Stanley Kunitz
1976-1978: Robert Hayden
1978-1980: William Meredith
1981-1982: Maxine Kumin

1982-1984: Anthony Hecht
1984-1985: Robert Fitzgerald (limited by health) and
　　　　　Reed Whittemore (interim consultant)
1985-1986: Gwendolyn Brooks
1986-1987: Robert Penn Warren (first poet to be
　　　　　designated Poet Laureate Consultant in Poetry)
1987-1988: Richard Wilbur
1988-1990: Howard Nemerov
1990-1991: Mark Strand
1991-1992: Joseph Brodsky
1992-1993: Mona Van Duyn
1993-1995: Rita Dove
1995-1997: Robert Hass
1997-2000: Robert Pinsky
1999-2000: Rita Dove, Louise Glück, and W. S.
　　　　　Merwin (special consultants for Library of
　　　　　Congress bicentennial)
2000-2001: Stanley Kunitz
2001-2003: Billy Collins
2003-2004: Louise Glück
2004-2006: Ted Kooser
2006-2007: Donald Hall
2007-2008: Charles Simic
2008-2010: Kay Ryan
2010-　　: W. S. Merwin

Poet Laureate of the United Kingdom of Great Britain and Northern Ireland

The British Poet Laureate, originally an appointment for life, is now a ten-year term. John Dryden was the first official laureate. Carol Ann Duffy, in 2009, became the first woman appointed to the position.

1591-1599: Edmund Spenser
1599-1619: Samuel Daniel
1619-1637: Ben Jonson
1638-1668: William Davenant
1668-1689: John Dryden
1689-1692: Thomas Shadwell
1692-1715: Nahum Tate
1715-1718: Nicholas Rowe
1718-1730: Laurence Eusden
1730-1757: Colley Cibber
1757-1785: William Whitehead
1785-1790: Thomas Warton

1790-1813: Henry James Pye
1813-1843: Robert Southey
1843-1850: William Wordsworth
1850-1892: Alfred, Lord Tennyson
1896-1913: Alfred Austin
1913-1930: Robert Bridges
1930-1967: John Masefield
1967-1972: Cecil Day Lewis
1972-1984: Sir John Betjeman
1984-1998: Ted Hughes
1999-2009: Andrew Motion
2009-   : Carol Ann Duffy

Pulitzer Prize in Poetry

Awarded by Columbia University's Graduate School of Journalism to honor an American poet who has published a distinguished collection of poetry.

1918: Sara Teasdale—*Love Songs*
1919: Margaret Widdemer—*Old Road to Paradise* and Carl Sandburg—*Cornhuskers*
1920: no award
1921: no award
1922: Edwin Arlington Robinson—*Collected Poems*
1923: Edna St. Vincent Millay—*The Ballad of the Harp-Weaver*
1924: Robert Frost—*New Hampshire: A Poem with Notes and Grace Notes*
1925: Edwin Arlington Robinson—*The Man Who Died Twice*
1926: Amy Lowell—*What's O'Clock*
1927: Leonora Speyer—*Fiddler's Farewell*
1928: Edwin Arlington Robinson—*Tristram*
1929: Stephen Vincent Benét—*John Brown's Body*
1930: Conrad Aiken—*Selected Poems*
1931: Robert Frost—*Collected Poems*
1932: George Dillon—*The Flowering Stone*
1933: Archibald MacLeish—*Conquistador*
1934: Robert Hillyer—*Collected Verse*
1935: Audrey Wurdemann—*Bright Ambush*

1936: Robert P. Tristram Coffin—*Strange Holiness*
1937: Robert Frost—*A Further Range*
1938: Marya Zaturenska—*Cold Morning Sky*
1939: John Gould Fletcher—*Selected Poems*
1940: Mark Van Doren—*Selected Poems*
1941: Leonard Bacon—*Sunderland Capture*
1942: William Rose Benet—*The Dust Which Is God*
1943: Robert Frost—*A Witness Tree*
1944: Stephen Vincent Benét—*Western Star*
1945: Karl Shapiro—*V-Letter and Other Poems*
1946: no award
1947: Robert Lowell—*Lord Weary's Castle*
1948: W. H. Auden—*The Age of Anxiety*
1949: Peter Viereck—*Terror and Decorum*
1950: Gwendolyn Brooks—*Annie Allen*
1951: Carl Sandburg—*Complete Poems*
1952: Marianne Moore—*Collected Poems*
1953: Archibald MacLeish—*Collected Poems, 1917-1952*
1954: Theodore Roethke—*The Waking*
1955: Wallace Stevens—*Collected Poems*
1956: Elizabeth Bishop—*Poems: North and South*

1957: Richard Wilbur—*Things of This World*

1958: Robert Penn Warren—*Promises: Poems, 1954-1956*

1959: Stanley Kunitz—*Selected Poems, 1928-1958*

1960: W. D. Snodgrass—*Heart's Needle*

1961: Phyllis McGinley—*Times Three: Selected Verse from Three Decades*

1962: Alan Dugan—*Poems*

1963: William Carlos Williams—*Pictures from Breughel*

1964: Louis Simpson—*At the End of the Open Road*

1965: John Berryman—*Seventy-seven Dream Songs*

1966: Richard Eberhart—*Selected Poems*

1967: Anne Sexton—*Live or Die*

1968: Anthony Hecht—*The Hard Hours*

1969: George Oppen—*Of Being Numerous*

1970: Richard Howard—*Untitled Subjects*

1971: W. S. Merwin—*The Carrier of Ladders*

1972: James Wright—*Collected Poems*

1973: Maxine Kumin—*Up Country*

1974: Robert Lowell—*The Dolphin*

1975: Gary Snyder—*Turtle Island*

1976: John Ashbery—*Self-Portrait in a Convex Mirror*

1977: James Merrill—*Divine Comedies*

1978: Howard Nemerov—*Collected Poems*

1979: Robert Penn Warren—*Now and Then*

1980: Donald Justice—*Selected Poems*

1981: James Schuyler—*The Morning of the Poem*

1982: Sylvia Plath—*The Collected Poems*

1983: Galway Kinnell—*Selected Poems*

1984: Mary Oliver—*American Primitive*

1985: Carolyn Kizer—*Yin*

1986: Henry Taylor—*The Flying Change*

1987: Rita Dove—*Thomas and Beulah*

1988: William Meredith—*Partial Accounts: New and Selected Poems*

1989: Richard Wilbur—*New and Collected Poems*

1990: Charles Simic—*The World Doesn't End*

1991: Mona Van Duyn—*Near Changes*

1992: James Tate—*Selected Poems*

1993: Louise Glück—*The Wild Iris*

1994: Yusef Komunyakaa—*Neon Vernacular: New and Selected Poems*

1995: Philip Levine—*The Simple Truth*

1996: Jorie Graham—*The Dream of the Unified Field*

1997: Lisel Mueller—*Alive Together: New and Selected Poems*

1998: Charles Wright—*Black Zodiac*

1999: Mark Strand—*Blizzard of One*

2000: C. K. Williams—*Repair*

2001: Stephen Dunn—*Different Hours*

2002: Carl Dennis—*Practical Gods*

2003: Paul Muldoon—*Moy Sand and Gravel*

2004: Franz Wright—*Walking to Martha's Vineyard*

2005: Ted Kooser—*Delights and Shadows*

2006: Claudia Emerson—*Late Wife*

2007: Natasha Trethewey—*Native Guard*

2008: Robert Hass—*Time and Materials*

2009: W. S. Merwin—*The Shadow of Sirius*

2010: Rae Armantrout—*Versed*

QUEEN'S GOLD MEDAL FOR POETRY

A special committee, selected and chaired by the British poet laureate, selects for this medal a poet from any nation or realm of the British Commonwealth.

1934: Laurence Whistler

1937: W. H. Auden

1940: Michael Thwaites

1952: Andrew Young

1953: Arthur Waley

1954: Ralph Hodgson

1955: Ruth Pitter

1956: Edmund Blunden

1957: Siegfried Sassoon

1959: Frances Cornford

1960: John Betjeman

1962: Christopher Fry

1963: William Plomer

1964: R. S. Thomas

1965: Philip Larkin

1967: Charles Causley

1968: Robert Graves

1969: Stevie Smith

1970: Roy Fuller
1971: Stephen Spender
1973: John Heath-Stubbs
1974: Ted Hughes
1977: Norman Nicholson
1981: D. J. Enright
1986: Norman MacCaig
1988: Derek Walcott
1989: Allen Curnow
1990: Sorley Maclean
1991: Judith Wright

1992: Kathleen Raine
1996: Peter Redgrove
1998: Les Murray
2000: Edwin Morgan
2001: Michael Longley
2002: Peter Porter
2003: U. A. Fanthorpe
2004: Hugo Williams
2006: Fleur Adcock
2007: James Fenton
2010: Don Paterson

QUEENSLAND PREMIER'S LITERARY AWARDS

Inaugurated in 1999, the Queensland Premier's Literary Awards are a leading literary awards program within Australia, with prizes in more than fourteen categories. The Arts Queensland Judith Wright Calanthe Award is given each year for the best poetry collection.

2004: Judith Beveridge—*Wolf Notes*
2005: Sarah Day—*The Ship*
2006: John Kinsella—*The New Arcadia*
2007: Laurie Duggan—*The Passenger*

2008: David Malouf—*Typewriter Music*
2009: Emma Jones—*The Striped World*
2010: Peter Boyle—*Apo crypha*

JUAN RULFO PRIZE FOR LATIN AMERICAN AND CARIBBEAN LITERATURE

The Guadalajara International Book Fair in Mexico presents its annual literary award to a writer from the Americas who writes in Spanish, Portuguese, French, or English. Award organizers include Mexico's National Council for Culture and Arts and the University of Guadalajara. The list below includes only poets who have received the award.

1991: Nicanor Parra (Chile)
1993: Eliseo Diego (Cuba)
1998: Olga Orozco (Argentina)
2000: Juan Gelman (Argentina)
2002: Cintio Vitier (Cuba)

2004: Juan Goytisolo (Spain)
2005: Tomás Segovia (Mexico)
2007: Fernando del Paso (Mexico)
2009: Rafael Cadenas (Venezuela)

SHELLEY MEMORIAL AWARD

Awarded by the Poetry Society of America to an American poet on the basis of genius and need.

1929: Conrad Aiken
1930: Lizette Woodworth Reese
1931: Archibald MacLeish
1932: no award
1933: Lola Ridge and Frances Frost

1934: Lola Ridge and Marya Zaturenska
1935: Josephine Miles
1936: Charlotte Wilder and Ben Belitt
1937: Lincoln Fitzell
1938: Robert Francis and Harry Brown

1939: Herbert Bruncken and Winfield T. Scott
1940: Marianne Moore
1941: Ridgely Torrence
1942: Robert Penn Warren
1943: Edgar Lee Masters
1944: E. E. Cummings
1945: Karl Shapiro
1946: Rolfe Humphries
1947: Janet Lewis
1948: John Berryman
1949: Louis Kent
1950: Jeremy Ingalls
1951: Richard Eberhart
1952: Elizabeth Bishop
1953: Kenneth Patchen
1954: Leonie Adams
1955: Robert Fitzgerald
1956: George Abbe
1957: Kenneth Rexroth
1958: Rose Garcia Villa
1959: Delmore Schwartz
1960: Robinson Jeffers
1961: Theodore Roethke
1962: Eric Barker
1963: William Stafford
1964: Ruth Stone
1965: David Ignatow
1966: Anne Sexton
1967: May Swenson
1968: Anne Stanford
1969: X. J. Kennedy and Mary Oliver
1970: Adrienne Rich and Louise Townsend Nicholl
1971: Galway Kinnell
1972: John Ashbery and Richard Wilbur
1973: W. S. Merwin
1974: Edward Field

1975: Gwendolyn Brooks
1976: Muriel Rukeyser
1977: Jane Cooper and William Everson
1978: Hayden Carruth
1979: Julia Randall
1980: Robert Creeley
1981: Alan Dugan
1982: Jon Anderson and Leo Connellan
1983: Denise Levertov and Robert Duncan
1984: Etheridge Knight
1986: Gary Snyder
1987: Mona Van Duyn
1988: Dennis Schmitz
1989: no award
1990: Thomas McGrath and Theodore Weiss
1991: Shirley Kaufman
1992: Lucille Clifton
1993: Josephine Jacobsen
1994: Kenneth Koch and Cathy Song
1995: Stanley Kunitz
1996: Robert Pinsky and Anne Waldman
1997: Frank Bidart
1998: Eleanor Ross Taylor
1999: Tom Sleigh
2000: Jean Valentine
2001: Alice Notley and Michael Palmer
2002: Angela Jackson and Marie Ponsot
2003: James McMichael
2004: Yusef Komunyakaa
2005: Lyn Hejinian
2006: George Stanley
2007: Kimiko Hahn
2008: Ed Roberson
2009: Ron Padgett and Gary Young
2010: Kenneth Irby and Eileen Myles

WALLACE STEVENS AWARD

Awarded by the Academy of American Poets to a poet for outstanding and proven mastery of the art of poetry.

1994: W. S. Merwin
1995: James Tate

1996: Adrienne Rich
1997: Anthony Hecht

1998: A. R. Ammons
1999: Jackson MacLow
2000: Frank Bidart
2001: John Ashbery
2002: Ruth Stone
2003: Richard Wilbur

2004: Mark Strand
2005: Gerald Stern
2006: Michael Palmer
2007: Charles Simic
2008: Louise Glück
2009: Jean Valentine

KINGSLEY TUFTS POETRY AWARD

Claremont Graduate University presents the annual Kingsley Tufts Poetry Award for a single collection of a poet's work.

1993: Susan Mitchell—*Rapture*
1994: Yusef Komunyakaa—*Neon Vernacular*
1995: Thomas Lux—*Split Horizon*
1996: Deborah Digges—*Rough Music*
1997: Campbell McGrath—*Spring Comes to Chicago*
1998: John Koethe—*Falling Water*
1999: B. H. Fairchild—*The Art of the Lathe*
2000: Robert Wrigley—*Reign of Snakes*
2001: Alan Shapiro—*The Dead Alive and Busy*

2002: Carl Phillips—*The Tether*
2003: Linda Gregerson—*Waterborne*
2004: Henri Cole—*Middle Earth*
2005: Michael Ryan—*New and Selected Poems*
2006: Lucia Perillo—*Luck Is Luck*
2007: Rodney Jones—*Salvation Blues*
2008: Tom Sleigh—*Space Walk*
2009: Matthea Harvey—*Modern Life*
2010: D. A. Powell—*Chronic*

TIN UJEVIĆ AWARD

The Tin Ujević Award is an award given for contributions to Croatian poetry. Founded in 1980 and awarded by the Croatian Writers' Society, it is considered the most prestigious such award in Croatia.

1981: Nikica Petrak—"Tiha knjiga"
1982: Slavko Mihalić—"Pohvala praznom džepu"
1983: Irena Vrkljan—"U koži moje sestre"
1984: Nikola Milićević—"Nepovrat"
1985: Branimir Bošnjak—"Semanti ka gladovanja"
1986: Igor Zidić—"Strijela od stakla"
1987: Dragutin Tadijanović—"Kruh svagdanji"
1988: Tonko Maroević—"Trag roga ne bez vraga"
1989: Tonći Petrasov Marović—"Moći ne govoriti"
1990: Luko Paljetak—"Snižena vrata"
1991: Vlado Gotovac—"Crna kazaljka"
1992: Zvonimir Golob—"Rana"
1993: Mate Ganza—"Knjiga bdjenja"
1994: Dražen Katunarić—"Nebo/Zemlja"
1995: Vladimir Pavlović—"Gral"

1996: Dubravko Horvatić—"Ratnoa noć"
1997: Boris Domagoj Biletić—"Radovi na nekropoli"
1998: Gordana Benić—"Laterna magica"
1999: Andrijana Škunca—"Novaljski svjetlopis"
2000: Mario Suško—"Versus axsul"
2001: Ivan Slamnig—"Ranjeni tenk" (posthumous)
2002: Petar Gudelj—"Po zraku i po vodi"
2003: Vesna Parun—"Suze putuju"
2004: Alojzije Majetić—"Odmicanje pau ine"
2005: Borben Vladović—"Tijat"
2006: Željko Knežević—"Kopito trajnoga konja"
2007: Ante Stamać—"Vrijeme, vrijeme"
2008: Miroslav Slavko Mađer—"Stihovi dugih naziva"
2009: Tomislav Marijan Bilosnić—"Molitve"

WALT WHITMAN AWARD

Awarded by the Academy of American Poets to a poet for the publication of a distinguished first collection of poetry.

1975: Reg Saner—*Climbing into the Roots*

1976: Laura Gilpin—*The Hocus-Pocus of the Universe*

1977: Lauren Shakely—*Guilty Bystander*

1978: Karen Snow—*Wonders*

1979: David Bottoms—*Shooting Rats at the Bibb County Dump*

1980: Jared Carter—*Work, for the Night Is Coming*

1981: Alberto Ríos—*Whispering to Fool the Wind*

1982: Anthony Petrosky—*Jurgis Petraskas*

1983: Christopher Gilbert—*Across the Mutual Landscape*

1984: Eric Pankey—*For the New Year*

1985: Christianne Balk—*Bindweed*

1986: Chris Llewellyn—*Fragments from the Fire*

1987: Judith Baumel—*The Weight of Numbers*

1988: April Bernard—*Blackbird Bye Bye*

1989: Martha Hollander—*The Game of Statues*

1990: Elaine Terranova—*The Cult of the Right Hand*

1991: Greg Glazner—*From the Iron Chair*

1992: Stephen Yenser—*The Fire in All Things*

1993: Alison Hawthorne Deming—*Science and Other Poems*

1994: Jan Richman—*Because the Brain Can Be Talked into Anything*

1995: Nicole Cooley—*Resurrection*

1996: Joshua Clover—*Madonna anno domini*

1997: Barbara Ras—*Bite Every Sorrow*

1998: Jan Heller Levi—*Once I Gazed at You in Wonder*

1999: Judy Jordan—*Carolina Ghost Woods*

2000: Ben Doyle—*Radio, Radio*

2001: John Canaday—*The Invisible World*

2002: Sue Kwock Kim—*Notes from the Divided Country*

2003: Tony Tost—*Invisible Bride*

2004: Geri Doran—*Resin*

2005: Mary Rose O'Reilley—*Half Wild*

2006: Anne Pierson Wiese—*Floating City*

2007: Sally Van Doren—*Sex at Noon Taxes*

2008: Jonathan Thirkield—*The Walker's Corridor*

2009: J. Michael Martinez—*Heredities*

2010: Carl Adamshick—*Curses and Wishes*

YALE SERIES OF YOUNGER POETS

This annual event of Yale University Press aims to publish the first collection of a promising American poet. Founded in 1919, it is the oldest annual literary award in the United States. Judges have included Stephen Vincent Benét (1933-1942), Archibald MacLeish (1944-1946), W. H. Auden (1947-1959), Stanley Kunitz (1969-1977), W. S. Merwin (1998-2003), Louise Glück (2003-2010), and Carl Phillips (2011-   ). Years reflect publication dates.

1919: John Chipman—*Farrar Forgotten Shrines*

1919: Howard Buck—*The Tempering*

1920: Darl MacLeod Boyle—*Where Lilith Dances*

1920: Thomas Caldecot Chubb—*The White God, and Other Poems*

1920: David Osborne Hamilton—*Four Gardens*

1920: Alfred Raymond Bellinger—*Spires and Poplars*

1921: Hervey Allen—*Wampum and Old Gold*

1921: Viola C. White—*Horizons*

1921: Oscar Williams—*Golden Darkness*

1921: Theodore H. Banks, Jr.—*Wild Geese*

1922: Bernard Raymund—*Hidden Waters*

1922: Medora C. Addison—*Dreams and a Sword*

1922: Paul Tanaquil—*Attitudes*

1922: Harold Vinal—*White April*

1923: Marion M. Boyd—*Silver Wands*

1923: Amos Niven Wilder—*Battle-Retrospect*

1923: Beatrice E. Harmon—*Mosaics*

1923: Dean B. Lyman, Jr.—*The Last Lutanist*

1924: Elizabeth Jessup—*Blake Up and Down*

1925: Dorothy E. Reid—*Coach into Pumpkin*

1926: Eleanor Slater—*Quest*

1926: Thomas Hornsby Ferril—*High Passage*

1927: Lindley Williams Hubbell—*Dark Pavilion*

1928: Ted Olson—*A Stranger and Afraid*

1928: Francis Claiborne Mason—*This Unchanging Mask*

1928: Mildred Bowers—*Twist o' Smoke*

1929: Frances M. Frost—*Hemlock Wall*

1929: Henri Faust—*Half-Light and Overture*

1930: Louise Owen—*Virtuosa*

1931: Dorothy Belle Flanagan—*Dark Certainty*

1932: Paul Engle—*Worn Earth*

1933: Shirley Barker—*The Dark Hills Under*

1934: James Agee—*Permit Me Voyage*

1935: Muriel Rukeyser—*Theory of Flight*

1936: Edward Weismiller—*The Deer Come Down*

1937: Margaret Haley—*The Gardener Mind*

1938: Joy Davidman—*Letter to a Comrade*

1939: Reuel Denney—*The Connecticut River, and Other Poems*

1940: Norman Rosten—*Return Again, Traveler*

1941: Jeremy Ingalls—*The Metaphysical Sword*

1942: Margaret Walker—*For My People*

1944: William Meredith—*Love Letters from an Impossible Land*

1945: Charles E. Butler—*Cut Is the Branch*

1946: Eve Merriam—*Family Circle*

1947: Joan Murray—*Poems*

1948: Robert Horan—*A Beginning*

1949: Rosalie Moore—*The Grasshopper's Man, and Other Poems*

1951: Adrienne Rich—*A Change of World*

1952: W. S. Merwin—*A Mask for Janus*

1953: Edgar Bogardus—*Various Jangling Keys*

1954: Daniel Hoffman—*An Armada of Thirty Whales*

1956: John Ashbery—*Some Trees*

1957: James Wright—*The Green Wall*

1958: John Hollander—*A Crackling of Thorns*

1959: William Dickey—*Of the Festivity*

1960: George Starbuck—*Bone Thoughts*

1961: Alan Dugan—*Poems*

1962: Jack Gilbert—*Views of Jeopardy*

1963: Sandra Hochman—*Manhattan Pastures*

1964: Peter Davison—*The Breaking of the Day*

1965: Jean Valentine—*Dream Barker*

1967: James Tate—*The Lost Pilot*

1968: Helen Chasin—*Coming Close, and Other Poems*

1969: Judith Johnson—*Sherwin Uranium Poems*

1970: Hugh Seidman—*Collecting Evidence*

1971: Peter Klappert—*Lugging Vegetables to Nantucket*

1972: Michael Casey—*Obscenities*

1973: Robert Hass—*Field Guide*

1974: Michael Ryan—*Threats Instead of Trees*

1975: Maura Stanton—*Snow on Snow*

1976: Carolyn Forché—*Gathering the Tribes*

1977: Olga Broumas—*Beginning with O*

1978: Bin Ramke—*The Difference Between Night and Day*

1979: Leslie Ullman—*Natural Histories*

1980: William Virgil Davis—*One Way to Reconstruct the Scene*

1981: John Bensko—*Green Soldiers*

1982: David Wojahn—*Icehouse Lights*

1983: Cathy Song—*Picture Bride*

1984: Richard Kenney—*The Evolution of the Flightless Bird*

1985: Pamela Alexander—*Navigable Waterways*

1986: George Bradley—*Terms to Be Met*

1987: Julie Agoos—*Above the Land*

1988: Brigit Pegeen Kelly—*To the Place of Trumpets*

1989: Thomas Bolt—*Out of the Woods*

1990: Daniel Hall—*Hermit with Landscape*

1991: Christiane Jacox Kyle—*Bears Dancing in the Northern Air*

1992: Nicholas Samaras—*Hands of the Saddlemaker*

1993: Jody Gladding—*Stone Crop*

1994: Valerie Wohlfeld—*Thinking the World Visible*

1995: Tony Crunk—*Living in the Resurrection*

1996: Ellen Hinsey—*Cities of Memory*

1997: Talvikki Ansel—*My Shining Archipelago*

1999: Craig Arnold—*Shells*

2000: Davis McCombs—*Ultima Thule*

2001: Maurice Manning—*Laurence Booth's Book of Visions*

2002: Sean Singer—*Discography*

2003: Loren Goodman—*Famous Americans*

2004: Peter Streckfus—*The Cuckoo*

2005: Richard Siken—*Crush*

2006: Jay Hopler—*Green Squall*
2007: Jessica Fisher—*Frail-Craft*
2008: Fady Joudah—*The Earth in the Attic*

2009: Arda Collins—*It Is Daylight*
2010: Ken Chen—*Juvenilia*
2011: Katherine Larson—*Radial Symmetry*

INDEXES

GEOGRAPHICAL INDEX OF ESSAYS

AFRICA
African Poetry, 15
Postcolonial Criticism, 769
Postcolonial Poetry, 500

ASIA. *See* **CHINA; INDIA; JAPAN; TIBET**

AUSTRALIA
Australian and New Zealand Poetry, 30
Postcolonial Criticism, 769
Postcolonial Poetry, 500

BRAZIL
Latin American Poetry, 435

CANADA
Canadian Poetry, 37
Postcolonial Criticism, 769
Postcolonial Poetry, 500

CHILE
Latin American Poetry, 435

CHINA
Chinese Poetry, 54
Tibetan Poetry, 604

CROATIA
Croatian Poetry, 71

CZECH REPUBLIC. *See also* **SLOVAKIA**
Czech Poetry, 78

EL SALVADOR
Latin American Poetry, 435

ENGLAND
Confessional Poets, 668

English and American Poetry in the Nineteenth Century, 174
English and American Poetry in the Twentieth Century, 185
English and Continental Poetry in the Fourteenth Century, 98
English Poetry in the Eighteenth Century, 160
English Poetry in the Fifteenth Century, 120
English Poetry in the Seventeenth Century, 144
English Poetry in the Sixteenth Century, 130
Green Movement Poets, 690
Imagists, 644
Metaphysical Poets, 615
Modernists, 650
Movement Poets, 679
Postcolonial Criticism, 769
Restoration Poetry, 620
Romantic Poets, 626

EUROPE
European Oral and Epic Traditions, 214

FINLAND
Scandinavian Poetry, 526

FRANCE
French Poetry Since 1700, 254
French Poetry to 1700, 232
French Symbolists, 639

GERMANY
East German Poetry, 87
German Poetry Since Reunification, 315

German Poetry to 1800, 283
German Poetry: 1800 to Reunification, 298

GREAT BRITAIN. *See also* **ENGLAND**
Confessional Poets, 668
English and American Poetry in the Nineteenth Century, 174
English and American Poetry in the Twentieth Century, 185
English and Continental Poetry in the Fourteenth Century, 98
English Poetry in the Eighteenth Century, 160
English Poetry in the Fifteenth Century, 120
English Poetry in the Seventeenth Century, 144
English Poetry in the Sixteenth Century, 130
Green Movement Poets, 690
Imagists, 644
Metaphysical Poets, 615
Modernists, 650
Movement Poets, 679
Postcolonial Criticism, 769
Restoration Poetry, 620
Romantic Poets, 626

GREECE
Greek Poetry in Antiquity, 320
Greek Poetry Since 1820, 331
Macedonian Poetry, 475

HUNGARY
Hungarian Poetry, 352

INDIA
Indian English Poetry, 365
Postcolonial Poetry, 500

ITALY

Italian Poetry Since 1800, 393

Italian Poetry to 1800, 377

JAPAN

Japanese Poetry Since 1800, 427

Japanese Poetry to 1800, 412

LATIN AMERICA

Latin American Poetry, 435

MEXICO

Latin American Poetry, 435

NEW ZEALAND

Australian and New Zealand
    Poetry, 30

Postcolonial Criticism, 769

NICARAGUA

Latin American Poetry, 435

PERU

Latin American Poetry, 435

POLAND

Polish Poetry, 489

ROMAN EMPIRE

Latin Poetry, 441

RUSSIA

Russian Poetry, 509

SERBIA

Macedonian Poetry, 475

Serbian Poetry, 566

SLOVAKIA. *See also* **CZECH
    REPUBLIC**

Slovak Poetry, 573

SLOVENIA

Slovenian Poetry, 579

SOVIET UNION. *See* **RUSSIA**

SPAIN

Catalan Poetry, 48

Spanish Poetry Since 1400, 592

Spanish Poetry to 1400, 583

SWEDEN

Scandinavian Poetry, 526

TIBET

Tibetan Poetry, 604

UNITED STATES

African American Poetry, 3

Asian American Poetry, 21

Beat Poets, 661

Black Mountain School, 684

Confessional Poets, 668

English and American Poetry in
    the Nineteenth Century, 174

English and American Poetry in
    the Twentieth Century, 185

Fireside Poets, 633

Green Movement Poets, 690

Harlem Renaissance, 655

Imagists, 644

Latino Poetry, 466

Metaphysical Poets, 615

Modernists, 650

Native American Poetry, 478

New York School, 674

Postcolonial Criticism, 769

WEST INDIES

Caribbean Poetry, 43

Postcolonial Poetry, 500

YUGOSLAVIA. *See also*
    **CROATIA; SERBIA;
    SLOVENIA**

Macedonian Poetry, 475

Critical Survey of Poetry Series: Master List of Contents

The Critical Survey of Poetry, Fourth Edition, *profiles more than eight hundred poets in four subsets:* American Poets; British, Irish, and Commonwealth Poets; European Poets; *and* World Poets. *Although some individuals could have been included in more than one subset, each poet appears in only one subset. A fifth subset,* Topical Essays, *includes more than seventy overviews covering geographical areas, historical periods, movements, and critical approaches.*

AMERICAN POETS

Volume 1

Publisher's Note v
Contributors ix
Contents. xv
Complete List of
    Contents xvii
Pronunciation Key xxiii

Diane Ackerman 1
Léonie Adams 4
Ai. 8
Conrad Aiken 12
Elizabeth Alexander 17
Sherman Alexie. 21
Agha Shahid Ali 24
Paula Gunn Allen 27
Julia Alvarez 31
A. R. Ammons 37
Maggie Anderson. 43
Maya Angelou 46
James Applewhite. 51
John Ashbery 55
Rose Ausländer 65

Jimmy Santiago Baca. . . . 71
David Baker. 77
John Balaban 81
Mary Jo Bang 85
Amiri Baraka 89
Mary Barnard 100
Paul Beatty 107
Robin Becker 110
Ben Belitt 114

Marvin Bell 119
Stephen Vincent Benét . . . 124
William Rose Benét 128
Charles Bernstein 132
Daniel Berrigan 137
Ted Berrigan. 143
Wendell Berry 146
John Berryman 155
Frank Bidart 162
Elizabeth Bishop 169
John Peale Bishop. 177
Paul Blackburn 180
Robert Bly 188
Louise Bogan 197
Arna Bontemps 205
Philip Booth 209
David Bottoms. 216
Edgar Bowers 219
Anne Bradstreet 223
Edward Kamau
    Brathwaite 228
Richard Brautigan 239
William Bronk. 243
Gwendolyn Brooks 247
Sterling A. Brown 254
William Cullen Bryant . . . 259
Charles Bukowski 264
Witter Bynner 274

Hayden Carruth 278
Raymond Carver 284
Turner Cassity 291
Lorna Dee Cervantes 298

Fred Chappell 303
Marilyn Chin 307
John Ciardi 312
Sandra Cisneros 318
Amy Clampitt 322
Lucille Clifton 326
Andrei Codrescu. 331
Henri Cole. 333
Michael Collier 336
Billy Collins. 341
Cid Corman 347
Alfred Corn 352
Gregory Corso. 356
Henri Coulette. 362
Malcolm Cowley 366
Louis Coxe 375
Hart Crane 379
Stephen Crane 387
Robert Creeley. 392
Victor Hernández Cruz . . . 400
Countée Cullen 404
E. E. Cummings 410
J. V. Cunningham 417

Philip Dacey. 425
Robert Dana 430
Peter Davison 437
Carl Dennis 441
Toi Derricotte 444
James Dickey 448
Emily Dickinson. 455
Diane di Prima. 464
Owen Dodson 471

Edward Dorn 474
Mark Doty 481
Rita Dove 486
Norman Dubie 493
Alan Dugan 498
Paul Laurence Dunbar 502
Robert Duncan 509
Stephen Dunn 517

Cornelius Eady 521
Richard Eberhart 526
W. D. Ehrhart 532
James A. Emanuel 538
Claudia Emerson 541
Ralph Waldo Emerson 544
Louise Erdrich 553
Martín Espada 559
Mari Evans 563
William Everson 567

B. H. Fairchild 579
Kenneth Fearing 582
Irving Feldman 588
Beth Ann Fennelly 591
Lawrence Ferlinghetti 593
Edward Field 602

Volume 2
Contents xxxi
Complete List of
   Contents xxxiii
Pronunciation Key xxxix

Roland Flint 607
Carolyn Forché 611
Philip Freneau 618
Robert Frost 625
Alice Fulton 633

Tess Gallagher 639
Brendan Galvin 644
Isabella Gardner 653
George Garrett 656
Amy Gerstler 660
Kahlil Gibran 663

Margaret Gibson 670
Jack Gilbert 673
Allen Ginsberg 677
Dana Gioia 688
Nikki Giovanni 692
Diane Glancy 702
Mel Glenn 706
Louise Glück 710
Albert Goldbarth 719
Jorie Graham 725
Linda Gregerson 732
Linda Gregg 735
Horace Gregory 738
Eamon Grennan 741
Barbara Guest 745
Edgar A. Guest 748

H. D. 754
Marilyn Hacker 761
Kimiko Hahn 768
John Meade Haines 772
Donald Hall 775
Patricia Hampl 785
Joy Harjo 789
Michael S. Harper 794
Jim Harrison 802
Robert Hass 814
Robert Hayden 820
Anthony Hecht 826
Lyn Hejinian 836
William Heyen 841
Robert Hillyer 850
Edward Hirsch 853
Jane Hirshfield 858
Daniel Hoffman 863
Linda Hogan 871
John Hollander 877
Anselm Hollo 887
Oliver Wendell Holmes . . . 893
Garrett Kaoru Hongo 900
George Moses Horton 905
Richard Howard 909
Susan Howe 913
Barbara Howes 921
Andrew Hudgins 924

Langston Hughes 927
Richard Hugo 934
Erica Hunt 938

David Ignatow 941

Josephine Jacobsen 950
Mark Jarman 953
Randall Jarrell 957
Robinson Jeffers 963
James Weldon Johnson . . . 972
Ronald Johnson 976
June Jordan 981
Donald Justice 986

Mary Karr 993
Julia Kasdorf 996
Laura Kasischke 999
Bob Kaufman 1002
Weldon Kees 1006
Brigit Pegeen Kelly 1012
Robert Kelly 1015
X. J. Kennedy 1020
Jane Kenyon 1028
Galway Kinnell 1033
David Kirby 1039
Lincoln Kirstein 1042
Carolyn Kizer 1046
Etheridge Knight 1053
Kenneth Koch 1058
Yusef Komunyakaa 1064
Ted Kooser 1070
Maxine Kumin 1073
Stanley Kunitz 1083

Sidney Lanier 1095
Li-Young Lee 1102
Brad Leithauser 1108
Denise Levertov 1111
Philip Levine 1120
Larry Levis 1127
Janet Lewis 1132
Lyn Lifshin 1136
Sarah Lindsay 1143
Vachel Lindsay 1146
John Logan 1153

Henry Wadsworth
  Longfellow 1157
Audre Lorde 1166
Amy Lowell 1172
James Russell Lowell . . . 1180
Robert Lowell 1187
Mina Loy 1200
Wing Tek Lum 1204

Volume 3
Contents xlvii
Complete List of
  Contents xlix
Pronunciation Key lv

Michael McClure 1207
Cynthia Macdonald 1211
Walt McDonald 1215
Phyllis McGinley 1221
Thomas McGrath 1225
Heather McHugh 1230
Claude McKay 1234
Nathaniel Mackey 1241
Archibald MacLeish 1244
James McMichael 1255
Sandra McPherson 1258
Haki R. Madhubuti 1265
Edwin Markham 1274
Edgar Lee Masters 1278
William Matthews 1284
Peter Meinke 1290
Herman Melville 1294
Samuel Menashe 1302
William Meredith 1308
James Merrill 1317
Thomas Merton 1325
W. S. Merwin 1331
Josephine Miles 1340
Edna St. Vincent Millay . . . 1344
Vassar Miller 1349
James Masao Mitsui 1354
N. Scott Momaday 1358
Marianne Moore 1364
Pat Mora 1371
Howard Moss 1375

Thylias Moss 1380
Lisel Mueller 1383
Harryette Mullen 1387
David Mura 1390
Carol Muske 1396

Ogden Nash 1401
John G. Neihardt 1405
Howard Nemerov 1409
Lorine Niedecker 1415
John Frederick Nims 1421
Kathleen Norris 1428
Alice Notley 1431
Naomi Shihab Nye 1435

Joyce Carol Oates 1443
Frank O'Hara 1451
Sharon Olds 1456
Mary Oliver 1463
Charles Olson 1469
George Oppen 1477
Joel Oppenheimer 1481
Gregory Orr 1485
Simon Ortiz 1493
Judith Ortiz Cofer 1499
Alicia Suskin Ostriker . . . 1502

Grace Paley 1506
Dorothy Parker 1509
Linda Pastan 1514
Kenneth Patchen 1520
Molly Peacock 1525
Carl Phillips 1529
Marge Piercy 1532
Robert Pinsky 1538
Sylvia Plath 1547
Stanley Plumly 1556
Edgar Allan Poe 1561
Marie Ponsot 1569
Anne Porter 1573
Ezra Pound 1577
Reynolds Price 1586

Carl Rakosi 1590
Dudley Randall 1595

Claudia Rankine 1602
John Crowe Ransom 1605
Ishmael Reed 1612
Lizette Woodworth
  Reese 1616
Kenneth Rexroth 1621
Charles Reznikoff 1627
Adrienne Rich 1633
Laura Riding 1642
James Whitcomb Riley . . . 1645
Alberto Ríos 1654
Tomás Rivera 1657
Edwin Arlington
  Robinson 1660
Carolyn M. Rodgers 1668
Theodore Roethke 1671
Pattiann Rogers 1679
Edwin Rolfe 1682
Muriel Rukeyser 1686

David St. John 1693
Sonia Sanchez 1698
Carl Sandburg 1704
Sherod Santos 1711
May Sarton 1714
Leslie Scalapino 1724
Gjertrud
  Schnackenberg 1728
James Schuyler 1732
Delmore Schwartz 1738
Winfield Townley
  Scott 1746
Alan Seeger 1750
Anne Sexton 1753
Alan Shapiro 1759
Karl Shapiro 1764
Enid Shomer 1769
Jane Shore 1773
Leslie Marmon Silko 1777
Shel Silverstein 1781
Charles Simic 1785
Louis Simpson 1793
L. E. Sissman 1802
David Slavitt 1809
Dave Smith 1817

Volume 4

Contents lxi
Complete List of
   Contents lxiii
Pronunciation Key. lxix

William Jay Smith 1825
W. D. Snodgrass 1831
Gary Snyder 1840
Cathy Song. 1853
Gilbert Sorrentino 1858
Gary Soto. 1862
Jack Spicer 1868
William Stafford 1872
Timothy Steele 1881
Gertrude Stein 1885
Gerald Stern 1893
Wallace Stevens 1905
James Still 1913
Mark Strand 1918
Lucien Stryk 1927
Cole Swensen 1931
May Swenson 1934

Allen Tate 1941
James Tate 1947
Edward Taylor 1959
Henry Taylor 1968
Sara Teasdale. 1974
Henry David Thoreau . . . 1977
Melvin B. Tolson. 1984
Jean Toomer 1988
Natasha Trethewey. 1995
Frederick Goddard
   Tuckerman 1998
Chase Twichell. 2002

Louis Untermeyer 2007
John Updike 2016

Jean Valentine 2024
Mark Van Doren 2027
Mona Van Duyn 2032
Jones Very 2039
Peter Viereck. 2042
José García Villa 2048
Ellen Bryant Voigt 2054

David Wagoner. 2059
Diane Wakoski 2068
Anne Waldman. 2076
Alice Walker 2080
Margaret Walker 2086
Ronald Wallace. 2090
Robert Penn Warren 2094
Bruce Weigl 2102
James Welch 2107
Philip Whalen 2111
Phillis Wheatley 2114
John Hall Wheelock 2123
John Wheelwright 2126
Walt Whitman 2130
Reed Whittemore. 2140
John Greenleaf
   Whittier. 2144
Richard Wilbur. 2151
C. K. Williams 2161
Miller Williams 2168
Sherley Anne
   Williams 2172
William Carlos
   Williams 2175
Yvor Winters. 2184

David Wojahn 2190
Baron Wormser 2196
C. D. Wright 2203
Charles Wright. 2207
Franz Wright. 2217
James Wright. 2221
Jay Wright 2231
Elinor Wylie 2240

Mitsuye Yamada 2244
Al Young. 2248
Dean Young 2257

Paul Zimmer 2261
Louis Zukofsky 2265

RESOURCES

Explicating Poetry 2273
Language and
   Linguistics 2282
Glossary of Poetical
   Terms 2294
Bibliography 2307
Guide to Online
   Resources. 2314
Time Line 2318
Major Awards 2321
Chronological List
   of Poets 2334

INDEXES

Categorized Index
   of Poets 2341
Master List of
   Contents. 2357
Subject Index. 2369

BRITISH, IRISH, AND COMMONWEALTH POETS

Volume 1

Publisher's Note v
Contributors ix
Contents xiii

Complete List of
   Contents xv
Pronunciation Key xix

Dannie Abse 1
Joseph Addison 7
Æ 13
Richard Aldington 17

William Allingham 23
Matthew Arnold 30
Margaret Atwood 37
W. H. Auden 47

Thomas Lovell Beddoes . . . 56
Patricia Beer 60
Aphra Behn 66
Hilaire Belloc 73
John Betjeman 80
Earle Birney 86
William Blake 91
Edmund Blunden 104
Eavan Boland 108
William Lisle Bowles . . . 119
Nicholas Breton 124
Robert Bridges 131
Emily Brontë 137
Rupert Brooke 144
Elizabeth Barrett
    Browning 149
Robert Browning 158
Basil Bunting 168
Robert Burns 173
Samuel Butler 180
Lord Byron 186

Cædmon 197
Thomas Campion 202
Thomas Carew 208
Lewis Carroll 213
Anne Carson 225
George Chapman 228
Thomas Chatterton 235
Geoffrey Chaucer 243
John Clare 254
Austin Clarke 261
Arthur Hugh Clough . . . 266
Leonard Cohen 272
Samuel Taylor
    Coleridge 276
William Collins 287
Padraic Colum 292
William Congreve 296
Henry Constable 301

Charles Cotton 306
Abraham Cowley 312
William Cowper 320
George Crabbe 327
Richard Crashaw 337
Cynewulf 344

Samuel Daniel 352
George Darley 359
Sir William
    Davenant 362
Donald Davie 367
Sir John Davies 375
Cecil Day Lewis 384
Thomas Dekker 390
Walter de la Mare 398
John Donne 405
Michael Drayton 417
William Drummond of
    Hawthornden 424
John Dryden 433
William Dunbar 442
Lawrence Durrell 451

T. S. Eliot 458
William Empson 468
Sir George Etherege 476

Volume 2
Contents xxvii
Complete List of
    Contents xxix
Pronunciation Key xxxiii

Sir Richard Fanshawe 481
James Fenton 487
Anne Finch 491
Edward FitzGerald 495
Roy Fuller 500

George Gascoigne 505
John Gay 512
Oliver Goldsmith 520
John Gower 525

Robert Graves 534
Thomas Gray 542
Robert Greene 548
Fulke Greville 555
Thom Gunn 560
Ivor Gurney 568

Arthur Henry Hallam 575
Thomas Hardy 579
Tony Harrison 588
Seamus Heaney 594
Anne Hébert 605
Felicia Dorothea
    Hemans 609
Robert Henryson 612
George Herbert 617
Robert Herrick 626
John Heywood 635
Geoffrey Hill 641
Thomas Hood 650
A. D. Hope 660
Gerard Manley Hopkins . . . 666
A. E. Housman 677
Ted Hughes 686
Leigh Hunt 694

Samuel Johnson 700
David Jones 707
Ben Jonson 711
James Joyce 719

Patrick Kavanagh 726
John Keats 731
Henry King 743
Thomas Kinsella 751
Rudyard Kipling 760

Charles Lamb 768
Walter Savage Landor 774
William Langland 780
Philip Larkin 786
D. H. Lawrence 795
Layamon 803
Irving Layton 808
Edward Lear 812

Thomas Lodge. 817
Christopher Logue. 823
Richard Lovelace 827
John Lydgate 832

George MacBeth. 841
Hugh MacDiarmid. 846
Louis MacNeice. 854
James Clarence Mangan. . . 866
Christopher Marlowe 870
Andrew Marvell 877
John Masefield 885
George Meredith 890
Charlotte Mew. 894
Christopher Middleton . . . 898
John Milton 905
John Montague 914
William Morris 924
Edwin Muir 933
Paul Muldoon 937
Les A. Murray. 946

Thomas Nashe. 953
Margaret Cavendish,
    duchess of Newcastle. . . 958
Nuala Ní Dhomhnaill 964

Volume 3
Contents xli
Complete List of
    Contents xliii
Pronunciation Key xlvii

John Oldham 969
Michael Ondaatje 973
Wilfred Owen 977

Coventry Patmore 983
Pearl-Poet 991
Harold Pinter. 1001
Alexander Pope 1005
E. J. Pratt. 1016

F. T. Prince 1021
Matthew Prior 1026

Francis Quarles. 1031

Sir Walter Ralegh 1037
Henry Reed. 1043
John Wilmot, earl of
    Rochester 1048
Isaac Rosenberg 1055
Christina Rossetti 1060
Dante Gabriel Rossetti . . . 1065

Thomas Sackville 1074
Siegfried Sassoon 1080
Sir Walter Scott 1087
Sir Charles Sedley 1094
Robert W. Service 1099
William Shakespeare. . . . 1105
Percy Bysshe Shelley . . . 1112
Sir Philip Sidney 1126
Sir Robert Sidney 1135
Jon Silkin. 1141
Edith Sitwell 1145
John Skelton 1153
Christopher Smart 1159
Stevie Smith 1164
Robert Southey. 1171
Robert Southwell. 1178
Stephen Spender 1183
Edmund Spenser 1191
Robert Louis
    Stevenson 1201
Sir John Suckling 1206
Henry Howard, earl of
    Surrey 1212
Jonathan Swift 1218
Algernon Charles
    Swinburne 1227

Alfred, Lord Tennyson. . . 1236
Dylan Thomas 1245

Edward Thomas 1252
R. S. Thomas. 1257
James Thomson 1260
James Thomson 1264
Charles Tomlinson 1268
Thomas Traherne. 1277

Henry Vaughan. 1284

Edmund Waller. 1290
Isaac Watts 1297
Oscar Wilde 1303
William Wordsworth 1310
Sir Thomas Wyatt 1322

William Butler
    Yeats 1330
Edward Young 1349

RESOURCES
Explicating Poetry 1357
Language and
    Linguistics 1366
Glossary of Poetical
    Terms 1378
Bibliography 1391
Guide to Online
    Resources 1401
Time Line 1405
Major Awards 1408
Chronological List
    of Poets 1415

INDEXES
Geographical Index
    of Poets 1421
Categorized Index
    of Poets 1425
Master List of
    Contents. 1437
Subject Index. 1448

EUROPEAN POETS

Volume 1

Publisher's Note v
Contributors ix
Contents xiii
Complete List of Contents. . . xv
Pronunciation Key xix

Endre Ady 1
Rafael Alberti 6
Vicente Aleixandre 12
Anacreon 17
Guillaume Apollinaire 22
Apollonius Rhodius. 30
Louis Aragon 35
János Arany. 42
Archilochus. 50
Ludovico Ariosto 56
Hans Arp 62

Mihály Babits. 68
Ingeborg Bachmann 72
Stanisław Barańczak 77
Charles Baudelaire 80
Samuel Beckett 87
Gustavo Adolfo Bécquer . . . 95
Pietro Bembo 101
Gottfried Benn. 107
Thomas Bernhard 112
Wolf Biermann 119
Johannes Bobrowski. 126
Giovanni Boccaccio 131
Matteo Maria Boiardo. . . . 135
Nicolas
　　Boileau-Despréaux. . . . 138
Yves Bonnefoy 142
Bertolt Brecht 149
André Breton 157
Breyten Breytenbach 162

Pedro Calderón de
　　la Barca. 170
Callimachus 175
Luís de Camões 180

Giosuè Carducci. 185
Rosalía de Castro 190
Catullus 197
Constantine P. Cavafy 204
Guido Cavalcanti 210
Paul Celan 214
Luis Cernuda 220
René Char 226
Charles d'Orléans 230
Alain Chartier 236
Christine de Pizan 240
Paul Claudel 244
Jean Cocteau. 253
Tristan Corbière 260

Gabriele D'Annunzio 264
Dante 270
Joachim du Bellay. 289
Jovan Dučić 292

Joseph von Eichendorff . . . 299
Gunnar Ekelöf. 306
Paul Éluard 313
Odysseus Elytis 317
Hans Magnus
　　Enzensberger. 323

J. V. Foix. 329
Jean Follain 335
Ugo Foscolo 340
Girolamo Fracastoro. 345

Federico García Lorca. . . . 355
Garcilaso de la Vega. 362
Théophile Gautier 368
Stefan George 377
Guido Gezelle 384
Giuseppe Giusti 391
Johann Wolfgang
　　von Goethe. 396
Eugen Gomringer 405
Luis de Góngora
　　y Argote 410

Gottfried von Strassburg. . . 415
Günter Grass. 418
Guillaume de Lorris
　　and Jean de Meung . . . 424
Jorge Guillén 430

Volume 2

Contents xxvii
Complete List of
　　Contents xxix
Pronunciation Key. xxxiii

Paavo Haavikko 435
Hartmann von Aue 441
Piet Hein. 447
Heinrich Heine 451
Zbigniew Herbert 458
Hesiod 465
Hermann Hesse 471
Hugo von Hofmannsthal. . . 478
Friedrich Hölderlin 485
Miroslav Holub 492
Arno Holz 497
Homer 502
Horace 510
Victor Hugo 518

Gyula Illyés 528

Juan Ramón Jiménez 533
Saint John of the Cross . . . 539
Judah ha-Levi 549
Juvenal. 553

Nikos Kazantzakis. 557
Karl Kraus. 563
Reiner Kunze 570

Jean de La Fontaine 577
Jules Laforgue. 584
Alphonse de Lamartine . . . 591
Luis de León. 597

Leonidas of Tarentum 602
Giacomo Leopardi. 607
Elias Lönnrot 617
Lucan 621
Lucretius. 627

Antonio Machado 633
François de Malherbe . . . 639
Stéphane Mallarmé 644
Itzik Manger. 650
Jorge Manrique 657
Alessandro Manzoni. . . . 660
Marie de France 666
Giambattista Marino. . . . 674
Martial. 678
Harry Martinson. 681
Meleager. 685
Henri Michaux. 688
Michelangelo 694
Adam Mickiewicz 702
Czesław Miłosz 709
Eugenio Montale 721
Christian Morgenstern. . . 727
Eduard Mörike. 732
Alfred de Musset 736

Gérard de Nerval 741
Novalis. 748

Blas de Otero 757
Ovid 763

Giovanni Pascoli. 771
Pier Paolo Pasolini 776
Cesare Pavese 783
Miodrag Pavlović 786
Charles-Pierre Péguy . . . 791
Nikos Pentzikis 797
Saint-John Perse. 801
Persius. 806
Fernando Pessoa. 811
Sándor Petőfi 816
Petrarch 828
Pindar 836
Poliziano. 841

Francis Ponge 848
Vasko Popa 856

Volume 3
Contents xli
Complete List of
   Contents xliii
Pronunciation Key xlvii

Jacques Prévert 861
Sextus Propertius 866

Salvatore Quasimodo 873

Miklós Radnóti 879
Pierre Reverdy. 883
Rainer Maria Rilke 889
Arthur Rimbaud 897
Yannis Ritsos 904
Pierre de Ronsard 912
Tadeusz Różewicz. 917

Umberto Saba 925
Nelly Sachs 930
Pedro Salinas 936
Sappho. 941
Friedrich Schiller 949
George Seferis. 957
Jaroslav Seifert 961
Antoni Słonimski 968
Juliusz Słowacki. 972
Edith Södergran 981
Dionysios Solomos 987
Gaspara Stampa 993
Statius 998
Anna Swir 1004
Wisława Szymborska . . . 1007

Torquato Tasso 1014
Esaias Tegnér. 1020
Theocritus 1023
Theognis 1029
Georg Trakl 1033
Tomas Tranströmer. . . . 1039
Tristan Tzara 1044

Miguel de Unamuno
   y Jugo 1051
Giuseppe Ungaretti. 1056

Paul Valéry. 1065
Lope de Vega Carpio. . . . 1073
Vergil 1080
Émile Verhaeren 1089
Paul Verlaine 1093
Alfred de Vigny 1099
François Villon. 1106
Mihály Vörösmarty 1112
Walther von der
   Vogelweide 1119

Adam Ważyk. 1126
Wolfram von
   Eschenbach 1130

Adam Zagajewski 1137
Stefan Zweig 1141

RESOURCES
Explicating Poetry 1151
Language and
   Linguistics 1160
Glossary of Poetical
   Terms 1172
Bibliography 1185
Guide to Online
   Resources 1199
Time Line 1202
Major Awards 1205
Chronological List
   of Poets 1211

INDEXES
Geographical Index
   of Poets 1217
Categorized Index
   of Poets 1220
Master List of
   Contents. 1229
Subject Index. 1240

WORLD POETS

Publisher's Note v
Contributors ix
Contents xi
Pronunciation Key xiii

Chinua Achebe 1
Anna Akhmatova 3
Claribel Alegría 9
Yehuda Amichai 14
Innokenty Annensky 21
Kofi Awoonor 25

Aleksandr Blok 33
Jorge Luis Borges 39
Joseph Brodsky 44

Ernesto Cardenal 52
Aimé Césaire 56
Michelle Cliff 61
Sor Juana Inés de la Cruz . . 64

Rubén Darío 71
Carlos Drummond de
    Andrade 76
Du Fu 84

Sergei Esenin 90

Firdusi 96

Enrique González
    Martínez 101

Hafiz 108
José Hernández 114
Nazim Hikmet 117

Issa 126

Vladislav Khodasevich . . . 133
Ko Un 138

Mikhail Lermontov 142
Li Bo 150
Li Qingzhao 157

Osip Mandelstam 163
Matsuo Bashō 170
Vladimir
    Mayakovsky . . . 176
Meng Haoran 182
Gabriela Mistral 185
Kenji Miyazawa 191

Pablo Neruda 196

Christopher Okigbo 205
Omar Khayyám 208

Dan Pagis 213
Nicanor Parra 216
Boris Pasternak 222
Octavio Paz 230
Alexander Pushkin 236

Alfonso Reyes 245
Ruan Ji 250
Jalāl al-Dīn Rūmī 255

Saʿdi 260
Léopold Senghor 264
Vikram Seth 272
Wole Soyinka 276

Rabindranath Tagore . . . 281
Tao Qian 288
Marina Tsvetayeva 293

César Vallejo 300
Vālmīki 308
Andrei Voznesensky 311

Derek Walcott 317
Wang Wei 326

Xie Lingyun 334

Yevgeny Yevtushenko 339
Yosano Akiko 349

Daisy Zamora 354

RESOURCES
Explicating Poetry 359
Language and
    Linguistics 368
Glossary of Poetical
    Terms 380
Bibliography 393
Guide to Online
    Resources 403
Time Line 406
Major Awards 408
Chronological List
    of Poets 413

INDEXES
Geographical Index
    of Poets 417
Categorized Index
    of Poets 419
Master List of
    Contents 423
Subject Index 434

TOPICAL ESSAYS

Volume 1

Publisher's Note v
Contributors ix
Contents xi
Complete List of
    Contents xiii

POETRY AROUND
THE WORLD

African American Poetry . . . 3
African Poetry 15
Asian American Poetry 21
Australian and New
    Zealand Poetry 30
Canadian Poetry 37
Caribbean Poetry 43
Catalan Poetry 48
Chinese Poetry 54
Croatian Poetry 71
Czech Poetry 78
East German Poetry 87
English and Continental
    Poetry in the
    Fourteenth Century 98
English Poetry in the
    Fifteenth Century 120
English Poetry in the
    Sixteenth Century 130
English Poetry in the
    Seventeenth Century . . . 144
English Poetry in the
    Eighteenth Century . . . 160
English and American
    Poetry in the
    Nineteenth Century . . . 174
English and American
    Poetry in the
    Twentieth Century 185
European Oral and Epic
    Traditions 214
French Poetry to 1700 232

French Poetry
    Since 1700 254
German Poetry to 1800 . . . 283
German Poetry: 1800 to
    Reunification 298
German Poetry Since
    Reunification 315
Greek Poetry in
    Antiquity 320
Greek Poetry
    Since 1820 331
Hungarian Poetry 352
Indian English Poetry 365
Italian Poetry to 1800 377
Italian Poetry
    Since 1800 393
Japanese Poetry
    to 1800 412
Japanese Poetry
    Since 1800 427
Latin American Poetry . . . 435
Latin Poetry 441
Latino Poetry 466

Volume 2

Contents xxi
Complete List
    of Contents xxiii

POETRY AROUND
THE WORLD (*cont.*)

Macedonian Poetry 475
Native American Poetry . . . 478
Polish Poetry 489
Postcolonial Poetry 500
Russian Poetry 509
Scandinavian Poetry 526
Serbian Poetry 566
Slovak Poetry 573
Slovenian Poetry 579

Spanish Poetry
    to 1400 583
Spanish Poetry
    Since 1400 592
Tibetan Poetry 604

LITERARY MOVEMENTS

Metaphysical Poets 615
Restoration Poetry 620
Romantic Poets 626
Fireside Poets 633
French Symbolists 639
Imagists 644
Modernists 650
Harlem Renaissance 655
Beat Poets 661
Confessional Poets 668
New York School 674
Movement Poets 679
Black Mountain School . . . 684
Green Movement Poets . . . 690

CRITICISM AND THEORY

Criticism from Plato
    to Eliot 699
Archetypal and
    Psychological
    Criticism 719
Cultural Criticism 731
Feminist Criticism 736
Formalistic Criticism 743
Linguistic Criticism 750
Marxist Criticism 760
New Historicism 764
Postcolonial
    Criticism 769
Queer Theory 774
Structuralist and
    Poststructuralist
    Criticism 780

RESOURCES
Explicating Poetry 789
Language and
    Linguistics 798
Glossary of Poetical
    Terms 810

Bibliography 823
Guide to Online
    Resources 851
Time Line 856
Major Awards 865

INDEXES
Geographical Index
    of Essays 893
Master List
    of Contents 895
Subject Index 906

CUMULATIVE INDEXES

Publisher's Note v
Contributors vii
Contents xix

RESOURCES
Bibliography 3
Guide to Online
    Resources 31
Time Line 36
Major Awards 45
Chronological List
    of Poets 71

INDEXES
Categorized Index of
    Poets and Essays 85
Geographical Index of
    Poets and Essays 121
Master List
    of Contents 133
Subject Index 145

SUBJECT INDEX

All personages whose names appear in **boldface type** in this index are the subject of articles in *Critical Survey of Poetry, Fourth Edition.*

"Aboriginal Charter of Rights" (Walker), 503

Aboriginal poetry, Australia, 503

Absalom and Achitophel (Dryden), 156, 622

Absurdist poets, 522

Academy of American Poets Fellowship, 865

Accademia dell'Arcadia, 387

Accentual meter, defined, 810

Accentual-syllabic meter, defined, 810

Achebe, Chinua, 770

Acmeism, 518

Addison, Joseph, 706

Adonais Prize for Poetry, 866

Adone, L' (Marino), 386

Adorno, Theodor, 311

Ady, Endre, 358

Africa. *See* Geographical Index

African American poetry, 3-14, 209

African poetry, 15-20, 506

Afro-Caribbean poetry, 43

Åkesson, Sonja, 555

Akhmatova, Anna, 519

Alagherius, Durante. *See* Dante

Alcaeus, 223, 321

Alcman, 224, 322

Alcuin, 462

Aldington, Edward Godfree. *See* Aldington, Richard

Aldington, Richard, 188, 646

Aleixandre, Vicente, 600

Aleksandrov, Josip Murn, 580

Alepoudhelis, Odysseus. *See* Elytis, Odysseus

Aleramo, Sibilla, 397

Alexie, Sherman, 486

Alfieri, Vittorio, 389

Alfred, Lord Tennyson. *See* Tennyson, Alfred, Lord

Algarín, Miguel, 468

Ali, Agha Shahid, 374

Alighieri, Dante. *See* Dante

All My Pretty Ones (Sexton), 671

Allegory, defined, 810

Allegory, England, 133

Allen, Paula Gunn, 483

Alliteration, defined, 810

Alliterative revival, 105

Allusion, defined, 810

Alonso, Dámaso, 600

Alvarez, Julia, 473

Ambivalence, moral, 193

Ambrogini, Angelo. *See* Poliziano

American Indian poetry. *See* Native American poetry

American Indian Poetry. See *Path on the Rainbow, The*

American poetry; nineteenth century, 174-184; twentieth century, 185-206, 208-213

Americas Review (journal), 466

Amis, Aphara. *See* Behn, Aphra

Anacreon, 322

Anacrusis, defined, 810

"Anaesthetic Criticism" (Crews), 727

Anagnostakis, Manolis, 348

Anapest, defined, 810

Anaphora, defined, 810

Anatomy of Criticism (Frye), 721

Ancel, Paul. *See* Celan, Paul

Andersson, Claes, 560

Andrei Bely Prize, 867

Andreyevna Gorenko, Anna. *See* Akhmatova, Anna

Anglophone poetry, Africa, 16

Angry Penguin movement, 32

Anile, Antonino, 406

Annensky, Innokenty, 518

Anthology of New York Poets, A (anthology), 675

Antschel, Paul. *See* Celan, Paul

Aphra Bayn. *See* Behn, Aphra

Apollinaire, Guillaume, 272

Apollonius Rhodius, 328

Approximate rhyme, defined, 810

Apuleius, Lucius, 457

Aragon, Louis, 274

Arany, János, 357

Archetypal criticism, 719-730

Archetype, 192, 719

Archetype, defined, 810

Archilochus, 222, 321

Argote, Luis de Góngora y. *See* Góngora y Argote, Luis de

Aribau, Bonaventura Carles, 51

Ariel (Plath), 670

Ariosto, Ludovico, 383; *Orlando Furioso,* 383

Aristotle, 700, 743; *Poetics,* 700

Ariwara no Narihira, 416

Arnold, Matthew, 712; *Culture and Anarchy,* 731; "The Study of Poetry," 713

Aronpuro, Kari, 559

Ars poetica. See Art of Poetry, The (Horace)

Art for art's sake, 264; Italy, 393; Parnassians, 639

Art of Poetry, The (Horace), 702

"Art poétique, L'" (Verlaine), 642

Arthurian legends, 103, 286

Arvon, Henri, 761

Ashbery, John, 674; *A Wave,* 676

Asian American poetry, 21-29, 209

Asian-influenced poetry, 192

Aškerc, Anton, 580

Aspenström, Werner, 549

Astrea. *See* Behn, Aphra

Astrov, Margot, 481

Atterbom, P. D. A., 534

Atwood, Margaret, 40, 502

Aubade, defined, 810

Auden, W. H., 653

Aue, Hartmann von. *See* Hartmann von Aue

Augustan Age, Roman, 450

Augustine, Saint, 459

Ausonius, Decimus Magnus, 460

Austin, J. L., 757

Australia. *See* Geographical Index

Australian poetry, 30-36, 500

Avant-garde poets; Italy, 410; Japan, 429

Awards, 865-889

Axion Esti, The (Elytis), 344

Ayala, Pedro López de, 590

Azorín, 598

Babits, Mihály, 359

Bachmann, Ingeborg, 311

Baggesen, Jens, 533

Bai hua (Chinese vernacular), 55

Bajza, Jozef Ignác, 574

Bakhtin, Mikhail, 760

Balassi, Bálint, 353

Ballade (poetic form), 244

Ballade (poetic form), defined, 811

Ballads; England, 167; fifteenth century, 125; Scandinavian, 528

Ballads, defined, 811

Balmont, Konstantin, 517

Banville, Théodore de, 265

Baraka, Amiri, 3

Barbour, John, 109

Bard poetry, Russia, 524

Bar-do thos-sgrol. See Tibetan Book of the Dead, The

Barker, Jane, 624

Barnes, Jim, 692

Baronet Scott, First. *See* Scott, Sir Walter

Baroque poetry, 151; France, 251; Germany, 292; Hungary, 353; Poland, 490; Sweden, 530

Base meter, defined, 811

Bashō. *See* Matsuo Bashō

"Bateau ivre, Le." *See* "Drunken Boat, The"

Batiushkov, Konstantin, 511

Baudelaire, Charles, 266, 640, 753; "Correspondences," 640; *Flowers of Evil*, 266

Baudouin, Marcel and Pierre. *See* Péguy, Charles-Pierre

Beat generation, 203, 661-667

Beatnik, definition of, 665

Beauvoir, Simone de, 774

Becher, Johannes R., 307

Bécquer, Gustavo Adolfo, 597

Behn, Aphra, 624

Bei Dao, 67

Belinsky, Vissarion, 515

Bellay, Joachim du. *See* Du Bellay, Joachim

Bellman, Carl Michael, 531

Bembo, Pietro, 398

Benediktsson, Einar, 541

Bengali poetry. *See* Indian English poetry

Benjamin, Walter, 760

Benn, Gottfried, 307

Bennett, Louise, 44

Beowulf, 225

Berggren, Tobias, 554

Bernolák, Antonín, 574

Bernolák movement, 574

Berry, Wendell, 692

Berryman, John, 197; *The Dream Songs*, 198

Bertin, Antoine, 258

Betocchi, Carlo, 406

Bhatt, Sujata, 375

Biedermeier, 299

Biernat of Lublin, 489

Bilingual Review (journal), 466

Biographia Literaria (Coleridge), 710

Biography (Milarepa), 609

Birthday Letters (Hughes), 198

Bitterfeld movement, 88

Bjartmarsson, Sigfús, 562

Björling, Gunnar, 545

Bjørnson, Bjørnstjerne, 538

Bjørnvig, Thorkild, 551

Black Arts movement, 6-7. *See also* Harlem Renaissance

Black Fire (anthology), 7

Black Mountain School, 684-689

Black Skin, White Masks (Fanon), 770

Blackburn, Paul, 688

Blake, William, 166, 177, 631; Beat generation, 662; "The Sick Rose," 720

Blank verse, defined, 811

Blok, Aleksandr, 518

Bloomfield, Leonard, 750

Bo Juyi, 62

Boccaccio, Giovanni, 102, 380

Bodmer, Johann Jakob, 294

Boethius, 461

Bohemia, 78

Boiardo, Matteo Maria, 382; *Orlando Innamorato*, 383

Boileau-Despréaux, Nicolas, 251

Bolan, Eavan, 210

Bollingen Prize in Poetry, 867

"Bonjour Monsieur Soutine" (Kiwus), 316

Bonnefoy, Yves, 280

Book of Good Love, The (Juan Ruiz), 588

Book of Songs, The (anthology), 56

Borchers, Elisabeth, 312, 317

Boscán, Juan, 592

Boye, Karin, 544

Bracken, Thomas, 35

Bradstreet, Anne, 154, 200

Brandes, Georg, 537

Brandt, Jørgen Gustava, 563

Brant, Sebastian, 288

Brathwaite, Edward Kamau, 45

Brazil. *See* Geographical Index

"Breaking Silence" (Mirikitani), 23

Brecht, Bertolt, 309

Breitinger, Johann Jakob, 294

Brentano, Clemens, 299

Breton, André, 274

Bridel, Bedřich, 80

Bridge, The (Crane), 196

Britting, Georg, 309

Brodsky, Joseph, 523

Brooks, Gwendolyn, 6

Brorson, Hans Adolph, 531

Brown, James Willie. *See*
    Komunyakaa, Yusef

Bruchac, Joseph, 486

Bryant, William Cullen, 636

Buch von der deutschen Poeterey, Das
    (Opitz), 292

Buchanan, George, 463

Bull, Olaf, 542

Burguillos, Tomé de. *See* Vega
    Carpio, Lope de

Burns, Robert, 170, 177

Butler, Judith, 774

Butler, Samuel, 622; *Hudibras*, 622

Bylina (poetic form), 509

Byron, Lord, 178, 631

"Byzantium" (Yeats), 193

Cadence, defined, 811

Caedmon, 226

Caesar, 449

Caesura, defined, 811

Cai Yan, 59

Calligrammes (Apollinaire), 273

Callimachus, 328

Calpurnius Siculus, Titus, 456

Camerata dei Bardi, 385

Campana, Dino, 402

Campbell, Roy, 501

Canada. *See* Geographical Index

Canadian poetry, 37-42, 501

Cankar, Ivan, 580

"Canonization, The" (Donne), 746

Cantar de mío Cid. See *Poem of the
    Cid*

Canterbury Tales, The (Chaucer), 113

Cantigas (poetic form), 584

Cantos (Pound), 195

Cao Zhi, 59

Carducci, Giosuè, 393

Caribbean poetry, 43-47

Carlyle, Thomas, 731

Carner, Josep, 52

Carol (lyric form), 124

Carolingian Revival, 462

Carpelan, Bo, 553

Carpio, Lope de Vega. *See* Vega
    Carpio, Lope de

Carroll, Lewis; "Jabberwocky," 804

Carson, Anne, 40

Carus, Titus Lucretius. *See* Lucretius

Casal, Lourdes, 471

Cassiodorus, 462

"Cat, The" (Baudelaire), 641

Catalan poetry, 48-53

Catharsis, defined, 701

Catullus, 449

Caudwell, Christopher, 760

Cavafy, Constantine P., 335

Čech, Svatopluk, 82

Celan, Paul, 311

Cendrars, Blaise, 270

Cervantes Prize, 869

Chanson de Roland. See *Song of
    Roland, The*

Chansons de geste, 233

Chants de Maldoror (Ducasse), 266

Char, René, 279

Charles d'Orléans, 123, 244

"Chat, Le." *See* "Cat, The"

Chatterton, Thomas, 628

Chattopadhyaya, Harindranath, 371

Chaucer, Geoffrey, 113, 120; *The
    Canterbury Tales*, 113

Chaulieu, Guillaume Amfrye, Abbe
    de, 255

Chedid, Andrée, 280

Chénier, André-Marie, 258

Chi, Juan. *See* Ruan Ji

Chiabrera, Gabriello, 386

Chicano poetry, 466-474

Children's/young adult poetry,
    eighteenth century, 168

Chile. *See* Geographical Index

China. *See* Geographical Index

Chinese American poetry, 21

Chinese poetry, 54-70

Chōka, 413

Chomsky, Noam, 753

Choral poetry, 224

Chrétien de Troyes, 239

Christensen, Inger, 563

Christopher Brennan Award, 868

Chronicle of the Cid. See *Poem of the
    Cid*

Chu ci (poetic form), 58

Churchill, Charles, 170

Cicero, 449

Cinq Grandes Odes. See *Five Great
    Odes*

Cinquain, defined, 811

Cinto, Mossén. *See* Verdaguer, Jacint

Classical period, ancient Greece, 322

Classical period, China, 55

Classicism, 149

Classicism, defined, 811

Claudel, Paul, 271; *Five Great Odes*,
    271

Claudian, 460

Claussen, Sophus, 539

Clavijo Uva, 470

Clopinel, Jehan. *See* Jean de Meung

Cocteau, Jean, 275

Coleridge, Samuel Taylor, 178, 630,
    710; *Biographia Lilteraria*, 710

*Collected Poems of Frank O'Hara,
    The* (O'Hara), 676

*Collected Poems of Kenneth Koch,
    The* (Koch), 677

*Collections of Ten Thousand Leaves,
    The*. See *Manyoshu, The*

Collins, William, 169

Colonialism; Africa, 15; beginning of, 769; British, 500; Caribbean, 43

Colonna, Vittoria, 386

Commonwealth literature, defined, 500

Commonwealth studies. *See* Postcolonialism

"Composed upon Westminster Bridge, September 3, 1802" (Wordsworth), 746

Conceit, defined, 148, 811

Conceptismo, 594

Concrete poetry, 317; Germany, 312; Scandinavia, 554

Confederation poets (Canada), 39

Confessio Amantis (Gower), 112

Confessional poetry, 200, 668-673

Connotation, defined, 811

Consonance, defined, 812

Consonants, defined, 812

Contemplations, Les (Hugo), 263

Continental poetry; fourteenth century, 98-119

Controlling image, defined, 812

Controlling metaphor, defined, 812

Cope, Wendy, 209

Corbière, Tristan, 642

"Correspondences" (Baudelaire), 640

Costa i Llobera, Miquel, 51

Costumbrismo, 598

Country and the City, The (Williams), 734

Couplet, defined, 812

Course in General Linguistics (Saussure), 750

Courtly love, 238

Cowper, William, 170

Crabbe, George, 170

Crane, Hart, 196; *The Bridge*, 196

Creeley, Robert, 687

Crepuscular poets, 400

Crews, Frederick, 726

Criticism; archetypal, 719-730; cultural, 731-735; dialectical, 761; England, 132; feminist, 736-742;

formalist, 743-749; history of, 699-718; linguistic, 750-759; Marxist, 733, 760-763; postcolonial, 769-773; postmodern, 733; poststructuralist, 733, 780-786; psychological, 719-730; structuralist, 780-786

Croatian poetry, 71-77

Cronyn, George W., 481

Crow (Hughes), 198

Cruz, Sor Juana Inés de la, 149, 435, 595

Crystal, David, 757

Csokonai Vitéz, Mihály, 355

Csoori, Sandor, 362

Cuban American poetry, 466-474

Cullen, Countée, 657

Culler, Jonathan, 821

Culteranismo, 594

Cultural criticism, 731-735

Cultural studies, 733, 760

Culture, defined, 731

Culture and Anarchy (Arnold), 731

Curnow, Allen, 35

Curtis, Natalie, 481

Cynewulf, 226

Czech poetry, 78-86

Czechowski, Heinz, 317

Dactyl, defined, 812

Dadaism, 273, 651

D'Aguiar, Fred, 46

Dahlstierna, Gunno, 530

Dalai Lama, Sixth, 609

Dalin, Olaf von, 530

"Dance of the Sevin Deidly Synnis, The" (Dunbar), 128

D'Annunzio, Gabriele, 396

Danrin school, 423

Dante, 101, 378, 464

Darío, Rubén, 436

Daruwalla, Keki N., 374

Das, Kamala, 373, 505

Dauenhauer, Nora Marks, 482

Davičo, Oskar, 570

Davison, Lawrence H. *See* Lawrence, D. H.

Dawe, Bruce, 33

De poetica. See Poetics (Aristotle)

Decadent poets, 187, 639; Czech, 83; France, 269; Poland, 495; Russia, 517

Deconstruction, 208, 782

Deconstruction, defined, 813

Decorum, defined, 702

Deep Image poetry, 191

Defence and Illustration of the French Language, The (Du Bellay), 248

Defence of Poesie (Sidney), 132, 703

Defence of Poetry, A (Shelley), 711

Défense et illustration de la langue française, La. See Defence and Illustration of the French Language, The

Deguy, Michel, 280

Delille, Jacques, 257

Della Valle, Federico, 387

De Mehun, Jean. *See* Jean de Meung

Demetz, Peter, 761

De Meung, Jean. *See* Jean de Meung

Demoticism (Greek vernacular), 331

Denby, Edwin, 674

Denotation, defined, 813

Depressed foot, defined, 813

Depth psychology, 719

De Robertis, Giuseppe, 401

Derozio, Henry, 367

Derrida, Jacques, 775, 782, 813

Derzhavin, Gavrila, 511

Desconhort, Lo (Lull), 49

Desmond, Gail Whang, 24

Desnos, Robert, 274

De Souza, Goan Eunice, 373

Despréau, Monsieur. *See* Boileau-Despréaux, Nicolas

Deuxième Sexe, Le. See Second Sex, The

Diachrony (linguistics), 781

Dialectical criticism, 761

Dickinson, Emily, 191

Diction, defined, 813

Didactic poetry, 108; England, 165;
    France, 256

Diego, Gerardo, 601

Dieresis, defined, 813

Différance (literary term), 783

Di Giacomo, Salvatore, 398

Diktonius, Elmer, 545

Dimoula, Kiki, 350

Discontinuity; German
    expressionism, 306; modernism,
    194

Discourse; gendered, 739; New
    Historicism, 767

Dodgson, Charles Lutwidge. *See*
    Carroll, Lewis

Doha. *See* Tantric songs

Dolce stil nuovo, 50, 378

Domin, Hilde, 313

Donne, John, 144; "The
    Canonization," 746

Doolittle, Hilda. *See* H. D.

Dorn, Edward, 687

Douglas, Gavin, 128

Drachmann, Holger, 537

Dramatic dialogue, defined, 813

Dramatic monologue, defined, 813

Dream Songs, The (Berryman), 198

Droste-Hülshoff, Annette von, 300

"Drunken Boat, The" (Rimbaud), 641

Dryden, John, 144, 622, 705; *Absalom
    and Achitophel*, 156, 622; *Mac
    Flecknoe*, 622; "Preface to *Fables
    Ancient and Modern*," 705

Du Bellay, Joachim, 248, 463; *The
    Defence and Illustration of the
    French Language*, 248

Du Bouchet, André, 279

Du Fu, 61

Du Mu, 62

Ducasse, Isidore-Lucien, 266

Dučić, Jovan, 569

Dudley, Anne. *See* Bradstreet, Anne

Duffy, Carol Ann, 210

Dunbar, Paul Laurence, 4

Dunbar, William, 127; "The Dance of
    the Sevin Deidly Synnis," 128

Duncan, Robert, 687

Dunlop, Eliza Hamilton, 31

Dupin, Jacques, 279

Duration, defined, 813

Dutt, Michael Madhusudan, 368

Dutt, Toru, 368

Dynamics of Literary Response, The
    (Holland), 724

Eagleton, Terry, 761

East German poetry, 87-97, 315

Eberhart, Richard, 664

Ecofeminism, 693

Eddic poetry, 227, 526

Edward Symmes, Robert. *See*
    Duncan, Robert

Edwards, Eli. *See* McKay, Claude

Egill Skallagrímsson, 527

Ego psychology, 723

Eich, Günther, 308

Eichendorff, Joseph von, 299

Eigner, Larry, 687

Ekelöf, Gunnar, 544

Ekelund, Vilhelm, 541

El Salvador. *See* Geographical Index

Elegies; ancient Greece, 323;
    England, 162

Elegy, defined, 813

Eliot, T. S., 189, 652, 715; *On Poetry
    and Poets*, 715; *The Use of Poetry
    and the Use of Criticism*, 715

Elision, defined, 813

Elizabethan Age, 136

Elmslie, Kenward, 674

Éluard, Paul, 274

Elytis, Odysseus, 342; *The Axion Esti*,
    344

Embirikos, Andreas, 342

Emblem poetry, 149

Emerson, Ralph Waldo, 179

Empedocles, 326

Emphasis, defined, 813

Enckell, Rabbe, 546

End-stop, defined, 813

Engels, Friedrich, 760

England. *See* Geographical Index

English poetry; fourteenth century,
    98-119; fifteenth century, 120-
    129; sixteenth century, 130-143;
    seventeenth century, 144-159;
    eighteenth century, 160-173;
    nineteenth century, 174-184;
    twentieth century, 185-206, 208-
    213

Engo (poetic technique), 417

Enlightenment; Hungary, 354; Italy,
    388; Poland, 492

Ennius, Quintus, 446

Envoy, defined, 814

Enzensberger, Hans Magnus, 311

Epic, defined, 814

Epics; England, 161; Europe, 214-
    231; Poland, 494; Scandinavia,
    529; Serbia, 566; Tibet, 607

Epicureanism, 453

Epigrams; ancient Greece, 329;
    England, 162; Martial, 456

Epistles; ancient Greece, 453;
    England, 162

Epitaphios (Ritsos), 345

Epstein, Edmund L., 751

Erb, Elke, 315

Erba, Luciano, 410

Erben, Karel Jaromír, 81

Erdrich, Louise, 484

Erlingsson, Thorsteinn, 537

Erotic poetry, 293; England, 137

Eschenbach, Wolfram von. *See*
    Wolfram von Eschenbach

Esenin, Sergei, 520

Espriu, Salvador, 52

Espronceda, José de, 597

Essay on Criticism, An (Pope), 163,
    706

Etherege, Sir George, 621

Ethnopoetics, 481

Eugen, Berthold. *See* Brecht, Bertolt

Evans, Mari, 8

Ewald, Johannes, 533

Existentialism, 203; France, 277

Explication process, 789-797

Expressionism, 305

Extended metaphor, defined, 814

Exteriorismo (poetic technique), 438

Eye rhyme, defined, 814

Ezekiel, Nissim, 372, 506

Fables; England, 162; Spain, 596

Fables (Henryson), 127

Fables choisies, mises en vers. See
   Fables Written in Verse

Fables Written in Verse (La Fontaine),
   252

Fabliau, defined, 814

Fabliaux, 240

Faccio, Rina. *See* Aleramo, Sibilla

Falkner, Gerhard, 317

Fallacy; affective, 747; intentional, 747

Falling rhyme, defined, 814

Falling rhythm, defined, 814

Fanon, Frantz, 770

Feminine rhyme, defined, 814

Feminist criticism, 736-742

Feminist criticism, defined, 814

Feminist poets; Africa, 17; Germany,
   316; India, 374; Mexico, 438;
   Scandinavia, 555

Ferlin, Nils, 543

Ferlinghetti, Lawrence, 665

Field, Barron, 30

Fifty Poems (Meleager). *See Garland*

Filipino American poetry, 25

Finland. *See* Geographical Index

Fireside poets, 633-638

First Fruits of Australian Poetry
   (Field), 30

First person, defined, 814

Fischer, Ernst, 761

Five Great Odes (Claudel), 271

Flaccus, Aulus Persius. *See* Persius

Fletcher, Giles, 152

Fletcher, John Gould, 647

Flint, F. S., 648

Flowers of Evil (Baudelaire), 266

Foix, J. V., 52

Folk poetry; China, 56; Croatia, 73;
   Czech, 80; Germany, 295; Greece,
   332; Hungary, 356; India, 370;
   Macedonia, 475; and Adam
   Mickiewicz, 493; Russia, 520;
   Scandinavia, 528; Serbia, 566;
   Tibet, 608

Fontaine, Jean de La. *See* La
   Fontaine, Jean de

Foot/feet, defined, 814

Form, defined, 815

Formalism, Russian, defined, 815

Formalist criticism, 743-749

Forssell, Lars, 550

Fort, Paul, 270

Fortunatus, Venantius, 462

Foster, Joy. *See* Harjo, Joy

Foucault, Michel, 766, 776

Found poetry, defined, 815

Fowler, Roger, 758

France. *See* Geographical Index

Francis, Paula Marie. *See* Allen,
   Paula Gunn

Francophone poetry; Africa, 16;
   Canada, 37

Frank, Joseph, 780

Franzén, Frans Mikael, 532

Frazer, Sir James George, 719

Fredmans epistlar (Bellman), 532

Fredmans sånger (Bellman), 532

Free verse, defined, 815

French poetry; origins to seventeenth
   century, 232-253; eighteenth
   century to present, 254-282

Freud, Sigmund, 720

Fröding, Gustaf, 538

Fronto, Marcus Cornelius, 457

Frost, Robert, 653

Frost Medal, 870

Frostenson, Katarina, 556

Frye, Northrop, 719, 810

Fu (poetic form), 58

Fu, Du. *See* Du Fu

Fujiwara Teika, 419

Furtado, Joseph, 372

Futurism, 651; Italy, 401; Poland,
   497; Russia, 520

Gadara, Meleager of. *See* Meleager

Gallus, 451

García Lorca, Federico, 600

Garcilaso de la Vega, 593

Gardons, S. S. *See* Snodgrass, W. D.

Garland (Meleager), 329

Gascoigne, George, 136

Gautier, Théophile, 264

Gawain poems, 104

Gawain-Poet. *See* Pearl-Poet

Geijer, Erik Gustaf, 535

Gellius, Aulus, 457

Gender; feminist criticism, 736;
   performance of, 777; queer theory,
   774; social construction of, 777

Generation of '98, 598

Generation of '27, 598

Generation of '68, 498

Genius versus wit, 166

Georg Büchner Prize, 869

George, Stefan, 304

Georgian poetry, 187

German Democratic Republic poetry.
   See East German poetry

German poetry; origins to nineteenth
   century, 283-297; nineteenth
   century to Reunification, 298-314;
   Reunification to present, 315-319

Germany. *See* Geographical Index

*Gerusalemme liberata. See Jerusalem
   Delivered*

Ge-sar epic, 607

Ghazal, defined, 815

Ghose, Kasiprasad, 367

Ghose, Manmohan, 371

Ghose, Sri Aurobindo, 369

Gilbert, Anne Hart, 43

Gilbert, Nicolas-Joseph-Laurent, 257

Ginsberg, Allen, 662; "Howl," 663

Giovanni, Nikki, 11; "Nikki-Rosa," 11

Gjuzel, Bogomil, 476

Glatter, Miklós. *See* Radnóti, Miklós

Glu (poetic form), 608

Gnomic verse, defined, 815

God Defend New Zealand (Bracken), 35

Goethe, Johann Wolfgang von, 295

Golden age, China, 60

Golden Bough, The (Frazer), 719

Golden Wreath Award, 871

Goldsmith, Oliver, 169

"Golf Links, The" (Cleghorn), 762

Golob, Zvonimir, 76

Goncourt Prize in Poetry, 872

Góngora y Argote, Luis de, 594, 618

Gongorism, 594, 618

Gonzaga, Russell, 26

Gonzales, Rodolfo, 468

Gonzalo de Berceo, 586

Googe, Barnabe, 135

Gordon, Adam Lindsay, 31

Gordon, George. *See* Byron, Lord

Gothic literature, 167

Gotovac, Vlado, 76

Gottsched, Johann Christoph, 294

Gourmont, Remy de, 640

Governor General's Literary Awards (English-language poetry), 872

Governor General's Literary Awards (French-language poetry), 872

Govoni, Corrado, 400

Gower, John; *Confessio Amantis*, 112

Gozzano, Guido, 400

Grace Leven Prize for Poetry, 876

Grainger, James, 43

Grammar and language, 753

Gramsci, Antonio, 760

Graveyard school, 628

Gray, Thomas, 169

Great Britain. *See* Geographical Index

Greece. *See* Geographical Index

Greek poetry; antiquity, 215, 320-330; since 1820, 331-351

Green movement, 690-695

Greenblatt, Stephen, 764

Gregorčič, Simon, 580

Grieg, Nordahl, 547

Griffin Poetry Prize, 873

Grindel, Eugène. *See* Éluard, Paul

Grove Day, A., 481

Grünbein, Durs, 318

Grundtvig, N. F. S., 534

Gryphius, Andreas, 292

Guarini, Battista, 385

Guest, Barbara, 674

Guillaume de Lorris; *The Romance of the Rose*, 240

Guitar and Concertina (Fröding), 538

Gujarati poetry. *See* Indian English poetry

Gullberg, Hjalmar, 543

Gumilyov, Nikolay, 518

Gundulić, Ivan, 72

Gunnarsson, Pétur, 561

Gushi (poetic form), 59

Gustafsson, Lars, 555

Guthmundsson, Tómas, 548

Gynocriticism, 736

Gyöngyösi, István, 354

H. D., 188, 647

Haavikko, Paavo, 552

Haavio, Martti. *See* Mustapää, P.

Hagedorn, Jessica, 25

Hagiwara Sakutarō, 429

Hahn, Ulla, 316

Haikai no renga, 422

Haiku, 420, 427

Haiku, defined, 815

Håkansson, Björn, 554

Halliday, M. A. K., 755

Hamri, Thorsteinn frá, 561

Han Yu, 62

Hara Shirō, 433

Hardenberg, Friedrich von. *See* Novalis

Harding, Gunnar, 555

Hardy, Thomas, 190

Harjo, Joy, 484, 694

Harlem Renaissance, 5, 655-660

Harpur, Charles, 30

Harris, Max, 32

Hart sisters, 43

Hartmann von Aue, 286

Harvey, Anne Gray. *See* Sexton, Anne

Hauge, Olav H., 556

Haugen, Paal-Helge, 558

Hault, Jean du. *See* Éluard, Paul

Havlíček Borovský, Karel, 81

Hawkes, Terence, 751

Hayden, Robert, 11

Heaney, Seamus, 199; *North*, 199

Heart's Needle (Snodgrass), 201, 669

Hebbel, Friedrich, 302

Heidenstam, Verner von, 538

Heine, Heinrich, 301

Hellaakoski, Aaro, 546

Hellenistic poets, 328

Henryson, Robert, 127; *Fables*, 127

Herder, Johann Gottfried, 295

Heredia, José-Maria de (French poet), 265

Hermeticism; Germany, 311; Italy, 405

Hermodsson, Elisabet, 555

Hernández, José, 435

Hernández, Miguel, 601

Herrick, Robert, 150

Hervent, Maurice. *See* Éluard, Paul

Hesiod, 221, 320; *Theogony*, 222; *Works and Days*, 222

Heyduk, Adolf, 82

Heym, Georg, 306

Hill, Archibald A., 751

Hill, Geoffrey, 198; *Mercian Hymns*, 198; *The Triumph of Love*, 199

Hindi poetry. *See* Indian English poetry

Historical criticism, defined, 815

Historical poetry; England, 140; Middle English, 109; modern Greek, 336

Hitomaro. *See* Kakinomoto Hitomaro

Hobbes, Thomas, 153

Hoccleve, Thomas, 122

Hoddis, Jakob von, 306

Hofmannsthal, Hugo von, 304

Hofmannswaldau, Christian Hofmann von, 293

Hogan, Linda, 485, 692

Hoggart, Richard, 733

Hokku (poetic form), 424

Holan, Vladimír, 85

Holberg, Ludvig, 530

Hölderlin, Friedrich, 296

Holmes, Oliver Wendell, 637

Holmsen, Bjarne P. *See* Holz, Arno

Holz, Arno, 303

Homer, 217, 320; *Iliad*, 217; *Odyssey*, 217

Honkadori (poetic technique), 418

Hope, A. D., 502

Horace, 451, 702; *The Art of Poetry*, 702

"Howl" (Ginsberg), 663

Howling at the Moon (Hagiwara), 429

Huchel, Peter, 308

Hudibras (Butler), 622

Hugh Selwyn Mauberley (Pound), 195

Hughes, Langston, 658

Hughes, Ted, 198; *Birthday Letters*, 198; *Crow*, 198

Hugo, Victor, 262; *Les Contemplations*, 263

Huldén, Lars, 560

Humanism, 733; Germany, 290; Italy, 381; Spain, 592

Hundred-Thousand Songs (Milarepa), 609

Hungarian poetry, 352-364

Hymn to Liberty, The (Solomos), 332

Hymnen an die Nacht. See Hymns to the Night

Hymns; England, 168; Germany, 291; Homeric, 217, 320; Hungary, 352; Latin, 460; Scandinavia, 529; Slovakia, 573; Spain, 586

Hymns to the Night (Novalis), 298

Hyperbole, defined, 815

I Am Joaquín/Yo soy Joaquín (Gonzales), 468

Iamb, defined, 815

Iambic pentameter, defined, 815

Identical rhyme, defined, 815

Ideology, 761; of art, 304; cultural criticism, 764; defined, 760

"If We Must Die" (McKay), 44

Ihara Saikaku, 423

Iliad (Homer), 217

Ilić, Vojislav, 569

Illuminations (Rimbaud), 268

Illusion and Reality (Caudwell), 760

Illyés, Gyula, 361

Illyrian movement, 73

Imagery, defined, 815

Imaginative truth, 627

Imagism, 187, 644-649, 652

Imagistes, Des (anthology), 645, 652

Imnos is tin eleftheria. See Hymn to Liberty, The

Impermanence, 417

In a Free State (Naipaul), 772

India. *See* Geographical Index

Indian English poetry, 365-376

Indian poetry, 505

Indians' Book, The (anthology), 481

Indigenous poetry; Canada, 504; Commonwealth, 503

Interior monologue, defined, 816

Irigaray, Luce, 774

Irish poetry, 210

Irony, defined, 816

Ishikawa Takuboku, 428

Italian poetry; origins to nineteenth century, 377-392; nineteenth century to present, 393-411

Iyengar, K. R. Srinivasa, 367

"Jabberwocky" (Carroll), 804

Jaccottet, Philippe, 280

Jacob, Max, 275

Jacobsen, Jens Peter, 537

Jacobsen, Rolf, 551

Jahier, Piero, 401

Jakobson, Roman, 751, 781, 820

James I, 122

James Laughlin Award, 875

Jameson, Fredric, 761

Jammes, Francis, 270

Janevski, Slavko, 476

Japanese American poetry, 22

Japanese poetry; origins to nineteenth century, 412-426; nineteenth century to present, 427-434

Jazz poetry, 11

Jean de Meung; *The Romance of the Rose*, 240

Jenko, Simon, 580

Jensen, Johannes V., 542

Jerry, Bongo, 46

Jerusalem Delivered (Tasso), 384

Ji, Ruan. *See* Ruan Ji

Jigme, Hortsang, 610

Jiménez, Juan Ramón, 599

Jindyworobak movement, 32

Jnanpith Award, 874

Johannesen, Georg, 557

Johnson, Aphra. *See* Behn, Aphra

Johnson, Bengt Emil, 554

Johnson, Colin. *See* Narogin, Mudrooroo

Johnson, James Weldon, 4, 659

Johnson, Samuel, 169, 706; *The Lives of the Poets*, 706

Jokotoba (poetic technique), 417

Jónasson, Jóhannes B. *See* Kötlum, Jóhannes úr

Jones, LeRoi. *See* Baraka, Amiri

Jones, Sir William, 365

Jonson, Ben, 149

Jonsson, Thorsteinn. *See* Hamri, Thorsteinn frá

Jørgensen, Johannes, 539

József, Attila, 360

Juan Rulfo Prize for Latin American and Caribbean Literature. *See* Rulfo Prize for Latin American and Caribbean Literature

Juana, Sor. *See* Cruz, Sor Juana Inés de la
Jueju (poetic form), 60
Jugendstil, 303
Jugo, Miguel de Unamuno y. *See* Unamuno y Jugo, Miguel de
Juhász, Gyula, 359
Jung, Carl, 719, 810; literary criticism, 719
Juvenal, 456

Kabaphes, Konstantionos Petrou. *See* Cavafy, Constantine P.
Ka-bzhas (poetic form), 610
Kaichōon, 428
Kaila, Tiina, 559
Kailas, Uuno, 546
Kakekotoba (poetic technique), 417
Kakinomoto Hitomaro, 413
Kallimachos. *See* Callimachus
Kalvos, Andreas, 333
Kanshi (poetic form), 429
Kantemir, Antioch, 510
Karlfeldt, Erik Axel, 539
Karouzos, Nikos, 349
Karyotakis, Kostas, 339
Karyotakism, 339
Katolická Moderna, 83
Kazantzakis, Nikos, 346
Kazinczy, Ferenc, 354
Keats, John, 178, 630, 712
Kellgren, Johann Henrik, 532
Kenny, Maurice, 485
Kerouac, Jack, 206, 661; *Mexico City Blues*, 665
Kette, Dragotin, 580
Key-Åberg, Sandro, 550
Kharjas (poetic form), 583
Ki no Tsurayuki, 415
Killigrew, Anne, 624
Kim Tong Il, 24
Kincaid, Jamaica, 772
Kingo, Thomas, 530
Kingsley Tufts Poetry Award, 886
Kirstinä, Väinö, 558

Kiss, József, 358
Kiwus, Karin, 316
Kling, Thomas, 318
Klopstock, Friedrich Gottlieb, 294
Knudsen, Erik, 551
Koch, Kenneth, 674; *The Collected Poems of Kenneth Koch*, 677
Kochanowski, Jan, 490
Kokinshū (anthology), 415
Kölcsey, Ferenc, 356
Kolenic, Ivan, 577
Kollár, Ján, 81
Komachi. *See* Ono no Komachi
Komunyakaa, Yusef, 9
Koneski, Blaže, 476
Korean American poetry, 23
Kostrowitzki, Guillelmus Apollinaris de. *See* Apollinaire, Guillaume
Kosztolányi, Dezső, 359
Kötlum, Jóhannes úr, 549
Kowhai Gold (anthology), 35
Kraków Vanguard, 497
Král, Janko, 574
Kralická Bible, 79
Kranjčević, Silvije Strahimir, 74
Krasicki, Ignacy, 492
Krasiński, Zygmunt, 494
Krechel, Ursula, 316
Kristensen, Tom, 547
Krleža, Miroslav, 75
Krolow, Karl, 311
Kruchonykh, Aleksei, 520
Kynewulf. *See* Cynewulf

Labrunie, Gérard. *See* Nerval, Gérard de
Lacan, Jacques, 725
La Cour, Paul, 548
La Fontaine, Jean de, 252; *Fables Written in Verse*, 252
Laforgue, Jules, 269
Lagerkvist, Pär, 543
Lakoff, Robin, 739
Lamartine, Alphonse de, 260; *Poetical Meditations*, 260

Langgässer, Elisabeth, 309
Langland, William; *The Vision of William, Concerning Piers the Plowman*, 110
Language, 798-809; feminist criticism, 737
Language and Woman's Place (Lakoff), 739
Language poetry, 208
Langue (linguistics), 750
Langue d'oc (poetic form), 237
Larkin, Philip, 203, 682
Larsen, Marianne, 564
Larsson, Stig, 556
Lasker-Schüler, Else, 306
Latin America. *See* Geographical Index
Latin American poetry, 435-440
Latin poetry, 441-465
Latino poetry, 466-474
Lautréamont. *See* Ducasse, Isidore-Lucien
Lawrence, D. H., 648
Lawson, Henry, 32
Lde'u, 607
"Leaving Seoul" (Lew), 24
Leavis, F. R., 732, 743
Lebrun, Ponce-Denis Écouchard, 257
Leconte de Lisle, Charles-Marie, 265
Lee, Li-Young, 27
Léger, Alexis Saint-Léger. *See* Perse, Saint-John
Lehmann, Wilhelm, 309
Leino, Eino, 540
Lenau, Nikolaus, 301
Lenngren, Anna Maria, 532
Lenore Marshall Poetry Prize, 877
Léonard, Nicolas-Germain, 258
Lermontov, Mikhail, 513
Leśmian, Bolesław, 496
Levertov, Denise, 687
Lévi-Strauss, Claude, 753
Levin, Samuel, 754
Levstik, Fran, 580
Lew, Walter, 24

Li Bo, 60

Li Ch'ing-chao. *See* Li Qingzhao

Li Pai. *See* Li Bo

Li Po. *See* Li Bo

Li Qingzhao, 63

Li Sao, The (Qu Yuan), 58

Li Shangyin, 62

Li Taibo. *See* Li Bo

Li T'ai-pai. *See* Li Bo

Li T'ai-po. *See* Li Bo

Li-Young Lee. *See* Lee, Li-Young

Liberation poetry, Africa, 16

Libro de buen amor. See Book of
　Good Love, The

Lichtenstein, Alfred, 308

Life Studies (Lowell), 201, 668

Liliencron, Detlev von, 303

Lim, Genny, 22

Limerick, defined, 816

Lindegren, Erik, 549

Line, defined, 816

Linguistic criticism, 750-759

Linguistics, 798-809

Literature as "criticism of life," 713

Literature as Social Discourse
　(Fowler), 758

Lives of the Poets, The (Johnson), 706

Livius Andronicus, Lucius, 446

Livy, 452

Loerke, Oskar, 309

Loges, François des. *See* Villon,
　François

Lomonosov, Mikhail, 510

Longfellow, Henry Wadsworth, 633;
　"A Psalm of Life," 761

Longinus, 702; *On the Sublime,* 702

Lönnrot, Elias, 529

Lorca, Federico García. *See* García
　Lorca, Federico

Lord, Albert B., 218

Lord Tennyson, Alfred. *See*
　Tennyson, Alfred, Lord

Lorde, Audre, 8

Lorris, Guillaume de. *See* Guillaume
　de Lorris

Loury, Guillaume de. *See* Guillaume
　de Lorris

"Love Songs of the Sixth Dalai
　Lama," 609

Løveid, Cecilie, 558

Lowell, Amy, 648, 652

Lowell, James Russell, 634

Lowell, Robert, 201, 668; *Life*
　Studies, 201, 668

"Lower East Side Poem, A" (Piñero),
　469

Lu You, 63

Lucas, Victoria. *See* Plath, Sylvia

Lucidor, Lasse, 530

Lucilius, Gaius, 447

Lucretius, 449

Lukáč, Emil Boleslav, 576

Lukács, Georg, 760

"Luke Havergal" (Robinson), 789

Lull, Raymond, 48

Lundkvist, Artur, 544

Lushi (poetic form), 60

Lusophone poetry, Africa, 16

Lutwidge Dodgson, Charles. *See*
　Carroll, Lewis

Luzán, Ignacio de, 595

Luzi, Mario, 406

Lydgate, John, 121

Lyric poetry; English, 162; French,
　237; German, 287; Indian, 372;
　Italian, 377; Native American, 478;
　Restoration, 620; Serbian, 566

Lyric poetry, defined, 816

Lyrics, Middle English, 107, 123

"Ma Rainey" (Brown), 12

Mac Flecknoe (Dryden), 622

McAuley, James, 33

Macedonian poetry, 475-477

McGuckian, Medbh, 210

Mácha, Karel Hynek, 81

Machado, Antonio, 598

Machar, Josef Svatopluk, 83

McKay, Claude, 44, 658; "If We Must
　Die," 44

Macpherson, James; *Ossian,* 628

Macrobius, Ambrosius Theodosius,
　459

Mad-song, defined, 816

Madame de Staël, 259

Madoc (Muldoon), 210

Máj. See May

Makars, 126

Makurakotoba (poetic technique),
　414

Mal du siècle, 260

Malherbe, François, 251

Malinowski, Ivan, 562

Mallarmé, Stéphane, 268, 643

Mallorcan school, 51

Malory, Sir Thomas, 125

Manathi poetry. *See* Indian English
　poetry

Mandelstam, Osip, 519

Manner, Eeva-Liisa, 552

Manninen, Otto, 540

Manyoshu, The (anthology), 412

Maoist poetry, 67

Maori poets, 504

Maragall, Juan, 51

March, Ausiàs, 50

Marginalization and literary works,
　734

Marian poems, 124

Marinetti, Filippo Tommaso, 401

Marinismo, 386, 618

Marino, Giambattista, 386, 618;
　L'Adone, 386

Marmon, Leslie. *See* Silko, Leslie
　Marmon

Maro, Publius Vergilius. *See* Vergil

Marot, Clément, 247

Martial, 456

Martian poetry, 208

Martin, Egbert, 44

Martinson, Harry, 544

Marulić, Marko, 71

Marx, Karl, 760

Marxism and Form (Jameson), 761

Marxist criticism, 733, 760-763

Marxist criticism, defined, 816

Mas, Josep Arseni Vicenç Foix i. *See* Foix, J. V.

Masaoka Shiki, 428

Masaoka Shiki International Haiku Prize, 878

Masculine rhyme, defined, 816

Matevski, Mateja, 476

Matsunaga Teitoku, 422

Matsuo Bashō, 423

Maximus Poems, The (Olson), 197

May (Mácha), 81

Mayakovsky, Vladimir, 520

Mažuranić, Ivan, 73

Medici, Lorenzo de', 381

Medieval poetry, Latin, 461

Méditations poétiques. See Poetical Meditations

Megara, Theognis of. *See* Theognis

Mehren, Stein, 556

Mehun, Jean de. *See* Jean de Meung

Meleager, 329; *Garland*, 329

Mercian Hymns (Hill), 198

Meredith, Louisa Anne, 31

Merezhkovsky, Dmitri, 516

Metaphor, defined, 816

Metaphysical poetry, 147, 615-619, 708, 744; twentieth century, 189

Metapoem, 278

Metastasio, Pietro, 387

Meter, defined, 817

Metonymy, defined, 817

Meung, Jean de. *See* Jean de Meung

Mexico. *See* Geographical Index

Mexico City Blues (Kerouac), 665

Meyer, Conrad Ferdinand, 302

Mgur (poetic form), 608

Michaux, Henri, 277

Mickiewicz, Adam, 493; *Pan Tadeusz*, 494

Miguel de Cervantes Prize. *See* Cervantes Prize

Mihalić, Slavko, 75

Milarepa, 609

Miljković, Branko, 571

Miller, J. Hillis, 818

Millevoye, Charles-Hubert, 258

Milton, John, 623; *Paradise Lost*, 623

Mimesis, 699, 701

Minjian poets, 68

Minne (poetic form), 287

Mirikitani, Janice, 23

Mirror (Roig), 50

Misty poetry, 67

Miyazawa Kenji, 430

Mnemonic verse, defined, 817

Modern Poetry and the Tradition (Brooks), 744

Moderna, 74, 575

Modernism, 12, 185, 650-654; Canadian, 39; Catalan, 51; Croatian, 74; Czech, 83; Finno-Swedish, 545; German, 310; Indian English, 372; Russian, 516; Slovenian, 580

Modernism, defined, 817

Modernismo, 435, 598

"Moïse" (Vigny), 261

Mokichi. *See* Saitō Mokichi

Momaday, N. Scott, 482

Montale, Eugenio, 403

Montcorbier, François de. *See* Villon, François

Monti, Vincenzo, 390

Moonlight Sonata, The (Ritsos), 346

Moore, Marianne, 653

Mora, Pat, 471

Moraes, Dom, 374

Morall Fabillis of Esope, the Phrygian, The. See Fables (Henryson)

Moratín, Nicolás Fernández de, 595

More, Henry, 149

Moréas, Jean, 639

Mori Ōgai, 428

Mörike, Eduard, 300

Morley, Hilda, 689

Mossén Cinto. *See* Verdaguer, Jacint

Most Delightful History of Reynard the Fox. See Roman de Renart

Movement poets, 203, 679-683

Muldoon, Paul, 209; *Madoc*, 210

Multiculturalism, defined, 817

Murray, Les A., 33, 502

Musset, Alfred de, 262

Mustapää, P., 546

Myrtle, Marmaduke. *See* Addison, Joseph

Mysticism, Germany, 289

Myth, 192

Myth, defined, 817

Myth criticism, defined, 817

Mythistorema (Seferis), 340

Naevius, Gnaeus, 446

Naidu, Sarojini, 369, 505

Naipaul, V. S., 772

Narihira. *See* Ariwara no Narihira

Narogin, Mudrooroo, 504

Narrator, defined, 817

National Book Award in Poetry, 878

National Socialism, 310

Native American poetry, 209, 478-488

Natsume Sōseki, 429

Naturalism, 182; Germany, 303; Russia, 515; Scandinavia, 537

Nature poetry; Denmark, 531; East Germany, 93; England, 165, 628; France, 260; Germany, 308; United States, 180

Nazor, Vladimir, 74

Neal, Larry, 7

Necessity of Art, The (Fischer), 761

Negri, Ada, 407

Negritude, 16

Nekrasov, Nikolai, 515

Nemesianus, 457

Neoclassicism, 156; criticism, 705; Italy, 391; Latin America, 435

Neo-Hermeticism, 409

Neorealism, Italy, 409

Neoterics, 450

Nepos, Cornelius, 449

Neruda, Jan, 82

Nerval, Gérard de, 265

Neustadt International Prize, 879

New Black Renaissance. *See* Black Arts movement

New Criticism, 193, 715, 733

New Criticism, defined, 817

New Historicism, 764-768

New Humanism, 732

New Lines (anthology), 681

New Negro movement. *See* Harlem Renaissance

New Poetry, The (anthology), 682

New populists, Hungary, 361

New School of Athens, 334

New Science, 154

New Simplicity, 553

New Subjectivity, 312

New York Intellectuals, 732

New York School, 191, 674-678

New Zealand. *See* Geographical Index

New Zealand poetry, 30-36, 502

Nezval, Vítězslav, 85

Ngugi Wa Thiong'o, 771

Niatum, Duane, 482

Nibelungenlied, 228, 286

Nicaragua. *See* Geographical Index

Nichols, Grace, 46

Nike Award, 880

"Nikki-Rosa" (Giovanni), 11

Nishiwaki Junsaburō, 429

Nishiyama Sōin, 423

Njegoš, Petar Petrović, 567

Nobel Prize in Literature, 880

Noël, Bernard, 280

Noonuccal, Oodgeroo. *See* Walker, Kath

Nordbrandt, Henrik, 564

Nordenflycht, Hedvig Charlotta, 531

Nordic poetry. *See* Scandinavian poetry

Norén, Lars, 555

North (Heaney), 199

Norwid, Kamil, 494

Novak, Helga M., 317

Novalis, 298; *Hymns to the Night*, 298

Novísimos, 601

Nuyorican poetry, 466-474

Oaten, Edward Farley, 366

Object poem, 305

Object-relations theory, 725

Obrestad, Tor, 557

Occasional verse, 817

Octave, defined, 818

"Ode to George Haldane, Governor of the Island of Jamaica, An" (Williams), 43

Odes, 818

Odes, England, 161

Odyssey (Homer), 217

Oehlenschläger, Adam Gottlob, 533

O'Hara, Frank, 674; *The Collected Poems of Frank O'Hara*, 676

Okigbo, Christopher, 507

Økland, Einar, 557

Okura. *See* Yamanoe Okura

Olson, Charles, 197, 686; *The Maximus Poems*, 197; "Projective Verse," 205

On Poetry and Poets (Eliot), 715

"On the Abolition of the English Department" (Ngugi Wa Thiong'o et al.), 771

On the Sublime (Longinus), 702

Ondaatje, Michael, 40

Ono no Komachi, 416

Onofri, Arturo, 401

Opitz, Martin, 292

Oppenheimer, Joel, 688

"Opportunity" (Sill), 762

Oral tradition; Africa, 15; Croatia, 218; Europe, 214-231; Native American, 478; Russia, 509; Serbia, 218

Organic form, 743

Orientalism (Said), 769

Orlando Furioso (Ariosto), 383

Orlando Innamorato (Boiardo), 383

Orléans, Charles d'. *See* Charles d'Orléans

Ørnsbo, Jess, 562

Országh-Hviezdoslav, Pavol, 575

Ortega y Gasset, José, 599

Ortiz, Simon, 483

Osman (Gundulić), 72

Ossian (Macpherson), 628

Ōtomo Tabito, 415

Ōtomo Yakamochi, 415

Ottava rima, defined, 818

Ouwe, Hartmann von. *See* Hartmann von Aue

Ouyang Xiu, 62

Øverland, Arnulf, 546

Owuor-Anyumba, Henry, 771

Oxymoron, defined, 818

Padmasambhava, 605

Palamas, Kostis, 334

Palm, Göran, 554

Pálsson, Sigurður, 561

Paludan-Müller, Frederik, 535

Pan Tadeusz (Mickiewicz), 494

Pannonius, Janus, 353

Pantoum, defined, 818

Paradise Lost (Milton), 623

Paradox, defined, 818

Parallelism, 752

Parini, Giuseppe, 388

Parmenides, 325

Parnassianism, 264, 639

Parny, Évariste-Désiré de Forges de, 258

Parole (linguistics), 750

Paros, Archilochus of. *See* Archilochus

Parra, Nicanor, 438

Parry, Miilman, 218

Parun, Vesna, 75

Parzival (Wolfram von Eschenbach), 287

Pascarella, Cesare, 399

Pascoli, Giovanni, 395

Pasolini, Pier Paolo, 400

Pasternak, Boris, 521
Paterson (Williams), 196
Path on the Rainbow, The
 (anthology), 481
"Pàtria, La" (Aribau), 51
Patriotic verse, German, 299
Pavlović, Miodrag, 570
Pavlovski, Radovan, 476
Paz, Octavio, 438
P'Bitek, Okot, 507
Pearl (Pearl-Poet), 108
Pearl-Poet, 108; _Pearl_, 108; _Sir
 Gawain and the Green Knight_,
 111
Peau noire, masques blancs. See
 Black Skin, White Masks
Péguy, Charles-Pierre, 271
PEN/Voelcker Award for Poetry, 881
Pentameter, defined, 818
Pérez Firmat, Gustavo, 472
Performance poetry, 27
Peri hypsous. See _On the Sublime_
Periphrasis, defined, 818
Perse, Saint-John, 277
Persius, 456
Peru. _See_ Geographical Index
Petersen, Nis, 548
Petőfi, Sándor, 357
Petrarch, 102, 379
Petrarchan sonnet, 136
Petri, György, 362
Petrou Kabaphes, Konstantionos. _See_
 Cavafy, Constantine P.
Pétursson, Hannes, 553
Phaedrus, 456
Phallocentricism, 737
Phenomenological criticism, defined,
 818
Phenomenological psychology, 727
Philips, Katherine, 624
Philosophes, 254
Philosophical poetry, ancient Greece,
 324
Pian wen (poetic form), 60
Piers Plowman. See _Vision of_

_William, Concerning Piers the
 Plowman, The_
Pietri, Pedro, 470
Pindar, 327
Pindaros. _See_ Pindar
Pindarus. _See_ Pindar
Piñero, Miguel, 466
Pinson, Barbara Ann. _See_ Guest,
 Barbara
Plain style, 134
Plath, Sylvia, 202, 670; _Ariel_, 670
Plato, 700; _Republic_, 700
Pléiade poets, 248, 463
Pleynet, Marcelin, 278
Podjavorinská, Ludmila, 575
Poem of the Cid (anonymous), 584
Poem sequence, 194
Poema de Fernán González
 (anonymous), 588
Poet, Pearl. _See_ Pearl-Poet
Poet Laureate Consultant in Poetry,
 881
Poet Laureate of the United Kingdom
 of Great Britain and Northern
 Ireland, 882
Poetic diction, 709
Poetic Edda, 226
Poetic function, 781
Poetical Meditations (Lamartine),
 260
Poetical terms, 810-822
Poetics; defined, 700; France, 276;
 German Enlightenment, 294;
 Marxist criticism, 761; modern,
 194, 715, 750; Octavio Paz, 438;
 Romanticism, 298; Scandinavia,
 554; Spain, 595; Symbolism, 643
Poetics (Aristotle), 700, 743
Poetry; literary canon, 734; as
 literature, 703; psychology, 744;
 science, 744
Poetry (magazine), 645
Poiesis, 701
Point of view, defined, 818
Poli, Umberto. _See_ Saba, Umberto

Polish poetry, 489-499
Politeia. See _Republic_ (Plato)
Politian. _See_ Poliziano
Political poetry; China, 56; East
 Germany, 91; Germany, 299, 311;
 postwar Japan, 431; Middle
 English, 109; nineteenth century
 Poland, 493; Serbia, 569; Soviet
 Union, 524; Sweden, 554
Poliziano, 381, 463
Pondicherry school, 372
Ponge, Francis, 278
Popa, Vasko, 570
Pope, Alexander, 163, 706; _An Essay
 on Criticism_, 706
Porter, Countée LeRoy. _See_ Cullen,
 Countée
Postcolonial criticism, 769-773
Postcolonial poetry, 211, 500-508;
 Africa, 16, 770; Caribbean, 46,
 772; India, 772; Pakistan, 772
Postcolonialism, defined, 818
Postmodernism, 207; Canada, 40;
 Latin America, 436; Scandinavia,
 556
Postmodernism, defined, 818
Poststructuralism, 784
Poststructuralist criticism, 733, 780-
 786
Poulet, Georges, 818
Pound, Ezra, 188, 652, 784; _Cantos_,
 195; _Homage to Sextus
 Propertius_, 195; _Hugh Selwyn
 Mauberley_, 195
Praise poetry, 15
Pratt, Mary Louise, 758
Précieux poets, 251
"Preface to _Fables Ancient and
 Modern_" (Dryden), 705
Preface to _Lyrical Ballads_
 (Wordsworth), 708
Pre-Raphaelites, 183
Pre-Romanticism, France, 258
Prešeren, France, 579
Prévert, Jacques, 275

Primitivism, 168; Sweden, 544

Profil group, 557

Projective verse, 197

"Projective Verse" (Olson), 205

Proletarian poetry, 84

Prose poem, defined, 818

Prose poetry, 266

Protagoras (Simonides), 325

Provençal poetry, 48

Prudhomme, René François Armand. *See* Prudhomme, Sully

Prudhomme, Sully, 265

"Psalm of Life, A" (Longfellow), 761

Psappho. *See* Sappho

Psychoanalysis, 722

Psychological criticism, 719-730

Psychological criticism, defined, 819

Puerto Rican Obituary (Pietri), 470

Puerto Rican poetry. *See* Nuyorican poetry

Pueyrredón, José Rafael Hernández y. *See* Hernández, José

Pulci, Luigi, 382

Pulitzer Prize in Poetry, 882

Pun, defined, 819

Punjabi poetry. *See* Indian English poetry

Purdy, Al, 502

"Pure and Impure Poetry" (Warren), 744

Pushkin, Alexander, 512

Pyrrhus, defined, 819

Qu Yuan, 58

Quasimodo, Salvatore, 404

Quatrain, defined, 819

Queen's Gold Medal for Poetry, 883

Queer, defined, 775

Queer theory, 774-779

Quevedo y Villegas, Francisco Gómez de, 594

Quintilian, 455

Racin, Kosta, 475

Racine, Louis, 256

Radishchev, Aleksandr, 511

Radnóti, Miklós, 360

Raičković, Stevan, 571

Raine, Craig, 208

Rakić, Milan, 569

Rambouillet, marquise de, 251

Realism; Croatia, 74; Germany, 302; Scandinavia, 537

Realism, defined, 819

Rèbora, Clemente, 406

Reed, E. *See* Evans, Mari

Regional poetry, Italy, 397

Régnier, Henri de, 269

Regular meter, defined, 819

Rej, Mikolaj, 489

"Relationship of the Poet to Daydreaming, The" (Freud), 722

Relative stress, defined, 819

Religious poetry; England, 138, 149, 168; France, 256; Hungary, 353; Iceland, 527; Italy, 377, 406; Poland, 489

Renaissance; Catalan, 49; criticism, 703; Croatia, 72; England, 145; France, 245; Hungary, 352; Italy, 381; Latin poetry, 463; Poland, 489

Renaixença, 51

Renga (poetic form), 420

Renga (Tomlinson et al.), 200

Republic (Plato), 700

Resistance poetry; Italy, 407

Resolution, defined, 819

Restoration poetry, 620-625

Restorative poetry, Native American, 479

Reuterswärd, Carl Fredrik, 554

Revard, Carter, 485

Reverdy, Pierre, 275

Reviczky, Gyula, 358

Revista Bilingüe, La (journal), 466

Revista Chicano-Riqueña (journal), 466

Rexroth, Kenneth, 663

Rhetorical poetry, 292

Rhétoriqueurs, 247

Rhodius, Apollonius. *See* Apollonius Rhodius

Rhyme, 752

Rhyme, defined, 819

Rhyme scheme, defined, 819

Rhymes (Petrarch), 380

Riba, Carles, 52

Rifbjerg, Klaus, 562

Riffaterre, Michael, 752

Rilke, Rainer Maria, 304

Rimado de palaçio (Ayala), 590

Rimbaud, Arthur, 268, 641; *Illuminations*, 268; *A Season in Hell*, 268

Rime royal, defined, 820

Rímur (poetic form), 529

Ritsos, Yannis, 345; *Epitaphios*, 345; *The Moonlight Sonata*, 346

Ritual poetry, Native American, 479

Robinson, Edwin Arlington; "Luke Havergal," 789

Rochester, John Wilmot, earl of, 620

Roiç de Corella, Joan, 50

Roig, Jaume, 50

Roland, Alan, 726

Roman de la rose. See *Romance of the Rose, The*

Roman de Renart, 241

Roman period, Greece, 329

Romance of the Rose, The (Guillaume de Lorris and Jean de Meung), 240

Romances; England, 124; France, 239; Germany, 286; Middle English, 105

Romances sans paroles. See *Romances Without Words*

Romances Without Words (Verlaine), 268

Romano, Enotrio. *See* Carducci, Giosuè

Romanticism; criticism, 708; Croatian, 73; Czech poetry, 81; definition of, 298; England, 176,

626-632; France, 258; Germany, 298; Hungary, 355; Poland, 492; Scandinavia, 533; Serbia, 567; Slovakia, 574; Spain, 597; twentieth century, 191
Romanticism, defined, 820
Romero, Alberto, 471
Rondeau, defined, 820
Rondisti, 407
Ronsard, Pierre de, 247
Room of One's Own, A (Woolf), 738
Rose, Wendy, 485
Rossetti, Dante Gabriel, 183
Rossi, Matti, 559
Roucher, Jean-Antoine, 257
Rousseau, Jean-Baptiste, 255
Roux, Paul-Pierre. *See* Saint-Pol-Roux
Ruan Ji, 59
Rubaiyat stanza, defined, 820
Rúfus, Milan, 577
Ruiz, José Martínez. *See* Azorín
Rulfo Prize for Latin American and Caribbean Literature, 884
"Runagate Runagate" (Hayden), 11
Runius, Johan, 530
Rushdie, Salman, 772
Ruskin, John, 731
Russian poetry, 509-525
Ruth Lilly Poetry Prize, 877

Saarikoski, Pentti, 558
Saavedra, Ángel de, 597
Saba, Umberto, 404
Sackville, Charles, earl of Dorset, 620
Sahtouris, Miltos, 349
Said, Edward W., 769
Saikaku. *See* Ihara Saikaku
"Sailing to Byzantium" (Yeats), 193
Saint-Lambert, Jean-François, marquis de, 256
Saint-Pol-Roux, 270
Saitō Mokichi, 428
Salamancan poets, 593
Salinas, Pedro, 600

Salustri, Carlo Alberto, 399
San Francisco Renaissance, 663
Sanchez, Carol Lee, 483
Sánchez, Ricardo, 468
Sanders, Ed, 675
Sannazzaro, Jacopo, 382
Sanqu (poetic form), 64
Sant Jordi, Jordi de, 49
Santillana, Juana Inés de Asbaje y Ramírez de. *See* Cruz, Sor Juana Inés de la
Sappho, 223, 321
Sarmiento, Félix Rubén García. *See* Darío, Rubén
Saroyan, Aram, 675
Sartorius, Joachim, 317
Sarvig, Ole, 550
Sa-skya Pandita, 608
Satiric poetry; England, 138, 161; Latin, 456; Restoration, 156, 621
Satirical poetry; England, 163
Satura (poetic form), 443
Sauser, Frédéric. *See* Cendrars, Blaise
Saussure, Ferdinand de, 750, 775, 780
Scandinavian poetry, 526-565
Scansion, defined, 820
Scapigliatura movement, 393
Scar literature (China), 67
Schade, Jens August, 548
Schiller, Friedrich, 296
Schlauch, Margaret, 761
Schuyler, James, 674
Schwartz, Delmore, 669
Scott, First Baronet. *See* Scott, Sir Walter
Scott, Sir Walter, 178, 629
Scribleruls Club, 163
Scudéry, Madeleine de, 252
Searle, John R., 757
Season in Hell, A (Rimbaud), 268
Seasons, The (Thomson), 165
Second Sex, The (Beauvoir), 737
Second Vanguard, 497
Sedgwick, Eve Kosofsky, 774

Seferiades, Giorgos Stylianou. *See* Seferis, George
Seferis, George, 340
Seguidilla, defined, 820
Seifert, Jaroslav, 85
Sem Tov, Rabbi, 590
Semiotics, defined, 820
Semonides, 321
Sensibility movement, 165
Serbia. *See* Geographical Index
Serbian poetry, 566-572
Sestet, defined, 820
Sestina, defined, 820
Seth, Vikram, 374
Settler poets, 500
Sevillan poets, 593
Sexton, Anne, 671; *All My Pretty Ones*, 671
Seymour, Arthur J., 45
Sgrung, 607
Shakespearean Negotiations (Greenblatt), 764
Shelley, Percy Bysshe, 178, 630, 711; *A Defence of Poetry*, 711
Shelley Memorial Award, 884
Shelton, John. *See* Skelton, John
Shi (poetic form), 59
Shijing. *See* Book of Songs, The
Shiki. *See* Masaoka Shiki
Shinkokinshū (anthology), 418
Shintaisho (anthology), 427
Shiraishi Kazuko, 432
Shōfū, 423
Showalter, Elaine C., 736
"Shrapnel Shards on Blue Water" (Thuy), 27
Sia, Beau, 22
Sicilian school, 378
"Sick Rose, The" (Blake), 720
Sidney, Sir Philip; *Defence of Poesie*, 132, 703
Signifiers and signifieds, 726, 775, 780
Sigurthsson, Stefán, 548
Sikelianos, Angelos, 337

Silko, Leslie Marmon, 483

Silver Age; Latin poetry, 453;
    Russian, 516

Sima Xiangru, 59

Šimić, Antun Branko, 75

Simile, defined, 820

Simonides, 325

Sinclair, John, 756

Sinisgalli, Leonardo, 406

Sinopoulos, Takis, 347

Sir Gawain and the Green Knight
    (Pearl-Poet), 111

Sishui (Wen Yidou), 66

Sitwell, Edith, 187

Sitwellian poetry, 187

Sjöberg, Birger, 543

Skaldic poetry, 527

Skamander, 496

Skelton, John, 133

Skolia, 323

Sládkovič, Andrej, 575

Slamnig, Ivan, 76

Slaviček, Milivoj, 75

Slávy dcera (Kollár), 81

Slessor, Kenneth, 32

Slovak poetry, 573-578

Slovenian poetry, 579-582

Slovo o polku Igoreve. See *Tale of the*
    Armament of Igor, The

Słowacki, Juliusz, 494

Smith, Henry Lee, Jr., 750

Smith, John Allyn. *See* Berryman,
    John

Smrek, Ján, 576

Snodgrass, W. D., 201, 669; *Heart's*
    Needle, 201, 669

Snoilsky, Carl, 536

Snyder, Gary, 206

Social Realism, China, 66

Socialist Realism, 84; Hungary, 361

Society of the Temple, 255

Sociolinguistics, 758

Södergran, Edith, 545

Sōgi, 421

Soledades. See *Solitudes, The*

Solitudes, The (Góngora), 594

Solitudes of Don Luis de Góngora.
    See *Solitudes, The*

Šoljan, Antun, 76

Solomos, Dionysios, 331

Solon, 224

Solovyov, Vladimir, 517

Song, Cathy, 25

Song ci (poetic form), 58

Song of Roland, The (anonymous),
    229, 234

Songs; Native American, 478; Soviet
    Russia, 524; Swedish, 531

Sonne, Jørgen, 562

Sonnet, defined, 820

Sonnet; England, 137

Sonnevi, Göran, 554

Sophists, 325

Šopov, Aco, 476

Sor Juana. *See* Cruz, Sor Juana Inés
    de la

Sōseki. *See* Natsume Sōseki

Soto, Gary, 471

South African poetry, 504

Southeast Asian American poetry, 26

"Souvenirs" (Hagedorn), 25

Soyinka, Wole, 506

Spain. *See* Geographical Index

Spanish poetry; origins to fifteenth
    century, 583-591; fifteenth
    century to present, 592-603

"Spatial Form in Modern Literature"
    (Frank), 780

Spatiality, 780, 783

Speech act theory, 757

Spenser, Edmund, 139, 146

Spill o llibre de les dones. See *Mirror*

Spivak, Gayatri Chakravorty, 739

Split foot, defined, 821

Spondee, defined, 821

Sprung rhythm, defined, 821

Stadler, Ernst, 307

Stagnelius, Erik Johan, 534

Stampa, Gaspara, 386

Stanza, defined, 821

Stéfan, Jude, 280

Stefánsson, Davíth, 548

Steinarr, Steinn, 553

Stephanos. See *Garland*

Stephansson, Stephan G., 541

Stevens, Wallace, 653

Stewart, Harold, 33

Storm, Theodor, 302

Stramm, August, 308

Stritar, Josip, 580

Strophe (poetic form), 299

Structuralism, defined, 780, 821

Structuralist criticism, 780-786

Stub, Ambrosius, 531

"Study of Poetry, The" (Arnold),
    713

Štúr, Ludovít, 574

Style in Language (Sebeok), 751

Stylistic analysis, 756

Stylistic devices, 753

Stylistics, 750

Su Dongpo, 63

Subhasitaratnanidhi (Sa-skya
    Pandita), 608

Substitution, defined, 821

Sugar-Cane, The (Grainger), 43

Suhrawardy, Shahid, 372

Supervielle, Jules, 275

Surrealism, 191; Czech, 84; definition
    of, 273; France, 273; Greece, 342;
    Scandinavia, 555; Slovakia, 576

Sweden. *See* Geographical Index

Syllabic meter, defined, 821

Symbol, defined, 821

Symbolism, 188, 267, 639-643;
    Denmark, 539; Germany, 304;
    Russia, 518

Symbolist Movement in Literature,
    The (Symons), 189

Symons, Arthur, 189

Synchrony (linguistics), 781

Synecdoche, defined, 822

Synesthesia and Symbolist poetry,
    641

Syntactic Structures (Chomsky), 753

Szabó, Lőrinc, 360

Szarzyński, Mikolaj Sep, 490

Szymborska, Wisława, 498

T. S. Eliot Prize, 870

Taban lo Liyong, 771

Tabermann, Tommy, 559

Tabito. *See* Ōtomo Tabito

Tagore, Rabindranath, 371

Takamura Kōtarō, 430

Takuboku. *See* Ishikawa Takuboku

Tale of the Armament of Igor, The
    (anonymous), 509

Taller generation, 438

Tamil poetry. *See* Indian English
    poetry

Tanikawa Shuntarō, 431

Tanka, 413

Tantric songs, 608

Tao Qian, 60

Tasso, Torquato, 384

Tate, Allen; "Tension in Poetry," 744

Tegnér, Esaias, 535

Teitoku. *See* Matsunaga Teitoku

Telquelistes, 276

Temporality, 780, 783

Ten Thousand Leaves, The. See
    Manyoshu, The

Tennyson, Alfred, Lord, 180

"Tension in Poetry" (Tate), 744

Tercet, defined, 822

Terza rima, defined, 822

Thakur, Rabindranath. *See* Tagore,
    Rabindranath

Theme, defined, 822

Theognis, 224, 322

Theogony (Hesiod), 222

Theory of Literature (Wellek and
    Warren), 746

Third person, defined, 822

Thomas, Antoine-Léonard, 257

Thomsen, Søren Ulrik, 564

Thomson, James (1700-1748), 165;
    The Seasons, 165

Thorild, Thomas, 532

Thorne, J. P., 754

Thuy, Le Thi Diem, 26

Thwaites, Elizabeth Hart, 43

Tibetan Book of the Dead, The
    (Padmasambhava), 605

Tibetan poetry, 604-611

Tibullinus. *See* Parny, Évariste-Désiré
    de Forges de

Tin Ujević Award, 886

Tish poets, 40

Tomlinson, Charles; *Renga*, 200

Tone, defined, 822

Tóth, Árpád, 359

Tottel's Miscellany (anthology), 134

*Toward a Speech Act Theory of
    Literary Discourse* (Pratt), 758

Trakl, Georg, 306

Transcendentalism, 179

Transformational poetry, Native
    American, 480

Translation; Indian English poetry,
    369; Native American poetry, 481

Tranströmer, Tomas, 550

Trapassi, Pietro. *See* Metastasio,
    Pietro

Traverseger, George L., 750

Trembecki, Stanisław, 492

Tribe of Ben, 150

Trilling, Lionel, 732

Triumph of Love, The (Hill), 199

Trochee, defined, 822

Troubador poetry, 237

Trouvères (poetic style), 239

Truncation, defined, 822

Tsangyang Gyatso. *See* Dalai Lama,
    Sixth

Tsoai-talee. *See* Momaday, N. Scott

Tsuki ni hoeru. See *Howling at the
    Moon*

Tsvetayeva, Marina, 521

Tu Fu. *See* Du Fu

Tullin, Christian Braunmann, 531

Turberville, George, 136

Turoldo, David Maria, 407

Tuwhare, Hone, 34

Twelve Words of the Gypsy, The
    (Palamas), 335

Tyutchev, Fyodor, 515

Ueda Bin, 428

Ujević, Tin, 75

Ultraísmo, 437

Unamuno y Jugo, Miguel de, 598

Ungaretti, Giuseppe, 402

United States. *See* Geographical
    Index

Urdu poetry. *See* Indian English
    poetry

*Use of Poetry and the Use of
    Criticism, The* (Eliot), 715

Vajda, János, 358

Vakalo, Eleni, 349

Valéry, Paul, 272, 639

Varnalis, Kostas, 338

Varro, 449

Vega, Garcilaso de la. *See* Garcilaso
    de la Vega

Vega Carpio, Lope de, 594

Venison, Alfred. *See* Pound, Ezra

Vennberg, Karl, 549

Verdaguer, Jacint, 51

Vergil, 451

Verhaeren, Émile, 269

Verismo, 393

Verlaine, Paul, 267, 642; *Romances
    Without Words*, 268

Vernacular poetry; England, 131;
    Italy, 377; Latin, 464

Verse, defined, 822

Verse drama, defined, 822

Verse paragraph, defined, 822

Verset claudélien (poetic form), 271

Versus fescennini (poetic form), 443

Versus saturnius (poetic form), 443

Vesaas, Tarjei, 551

Victor, Comte de Vigny, Alfred. *See*
    Vigny, Alfred de

Victorian era, 180; criticism, 712;
    reaction against, 186

Victory odes, 327

Vigny, Alfred de, 261; "Moïse," 261

Villa, José García, 25

Villancicos (poetic form), 584

Villanelle, defined, 822

Villion, François, 244

Virgil. *See* Vergil

Vision of William, Concerning Piers the Plowman, The (Langland), 110

Vizenor, Gerald R., 484

Vociani, 401

Vodnik, Valentin, 579

Vogelweide, Walther von der. *See* Walther von der Vogelweide

Vold, Jan Erik, 557

Volkslied, 289

Voltaire, 255

Von Aue, Hartmann. *See* Hartmann von Aue

Von Hofmannsthal, Hugo. *See* Hofmannsthal, Hugo von

Vormärz, 300

Vörösmarty, Mihály, 356

Voznesensky, Andrei, 522

Vrchlický, Jaroslav, 83

Walcott, Derek, 45, 211, 505

Walker, Kath, 503

Wallace Stevens Award, 885

Waller, Edmund, 150

Walt Whitman Award, 887

Walther von der Vogelweide, 287

Wang Anshi, 63

Wang Wei, 60, 62

War poetry; ancient Greece, 324; France, 271; Greece, 344; Norway, 547

Warren, Austin, 746

Warren, Robert Penn; "Pure and Impure Poetry," 744

Waste Land, The (Eliot), 189

Watts, Isaac, 168

Wave, A (Ashbery), 676

Welhaven, Johan Sebastian, 536

Wellek, René, 746

Wen Yiduo, 66

Wenli (classical Chinese writing), 55

Wenyan (literary Chinese writing), 55

Werfel, Franz, 307

Wergeland, Henrik, 536

West Indian poetry. *See* Caribbean poetry

West Indies. *See* Geographical Index

Wheatley, Phillis, 3

Whitehall, Harold, 751

Whitman, Walt, 190; Beat generation, 205

Whittier, John Greenleaf, 635

Wieners, John, 688

Williams, Francis, 43

Williams, Jonathan, 688

Williams, Raymond, 734, 761

Williams, William Carlos, 196, 653; *Paterson*, 196

Wilmot, John, earl of Rochester. *See* Rochester, John Wilmot, earl of

Winther, Christian, 535

Wit, defined, 708

Wivallius, Lars, 529

Wolfram von Eschenbach, 287; *Parzival*, 287

Women poets, 210; Africa, 18; Australia, 31; Germany, 312; India, 373; Italy, 386

Woolf, Virginia; *A Room of One's Own*, 738

Wordsworth, William, 177, 628, 708; "Composed upon Westminster Bridge, September 3, 1802," 746; Preface to *Lyrical Ballads*, 708

"Work" (Cook), 762

Works and Days (Hesiod), 222

World Anthology, The (anthology), 675

Wright, Judith, 33, 502

Xin yuefu (poetic form), 62

Yakamochi. *See* Ōtomo Yakamochi

Yale Series of Younger Poets, 887

Yamanoe Okura, 414

Yeats, William Butler, 652; "Byzantium," 193; "Sailing to Byzantium," 193

Yevtushenko, Yevgeny, 522

Yo soy Joaquín. See *I Am Joaquín/Yo soy Joaquín*

Yonghuai shi (poetic form), 59

Yosano Akiko, 428

Young Poland poetry, 495

Yuan Zhen, 62

Yuefu (poetic form), 59

Yūgen, 419

Yugloslavia. *See* Geographical Index

Zanzotto, Andrea, 409

Zepeda, Ofelia, 486

Zhukovsky, Vasily, 511

Zmaj, Jovan Jovanović, 568

Zrínyi, Miklós, 353

Župančič, Oton, 581